Contents

8 Tahiti   215

9 Moorea   250

10 Bora Bora   271

⑭ American Samoa   398

⑮ The Kingdom of Tonga   412

Appendix: The South Pacific in Depth   450

Index   457

List of Maps

To my father,

*with love and with grateful thanks for supporting my
being a writer rather than a lawyer*

Acknowledgments

I owe a debt of gratitude to many individuals and organizations without whose help this book would have been impossible to research and write. You will become acquainted with many of them in these pages, and it will be your good fortune if you meet them in the islands.

My good fortune was to be assisted on this edition by Valerie Haeder, who had the enviable task of reporting on Fiji's beautiful Yasawa Islands. You will read her well-chosen words in chapter 5.

I am particularly grateful to Dany Panero, Vaiani Raoulx, Al Keahi, Jonathan Reap, and Leila Laille of Tahiti Tourisme; Cherill Watson, Ili Matatolu, Keti Wagavonovono, Susan Bejeckian, and Thomas Valentine of the Fiji Visitors Bureau; Papatua Papatua of the Cook Islands Tourism Corporation; Sonja Hunter of the Samoa Tourism Authority; Virginia F. Samuelu of the American Samoa Office of Tourism; and Edgar Cocker, Bruno Toke, and Sandradee Fonua of the Tonga Visitors Bureau.

My deep personal thanks go to Connie Haeder, Curtis and Judy Moore, Anne Simon, Suzanne McIntosh, Nancy Monseaux, and Max Parrish, who have tended the home fires while I was away in paradise; to Bill and Donna Wilder, who started all this by introducing me to Tahiti and Moorea; to my sister, Jean Goodwin Santa-Maria, who has consistently given much-needed moral support; to Dick Beaulieu, always a font of information, advice, and ice-cold Fiji Bitters; and to David Hunt, with whom I have shared many a pleasant Sunday in Tonga.

I am truly blessed to have all of them in my life.

—Bill Goodwin

An Invitation to the Reader

In researching this book, we discovered many wonderful places—hotels, restaurants, shops, and more. We're sure you'll find others. Please tell us about them, so we can share the information with your fellow travelers in upcoming editions. If you were disappointed with a recommendation, we'd love to know that, too. Please write to:

Frommer's South Pacific, 11th Edition
Wiley Publishing, Inc. • 111 River St. • Hoboken, NJ 07030-5774

An Additional Note

Please be advised that travel information is subject to change at any time—and this is especially true of prices. We therefore suggest that you write or call ahead for confirmation when making your travel plans. The authors, editors, and publisher cannot be held responsible for the experiences of readers while traveling. Your safety is important to us, however, so we encourage you to stay alert and be aware of your surroundings. Keep a close eye on cameras, purses, and wallets, all favorite targets of thieves and pickpockets.

About the Author

Bill Goodwin is one of the world's experts on travel to the South Pacific. Before falling in love with the islands, he was an award-winning newspaper reporter and then legal counsel and speechwriter for two influential U.S. senators—Sam Nunn of Georgia and the late Sam Ervin of North Carolina. In 1977 he and a friend sailed a 41-foot yacht from Annapolis, Maryland, to Tahiti. He left the boat in Papeete and, with girlfriend and backpack, spent more than a year exploring French Polynesia, American Samoa, Samoa, Tonga, Fiji, New Zealand, and Australia. Altogether he has spent several years in the South Pacific, including one researching and writing the first edition of this book in 1986–87. More recently, he is the author of *Frommer's Tahiti & French Polynesia* and *Frommer's Fiji,* which expand on the coverage in this book. At home, he also is the author of *Frommer's Virginia.* Visit him at www.billgoodwin.com.

Other Great Guides for Your Trip:

Frommer's Tahiti & French Polynesia
Frommer's Fiji
Frommer's Australia
Frommer's New Zealand
Frommer's Southeast Asia

Frommer's Star Ratings, Icons & Abbreviations

Every hotel, restaurant, and attraction listing in this guide has been ranked for quality, value, service, amenities, and special features using a **star-rating system.** In country, state, and regional guides, we also rate towns and regions to help you narrow down your choices and budget your time accordingly. Hotels and restaurants are rated on a scale of zero (recommended) to three stars (exceptional). Attractions, shopping, nightlife, towns, and regions are rated according to the following scale: zero stars (recommended), one star (highly recommended), two stars (very highly recommended), and three stars (must-see).

In addition to the star-rating system, we also use **seven feature icons** that point you to the great deals, in-the-know advice, and unique experiences that separate travelers from tourists. Throughout the book, look for:

Finds	Special finds—those places only insiders know about
Fun Fact	Fun facts—details that make travelers more informed and their trips more fun
Kids	Best bets for kids and advice for the whole family
Moments	Special moments—those experiences that memories are made of
Overrated	Places or experiences not worth your time or money
Tips	Insider tips—great ways to save time and money
Value	Great values—where to get the best deals

The following **abbreviations** are used for credit cards:

AE	American Express	V	Visa
DC	Diners Club	MC	MasterCard

Frommers.com

Now that you have this guidebook to help you plan a great trip, visit our website at **www. frommers.com** for additional travel information on more than 4,000 destinations. We update features regularly to give you instant access to the most current trip-planning information available. At Frommers.com, you'll find scoops on the best airfares, lodging rates, and car rental bargains. You can even book your travel online through our reliable travel booking partners. Other popular features include:

- Online updates of our most popular guidebooks
- Vacation sweepstakes and contest giveaways
- Newsletters highlighting the hottest travel trends
- Podcasts, interactive maps, and up-to-the-minute events listings
- Opinionated blog entries by Arthur Frommer himself
- Online travel message boards with featured travel discussions

What's New in the South Pacific

The South Pacific islands continue to develop at a rapid pace, with more resorts and restaurants being added all the time. Here's a recap of the major changes since I prepared the previous edition of *Frommer's South Pacific*. Much of this information originally appeared on my website, **www.billgoodwin.com,** where I post updates as soon as they happen.

PLANNING YOUR TRIP
Air New Zealand has stopped flying its historic "Coral Route" between Tahiti, the Cook Islands, and Fiji. **Air Tahiti,** French Polynesia's domestic carrier, flies between Tahiti and Rarotonga, but there is no more east-west shortcut between Fiji and the Cooks.

Air New Zealand now goes nonstop between Los Angeles and Rarotonga, but no longer flies its own planes from Los Angeles to Tahiti and Fiji. Instead, it code-shares these routes with **Air Tahiti Nui** and **Air Pacific,** respectively.

Formerly nonstop, Air Tahiti Nui flights from New York's JFK International Airport now stop in Los Angeles to and from Papeete.

See chapter 2 for complete trip-planning information.

FIJI
I spent nearly 2 months in Fiji researching this book and saw little evidence of the coup that deposed the elected government on December 5, 2006. From a traveler's viewpoint, everything was operating normally.

Air Pacific has taken over **Sun Air** and is flying within Fiji as **Pacific Sun** airlines. They share reservation offices.

Fiji's first overwater bungalows are at the upscale, spa-equipped **Likuliku Lagoon Resort,** on Malolo Island off Nadi (✆ 672-0978; www.likulikulagoon.com). Exquisitely designed in Fijian style, its 10 overwater and 36 beachfront *bures* are in a half-moon bay on the western side of Malolo Island. Only couples need apply.

Denarau Island has two new hotels: **The Fiji Beach Resort and Spa Managed by Hilton** (✆ 675-6800; www.hilton.com), and the **Radisson Resort Fiji** (✆ 675-1246; www.radisson.com/fiji). The Radisson's swimming pool complex is outstanding.

Budget-minded travelers have a new choices on Wailoaloa Beach: **Smugglers Cove Beach Resort & Hotel** (✆ 672-6578; www.smugglersbeachfiji.com), has rooms equipped with TVs, phones, and other modern amenities.

The Yasawa Islands continue to develop with the addition of **Navutu Stars Resort** in the Yasawa Islands (✆ 664-0553; www.navutustarsfiji), a nine-unit property with a swimming pool, spa, and yoga retreat; and **Nanuya Island Resort** (✆ 666-6322; www.nanuyafiji.com), beside one of the best beaches in Fiji.

In Pacific Harbour, the backpacker-oriented **Tsulu Beach Bunkhouse** (✆ 345-0065; www.tsulu.com) has opened as part of the **Arts Village** (www.artsvillage.com), offering inexpensive apartments, rooms, and a dormitory. Nearby, **The Uprising**

Beach Resort (© 345-2200; www. uprisingbeachresort.com) is on the beach and has a 24-bunk "treehouse" dorm as well as 12 spacious bungalows.

See chapters 4 through 6 for complete information on Fiji.

TAHITI & FRENCH POLYNESIA

Princess Cruises www.princesscruises. com) will be operating the *Tahitian Princess* on 7- and 10-night cruises in French Polynesia only until late 2009. Its identical sister ship, the *Pacific Princess,* may cruise in French Polynesia thereafter (check the line's website for more information).

The 170-passenger tall ship *Star Flyer* makes 7- 10- and 11-day cruises from Papeete through the Society and Tuamotu islands. It's operated by **Star Clippers** (© 800/442-0552; www.starclippers. com).

In Papeete, the **Musée de la Perle Robert Wan** (Robert Wan Pearl Museum) has moved to Boulevard Pomare at rue l'Aarthémise, opposite the Eglise Evangélique. Admission is free.

The modern **Tahiti Airport Motel** (© 50.40.00; www.tahitiairportmotel. com) overlooks the runways of Tahiti-Faaa International Airport. The 42 air-conditioned units are minimally decorated but have TVs, phones, fridges, wireless Internet access, and private bathrooms.

Fare Suisse (© 42.00.30; www. fare-suisse.com) is a four-room guest-house on rue des Poilus Tahitiens, in the Paofai neighborhood, and is within walking distance of the Papeete waterfront.

In a 126-year-old house about 6 blocks inland from the Moorea Ferry docks, the **Teamo Hostel,** on rue du Pont-Neuf (© 42.00.35; teamohostel@mail.pf), has added TVs and air conditioners to its rooms and dorms.

The Jack Nicklaus–designed **Moorea Green Pearl Golf Club,** at Temae near the airport (© 56.27.32; www.mooreagolf-resort.com), is French Polynesia's second course.

The **Sofitel Moorea Beach Resort** (© 800/763-4835; www.accorhotels. com), formerly the Sofitel Ia Ora Moorea, has been extensively renovated and is now the top choice on Tahiti's sister isle.

Among the super-luxurious amenities at the **St. Regis Resort Bora Bora** (© 800/ 782-9488 or 60-33-96; www.starwood spacollection.com) is a 13,000-square-foot spa on its own islet. The 100 super-luxe guest quarters range from house-size bungalows to the Royal Estate, where Nicole Kidman and Keith Urban spent their honeymoon.

Almost over the top is the **InterContinental Resort and Thalasso Spa Bora Bora** (© 800/327-0200 or 60-49-00; www.boraboraspa.intercontinental.com). The entire resort is the world's first to be air-conditioned using cold seawater pumped from 2,500 feet down in the ocean. The saltwater is reheated for the spa's unique treatments, some dispensed in over-water rooms with glass floors for fish-viewing. The wedding chapel is also over the lagoon.

On Huahine, you may think you're staying at a tented safari camp in Kenya if you opt for the **Fare Ie** (© 60.63.77; www.tahitisafari.com). It has well-equipped tents perched beside a beach north of Fare, Huahine's main town, and near Parea, on the island's southern end.

Relais Mahana (www.relaismahana. com) has reopened after nearly $4 million in renovations.

In the Tuamotu Archipelago, the charming **Relais Royal Tikehau** (© 96. 23.37; www.royaltikehau.pf) has four rooms and seven bungalows on a small islet near the main island.

See chapters 7 through 11 for complete information on French Polynesia.

RAROTONGA & THE COOK ISLANDS

The luxurious Reflections on Rarotonga and Rumours of Romance have merged into **Rumours of Romance Luxury**

Villas & Spa (© 22-551; www.rumours-rarotonga.com). As the name implies, it now has a spa.

The **Little Polynesian** (© 24-280; www.littlepolynesian.com) has reopened after a massive renovation added a swimming pool, outdoor restaurant, and 10 spacious beachside bungalows.

Joining Rarotonga's upscale bungalows are six luxurious units at **Sea Change Villas,** on the south coast (© 22-532; www.sea-change-rarotonga.com). There's no restaurant, but the Salt Water Cafe is nearby.

Rarotonga Backpackers (© 21-590; www.rarotongabackpackers.com) has added four cottages, eight rooms, a dormitory, and a swimming pool beside the beach on the west coast.

See chapter 12 for complete information about the Cook Islands.

SAMOA

The 18-hole **Le Penina Golf Course** (© 770-4653) wraps around Aggie Grey's Lagoon, Beach Resort & Spa.

On the western tip of Upolu Island, **Le Vasa Resort** (© 46-028; www.levasaresort.com) has 11 comfortable bungalows plus a swimming pool and a small, but picturesque, beach.

Coconuts Beach Club has changed its name to **Coconuts Beach Club Resort & Spa** following installation of a full-service spa. The resort also has remodeled its overwater bungalows, expanding them by 20% and adding shaded areas to their decks.

On Savai'i, Kuki and Sara Retzlaff have rebuilt their **Le Lagoto Beach Resort** into a terrific boutique hotel. Most of their 12 units are in Samoan-style *fales,* with intricately lashed ceilings. An infinity pool augments the fine beach.

See chapter 13 for complete information on Samoa.

AMERICAN SAMOA

The **Sadie Thompson Inn** and **Sadie's by the Sea** now have a joint website:

www.sadieshotels.com. Sadie's by the Sea (© 633-5900) was part of the old Rainmaker Hotel until recently. It's the only American Samoan hotel on a beach.

See chapter 14 for complete information on American Samoa.

THE KINGDOM OF TONGA

King Taufa'ahau Tupou IV died in September 2006 at age 88. His son, King George Topou V, assumed the throne.

Downtown Nuku'alofa is open to the public after a pro-democracy demonstration turned into a riot in November 2006. The rubble has been cleaned up, leaving several vacant downtown blocks.

Domestic air travel has been in a state of flux, with only **Airlines Tonga** flying from Tongatapu to Hapai'i and Vava'u (through a local partnership with **Teta Tours;** © 676/23-690 or 24-506; www.tetatourstonga.to). The situation has stabilized a bit with the arrival of **Chathams Pacific—The Friendly Islands Airline** (© 28-000; www.chathamspacific.com), which began operating in April 2008. Its one-way fares from Tongatapu are T$278 (US$139; £70) to Vava'u and T$173 (US$87; £43) to Ha'apai.

The **International Dateline Hotel** (www.datelinehotel.com) has renovated the rooms in its two original wings. Despite super-hard beds in the old wings, it is once again worthy of consideration.

Beachside accommodation is available on Tongatapu at **White Sands** (© 878-9383; www.whitesandstonga.com), on the west coast.

Up in Vava'u, the English-owned **Reef Resort** has four bungalows out on an island in the magnificent lagoon (© 47-156; www.reefresortvavau.com), while the **Mystic Sands Beachfront Bungalows** (© 59-323; www.mysticsands.net) provides cottages for travelers of moderate means.

See chapter 15 for complete information on the Kingdom of Tonga.

1

The Best of the South Pacific

Tahiti, Fiji, Samoa, Rarotonga, and Tonga have conjured up romantic images of an earthly paradise since European sailors brought home tales of their tropical splendor and uninhabited people in the 1760s. My own love affair with the South Pacific doesn't go back *quite* that far, but when I did wash ashore, I quickly understood why these remote outposts came to have such a reputation. These are some of the most beautiful islands in the world—if not *the* most beautiful. They are blessed with some of the most gorgeous beaches the planet has to offer, and their lagoons offer some of the globe's most fabulous diving and snorkeling.

Picking the best of the South Pacific is no easy task. I cannot, for example, choose the friendliest island, for these islanders are among the most welcoming folks on earth. Their fabled history has provided fodder for famous books and films, their culture inspires hedonistic dreams, and their big smiles and genuine hospitality are prime attractions everywhere in the South Pacific.

In this chapter, I point out the best of the best—not necessarily to pass qualitative judgment, but to help you choose among many options. I list them here in the order in which they appear in the book.

For a preview of each South Pacific country, see "The Islands in Brief" in chapter 2.

1 The Most Beautiful Islands

"In the South Seas," Rupert Brooke wrote in 1914, "the Creator seems to have laid himself out to show what He can do." How right the poet was, for all across the South Pacific lie some of the world's most dramatically beautiful islands. In my opinion, the best of the lot have jagged mountain peaks plunging into aquamarine lagoons. Here are some of them:

- **The Yasawa Islands** (Fiji): This chain of long, narrow islands off the northwest coast of Viti Levu, Fiji's main island, ranks as the South Pacific's hottest destination of late, and in all price ranges. The Yasawas have some of the region's best beaches. Despite the inroads of tourism, however, the group remains mostly populated by Fijians, who live in traditional villages. See chapter 5.

- **Ovalau** (Fiji): The sheer cliffs of Ovalau kept the town of Levuka from becoming Fiji's modern capital, but they create a dramatic backdrop to an old South Seas town little-changed in the past century. Ovalau has no good beaches, which means it has no resorts to alter its landscape. See "A Side Trip Back in Time to Levuka," in chapter 5.

- **Qamea and Matagi Islands** (Fiji): These little jewels off the northern coast of Taveuni are lushly beautiful, with their shorelines either dropping precipitously into the surrounding waters or forming bays with idyllic beaches. See "Resorts on Qamea & Matagi Islands," in chapter 6.

- **Moorea** (French Polynesia): I think Moorea is the most beautiful island in the world. Nothing compares with its sawtooth ridges and the dark-green hulk of Mount Rotui separating Cook's and Opunohu bays. The view from Tahiti of Moorea's skyline is unforgettable. See chapter 9.
- **Bora Bora** (French Polynesia): The late James Michener thought that Bora Bora was the most beautiful island in the world. Although tourism has turned this gem into a sort of South Seas Disneyland, development hasn't altered the beauty of Bora Bora's basaltic tombstone, towering over a lagoon that ranges in color from yellow to deep blue. See chapter 10.
- **Rarotonga** (Cook Islands): Only 32km (20 miles) around, the capital of the Cook Islands boasts the beauty of Tahiti—with hints of Moorea. See chapter 12.
- **Aitutaki** (Cook Islands): A junior version of Bora Bora, Aitutaki sits at the apex of a colorful lagoon, which, from the air, looks like a turquoise carpet laid on the deep blue sea. See "Aitutaki," in chapter 12.
- **Upolu** (Samoa): Robert Louis Stevenson was so enraptured with Samoa that he spent the last 5 years of his life in the hills of Upolu. The

eastern part of the island is ruggedly beautiful, especially in Aliepata, where a cliff virtually drops down to one of the region's most spectacular beaches. See "Exploring Apia & the Rest of Upolu," in chapter 13.
- **Savai'i** (Samoa): One of the largest Polynesian islands, this great volcanic shield slopes gently to gorgeous beaches on its eastern and northern sides. There are no towns on Savai'i, only traditional Samoan villages interspersed among rainforests, which adds to its unspoiled beauty. See "Savai'i," in chapter 13.
- **Tutuila** (American Samoa): A primary reason to go to American Samoa is to see the physical beauty of Tutuila and its magnificent harbor at Pago Pago. If you can ignore the canneries and stacks of shipping containers, this island is right up there with Moorea. See chapter 14.
- **Vava'u** (Tonga): One of the South Pacific's best yachting destinations, hilly Vava'u is shaped like a jellyfish, with small islands instead of tentacles trailing off into a quiet lagoon. Waterways cut into the center of the main island, creating the picturesque and perfectly protected Port of Refuge. See "Vava'u," in chapter 15.

2 The Best Beaches

Because all but a few South Pacific islands are surrounded by coral reefs, there are few surf beaches. Tahiti has a few, but they all have heat-absorbing black volcanic sand. Otherwise, most islands (and all but a few resorts) have bathtublike lagoons that lap on coral sands draped by palms. Fortunately for the environmentalists among us, some of the most spectacular beaches are on remote islands and are protected from development by the islanders' devotion to their cultures and villages' land rights. Here are a few that stand out:

- **The Yasawa Islands** (Fiji): This gorgeous chain of islands off northwest Fiji has some of the best beaches I've ever seen. One on Yasawa Island, northernmost in the chain, is a long expanse of deep sand broken by a teapotlike rock outcrop, which also separates two Fijian villages. There are other great beaches at Yasawa Island Resort, Oarsmans Bay Lodge, and Nanuya Island Resort. See "The Mamanuca & Yasawa Islands," in chapter 5.

- **Horseshoe Bay** (Matagi Island, Fiji): Home of one of the region's best resorts, Matagi is an extinct volcano whose crater fell away on one side and formed picturesque Horseshoe Bay. The half-moon beach at its head is one of the finest in the islands. See "Resorts on Qamea & Matagi Islands," in chapter 6.
- **Temae Plage Publique** (Moorea, French Polynesia): The northeastern coast of Moorea is fringed by a stretch of white-sand beach, which commands a glorious view across a speckled lagoon to Tahiti, sitting on the horizon across the Sea of the Moon. See "Exploring Moorea," in chapter 9.
- **Matira Beach** (Bora Bora, French Polynesia): Beginning at the Hotel Bora Bora, this fine ribbon of sand stretches around Matira Point, which forms the island's southern extremity, all the way to the Club Med. The eastern side has views of the islands of Raiatea and Tahaa. See "Exploring Bora Bora," in chapter 10.
- **Avea Beach** (Huahine, French Polynesia): My favorite resort beach is at Relais Mahana, a small hotel on Auea Bay near Huahine's southern end. Trees grow along the beach, which slopes into a lagoon deep enough for swimming at any tide. It's a perfect and safe place to snorkel, and the lagoon here is protected from the trade winds, making it safe for sailing. See "Where to Stay on Huahine," in chapter 11.
- **Titikaveka Beach** (Rarotonga, Cook Islands): On Rarotonga's southern coast, Titikaveka is blessed with palm

trees draped over a long beach of brilliant white sand, and the lagoon here is the island's best for swimming and snorkeling. See "Exploring Rarotonga" in chapter 12.
- **One Foot Island** (Aitutaki, Cook Islands): The sands on the islets surrounding Aitutaki gleam pure white, like talcum. Tiny One Foot Island has the best beach here, with part of it along a channel whose coral bottom is scoured clean by strong tidal currents. Another stretch runs out to a sandbar known as Nude Island—a reference not to clothes but to a lack of vegetation. See "Exploring Aitutaki," in chapter 12.
- **Lalomanu Beach** (Upolu, Samoa): On the southeastern corner of Upolu, a clifflike mountain forms a dramatic backdrop to the deep sands of Lolomanu Beach, which faces a group of small islets offshore. This is a great place to stay in an open-air beach *fale*. See "Exploring Apia & the Rest of Upolu," in chapter 13.
- **Return to Paradise Beach** (Upolu, Samoa): This idyllic stretch of white sand and black rocks overhung by coconut palms gets its name from *Return to Paradise*, the 1953 Gary Cooper movie filmed here. See "Exploring Apia & the Rest of Upolu," in chapter 13.
- **Manase Beach** (Savai'i, Samoa): The long stretch of white sand fronting Manase village on the north shore of Savai'i is another extraordinary place to spend a night in an open-air beach fale. See "Savai'i," in chapter 13.

3 The Best Honeymoon Resorts

Honeymooning or not, the South Pacific is a marvelous place for romantic escapes. After all, romance and the islands have gone hand-in-hand since the bare-breasted

young women of Tahiti gave rousing welcomes to the 18th-century European explorers.

I've never stayed anywhere as romantic as a thatch-roof bungalow, especially one built on stilts over a lagoon, with a glass panel in its floor for viewing fish that swim below you, and steps leading into the warm waters. You'll find lots of these in French Polynesia—especially on Bora Bora, the South Pacific's most famous honeymoon destination—and a handful more in Fiji, the Cook Islands, and Samoa.

One caveat is in order: Many overwater bungalows are relatively close together, meaning that your honeymooning next-door neighbors will be within earshot if not eyeshot. Therefore, if you're seeking a high degree of privacy and seclusion, they won't be your best choice. Look instead to a growing number of super-private honeymoon "villas"—many with their own swimming pools and hot tubs.

Also, many of the South Pacific's small, relatively remote offshore resorts fall into another category: Best Places to Get Away from It All. They are so romantic that a friend of mine says her ideal wedding would be to rent an entire small resort in Fiji, take her wedding party with her, get married in Fijian costume beside the beach, and make her honeymoon a diving vacation. Most resorts in this book are aware of such desires, and they offer wedding packages complete with traditional ceremony and costumes (see the "Getting Hitched in the Islands" box, later in this chapter).

Here's my choice of the best honeymoon resorts. With few exceptions, they all have full-service spas.

FIJI

Fiji has one of the world's finest collections of small offshore resorts. These have two advantages over their French Polynesian competitors. First, many have fewer than 20 bungalows each instead of the 40 or more found at the French Polynesian resorts, which means they are usually more widely spaced than their Tahitian

cousins. Second, they are on islands all by themselves. Together, these two advantages multiply the privacy factor.

Several hotels in the Mamanuca Islands off Nadi appeal to honeymooners. Tops is the exquisitely designed **Likuliku Lagoon Resort,** the first in Fiji with overwater bungalows (p. 123). **Tokoriki Island Resort** has five bungalows with their own plunge pools (p. 124). It's less luxurious, but **Matamanoa Island Resort** caters exclusively to couples and is a good choice for cost-conscious honeymooners. See p. 126.

Yasawa Island Resort and Spa sits on one of the prettiest beaches and has a low-key, friendly ambience. It has large bungalows, the choice being the secluded honeymoon unit sitting by its own beach; it even has its own pool. See p. 128.

Also in the Yasawa Islands is the less expensive **Navutu Stars Resort,** which has a spa and yoga sessions in addition to fine food. See p. 129.

In central Fiji off Suva, **The Wakaya Club** is generally considered Fiji's top resort. It has the country's largest bungalows, plus a palatial mansion with its own pool, perched high atop a ridge. You might see a movie star or two relaxing at Wakaya. See p. 157.

At Savusavu in northern Fiji, **Jean-Michel Cousteau Fiji Islands Resort** is the South Pacific's best family hotel, but a beautiful villa with its own swimming pool is hidden away from the kids. See p. 169. Motivational speaker Anthony Robbin's luxurious **Namale Resort** also has private, pool-equipped villas plus a bowling alley, golf simulator, and a ton of other toys. See p. 171.

At the other extreme, Taveuni's low-key, three-unit **Coconut Grove Beachfront Cottages** is one of Fiji's best bargains. See p. 179. Most bungalows at **Maravu Plantation Beach Resort & Spa** come equipped with hot tubs, and a honeymoon unit is built up in a tree. See p. 180.

So is one of the widely spaced bunga-lows at **Matangi Island Resort,** off Tave-uni, where two more are carved into the side of a cliff. They all have outdoor bath-rooms. See p. 184. Among my favorite places are the charming, old South Seas–style bungalows and the stunning central building at **Qamea Resort and Spa.** Lanterns romantically light the 52-foot-high thatched roof of Qamea's main building. See p. 185.

FRENCH POLYNESIA

The resorts in French Polynesia have the region's widest selection of overwater bungalows.

On Tahiti, which most visitors now consider a way station to the other islands, the **InterContinental Tahiti Beachcomber Resort** has overwater bun-galows that face the outline of Moorea across the Sea of the Moon. See p. 239. Some of those at **Le Meridien Tahiti** also have this view. See p. 239.

On Moorea, the overwater units at the **Club Bali Hai** are the among the old-est—and the least expensive—in the islands. They lack most modern ameni-ties, but they enjoy an unparalleled view of the jagged mountains surrounding Cook's Bay. See p. 263. Some overwater units at the **Sofitel Moorea Beach Resort** face Tahiti across the Sea of the Moon, and they're built over Moorea's most colorful lagoon. See p. 264. The **Moorea Pearl Resort** has a few perched on the edge of the clifflike reef, making for superb snorkeling right off your front deck. See p. 264.

Bora Bora has several hundred overwa-ter bungalows. The newest and largest are at the super-luxurious **St. Regis Resort Bora Bora,** where Nicole Kidman and Keith Urban spent their honeymoon in the enormous Royal Estate (p. 284). Also huge are the units at **InterContinental Resort and Thalasso Spa Bora Bora,** where you can watch fish swim beneath your overwater treatment room while get-ting a massage in the South Pacific's top spa (p. 282).

Units at the **Bora Bora Nui Resort** also are large and luxurious, although they don't look out to pillarlike Mount Otemanu rising across the famous lagoon (p. 280). For that signature vista, you can stay at the **Sofitel Motu** (p. 283) or at the venerable **Hotel Bora Bora** (p. 281). The Hotel Bora Bora also has luxurious bun-galows boasting their own courtyards with swimming pools. Equally private, though less luxe, are the garden units at the **Bora Bora Pearl Beach Resort;** you can cavort in their wall-enclosed patios, which have sun decks and splash pools. See p. 280. The smaller, but well-appointed, overwater units at the friendly **Hotel Maitai Polynesia** are the least expensive on Bora Bora. See p. 284.

On Huahine, units at the **Te Tiare Beach Resort** have some of the largest decks of any overwater bungalows (one side is shaded by a thatched roof). See p. 296.

The most charming of French Polyne-sia's overwater units are at the **Le Taha'a Private Island & Spa,** a luxurious resort on a small islet off Tahaa. Some of these espy Bora Bora on the horizon. See p. 304.

Out at the huge atoll known as Ran-giroa, in the Tuamotu archipelago, **Hotel Kia Ora** has bungalows over the world's second-largest lagoon. See p. 309. On the adjacent atoll, overwater bungalows at the **Tikehau Pearl Beach Resort** sit over the rip tides in a pass that lets the sea into the lagoon. See p. 311. On Manihi atoll, units at the **Manihi Pearl Beach Resort** are cooled by the almost con-stantly blowing trade winds. Isolated on their own islets, the Pearl Beach resorts on Tikihau and Manihi more closely approximate the privacy of Fiji's remote offshore resorts than any others in French Polynesia. See p. 312.

Getting Hitched in the Islands

These romantic islands are marvelous places to get married, although getting *legally* hitched is relatively easy only in Fiji, the Cook Islands, and Samoa. It's impractical in French Polynesia and American Samoa, which require 30-day residencies prior to getting a marriage license, and more difficult in Tonga, which requires 6 months. Legal or not, many couples still opt for island wedding ceremonies during their honeymoons. Many resorts will take care of the formalities and organize traditional ceremonies, on the beach as you prefer. Their wedding coordinators will tell you what documents you will need to bring (or send in advance) and what local formalities you will need to execute. Do not even think of making the arrangements yourself.

THE COOK ISLANDS

Generally you will spend less on your honeymoon in Rarotonga and the Cook Islands than in nearby French Polynesia.

Up in Aitutaki, you can stay in an overwater bungalow at the **Aitutaki Lagoon Resort & Spa,** which has one of the most cleverly designed "villas" in the islands (you roll off your daybed into your own pool and swim to your own hot tub!). See p. 355. The stunning **Pacific Resort Aitutaki** has bungalows down by the beach and hidden away among old-growth forest on a headland. **Etu Moana Beach Villas** lacks a restaurant, but its bungalows are within walking distance of one. See p. 355.

The most luxurious digs on Rarotonga are at **Rumours of Romance Luxury Villas & Spa,** where one unit has its own movie theater. They are not, however, individual bungalows. See p. 340. Nor are those at **Sea Change Villas,** but the beachside units have their own pools. See p. 342. My favorite bungalows are the spacious and charming units at **Rarotonga Beach Bungalows,** sitting beside the island's best beach and lagoon. See p. 342. Nearby, the **Little Polynesian** now has 10 spacious beachside bungalows and a pool (see p. 341), as does **Royale Takitumu Villas** (see p. 342). The best family resort in the Cooks, the **Rarotongan Beach Resort & Spa,** also has a luxurious honeymoon villa with pool hidden from the throngs. Even more private villas are across the road. See p. 344. **Crown Beach Resort,** the top small full-service hotel on Rarotonga, has hot tubs in the porches on its beachside units and has added 16 private villas with pools. See p. 343.

SAMOA

Often overshadowed by its South Pacific neighbors, independent Samoa has much to offer honeymooners, especially those without unlimited funds.

On Upolu's south coast, **Coconuts Beach Club & Spa** has Samoa's only overwater bungalows, and three villas with rock-wall bathrooms. See p. 388. Nearby, **Sinalei Reef Resort & Spa** has a spa, a 9-hole golf course, and individual bungalows. The honeymoon units sit beside their own beach. See p. 390.

Although it does not have bungalows, **Aggie Grey's Lagoon, Beach Resort & Spa** does sport a full-service spa, and it's surrounded by the sea and an 18-hole golf course. See p. 388.

On Savai'i, **Le Lagoto Beach Resort** has a dozen Samoan-style *fales* with intricately lashed ceilings. An infinity pool augments the fine beach. See p. 395.

4 The Best Family Vacations

There are no Disney Worlds or other such attractions in the islands. That's not to say that children won't have a fine time, for more resorts are making provisions for families. Kids will enjoy themselves most if they like being around the water.

A family can vacation in style and comfort at resorts like the big resorts on Denarau Island in Fiji, or Shangri-la's Fijian Resort on the Coral Coast, but here are some of the best smaller establishments that welcome families.

- **Castaway Island Resort** (Mamanuca Islands, Fiji): One of Fiji's oldest resorts but thoroughly refurbished, Castaway has plenty to keep both adults and children occupied, from a wide array of watersports to a kids' playroom and a nursery. There's even a nurse on duty. See p. 123.

- **Jean-Michel Cousteau Fiji Islands Resort** (Savusavu, Fiji): The South Pacific's finest family resort encourages parents to enroll their kids in an exceptional environmental education program. It keeps the youngsters educated and entertained from sunup to bedtime. See p. 169.

- **Le Meridien Bora Bora** (Bora Bora, French Polynesia): Most resorts in French Polynesia are designed for romance, not children. The notable exception is Le Meridien Bora Bora, which has a shallow, lakelike lagoon where children can safely swim with young sea turtles bred in the resort's conservation program. See p. 282.

- **St. Regis Resort Bora Bora** (Bora Bora, French Polynesia): Well-heeled children will feel right at home playing in the St. Regis's state-of-the-art *Hono Iti* (Little Turtle) kids' club, where computers come equipped with high-speed Internet access and educational software. See p. 284.

- **The Rarotongan Beach Resort & Spa** (Rarotonga, Cook Islands): Rising like a phoenix after years of neglect, this is now the best international-standard resort on Rarotonga. Although it caters to everyone from honeymooners to families, the children's program is tops in the Cook Islands. See p. 344.

5 The Best Cultural Experiences

The South Pacific Islanders are proud of their ancient Polynesian and Fijian cultures, and they eagerly inform anyone who asks about their ancient and modern ways. Here are some of the best ways to learn about the islanders and their lifestyles:

- **Fijian Village Visits** (Fiji): Many tours from Nadi and most offshore resorts include visits to traditional Fijian villages, whose residents stage welcoming ceremonies (featuring the slightly narcotic drink *kava*) and then show visitors around and explain how the old and the new combine in today's villages. See "Sightseeing Tours" in chapter 5.

- **Tiki Theatre Village** (Moorea, French Polynesia): Built to resemble a pre-European Tahitian village, this cultural center has demonstrations of crafts and puts on a nightly dance show and feast. It's a bit commercial, and the staff isn't always fluent in English, but this is the only place in French Polynesia where one can sample the old ways. See "Exploring Moorea," in chapter 9.

- **Rarotonga** (Cook Islands): In addition to offering some of the region's most laid-back beach vacations, the people of Rarotonga go out of their way to let visitors know about their unique Cook Islands way of life. A morning spent at the **Cook Islands Cultural Village** and on a **cultural tour** of the island is an excellent educational experience. For a look at flora and fauna, and their traditional uses, **Pa's Cross-Island Mountain Trek** cannot be topped. See "Exploring Rarotonga" in chapter 12.

- **Samoa:** The entire country serves as a cultural storehouse of *fa'a Samoa*, the traditional Samoan way of life. Most Samoans still live in villages featuring *fales* (oval houses), some of which have stood for centuries—although tin roofs have replaced thatch. The island of Savai'i is especially well preserved. A highlight of any visit to Savai'i should be a **tour** with Warren Jopling, a

retired Australian geologist who has lived on Samoa's largest island for many years. Not only does he know the forbidding lava fields like the back of his hand, but everyone on Savai'i knows him, which helps make his cultural commentaries extremely informative. See "Savai'i," in chapter 13.

- **Tongan National Cultural Centre** (Nuku'alofa, Tonga): Artisans turn out classic Tongan crafts, and a museum exhibits Tongan history, including the robe worn by Queen Salote at the coronation of Queen Elizabeth II in 1953; and the carcass of Tui Malila, a Galápagos turtle that Captain Cook reputedly gave to the king of Tonga in 1777, which lived until 1968. The center has island-night dance shows and feasts with traditional food. See "Exploring Tongatapu," in chapter 15.

6 The Best of the Old South Seas

Many South Pacific islands are developing rapidly, with modern, fast-paced cities replacing sleepy backwater ports, such as those at Papeete in French Polynesia and Suva in Fiji. However, there are still many remnants of the old South Sea days of coconut planters, beach bums, and missionaries.

- **Levuka** (Ovalau Island, Fiji): No other town has remained the same after a century as has Levuka, Fiji's first European-style town and its original colonial capital in the 1870s. Levuka looks very much as it did when the government moved to Suva in 1882, with a row of clapboard general stores along picturesque Beach Street. See "A Side Trip Back in Time to Levuka," in chapter 5.

- **Taveuni Island** (Northern Fiji): Like Savai'i, Fiji's third-largest and lushest island has changed little since Europeans started coconut plantations in

the 1860s. With the largest remaining population of indigenous plants and animals in the South Pacific, Taveuni is a nature lover's delight. See "Taveuni," in chapter 6.

- **Huahine** (French Polynesia): Of the French Polynesian islands frequented by visitors, Huahine has been the least affected by tourism, and its residents are still likely to give you an unprompted Tahitian greeting, *"Ia orana!"* As on Aitutaki, agriculture is still king on Huahine, which makes it the "Island of Fruits." There are ancient *marae* (temples) to visit, and the only town, tiny Fare, is little more than a collection of Chinese shops fronting the island's wharf, which comes to life when ships pull in. See "Huahine," in chapter 11.

- **Aitutaki** (Cook Islands): Although it is now one of the hottest destinations in the South Pacific, the little island of Aitutaki is still very much old Polynesia, with most of its residents farming and fishing for a living. The crystal-clear lagoon is something to behold. See "Aitutaki," in chapter 12.

- **Apia** (Samoa): Despite a sea wall along what used to be a beach and two high-rises sitting on reclaimed land, a number of clapboard buildings and 19th-century churches make Apia look much as it did when Robert Louis Stevenson settled here in 1889. See "Exploring Apia & the Rest of Upolu," in chapter 13.
- **Savai'i** (Samoa): One of the largest of all Polynesian islands, this great volcanic shield also is one of the least populated, with the oval-shaped houses of traditional villages sitting beside freshwater bathing pools fed by underground springs. See "Savai'i," in chapter 13.
- **Neiafu** (Vava'u, Tonga): Although Nuku'alofa, the capital on the main island of Tongatapu, gets most of the ink about Tonga, the little village of Neiafu, on the sailor's paradise of Vava'u, has remained untouched by development. Built by convicted adulteresses, the Road of the Doves still winds above the dramatic Port of Refuge, just as it did in 1875. See "Vava'u," in chapter 15.

7 The Best Dining Experiences

You won't be stuck eating island-style food cooked in an earth oven (see "Tips on Dining," in chapter 2), for the islands have some restaurants of remarkably high caliber. Here are a few of my favorites.

- **Nadina Authentic Fijian Restaurant** (Nadi, Fiji): Most resorts serve native food on buffets at their island night feasts, but this little restaurant serves great Fijian fare all the time, including *miti,* the tender young shoots of the wood fern, served with coconut milk. See p. 118.
- **Vilisite's Seafood Restaurant** (The Coral Coast, Fiji): This seaside restaurant, owned and operated by a friendly Fijian woman named Vilisite, doesn't look like much from the outside, but it offers a handful of excellent seafood meals to augment a terrific view along Fiji's Coral Coast from the veranda. See p. 141.
- **Old Mill Cottage** (Suva, Fiji): Diplomats and government workers pack this old colonial cottage at breakfast and lunch for some of the region's least-expensive local fare. Offerings range from English-style roast chicken with mashed potatoes and peas to Fijian-style *palusami* (fresh fish wrapped in taro leaves and steamed in coconut milk). See p. 160.
- **L'O a la Bouche** (Papeete, Tahiti): The chefs at this sophisticated bistro in the heart of Papeete range far from traditional French fare to items from Spain, Italy, and other countries. They're also good at coming up with creative spins using local ingredients. It's one of the best restaurants in French Polynesia. See p. 246.
- **Le Lotus** (Papeete, Tahiti): The most romantic setting of any South Pacific restaurant is in this overwater dining room at the Tahiti Beachcomber Inter-Continental Resort. Even if the food weren't gourmet and the service weren't efficient and unobtrusive, the view of Moorea on a moonlit night makes an evening here special. See p. 245.
- **Les Roulottes** (Papeete, French Polynesia): The Papeete waterfront turns into a carnival when meal wagons set up shop after dark, offering char-grilled steaks with french fries and a variety of other inexpensive fare. Most other islands have them, too. See p. 244.

- **Le Mayflower** (Moorea, French Polynesia): You'll want to write home about the lobster ravioli in cream sauce at this moderately priced roadside restaurant, Moorea's best. It's excellent value in expensive French Polynesia. See p. 269.

- **Bloody Mary's Restaurant & Bar** (Bora Bora, French Polynesia): A fun evening at the South Pacific's most famous restaurant is a must when on Bora Bora. That's because Bloody's offers the most unique and charming dining experience in the islands. Come early for a drink at the friendly bar, and then pick your fresh seafood from atop a huge tray of ice. After eating heavy French fare elsewhere for a few days, the sauceless fish from the grill will seem downright refreshing. See p. 287.

- **La Villa Mahana** (Bora Bora, French Polynesia): Corsican chef Damien Rinaldi Devio also offers relief from traditional French sauces at his little restaurant, where he uses exotic spices to enliven fresh fish and beef dishes. See p. 288.

- **Tamarind House Restaurant & Bar** (Rarotonga, Cook Islands): Noted restaurateur and cookbook author Sue Carruthers brings the seasonings of her native Kenya to this charmer in a seaside colonial house. See p. 349.

- **Sails at Mulinu'u** (Apia, Samoa): Ian and Lyvia Black own one of the South Pacific's best casual restaurants beside Apia Harbour on the Mulinu'u Peninsula. Most likely your table will be under the stars. See p. 392.

- **Seaview Restaurant** (Nuku'alofa, Tonga): In a country where restaurants come and go, this Austrian-owned establishment, in an old waterfront home, has long provided Nuku'alofa's best cuisine. Tonga is the last island nation with a reliable supply of spiny tropical lobsters, so have one here. See p. 437.

8 The Best Island Nights

Don't come to the South Pacific islands expecting opera and ballet, or Las Vegas–style floor shows, either. Other than pub-crawling to bars and nightclubs with music for dancing, evening entertainment here consists primarily of island nights, which invariably feature feasts of island foods followed by traditional dancing.

In the cases of French Polynesia and the Cook Islands, of course, the hip-swinging traditional dances are world famous. They are not as lewd and lascivious today as they were in the days before the missionaries arrived, but they still have plenty of suggestive movements to the primordial beat of drums. By contrast, dancing in Fiji, Tonga, and the Samoas is much more reserved, with graceful movements, terrific harmony, and occasional action in a war or fire dance.

- **French Polynesia:** Hotels are the places to see Tahitian dancing. The resorts rely on village groups to perform a few times a week. The very best shows are during the annual *Heiva i Tahiti* festival in July; the winners then tour the other islands in August for minifestivals at the resorts. See "Island Nights," in chapters 8 through 10.

- **The Cook Islands:** Although the Tahitians are more famous for their dancing than the Cook Islanders, many of their original movements were quashed by the missionaries in the early 19th century. By the time the French took over in 1841 and allowed dancing again, the Tahitians had forgotten many of the old movements. They turned to the Cook Islands, where dancing was—and still

Weekend Pub-Crawling

Fundamentalist Christians may own Sundays in the islands, but Friday and Saturday nights definitely belong to the sinners. That's because bar-hopping—or **pub-crawling** as it's known here—is *the* thing to do after dark on weekends. Every island has its favorite bars, which are packed until the wee hours on Friday night, until midnight on Saturday. There's a dark side, however, for fights can break out, and drunken driving is a problem on those nights.

is—the thing to do when the sun goes down. There's an island night show every evening except Sunday on Rarotonga. The best troupes usually perform at the Edgewater Resort and the Rarotongan Beach Resort. See "Island Nights on Rarotonga," in chapter 12.

- **Samoa:** Among the great shows in the South Pacific are *fiafia* nights in the main building at Aggie Grey's Hotel & Bungalows in Apia. The show culminates in a fire dance around the adjacent pool. See "Island Nights on Upolu," in chapter 13.

- **Tonga:** The shows at the Tongan National Cultural Centre are unique, with expert commentary before each dance, explaining its movements and their meanings. That's a big help, since all songs throughout the South Pacific are in the native languages. See "Island Nights on Tongatapu," in chapter 15.

9 The Best Buys

Take some extra money along, for you'll spend it on handicrafts, black pearls, and tropical clothing.

For the locations of the best shops, see the shopping sections in chapters 5 through 15.

- **Black Pearls:** Few people will escape French Polynesia or the Cook Islands without buying at least one black pearl. That's because the clearwater lagoons of French Polynesia's Tuamotu archipelago and the Manihiki and Penrhyn atolls in the Cook Islands are the world's largest producers of the beautiful dark orbs, and they're being harvested in Fiji, too. See chapters 8, 9, 10, and 12.

- **Handicrafts:** Although many of the items you will see in island souvenir shops are actually made in Asia, locally produced handicrafts are the South Pacific's best buys. The most widespread are hats, mats, and baskets woven of *pandanus* or other

fibers, usually by women who have maintained this ancient art to a high degree. Tonga has the widest selection of woven items, although Samoa and Fiji are making comebacks. The finely woven mats made in Tonga and the Samoas are still highly valued as ceremonial possessions and are seldom for sale to tourists. See chapters 5, 13, and 15.

Before the coming of European traders and printed cotton, the South Pacific islanders wore garments made from the beaten bark of the paper mulberry tree. The making of this bark cloth, known as *tapa,* is another preserved art in Tonga, Samoa (where it is called *siapo*), and Fiji (where it is known as *masi*). The cloth is painted with dyes made from natural substances, usually in geometric designs that have ancestries dating back thousands of years. Tapa is an excellent souvenir because it can be folded and brought back in a suitcase. See chapters 5, 13, and 15.

Woodcarvings are also popular. Spears, war clubs, knives made from sharks' teeth, canoe prows, and cannibal forks are some examples. Many carvings, however, tend to be produced for the tourist trade and can lack the imagery of bygone days, and some may be machine-produced. Carved tikis are found in most South Pacific countries, but many of them resemble the figures of the New Zealand Maoris rather than figures indigenous to those countries. The carvings from Fiji and the Marquesas Islands of French Polynesia are the best of the lot. See chapters 5 and 8 through 12.

- **Tropical Clothing:** Colorful hand-screened, -blocked, and -dyed fabrics are popular in the islands for making dresses or the wraparound skirt known as *pareu* in Tahiti and Rarotonga, *lava-lava* in the Samoas and Tonga, and *sulu* in Fiji. Heat-sensitive dyes are hand-applied to gauzelike cotton, which is laid in the sun for several hours. Flowers, leaves, and other designs are placed on the fabric, and as the heat of the sun darkens and sets the dyes, the shadows from these objects leave their images on the finished product. See chapters 5 through 15.

10 The Best Diving & Snorkeling

All the islands have excellent scuba diving and snorkeling, and all but a few of the resorts either have their own dive operations or can make arrangements with a local company. Here are the best:

- **Fiji:** With nutrient-rich waters welling up from the Tonga Trench offshore and being carried by strong currents funneling through narrow passages, Fiji is famous for some of the world's most colorful soft corals. This is especially true of the Somosomo Strait between Vanua Levu and Taveuni in northern Fiji, home of the Rainbow Reef and its Great White Wall. The Beqa Lagoon is also famous for having plentiful soft corals. See chapters 5 and 6.
- **Rangiroa and Fakarava** (French Polynesia): Like those surrounding most populated islands, some lagoons in French Polynesia have been relatively "fished out" over the years. That's not to say that diving in such places as Moorea and Bora Bora can't be world-class, but the best is at Rangiroa and Fakarava in the Tuamotu Archipelago. They are more famous for their sea life, including sharks, than colorful soft corals. Go to Rangiroa to see sharks; to Fakarava for more fish than you ever imagined existed. See chapter 11.
- **Tonga:** The north shore of the main island of Tongatapu fronts a huge lagoon, where the government has made national parks of the Hakaumama'o and Malinoa reefs. The best diving in Tonga is around Ha'apai and Vava'u. See "Ha'apai" and "Vava'u," in chapter 15.

11 The Best Sailing

One would think that the South Pacific is a yachting paradise, and it certainly gets more than its share of cruising boats on holiday from Australia and New Zealand or heading around the world (the region is on the safest circumnavigation route). However, the reefs in most places make sailing a precarious undertaking, so yachting is not that widespread. It has only recently gained a toehold in Fiji.

There are only two places where you can charter a yacht and sail it yourself:

- **Raiatea** (French Polynesia): Firms have charter fleets based in Raiatea in the Leeward Islands of French Polynesia. Raiatea shares a lagoon with Tahaa, a hilly island indented with long bays that shelter numerous anchorages. Boats can be sailed completely around Tahaa without leaving the lagoon, and Bora Bora and Huahine are just 32km (20 miles) away over blue water. See "Raiatea & Tahaa," in chapter 11.

- **Vava'u** (Tonga): The second most popular yachting spot, Vava'u is virtually serrated by such well-protected bays as the Port of Refuge. Chains of small islands trail off the south side of Vava'u like the tentacles of a jellyfish, creating large, quiet cruising grounds. Many anchorages are off deserted islands with their own beaches. See "Vava'u," in chapter 15.

12 The Best Offbeat Travel Experiences

Some cynics might say that a visit to the South Pacific itself is an offbeat experience, but there are a few things to do that are even more unusual.

- **Getting Asked to Dance** (everywhere): I've seen so many traditional South Pacific dance shows that I now stand by the rear door, ready to beat a quick escape before those lovely young women in grass skirts can grab my hand and force me to make a fool of myself trying to gyrate my hips up on the stage. It's part of the tourist experience at all resorts, and it's all in good fun.

- **Swimming with the Sharks** (Bora Bora, French Polynesia): A key attraction in Bora Bora's magnificent lagoon is to snorkel with a guide, who actually feeds a school of sharks as they thrash around in a frenzy. I prefer to leave this one to the Discovery Channel. See "Exploring Bora Bora," in chapter 10.

- **Riding the Rip** (Rangiroa and Manihi, French Polynesia): Snorkelers will never forget the flying sensation as they ride the strong currents ripping through a pass into the lagoons at Rangiroa and Manihi. See "Rangiroa" and "Manihi," in chapter 11.

- **Sleeping in a Beach Fale** (Samoa): Even if you don't like to camp, you'll enjoy every minute spent in one of Samoa's beach fales—little thatched-roof buildings beside one of that country's lovely beaches. Forget privacy, since most are open-sided in traditional Samoan fashion. But why block the view? And the neighbors you meet could become lifetime friends. See "Where to Stay on Upolu" and "Where to Stay & Dine on Savai'i," in chapter 13.

- **Worshipping with the King** (Nuku'alofa, Tonga): It's not every day you get to see a real-life king, but you can in Tonga. In fact, you can even go to church with him on Sunday, or perhaps watch him ride by in his big, black SUV other days of the week. See "How To Survive Sunday in Tonga," in chapter 15.

- **Cave Swimming** (Samoa and Tonga): Boats can go into Swallows Cave on one of the small islands that make up Vava'u, but you have to don masks and snorkels and follow a guide underwater into Mariner's Cave, whose only light comes from the passage you just swam through. See "Exploring Vava'u," in chapter 15. You also have to swim underwater into the Piula Cave Pool in Samoa. See "Exploring Apia & the Rest of Upolu," in chapter 13.

2

Planning Your Trip to the South Pacific

The countries in this relatively safe region are all developing nations, in some cases quite rapidly developing. Every year sees new resorts, tours, restaurants, and other facilities. In other words, change is in the air out here, so wise planning is essential to get the most out of your time and money in this vast and varied modern paradise.

Fiji, Tahiti and French Polynesia, the Cook Islands, Samoa, American Samoa, and the Kingdom of Tonga have their own sources of information, entry requirements, currency, government, customs, laws, internal transportation, styles of accommodation, and food. In this chapter I give a brief description of the islands and tell you how to plan your trip in general. This information augments, but is not a substitute for, the chapters devoted to each destination.

1 The Islands in Brief

Most of the islands covered in this book are part of the Polynesian Triangle, which stretches across the vast Pacific Ocean from Hawaii to New Zealand to Easter Island. With the exception of Fiji, they are variations on an overall cultural theme. Each has its own identity, yet each is fundamentally Polynesian. Sitting on the border between Polynesia and the Melanesian islands to the west, Fiji has its own culture blending elements from both areas. The Fijians also share their islands with East Indians, who add a starkly contrasting culture to the mix.

Let's take a quick tour to see what each island country or territory contributes to this smorgasbord.

FIJI

Because its international airport at **Nadi** is the region's major transportation hub, Fiji is a prime place with which to begin or end a trip to the South Pacific. In fact, more than twice as many people visit Fiji each year as come to any other South Pacific island destination.

This lush country of 300-plus islands has something for everyone—from lying on some of the region's best beaches to

---

Impressions

The South Pacific is memorable because when you are in the islands you simply cannot ignore nature. You cannot avoid looking up at the stars, large as apples on a new tree. You cannot deafen your ear to the thunder of the surf. The bright sands, the screaming birds, and the wild winds are always with you.
—James A. Michener, *Return to Paradise*, 1951

The South Pacific

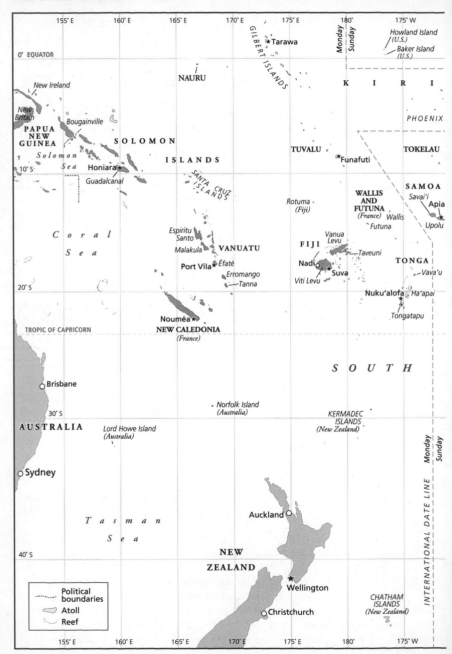

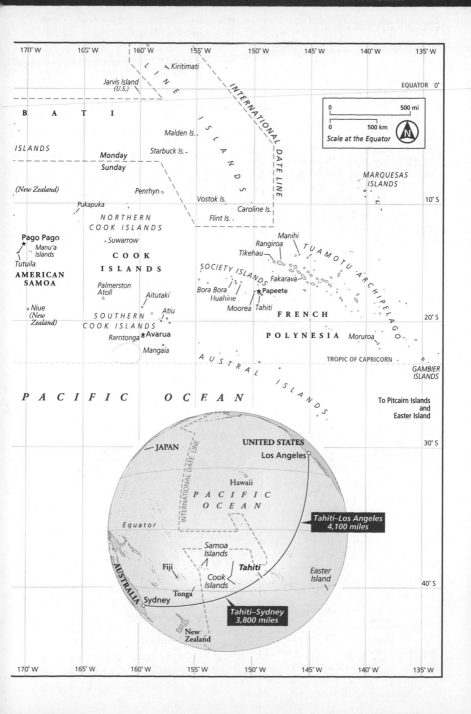

diving on some of the world's most colorful reefs, from cruising to intriguing outer islands to hiking into the mountainous interior.

Although its beaches aren't the best in Fiji, the Nadi area is home to **Denarau Island,** a tropical resort with an 18-hole golf course, a tennis center, a marina, several large hotels, and a small shopping mall. From Denarau you can cruise out to the **Mamanuca** and **Yasawa** islands, all little specks of land that are home to fine beaches, a host of watersports, and a wide range of offshore resorts.

The Queen's Road goes south from Nadi to the **Coral Coast,** Fiji's first resort area and still host to several family-oriented resorts, and to **Pacific Harbour,** site of a cultural center and golf course. Known as the Adventure Capital of Fiji, Pacific Harbour is the departure point for rafting trips on the Navua River and to the island of **Beqa** (pronounced *Beng*-ga), whose surrounding lagoon proffers some of its best diving and snorkeling.

The Queen's Road ends in **Suva,** Fiji's cosmopolitan capital city. Suva gives a glimpse through its rainy climate of the era when Great Britain ruled here. A 10-minute flight from nearby Nausori Airport will whisk you to the island of **Ovalau,** where the country's first European-style town, **Levuka,** still looks like it did in the late 1800s, before the government moved the capital to Suva.

Up in Northern Fiji, **Savusavu** and **Taveuni** will transport you back in time to the Fiji of colonial coconut plantations. Between them lies the **Somosomo Strait,** home to the Great White Wall and its Rainbow Reef, as well as other world-class dive sites.

Fiji has the South Pacific's most fascinating mix of peoples. A bit more than half the population are friendly, easygoing Fijians, most of whom still live in traditional villages surrounded by vegetable gardens. About 38% are industrious—and sometimes abrasive—Fiji Indians whose ancestors came from India to work the sugar-cane plantations that make Fiji the most self-sufficient of the South Pacific countries. Although the contrasting cultures have resulted in political unrest and four coups since 1987, it also makes this an interesting place to get into a conversation.

FRENCH POLYNESIA

If there is a "major league" of dramatically beautiful islands, then Tahiti and her French Polynesian sisters dominate it. This is especially true of **Moorea** and **Bora Bora,** which provide Hollywood with many of its choice "stock shots" of glorious tropical settings. Moorea's jagged, shark's-teeth ridges serrate the horizon like the back of some primordial dinosaur resting on the sea just 20km (12 miles) west of Tahiti. One of the world's most romantic honeymoon destinations, Bora Bora is famous for its world-class lagoon, out of which rises the main island topped by the dramatic, tombstonelike Mt. Otemanu.

High and well watered, **Tahiti** is the largest of the French Polynesian islands and was the first to be discovered by European explorers in the late 18th century. A great majority of the territory's population lives on Tahiti, especially in and around **Papeete,** the capital. Today this busy little city has so many cars, trucks, and motor scooters that it can take up to 2 hours to commute to work from the outlying regions. Although Papeete has lost much of its old South Seas charm, Tahiti's rural areas still display aspects of traditional Polynesia.

Even more of Old Polynesia exists on the territory's third-most-beautiful island, **Huahine,** which locals call "wild" because of its undeveloped status. Here you can explore some of the region's most important archaeological sites. The adjacent islands of **Raiatea** and **Tahaa** are even more natural. The two islands are enclosed by one large lagoon, making them French Polynesia's prime sailing grounds.

Off to the northeast, the line of atolls known as the **Tuamotu Archipelago** boasts French Polynesia's top scuba diving destinations. **Rangiroa,** which encloses the world's second-largest lagoon, is known for its clear waters, which are home to thousands of sharks. Sitting next to Rangiroa, **Tikehau** is considerably smaller, and its one international-standard resort sits on an islet all to itself. Also much smaller and shallower than the lagoon at Rangiroa, the fish-filled lagoon at **Manihi** makes it the world's largest producer of black pearls. Farther afield, **Fakarava** possesses the world's third-largest lagoon, most of it a marine preserve.

Even farther afield are the beautiful **Marquesas Islands,** made famous by TV's *Survivor* series.

Thanks to tons of francs poured in by the French government, the territory is the most developed, and has the highest standard of living, of any South Pacific island country. The flip side of that is that everyone pays high prices for almost everything, residents and visitors alike. Indeed, French Polynesia is the most expensive South Pacific destination. As one resident of these gorgeous islands says, "Here, you must pay for the view."

THE COOK ISLANDS

Only 800km (497 miles) west of Tahiti (virtually next door in this part of the world), the tiny Cook Islands have much in common with French Polynesia, both in physical beauty and people.

Barely 32km (20 miles) around, **Rarotonga** is a miniature Tahiti in terms of its mountains, beaches, and reefs—but in terms of development, it's like Tahiti was some 50 years ago. Unlike Papeete, however, the capital of the Cook Islands, **Avarua,** remains a quiet little backwater, a picturesque village without a stoplight. Yet no other South Pacific destination has as many hotels, restaurants, daytime activities, and nightclubs packed into so small a space as does Rarotonga.

Among the outer islands, **Aitutaki** bears the same relationship to Rarotonga as Bora Bora does to Tahiti. A small central island sits at the apex of a shallow but spectacular aquamarine lagoon fringed by some of the region's whitest, talcumlike sand beaches. Long a backwater, Aitutaki is now a thriving destination. It's worth at least a day trip to Aitutaki just to take a lagoon excursion out to the little islands fringing the reef.

The Cook Islanders share with the Tahitians a fun-loving lifestyle, many old Polynesian legends and gods, and about 60% of their native language. The Cooks were governed by New Zealand from 1901 until 1965 and still are associated with New Zealand. Consequently, most Cook Islanders speak English fluently, which makes it easy for English-speaking travelers to take advantage of the South Pacific's most informative cultural tours and exhibits. They also pay less for almost everything and use the New Zealand dollar as their local currency, which means the Cooks are more affordable than French Polynesia.

SAMOA

Once known as Western Samoa, the independent nation of **Samoa** is like a cultural museum, especially when compared with its much smaller cousin, **American Samoa.** The peoples of both are related by family and tradition, if not by politics. Samoan culture still exists in the American islands, and it is preserved to a remarkable degree in Samoa, relatively unchanged by modern materialism. Traditional Samoan villages, with their turtle-shaped houses, rest peacefully along the coasts of the two main western Samoan islands, **Upolu** and **Savai'i.** Although Samoa has been experiencing a good economy, time seems to have forgotten some of the weather-beaten, clapboard buildings that distinguish

Apia, the country's picturesque capital. Although tourism is not a major industry, the country has three luxury beach resorts from which you can fan out and meet the friendly Samoans. Experiencing their culture and visiting their truly remarkable and undeveloped beaches (one of which was the setting for the Gary Cooper movie *Return to Paradise*) are highlights of any visit. You can even sleep right on the sands in one of the country's numerous beach *fales* (small, open-air huts).

AMERICAN SAMOA

Tutuila, the main island in American Samoa, rivals the dramatic beauty of Moorea and Bora Bora in French Polynesia. The mountains drop straight down into fabled **Pago Pago,** the finest harbor in the South Pacific and the main reason that the United States has had a presence there since 1890. This American influence has resulted in a blend of cultures: the Samoan emphasis on extended families and communal ownership of property, especially land, and the Western desire for business and progress. The result of the latter is that Pago Pago harbor is dominated—and polluted—by two large tuna canneries, and large stacks of shipping containers often block the splendid views. The road around the harbor is often clogged with vehicles as American Samoans rush past their traditional villages on their way to American-style shopping centers.

TONGA

From his Victorian palace in **Nuku'alofa,** King George V of Tonga rules over a nobility that carries European titles but is in reality a pure Polynesian system of high chiefs. Despite grumbling among his subjects in recent years (some of them rioted in 2006, burning much of the capital), the king, his family, and the nobles control the government and all the land, of which they are obligated to provide 3.4 hectares (8½ acres) to every Tongan adult male.

While the relatively flat main island of **Tongatapu** offers little in the way of dramatic beauty, the adjacent lagoon provides excellent boating, snorkeling, fishing, and diving. By contrast, hilly **Vava'u** presents long and narrow fjords and a plethora of deserted islands; these features make it one of the South Pacific's leading yachting and whale-watching centers. **Neiafu,** the only town on Vava'u, is a reminder of the old days of traders and beach bums.

Indeed, Tonga is the heart of the South Pacific "Bible Belt." Things are slow on Sunday in most island countries, but they stop almost completely in Tonga—except for church, picnics at the beautiful beaches, and escapes to resorts on tiny islets offshore.

2 Visitor Information & Maps

The best sources for data and maps about the specific island countries are their tourist information offices. See "Visitor Information & Maps," in chapters 4, 7, 12, 13, 14, and 15 for details.

A good source for general information is **www.spto.org** (formerly the South Pacific Tourism Organization), P.O. Box 13119, Suva, Fiji Islands (© **679/330-4177** in Fiji.

The U.S. Department of State maintains a **Travel Advisory** (© **202/647-5225;** http://travel.state.gov) to keep you abreast of political or other problems throughout the world and posts travel warnings and other timely information.

The East-West Center at the University of Hawaii gathers news from throughout the islands on its **Pacific Islands Report** website, http://pidp.east westcenter.org/pireport. It's an excellent source for breaking news, and it has links to newspapers, news services, universities, and other useful sites.

Other useful sites for regional news are posted by the Hawaii-based *Pacific Magazine* (www.pacificmagazine.net) and Fiji-based *Islands Business Magazine* (www.islandsbusiness.com).

The best place to order quality maps of the region is from Maptown Ltd. (www.maptown.com). The Perry-Castañeda Library at the University of Texas at Austin posts free maps of the region on its website at www.lib.utexas.edu/maps/australia.html. Other free sources are www.mapsouthpacific.com, www.mapspacific.com, and www.worldatlas.com.

3 Entry Requirements

PASSPORTS

All South Pacific countries require each new arrival to have a **passport** that will be valid for 6 months beyond the duration of the visit, as well as an onward or return airline ticket. See chapters 4, 7, 12, 13, 14, and 15 for details about each country's entry requirements. For an up-to-date, country-by-country listing of passport requirements around the world, go to the "Foreign Entry Requirement" Web page of the U.S. Department of State at **http://travel.state.gov**.

For information on how to get a passport, go to "Passports," in the "Fast Facts" section at the end of this chapter.

I always keep a copy of the critical pages, with my passport number, in a separate place. The United States has embassies in Fiji and Samoa. The governor of American Samoa can issue a temporary U.S. replacement passport. Australia, New Zealand, and the United Kingdom have high commissioners in Fiji, Samoa, and Tonga.

Note that *every* individual who travels by air must have his or her own passport, regardless of age.

CUSTOMS

For information on what you can bring into and take out of the islands, go to **"Customs"** in the **"Fast Facts"** section of this chapter.

MEDICAL REQUIREMENTS

The only vaccination required anywhere in the South Pacific is for yellow fever, and then only if you're coming from an infected area of South America or Africa.

4 When to Go

THE CLIMATE

The South Pacific islands covered in this book lie within the tropics. Compared to the pronounced winters and summers of the temperate zones, there is little variation from one island group to the next: They are warm and humid all year.

Although local weather patterns have changed in the past 20 years, making conditions less predictable, local residents recognize a cooler and more comfortable **dry season** during the austral winter, from May to October. The winter trade wind blows fairly steadily during these months, bringing generally fine tropical weather throughout the area. Rarotonga in the Cook Islands and Tongatapu in Tonga are farther from the equator and see cooler temperatures. Breezy wintertime nights can feel chilly in those islands. See "When to Go," in the country chapters, for temperature ranges.

The austral summer from November through April is the warmer and more humid **wet season.** Low-pressure troughs and tropical depressions can bring several days of rain at a time, but usually heavy rain showers are followed by periods of intense sunshine. An air-conditioned hotel room or bungalow will feel like heaven during this time of year. This is also the season for tropical cyclones (hurricanes),

⟨Moments⟩ When the Moon Is Full

The islands are extraordinarily beautiful anytime, especially so at solstice time in late September and late March, when the sun's rays hit the lagoons at just the right angle to highlight the gorgeous colors out in the lagoons. The play of moonlight on the water, and the black silhouettes the mountains cast against the sky, make them even more magical when the moon is full. Keep that in mind when planning your trip—especially if it's your honeymoon.

which can be devastating and should never be taken lightly. Fortunately, they usually move fast enough that their major effect on visitors is a day or two of heavy rain and wind. If you're caught in one, the hotel employees are experts on what to do to ensure your safety.

Another factor to consider is the part of an island that you'll visit. Because moist trade winds often blow from the east, the eastern sides of the high, mountainous islands tend to be wetter all year than the western sides.

Also bear in mind that the higher the altitude, the lower the temperature. If you're going up in the mountains, be prepared for much cooler weather than you'd have on the coast.

THE BUSY SEASON

July and August are the busiest tourist months in the South Pacific. That's when Australians and New Zealanders visit the islands to escape the cold back home. It's also when residents of Tahiti head to their own outer islands, in keeping with the traditional July-August holiday break in France. Many Europeans also visit the islands during this time.

There also are busy miniseasons at school holiday time in Australia and New Zealand. These periods vary, but in general they are from the end of March

through the middle of April, 2 weeks in late May, 2 weeks at the beginning of July, 2 weeks in the middle of September, and from mid-December until mid-January. You can get a list of Australian holidays at **www.oztourism.com.au** (click on the "Holiday dates" link); for New Zealand go to **www.tourism.org.nz** (the "Utilities and Holidays" link).

Some South Pacific hoteliers raise their rates during the busy periods.

Christmas through the middle of January is a good time to get a hotel reservation in the South Pacific, but airline seats can be hard to come by, as thousands of islanders fly home from overseas.

HOLIDAYS & SPECIAL EVENTS

The chapters of this book list each country's festivals and special events, which can change the nature of a visit to the South Pacific. The annual *Heiva Nui* in French Polynesia, the Heilala Festival in Tonga, and the National Self Governing Commemoration in Rarotonga are just three examples, and every country has at least one such major celebration. These are the best times to see traditional dancing, arts, and sporting events. Be sure to make your reservations well in advance if you want to visit at celebration time, for hotel rooms and airline seats can be in short supply.

5 Getting There & Getting Around

The only practical way to, from, and among the islands is by air. Even though you can board a jetliner in Los Angeles or

Sydney in the evening and be strolling under the palm trees of Tahiti by the crack of dawn, the distances are quite vast. So be prepared for long flights: 10½ hours or more from Los Angeles to Fiji, 7½ hours to Tahiti from Los Angeles or Sydney. It takes even longer from the U.K. and Europe.

Because populations are small, flights are not nearly as frequent to and among the islands as we Westerners are used to at home. There may be only one flight weekly between some countries, and flights scheduled today may be eliminated tomorrow. The local airlines have relatively few planes, so mechanical problems can cause delays.

Only a handful of the outer-island airstrips are lighted, so there are few connecting flights after dark. Consult a travel agent or contact the airlines to find out what's happening at present. See the "Getting Around" sections in the following chapters for details.

THE AIRPORTS

Each island country has just one main international airport: **Nadi (NAN)** in Fiji; **Papeete (PPT)** on Tahiti in French Polynesia; **Rarotonga (RAR)** in the Cook Islands; **Apia (APW)** in Samoa; **Pago Pago (PPG)** in American Samoa; and **Tongatapu (TBU),** the main island in Tonga. Only Nadi (pronounced *Nahn-dee*) has enough international traffic to be considered a regional hub.

THE AIRLINES

Here, in alphabetical order, are the airlines with service to the islands (their phone numbers are in the U.S. unless otherwise noted):

- **Air New Zealand** (© **800/262-1234** or 310/615-1111; www.airnewzealand.com) flies between Auckland and all the island countries. It serves many other New Zealand cities and several in Australia, so Kiwis and Aussies can reach the islands either nonstop or by changing planes in Auckland. It's the only airline flying nonstop from Los Angeles to the

Cook Islands, Samoa, and Tonga (the planes stop there on their way between Los Angeles and Auckland). It has service from Los Angeles to Fiji and Tahiti, although the planes are flown by Air Pacific and Air Tahiti Nui (see below), on a code-share basis. It links the U.K. and Europe to Los Angeles, where passengers connect to the islands. It also flies from Japan, Hong Kong, Singapore, Seoul, Taipei, and Beijing to Auckland, with connections from there to the islands. It is a member of the Star Alliance, which includes United Airlines and several other carriers.

- **Air France** (© **800/321-4538;** www.airfrance.com) flies to Tahiti from Paris, and from London to Los Angeles, where you can connect to Tahiti.

- **Air Pacific** (© **800/227-4446;** www.airpacific.com), Fiji's international airline, has extensive service to Nadi from Sydney, Brisbane, and Melbourne in Australia, and Auckland, Wellington, and Christchurch in New Zealand. It flies its own planes 6 days a week between Nadi and Los Angeles, a service it code-shares with Air New Zealand (see above) and Qantas (see below), and once weekly between Vancouver, B.C., and Nadi via Honolulu. One of its Nadi–Honolulu flights stops in Christmas Island in the central Pacific. It code-shares with American Airlines, which provides feeder service from many U.S. and Canadian cities to Los Angeles. Within the region, it links Nadi to Samoa and Tonga, and it goes west to Vanuatu and Solomon Islands. It also provides nonstop service between Fiji and Japan.

- **Air Tahiti Nui** (© **877/824-4846;** www.airtahitinui.com), French Polynesia's national airline, has more flights—all on relatively new Airbus planes—between Tahiti and Los

> **Tips Reserve Early & Reconfirm**
>
> Planes do not always fly between all the island countries every day in this sparsely populated, far-flung region. When planning your trip, therefore, first find out the airlines' schedules, which will determine the dates you can travel. By all means book your domestic inter-island flights well in advance. You may not get on a plane at all if you wait until you arrive in the islands to take care of this important chore.
>
> Although it's unnecessary for international flights, and for domestic flights within French Polynesia, **always reconfirm** your return flight as soon as you arrive on an outer island within Fiji, the Cook Islands, Samoa, American Samoa, and Tonga. Avoid booking a return flight from an outer island on the same day your international flight is due to leave for home; give yourself plenty of leeway in case the weather or mechanical or scheduling problems prevent the plane from getting to and from the outer island on time.

Angeles than any other airline. Some of those depart early afternoon California time and arrive in Papeete before dark, so you can connect to Moorea that evening. Most return flights are overnight, but you arrive in Los Angeles early enough in the morning to make convenient connections. It also flies between New York's John F. Kennedy International Airport and Papeete. On the other end, the New York–Tahiti plane keeps going to Sydney in Australia. Air Tahiti Nui also links Paris, Tokyo, and Auckland to Papeete, and it has service between Paris and Tahiti via Los Angeles.

- **Airlines Tonga** (© **26-125** in Tonga; tetatour@kalianet.to), the only domestic carrier in Tonga, has been flying twice a week between Nadi and Vava'u, which would be handy for whale-watchers and sailors headed to Vava'u. This service can be difficult to book, however, so let your whale-watching or yacht charter firms make your flight arrangements. See "Getting Around," in chapter 15.
- **Hawaiian Airlines** (© **800/367-5320** in the continental U.S., Alaska, and Canada, or 808/838-1555 in

Honolulu; www.hawaiianair.com) flies from Los Angeles, San Francisco, Portland, and Seattle to Tahiti and to American Samoa. You must change planes in Honolulu, which can result in delays and even an unexpected Hawaiian layover. Samoans heavily book the Pago Pago flights from June through August and during holiday periods, so make your reservations as soon as possible.

- **Korean Air** (© **800/438-5000;** www.koreanair.com) has service between Seoul and Fiji. Although it's a longer distance, a connection through Seoul can be quicker from the U.K. and Europe than flying through Los Angeles.
- **LAN Chile** (© **800/735-5526;** www.lan.com) flies at least weekly between Santiago, Chile, and Tahiti by way of Easter Island.
- **Pacific Blue** (© **13-16-45** in Australia; 0800/67-0000 in New Zealand; www.flypacificblue.com), the international subsidiary of the Australian cut-rate airline Virgin Blue (itself an offshoot of Sir Richard Branson's Virgin Atlantic), has low-fare service from Australia and New Zealand to Fiji, the Cook Islands, and Tonga. It also flies

to Samoa as Polynesian Blue (see below).

- **Polynesian Airlines** (© 21-261 in Samoa; www.polynesianairlines.com), the national carrier of Samoa, connects its home base at Apia to American Samoa.
- **Polynesian Blue** (© 13-16-45 in Australia; 0800/67-0000 in New Zealand; www.polynesianblue.com), a successful joint venture between Polynesian Airlines and Pacific Blue, has low-fare service to Samoa from Sydney and Auckland.
- **Qantas Airways** (© 800/227-4500; www.qantas.com), the Australian carrier, has flights from several Australian cities and Fiji, and between Los Angeles and Fiji (its Fiji-bound passengers fly on Air Pacific planes).

FLYING FOR LESS: TIPS FOR GETTING THE BEST AIRFARE

Many tour operators specializing in the South Pacific will sell discounted airfare with or without hotel accommodations. I list some of the best under "Packages for the Independent Traveler," later in this chapter. Always check with them.

Here are some other tips:

- You may pay a fraction of the full fare passengers if you can book your ticket either **long in advance or at the last minute,** or **fly midweek** or **at less-trafficked times.** If your schedule is flexible, say so, and ask if you can secure a cheaper fare by changing your flight plans.
- Search **the Internet** for cheap fares. The most popular online travel sites are **Travelocity.com** (www.travelocity. co.uk); **Expedia.com** (www.expedia. co.uk and www.expedia.ca); and **Orbitz.com.** In the U.K., go to **Travelsupermarket** (© 0845/345-5708; www.travelsupermarket.com), a search engine that offers flight comparisons for the budget airlines whose

seats often end up in bucket-shop sales. Other websites for booking airline tickets online include **Cheapflights.com, SmarterTravel. com, Priceline.com,** and **Opodo** (www.opodo.co.uk). Meta-search sites (which find and then direct you to airline and hotel websites for booking) include **Sidestep.com** and **Kayak. com.** In addition, most **airlines** offer online-only fares through their websites. British travelers should check **Flights International** (© 0800/ 0187050; www.flights-international. com) for deals on flights all over the world.

- Keep an eye on local newspapers for **promotional specials** or **fare wars,** when airlines lower prices on their most popular routes.
- Try to book a ticket **in its country of origin.** If you're planning a one-way flight from London to Fiji, a U.K.-based travel agent will probably have the lowest fares. For foreign travelers on multileg trips, book in the country of the first leg; for example, book New York–Fiji–Sydney–New York in the U.S.
- **Consolidators,** also known as bucket shops, are wholesale brokers in the airline-ticket game. Consolidators buy deeply discounted tickets ("distressed" inventories of unsold seats) from airlines and sell them to online ticket agencies, travel agents, tour operators, corporations, and, to a lesser degree, the general public. Consolidators advertise in Sunday newspaper travel sections, both in the U.S. and the U.K. They can be great sources for cheap international tickets. On the down side, bucket shop tickets are often rigged with restrictions, such as stiff cancellation penalties (as high as 50%–75% of the ticket price). And keep in mind that most of what you see advertised is of

limited availability. Several reliable consolidators are worldwide and available online. **STA Travel** (www.statravel.com) has been the world's leading consolidator for students since purchasing Council Travel, but their fares are competitive for travelers of all ages. **Flights.com** (© 800/TRAV-800 [872-8800]; www.flights.com) has excellent fares worldwide. They also have "local" websites in 12 countries. **FlyCheap** (© 800/FLY-CHEAP [359-24327]; www.1800flycheap.com) has good fares to sunny destinations. **Air Tickets Direct** (© 800/778-3447; www.airticketsdirect.com) is based in Montreal.

- Join **frequent-flier clubs.** Frequent-flier membership doesn't cost a cent, but it does entitle you to free tickets or upgrades when you amass the airline's required number of frequent-flier points. You don't even have to fly to earn points; **frequent-flier credit cards** can earn you thousands of miles for doing your everyday shopping. Frankly, credit card miles have very low priority, so good luck trying to cash them in. Also keep in mind that award seats are limited, seats on popular routes are hard to snag, and more and more major airlines are cutting their expiration periods for mileage points—so check your airline's frequent-flier program so you don't lose your miles before you use them. *Inside tip:* Award seats are offered almost a year in advance, but seats also open up at the last minute, so if your travel plans are flexible, you may strike gold. To play the frequent-flier game to your best advantage, consult the community bulletin boards on **FlyerTalk** (www.flyertalk.com) or go to Randy Petersen's **Inside Flyer** (www.insideflyer.com). Petersen and friends review all the programs in detail and post regular updates on changes in policies and trends.

BAGGAGE ALLOWANCES

How many bags you can carry on board and check (and how much they can weigh) can vary by airline, so check with your chosen carrier before packing.

Only one rule is set in stone: Passengers on flights to or from the continental United States may check two bags each weighing up to 30 kilograms (66 lb.), with total dimensions (height, width, and length) of both not exceeding 158cm (62 in.). The allowance on flights to and from Hawaii and the South Pacific may be limited to 30 kilograms (66 lb.) per economy class passengers, 32 kilograms (70 lb.) for first and business class.

Although domestic U.S. allowances may be less, you can check this much baggage if you're connecting to an international flight. United Airlines and other U.S. carriers now charge extra for more than one checked bag, so make sure they know you're connecting to an international flight.

In general, first-class passengers on other international flights are entitled to 40 kilograms (88 lb.) of checked luggage, business-class passengers to 30 kilograms (66 lb.), and coach passengers to 20 kilograms (44 lb.). Some airlines, such as Air New Zealand and Air Pacific, strictly enforce these limits and make you pay for each kilogram over the maximum. So does Air Tahiti on its flights between Papeete and the Cook Islands.

In addition to a handbag or purse, most international passengers are permitted one carry-on, with total measurements not exceeding 115 centimeters (45 in.). Carry-on hoarders can stuff all sorts of things into a laptop bag; as long as it has a laptop in it, it's still considered a personal item (remember, however, you must remove your laptop and pass it through security separately).

Tips Getting Through the Airport

- Arrive at the airport at least 1 hour before a domestic flight and 2 hours before an international flight. You can check the average wait times at your airport by going to the TSA **Security Checkpoint Wait Times** site (http://waittime.tsa.dhs.gov).
- Know what you can carry on and what you can't. For the latest updates on items you are prohibited to bring in carry-on luggage, go to **www.tsa. gov/travelers/airtravel**.
- Beat the ticket-counter lines by using the self-service electronic ticket kiosks at the airport or even printing out your boarding pass at home from the airline website. Using curbside check-in is also a smart way to avoid lines, although this may not work for international flights.
- Help speed up security before you're screened. Remove jackets, shoes, belt buckles, heavy jewelry, and watches and place them either in your carry-on luggage or the security bins provided. Place keys, coins, cell-phones, and pagers in a security bin. If you have metallic body parts, carry a note from your doctor. Each passenger can carry on a 1-quart (1L) size clear plastic bag with zip top containing 3.4 ounces (100mL) or less bottles of liquids. Otherwise, keep liquids in checked baggage.
- Make sure the batteries in your camera, iPod, laptop, and other electronic gear are charged, in case you are asked to turn them on.
- Use a TSA-approved lock for your checked luggage. Travel Sentry certified locks are widely available at luggage or travel shops, at Brookstone stores (or online at www.brookstone.com), and at office supply stores such as Staples, Office Depot, and OfficeMax.

Note: Many domestic air carriers in the islands limit their baggage allowance to 10 kilograms (22 lb.), which I point out in the following chapters. Check with the individual airlines to avoid showing up at the check-in counter with too much luggage. Most hotels in the main towns have storage facilities where you can leave your extra bags during side trips.

LONG-HAUL FLIGHTS: HOW TO STAY COMFORTABLE

Australians and New Zealanders have relatively short flights to the islands. The rest of us will spend considerable time flying. Here are some tips on how to stay comfortable for the long haul:

- Your choice of airline and airplane will affect your leg room. Find more details about U.S. airlines at **www. seatguru.com**. For international airlines, Skytrax has posted a list of average seat pitches at **www.airline quality.com**.
- Emergency exit seats and bulkhead seats typically have the most legroom. Emergency exit seats are usually left unassigned until the day of a flight (to ensure that someone able-bodied fills the seats); it's worth getting to the ticket counter early to snag one of these for a long flight. Many passengers find that bulkhead seating (the row facing the wall at the front of the cabin) offers more legroom, but keep

Tips Coping with Jet Lag

Except for Air Tahiti Nui's afternoon departures from Los Angeles bound for the islands (see "The Airlines"), flights from North America, including connecting flights from the U.K. and Europe, leave after dark, which means you will fly overnight and cross at least two time zones. For those of us traveling from the Northern Hemisphere, this invariably translates into jet lag. Here are some tips for combating this malady:

- **Reset your watch** to your destination time before you board the plane.
- **Drink lots of water** before, during, and after your flight. Avoid alcohol.
- **Exercise and sleep well** for a few days before your trip.
- Daylight is the key to resetting your body clock. At the website for **Outside In** (www.bodyclock.com), you can get a customized plan of when to seek and avoid light.
- If you need help getting to sleep and staying asleep, some doctors recommend taking melatonin or Ambien—but not together. Take 2 to 5 milligrams of melatonin about 2 hours before your planned bedtime.

in mind that bulkhead seats have no storage space on the floor in front of you.

- To have two seats for yourself in a three-seat row, try for an aisle seat in a center section toward the back of coach. If you're traveling with a companion, book an aisle and a window seat. Middle seats are usually booked last, so chances are good you'll end up with three seats to yourselves. And in the event that a third passenger is assigned the middle seat, he or she will probably be more than happy to trade for a window or an aisle.
- Ask about entertainment options. Many airlines offer seatback video systems where you get to choose your movies or play video games—but only on some of their planes. (Boeing 777s are your best bet.)
- To sleep, avoid the last row of any section or the row in front of an

emergency exit, as these seats are the least likely to recline. Avoid seats near toilet areas. Avoid seats in the back of many jets—these can be narrower than those in the rest of coach. Or reserve a window seat so you can rest your head and avoid being bumped in the aisle.

- Get up, walk around, and stretch every 60 to 90 minutes to keep your blood flowing. This helps avoid **deep-vein thrombosis.** See the box "Avoiding 'Economy Class Syndrome,'" on p. 37.
- Drink water before, during, and after your flight to combat the lack of humidity in airplane cabins. Avoid alcohol, which will dehydrate you.
- When flying with kids, don't forget to carry on toys, books, pacifiers, and snacks and chewing gum to help them relieve ear pressure buildup during ascent and descent.

6 General Travel Resources

MONEY & COSTS

I always bring a mix of cash, credit and debit cards, and traveler's checks. It's

impractical to change cash into most island currencies before leaving home, so my first stop upon arrival is at an airport

ATM or exchange counter to get enough local cash to cover airport incidentals, tipping, and hotel transfer.

How much money you will need depends to a large extent on which islands you decide to visit and which currency you use. French Polynesia is far and away the most expensive, with costs comparable to or exceeding most major U.S. cities. This is especially so for those of us spending depressed U.S. dollars, because the French Polynesian currency is pegged to the Euro. Prices are more reasonable in the Cook Islands, though they will seem relatively expensive to New Zealanders. Samoa and Tonga are the least expensive, with Fiji in between. Overall, the islands will cost more than most Southeast Asian destinations.

CURRENCIES

The Cook Islands use **New Zealand dollars** (NZ$ in this book, or NZD in bank lingo), and American Samoa spends **U.S. dollars** (US$, or USD). Other South Pacific countries have their own currencies—**Fiji dollars** (F$ or FID), **French Pacific francs** (CFP or XFP), **Samoan tala** (S$, WST, or SAT), and **Tongan pa'anga** (T$ or TOP). See "Money" in the country chapters.

To find up-to-the-minute exchange rates, go to **www.xe.com**.

U.S., Australian, and New Zealand dollars are widely accepted (euros, too, in French Polynesia), and the local banks will change other major currencies.

You'll get a better exchange rate at a bank or currency exchange shop than at a hotel or store. Most banks charge a set fee to change notes and traveler's checks, which can wipe out the advantage if you're changing small denominations.

ATMS

Automated teller machines (ATMs), sometimes referred to as "cash machines" or "cashpoints," are becoming more widespread in the islands and are the easiest way to get local currency. I tell you in the "Fast Facts" section whether an island has ATM machines. Be sure to read this information—or check with the banks or tourist offices in the main towns—before heading off cashless to an outer island.

The **Cirrus** (© 800/424-7787; www. mastercard.com) and **PLUS** (© 800/843-7587; www.visa.com) networks are present in the islands.

I carry two debit (that is, "cash" or "check") cards so that if one doesn't work in a bank's ATM, I have a backup. I use them to get local cash for two reasons: I get a better exchange rate than if I had changed traveler's checks, and I avoid the local banks' exchange fees.

Visa and MasterCard tack a 1% currency conversion fee to every debit card withdrawal, and many banks add up to 5% as their own "foreign transaction fee." In addition, many banks impose a fee every time you use a card at another bank's ATM, and that fee can be even higher for international transactions (up

---

Tips Small Change

When I change money (or after I've withdrawn local currency from an ATM), I ask for some small bills, as petty cash comes in handy for public transportation (South Pacific taxi drivers never seem to have change for large bills). I keep my small money separate from my larger bills, so it's readily accessible while my big notes are less of a target for thieves. I also go first to WestPac Bank's ATMs, which usually dispense smaller notes than those at ANZ Bank (they are the major banks out here).

to $5 or more). Ask your bank about its international withdrawal fees.

Be sure you know your **personal identification number (PIN)** for each card before you leave home, and be sure to find out your daily withdrawal limit before you depart. Four-digit PINs work in the islands.

CREDIT CARDS

You can withdraw cash advances from your credit cards at banks or ATMs, but high withdrawal fees make credit card cash advances a pricey way to get cash. In addition to the fees, you'll pay interest from the moment of your withdrawal, even if you pay your bills on time.

On the other hand, you can use MasterCard and Visa cards to charge your expenses at most island hotels, car-rental companies, restaurants, and large shops. Many also accept American Express. Only the major hotels and car-rental firms accept Diners Club, however; and none takes Discover cards. Always ask first, and when you're away from the main towns, don't count on putting anything on plastic.

Also, note that many banks now assess a 1% to 3% "transaction fee" on **all** charges you incur abroad (whether you're using the local currency or your native currency). I use my Capital One credit card because it charges no foreign transaction fee, nor does it have an annual fee. Read your card member agreement—or call the customer service department—for charges.

TRAVELER'S CHECKS

I seldom use them, but I carry a few hundred U.S. dollars in traveler's checks in case the local ATM runs out of cash or is on the blink. You can get traveler's checks at most banks in denominations of $20, $50, $100, $500, and sometimes $1,000. Generally, you'll pay a service charge ranging from 1% to 4%.

The most popular traveler's checks are offered by **American Express** (© 800/807-6233 or © 800/221-7282 for card holders—this number accepts collect calls, offers service in several foreign languages, and exempts Amex gold and platinum cardholders from the 1% fee.); **Visa** (© 800/732-1322)—AAA members can obtain Visa checks for a $9.95 fee (for checks up to $1,500) at most AAA offices or by calling © 866/339-3378; and **MasterCard** (© 800/223-9920).

Be sure to keep a record of the traveler's checks serial numbers separate from your checks in the event that they are stolen or lost. You'll get a refund faster if you know the numbers.

TRAVEL INSURANCE

I buy travel insurance for my South Pacific trips for three prime reasons. First, the airlines out here have relatively few planes, thus the chances of a canceled or delayed flight are greater than in more populous areas of the world. Second, health care is not up to Western standards in most islands, so I like the idea of having medical evacuation coverage in case of an emergency. And third, there always is a chance that hurricanes or other unforeseen events can seriously disrupt my travel plans between November and March.

Check your existing insurance policies and credit card coverage before you buy

---

Tips Credit Card Add-Ons

Many island businesses add 3% to 5% to your bill if you use a credit card, while others may offer a similar discount for cash payments. Credit card issuers frown on the add-ons, but the locals do it anyway. Always ask if there's an add-on or discount.

Tips Getting Rid of Your Leftover Currency

Use your leftover currency to pay part of your hotel bill when leaving the South Pacific. Put the rest on your credit card. It will save you the trouble of having to change it at the airport.

---

travel insurance. You may already be covered for lost luggage, cancelled tickets or medical expenses.

The cost of travel insurance varies widely, depending on the destination, the cost and length of your trip, your age and health, and the type of trip you're taking, but expect to pay between 5% and 8% of the vacation itself. You can get estimates from various providers through **Insure-MyTrip.com**. Enter your trip cost and dates, your age, and other information, for prices from more than a dozen companies.

The major U.S. travel insurers are **Access America** (© 866/807-3982; www.accessamerica.com); **Travel Guard International** (© 800/826-4919; www.travelguard.com); **Travel Insured International** (© 800/243-3174; www.travelinsured.com); **Travelex Insurance Services** (© 888/457-4602; www.travelexinsurance.com); and **Travel Assistance International** (© 800/821-2828 or 202/331-1596; www.travelassistance.com). The latter is a U.S. agent for **Europ Assistance** (www.europ-assistance.com), one of the largest worldwide travel insurers.

U.K. citizens and their families who make more than one trip abroad per year may find an annual travel insurance policy works out cheaper. Check **www.money supermarket.com**, which compares prices across a range of providers for single- and multitrip policies.

Most big travel agents offer their own insurance and will probably try to sell you their package when you book a holiday. Think before you sign. **Britain's Consumers' Association** recommends that you insist on seeing the policy and reading the fine print before buying travel insurance. **The Association of British Insurers** (© 020/7600-3333; www.abi.org.uk) gives advice by phone and publishes *Holiday Insurance*, a free guide to policy provisions and prices. You might also shop around for better deals: Try **Columbus Direct** (© 0870/033-9988; www.columbusdirect.net).

TRIP-CANCELLATION INSURANCE

Trip-cancellation insurance will help retrieve your money if you have to back out of a trip or depart early, or if your travel supplier goes bankrupt. Trip cancellation traditionally covers such events as sickness, natural disasters, and Department of State advisories. The latest news in trip-cancellation insurance is the availability of **expanded hurricane coverage** and the **"any-reason"** coverage—which costs more but covers cancellations made for any reason. You won't get back 100% of your prepaid trip cost, but you'll be refunded a substantial portion. **Travel-Safe** (© 888/885-7233; www.travelsafe.com) offers both types. Expedia offers any-reason cancellation coverage for its air-hotel packages.

MEDICAL INSURANCE

I always buy a travel insurance policy that includes both health coverage and medical evacuation in case of life-threatening injury or illness. Otherwise, the cost of a flying ambulance would wipe out my life's savings.

Most U.S. health plans (including Medicare and Medicaid) do not provide coverage outside the United States, and the ones that do often require you to pay for services upfront and reimburse you only after you return home.

If you require additional medical insurance, try **MEDEX Assistance** (② 410/453-6300; www.medexassist.com) or **Travel Assistance International** (② 800/821-2828; www.travelassistance.com), the U.S. agent for **Europ Assistance** (www.europ-assistance.com). **American Express** (www.americanexpress.com) cardholders can sign up for a standing travel policy providing health and medical evacuation coverage whenever they are more than 150 miles from home.

Canadians should check with their provincial health plan offices or call **Health Canada** (② 866/225-0709; www.hc-sc.gc.ca) to find out the extent of their coverage and what documentation and receipts they must present in case they are treated overseas.

LOST-LUGGAGE INSURANCE

On international flights (including U.S. portions of international trips), baggage coverage is limited to approximately $9.07 per pound, up to about $635 per checked bag. If you plan to check items more valuable than what's covered by the standard liability, see if your homeowner's policy covers your valuables, get baggage insurance as part of your travel-insurance package, or buy Travel Guard's "BagTrak" product.

If your luggage is lost, immediately file a lost-luggage claim at the airport, detailing the luggage contents. Most airlines require that you report delayed, damaged, or lost baggage within 4 hours of arrival. The airlines are required to

deliver luggage, once found, directly to your house or destination free of charge.

CAR-RENTAL INSURANCE

Your own auto insurance policy may cover you for loss or damage to the car and liability in case a passenger is injured. The credit card you used to rent the car also may provide some coverage. Check your own insurance policy, the rental company policy, and your credit card coverage for the extent of coverage.

Even if you have such coverage, rental car companies in the islands are likely to require that you pay for any damages on the scene and sort it out with your insurer or credit card company when you get home. Given the hassles this can cause, I always buy the collision damage waiver and liability policies offered by the local companies. It adds to the cost, but it's a small price to pay for peace of mind.

HEALTH
STAYING HEALTHY

The South Pacific islands covered in this book pose no major health problems for most travelers, although it's a good idea to have your tetanus, hepatitis-A, and hepatitis-B vaccinations up to date.

If you have a chronic condition, check with your doctor before visiting the islands. For such conditions as epilepsy, diabetes, or heart problems, wear a **Medic Alert Identification Tag** (② 800/825-3785; www.medicalert.org), which will alert doctors to your condition and give them access to your records through MedicAlert's 24-hour hot line.

And don't forget **sunglasses** and an extra pair of **contact lenses** or **prescription glasses.** You can easily replace your

---

Tips Band-Aids

Cuts, scratches, and all open sores should be treated promptly in the tropics. I always carry a tube of antibacterial ointment and a small package of adhesive bandages such as Band-Aids.

> ## ⌜Tips⌝ Multitudes of Animals
>
> Don't bother complaining to me about the multitude of dogs, chickens, pigs, and squawking myna birds running loose, even in the finest restaurants. They are as much a part of life as the islanders themselves. And don't be frightened by those little **geckos** (lizards) crawling around the rafters of even the most expensive bungalows. They're harmless to us humans but lethal to insects.

contacts and prescription lenses only in French Polynesia, the Cook Islands, and Fiji.

Contact the **International Association for Medical Assistance to Travelers** (IAMAT) (℃ **716/754-4883** or, in Canada, 416/652-0137; www.iamat.org) for tips on travel and health concerns in the countries you're visiting, and for lists of local, English-speaking doctors. The United States **Centers for Disease Control and Prevention** (℃ **800/311-3435;** www.cdc.gov) provides up-to-date information on health hazards by region or country and offers tips on food safety. **Travel Health Online** (www.tripprep. com), sponsored by a consortium of travel medicine practitioners, may also offer helpful advice on traveling abroad. You can find listings of reliable medical clinics overseas at the **International Society of Travel Medicine** (www.istm.org).

COMMON AILMENTS
Among minor illnesses, the islands have the common cold and occasional outbreaks of influenza and conjunctivitis (pink eye).

TROPICAL ILLNESSES There are plenty of mosquitoes but they do not carry deadly endemic diseases such as malaria. From time to time the islands will experience an outbreak of **dengue fever,** a viral disease borne by the *Adës aegypti* mosquito, which lives indoors and bites only during daylight hours. Dengue seldom is fatal in adults, but you should take extra precautions to keep children from being bitten by mosquitoes if the

disease is present. (Other precautions should be taken if you are traveling with children; see "Specialized Travel Resources," below.)

BUGS, BITES & OTHER WILDLIFE CONCERNS YOU WILL FIND THAT WE COOK ISLANDERS ARE AMONG THE FRIENDLIEST PEOPLE IN THE SOUTH PACIFIC, a sign in a Cook Island resort advises its guests. AMONGST ALL THE FRIENDLY PEOPLE, WE ALSO HAVE THE FRIENDLIEST ANTS, ROACHES, GECKOS, CRABS, AND INSECTS, WHO ARE ALL DYING TO MAKE YOUR ACQUAINTANCE.

Indeed, the South Pacific islands have multitudes of mosquitoes, roaches, ants, houseflies, and other insects. **Ants** are omnipresent here, so don't leave crumbs or dirty dishes lying around your room. Many beaches and swampy areas also have invisible **sand flies**—the dreaded "no-see-ums" or "no-nos"—which bite the ankles around daybreak and dusk.

Insect repellent is widely available. The most effective contain a high percentage of deet (N,N-diethyl-m-toluamide).

I light a mosquito coil in my non-air-conditioned rooms at dusk to keep the pests from flying in, and I start another at bedtime. Grocery stores throughout the islands carry these inexpensive coils. I have found the Fish brand coils, made by the appropriately named Blood Protection Company, to work best.

SUN EXPOSURE The tropical sun in the islands can be brutal, even on what seems like an overcast day. Accordingly, it's important to use sunscreen whenever

Tips Be Careful in the Water

Most of the South Pacific's marine creatures are harmless to humans, but there are some to avoid. Always **seek local advice** before snorkeling or swimming in a lagoon away from the hotel beaches. Many diving operators conduct snorkeling tours. If you don't know what you're doing, go with them.

Wash and apply a good antiseptic or antibacterial ointment to all **coral cuts and scrapes** as soon as possible.

Because coral cannot grow in fresh water, the flow of rivers and streams into the lagoon creates narrow channels, known as **passes,** through the reef. Currents can be very strong in the passes, so stay in the protected, shallow water of the inner lagoons.

Sharks are curious beasts that are attracted by bright objects such as watches and knives, so be careful what you wear in the water. Don't swim in areas where sewage or edible wastes are dumped, and never swim alone if you have any suspicion that sharks might be present. If you do see a shark, don't splash in the water or urinate. Calmly retreat and get out of the water as quickly as you can, without creating a disturbance.

Those round things on the rocks and reefs that look like pin cushions are **sea urchins,** and their calcium spikes can be more painful than needles. A sea-urchin puncture can result in burning, aching, swelling, and discoloration (black or purple) around the area where the spines entered your skin. The best thing to do is to pull any protruding spines out. The body will absorb the spines within 24 hours to 3 weeks, or the remainder of the spines will work themselves out. Contrary to popular advice, do not urinate or pour vinegar on the embedded spines—this will not help.

Jellyfish stings can hurt like the devil but are seldom life-threatening. You need to get any visible tentacles off your body right away, but not with your hands, unless you are wearing gloves. Use a stick or anything else that is handy. Then rinse the sting with salt- or freshwater, and apply ice to prevent swelling and to help control the pain. If you can find it at an island grocery store, Adolph's Meat Tenderizer is a great antidote.

The **stone fish** is so named because it looks like a piece of stone or coral as it lies buried in the sand on the lagoon bottom with only its back and 13 venomous spikes sticking out. Its venom can cause paralysis and even death. You'll know by the intense pain if you've been stuck. Serum is available, so get to a hospital at once.

Sea snakes, cone shells, crown-of-thorns starfish, moray eels, lionfish, and **demon stingers** can also be painful, if not deadly. The last thing any of them wants to do is to tangle with a human, so keep your hands to yourself.

you're outdoors, especially at midday. This is particularly true for children.

HIV/AIDS Throughout the islands, sexual relations before marriage—heterosexual, homosexual, and bisexual—are more or less accepted (abstinence campaigns fall on deaf ears here). Both male and female prostitution is common in the larger towns. HIV is present in the islands, so if you intend to engage in sex with strangers, you should exercise *at least* the same caution in choosing them, and in practicing safe sex, as you would at home.

WHAT TO DO IF YOU GET SICK AWAY FROM HOME

Hospitals and clinics are widespread in the South Pacific, but the quality varies a great deal from place to place. You can get a broken bone set and a coral scrape tended, but treating more serious ailments likely will be beyond the capability of the local hospital everywhere except in Tahiti. I list hospitals and emergency numbers under "Fast Facts," in the country chapters.

You may have to pay all medical costs upfront and be reimbursed later. Medicare and Medicaid do not provide coverage for medical costs outside the U.S. Before leaving home, find out what medical services your health insurance covers. To protect yourself, consider buying medical travel insurance (see "Medical Insurance," under "Travel Insurance," above).

Very few health insurance plans pay for medical evacuation back to the U.S., the U.K., or Europe (which can cost $10,000 and up). A number of companies offer medical evacuation services anywhere in the world. If you're ever hospitalized more than 150 miles from home, **Medjet Assist** (© **800/527-7478;** www.medjet assistance.com) will pick you up and fly you to the hospital of your choice virtually anywhere in the world in a medically equipped and staffed aircraft 24 hours day, 7 days a week. Annual memberships are $225 individual, $350 family; you can also purchase short-term memberships.

U.K. nationals will need a **European Health Insurance Card (EHIC)** to receive free or reduced-cost health benefits during a visit to a European Economic Area (EEA) country (European Union countries plus Iceland, Liechtenstein, and Norway) or Switzerland. The European Health Insurance Card replaces the E111 form, which is no longer valid. For advice, ask at your local post office or see **www.dh.gov.uk/travellers**.

All the islands have pharmacies and drug stores which carry over-the-counter and **prescription medications.** Most medications can be purchased without a prescription, but bring your own medications (in your carry-on luggage), in their original containers. Also bring along copies of your prescriptions in case you lose your pills or run out. Carry the generic name of medicines, because local pharmacies primarily carry medications manufactured in France, Australia, and New Zealand, and the brand names might be different than in the United States.

Avoiding "Economy-Class Syndrome"

Deep-vein thrombosis, or as it's known in the world of flying, "economy-class syndrome," is a blood clot that develops in a deep vein. It's a potentially deadly condition that can be caused by sitting in cramped conditions—such as an airplane cabin—for too long. During a long-haul flight, get up, walk around, and stretch your legs every 60 to 90 minutes. Other preventative measures include frequent flexing of the legs while sitting, drinking lots of water, and avoiding alcohol and sleeping pills. If you have a history of deep vein thrombosis, heart disease, or another condition that puts you at high risk, some experts recommend wearing compression stockings or taking anticoagulants when you fly; always ask your physician about the best course for you. Symptoms of deep vein thrombosis include leg pain or swelling, or even shortness of breath.

Healthy Travels to You

The following government websites offer up-to-date health-related travel advice.

- **Australia:** www.smartraveller.gov.au
- **Canada:** www.hc-sc.gc.ca/index_e.html
- **U.K.:** www.dh.gov.uk/en/Healthcare/Healthadvicefortravellers/index.htm
- **U.S.:** www.cdc.gov/travel

STAYING SAFE

While international terrorism is a threat throughout the world, the South Pacific islands are among the planet's safest destinations. Tight security procedures are in effect at the major airports, but once you're on the outer islands, you are unlikely to see a metal detector, nor is anyone likely to inspect your carry-on.

The region has seen increasing property theft in recent years, however, including occasional break-ins at hotel rooms and resort bungalows. Although street crimes against tourists are still relatively rare, friends of mine who live here don't stroll off Papeete's busy boulevard Pomare after dark, and they keep a sharp eye peeled everywhere in Fiji. For that matter, you should stay alert wherever you are after dusk.

Don't leave valuable items in your hotel room, in your rental car, or unattended. See the "Fast Facts" sections in the following chapters for specific precautions.

Women should not wander alone on deserted beaches any time, as some Polynesian men may consider such behavior to be an invitation for instant amorous activity.

When heading outdoors, keep in mind that injuries often occur when people fail to follow instructions. Hike only in designated areas, swim and snorkel only where you see other people swimming and snorkeling, follow the marine charts if piloting your own boat, carry rain gear, and wear a life jacket when canoeing or rafting. Mountain weather can be fickle at any time. Watch out for sudden storms that can leave you drenched and send bolts of lightning your way.

7 Specialized Travel Resources

TRAVELERS WITH DISABILITIES

Most disabilities shouldn't stop anyone from traveling, even in the South Pacific islands, where ramps, handles, accessible toilets, automatic opening doors, telephones at convenient heights, and other helpful aids in Western countries are just beginning to appear.

Some hotels provide rooms specially equipped for people with disabilities. Such improvements are ongoing; I have pointed out some of them in this book, but inquire when making a reservation whether such rooms are available.

The major international airlines make special arrangements for handicapped persons. Be sure to tell them of your needs when you reserve. Although most local airlines use small planes that are not equipped for disabled passengers, their staffs go out of their way to help everyone get in and out of the craft.

Organizations that offer a vast range of resources and assistance to disabled travelers include **MossRehab** (© 800/ **CALL-MOSS** [225-56677]; www.moss resourcenet.org); the **American Foundation for the Blind (AFB)** (© 800/ **232-5463;** www.afb.org); and **SATH (Society for Accessible Travel & Hospitality)** (© 212/447-7284; www.sath. org). **AirAmbulanceCard.com** is now partnered with SATH and allows you to preselect top-notch hospitals in case of an emergency. **Access-Able Travel Source** (© **303/ 232-2979;** www.access-able.com) offers a database on travel agents from around the world with experience in accessible travel; destination-specific access information; and links to such resources as service animals, equipment rentals, and access guides.

Many travel agencies offer customized tours and itineraries for travelers with disabilities. Among them are **Flying Wheels Travel** (© **507/451-5005;** www.flying wheelstravel.com); and **Accessible Journeys** ((© **800/846-4537** or 610/521-0339; www.disabilitytravel.com).

Flying with Disability (www.flying-with-disability.org) is a comprehensive information source on airplane travel.

Avis Rent a Car (© **888/879-4273**) has an "Avis Access" program that offers services for customers with special travel needs. These include specially outfitted vehicles with swivel seats, spinner knobs, and hand controls; mobility scooter rentals; and accessible bus service. Be sure to reserve well in advance.

Also check out the quarterly magazine *Emerging Horizons* (www.emerging horizons.com), available by subscription ($17 per year in the U.S.; $22 outside U.S). The "Accessible Travel" link at **Mobility-Advisor.com** offers a variety of travel resources to disabled persons.

British travelers should contact **Holiday Care** (© **0845/124-9971** in UK only; www.holidaycare.org.uk) to access a range of travel information and resources for disabled and elderly people.

GAY & LESBIAN TRAVELERS

Although homosexuality is officially frowned upon by local laws and by some local religious leaders, especially in Fiji, an old Polynesian custom makes the South Pacific a relatively friendly destination for gay men.

In the islands, many families with a shortage of female offspring rear young boys as girls, or at least relegate them to female chores around the home and village. These males-raised-as-girls are known as *mahus* in Tahiti, *magus* in Samoa, and *fakaleitis* in Tonga. Some of them grow up to be heterosexual; others become homosexual or bisexual and, often appearing publicly in women's attire, actively seek the company of tourists. Some dance the female parts in traditional island night shows. You'll see them throughout the islands; many hold jobs in hotels and restaurants.

On the other hand, women were not considered equal in this respect in ancient times, and lesbianism was discouraged.

The International Gay & Lesbian Travel Association (IGLTA) (© **800/ 448-8550** or 954/776-2626; fax 954/776-3303; www.iglta.org) is the trade association for the gay and lesbian travel industry, and offers an online directory of gay and lesbian-friendly travel businesses; go to their website and click on "Members."

Many agencies offer tours and travel itineraries specifically for gay and lesbian travelers. **MIM Travel** (© **877/844-8055;** www.gay-travel-by-mim.com) recently had a gay cruise aboard the *Tahitian Princess,* while **Now, Voyager** (© **800/255-6951;** www.nowvoyager. com) had one on the *Star Flyer* (both in French Polynesia; see chapter 7). Also check out **Above and Beyond Tours** (© **800/397-2681;** www.abovebeyond tours.com), a gay Australia tour specialist, and **Olivia** (© **800/631-6277;** www. olivia.com), offering lesbian cruises and resort vacations.

Gay.com Travel (© **800/929-2268** or 415/644-8044; www.gay.com/travel or www.outandabout.com) is an excellent online successor to the popular *Out & About* print magazine. It provides regularly updated information about gay-owned, gay-oriented, and gay-friendly lodging, dining, sightseeing, nightlife, and shopping establishments in every important destination worldwide. British travelers should click on the "Travel" link at **www.uk.gay.com** for advice and gay-friendly trip ideas.

The Canadian website **GayTraveler** (gaytraveler.ca) offers ideas and advice for gay travel all over the world.

The following travel guides are available at many bookstores, or you can order them online: *Spartacus International Gay Guide, 37th Edition* (Bruno Gmünder Verlag; www.spartacusworld. com/gayguide) and the *Damron* guides (www.damron.com), with books for gay men and lesbians.

SENIOR TRAVEL

Children are cared for in the South Pacific's extended family systems, and so are senior citizens. Most islanders live with their families from birth to death. Consequently, local governments don't provide programs and other benefits for persons of retirement age. You won't find many senior citizen discounts. Children get them; seniors don't.

Nevertheless, mention the fact that you're a senior citizen when you first make your travel reservations. Some airlines and many chain hotels offer discounts for seniors.

Elderhostel, 75 Federal St., Boston, MA 02110-1941 (© **877/426-8056;** www.elderhostel.org), arranges study programs for those ages 55 and older (and a spouse or companion of any age) in the United States and in more than 80 countries. Most include airfare, modest accommodations, meals, and tuition. One recent trip included a 2-week cruise to the Marquesas Islands in French Polynesia.

Members of **AARP,** 601 E St. NW, Washington, DC 20049 (© **888/687-2277** or 202/434-2277; www.aarp.org), get discounts on hotels, airfares, and car rentals. AARP offers members a wide range of benefits, including *AARP: The Magazine* and a monthly newsletter. Anyone over 50 can join.

FAMILY TRAVEL

The islanders adore infants and young children, but childhood does not last as long in the South Pacific as it does in Western societies. As soon as they are capable, children are put to work, first caring for their younger siblings and cousins and helping out with household chores, later tending the village gardens. It's only as teenagers, and then only if they leave their villages for town, that they know unemployment in the Western sense. Accordingly, few towns and villages have children's facilities, such as playgrounds, outside school property.

On the other hand, the islanders invariably love children and are very good at babysitting. Just make sure you get one who speaks English. The hotels can take care of this for you.

The larger hotels in Fiji and the Cook Islands cater to Australian and New Zealander families with ample activities for all ages. Even some smaller resorts, such as **Jean-Michel Cousteau Fiji Islands Resort** in northern Fiji, welcome families (see chapter 6). Although most are oriented for couples, many French Polynesian resorts also welcome children. Best is the **Le Meridien Bora Bora** (see chapter 10).

Some resorts do not accept children at all; I point those out in the establishment listings, but you should ask to make sure. Even if they do, check whether the hotel can provide cribs and other needs, and if they have children's menus.

Disposable diapers, cotton swabs (known as Buds, not Q-Tips), and baby food are sold in many main-town stores, but you should take along a supply of such items as children's aspirin, a thermometer, adhesive bandages, and special medications. Make sure your children's vaccinations are up-to-date. If your children are very small, perhaps you should discuss your travel plans with your family doctor. Remember to protect youngsters with ample sunscreen.

Other tips: Some tropical plants and animals may resemble rocks or vegetation, so teach your youngsters to avoid touching or brushing up against rocks, seaweed, and other objects. If your children are prone to swimmer's ear, use vinegar or preventive drops before they go swimming in freshwater streams or lakes. Have them shower soon after swimming or suffering cuts or abrasions.

Rascals in Paradise, One Daniel Burnham Court, Suite 105-C, San Francisco, CA 94107 (℃ **415/921-7000;** fax 415/921-7050; www.rascalsinparadise.com), specializes in organizing South Pacific tours for families with kids, including visits with local families and children.

Adventures Abroad (℃ **800/665-3998;** www.adventures-abroad.com) organizes 1-week family sightseeing tours around Viti Levu in Fiji, including village and market village visits.

WOMEN TRAVELERS

The South Pacific islands are relatively safe for women traveling alone, but don't let the charm of warm nights and smiling faces lull you into any less caution than you would exercise at home. *Do not* wander alone on deserted beaches. In the old days this was an invitation for sex. If that's what you want today, then that's what you're likely to get. Otherwise, it could result in your being raped.

And don't hitchhike alone, either.

Check out the award-winning website **Journeywoman** (www.journeywoman.com), a "real life" women's travel-information network where you can sign up for a free e-mail newsletter and get advice on everything from etiquette and dress to safety. The travel guide *Safety and Security for Women Who Travel* by Sheila Swan and Peter Laufer (Travelers' Tales Guides), offering common-sense tips on safe travel, was updated in 2004.

AFRICAN-AMERICAN TRAVELERS

Among general sources for African-American travelers, **Black Travel Online** (www.blacktravelonline.com) posts news on upcoming events and includes links to articles and travel-booking sites. **Soul of America** (www.soulofamerica.com) is a comprehensive website, with travel tips, event and family reunion postings, and sections on historically black beach resorts and active vacations.

Agencies and organizations that provide resources for black travelers include: **Rodgers Travel** (℃ **800/825-1775;** www.rodgerstravel.com); the **African American Association of Innkeepers International** (℃ **877/422-5777;** www.africanamericaninns.com); and **Henderson Travel & Tours** (℃ **800/327-2309** or 301/650-5700; www.hendersontravel.com), which has specialized in trips to Africa since 1957.

Go Girl: The Black Woman's Guide to Travel & Adventure (Eighth Mountain Press) is a compilation of travel essays by writers including Jill Nelson and Audre Lorde. *The African-American Travel Guide* by Wayne C. Robinson (Hunter Publishing; www.hunterpublishing.com) was published in 1997, so it may be somewhat dated. The well-done *Pathfinders Magazine* (℃ **877/977-PATH** [7284]; www.pathfinderstravel.com) includes articles on everything from Rio de Janeiro to Ghana to upcoming ski, diving, golf, and tennis trips.

STUDENT TRAVEL

The South Pacific islands have one of the most developed backpacker industries in the world, especially in Fiji and the Cook Islands.

You won't find any student discounts, however, so a student ID card won't do you much good in the islands. If you're going on to New Zealand and Australia, you'd be wise to get an **international student I.D. card** from the **International Student Travel Confederation (ISTC)** (www.istc.org), which offers savings on plane tickets. It also provides basic health and life insurance and a 24-hour help line. You can apply for the card online or in person at **STA Travel** (© 800/ 781-4040 in North America; www.sta travel.com), the biggest student travel agency in the world; check out the website to locate STA Travel offices worldwide.

If you're no longer a student but are still under 26, you can get an **International Youth Travel Card (IYTC)** for the same price from the same people. The card offers some discounts (but not on museum admissions).

Travel CUTS (© 800/667-2887 or 416/614-2887; www.travelcuts.com) offers similar services for Canada and U.S. residents. Irish students may prefer to turn to **USIT** (© 01/602-1904; www. usitnow.ie), an Ireland-based specialist in student, youth, and independent travel.

Both high school and university students can participate in summer community service programs in Fiji organized by **Rustic Pathways** (© 800/321-4353; www.rusticpathways.com).

SINGLE TRAVELERS

Having traveled alone through the South Pacific for more years than I care to admit, I can tell you it's a great place to be unattached. After all, this is the land of smiles and genuine warmth toward strangers. The attitude soon infects visitors: All I've ever had to do to meet my fellow travelers is wander into a hotel bar, order a beer, and ask the persons next to me where they are from and what they have done in Fiji, Tahiti, and so on.

The two hottest destinations for singles—especially those of backpacking age—are Fiji and the Cook Islands. Fiji has dozens of resorts aimed at this low-budget market.

Even couples-oriented French Polynesia has a playground especially suited to singles: The **Club Med** on Bora Bora (see chapter 10).

Unfortunately, the solo traveler is often forced to pay a "single supplement" charged by many resorts, cruise lines, and tours for the privilege of sleeping alone.

TravelChums (© 212/799-6464; www.travelchums.com) is an Internet-only travel-companion-matching service hosted by respected New York–based Shaw Guides travel service.

Based in Canada, **Travel Buddies Singles Travel Club** (© 800/998-9099; www.travelbuddiesworldwide.com) runs small, intimate, single-friendly group trips and will match you with a roommate free of charge and save you the cost of single supplements.

TRAVELING WITH PETS

Don't even *think* about bringing your pet. Every country will quarantine Fido until you are ready to fly home.

8 Sustainable Tourism/Ecotourism

Climate change and rising sea levels resulting from global warming are having a noticeable impact on the South Pacific islands. Natives I have known for more than 30 years tell me the seasons are now unpredictable (it's more likely to rain in the dry season, and vice versa), and the tides are higher than ever (in some places the lagoons lap on shore at high tide rather than the beach). Indeed, most islanders don't want to hear any corporate-induced spin about there being

Frommers.com: The Complete Travel Resource

It should go without saying, but I highly recommend **Frommers.com**, voted Best Travel Site by *PC Magazine*. We think you'll find our expert advice and tips; independent reviews of hotels, restaurants, attractions, and preferred shopping and nightlife venues; vacation giveaways; and an online booking tool indispensable before, during, and after your travels. We publish the complete contents of over 128 travel guides in our **Destinations** section covering nearly 3,800 places worldwide to help you plan your trip. Each weekday, we publish original articles reporting on **Deals and News** via our free **Frommers.com Newsletter** to help you save time and money and travel smarter. We're betting you'll find our new **Events** listings (**http://events.frommers.com**) an invaluable resource; it's an up-to-the-minute roster of what's happening everywhere—including concerts, festivals, lectures, and more. We've also added weekly **podcasts, interactive maps,** and hundreds of new images across the site. Check out our **Travel Talk** area, featuring **message boards** where you can join in conversations with thousands of fellow travelers and post your own trip report.

no evidence of global warming and its consequences. They know it's true from firsthand experience.

Carbon emissions, the prime cause of global warming, are released into the atmosphere each time you take a flight or drive a car. You can help neutralize this danger to our planet through "carbon offsetting"—paying someone to reduce your carbon emissions by the same amount you've added. Carbon offsets can be purchased in the U.S. from companies such as **Carbonfund.org** and **TerraPass** (www.terrapass.org), and from **Climate Care** (www.climatecare.org) in the U.K.

Although one could argue that any vacation that includes an airplane flight can't be truly "green," you can go on holiday and still contribute positively to the environment. You can offset carbon emissions from your flight in other ways. Choose companies that embrace responsible development practices, helping preserve destinations for the future by working alongside local people. An increasing number of sustainable tourism

initiatives can help you plan a trip and leave as small a "footprint" as possible on the places you visit.

Responsible Travel (www.responsibletravel.com) is a great source of sustainable travel ideas run by a spokesperson for responsible tourism in the travel industry. **Sustainable Travel International** (www.sustainabletravelinternational.org) promotes responsible tourism practices and issues a Green Gear & Gift Guide.

You can find eco-friendly travel tips, statistics, and touring companies and associations—listed by destination under "Travel Choice"—at the TIES website, **www.ecotourism.org. Ecotravel.com** is part online magazine and part eco-directory that lets you search for touring companies in several categories (water-based, land-based, spiritually oriented, and so on).

In the U.K., **Tourism Concern** (www.tourismconcern.org.uk) works to reduce social and environmental problems connected to tourism and find ways of improving tourism so that local benefits are increased.

The **Association of Independent Tour Operators (AITO)** (www.aito.co.uk) is a group of interesting specialist operators leading the field in making holidays sustainable.

For information about the ethics of swimming with dolphins and other outdoor activities, visit the **Whale and Dolphin Conservation Society** (www.wdcs.org) and **Tread Lightly** (www.treadlightly.org).

9 Staying Connected

TELEPHONES

Each island country has its own telephone system. Most are operated by local monopolies and are relatively expensive by Western standards. You can directly dial into and out of all the islands. See the "Fast Facts" section in each country chapter for details about how to use the local systems.

CELLPHONES

Known as "mobiles" here, cellphones are prevalent throughout the islands. No international wireless company operates in the South Pacific, and many American phones won't work because all the islands use the Global System for Mobiles (GSM) technology. Although the technology is gaining in popularity worldwide, only T-Mobile and AT&T Wireless use GSM in the U.S. In Canada, Microcell and some Rogers customers are GSM. All Europeans and most Australians use GSM. Call your wireless company to see if your phone is GSM.

If you do have a GSM phone, you may be able to use it in the islands if your provider has a roaming agreement with the local phone companies. Just call your wireless operator and ask for "international roaming" to be activated on your account.

If it doesn't, you may still use your phone (1) if it transmits and receives on the 900 mHz band; (2) if it has been "unlocked" from its SIM card, the removable computer chip which stores your and your provider's information; and (3) if you rent or buy a local SIM card.

The **Travel Insider** (www.thetravelinsider.info) has an excellent explanation of all this as well as a phone unlocking service. Click on "Road Warrior Resources" and "International Cellphone Service."

Renting a phone or SIM card is easy in the islands. In fact, one of the first things you'll see after clearing Customs at Nadi airport in Fiji is a mobile phone rental booth. See "Fast Facts" in each country chapter.

North Americans can rent a phone or SIM card before leaving home from **InTouch USA** (© **800/872-7626;** www.intouchglobal.com) or **RoadPost** (© **888/290-1606** or 905/272-5665; www.roadpost.com). InTouch will also, for free, advise you on whether your existing phone will work overseas; simply call © **703/222-7161** between 9am and 4pm EST, or go to **www.intouchglobal.com/travel.htm.**

INTERNET/E-MAIL

E-mail is as much a part of life in the South Pacific as it is anywhere else these days, but most Internet connections are relatively slow. High-speed access is growing, but at best, the ADSL systems operate at 512kb per second. That's a snail's pace compared to the 3 megabytes or more in most Western countries.

Access is relatively expensive. Most local Internet service providers (ISP) charge by the minute rather than by the month, and many hotels slap a large fee on top of that. (My Internet and phone bills for checking my e-mail and bank sites from Tahiti have topped US$50!)

Online Traveler's Toolbox

Veteran travelers usually carry some essential items to make their trips easier. Following is a selection of handy online tools to bookmark and use.

- **Airplane Food** (www.airlinemeals.net)
- **Airplane Seating** (www.seatguru.com; www.airlinequality.com)
- **Foreign Languages for Travelers** (www.travlang.com)
- **Maps** (www.mapsouthpacific.com; www.maps-pacific.com; www.world atlas.com)
- **Time and Date** (www.timeanddate.com)
- **Travel Warnings** (www.travel.state.gov; www.fco.gov.uk/travel; www.voyage.gc.ca; www.dfat.gov.au/consular/advice)
- **Universal Currency Converter** (www.xe.com/ucc)
- **Visa ATM Locator** (www.visa.com), **MasterCard ATM Locator** (www.mastercard.com)
- **Weather** (www.met.gov.fj; www.meteo.pf; www.intellicast.com; www.weather.com; www.accuweather.com; www.wunderground.com)

WITHOUT YOUR OWN COMPUTER

The easiest way to get your e-mail on the Web is at your hotel, resort, or hostel. Most have computers for guest use. Or you can go to one of the numerous cybercafes in the islands. See "Fast Facts" in the country chapters.

WITH YOUR OWN COMPUTER

Because no major international ISP has a local access number in the islands, you can't just plug in your laptop, program in the local access number, and go online as you would at home. Nor will you find **Wi-Fi** (wireless fidelity) in most hotels. On the other hand, you can use your own computer from any hotel room with a phone, provided you sign up for a **temporary local Internet access account.** For details see "Fast Facts," in the destination chapters.

There are a growing number of Wi-Fi hotspots in the islands. Many are in coffee shops or hotel bars, so you can sip a cuppa or a cold one while answering your e-mail. The hotspots are not free, and some require that you purchase a prepaid usage card. See the "Fast Facts" section in each country chapter for locations.

Along with your laptop, be sure to bring a **connection kit** of the right power, plus phone adapters (French in French Polynesia, American in American Samoa, Australian elsewhere) and a spare phone cord.

10 Packages for the Independent Traveler

In addition to searching for the lowest airfare, you may want to consider booking your flight as part of a travel package. Buying a package is a way to get the airfare, accommodations, and other elements of your trip (such as car rentals, airport transfers, and even meals and activities) at the same time and often at discounted prices—kind of like one-stop shopping. In fact, package tours usually provide the best bargains, especially to expensive French Polynesia.

Package tours are not the same thing as escorted tours, which are structured tours with a group leader. Few escorted tours go to the South Pacific islands except as add-ons to tours primarily of Australia and New Zealand.

The costs are kept down because wholesale tour operators (known as wholesalers in the travel industry) can make volume bookings on the airlines and at the hotels. Packages traditionally were then sold through retail travel agents, but many wholesalers now deal directly with the public, thus passing savings along to you, rather than part of their commissions to retail agents.

Travel packages are listed in the travel section of many Sunday newspapers. Or check ads in magazines such as *Arthur Frommer's Budget Travel Magazine, Travel & Leisure, National Geographic Traveler,* and *Condé Nast Traveler.*

Airlines frequently offer air-and-hotel packages, so check the Web sites of **Air New Zealand** (www.airnewzealand.com/vacations) **Air Pacific** (www.airpacific.com), **Air Tahiti Nui** (www.airtahitinui.com), **Qantas Airlines** www.qantasvacations.com), and the other South Pacific carriers.

Some local tourism information offices have information about agencies selling packages to their countries. For example, **Tahiti Tourisme** (see "Visitor Information & Maps," in chapter 7) provides links to many money-saving packages to French Polynesia on its North American website (www.tahiti-tourisme.com).

INTERNATIONAL TOUR AGENTS

Following in alphabetical order are some reputable American-based companies selling package tours. Some will discount air tickets and hotel rooms separately; that is, not as part of a package. Be sure to shop for the best deal among them.

- **Blue Pacific Vacations** (℗ 800/798-0590; www.bluepacificvacations.com), a division of France Vacations, is headed by John Biggerstaff and Ken Jordan, two veterans of Tahiti

tourism. They will customize tours to most French Polynesian islands.
- **Brendan Worldwide Vacations** (℗ 800/421-8446 or 818/785-9696; www.brendanvacations.com) provides packages to Fiji and French Polynesia.
- **Costco Travel** (℗ 877/849-2730; www.costco.com) sells island packages to Costco members. The agency was a South Pacific specialist before Costco bought it.
- **GoGo Worldwide Vacations** (℗ 617/734-2350; www.gogovacationdeals.com), headquartered in Massachusetts, specializes in French Polynesia.
- **Go-Today** (℗ 800/227-3235; www.go-today.com), based in Washington State, offers discount-priced packages to Fiji, French Polynesia, and the Cook Islands.
- **Islands in the Sun** (℗ 800/828-6877 or 310/536-0051; www.islandsinthesun.com), the largest and oldest South Pacific specialist, offers packages to all the islands.
- **Jetabout Island Vacations** (℗ 800/348-8145; www.jetabouttahitivacations.com) of El Segundo, California, offers a wide variety of packages to Fiji and Tahiti. It's the U.S. representative of Qantas Vacations.
- **Journey Pacific** (℗ 800/704-7094; www.journeypacific.com) is a Las Vegas–based agency offering packages to all of the islands.
- **Newmans South Pacific Vacations** (℗ 800/421-3326; www.newmansvacations.com) offers packages to the islands, including Samoa and Tonga. It's a long-established New Zealand company.
- **Pacific Destination Center** (℗ 800/227-5317; www.pacific-destinations.com) is owned and operated by Australian-born Janette Ryan, who offers some good deals to the islands.

Tips **Ask Before You Go**

Before you invest in a package deal or an escorted tour:
- Always ask about the **cancellation policy**. Can you get your money back? Is there a deposit required?
- Ask about the **accommodations choices and prices** for each. Then look up the hotels' reviews in a Frommer's guide and check their rates online for your specific dates of travel. Also find out what types of rooms are offered.
- Discuss what is included in the **price** (transportation, meals, tips, airport transfers, and so on).
- Finally, look for **hidden expenses**. Ask whether airport departure fees and taxes, for example, are included in the total cost—they rarely are.

- **Pacific for Less** (© 800/915-2776; www.pacific-for-less.com), based in Hawaii, has reasonably priced packages to French Polynesia, although its specialty is high-end honeymoons.
- **Pleasant Holidays** (© 800/742-9244; www.pleasantholidays.com), a huge company best known for its Pleasant Hawaiian and Pleasant Mexico operations, offers packages to Fiji and French Polynesia.
- **South Pacific Direct** (www.south pacificdirect.com) is an Internet-only firm offering deals to all the islands.
- **South Seas Adventures** (© 800/576-7327; www.south-seas-adventures. com) has packages to Samoa and Tonga as well as Fiji, French Polynesia, and the Cook Islands.
- **Swain Tahiti Tours** (© 800/22-SWAIN [227-9246]; www.swain tours.com) obviously knows a lot about Tahiti and French Polynesia, but it also sells packages to Fiji and the Cook Islands.
- **Sunspots International** (© 800/334-5623 or 503/666-3893; www. sunspotsintl.com), based in Portland, Oregon, has trips to all the islands. It has particular expertise in the Cook Islands, Samoa, and Tonga.

- **Tahiti Discount Travel** (© 877/426-7262; www.tahiti-discount travel.com) is owned by former employees of the defunct Discover Wholesale Travel, once the leader in budget packages. Today they arrange some of the lowest-priced packages to French Polynesia.
- **Tahiti Legends** (© 800/200-1213; www.tahiti-legends.com) is run by former officials of Islands in the Sun. It sells tours to French Polynesia, the Cook Islands, and Fiji under the names **Pacific Legends** (www.pacific legends.com).
- **Tahiti Vacations** (© 800/553-3477; www.tahitivacation.com), a subsidiary of Air Tahiti, French Polynesia's domestic airline, specializes in French Polynesia but also has packages to Fiji, the Cook Islands, and Tonga. It frequently offers the least-expensive packages available to Tahiti and Moorea.
- **Travel Arrangements Ltd.** (© 800/392-8213; www.southpacific reservations.com) is operated by Fiji-born Ron Hunt, a veteran South Pacific travel agent based in California. He sells packages to all the islands and specializes in designing

itineraries (and weddings) to suit your whims and pocketbook.

- **Travelwizard** (© 800/330-8820; www.travelwizard.com) specializes in designing luxury travel packages to all the islands but also has less expensive offerings. It also has adventure, diving, and surfing trips to Fiji and French Polynesia.

Other companies have adventure travel packages combining outdoor activities with accommodations. See "The Active Traveler," later in this chapter.

LOCAL TOUR OPERATORS

Another tactic is to check with the South Pacific **inbound tour operators.** These companies are in the islands and usually put together the local elements of tour packages such as hotel rooms and airport transfers. They have the advantage of being on the scene and thus familiar with the local airlines and hotels. Some sell directly to inbound visitors as well as other tour companies.

In Fiji, two small companies specialize in discount travel arrangements: **Impulse**

Fiji (© 800/953-7595 in the U.S.; 672-0600 in Fiji; www.impulsefiji.com) and **Sun Vacations** (© 672-4273 in Fiji; www.sunvacationsfiji.com).

In French Polynesia, **Tahiti Nui Travel** (© 46.40.10 in Tahiti; www.tahitinuitravel.com) has a variety of local packages, while **True Tahiti Vacations** (© 310/464-1490 in the U.S.; www.truetahitivacation.com) is operated by American-born Laurel Samuela, who lives on Moorea.

In the Cook Islands, **Island Hopper Vacations** (© 22-026 in Rarotonga; www.islandhoppervacations.com) books hotels and puts together local packages, as does **Jetsave Travel** (© 27-707 in Rarotonga; www.jetsave.co.ck), which is owned by American ex-pat Malynnda Morrisette, who lives in the Cooks.

Oceania Travel & Tours is good in Samoa (© 24-443 in Apia, inside the Hotel Kitano in Tusatala.

In Tonga, I highly recommend **Pacific Travel Marketing** (© 28-304; sales@ pacifictravelmarketing.afe.to) for both hotel and airline reservations.

11 Escorted General-Interest Tours

Escorted tours are structured group tours, with a group leader (I prefer the old-fashioned term "tour guide"). The price usually includes everything from airfare to hotels, meals, tours, admission costs, and local transportation.

Escorted tours are not a big part of the business in these small islands, where it's easy to find your way around and book local tours and activities. Most of the travel agents I mention under "Packages for the Independent Traveler," above, will have someone meet and greet you at the airport upon arrival, take you to your hotel, and make sure you get on any prearranged tours and activities, but you will not have a tour guide.

Some tour companies add a short stopover in Fiji or Tahiti to their escorted tours

of Australia and New Zealand, but these may not include a guide for the island portion. Leaders in this add-on feature include **Tauck Tours** (© 800/788-7885; www.tauck.com), **Qantas Vacations** (© 800/641-8772; www.qantasvacations.com), **Australia Escorted Tours** (© 888/333-6607; www.australia-escorted-tours.com), and **Abercrombie & Kent** (© 800/652-7986; www.abercrombiekent.com), which adds Fiji and French Polynesia to its high-end escorted tours. Otherwise, I recommend getting a travel agent to track down an escorted tour.

Despite the fact that escorted tours require big deposits and predetermine hotels, restaurants, and itineraries, many people derive security and peace of mind from the structure they offer. Escorted tours let travelers sit back and enjoy the trip without having to drive or worry about details. They're convenient for people with limited mobility and they can be a great way to make new friends. On the downside, you'll have little opportunity for serendipitous interactions with locals. The tours can be jam-packed with activities, leaving little room for individual sightseeing, whim, or adventure—plus they often focus on the heavily touristed sites, so you miss out on many a lesser-known gem.

12 Special-Interest Trips

Although outdoor activities take first place in the islands (see "The Active Traveler," below), you can also spend your time learning a new craft, exploring the reefs as part of a conservation project, and whale- and dolphin-watching.

BIRD-WATCHING

Avid bird-watchers are likely to see terns, boobies, herons, petrols, noddies, and many other seabirds throughout the islands. French Polynesia alone has 28 species of breeding seabirds, making memorable a visit to Motu Puarua and Motu Oeone, tiny islets out in Tikihau's lagoon, where noddies and snowy white fairy terns nest (see chapter 11).

The number and variety of land birds diminishes as you go eastward. Most live in the bush away from settlements and the accompanying cats, dogs, and rats, so you will need to head into the bush for the best watching.

With 26 endemic species, Fiji has more diversity than the other island countries. Many are on display in **Kula Eco Park** (© 650-0505; www.fijiwild.com), on Fiji's Coral Coast (see chapter 5). **Taveuni** island is best for watching in Fiji, with more than 100 species including the rare orange dove, which lives high on Des Veux Peak. **Savusavu** on Vanua Levu is also good, especially the nearby Waisali Rainforest Reserve. **Daku Resort** in Savusavu (© 885-0046; www.daku resort.com) hosts bird-watching tours hosted by veteran Fiji watcher Robin Mercer. See chapter 6.

In French Polynesia, **Société d'Ornithologie de Polynésie** (Ornithological Society of Polynesia; © 50.62.09; www.manu.pf) lists local birds on its website.

In the Cook Islands, the **Takitumu Conservation Area** on Rarotonga is home to the rare kakeroi, which has recovered from near-extinction status. See chapter 12.

A few companies have bird-watching tours to the South Pacific, including the U.K.-based **Bird Quest** (© 44/1254-826317; www.birdquest.co.uk) and **Birdwatching Breaks** (© 44/1381-610495; www.birdwatchingbreaks.com).

EDUCATIONAL COURSES

In addition to bird-watching, **Daku Resort,** in northern Fiji (© 885-0046; www.dakuresort.com) hosts weeklong courses in such subjects as novel writing, sketching, painting, quilting, and gospel singing. The courses are organized by creative-writing teacher Delia Rothnie-Jones (she and husband John own the resort). They have special package rates for the courses and will help you arrange air transportation to Fiji. See chapter 6.

ECOTRAVEL TOURS

The **Oceanic Society** (© 800/326-7491; www.oceanicsociety.org), an award-winning organization based in California, has natural history and eco-tourism expeditions to the islands. A naturalist accompanies its annual 11-day snorkeling trip to the pristine reefs off Taveuni and Namena islands in northern

Fiji (see chapter 6). The trip includes village visits and bird-watching.

Seacology (© 510/559-3505; www.seacology.org), a California-based organization dedicated to preserving island cultures and environments, has an annual trip to Jean-Michel Cousteau Fiji Islands Resort and occasionally to Samoa.

Fiji Adventures (© 888/418-4461; www.fijiadventures.com) offers several packages, one of which combines several cultural activities offered in Fiji such as river rafting, cave and waterfall visits, and a trip into Viti Levu's interior. The packages do not include airfare, but they save you from having to arrange each activity after you arrive in Fiji.

Formerly known as Tui Tai Adventure Cruises, environmentally and culturally friendly **Active Fiji** (www.tuitai.com, or www.activefiji.com) uses a 140-foot sailing schooner to explore out-of-the-way islands in northern Fiji. The boat goes to Fijian villages and carries bikes as well snorkeling and diving gear. See chapter 6.

Based in London but with an office in the U.S., the nonprofit **Greenforce** (© 0207/470-8888 in London, 740/416-4016 in the U.S.; www.greenforce.org) sends expeditions to help survey Fiji's coral reefs for the World Conservation Society. They'll even teach you to dive while you're there. The trips last from 6 to 10 weeks. Check the website for prices.

WHALE & DOLPHIN WATCHING

Whale- and dolphin-watching are popular activities throughout the South Pacific. Dolphins live here year-round, and humpback whales escape the cold of Antarctica and spend from July until October giving birth to their calves in the tropical South Pacific. They can be seen swimming off many islands, but the prime whale-watching venue is off Vava'u, in Tonga, where you can actually swim in the water alongside these magnificent mammals. Several companies on Vava'u will organize visits (see chapter 15).

The California-based **Oceanic Society** (© 800/326-7491; www.oceanicsociety.org) has 1-week whale-watching trips to Tonga in September. Cost is about US$3,000 per person. You must be experienced snorkeler to swim with the whales.

The best dolphin-watching experiences are on Moorea in French Polynesia, where American marine biologist **Dr. Michael Poole** leads daylong excursions to visit some of the 150 spinner dolphins he has identified as regular residents. Honeymooners love to have their pictures taken while swimming with the intelligent mammals in a fenced-in area at **Moorea Dolphin Center,** at the InterContinental Resort & Spa Moorea. See chapter 9 for details.

13 The Active Traveler

The South Pacific islands are a dream if you're an active traveler, and especially if you're into diving, snorkeling, swimming, boating, and other watersports. You can also play golf and tennis, or hike into the jungle-clad mountainous interiors of the islands. Kayaking is popular everywhere, and Fiji has river rafting. There's good biking along the many roads skirting colorful lagoons. You can engage in these activities everywhere, although some islands are better than others. I point out the best in the following chapters, but here's a brief rundown of my favorites.

Some travel companies have tours combining several outdoor activities in one trip, especially to Fiji, which has the widest variety of outdoor activities. For example, Colorado-based **The World Outdoors** (© 800/488-8483; www.theworldoutdoors.com) includes mountain biking, hiking, river rafting, sea kayaking, snorkeling, and sailing in its "Fiji Multi-Sport" tour. **Travelwizard** (© 800/330-8820; www.travelwizard.com) sells diving and surfing packages to Fiji and French Polynesia. Likewise, **Fiji Adventures** © 888/418-4461; www.fijiadventures.com) has diving, surfing, river rafting, and windsurfing expeditions to Fiji. On the Web, **Gordon's Guide** (www.gordonsguide.com) compiles adventure tours from around the world. It's a good place to search for South Pacific adventure trips. Save time by searching for a specific destination.

BIKING
Relatively flat roads circle most of the islands I cover in this book, making for easy, scenic bike riding. In fact, bicycles are one of my favorite means of getting around. It's simple and inexpensive to rent bikes on all the islands in French Polynesia, the Cook Islands, Samoa, and Tonga. In fact, many hotels and resorts provide bikes for their guests to use.

In Fiji, **Active Fiji** (www.activefiji.com or www.tuitai.com), formerly known as Tui Tai Adventure Cruises, carries mountain bikes on its eco-cruises. See chapter 6.

DIVING & SNORKELING
Most of the islands have good to great diving and snorkeling. Almost every lagoon-side resort has a dive operator, and many will let snorkelers go along.

Fiji is on every diver's list of world-class destinations for colorful soft corals. See "Diving in Fiji" in chapter 4. This is especially true in northern Fiji, where nutrient-rich waters bathe the reefs in the Somosomo Strait, between Vanua Levu and Taveuni islands. Here you'll find Rainbow Reef and its Great White Wall. See chapter 6. More colorful corals exist off northern Viti Levu and in the Beqa Lagoon, off the island's southern coast. You can watch sharks being fed off Pacific Harbour. See chapter 5. Liveaboard dive boats operate in Fiji, too.

French Polynesia is famous for its bountiful sea life, from tropical fish to hammerhead sharks. You'll see plenty of creatures at Moorea, Bora Bora, Huahine, and Raiatea-Tahaa, but the best diving and snorkeling are in the huge lagoons of Rangiroa, Tikehau, Manihi, and Fakarava in the Tuamotu Islands. See chapters 9, 10, and 11.

The shallow lagoons in the Cook Islands and the Samoas are fine for snorkeling, but most diving is in open water outside the reef, where you'll see ample sea life swimming in caves and canyons. Tonga offers a mix, with lagoon diving off Tongatapu and Vava'u and open-water dives off the island of Eu'a. See chapters 12, 13, and 15.

Most resorts offer dive packages to their guests, and the American-based **PADI Travel Network** (© 800/729-7234; www.padi.com) puts together packages for divers of all levels.

DEEP-SEA FISHING
Charter boats in every country will take you in search of marlin, swordfish, tuna, mahimahi, and other game fish. For example, a lucky Australian angler recently snagged a record-breaking 328.8kg (725 lb.) black marlin off Vava'u in Tonga, which to my mind is the best place to go deep-sea fishing in the islands (see chapter 15).

In French Polynesia you can cast your line while living in relative luxury in the Tuamotu Archipelago aboard **Haumana Cruises** (www.tahiti-haumana-cruises.com), which uses a 17-cabin yacht.

GOLF & TENNIS
Most islands have at least one golf course, and some hotels and resorts have tennis courts, but generally this is not the place for a golf and tennis vacation.

Notable exceptions are in Fiji, where **Denarau Golf & Racquet Club** is a modern complex with an 18-hole resort course and 10 tennis courts. Fiji is home to the region's most picturesque course, **The Pearl Championship Golf Course & Country** at Pacific Harbour. See chapter 5.

French Polynesia has an 18-hole set of links on Moorea to complement the venerable **Olivier Breaud International Golf Course,** on the south coast of Tahiti. See chapters 9 and 8, respectively. The Cook Islands have two 9-hole courses, one on Rarotonga and one on Aitutaki. Both are famous for their antenna guy-wire obstacles, which are in play. See chapter 12. Samoa has three courses, the newest wrapping around Aggie Grey's Lagoon, Beach Resort & Spa. See chapter 13. Tonga has one flat course. See chapter 15.

HIKING

These aren't the Rocky Mountains, nor are there blazed trails out here, but hiking in the islands is a lot of fun.

In Fiji you can trek into the mountains and stop at—or stay in—native Fijian villages. **Adventures Fiji,** an arm of Fiji's Rosie the Travel Service (www.rosiefiji. com), has guided hikes ranging from 1 to 10 days into the mountains of Viti Levu, with meals and accommodations provided by Fijian villagers. See chapter 5. On Taveuni island, you can hike a spectacular **Lavena Coastal Walk** to a waterfall or up to **Lake Tagimaucia,** in a crater at an altitude of more than 800m (2,700 ft.). It's home to the rare *tagimaucia* flower. See chapter 6.

Tahiti and Moorea have several trails into the highlands, some of which run along spectacular ridges. You'll need a guide for the best hikes, but you can easily hire them on both islands. See chapters 8 and 9.

Rarotonga in the Cook Islands is famous for its **Cross-Island Trek,** which runs across the mountains from coast-to-coast. See chapter 12.

Samoa has several excellent walks, including a breathtaking coastal trail in **O le Pup-Pue National Park** and a strenuous trek to the mountaintop **Lake Lanoto'o.** See chapter 13. Likewise, you'll find stunning scenery along the trails in the **National Park of American Samoa.** See chapter 14.

HORSEBACK RIDING

Although I prefer sipping a cold drink, a great way to experience a South Pacific sunset is from the back of a horse while riding along a beach. You can do just that in Fiji (see chapters 5 and 6), on Moorea and Huahine in French Polynesia (see chapters 9 and 11), and on Rarotonga in the Cook Islands (see chapter 12).

The ranches on Moorea and Huahine have daytime rides into the mountains.

KAYAKING

All but a few beachfront resorts have canoes, kayaks, small sailboats, sailboards, and other toys for their guests' amusement. As most of these properties sit beside lagoons, using these craft is not only fun, it's relatively safe. They are most fun where you can paddle or sail across the lagoon to uninhabited islets out on the reef, such as on Moorea's northwest coast and off Muri Beach on Rarotonga in the Cook Islands. See chapters 9 and 12, respectively.

Sea kayaking is popular throughout the islands, especially among Fiji's small islands. **Tamarillo Tropical Expeditions** (© **877/682-5433** in the U.S., 4/2399-855 in New Zealand; www.tamarillo. co.nz) has guided 5- to 9-day kayak trips along the shore of Fiji's Kadavu island. See chapters 5 and 6.

In Samoa, you can take kayak tours of a mangrove estuary and the small islands of Manono and Apolima. See chapter 13.

In Tonga, **Friendly Islands Kayak Company** (www.fikco.com) leads trips through Vava'u's multitude of islets. See chapter 15.

RIVER RAFTING

Only Fiji has rivers long enough and swift enough for white-water rafting. The best is the Navua River on Viti Levu, which starts in the mountainous interior and flows swiftly down to a flat delta on the island's south coast. Local companies offer trips using traditional *bilibilis* (bamboo rafts) on the lower, slow-flowing section of the river. The American-based **Rivers Fiji** (ⓒ 800/346-6277; www.riversfiji.com) uses inflatable rafts for white-water trips up in the highlands. See chapter 5.

SAILING

The region's reef-strewn waters make charter-boat sailing a precarious undertaking. The exceptions are the Leeward Islands in French Polynesia and Vava'u in Tonga, where you can rent sailboats with or without skippers. **The Moorings** (ⓒ 800/535-7289; www.moorings.com), one of the world's leading yacht charter companies, has operations at both locations. See chapters 11 and 15.

SURFING

The islands have some world-famous surfing spots such as Frigates Passage in Fiji and Teahupoo on Tahiti (see chapters 5 and 8, respectively). All the best are reef breaks; that is, the surf crashes out on coral reefs instead of on sandy beaches. These are no places for beginners, as you could suffer serious injury by landing on a razor-sharp coral reef. (Or as one of my island friends puts it, "You'll become hamburger in a hurry.")

The surf pounds directly on beaches on Tahiti, where you can learn to surf with *Ecole de Surf Tura'i Mataare* (**Tahiti Surf School**) (ⓒ 41.91.37; www.tahitisurfschool.info). See chapter 8.

14 Tips on Accommodations

The South Pacific has a wide range of accommodations, from resort hotels on their own islands to mom and pop guesthouses and bunk-bedded dorms.

TYPES OF ROOMS

My favorite type of hotel accommodates its guests in individual bungalows set in a coconut grove beside a sandy beach and quiet lagoon. If that's not the quintessential definition of the South Seas, then I don't know what is!

Hotels of this style are widespread in the South Pacific. Some in Fiji, French Polynesia, the Cook Islands, and Samoa feature super-romantic bungalows actually standing on stilts over the reef (although I should point out that some of these overwater units tend to be close together and less private than bungalows ashore elsewhere). Others are as basic as camping out. In between they vary in size, furnishings, and comfort. In all, you enjoy your own place. The bungalows are usually built or accented with thatch and other native materials but they contain most modern conveniences.

An increasing number of these accommodations are air-conditioned, which is a definite plus during the humid summer months from November through March. All but a few bungalows have ceiling fans, which usually will keep you comfortable during the rest of the year.

With the exception of French Polynesia, the major tourist markets for the island countries are Australia and New Zealand. Accordingly, the vast majority of hotels are tailored to Aussie and Kiwi tastes, expectations, and uses of the English language.

Unlike the usual U.S. hotel room, which likely has two huge beds, the standard Down Under room has a double or queen-size bed and a single bed that also serves as a settee. The room may or may not have a bathtub but always has a shower. There will be tea, instant coffee, sugar, creamer, and an electric jug to heat

---

Tips **It Could Pay to Ask for a Local Rate or Discount**

It never hurts to ask politely for a discounted or local hotel rate. Many South Pacific hotels have **local rates** for islanders, which they may extend to visitors if business is slow. Most pay travel agents and wholesalers 20% or more of their rates for sending clients their way, and some may give you the benefit of at least part of this commission if you book directly instead of going through an airline or travel agent. Some wholesale travel agents reduce the commission and sell directly to the public; see my list under "Packages for the Independent Traveler," earlier in this chapter.

---

water (that's usually what I mean by "coffeemaker" in my hotel descriptions). Televisions and telephones are numerous but not universal, but most hotels have clock radios whose selections are limited to the few stations on the island.

Rooms are known to South Pacific reservation desks as **singles** if one person books them, regardless of the number and size of beds they have. Singles are slightly less expensive than other rooms. A unit is a **double** if it has a double bed and is reserved for two persons who intend to sleep together in that bed. On the other hand, a **twin** has two twin beds; it is known as a **shared twin** if two unmarried people book them and don't intend to sleep together. Third and fourth occupants of any room are usually charged a few dollars on top of the double or shared twin rates.

Some hotel rooms, especially in Rarotonga and the Cook Islands, have kitchenettes equipped with a small refrigerator (the "fridge"), hot plates (the "cooker"), a water heater (the "jug"), pots, pans, crockery, and utensils. Having a kitchenette can result in quite a saving on breakfasts and light meals.

SURFING FOR HOTELS

The best independent website for South Pacific hotel discount shopping is Fiji-based **Travelmaxia.com**, where scores of properties throughout the region post their specials. You can search by country

for resorts, hotels, bed-and-breakfasts, dive operators, and cruises.

The Australian-based **Whotif.com** (© **300/88 7979**, 866/514-3281 in the U.S., 0845/458-4567 in the U.K.; www. whotif.com) discounts rooms in Fiji, French Polynesia, and the Cook Islands.

Headquartered in London, **Pacific-Resorts.com** often has discounted rates for resorts in all the islands.

Backpackers and other budget travelers can book inexpensive rooms and dorm beds at hostels in most island countries at **www.hostelworld.com**.

In addition to the big online travel booking sites **Travelocity, Expedia, Orbitz, Priceline,** and **Hotwire,** you can book hotels through **Hotels.com; Quikbook** (www.quikbook.com); and **Travelaxe** (www.travelaxe.net).

Frankly, I always go to the hotels' own sites before booking, as many now offer their own Internet specials, which often beat the big-site prices.

Other websites have reviews and comments about accommodations worldwise. **HotelChatter.com** is a daily webzine offering coverage and critiques. Go to **TripAdvisor.com** or **HotelShark.com** for independent consumer reviews of hotels and resort properties. (Anyone can post reviews on these sites, including hotel owners themselves and "guests" who have never stayed at a property, so I read them with a proverbial grain of salt.)

It's a good idea to **get a confirmation number** and **make a printout** of any online booking transaction.

SAVING ON YOUR HOTEL ROOM

The rate ranges quoted in this book are known as **rack rates,** or published rates; that is, the maximum a property charges for a room. Rack rates remain the best way of comparing prices, but they are becoming less meaningful as more and more hotels change their rates almost daily depending on how many people are booked in for a particular night. They change so frequently, in fact, that many hotels refuse to divulge their rack rates to travel writers like me. In other words, you may not know what the price of a room is until you call the hotel or book online for a particular date.

You may be able to save on hotel rooms by booking them through the airlines and international and local travel agencies (see my lists under "Packages for the Independent Traveler," above).

Here some other money-saving tips:

- **Ask about special rates or other discounts.** At chain motels, you may qualify for corporate, student, military, senior, frequent flier, union, or other discounts.
- **Dial direct.** When booking a room in a chain hotel, you'll often get a better deal by calling the individual hotel's reservation desk rather than the chain's main number.
- **Book online.** Many hotels offer Internet-only discounts, or supply rooms to Priceline, Hotwire, or Expedia at rates much lower than the ones

you can get through the hotel itself. Be sure to check the individual hotel's site for discounts and specials.

- **Remember the law of supply and demand.** You can save on hotel rooms by traveling in a destination's off-season or shoulder seasons, when rates typically drop, even at luxury properties.
- **Look into group or long-stay discounts.** If you come as part of a large group, you should be able to negotiate a bargain rate. Likewise, if you're planning a long stay (at least 5 days), you might qualify for a discount. As a general rule, expect 1 night free after a 7-night stay.
- **Sidestep excess surcharges and hidden costs.** Many hotels have adopted the practice of nickel-and-diming their guests with opaque surcharges. When you book a room, ask what is included in the room rate, and what is extra. Avoid dialing direct from hotel phones, which can have exorbitant rates. And don't be tempted by the room's minibar offerings: Most hotels charge through the nose for water, soda, and snacks. Finally, ask about local taxes and service charges, which can increase the cost of a room by 15% or more.
- Consider your hotel's meal plan. You will have no choice but to buy a plan at a remote offshore resort, from which it's impossible to stroll over to a nearby restaurant. Unless you're staying out on such a rock, it makes sense to choose a **Continental Plan (CP),** which includes breakfast only, or a **European Plan (EP),** which

---

> *Tips* **Bring a Face Cloth**
>
> All South Pacific hotels and resorts supply bath and hand towels, but many do not have face towels (or wash cloths) in their bathrooms. Just in case, bring your own.

Fun Fact Island Time vs. Island Service

There's an old story about a 19th-century planter who promised a South Pacific islander a weekly wage and a pension if he would come to work on his copra plantation. *Copra* is dried coconut meat, from which oil is pressed for use in soaps, cosmetics, and other products. Hours of backbreaking labor are required to chop open the coconuts and extract the meat by hand.

The islander was sitting by the lagoon, eating fruit he had picked from nearby trees while hauling in one fish after another. "Let me make sure I understand you," said the islander. "You want me to break my back working for you for 30 years. Then you'll pay me a pension so I can come back here and spend the rest of my life sitting by the lagoon, eating fruit from my trees and the fish I catch? I may not be sophisticated, but I am not stupid."

The islander's response reflects an attitude still prevalent in the South Pacific, where many people don't have to work in the Western sense. Here life moves at a slow pace. The locals call it "island time."

Consequently, do not expect the same level of service rendered in most hotels and restaurants back home. The slowness is not slothful inattention; it's just the way things are done here. Your drink will come in due course. If you must have it immediately, order it at the bar. Otherwise, relax with your friendly hosts and enjoy their charming company.

doesn't include any meals and allows you maximum flexibility. A **Modified American Plan (MAP)** includes breakfast and one meal. I thoroughly enjoy dining out and sampling local cuisine, so I usually avoid the **American Plan (AP),** which includes three meals.

- **Book an efficiency,** or a "self-contained unit," as rooms with cooking facilities are known in this part of the world. A kitchenette allows you to cook your own meals. This is a big money saver, especially for families on long stays.
- **Consider enrolling in hotel chains' "frequent-stay" programs,** which are upping the ante lately to win the loyalty of repeat customers. Frequent guests can accumulate points or credits to earn free hotel nights, airline miles, amenities, merchandise, tickets to concerts and events, and

discounts on sporting facilities. Many chain hotels partner with other hotel chains, car-rental firms, airlines, and credit card companies to give consumers additional incentive to do repeat business.

LANDING THE BEST ROOM

Somebody has to get the best room in the house. It might as well be you. You can start by joining the hotel's frequent-guest program, which may make you eligible for upgrades. A hotel-branded credit card usually gives its owner "silver" or "gold" status in frequent-guest programs for free.

If you aren't happy with your room when you arrive, ask for another one. Most lodgings will be willing to accommodate you.

Here are some other questions to ask before you book a room:

- What's the view like? If you're a cost-conscious traveler, you might be willing to pay less for a bungalow in the garden, especially if you don't plan to spend much time in the room.

- Does the room have air-conditioning or ceiling fans? An important consideration between November and March.
- What's included in the price? Your room may be moderately priced, but if you're charged for beach chairs, towels, sports equipment, and other amenities, you could end up spending more than you bargained for. Also ask if airport transfers and local hotel taxes are included in the quoted rate.
- How far is the room from the beach and other amenities, especially the bar if the hotel has nighttime entertainment?
- What is the cancellation policy?

15 Tips on Dining

Whether called an "island night" in the Cook Islands, *fiafia* in the Samoas, or *meke* in Fiji, traditional feasts and dance shows are essential after-dark ingredients throughout the South Pacific.

Before the Europeans arrived, the typical South Pacific diet consisted of bananas, coconuts, and other fruits. Staples were starchy breadfruit and root crops, such as taro, arrowroot, yams, and sweet potatoes. The reefs and lagoons provided abundant fish, lobsters, and clams to augment the meats provided by domesticated pigs, dogs, and chickens. Taro leaves and coconut cream served as complements. Corned beef has replaced dog on today's menu; otherwise, these same ingredients still make up the menus.

Like their ancestors, who had no crockery, today's islanders prepare their major meals in an earth oven, known as *himaa* in Tahiti, *lovo* in Fiji, and *imu* or *umu* elsewhere. Individual food items are wrapped in leaves, placed in the pit on a bed of heated stones, covered with more leaves and earth, and left to steam for several hours. The results are quite tasty, with the steam spreading the aroma of one ingredient to the others.

When the meal has finished cooking, the islanders uncover the oven, unwrap the food, and, using their fingers, set about eating their feast of *umukai* (island food) in a leisurely and convivial manner. Then they dance the night away.

You won't be stuck eating island-style food cooked in an earth oven, however, nor will you be limited to the rather bland tastes of New Zealanders and Australians, which predominate at many restaurants. Wherever the French go, fine food and wine are sure to follow, and French Polynesia is no exception. The East Indians brought curries to Fiji, and chefs trained there have spread those spicy offerings to the other islands. Many chefs in Tonga are from Germany and Italy and specialize in their own "native" food. Chinese cuisine of varying quality can be found everywhere.

FAST FACTS: The South Pacific

The facts in this section apply to the region in general. See the "Fast Facts" in the following chapters for information specific to each South Pacific island.

ATM Networks See "Money," p. 30.

Camera and Film Color print film and processing is available in all the main island towns. On the other hand, digital camera batteries are difficult to find

(I bring a spare). Make sure your digital camera battery charger will work on 220-volt electricity, which is common in the islands. Never pack film—exposed or unexposed—in checked bags, because the new, more powerful security scanners can fog film. The film you carry with you can be damaged by passenger scanners as well. X-ray damage is cumulative; the faster the film, and the more times you put it through a scanner, the more likely the damage. Film under 800 ASA is usually safe for up to five scans. On international flights, store your film in transparent baggies, so you can remove it easily before you go through scanners. On the other hand, **digital cameras** and storage cards are not affected by airport X-rays. Carry-on scanners will not damage **videotape** in video cameras, but the magnetic fields emitted by the walk-through security gateways and handheld inspection wands will. Always place your loaded camcorder on the screening conveyor belt or have it hand-inspected. Be sure your batteries are charged in all carry-on electronic gear, as you may be required to turn the device on to ensure that it's what it appears to be.

Cashpoints See "Money & Costs," p. 30.

Currency See "Money & Costs," p. 30.

Customs Each island country has its own Customs laws. See the "Fast Facts" sections in chapters 4, 7, 12, 13, 14, and 15.

What You Can Take Home from the South Pacific Some South Pacific governments restrict the export of antique carvings and other artifacts of historic value. If a piece looks old, check before you buy. Jewelry made of shells and of pink or black coral is available in many countries, as is scrimshaw, but items made of black coral and whalebone cannot legally be brought back to the United States and most other Western countries.

U.S. citizens who have been in the South Pacific for at least 48 hours are allowed to bring back, once every 30 days, US$800 worth of merchandise duty-free (US$1,200 from American Samoa). For specifics on what you can bring back and the corresponding fees, download the invaluable free pamphlet *Know Before You Go* online at **www.cbp.gov** (click on "Travel," and then click on "Know Before You Go! Online Brochure"). Or contact the **U.S. Customs & Border Protection (CBP)**, 1300 Pennsylvania Ave., NW, Washington, DC 20229 (© 877/287-8667) and request the pamphlet.

Canadian Citizens: For a clear summary of Canadian rules, write for the booklet *I Declare*, issued by the **Canada Border Services Agency** (© 800/461-9999 in Canada, or 204/983-3500; **www.cbsa-asfc.gc.ca**).

U.K. Citizens: For information, contact **HM Customs & Excise** at © 0845/010-9000 (from outside the U.K., 020/8929-0152), or consult their website at **www.hmce.gov.uk**.

Australian Citizens: A helpful brochure available from Australian consulates or Customs offices is *Know Before You Go*. For more information, call the **Australian Customs Service** at © 1300/363-263, or log on to **www.customs.gov.au**.

New Zealand Citizens: Most questions are answered in a free pamphlet available at New Zealand consulates and Customs offices: *New Zealand Customs Guide for Travellers, Notice no. 4*. For more information, contact **New**

Zealand Customs, The Customhouse, 17–21 Whitmore St., Box 2218, Wellington (© **04/473-6099** or 0800/428-786; **www.customs.govt.nz**).

Driving Rules See "Getting Around" in the specific country chapters.

Electricity American Samoa uses 110-volt current and flat, vertical plugs identical to those in the U.S. and Canada. Electricity in the other countries is 240-volt, 50 cycles. French Polynesia uses round French-style plugs, while Fiji, the Cook Islands, and Samoa use flat, angled plugs like those in Australia and New Zealand.

Health See "Health," under "General Travel Resources," earlier in this chapter and in the specific country chapters.

Holidays See "Holidays & Events," in the specific country chapters.

Internet Access See "Staying Connected," earlier in this chapter.

Lost & Found Be sure to tell all of your credit card companies the minute you discover your wallet has been lost or stolen and file a report at the nearest police precinct. Your credit card company or insurer may require a police report number or record of the loss. Most credit card companies have an emergency toll-free number to call if your card is lost or stolen; they may be able to wire you a cash advance immediately or deliver an emergency credit card in a day or two.

Measurements All South Pacific countries except American Samoa are on the metric system.

Passports Allow plenty of time before your trip to apply for a passport; processing normally takes 3 weeks but can take longer during busy periods (especially spring). And keep in mind that if you need a passport in a hurry, you'll pay a higher processing fee.

For Residents of Australia: You can pick up an application from your local post office or any branch of Passports Australia, but you must schedule an interview at the passport office to present your application materials. Call the **Australian Passport Information Service** at © **131-232**, or visit the government website at **www.passports.gov.au**.

For Residents of Canada: Passport applications are available at travel agencies throughout Canada or from the central **Passport Office,** Department of Foreign Affairs and International Trade, Ottawa, ON K1A 0G3 (© **800/567-6868**; www.ppt.gc.ca).

For Residents of Ireland: You can apply for a 10-year passport at the **Passport Office,** Setanta Centre, Molesworth Street, Dublin 2 (© **01/671-1633**; www.irl gov.ie/iveagh). Those under age 18 and over 65 must apply for a 3-year passport. You can also apply at 1A South Mall, Cork (© **021/272-525**) or at most main post offices.

For Residents of New Zealand: You can pick up a passport application at any New Zealand Passports Office or download it from their website. Contact the **Passports Office** at © **0800/225-050** in New Zealand or 04/474-8100, or log on to **www.passports.govt.nz**.

For Residents of the United Kingdom: To pick up an application for a standard 10-year passport (5-year passport for children under 16), visit your nearest passport office, major post office, or travel agency or contact the **United Kingdom Passport Service** at ⓒ 0870/521-0410 or search its website at **www. ukpa.gov.uk**.

For Residents of the United States: Whether you're applying in person or by mail, you can download passport applications from the U.S. Department of State website at **www.travel.state.gov**. To find your regional passport office, check the U.S. Department of State website or call the **National Passport Information Center** toll-free number (ⓒ 877/487-2778) for automated information.

Safety See "Staying Safe" under "General Travel Resources" earlier in this chapter and in the specific country chapters.

Smoking Although antismoking campaigns and hefty taxes have reduced the practice to a large extent, cigarette smoking is still more common in the islands, and especially in French Polynesia, than in most Western nations. Most office buildings and the airlines are smoke-free, but nonsmoking sections in restaurants are rare. Not all hotels have nonsmoking rooms, so don't assume you'll get a nonsmoking room without asking for one.

Taxes Hotel rooms are subject to tax everywhere, and most countries impose a hidden "value-added tax." See "Fast Facts" in the specific country chapters for details.

Time Zones See the "Fast Facts" sections in each specific country chapter for local time. The International Dateline runs north–south through the region, placing Fiji and Tonga in the same day as Australia and New Zealand. French Polynesia, the Cook Islands, and the Samoas are a day earlier.

Tipping Although tipping is considered contrary to the Polynesian and Melanesian traditions of hospitality and generosity, the practice is widely practiced in the islands. (TIPPING IS NOT ILLEGAL proclaims a sign in a Tahiti restaurant.) Nevertheless, you don't have to tip out here. That's not to say that a gratuity isn't in order for outstanding service. I usually give a small tip to porters who wrestle with my heavy international bags.

Useful Phone Numbers U.S. Department of State Travel Advisory (ⓒ 202/647-5225, manned 24 hrs.); U.S. Passport Agency (ⓒ 202/647-0518); U.S. Centers for Disease Control International Traveler's Hotline (ⓒ 404/332-4559).

Water Water from the tap is safe to drink in the city of Papeete on Tahiti, on parts of the island of Bora Bora, on Rarotonga in the Cook Islands, and in the main towns in Fiji. To avoid upsetting your intestines, buy bottled spring water at grocery stores (yes, Fiji Water really comes from Fiji). See "Fast Facts" in the following chapters for particulars.

3

Suggested South Pacific Itineraries

People often ask me where they should go in the South Pacific. Lacking the ability to read minds, I do not have an easy answer. In other words, it depends on what you want to see and do on your own vacation. What I can do is give you the benefit of my expertise so that you don't waste your valuable vacation time.

If you live in the United States, Canada, the U.K. or Europe, the long flights here and back mean you will burn a day getting here and a day returning home. Consequently, you should spend more than 1 week out here. If I had only 1 week, I would spend it in one island country, or even on one island. (Also I would pick only one if my primary goal is to spend as much time as possible in the water.) I suggest itineraries in this chapter which will do some degree of justice to the Cook Islands, the Samoas, and Tonga, which are smaller than Fiji and French Polynesia. I recommend 2 weeks for either of the latter.

The vast distances and the infrequent—in some cases nonexistent—air services between the islands make it difficult to see more than one or two South Pacific island countries in less than 3 weeks. You can see Samoa and Tonga in 2 weeks using Air New Zealand's weekly flights, which stop in both on their way between Auckland and Los Angeles. Air Pacific flies at least twice a week from Fiji to both Samoa and Tonga, but not between them, and Air Tahiti connects Papeete and Rarotonga in the Cook Islands. There are no other east-west flights among the islands. See "Getting There & Getting Around," in chapter 2, for transportation details.

However you construct your own itinerary, first find out the airlines' schedules and book all domestic inter-island flights well in advance. Do not wait until you arrive in the islands to take care of this important chore.

And remember the old travel agent's rule: Never stay at the most luxurious property first. In other words, anything after that will seem inferior, and you may come home disappointed.

1 2 Weeks in Fiji

This trip takes you to the highlights of Fiji. The Queens Road, a two-lane highway, links Nadi, the Coral Coast, and Suva, so you'll make this part of the trip overland. Bus connections are available, but I always rent a car in order to have the maximum flexibility. Ferries run from Suva to Taveuni and Savusavu, but don't even think about taking them. Fly instead.

Days ❶–❷: Relaxing in Nadi

Take the first day to recover from your international flight lounging around the pool, shopping in Nadi Town, or sightseeing. Spend Day 2 on land-based excursions, such as to the late Raymond Burr's **Garden of the Sleeping Giant** (p. 102); **Lautoka,** Fiji's second-largest city (p. 104); and **Viseisei Village,** the country's oldest native Fijian village (p. 102). Finish off with some more shopping and dinner in Nadi.

Days ❸–❹: Exploring the Coral Coast ⚔

Get up early and drive south to the Coral Coast, on the southern coast of Viti Levu, Fiji's mainland. Stop on the way at the **Sigatoka Sand Dunes National Park** (p. 133) and **Kula Eco Park** (p. 134), which I like because they give an interesting glimpse of Fiji's geology and wildlife. You can swim or snorkel in the afternoon, or hike to a waterfall with **Adventures in Paradise Fiji** (p. 134). Catch an evening show featuring the "fire walkers" from **Beqa Island** (p. 141).

Day ❺: Rafting on the Navua River ⚔⚔⚔

One of my favorite Fiji excursions is up the **Navua River,** which carves a dramatic gorge through Viti Levu's mountainous interior before spilling into a flood plain west of Suva. The usual trip takes you upriver on a fast speed boat but brings you back on a *bilibili* (bamboo raft). Or you can ride an inflatable boat over white waters with **Rivers Fiji** (p. 143).

Day ❻: Suva ⚔

On the way to Suva, Fiji's humid capital city, stop and see a presentation of native arts, crafts, and dancing at the **Pacific Harbour Arts Village,** the country's best cultural center (p. 142). Once in Suva, take a walking tour of downtown, ending at the **Fiji Museum** (p. 149). The city is the best place to do after-dark bar hopping (p. 160).

Day ❼: A Trip Back in Time to Levuka

A short trip from Suva to **Levuka** always highlights my visits to Fiji. The country's original capital, the old town has retained its 19th-century appearance, and its backdrop of sheer cliffs makes it one of the South Pacific's most beautiful towns. Get **Ovalau Watersports** (p. 158) to organize a morning walking tour and an afternoon excursion on Ovalau. Either catch the late afternoon flight back to Suva or overnight at the charming **Levuka Homestay** (p. 159).

Days ❽–❾: Exploring Taveuni ⚔⚔⚔

Take the early morning Air Fiji flight back to Nausori Airport near Suva and connect from there to **Taveuni,** Fiji's third-largest island. Famous for world-class diving on the **Great White Wall** and its **Rainbow Reef,** Taveuni also is a hiker's paradise. Stay near the airport, from where it's an easy trip to the waterfalls in **Bouma National Heritage Park** and the **Lavena Coastal Walk** (p. 177). The next day, hike to mountaintop **Lake Tagimaucia,** where you might see the rare flower of the same name.

Days ❿–⓫: Savusavu: "Little America"

Spend your first day exploring **Savusavu,** on Fiji's second-largest island, Vanua Levu. Although it is rapidly developing, the town still recalls its days as a 19th-century copra (coconut oil) port. Stroll along the harbor, have lunch at the **Bula-Re Cafe** (p. 173), and visit the famous **Savusavu Hot springs,** where Fijians still cook their evening meals (p. 172). Stop by **Curly's Cruising/Bosun's Locker** (p. 169) to rent a kayak or arrange an excursion to a Fijian village. If you have brought your children, stay at **Jean-Michel Cousteau Fiji Islands Resort** (p. 169), one of the South Pacific's top family resorts.

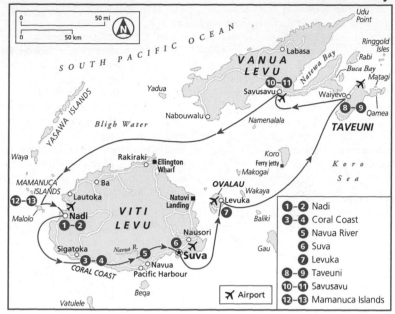

Days ⑫–⑬: An Island Retreat

Spending at least 1 night on a small island in the Mamanucas or Yasawas is almost an essential ingredient of any trip to Fiji, whether it's at the raucous **Beachcomber Island Resort** (p. 127), the family-oriented **Plantation Island Resort** (p. 126), a quiet couples-only hideaway like **Matamanoa Island Resort** (p. 126), the charming **Navutu Stars Resort** in the Yasawas, or one of the backpackers dotting the islands. They have much better beaches than you'll find on Viti Levu, and it'll give you a chance to rest for the trip home.

Day ⑭: Last-Minute Shopping in Nadi

If your homeward flight departs late at night, you can stay in the islands for an extra day. Otherwise spend your last day catching up on shopping or any excursions you might have missed in and around Nadi.

2 2 Weeks in Tahiti & French Polynesia

This itinerary takes you over the well-worn path through French Polynesia's Society Islands—Tahiti, Moorea, Huahine, and Bora Bora—plus a few days in Rangiroa, the largest atoll in the Tuamotu Archipelago. I suggest going to Rangiroa first because after the awesome mountainous beauty of the Society Islands, it may seem anticlimactic to end your trip at a flat atoll. Tikihau, Manihi, or Fakarava, its Tuamotuan sisters, are almost as good and are worthy alternatives to Rangiroa. If you have only 1 week, omit Rangiroa and head to Moorea first, then to Huahine and Bora Bora. If you're on an expensive honeymoon, you won't regret ending it at Le Taha'a Private Island & Spa (p. 304).

2 Weeks in Tahiti & French Polynesia

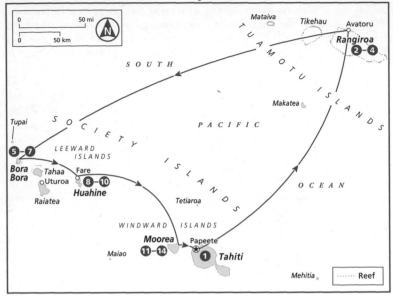

Day ❶: Circling Tahiti 🐾

Spend your first morning on a guided half-day **circle island** tour of Tahiti (p. 227). You won't have to drive or find your way around, so it's a good method of recovering while seeing the island. After a long French lunch, take a **walking tour** of downtown Papeete (p. 224). I like to stay in a hotel on Tahiti's west coast, where I can watch the sunset over Moorea, one of the region's most awe-inspiring sights.

Days ❷–❹: Riding the Rip on Rangiroa 🐾🐾

The world's second-largest lagoon demands a full-day excursion by boat to one of its two key sites: the **Pink Sands** or the **Blue Lagoon** (p. 308). My choice would be the Blue Lagoon, actually a small lagoon within the large lagoon. On another day, don your snorkel or diving gear and **ride the rip tide** through the main pass into the lagoon. Be sure to watch the dolphins playing in Ohotu Pass at sunset.

Days ❺–❼: Feeding the Sharks on Bora Bora 🐾🐾🐾

A nonstop flight from Rangiroa will bring you to beautiful **Bora Bora,** which many consider the world's most beautiful island. Spend part of your first day exploring the interior by four-wheel-drive **"safari expedition"** (p. 277). Devote a full day to a lagoon tour by boat, the top thing to do on Bora Bora. You'll get a fish-eye view of the island's dramatic peak, snorkel while watching your guide feed a school of reef sharks, and enjoy a fresh-fish lunch on a small islet on the fringing reef (p. 277).

Days ❽–❿: Old Polynesia on Huahine 🐾🐾

After the mile-a-minute activities on Bora Bora, **Huahine** will seem like a reserved Polynesian paradise. Spend your first day touring the historic *maraes* (ancient temples) at Maeva village with Paul Atallah of **Island Eco Tours** (p. 293). The next day tour the lagoon, swim, snorkel, or go horseback riding. I always have a sunset drink while watching the boats coming and going at **Fare,** the island's charming main town.

Days ⑪–⑭: Seeing the Sights on Moorea 🕿🕿🕿

While the lagoons are the highlights at Rangiroa and Bora Bora, the ruggedly gorgeous interior draws my eyes on **Moorea.** Whether it's on a regular guided tour, a four-wheel-drive safari excursion, or on your own, go up to the **Belvédère,** overlooking **Cook's** and **Opunohu** bays. Moorea's lagoon does have its good features, especially dolphin-watching excursions led by **Dr. Michael Poole** (p. 259). And don't miss a nighttime show at **Tiki Theatre Village,** one of the region's best cultural centers (p. 258). Moorea is only 7 minutes by plane from Tahiti, which makes it a snap to connect to Papeete and your flight home.

3 A Week in the Cook Islands

In many ways the Cook Islands are a microcosm of the South Pacific. Here in a small space are people as friendly as the Fijians, beautiful islands similar to those in French Polynesia, exposure to Polynesian culture rivaling that in Samoa and Tonga, and lots of outdoor activities. In other words, here you can easily see most of what the islands have to offer in 1 week. Since Rarotonga is less than a 2-hour flight from Tahiti, 3 from Fiji, this week can easily be added to your Fiji or French Polynesia visits.

Day ①: Arrival & Recovery on Rarotonga 🕿🕿🕿

My favorite thing to do after an all-night plane ride getting here is to head into **Avarua** for a cup of coffee at **The Cafe** (p. 348), then a stroll around the Cooks' little capital. Be sure to visit the **Cook Islands Library and Museum** (p. 331). Spend the afternoon recovering with a swim or a sail at **Muri Beach** (p. 333).

Day ②: Sampling Cook Islands Culture 🕿🕿🕿

The demonstrations at the **Cook Islands Cultural Village** and its guided tour around Rarotonga (p. 335) will take most of this day. Later on don't miss one of the region's best **island nights** (p. 350), featuring a feast and a lively dance show. If it's Friday or Saturday, make the obligatory "crawl" through Avarua's pubs (p. 350).

Day ③: A Walk Across Rarotonga 🕿🕿🕿

Plan to spend this morning hiking the **Cross-Island Track,** which literally traverses Rarotonga from north to south, passing the base of the famous **Needle** on the way. You will learn much as well as enjoy the views on a guided trek with **Pa's Nature Walks** (p. 335). If you're not up to walking and climbing, **Raro Safari Tours** will take you into the interior mountains via four-wheel-drive vehicle (p. 334).

Days ④–⑥: An Aitutaki Lagoon Excursion 🕿🕿🕿

On Day 4 take an early morning flight from Rarotonga to **Aitutaki.** Spend that afternoon exploring Aitutaki's main island, either on a guided tour or on your own via scooter or rental car. After sunset attend an island night buffet and dance show, preferably at **Samade on the Beach** (p. 358). Spend all of Day 5 on an excursion out on the lagoon, one of the South Pacific's most beautiful. You'll get to snorkel around tiny **One Foot Island,** one of my favorite things to do here. Have dinner at **Cafe Tupuna** (p. 358). Enjoy the morning of Day 6 on the beach before flying back to Rarotonga.

A Week in the Cook Islands

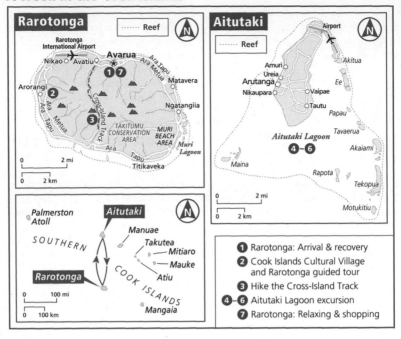

Day ❶ Rarotonga: Arrival & recovery
Day ❷ Cook Islands Cultural Village and Rarotonga guided tour
Day ❸ Hike the Cross-Island Track
Day ❹–❻ Aitutaki Lagoon excursion
Day ❼ Rarotonga: Relaxing & shopping

Day ❼: Relaxing & Shopping on Rarotonga

Spend the morning doing some shopping for black pearls, Tangaroa statues, and tropical clothing in Avarua (p. 337). In the afternoon head over to **Titikaveka** for Rarotonga's best snorkeling.

4 A Week in the Samoas

By being both Christian and conservative, Samoa and nearby American Samoa have maintained their traditional Polynesian cultures to a remarkable degree. I like this trip because it lets me examine the old way of life while still enjoying great beaches, reefs, and tropical scenery.

Day ❶: Arrival & Recovery on Upolu

Whether you stay in town or at a beachside resort, devote your first day to seeing **Apia,** the picturesque waterfront capital of independent Samoa. Stroll the promenade along the harbor and visit the nearby **Robert Louis Stevenson Museum & Grave,** where the great writer is buried on Mount Vaea overlooking Apia (p. 376). Don't miss a *fiafia* feast and show, especially at one of **Aggie Grey's** resorts (p. 392).

Day ❷: An Excursion to Lalomanu Beach ✹✹✹

Few South Pacific beaches combine great sand, a colorful lagoon, and a dramatic backdrop as does the one at **Lalomanu** village (p. 381), on the eastern end of Upolu, Samoa's main island. The drive there takes 2 hours, so leave early to enjoy a full day at the beach. You can also overnight beside the lagoon in a **beach fale** (p. 389).

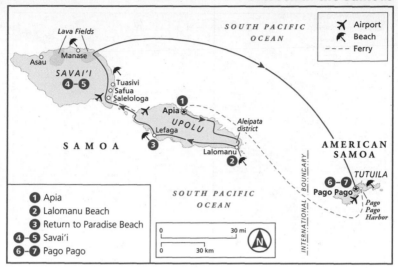

A Week in the Samoas

1 Apia
2 Lalomanu Beach
3 Return to Paradise Beach
4–5 Savai'i
6–7 Pago Pago

Day **3**: Return to Paradise Beach ⚘⚘⚘

In case you didn't get an eyeful at Lalomanu Beach, spend this day between the black rocks protruding at **Return to Paradise Beach,** on Upolu's southwestern coast, where Gary Cooper starred in the 1950s movie *Return to Paradise.*

Days **4–5**: Savai'i ⚘⚘⚘

Spend 1 of your 2 days on Samoa's undeveloped and fascinating "Big Island" exploring the **Virgin's Grave** and other sites on the Savai'i **lava fields** with Warren Jopling of **Safua Tours** (p. 393). Plan to stay in or near the north shore village of **Manase,** perhaps at the **Le Lagoto**

Beach Resort (see p. 395) or in an open-air beach fale beside Manase's magnificent white sands (p. 396).

Days **6–7**: A Slice of America in Pago Pago

Three good hotels now make this beautiful if somewhat commercialized American outpost worth a visit. Spend 1 day touring Tutuila's south shore, especially from the fabled harbor at **Pago Pago** to the island's eastern end. The winding road passes one gorgeous bay after another. After overnighting at **Sadie's by the Sea** (p. 410), devote your second day to hiking the **National Park of American Samoa** (p. 409).

5 A Week in Tonga

I approach the Kingdom of Tonga as two distinct destinations. On the one hand is the flat main island of Tongatapu, with its scruffy capital of Nuku'alofa, several historic sites worth observing out in the countryside, and little islets out in its harbor. On the other is hilly Vava'u, one of the South Pacific's sailing capitals. However you devise your own itinerary, give them equal time.

Day **1**: Exploring Nuku'alofa

Most hotels on Tongatapu are in Nuku'alofa, so use the capital as your base. Spend your first day seeing sights such as the **Royal Palace** and the **Royal Tombs** (p. 428), and visiting the **Tongan**

A Week in Tonga

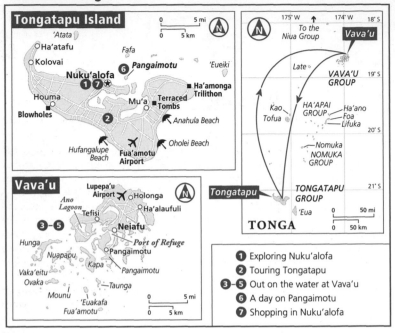

National Cultural Centre (p. 427). Don't miss dinner and a dance show at the center. Stop for coffee or lunch at **Friends Cafe** on the main street (p. 439).

Day 2: Touring Tongatapu

Spend your second day touring Tongatapu from end to end, with stops at the ancient **Ha'amonga Trilithon**, the **Blow Holes**, **Captain Cook's Landing Place**, and the exotic birds residing at the **Tongan Wildlife Centre** (p. 430). End up on the western shore, where you can sun and swim at **Ha'atafu** (p. 431).

Days 3–5: Out on the Water at Vava'u ✦✦✦

One of the region's most picturesque destinations, **Vava'u** merits at least 3 days. If you're an avid sailor, this is the safest place in the South Pacific to charter a yacht and explore the many small islets dotting the lagoon. Even if you aren't into boating, spend 1 day on a lagoon tour to **Swallows**

Cave and **Mariner's Cave** (p. 442). Vava'u also is the region's best place to go **whale-watching** from June through October (p. 443).

Day 6: A Day on Pangaimotu ✦✦

Especially if it's a Sunday when nearly everything closes, spend this day at **Pangaimotu Island Resort,** a few minutes off Nuku'alofa (p. 436). Hanging over a beach beside the country's best swimming lagoon, this ramshackle but charming establishment is my favorite South Pacific bar. You'll have lots of company out here on the Sabbath.

Day 7: Shopping for Handicrafts ✦✦✦

Tongans produce the South Pacific's best handicrafts, so spend most of your last day exploring the shops in Nuku'alofa, especially the **Langafonua Women's Association Handicraft Centre** (p. 433).

4

Introducing Fiji

The thing I love most about these 300-plus islands isn't their palm-draped beaches, their blue lagoons, or their rugged mountains. It is the enormous friendliness of the Fijian people.

You'll see why as soon as you get off the plane, clear Customs and Immigration, and are greeted by a procession of smiling faces, all of them exclaiming an enthusiastic *"Bula!"* That one word—"health" in Fijian—expresses the warmest and most heartfelt welcome I have ever received anywhere.

This country's great variety will also be immediately evident, for the taxi drivers who whisk us to our hotels and hostels are not Fijians of Melanesian heritage, but Indians whose ancestors migrated from such places as Calcutta and Madras. Now about 37% of the population, the Fiji Indians have played major roles in making their nation economically and politically independent.

But their presence has also resulted in racial animosity and four political coups, most recently in December 2006, during which the predominately Fijian army threw out elected governments.

Visitors have not directly been affected by the political tensions. The 2006 coup was peaceful. I spent the better part of 2 months in Fiji at the end of 2007, and from a traveler's point of view I saw no evidence that there had even been a coup. The primary impact was to stifle a tourism boom, during which record numbers of tourists arrived in Fiji and several new hotels and resorts were built. With business down, many establishments are offering deals on accommodations. All in all, this is a money-saving time to visit.

In the tourist areas—and especially on Fiji's marvelous offshore islets—you'll find gorgeous white-sand beaches bordered by curving coconut palms, azure lagoons and colorful reefs offering world-class scuba diving and snorkeling, green mountains sweeping to the sea, and a tropical climate in which to enjoy it all.

Fiji has something for every pocketbook. Its wide variety of accommodation ranges from deluxe resorts nestled in tropical gardens beside the beach to down-to-basics hostels that cater to the young and the young-at-heart. Out on its 300-plus islands is the largest and finest collection of small, Robinson Crusoe–like offshore resorts in the entire South Pacific—if not the world.

Regardless of where you stay and what you do, you are in for a memorable time. The friendly Fijians will see to that.

1 Fiji Today: The Regions in Brief

From a strategic position in the southwestern Pacific some 5,152km (3,200 miles) southwest of Honolulu and 3,156km (1,960 miles) northeast of Sydney, Fiji is the transportation and economic hub of the South Pacific islands. **Nadi International Airport** is the main connection point for flights going to the other island countries, and Fiji's capital city, **Suva,** is one of the region's prime shipping ports and headquarters of many regional organizations.

Given its size and diversity, any trip to Fiji requires careful planning to avoid disappointment. You could spend your entire vacation in Nadi, and although the tourism industry provides a host of activities to keep you busy there, you would miss what I consider are the best parts of Fiji. This is a country of more than 300 gorgeous islands, and I think you should try to experience more than one.

For visitors, Fiji is divided into several regions, each with its own special characteristics and appeal. Here's what each has to offer.

FIJI'S REGIONS IN BRIEF

The archipelago forms a horseshoe around the shallow, reef-strewn **Koro Sea,** much of which was dry land some 18,000 years ago during the last Ice Age. More than 300 islands and islets range in size from Viti Levu to tiny atolls that barely break the surface of the sea. The total land area is 18,187 sq. km (7,022 sq. miles).

ON VITI LEVU ISLAND

Known as the "mainland," **Viti Levu** island is 10 times the size of Tahiti, and Vanua Levu, the second-largest, is almost as big. **Suva,** the capital, lies 197km (122 miles) from Nadi airport; that's less than halfway around the island. In fact, at 10,803 sq. km (4,171 sq. miles), Viti Levu has more dry land than all the islands of French Polynesia.

With a few exceptions, Viti Levu does not have the best beaches in Fiji. Where it does have good sands, the reef offshore is more walkable than swimmable, especially at low tide. Look beyond Nadi and Viti Levu for good beaches and the best diving.

NADI   Most visitors arrive at Nadi International Airport, located among sugar cane fields on Viti Levu's dry western side. Known as **Nadi,** this area is the focal point of much of Fiji's tourism industry, and it's where many tourists traveling on package deals spend their time. There are a variety of hotels between the airport and predominately Indian **Nadi Town,** whose main industries are tourism and farming. Numerous handicraft, electronics, and clothing merchants wait to part you from your cash.

None of the airport hotels are on the beach, and even at **Denarau Island,** the country's major resort development, coastal mangrove forests make the beaches gray and the water offshore murky. There are many things to do in Nadi and Denarau Island, but I would make it a stopover on the way to someplace unless I had only a few days to spend here.

THE CORAL COAST   The **Queen's Road** runs around the south coast of Viti Levu through the resort area called the **Coral Coast.** Here you'll find comfortable hotels, luxury resorts, and fire-walking Fijians, but the beaches lead into very shallow lagoons. Most visitors staying on the Coast these days are tourists on packages. It's still a good choice for anyone who wants on-the-beach resort living while being able to conveniently see some of the country.

PACIFIC HARBOUR & BEQA ISLAND   About 48km (30 miles) west of Suva, Pacific Harbour was developed in the early 1970s as a resort complete with golf course, residences, shopping center, cultural center, and a seaside hotel. Because this area is in Viti Levu's rain belt, the project never reached its full potential. Nevertheless, it has the country's best cultural center, most scenic golf course, and excellent deep-sea fishing. It's also most convenient for river rafting on the **Navua**

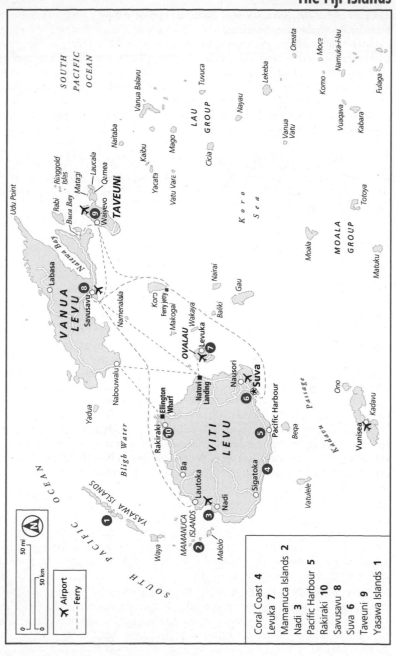

SOUTH PACIFIC OCEAN

Udu Point

SOUTH PACIFIC OCEAN

YASAWA ISLANDS

MAMANUCA ISLANDS

Waya

Malolo

Nabouwalu

Yadua

Bligh Water

Nadi

Lautoka

Ba

Rakiraki

Ellington Wharf

Sigatoka

VITI LEVU

Beqa

Pacific Harbour

Natovi Landing

Nausori

Suva

Pacific Harbour

Kadavu Passage

Vatulele

Ono

Vunisea

Kadavu

VANUA LEVU

Labasa

Savusavu

Natewa Bay

Namenalala

Namena

Nabouwalu

Rabi

Ringgold Isles

Buca Bay

Matagi

Laucala

Qemea

Waiyevo

TAVEUNI

OVALAU

Levuka

Koro

Ferry jetty

Makogai

Wakaya

Baliki

Nairai

Gau

Naitaba

Vanua Balavu

Yacata

Mago

Kaibu

Vatu Vara

Cicia

LAU GROUP

Nayau

Lekeba

Vanua Vatu

Omeata

Komo

Moce

Namuka-i-lau

Fulaga

Kabara

Vuaqava

Koro Sea

Moala

MOALA GROUP

Matuku

Totoya

Coral Coast **4**
Levuka **7**
Mamanuca Islands **2**
Nadi **3**
Pacific Harbour **5**
Rakiraki **10**
Savusavu **8**
Suva **6**
Taveuni **9**
Yasawa Islands **1**

✈ Airport
--- Ferry

50 mi
50 km

River, kayaking along the coast, and diving in lagoon surrounding **Beqa Island** (pronounced Beng-*ga*)—all of which make Pacific Harbour the self-anointed "Adventure Capital of Fiji."

NORTHERN VITI LEVU   An alternative driving route to Suva, the **King's Road** runs from Lautoka through the Sugar Belt of northern Viti Levu, passing through the predominately Indian towns of Ba and Tavua to **Rakiraki,** a Fijian village near the island's northernmost point and site of one of the country's few remaining colonial-era hotels. Jagged green mountains lend a gorgeous backdrop to the shoreline along the Rakiraki coast. Offshore, **Nananu-I-Ra Island** beckons windsurfers and budget-minded travelers, and the reefs are among Fiji's best for diving.

East of Rakiraki, the King's Road follows deep, mountain-bounded **Viti Levu Bay,** one of the most beautiful parts of Fiji. From the head of the bay, the road twists through the mountains, following the Wainbuka River, until it emerges near the east coast at Korovou. A left turn takes you to Natovi Wharf; and a right, to Suva. In other words, it's possible to drive or take buses all the way around Viti Levu via the Queen's and King's roads.

SUVA   The Queen's Road runs between Nadi Airport and **Suva,** Fiji's busy capital and one of the South Pacific's most cosmopolitan cities. The city had a population of 86,178, according to the 2007 census, but more than 300,000 are believed to live in the metropolitan area. Remnants of Fiji's century as a British possession and the presence of so many Indians give the town a certain air of the "Raj"—as if this were Agra or Bombay, not the boundary between Polynesia and Melanesia. On the other hand, Suva has high-rise buildings and lives at as fast a pace as can be found in the South Pacific west of Tahiti; this is no surprise because in many respects it's the bustling economic center of the region. The streets are filled with a melting-pot blend of Indians, Chinese, Fijians, other South Pacific islanders, "Europeans" (a term used in Fiji to mean persons of white skin, regardless of geographic origin), and individuals of mixed race.

> **Impressions**
>
> *There is no part of Fiji which is not civilized, although bush natives prefer a more naked kind of life.*
>
> —James A. Michener,
> *Return to Paradise*, 1951

ISLANDS OFF VITI LEVU

THE MAMANUCA ISLANDS   Beckoning off Nadi, the **Mamanuca Islands** offer day cruises and several offshore resorts of various sizes appealing to a broad spectrum of travelers, from swinging singles to quieter couples and families. Generally speaking, they are in the driest part of Fiji, which means sunshine most of the time. Some are flat atolls so small you can walk around them in 5 minutes. Others are hilly, grassy islands reminiscent of the Virgin Islands in the Caribbean. As the islands lie relatively close together, most offer excursions to the others. They also are close to Nadi, so you don't have to spend much extra money or time to get there.

THE YASAWA ISLANDS   A chain of gorgeous and relatively unspoiled islands stretching off north of the Mamanucas, the hilly **Yasawas** are blessed with the best beaches in Fiji. Two versions of *The Blue Lagoon* were filmed here. Young backpackers turned the Yasawas into one of the country's hottest destinations, but they now have resorts to fit every pocketbook.

Diving in Fiji

Fiji is famous among divers as being the "Soft Coral Capital of the World" because of the number and variety of colorful corals. These species grow well where moderate to heavy currents keep them fed, such as in the **Beqa Lagoon** south of Viti Levu and the **Somosomo Strait,** between Vanua Levu and Taveuni in northern Fiji, home of the **Great White Wall** and its **Rainbow Reef;** in turn, the corals attract a host of fish. As one example, more than 35 species of angelfish and butterfly fish swim in these waters.

The Great White Wall is covered—from between 23m and 60m (75–200 ft.) deep—with pale lavender corals, which appear almost snow-white underwater. Near Qamea and Matagi, off Taveuni, are the appropriately named **Purple Wall,** a straight drop from 9m to 24m (30–80 ft.), and Mariah's Cove, a small wall as colorful as the Rainbow Reef. Also in the north, **Magic Mountain,** on the Namena barrier reef around Moody's Namena, has hard corals on top and soft ones on the sides, which attract an enormous number of small fish and their predators. Magic Mountain is in the **Namena Marine Protected Reserve,** one of Fiji's top sites.

In Beqa Lagoon, the soft corals of **Frigate Passage** seem to fall over one another, and **Side Streets** has unusual orange coral. The nearby southern coast of Viti Levu has mostly hard corals, but you can go **shark diving** off Pacific Harbour (that is, the dive masters attract sharks by feeding them).

South of Viti Levu, **Kadavu** island is skirted by the **Great Astrolabe Reef,** known for its steep outside walls dotted with both soft and hard corals. The Astrolabe attracts Fiji's largest concentration of manta rays.

Even the heavily visited **Mamanuca Islands** off Nadi have their share of good sites, including **The Pinnacle,** a coral head rising 18m (59 ft.) from the lagoon floor, and a W-shaped protrusion from the outer reef. A drawback for some divers is that they don't have the Mamanuca sites all to themselves.

All but a few resorts in Fiji have dive operations on site, as I point out in the following chapters.

The best way to dive a lot of reefs in Fiji, especially Namena Marine Protected Reserve and others in Bligh Water between Viti Levu and Vanua Levu, is on a live-aboard dive boat. Most luxurious is the *NAI'A* (✆ **888/ 510-1593** in North America or 345-0382 in Fiji; www.naia.com.fj), a 120-foot motor-sailing yacht that can carry 18 persons in 9 staterooms. It's the favorite of every diver I know who lives in Fiji. Rates start at US$2,940 (£1,470) per person double occupancy for a 7-day cruise. Others are the two catamarans *Fiji Aggressor I and Fiji Aggressor II,* both operated by the U.S.-based Aggressor Fleet (✆ **800/348-2628** or 985/385-2628; www.aggressor. com). Rates begin at US$2,500 (£1,250) per person double occupancy.

BEQA ISLAND   A 30-minute boat ride off Pacific Harbour, rugged **Beqa** is best known for the **Beqa Lagoon,** one of Fiji's top diving destinations. Here you'll also find **Frigate Passage,** one of the world's best surfing spots (but not for novices, as the curling breakers slam onto the reef). Beqa has three comfortable hotels.

KADAVU   Fiji's third-largest island, **Kadavu** lies about 100km (62 miles) south of Viti Levu. It's a long and skinny island whose south shore is skirted by the **Great Astrolabe Reef,** another of Fiji's top diving destinations. On the north coast lie several kilometers of beautiful **Long Beach,** one of Fiji's finest. Ashore, its lack of mongooses, iguanas, and other imported predators makes it a heaven for indigenous wildlife and birds, including the endemic musk parrot, fantail, honeyeater, and whistling dove.

LEVUKA & OVALAU   East of Viti Levu, the picturesque island of **Ovalau** is home to the historic town of **Levuka,** which has changed little since its days as a boisterous whaling port and the first capital of a united Fiji in the 1800s. Few places in the South Pacific have retained their frontier facade as has this living museum.

NORTHERN FIJI

Vanua Levu, Taveuni, and their nearby islands are known locally as "The North" because they comprise Fiji's Northern Province. Over on Vanua Levu, Fiji's second-largest island, a little town with the exotic name **Savusavu** lies nestled in one of the region's most protected deep-water bays. Unlike Viti Levu, Savusavu and the Garden Isle of **Taveuni** are throwbacks to the old South Pacific, a land of copra plantations and small Fijian villages tucked away in the bush. Both have excellent places to stay, including fine resorts off Vanua Levu and near Taveuni's north coast on **Matagi** and **Qamea** islands. Vanua Levu and Taveuni have considerable amounts of freehold land; in fact, so many of my compatriots have bought parcels on southern Vanua Levu that Fijians now facetiously refer to Savusavu as "Little America."

GOVERNMENT

Fiji had a Westminster-style government before the 2006 coup. A 71-member parliament consisted of 23 seats reserved for Fijians, 19 for Indians, 1 for Rotuma (a Polynesian island north of Viti Levu), 3 for general electors (anyone who's a Fijian, Indian, or Rotuman), and 25 for any citizen, regardless of race. The Great Council of Chiefs picked the country's largely figurehead president, who presided over an appointed senate with relatively little power.

Since the coup the country has had an interim government headed by the military commander, navy Commodore Frank Bainimarama, who engineered the coup. Bainimarama threatened for most of 2006 to "clean up" the Fiji nationalist government of elected Prime Minister Laisenia Qarase, which he accused of being both corrupt and racist. His interim government includes Fiji Labour Party leader Mahendra Chaudhry as finance minister. Chaudhry was deposed as prime minister during the country's racially motivated insurrection in 2000 and was a key player in the coalition government removed by the first coup in 1987.

Bainimarama has agreed, in principle, to hold elections in 2009 after changes to the country's constitution, specifically removal of the race-based electoral system by which nationalist Fijians maintained a majority in parliament.

ECONOMY

Tourism is far and away Fiji's largest industry. Although visitors dropped off following the December 2006 coup, earlier record demand spurred a hotel construction boom. Sugar and garment manufacturing—Fiji's other economic mainstays—have also fallen off. Grown primarily by Indian farmers, the sugar cane is harvested between June and November and crushed in five aging sugar mills operated by the government-owned

Fiji Sugar Corporation; all the mills need repair and upgrading. The number of farmers has decreased since Fijian landowners have not renewed many of their land leases (some displaced farmers have moved into shanties around Suva). In addition, the country lost European Union sugar price supports and favorable trade preferences for garments sold to the United States and Australia.

Gold mining on northern Viti Levu also contributes to the economy, as do fishing, copra, timber, furniture, coffee (you'll get a rich, strong brew throughout the country), other consumer goods produced by small manufacturers (the Colgate toothpaste you buy in Fiji is made here), and the famous "Fiji" bottled water. Suva is also a major transshipment point for goods destined for other South Pacific islands. Remittances from Fijians working overseas also contribute significantly to the economy.

Unemployment is a persistent problem in Fiji. More than half the population is under 25, and there just aren't enough jobs being created for young people coming into the workforce. About 50% of all households live below the official poverty line or just above it. As a consequence, the country has seen a marked increase in burglaries, robberies, home invasions, and other crimes.

2 Fiji Yesterday: History 101

The Dutch navigator Abel Tasman sighted some of the Fiji Islands in the 1640s, and Capt. James Cook visited one of the southernmost islands in 1774. After the mutiny on HMS *Bounty* off Tonga in April 1789, Capt. William Bligh and his loyal crewmen sailed their longboat between Viti Levu and Vanua Levu, where they barely escaped capture by Fijians in speedy *druas* (war canoes). The passage between Viti Levu and Vanua Levu still is named Bligh Water.

European sandalwood, copra, and *bêche-de-mer* (sea cucumber) traders settled on Ovalau in the early 1820s and established the first urban-type town in Fiji at Levuka. They threw their lots with High Chief Cakobau of Bau, a tiny island off the eastern coast of Viti Levu. Cakobau never ruled all the islands, for Enele Ma'afu, a member of Tonga's royal family, invaded the Lau Group in 1848 and exerted control over eastern Fiji. Ma'afu made the conquered Fijian chiefs marry Tongan women, which helps explain why many of Fiji's high chiefs today appear as much Polynesian as Melanesian. Ma'afu also brought along Wesleyan missionaries from Tonga, thus giving the Methodist church a foothold in Fiji (it is still the major denomination here).

The early European settlers bought about 10% of the land from the Fijians, sometimes fraudulently and often for whiskey and guns (this freehold property is a sore point with some modern Fijians, who would like it back). Claims and counterclaims to land ownership swept Fiji to the brink of race war. To avoid anarchy, the Europeans established a national government at Levuka and named Cakobau king of Fiji. Three years later they forced Cakobau to cede the islands to Great Britain. The Deed of Cession making Fiji a British colony was signed on October 10, 1874.

Impressions

Many of the missionaries were eaten, leading an irreverent planter to suggest that they triumphed by infiltration.

—James A. Michener,
Return to Paradise, 1951

Britain sent Sir Arthur Gordon as the colony's first governor. He allowed the Fijian chiefs to govern their villages and districts as they had done before and to advise him through a Great Council of Chiefs. He declared that native Fijian lands could be leased but not sold. That decision, to this day, has helped to protect the Fijians, their land, and their customs, but it has also helped fuel animosity on the part of the land-deprived Indians.

> ## Impressions
>
> *A hundred years of prodding by the British have failed to make the Fijians see why they should work for money.*
>
> —James A. Michener, *Return to Paradise*, 1951

Gordon prohibited the planters from using Fijians as laborers (not that many of them had the slightest inclination to work for someone else). When the planters switched to sugar cane in the 1870s, Sir Arthur convinced them to import indentured servants from India. The first 463 East Indians arrived on May 14, 1879 (see "The Islanders," below).

FIJI BECOMES INDEPENDENT   Fiji's road to independence was anything but smooth. By the mid-20th century the Fiji Indians were highly organized, in political parties and trade unions, and they objected to a constitution that would institutionalize Fijian control of the government and Fijian ownership of most of the new nation's land. Key compromises were made in 1969, however, and on October 10, 1970—exactly 96 years after Cakobau signed the Deed of Cession—the Dominion of Fiji became an independent member of the British Commonwealth of Nations.

Under the 1970 constitution, Fiji had a Westminster-style Parliament consisting of an elected House of Representatives and a Senate composed of Fijian chiefs. For the first 17 years of independence, the Fijians maintained a majority—albeit a tenuous one—in the House of Representatives and control of the government under the leadership of the late Ratu Sir Kamisese Mara, the country's first prime minister.

Then, in a general election held in April 1987, a coalition of Indians and liberal Fijians voted Ratu Mara and his Alliance party out of power. Although a Fijian became prime minister, he named more Indians than Fijians to his cabinet.

RAMBO'S COUP   Shortly after the election, members of the predominantly Fijian army stormed into Parliament and overthrew the new government. It was the South Pacific's first military coup. The leader was Col. Sitiveni Rabuka (pronounced *Ram-bu-ka*), whom local wags quickly nicknamed "Rambo." A Fijian of nonchiefly lineage, Rabuka abrogated the 1970 constitution and declared Fiji to be an independent republic. In 1990, he promulgated a new constitution guaranteeing Fijians a parliamentary majority—thereby rankling the Indians. Rabuka's pro-Fijian party won the initial election, but he barely hung onto power in 1994 by forming a coalition with the European, Chinese, and mixed-race general-elector parliamentarians.

Rabuka also appointed a three-person Constitutional Review Commission, which proposed a new constitution. Ratified in 1998, it led to general elections in 1999. Supported by many Fijians, Labor Party leader Mahendra Chaudhry won an outright majority of parliament and became Fiji's first Indian prime minister.

THE 2000 INSURRECTION AND COUP   Chaudhry's tenure was short-lived, for in May 2000 a disgruntled Fijian businessman named George Speight led a gang of armed henchmen into parliament. Demanding the appointment of an all-Fijian government, they held Chaudhry and several members of parliament hostage for 56 days. While negotiating with Speight, Commodore Frank Bainimarama, Fiji's military chief, deposed Chaudhry and appointed an interim government headed by Fijian

---

(Fun Fact The Count Confounded

In 1917, Count Felix von Luckner arrived at Wakaya Island off Viti Levu in search of a replacement for his World War I German raider, the *Seeadler*, which had gone aground in the Cook Islands after shelling Papeete on Tahiti. A local constable became suspicious of the armed foreigners and notified the district police inspector. Only Europeans—not Fijians or Indians—could use firearms, so the inspector took a band of unarmed Fijians to Wakaya. Thinking he was up against a larger armed force, von Luckner unwittingly surrendered.

---

economist and banker Laisenia Qarase. Speight released his hostages after being promised amnesty, but the military arrested him 2 weeks later and charged him with treason. Convicted by a civilian court, his death sentence was later commuted to life in prison. Other participants, including members of Parliament, were convicted of lesser crimes and sent to jail.

Fiji's supreme court then ruled that the 1998 constitution was still in effect and ordered fresh parliamentary elections in 2001, when Qarase became the legal prime minister of a Fijian-dominated government. Chaudhry was returned to parliament as leader of the opposition. A Fiji nationalist, Qarase proposed a "Reconciliation, Tolerance, and Unity" bill, which opponents—including Bainimarama—claimed would grant amnesty to Speight and other participants in the 2000 insurrection. The proposed legislation was the most contentious issue in the general elections of May 2006, which returned Qarase to power.

THE 2006 COUP   Qarase further incensed the military by releasing some 200 coup participants from prison, and he continued to push his controversial reconciliation bill. He also proposed transferring ownership of Fiji's foreshore and lagoons from the government to indigenous seaside tribes, who would then be free to charge resorts, dive operators, fishers and others to use their lagoons and coastal waters. This proposal created a firestorm of protest from the tourism industry as well as from Fijians who do not live beside the sea—and thus presumably would have to pay to go fishing.

Bainimarama warned Qarase for most of 2006 that the military would take over if he did not abandon the proposals. On December 5—a date Fijians refer to as "5/12"—the military drove from Queen Elizabeth Barracks into Suva and took over. The coup was peaceful, and life outside tourism returned to normal quickly. The initial military roadblocks and checkpoints reduced Fiji's crime rate (it went back up when the soldiers were withdrawn, prompting some merchants to call for permanent checkpoints).

In addition to abandoning overtly racist government policies, Bainimarama has cracked down on corruption and uncontrolled government spending, which had become rampant under Qarase. He has opened Fiji's formerly monopolized communications industry to competition, which promises more over-the-air television channels (instead of one) and lower prices for phone and Internet services. He also has encouraged the thousands of Fiji Indian professionals who had fled the country to return home by letting them be permanent residents of Fiji as well as citizens of other nations (Fiji does not recognize dual citizenship).

3 The Islanders

The official 2007 census found Fiji's total population to be 827,900. Indigenous Fijians made up 57%, Fiji Indians 38%, and other Pacific islanders, Chinese, Europeans, and persons of mixed race the other 5%. Thanks to a high Fijian birth rate, the overall population has been rising slightly despite the country's losing thousands of Fiji Indians since the first military coup in 1987.

It's difficult to imagine peoples of two more contrasting cultures living side by side. "Fijians generally perceive Indians as mean and stingy, crafty and demanding to the extent of being considered greedy, inconsiderate and grasping, uncooperative, egotistic, and calculating," wrote Professor Asesela Ravuvu of the University of the South Pacific. "On the other hand," he said, "Indians see Fijians as *jungalis*—poor, backward, naive, foolish, and living on land they will not sell."

Given that these attitudes are not likely to change anytime soon, it is remarkable that Fijians and Fiji Indians actually manage to coexist. Politically correct Americans may take offense at some things they can hear said in Fiji because racial distinctions are a fact of life here, as you will notice on the country's Immigration entry form.

From a visitor's standpoint, the famously friendly Fijians give the country its laid-back South Seas charm while providing relatively good service at the hotels. For their

---

(Fun Fact   A Holy Meal

When meeting and talking to the smiling Fijians, it's difficult to imagine that hardly more than a century ago their ancestors were among the world's most ferocious cannibals. Today the only vestiges of this past are the four-pronged wooden cannibal forks sold in handicraft shops (they make interesting conversation pieces when used at home to serve hors d'oeuvres).

Yet in the early 1800s, the Fijians were so fierce that Europeans were slow to settle in the islands for fear of literally being turned into a meal. Back then, Fijian society was organized by tribes, which constantly warred with each other, usually with brutal vengeance. The winners hung captured enemy children by their feet from the rigging of their canoes, and they sometimes consecrated new buildings by burying live adult prisoners in holes dug for the support posts.

The ultimate insult, however, was to eat the enemy's flesh. Victorious chiefs were even said to cook and nibble on the fingers or tongues of the vanquished, relishing each bite while the victims watched in agony. "One man actually stood by my side and ate the very eyes out of a roasted skull he had, saying, 'Venaca, venaca,' that is, very good," wrote William Speiden, the purser on the U.S. exploring expedition that charted Fiji in 1840.

More than 100 white-skinned individuals ended up with their skulls smashed and their bodies baked in an earth oven, including the Rev. Thomas Baker, who attempted to convert the Viti Levu highlanders in 1867. Instead of converting, they killed the reverend, tossed his body into an oven, and made a meal of him.

"Grog" Etiquette

Known as *kava* elsewhere in the South Pacific, the slightly narcotic drink that Fijians call *yaqona* (yong-*go*-na) or "grog" rivals Fiji Bitter beer as the national drink. You will likely have half a coconut shell of grog offered—if not shoved in your face—beginning at your hotel's reception desk. Fiji has more grog shops than bars.

And thanks to the promotion of *kavalactone,* the active ingredient, as a health-food answer to stress and insomnia in the United States and elsewhere, growing the root is an important part of the economy in the South Pacific. When fears surfaced a few years ago that kava could be linked to liver disease, locals commented that if that were true, there would be few healthy livers in Fiji!

Yaqona has always played an important ceremonial role in Fijian life. No significant occasion takes place without it, and a *sevusevu* (welcoming) ceremony is usually held for tour groups visiting Fijian villages. Mats are placed on the floor, the participants gather in a circle, and the yaqona roots are mixed with water and strained through coconut husks into a carved wooden bowl, called a *tanoa.*

The ranking chief sits next to the tanoa during the welcoming ceremony. He extends in the direction of the guest of honor a cowrie shell attached to one leg of the bowl by a cord of woven coconut fiber. It's extremely impolite to cross the plane of the cord once it has been extended.

The guest of honor (in this case your tour guide) then offers a gift to the village (a kilogram or two of dried grog roots will do these days) and makes a speech explaining the purpose of his visit. The chief then passes the first cup of yaqona to the guest of honor, who claps once, takes the cup in both hands, and gulps down the entire cup of sawdust-tasting liquid in one swallow. Everyone else then claps three times.

Next, each chief drinks a cup, clapping once before bolting it down. Again, everyone else claps three times after each cup is drained. Except for the clapping and speeches, everyone remains silent throughout, a tradition easily understood considering kava's numbing effect on the lips and tongue.

part, the Fiji Indians make this an easy country to visit by providing excellent maintenance of facilities and efficient and inexpensive services, such as transportation.

The 1998 constitution makes everyone, regardless of his or her race, a Fiji Islander.

THE FIJIANS

Today's indigenous Fijians are descended from a Melanesian people who came from the west and began settling here around 500 B.C. Over time they replaced the Polynesians, whose ancestors had arrived some 1,000 years beforehand, but not before adopting much of Polynesian culture and intermarrying enough to give many Fijians lighter skin than that of most other Melanesians, especially in the islands of eastern Fiji near the Polynesian Kingdom of Tonga. (This is less the case in the west and among the hill dwellers, whose ancestors had less contact with Polynesians in ancient times.) Similar differences occur in terms of culture. For example, whereas Melanesians traditionally pick their chiefs by popular consensus, Fijian chiefs hold titles by heredity, in the Polynesian (or more precisely, Tongan) fashion.

Most Fijians still live in small villages along the coast and riverbanks or in the hills, and you will see some traditional thatch *bures*, or houses, scattered in the countryside away from the main roads. Members of each tribe cultivate and grow food crops in small "bush gardens" on plots of communally owned native land assigned to their families. More than 80% of the land in Fiji is communally owned by Fijians.

A majority of Fijians are Methodists, their forebears having been converted by Wesleyan missionaries who came to the islands in the 19th century. The Methodist Church is a powerful political force.

THE TABUA   The highest symbol of respect among Fijians is the tooth of the sperm whale, known as a *tabua* (pronounced tam-*bu*-a). Like large mother-of-pearl shells used in other parts of Melanesia, tabuas in ancient times played a role similar to that of money in modern society and still have various ceremonial uses. They are presented to chiefs as a sign of respect, given as gifts to arrange marriages, offered to friends to show sympathy after the death of a family member, and used as a means to seal a contract or another agreement. It is illegal to export a tabua out of Fiji; and even if you did, the international conventions on endangered species prohibit your bringing them into the United States and most other Western countries.

FIRE WALKING   Legend says that a Fijian god once repaid a favor to a warrior on Beqa island by giving him the ability to walk unharmed on fire. His descendants, all members of the Sawau tribe on Beqa, still walk across stones heated to white-hot by a bonfire—but usually for the entertainment of tourists at the hotels rather than for a particular religious purpose.

Traditionally, the participants—all male—had to abstain from women and coconuts for 2 weeks before the ceremony. If they partook of either, they would suffer burns to their feet. Naturally a priest (some would call him a witch doctor) would recite certain incantations to make sure the coals were hot and the gods were at bay and not angry enough to scorch the soles.

Today's fire walking is a bit touristy but still worth seeing. If you don't believe the stones are hot, go ahead and touch one of them—but do it gingerly.

Some Fiji Indians engage in fire walking, but it's strictly for religious purposes.

FIJIAN VILLAGE ETIQUETTE   Fijian villages are easy to visit, but keep in mind that to the people who live in them, the entire village—not just an individual's house—is home. In your native land, you wouldn't walk into a stranger's living room without being invited, so find someone and ask permission before traipsing into a village. The Fijians are accommodating people, and it's unlikely they will say no; in fact,

---

Impressions

It is doubtful if anyone but an Indian can dislike Fijians . . . They are one of the happiest peoples on earth and laugh constantly. Their joy in things is infectious; they love practical jokes, and in warfare they are without fear.
—James A. Michener, *Return to Paradise*, 1951

> **Moments Meeting the Friendly Fijians**
>
> The indigenous Fijians are justly renowned for their friendliness to strangers, and many Fiji Indians are as well-educated and informed as anyone in the South Pacific. Together, these two peoples are fun to meet, whether it be over a hotel desk or while riding with them in one of their fume-belching buses.

they may ask you to stay for a meal or stage a small yaqona ceremony in your honor (see the "'Grog' Etiquette" box above). They are very tied to tradition, so ask first.

If you are invited to stay or eat in the village, a small gift to the chief is appropriate; F$10 (US$6.50/£3.35) per person or a handful of dried kava root from the local market will do. The gift should be given to the chief or highest-ranking person present to accept it. Sometimes it helps to explain that it is a gift to the village and not payment for services rendered, especially if it's money you're giving.

Only chiefs are allowed to wear hats and sunglasses in Fijian villages, so it's good manners for visitors to take theirs off. Shoulders must be covered at all times. Fijians go barefoot and walk slightly stooped in their bures. Men sit cross-legged on the floor; women sit with their legs to the side. They don't point at one another with hands, fingers, or feet, nor do they touch each other's heads or hair. They greet each other and strangers with a big smile and a sincere "*Bula.*"

THE FIJI INDIANS

The *Leonidas,* a labor transport ship, arrived at Levuka from Calcutta on May 14, 1879, and landed 463 indentured servants destined to work Fiji's sugar cane fields. As more than 60,000 Indians would do over the next 37 years, these first immigrants signed agreements (*girmits,* they called them) requiring that they work in Fiji for 5 years; they would be free to return to India after 5 more years. Most of them labored in the cane fields for the initial term of their girmits, living in "coolie lines" of squalid shacks hardly better than the poverty-stricken conditions most left behind in India.

After the initial 5 years, however, they were free to seek work on their own. Many leased plots of land from the Fijians and began planting sugar cane or raising cattle. To this day most of Fiji's sugar crop, the country's most important agricultural export, is produced on small leased plots. Other Fiji Indians went into business in the growing cities and towns and, joined in the early 1900s by an influx of business-oriented Indians, founded Fiji's modern merchant and professional classes.

Of the immigrants who came from India between 1879 and 1916, when the indenturing system ended, some 85% were Hindus, 14% were Muslims, and the remaining 1% were Sikhs and Christians. Fiji offered these adventurers far more opportunities than caste-controlled India. In fact, the caste system was scrapped very quickly by the Hindus in Fiji, and, for the most part, the violent relations between Hindus and Muslims that racked India were put aside on the islands.

Only a small minority of the Fiji Indians went home after their girmits expired. They tended then—as now—to live in the towns and villages, and in the "Sugar Belt" along the drier north and west coasts of Viti Levu and Vanua Levu. Hindu and Sikh temples and Muslim mosques abound in these areas, and places such as Ba and Tavua look like small towns on the Indian subcontinent. On the southern coasts and in the mountains, the population is overwhelmingly Fijian. Fiji Indians constituted more

Impressions
The question of what to do with these clever Indians of Fiji is the most acute problem in the Pacific today. Within 10 years it will become a world concern.
                                        —James A. Michener, *Return to Paradise,* 1951

than half of Fiji's population prior to the 1987 coup, but emigration (not to India but to Australia, New Zealand, Canada, and the U.S.) reduced their share to 38% by 2007.

4 Languages

Fiji has three official languages. To oversimplify, the Fijians speak Fijian, the Indians speak Hindi, and they speak English to each other. Schoolchildren are taught in their native language until they are proficient (necessarily fluent) in English, which thereafter is the medium of instruction. Although you may not get into serious conversations in English with everyone, and you may have trouble understanding English with Fijian or Hindi accents, you should have little trouble getting around and enjoying the country.

FIJIAN

Fijian is similar to the Polynesian languages spoken in Tahiti, the Cook Islands, Samoa, and Tonga in that it uses vowel sounds similar to those in Latin, French, Italian, and Spanish: *a* as in b*a*d, *e* as in s*a*y, *i* as in b*ee*, *o* as in g*o*, and *u* as in kangar*oo*.

Some Fijian consonants, however, sound very different from their counterparts in English, Latin, or any other language. In devising a written form of Fijian, the early Wesleyan missionaries decided to use some familiar Roman consonants in unfamiliar ways. It would have been easier for English speakers to read Fijian had the missionaries used a combination of consonants—*th,* for example—for the Fijian sounds. Their main purpose, however, was to teach Fijians to read and write their own language. Because the Fijians separate all consonant sounds with vowels, writing two consonants together confused them.

The missionaries came up with the following usage: *b* sounds like *mb* (as in reme*mb*er), *c* sounds like *th* (as in *th*at), *d* sounds like *nd* (as in Su*nd*ay), *g* sounds like *ng* (as in si*ng*er), and *q* sounds like *ng + g* (as in fi*ng*er).

The unusual pronunciation is most evident in Fijian names such as Nadi, which is pronounced *Nahn-*di. There are many other names of people and places that are equally or even more confusing.

In addition, the letter *r* is rolled in an exaggerated fashion, like the Spanish *r* taken to extreme.

Here are some Fijian names with their unusual pronunciations:

Ba	mBah	**Labasa**	Lam-*ba*-sa
Bau	mBau	**Mamanuca**	Ma-ma-*nu*-tha
Beqa	*mBeng*-ga	**Nadi**	*Nahn*-di
Buca	*mBu*-tha	**Tabua**	*Tam*-bua
Cakobau	Thack-*om*-bau	**Toberua**	Tom-*bay*-rua
Korotogo	Ko-ro-*ton*-go	**Tubakula**	Toom-ba-*ku*-la

You are likely to hear these Fijian words and phrases used during your stay:

English	Fijian	Pronunciation
hello	**bula**	*boo*-lah
hello (formal)	**ni sa bula**	nee sahm *boo*-lah
good morning	**ni sa yadra**	nee sah *yand*-rah
good night	**ni sa moce**	nee sah *mo*-thay
thank you	**vinaka**	vee-*nah*-kah
thank you very much	**vinaka vaka levu**	vee-*nah*-kah *vah*-ka *lay*-voo
house/bungalow	**bure**	*boo*-ray
tapa cloth	**masi**	*mah*-see
sarong	**sulu**	*sue*-loo

FIJI HINDI

The common everyday language spoken among the Fiji Indians is a tongue peculiar to Fiji. Although it is based on Hindustani, it is different from that language as spoken in India. It grew out of the need for a common language among the immigrants who came from various parts of the subcontinent and spoke some of the many languages and dialects found in India and Pakistan. Thus it includes words from Hindi, Urdu, Tamil Nadu, a variety of Indian dialects, and even English and Fijian. You'll see what I mean by tuning into a Hindi radio station. If you want to impress the Fiji Indians, try these phrases in Fiji Hindi:

English	Fiji Hindi	Pronunciation
hello and good-bye	**namaste**	na-*mas*-tay
how are you?	**kaise?**	ka-*ee*-say
good	**accha**	*ach*-cha
I'm okay	**Thik hai**	teak high
right or okay	**rait**	right

5 Visitor Information & Maps

The **Fiji Visitors Bureau (FVB),** P.O. Box 9217, Nadi Airport, Fiji Islands (© **672 2433;** fax 672 0141; www.bulafiji.com), sends out maps, brochures, and other materials from its head office in the Colonial Plaza shopping center, on the Queens Road in Namaka, about halfway between Nadi Airport and Nadi Town. It also has an information desk in a historic colonial house at the corner of Thomson and Scott streets in the heart of Suva (© **330 2433**).

The FVB's award-winning website is a trove of up-to-date information and is linked to the home pages of the country's airlines, tour operators, attractions, and hotels. It also has a directory of e-mail addresses.

Other FVB offices are:

- **United States and Canada:** 5777 West Century Blvd., Ste. 220, Los Angeles, CA 90045 (© **800/932-3454** or 310/568-1616; fax 310/670-2318; www.bulafiji now.com)
- **Australia:** Level 12, St. Martins Tower, 31 Market St., Sydney, NSW 2000 (© **02/ 9264-3399;** fax 02/9264-3060; www.bulafiji-au.com)

> **(Tips) Beware of Unofficial "Tourist Information Centres"**
>
> When you see "Tourist Information Centre" in Nadi or elsewhere, it is most likely a travel agent or tour operator, whose staff will invariably steer you to its products. The only official, nonprofit tourist information centers are operated by the Fiji Visitors Bureau, at the Nadi and Suva locations listed above.

- **New Zealand:** 33 Scanlon St., Grey Lynn (P.O. Box 1179), Auckland (℃ 09/ 373-2533; fax 09/376-4720; info@bulafiji.co.nz)
- **Germany:** Petersburger Strasse 94, 10247 Berlin (℃ 30/4225-6026; fax 30/ 4225-6287; www.bulafiji.de).
- **Japan:** Noa Building, 14th Floor, 3–5, 2 Chome, Azabuudai, Minato-Ku, Tokyo 106 (℃ 03/3587-2038; fax 03/3587-2563; www.bulafiji-jp.com)
- **United Kingdom:** Lion House, 111 Hare Lane, Claygate, Surrey K1 0QF (℃ 0800/652-2158 or 1372/469-818; fax 1372 470057; fiji@ihml.com).

You can tune many hotel room TVs to the advertiser-supported **Visitor Information Network (VIN),** usually on channel 10, for tips about what to do and where to dine. The Fiji government's website is at **www.fiji.gov.fj**. See "Newspapers/Magazines" in "Fast Facts: Fiji," at the end of this chapter, for other useful sites.

Many bookstores and hotel gift shops in Fiji sell maps, and the Fiji telephone directory has colorful city and town maps in the front. See "Visitor Information & Maps," in chapter 2, for ordering maps before you leave home.

6 Entry Requirements

PASSPORTS & VISAS

All visitors must have a passport valid for 6 months beyond their visits and an onward or return airline ticket. See "Passports," in the "Fast Facts" section at the end of chapter 2, for information on how to get a passport.

Visitor permits good for stays of up to 4 months are issued upon arrival to citizens of the United States; all Commonwealth countries; most European, South American, and South Pacific island nations; and Mexico, Japan, Israel, Pakistan, South Korea, Thailand, Tunisia, and Turkey.

Citizens of all other countries must apply for visas in advance from the Fiji embassies or consulates. In the United States, contact the **Embassy of Fiji,** Ste. 710, 2000 M St. NW, Washington, DC 20007 (℃ 202/466-8320; fax 202/466-8325; www.fijiembassy.org). Other Fiji embassies or high commissions are in Canberra and Sydney, Australia; Wellington, New Zealand; London, England; Brussels, Belgium; Tokyo, Japan; Kuala Lumpur, Malaysia; Port Moresby, Papua New Guinea; New Delhi, India; and Beijing, China. Check your local phone book, or go to **www.fiji.gov.fj** and click on "Fiji Missions Overseas."

Persons wishing to remain longer than their initial permits must apply for extensions from the **Immigration Department,** whose primary offices are at the Nadi International Airport terminal (℃ 672 2454; www.fiji.gov.fj) and in the Labour Department building on Victoria Parade in downtown Suva (℃ 321 1775).

Vaccinations are not required unless you have been in a yellow fever or cholera area shortly before arriving in Fiji.

CUSTOMS

See "Fast Facts: Fiji" at the end of this chapter for what you can bring into Fiji and "Fast Facts: South Pacific" in chapter 2 for what you can bring home. *Note*: Fiji Customs inspectors will X-ray *all* of your luggage upon arrival.

7 When to Go

THE CLIMATE

Although global warming has made the climate more unpredictable than in the past, the prevailing southeast trade winds temper Fiji's warm, humid, tropical climate during most of the year. Nationally, average high temperatures range from 82°F (28°C) during the austral winter (June–Sept) to 88°F (31°C) during the summer months (Dec–Mar). Evenings average a warm and comfortable 70°F to 82°F (21°C–28°C) throughout the year.

The islands receive the most rain from November through March, but the amount depends on which side of each island the measurement is taken on. The north and west coasts tend to be drier and warmer, and the east and south coasts wetter (and somewhat cooler but more humid). Nadi, on the west side of Viti Levu, gets considerably less rain than does Suva, on the southeast side (some 200 in. a year), but its average temperatures are about 36°F (2°C) higher. Consequently, most of Fiji's resorts are on the western side of Viti Levu. Even during the wetter months, however, periods of intense tropical sunshine usually follow the rain showers.

Fiji is in the heart of the South Pacific cyclone belt and receives its share of hurricanes between November and April. Fiji's Meteorological Service is excellent at tracking hurricanes and issuing timely warnings, and the local travel industry is very adept at preparing for them. I've lived through a few Fiji cyclones, and I've never let the thought of one keep me from returning every chance I get.

The Fiji Meteorological Service (**www.met.gov.fj**) gives the current forecast.

Average Maximum Daytime Temperatures at Nadi

	Jan	Feb	Mar	Apr	May	June	July	Aug	Sept	Oct	Nov	Dec
Temp °F	89	89	88	87	86	85	83	84	85	86	88	89
Temp °C	32	32	31	31	30	29	29	29	29	30	31	31

HOLIDAYS & SPECIAL EVENTS

Unlike other South Pacific island countries, Fiji has no grand nationwide festival around which to plan a visit. Two local events worth noting are the annual **Hibiscus Festival** in Suva during mid-August and the **South Pacific World Music Festival,** which brings noted regional artists to Savusavu in November. Contact the Fiji Visitors Bureau or the Savusavu Tourism Association (**www.fiji-savusavu.com**) for details.

At press time, all banks, government offices, and most private businesses are closed for New Year's Day, Good Friday, Easter Saturday, Easter Monday, Ratu Sukuna Day (May 30 or the Mon closest thereto), The Prophet Mohammed's Birthday (a Mon in mid-July), Fiji Day (the Mon closest to Oct 10), Deepawali (the Indian festival of lights in late Oct or early Nov), Christmas Day, and December 26 (Boxing Day).

Banks take an additional holiday the first Monday in August, and some businesses also close for various Hindu and Muslim holy days. And if Fiji wins the annual Hong Kong Sevens rugby tournament, don't expect anyone to be at work the next day!

8 Money

The national currency is the Fiji dollar, which is divided into 100 cents and trades independently on the foreign exchange markets. The Fiji dollar is abbreviated "FID" by the banks and airlines, but I use **F$** in this book. Some hotels and resorts quote their rates in U.S. dollars, indicated here by **US$**.

HOW TO GET LOCAL CURRENCY   An **ANZ Bank** branch, in the international arrivals concourse at Nadi International Airport, is open 24 hours a day, 7 days a week. There's an ATM just outside the branch, where you can draw Fijian currency by using MasterCard or Visa credit or debit cards. **GlobalEX** has exchange counters (but no ATMs) in the arrivals concourse and near the departures door.

ANZ Bank, Westpac Bank, and Colonial National Bank have offices throughout the country where currency and traveler's checks can be exchanged. They all have ATMs at their Nadi and Suva offices and at their branches in Savusavu, and Colonial National Bank has an ATM on Taveuni. There's an ATM at the Nausori Airport terminal near Suva. Several large hotels on Viti Levu have ATMs in their lobbies. Elsewhere bring credit cards, cash, and traveler's checks. Banking hours nationwide are Monday to Thursday from 9:30am to 3pm and Friday from 9:30am to 4pm.

The Fiji Dollar, the U.S. & Canadian Dollar & the British Pound

At this writing, US$1 and the Canadian dollar (C$) = approximately F$1.54 (or, the other way around, F$1 = US65¢), which is the exchange rate I used to calculate the dollar values given in this book. **For British readers:** At this writing, £1 = approximately F$3 (or, F$1 = 33p), the rate used to calculate the pound values below. **Note:** International exchange rates fluctuate depending on economic and political factors. Thus, the values given in this table may not be the same when you travel to Fiji. Use the following table only as a guide. Find the current rates at **www.xe.com**.

F$	US$/C$	UK£	F$	US$/C$	UK£
0.25	0.16	0.08	15.00	9.75	4.88
0.50	0.33	0.16	20.00	13.00	6.50
0.75	0.49	0.24	25.00	16.25	8.13
1.00	0.65	0.33	30.00	19.50	9.75
2.00	1.30	0.65	35.00	22.75	11.38
3.00	1.95	0.98	40.00	26.00	13.00
4.00	2.60	1.30	45.00	29.25	14.63
5.00	3.25	1.63	50.00	32.50	16.25
6.00	3.90	1.95	75.00	48.75	24.38
7.00	4.55	2.28	100.00	65.00	32.50
8.00	5.20	2.60	125.00	81.25	40.63
9.00	5.85	2.93	150.00	97.50	48.75
10.00	6.50	3.25	200.00	130.00	65.00

You can get a better rate for traveler's checks at **GlobalEX** offices at Nadi Airport and in Nadi Town and Suva. See the "Fast Facts" sections in chapters 5 and 6 for specific currency exchange locations.

CREDIT CARDS   American Express, MasterCard, and Visa are widely accepted by the hotels, car-rental firms, travel and tour companies, large stores, and most restaurants. Don't count on using a Diners Club card outside the hotels. Leave your Discover card at home. Some businesses will add 3% to 5% to your bill if you use a credit card.

9 Getting There & Getting Around

GETTING THERE

Air New Zealand, Air Pacific, and **Qantas Airways** fly to **Nadi International Airport (NAN)** from North America, Australia, and New Zealand. **Pacific Blue** comes to Nadi from Australia and New Zealand, and **Korean Airlines** from Seoul. A few flights arrive from Samoa and Tonga at Suva's **Nausori Airport (SUV),** some 19km (12 miles). See "Getting There & Getting Around," in chapter 2, for details.

ARRIVING & DEPARTING

ARRIVING AT NADI   Nadi International Airport is on the western side of Viti Levu about 11km (7 miles) north of Nadi Town. Arriving passengers can purchase duty-free items at shops in the baggage claim area before clearing Customs (they are in fierce competition, so it will pay to comparison shop and ask for discounts). Imported liquor is expensive in Fiji, so if you drink, don't hesitate to buy two bottles here.

After Customs runs your bags through an X-ray machine, you emerge onto an air-conditioned concourse lined on both sides by airline offices, travel and tour companies, car-rental firms, and a 24-hour-a-day branch of the **ANZ Bank** (see "Money," above).

The Left Luggage counter at the far end of the departures concourse provides **baggage storage** for about F$3 to F$6 (US$1.95–US$3.90/£1–£2)) a day, depending on the size of the baggage. The counter is open 24 hours daily. The hotels all have baggage-storage rooms and will keep your extra stuff for free. The Left Luggage also has **showers** and rents towels.

A **post office,** in a separate building across the entry road from the main terminal, is open Monday to Friday from 8am to 4pm.

GETTING TO YOUR HOTEL FROM NADI AIRPORT   Representatives of the hotels and tour companies meet arriving visitors and provide free transportation to the hotels for those with reservations.

Taxis line up to the right outside the concourse. See the table under "Getting Around," below, for fares to the hotels. Only taxis painted yellow are allowed to take passengers from the airport. They have been inspected by the airport authority and are required to have air-conditioning, which most drivers will not voluntarily turn on.

Local buses to Nadi and Lautoka pass the airport on the Queen's Road every day. Walk straight out of the concourse, across the parking lot, and through the gate to the road. Driving in Fiji is on the left, so buses heading for Nadi and its hotels stop on the opposite side, next to Raffles' Gateway Hotel; those going to Lautoka stop on the airport side of the road. See "Getting Around Nadi," in chapter 5, for details.

DEPARTING FROM NADI   The Nadi domestic terminal and the international check-in counters are to the right of the arrival concourse as you exit Customs (or to the left, if you are arriving from the main road). There are **snack bars** near the domestic counters, including the excellent **Republic of Cappuccino.**

Fiji has no **departure tax** for either international or domestic flights. Nadi Airport has a modern, air-conditioned international departure lounge with a currency exchange counter, snack bar, showers, and the largest duty-free shops in the South Pacific. Duty-free prices, however, are higher here than you'll pay elsewhere in the country, and there is no haggling.

ARRIVING AT SUVA   Nausori Airport is on the flat plains of the Rewa River delta about 19km (12 miles) from downtown Suva. The small terminal has a snack bar and an ATM but few other amenities. Taxis between Nausori and downtown Suva cost about F$25 (US$16/£8) each way.

DEPARTING FROM SUVA   Nausori Airport has a small duty-free shop in its departure lounge but no currency exchange facility. Some of Air Pacific's flights between Nadi and Samoa and Tonga stop first at Nausori, where you will deplane and clear Immigration and Customs.

GETTING AROUND

Fiji has an extensive and reliable transportation network of airlines, rental cars, taxis, ferries, and both long-distance and local buses. This section deals primarily with getting from one island or major area to another; see the "Getting Around" sections in chapters 5 and 6 for details on transportation within the local areas.

BY PLANE & HELICOPTER

The easiest way to get around the country is to fly with **Pacific Sun** (© **800/ 294-4864** in the U.S. or 672 0888 in Nadi, 331 5755 in Suva; www.pacificsun. com.fj) or **Air Fiji** (© **877/247-3454** in the U.S., 0800/347 3624 in Fiji or 672 2521 in Nadi, 331 3666 in Suva; www.airfiji.com.fj) Both fly small planes from Nadi to the tourist destinations and have offices in the international arrivals concourse at Nadi International Airport and on Victoria Parade in Suva.

Pacific Sun is the domestic subsidiary of Air Pacific, Fiji's international airline (see "Getting There & Getting Around," in chapter 2), and the same offices handle both Air Pacific and Pacific Sun reservations.

One-way fares from Nadi as I write are about F$61 (US$40/£20) to Malololailai Island (Plantation Island and Musket Cove resorts); F$77 (US$50/£26) to Mana Island; F$135 (US$88/£44) to Suva; F$200 (US$130/£67) to Savusavu; and F$250 (US$162/£83) to Taveuni. Suva-Taveuni costs about F$250 (US$162/£83). You can save by booking roundtrip fares; ask the airlines for specifics. It also may pay to shop for the airlines' Internet specials (Pacific Sun often offers up to 40% discounts on its website). And always compare their fares, which can differ over the same route.

You can also save with four-flight **Air Pass** from Air Fiji. Any four flights cost US$270 (£135) if purchased in North America, F$517 (US$336/£172) elsewhere. The passes are not available in Fiji. Call or go to Air Fiji's website for details.

Pacific Islands Seaplanes (© **672 5644;** www.fijiseaplanes.com) provides charter service throughout Fiji in its small, Canadian-built floatplanes, which use wheels to

---

Tips **Avoid Backtracking**

Air Fiji's flights from Nadi and Suva to Taveuni stop in Savusavu going or coming, so don't let an uninformed travel agent book you back to Nadi or Suva in order to get from Taveuni to Savusavu.

> **Tips Weigh Your Bag & Reconfirm Your Flight**
>
> Baggage allowances on domestic flights may be 10 kilograms (22 lb.) instead of the 20 kilograms (44 lb.) on international flights. Check with the airlines to avoid showing up with too much luggage. *Always* reconfirm your domestic return flights as soon as possible after arriving. Also, check in when the airlines tell you to; planes sometimes arrive and depart a few minutes early.

take off from Nadi airport and floats to land on water at the offshore. In other words, you can connect directly at the airport. **Island Hoppers** (© 672 0140; www.helicopters.com.fj) also will whisk you to the Mamanucas in one of its helicopters. If you have to ask how much these rides cost, you can't afford it. I would let my choice of resort arrange my transfers and tell me how much it will cost.

Nadi and Nausori airports are the only lighted airstrips in the country, which means you don't fly domestically after dark. Many international flights arrive during the night, so a 1-night stay-over in Nadi may be necessary before you leave for another island.

BY RENTAL CAR

Rental cars are widely available in Fiji. Each company has its own pricing policy, and you can frequently find discounts, special deals, and some bargaining over long-term and long-distance use. All major companies, and a few not-so-major, have offices in the commercial concourse at Nadi International Airport, so it's easy to shop around. Most are open 7 days a week, some for 24 hours a day. Give careful consideration to how far you will drive; it's 197km (122 miles) from Nadi Airport to Suva, so an unlimited kilometer rate could work to your advantage if you plan to drive to Suva.

Avis (© 800/331-1212, or 672 2233 in Nadi; www.avis.com.fj) has more than 50% of the business here, and for good reason: The Toyota dealer is the local agent, so it has the newest and best-maintained fleet. In addition to the office at Nadi Airport, Avis can be found in Suva (© 331 3833), in Korolevu on the Coral Coast (© 653 0176), and at several hotels.

Thrifty Car Rental (© 800/367-2277, or 672 2935 in Nadi; www.thrifty.com), which is handled by Rosie the Travel Service, is my second choice, with rates and cars comparable to Avis's.

Other international agencies here are **Budget Rent-A-Car** (© 800/527-0700 or 672 2735; www.budget.com); **Hertz** (© 800/654-3131 or 672 3466; www.hertz.com), and **Europcar** (© 800/227-7368 or 672 5957; www.europcar.com).

The most reliable local companies are **Carpenters Rentals** (© 672 2772, or 332 8628 in Suva; rentals@carpenters.com.fj) and **Khan's Rental Cars** (© 679 0617 or 338 5033 in Suva; www.khansrental.com.fj). I do not rent from other "kick-the-tires" local companies.

Rates at all range from F$100 (US$65/£33) upwards per day with unlimited kilometers. Add about F$22 (US$14/£7.35) a day to reduce your collision damage liability. Your home **insurance** policy might cover any damages that occur in Fiji, but I recommend getting local coverage when you rent a car. Even if you do, the local policies require you to pay the first F$500 (US$325/£167) or more of damages in any event. Underbody and overhead damage is not covered, so go slow when crossing Fiji's innumerable "road humps"—and do not park under coconut trees!

> **_Tips_ Watch Out for Cows, Horses & Road Humps!**
>
> Most roads in Fiji are narrow, poorly maintained, and crooked. Not all local drivers are well trained, experienced, or skilled, and some of them (including bus drivers) go much too fast for the conditions. Consequently, you should **drive defensively** at all times. Constantly be alert for potholes, landslides, hairpin curves, and various stray animals—cows and horses are a very real danger, especially at night.
>
> Also keep an eye out for speed bumps known in Fiji as **road humps**. Most Fijian villages have them. Although big signs made to resemble traditional Fijian war clubs announce when you're entering and leaving villages on the Queen's Road, there are usually road humps between the clubs, so slow down! The humps are large enough to do serious damage to the bottom of a car, and no local rental insurance covers that.

All renters must be at least 21 years old, and a few companies require them to be at least 25 or have at least 2 years driving experience.

DRIVING RULES   Your valid home driver's license will be honored in Fiji. **Driving is on the left-hand side of the road. Seat belts** are mandatory. **Speed limits** are 80kmph (50 mph) on the open road and 50kmph (31 mph) in the towns and other built-up areas. It's illegal to drive while talking on a **cellphone.** You must **stop for pedestrians** in all marked crosswalks.

Driving under the influence of alcohol or other drugs is a criminal offense, and the police frequently throw up roadblocks and administer Breathalyzer tests to all drivers. Even if I have a rental, I take a taxi home after a session with friends at a local bar.

BY BUS

Appealing to backpackers and other cost-conscious travelers, **Feejee Experience** (© **672 5959;** www.feejeeexperience.com) runs a bus counter-clockwise around Viti Levu 4 days a week. The vehicles have local guides and stop for sightseeing and activities such as village visits, hiking, and river rafting. You buy a pass, which allows you to hop on and off the bus for up to 6 months. The "Hula Hoop" pass costs F$396 (US$257/£132) and includes the bus around Viti Levu. The "Lei Low" pass for F$558 (US$362/£186) adds a night in a dorm on Beachcomber Island Resort in the Mamanuca Islands off Nadi (see chapter 5). The "Hotel Lei" adds hotel accommodation for F$710 (US$461/£237) double occupancy, F$1,013 (US$658/£338) single occupancy. Otherwise, you must pay for your accommodations, although Feejee Experience will book and hold rooms or dorm beds at its preferred hostels, which include Mango Bay Resort on the Coral Coast, Raintree Lodge in Suva, and Volivoli Beach Resort in Rakiraki. You can get around by bus for a lot less, but you won't have the guides, the activities, or the companionship of young, often gorgeous fellow travelers.

Public buses are plentiful and inexpensive in Fiji, and it's possible to go all the way around Viti Levu on them. I did it once by taking the Fiji Express (see below) from Nadi to Suva one morning, a local express to Rakiraki the next morning, and then another express to Lautoka and a local back to Nadi.

The most comfortable bus between Nadi airport and Suva is the air-conditioned **Fiji Express** (© **672 3105** in Nadi, 331 2287 in Suva). One bus leaves Nadi airport daily at 7:30am and stops at the major hotels along the Queen's Road before arriving at Suva about 11:30am. It departs Suva at 4pm and returns to Nadi at 8pm. Another bus begins its daily runs at 7:30am from the Holiday Inn Suva and arrives in Nadi about 11:30am. It begins its return to Suva at 1pm, arriving in the capital about 5pm. One-way fares run up to F$20 (US$13/£6.65), depending on how far you go. You can book at any hotel tour desk.

Sunbeam Transport Ltd. (© **666 2822** in Lautoka, or 338 2704 in Suva) and **Pacific Transport Ltd.** (© **670 0044** in Nadi, or 330 4366 in Suva) operate express and regular buses all the way around Viti Levu. They stop at the domestic terminal at Nadi Airport and the markets at Nadi Town, Sigatoka, and Navua. The express buses take about 4 hours between Nadi and Suva, compared to 5 hours on the local "stages." These buses cater to local residents, do not take reservations, and have no air-conditioning. The Nadi-Suva fare is about F$10 (US$6.50/£3.35), express or local.

In addition to Sunbeam Transport Ltd., **Reliance Transport Bus Service** (© **666 3059** in Lautoka, or 338 2296 in Suva) and **Akbar Buses Ltd.** (© **669 4760** in Rakiraki) have express and local service between Lautoka and Suva via the King's Road. The Lautoka-Suva fare is about F$13 (US$8.45/£4.35).

Fume-belching **local buses** use the produce markets as their terminals. The older buses have side windows made of canvas panels that are rolled down during inclement weather (they usually fly out the sides and flap in the wind like great skirts). They run every few minutes along the Queen's Road between Lautoka and Nadi Town, passing the airport and most of the hotels and restaurants along the way (see "Getting Around Nadi," in chapter 5).

Minivans scoot along the Queen's Road between the Nadi Town market and the Suva Municipal Market. Those with yellow license tags with the prefix "LM" (licensed minivan) are regulated by the government. I avoid the others.

BY TAXI

Taxis are as abundant in Fiji as taxi meters are scarce. The Nadi Airport taxis are now required to have both meters, but the drivers do not always turn them on. Always settle on a fare to your destination before setting out (see the distance and fare chart below). Some drivers will complain about short fares and will badger you for more business later on during your stay; politely ignore these entreaties.

Not to be confused with minibuses, **"share taxis"** or "rolling taxis"—those not otherwise occupied—pick up passengers at bus stops and charge the bus fare. They are particularly good value on long-distance trips. A taxi returning to Suva, for example, will stop by the Nadi Town market and pick up a load of passengers at the bus fare rather than drive back to the capital empty. Ask around the local market bus stops if share taxis are available. You'll meet some wonderful Fijians that way.

Tips It Never Hurts to Bargain

In Nadi and on the Coral Coast, you will see the same taxi drivers outside your hotel every day. Usually they are paid on a salaried rather than a fare basis, so they may be willing to spend more time than usual showing you around. Also, they might charge less than the government-regulated fares for long-distance trips, such as from Nadi to the Coral Coast or Suva, because they would rather earn one big fare than several small ones. It never hurts to bargain politely.

Although the government sets all taxi fares, it has not raised them for several years despite skyrocketing fuel prices. They may be higher by the time you arrive. In the meantime, many drivers will ask for a few dollars more than the official fare. Even if they don't, I usually give them a small tip anyway—provided they haven't pestered me, refused to turn on the air conditioner, or blared loud music from their radios. The following are distances from Nadi International Airport via the Queen's Road and the official government-regulated taxi fares at press time:

From Nadi Airport to:	Km	Miles	Approx. Taxi Fare
Tanoa/Novotel Hotels	1.3	0.8	F$3.00/US$1.95/£1.00
Nomads Skylodge Hotel	3.3	2.0	F$4.00/US$2.60/£1.35
Mercure/Sandalwood Inn	5.2	3.2	F$5.00/US$3.25/£1.65
Nadi Town	9.0	5.6	F$10.00/US$6.50/£3.35)
Denarau Island	15.0	9.3	F$20.00/US$13.00/£6.65
Shangri-la's Fijian Resort and Spa	60.0	37.3	F$55.00/US$36.00/£18.00
Sigatoka	70.0	43.5	F$60.00/US$39.00/£20.00
Outrigger on the Lagoon Fiji	78.0	48.5	F$65.00/US$42.00/£22.00
Hideaway Resort	92.0	57.2	F$68.00/US$44.00/£23.00
The Warwick Fiji Resort & Spa	104.0	64.6	F$80.00/US$52.00/£27.00
Pacific Harbour	148.0	92.0	F$145.00/US$94.00/£48.00
Suva	197.0	122.4	F$165.00/US$107.00/£55.00

BY FERRY

Three reliable shuttle boats operated by Nadi-based **South Sea Cruises** (© 675 0500; www.ssc.com.fj) connect the Mamanuca and Yasawa islands to Denarau Island and Nadi. The *Tiger IV* and the *Cougar* make three runs daily through the Mamanucas, while the *Yasawa Express* goes to the Yasawas and back once a day. See "The Mamanuca & Yasawa Islands," in chapter 5, for details.

Vehicle- and passenger-carrying ferries also run between the main islands. Their schedules can change abruptly depending on the weather and the condition of the ships, however, so I don't recommend them unless you have unlimited time. Call the operators for the latest information.

Bligh Water Shipping Ltd. (© 331 8247 in Suva; 990 2032 in Lautoka; www. blighwatershipping.com.fj) operates the cleanest and most reliable ferries between Suva, Savusavu, and Taveuni, and between Lautoka and Savusavu. Its ferries are fully air-conditioned and have economy and first-class cabins. One departs Suva for Savusavu and Taveuni thrice weekly. Adult economy fare for the 11-hour run to Savusavu starts at F$63 (US$41/£21). Another ferry runs between Lautoka and Savusavu via the north coast of Viti Levu, going in one direction one day, the opposite way the next. Adult economy fares are F$60 (US$39/£20).

Patterson Shipping Services (© 331 5644 in Suva; patterson@connect.com.fj) has bus-ferry connections from Natovi Wharf (north of Suva on eastern Viti Levu) to Buresala Landing on Ovalau and to Nabouwalu on Vanua Levu. You connect by bus from Suva to Natovi, from Buresala to Levuka, and from Nabouwalu to Labasa (local buses connect Labasa to Savusavu). The Suva-Levuka fare costs about F$30

(US$19/£10), while the Suva-Labasa fare is about F$60 (US$39/£20). Patterson's office is in Ste. 1–2, Epworth House, Nina Street in Suva.

Based at Taveuni, the small ferry *Amazing Grace* (© **888 0320** on Taveuni, 927 1372 in Savusavu,) crosses the Somosomo Strait between Buca Bay on Vanua Levu and Waiyevo on Taveuni. One-way fare is F$25 (US$16/£8.35), including a bus ride from Savusavu to Buca Bay.

10 Tips on Dining

The Fijians in pre-European days steamed their food in an earth oven, known here as a *lovo*. They would use their fingers to eat the huge feasts (*mekes*), and then settle down to watch traditional dancing and perhaps polish off a few cups of yaqona.

The ingredients of a lovo meal are *buaka* (pig), *doa* (chicken), *ika* (fish), *mana* (lobster), *moci* (river shrimp), *kai* (freshwater mussels), and vegetables, such as dense *dalo* (taro root), spinachlike *rourou* (taro leaves), and *lumi* (seaweed). Most dishes are cooked in *lolo* (coconut milk). The most plentiful fish is the *walu*, or Spanish mackerel.

Fijians also make delicious *kokoda* (ko-*kon*-da), their version of fresh fish marinated in lime juice and mixed with fresh vegetables and coconut milk. Another Fijian specialty is *palusami,* a rich combination of meat or fish baked in banana leaves or foil with onions, taro leaves, and coconut milk.

> ⓘ *Tips* **Keep an Eye on Your Beer Mug**
>
> Bartenders in Fiji are taught to keep your beer mug full and your pockets empty—that is, they don't ask if you want another beer, they keep pouring until you tell them emphatically to stop.

Most resort hotels have mekes on their schedule of weekly events. Traditional Fijian dance shows follow the meals. Unlike the fast, hip-swinging, suggestive dancing of Tahiti and the Cook Islands, Fijians follow the custom of the Samoas and Tonga, with gentle movements taking second place to the harmony of their voices. Only in the spear-waving war dances do you see much action.

You will find Fijian-style dishes on many menus as well as Indian curries, which bodes well for vegetarians, since most Hindus here are vegetarian.

Most Fijian curries are on the mild side, but you can ask for it extra spicy and get it so hot you can't eat it. Curries are easy to figure out from the menu: lamb, goat, beef, chicken, vegetarian. If in doubt, ask the waiter or waitress. *Roti* is the round, lightly fried bread normally used to pick up your food (it is a hybrid of the round breads of India and Pakistan). *Puri* is a soft, puffy bread, and *papadam* is round, crispy, and chiplike. The meal may come on a round steel plate, with the curries, condiments, and rice in their own dishes arranged on the larger plate. The authentic method of dining is to dump the rice in the middle of the plate, add the smaller portions around it, and then mix them all together.

FAST FACTS: Fiji

The following facts apply to Fiji in general. For more specific information, see the "Fast Facts" sections in chapters 5 and 6. Also see "Fast Facts: South Pacific," at the end of chapter 2.

American Express   Fiji does not have a full-service American Express representative.

Area Codes   Fiji does not have domestic area codes. The country code for calling into Fiji is **679**.

Business Hours   Stores are generally open Monday to Saturday from 8am to 5pm, but many suburban stores stay open until 6pm and even 8pm. Sunday hours are from 8:30am to noon, although some tourist-oriented stores are open later. Shops in most hotels stay open until 9pm every day. Government office hours are Monday to Thursday from 8am to 4:30pm. Banking hours are Monday to Thursday 9:30am to 3pm, Friday 9:30am to 4pm.

Camera/Film   **Caines Photofast,** the largest processor of Kodak films, has shops in the main towns where you can also download and print digital photos.

Climate   See "When to Go," earlier in this chapter.

Customs   Fiji's **Customs allowances** are 200 cigarettes; 2 liters of liquor, beer, or wine; and F$400 (US$260/£133) worth of other goods in addition to personal belongings. Pornography is prohibited. Firearms and nonprescription narcotic drugs are strictly prohibited and subject to heavy fines and jail terms. Pets will be quarantined. Any fresh fruits and vegetables must be declared and are subject to inspection and fumigation. *Note:* Customs will X-ray *all* of your luggage upon arrival. See "Customs," in "Fast Facts: South Pacific" in chapter 2, for information about what you can bring home from Fiji. You will need advance permission to bring any animal into Fiji; if not, your pet will be quarantined.

Drug Laws   Marijuana is grown illegally up in the hills, but one drive past the Suva Gaol will convince you not to get caught buying it—or smuggling narcotics or dangerous drugs into Fiji.

Drugstores   The main towns have reasonably well-stocked pharmacies, or "chemists." Their medicines are likely to be from Australia or New Zealand. Many pharmacists will dispense medications without a prescription if you have your original bottle. The Morris Hedstrom department stores carry a wide range of toiletries, including Coppertone, Colgate, and many other familiar brands.

Electricity   Electric current in Fiji is 240 volts, 50 cycles. Many hotels have converters for 110-volt shavers, but these are not suitable for hair dryers. The plugs are the angled two-prong types used in Australia and New Zealand. Outlets have on/off switches mounted next to them.

Emergencies   The **police** emergency number is **917** throughout Fiji. The emergency telephone number for **fire** and **ambulance** is ⓒ **911.**

Embassies/Consulates   The **U.S. Embassy** is at 31 Loftus St., Suva (ⓒ **331 4466;** http://suva.usembassy.gov/reach_us.html). Other major diplomatic missions in Suva are **Australia,** 37 Princes Rd., Tamavua (ⓒ **338 2211); New Zealand,** 10th Floor, Reserve Bank of Fiji Bldg., Pratt St. (ⓒ **331 1422); United Kingdom,** Victoria House, 47 Gladstone Rd. (ⓒ **331 1033); Japan,** 2nd Floor, Dominion House, Thomson St. (ⓒ **330 2122); France,** 7th Floor, Dominion House, Thomson St. (ⓒ **331 2233); People's Republic of China,** 147 Queen Elizabeth Dr. (ⓒ **330 0215);** and **South Korea,** 8th Floor, Vanua House, Victoria Parade (ⓒ **330 0977).**

Etiquette & Customs See "Fijian Village Etiquette" and "'Grog' Etiquette," under "The Islanders," earlier in this chapter. Modest dress is the order of the day, particularly in the villages. As a rule, don't leave the hotel swimming pool or the beach in bathing suits or other skimpy attire. That includes low-slung pants and shorts that show everything from your navel down to your you-know-what. If you want to run around half-naked, go to Tahiti, where the French think it's cool. The Fijians do not.

Firearms Guns are illegal in Fiji, and persons found with them could be fined severely and sentenced to jail.

Gambling There are no casinos in Fiji, but you can play the local lottery.

Healthcare Medical and dental care in Fiji are not up to the standards common in the industrialized world. Most hotels have private physicians on call or can refer one. Doctors are listed at the beginning of the White Pages section of the Fiji telephone directory, under the heading "Medical Practitioners." See the "Fast Facts" sections in chapters 5 and 6 for specific doctors and clinics.

Hitchhiking Local residents seldom hitchhike, so the custom is not widespread, nor do I recommend it. Women traveling alone should never hitchhike in Fiji.

Holidays For more information, see "When to Go," earlier in this chapter.

Insects Fiji has no dangerous insects, and its plentiful mosquitoes do not carry malaria. The only dangerous animal is the bolo, a venomous snake that is docile and rarely seen.

Internet Access Most hotels and resorts have computers from which guests can send and receive e-mail and surf the Web. Cybercafes are widespread in Nadi and Suva, present in Savusavu. Although the interim government was moving to allow competition, at press time **Connect Internet Services** was Fiji's primary Internet service provider (© **670 7359** in Nadi, 330 0100 in Suva; www.connect.com.fj). No U.S. Internet service provider has a local access number in Fiji, and only a few hotels have wireless hotspots. If you bring your laptop, you can find a wireless hotspot at a coffee shop, or sign up for temporary dial-up access through Connect. See the "Fast Facts" section in chapter 5 for Connect's locations in Nadi Town and Suva. Connect charges F$15 (US$9.75/£5) for 1 month's access, plus F8¢ (US5¢; 3p) a minute, which will be billed to your hotel room. (Be careful, for some hotels add a huge service fee on top of these charges.) See "Staying Connected," in chapter 2, for more information.

Language English is an official language of Fiji and most residents can speak it to some degree. See "The Islanders," earlier in this chapter for useful Fijian and Hindi phrases.

Liquor Laws The legal drinking age is 21. Most grocery stores sell beer, spirits, and wines from Australia and New Zealand. Both beer and spirits are produced locally and are considerably less expensive than imported brands, which are taxed heavily. While local Bounty rum is okay, the other stuff is rot-gut. I bring quality brands of liquor with me. The locally brewed Fiji is served in a short bottle known as a Stubbie. Fiji Gold is a lighter lager than Fiji Bitter. Most bars also sell Australian and New Zealand beers.

Measurements Fiji is on the metric system. See the chart inside the front cover for details on converting metric measurements to nonmetric equivalents.

Mail All the main towns have post offices operated by Fiji Post, and there is a branch at Nadi International Airport, across the entry road from the terminal. Allow at least a week for delivery of airmail letters from Fiji. Surface mail to North America and Europe can take 2 months or more. Mail moves faster if you use "Fiji Islands" on envelopes and packages sent here. Post offices usually are open Monday to Friday from 8am to 4pm. **FedEx, UPS,** and **DHL Express** all have express service into and out of Fiji. It costs about F$2.30 (US/C$1.45) to send a 1-ounce letter via airmail to the U.S. or Canada; F$2.65 (88p) to Great Britain. Postcards cost F$.40 (26¢; 13p) by surface mail to all countries. You can calculate international airmail rates at **www.postfiji.com**.

Newspapers/Magazines Two national newspapers are published in English: the *Fiji Times* (www.fijitimes.com) and the *Fiji Sun* (www.sun.com.fj). Both appear daily and carry a few major stories from overseas. The international editions of *Time* and the leading Australian and New Zealand daily newspapers are available at some bookstores and hotel shops. Published monthly in Suva, the excellent *Island Business Magazine* (www.islandsbusiness.com) covers South Pacific regional news.

Police The nationwide emergency police number is ⓒ 917. The non-emergency numbers are ⓒ 670 0222 in Nadi, 334 3777 in Suva.

Radio & TV The Fijian government operates two nationwide AM radio networks with programming in Fijian and Hindi. Several private stations operate on the FM band in Suva and Nadi. The best is Radio Fiji Gold, which carries news bulletins on the hour and world, regional, and local news reports and weather bulletins daily at 7am and 6pm. The interim government has approved licenses for at least two more TV channels to join Fiji One, heretofore the country's sole over-the-air station. Fiji One has local news and weather at 6pm daily. The schedules are carried in the local newspapers. Many hotels have Sky TV, a pay system with the BBC, sports, and a few other channels.

Safety Property theft, armed robberies, burglaries, and home invasions are common. Caution is advised at all times, especially in Suva. Stick to the main streets everywhere after dark, and take a taxi back to your hotel if you're out late at night. Do not leave valuables in your hotel room or unattended elsewhere, including in rental cars and tour buses. Women should not wander alone on deserted beaches and should be extremely cautious about accepting a late-night lift back to their hotel or hostel.

Smoking Smoking is legally prohibited in many public buildings in Fiji but not at hotels, businesses, and restaurants. Ask for a nonsmoking room at your hotel and an outside table at restaurants.

Taxes Fiji imposes a 12.5% value-added tax (VAT) on most goods and services, which is included in most prices. These are known as "VAT-inclusive prices," or VIP. In addition, you will pay a 5% hotel tax. Hotels are not required to include the VAT and hotel tax in the rates they quote outside Fiji, so be sure to ask whether a quoted room rate includes all taxes and fees. You will not be entitled to a VAT refund when you leave the country.

Telephone Land-line telephone service is provided throughout the country by **Telecom Fiji Limited (TFL;** ✆ **112 233;** www.tfl.com.fj). Although calls are relatively expensive, it's a modern system.

To call Fiji: Dial the international access code (011 from the U.S.; 00 from the U.K., Ireland, or New Zealand; or 0011 from Australia), Fiji's country code **679,** and the local number (there are no area codes within Fiji).

To make international calls from within Fiji: First dial **00,** then the country code (U.S. or Canada 1, U.K. 44, Ireland 353, Australia 61, New Zealand 64), then the area code and phone number. Calls to most countries cost F60¢ (US39¢/20p) a minute when dialed directly. Frequent TFL promotions cut the price by 20% or more on nights and weekends.

Local access numbers: You cannot use a credit card to make calls in Fiji, but several international long-distance carriers have local access numbers their customers can call to access their international networks and use their company cards: **AT&T USA** (✆ 004 890 1001); **AT&T Canada** (✆ 004 890 1009); **Australia Telstra** (✆ 004 890 6101); **Australia Octopus** (✆ 004 890 6102); **Bell South** (✆ 004 890 1008); **BT** (✆ 004 890 4401); **BT Prepaid** (✆ 004 890 4402); **MCI** (✆ 004 890 1002); **New Zealand Telecom** (✆ 004 890 6401); **Sprint** (✆ 004 890 1003); **Teleglobe Canada** (✆ 004 890 1005); and **Verizon** (✆ 004 890 1007). These numbers can be dialed toll free from any land-line phone.

To make domestic calls within Fiji: No prefix or area code is required for domestic long distance calls, so dial the local number.

For directory assistance: Dial ✆ **011** for domestic information, ✆ **022** for international numbers. (On the Web, you can look up local numbers at **www. whitepages.com.fj** and **www.yellowpages.com.fj.**)

For operator assistance: Dial ✆ **010** for operator assistance in making a call.

Toll-free numbers: Local numbers beginning with **0800** are toll-free within Fiji, but calling a 1-800 number in the U.S. or Canada from Fiji is not toll-free. In fact, it costs the same as an overseas call.

Pay phones: Public phones are located at all post offices and in many other locations (look for Fijian war spears sticking out from plastic booths). You can make local, domestic long-distance ("trunk"), or international calls without operator assistance from any of them. They accept only prepaid Fiji Telecom **Telecards,** not coins. Post offices and many shops (including the gift shops in the Nadi Airport terminal) sell Telecards in denominations up to F$50 (US$32/£17). Scratch the tape off the back of the card to reveal your PIN number, which you must enter prior to placing a call.

Cellphones: Some international cellphone companies have roaming in Fiji; check to see if yours does. At press time, **Digicel Pacific** (www.digicelpacific. com) had been awarded a license to operate in Fiji, ending a monopoly held by **Vodaphone Fiji** (✆ **672 6226;** www.vodafone.com.fj), which rents both cellphones and GSM-compatible SIM cards. Vodaphone has a desk in the arrivals concourse at Nadi airport and offices in Nadi Town and Suva. The desk is staffed daily from 5am to 11pm and for major international flights. Phones cost F$6

(US$3.90/£2) a day to rent, SIM cards F$2 (US$1.30/65p) per day, plus F95¢ (US62¢/32p) per minute for outgoing calls to land lines, F52¢ (US34¢/17p) to other mobile phones. All incoming calls are free. Vodaphone will pre-authorize a credit of F$200 (US$130/£67) on your credit card, to which it will bill your rental and usage fees. An Australian firm, **Inkk Mobile,** sells phones and slightly discounted prepaid airtime over Vodaphone's network. The Tappoo department stores sell Inkk's phones and SIM cards.

See "Staying in Touch," in chapter 2, for more information.

Time Local time in Fiji is 12 hours ahead of Greenwich Mean Time. Although the 180° meridian passes through Taveuni, all of Fiji is west of the international date line, so it's one day ahead of the United States and shares the same day with Australia and New Zealand. Translated: When it's 5am on Tuesday in Fiji, it's noon on Monday in New York and 9am on Monday in Los Angeles. Fiji does not observe daylight saving time.

Tipping Tipping is discouraged throughout Fiji unless truly exceptional service has been rendered. That's not to say that the porter won't give you that where's-my-money look once he figures out you're an American.

Useful Phone Numbers See "Fast Facts: The South Pacific," in chapter 2, for useful international numbers.

Air Pacific/Pacific Sun: airlines ✆ 672 0888

Air Fiji: ✆ 0800/347-3624 toll free or 672 2521

Fiji Visitors Bureau: ✆ 672 2433 in Nadi, 330 2433 in Suva

Nadi Airport: flight arrival and departure information ✆ 672 7777

Water Except during periods of continuous heavy rain, the tap water in the main towns and at the resorts is safe to drink. Elsewhere I opt for the famous "Fiji" or other bottled waters, which are widely available at shops and hotels.

5

Viti Levu

Most of us begin our visits at Nadi International Airport, a modern facility among sugar cane fields on the dry western side of Viti Levu (Big Land), Fiji's largest island. The booming **Nadi** area is the focal point of much of Fiji's tourism industry, and it's where many tourists on package deals spend their time, especially on **Denarau Island,** the country's largest resort development. There are many things to do in Nadi, and it's the logical base from which to explore the rest of the country.

From Nadi, it's an easy hop over to the resorts out in the **Mamanuca Islands,** which have the beaches and clear lagoons the mainland lacks. Farther out, the even more beautiful, less developed, and increasingly popular **Yasawa Islands** have many of the best beaches in Fiji. The small, low-key cruise ships of **Blue Lagoon Cruises** ply the Yasawas, which have two of Fiji's most luxurious offshore resorts and some of its best backpacker retreats.

The Queen's Road heads south from Nadi to the **Coral Coast,** which has widely spaced resorts with gorgeous scenery and Fijian villages in between. Although its beaches are not as good as those on the offshore islands, the Coral Coast was Fiji's first major resort area and still attracts visitors in search of a beachside vacation on the mainland.

On the Queen's Road, between the Coral Coast and Suva, **Pacific Harbour** has Fiji's best cultural center and one of its two top golf courses. It also is the jumping-off point for white-water river rafting, kayaking excursions, and great diving in **Beqa Lagoon**—all of which give Pacific Harbour its title, "The Adventure Capital of Fiji."

With a population of about 100,000, often-rainy **Suva** is one of the South Pacific's largest and most cosmopolitan cities. Remnants of Fiji's century as a British possession and the presence of so many Indians give it a certain air of the colonial "Raj."

From Suva, you can go the other way around back to Nadi, along the King's Road from Lautoka, through the sugar cane fields of **northern Viti Levu,** where Rakiraki beckons, with its charming colonial-era hotel.

1 Nadi

You won't see much of the real Fiji if you spend your entire vacation in Nadi, but this area has more activities to keep you busy than any other part of the country. That's because the international airport and a dry climate combine to make it the country's main tourist center. The lagoon off Nadi is usually murky from runoff coming from the sugar cane fields, however, so this is not the ideal place in Fiji for a beach vacation.

Many visitors spend their entire holidays on pancake-flat **Denarau Island,** about 7km (4⅓ miles) west of Nadi Town. Only a narrow creek through a mangrove forest separates it from the mainland. Denarau is home to a huge real estate project officially known as **Denarau Island Resort Fiji** (www.denarau.com). To my mind—and many local folks'—it's a generic tropical resort development bearing little resemblance to Fiji. In fact, Denarau could be in Hawaii, Florida, or Australia's Gold Coast. It includes resort hotels, a 150-unit timeshare complex, homes and condos, an 18-hole golf course, and **Port Denarau,** a shopping center and marina where most of the area's cruises are based. The short bridge from the mainland whisks you from the Third World of Fiji into the First World.

By **"Nadi"** the locals mean the entire area around the international airport. It's the fastest-growing part of Fiji. New homes, stores, shopping centers, and office buildings are popping up along the 9km (5½ miles) of traffic-heavy Queen's Road between the airport and **Nadi Town,** a 7-block strip lined with handicraft, souvenir, and other stores as well as some of the country's better restaurants.

Many locals now do their shopping in **Namaka,** a rapidly developing commercial strip between Nadi Town and the airport. **Martintar,** another Queen's Road suburb, has a number of hotels, restaurants, and bars. From Martintar, a paved road leads to **Wailoaloa Beach,** a 1.5km-long (1-mile) stretch of gray sand, where a development known as **Newtown Beach** has several inexpensive hotels and hostels.

From Nadi, it's an easy 33km (20-mile) side trip to **Lautoka,** Fiji's second-largest city. Lautoka offers a genteel contrast to tourist-oriented Nadi Town.

GETTING AROUND NADI

All of Fiji's major **car-rental** firms have offices in the international arrival concourse of Nadi International Airport. See "Getting There & Getting Around," in chapter 4.

Westside Motorbike Rentals (© 672 6402; www.motorbikerentalsfiji.com) in Namaka, Martintar, Denarau Island, and Sigatoka rents scooters for F$79 (US$51/£26) including helmets and insurance. In my opinion, riding scooters in Fiji is *not* for novices.

Taxis gather outside the arrivals concourse at the airport and are stationed at the larger hotels. Ask the reception desk to call one, or contact **Taxi 2000** (© 672 1350), one of the more reliable companies whose cabs are radio-dispatched. The aggressive drivers will find you in Nadi Town. See the taxi fare chart on p. 92 in chapter 4.

I often take the **local buses,** which ply the Queen's Road between the markets in Nadi Town and Lautoka frequently during daylight, every 30 minutes after dark. Tell the driver where you're going; he'll tell you how much to pay when you board. Fares vary according to the length of the trip. No more than F65¢ (US42¢/22p) will take you anywhere between the airport and Nadi Town. **Westbus** (© 672 2917) runs a bus between the Nadi Town market and Denarau Island, where you can catch the free **Bula Bus** shuttle around the island from 7am to 11pm daily.

FAST FACTS: Nadi

The following facts apply specifically to Nadi and Lautoka. For more information, see "Fast Facts: Fiji," in chapter 4.

Bookstores The best bookstore is in the departures area of Nadi International Airport; it's open 24/7. Hotel boutiques also are the good places to buy magazines and books. Bookshops in town are actually stationery stores.

Camera/Film **Caines Photofast** has a film and 1-hour processing shop on Queen's Road in Nadi Town (© **670 1608**), and you download and print your digital photos there, too. Most of the hotel gift shops also sell film.

Currency Exchange **ANZ Bank, Westpac Bank,** and **Colonial National Bank** have offices with ATM machines in Namaka and on the Queen's Road in Nadi Town. ANZ and Westpac have ATMs at the Port Denarau marina on Denarau Island, and ANZ's airport office is open 24 hours a day. You'll get a better rate for currency and traveler's checks at the **GlobalEX** offices at the airport and on the Queen's Road in Nadi Town.

Drugstores Best stocked of three drugstores on the Queen's Road in Nadi is **Budget Pharmacy** (© **670 0064**). It has a branch in Namaka (© **672 2533**), and operates **Denarau Pharmacy** (© **675 0780**), in the Port Denarau complex.

Emergencies/Police The emergency phone number for **police** is © **917.** Dial © **911** for **fire** and **ambulance.** The Fiji **police** have stations at Nadi Town (© **670 0222**) and at the airport terminal (© **672 2222**).

Eyeglasses For optical needs, try **Eyesite,** on the Queen's Road in Nadi Town (© **670 7178**).

Healthcare The government-operated **Lautoka Hospital** (© **666 3337**) is the region's main facility. There is a **government medical clinic** in Nadi Town (© **670 0362**). **Dr. Ram Raju,** 2 Lodhia St., Nadi Town (© **670 0240** or 976333 mobile), has treated many visitors, including me. The private **Namaka Medical Center** (© **672 2228**) is open 24 hours a day and has doctors on call. Ask your hotel staff to recommend a **dentist** in private practice.

Information You can get brochures and other information from the tour companies in the arrivals concourse at Nadi Airport. The main office of **Fiji Visitors Bureau** (© **672 2433;** www.bulafiji.com) is in the Colonial Plaza shopping center, on the Queen's Road between Martintar and Namaka. Other so-called "Tourist Information Centres" are really travel agents or tour operators.

Internet Access All hotels and hostels have computers for their guests to access the Internet. There are Internet kiosks in the Nadi Airport terminal and several cybercafes on the Queen's Road in Nadi Town. On Denarau Island, the **Esquires** (© **675 0989**), in front of the Sheraton Denarau Villas, has free wireless access for its customers. Fiji's major provider, **Connect Internet Services** (© **670 7359**) has an office in Namaka, where you can sign up for temporary dial-up access (see "Fast Facts: Fiji" in chapter 4).

Laundry/Dry Cleaning **Flagstaff Laundry & Dry Cleaning** (© **672 2161**), on Northern Press Road in Martintar, has 1-day laundry and dry-cleaning.

Mail The Nadi post office, on Hospital Road near the south end of the market, is open Monday to Friday 8am to 4pm and Saturday 8am to noon. It has a well-stocked stationery store in the lobby. A small airport branch is across the main road from the terminal. It's open Monday to Friday from 8am to 4pm and Saturday from 8am to noon.

Water The tap water is safe to drink.

EXPLORING THE NADI AREA

Most hotel and hostel activity desks, or the reception-desk staff, will make reservations or arrangements for all activities.

You can easily waste a lot of time driving around this area without seeing much of anything, so I recommend at least a half-day guided sightseeing tour with a reputable company. Round-trip bus transportation from the Nadi area hotels is included in the price of the tours and outings; that is, a bus will pick you up within 30 minutes or so of the scheduled departure time for Nadi area trips, 1 hour or more for those on the Coral Coast. Children under 12 years of age pay half-fare on most activities.

ATTRACTIONS NORTH OF NADI

My favorite half-day tour goes north of Nadi Airport to the **Garden of the Sleeping Giant** ☀. The late Raymond Burr, star of TVs *Perry Mason* and *Ironside,* started this lovely, 50-acre orchid range in 1977 to house his private collection of tropical orchids (he once also owned Naitoba, a small island in the Lau Group). It sits at the base of "Sleeping Giant Mountain," whose profile forms the outline of a man fast asleep. There's much more here than orchids, and the guides will describe a variety of local plants and their uses. You can get here on your own by rental car or taxi. Look for the sign at Wailoko Road off the Queen's Road between Nadi and Lautoka. It's open Monday to Saturday from 9am to 5pm. Entrance fees are F$12 (US$7.80/£4) for adults, F$6 (US$3.90/£2) for children, including guided tour and a fruit drink.

From there the tour stops at historic **Viseisei Village,** on the Queen's Road about halfway between Nadi and Lautoka. One legend says that the first Fijians settled here. Today it's a typical, fairly prosperous Fijian village, with some modern houses and some shacks of concrete block and tin, a small handicrafts shop, and the usual road humps that bring traffic to a crawl.

Coral Sun Fiji (© 672 3105; www.coralsunfiji.com) charges about F$88 (US$57/£29) for its orchids and village tour.

SOUTH OF NADI: THE MOMI BATTERY

Installed during World War II to protect the main pass through the Great Sea Reef, the concrete bunkers and naval guns in **Momi Battery Historical Park** are now under the care of the **National Trust of Fiji** (© 330 1807), which operates the country's national parks and historical sites. The drive to the park is worth it for the splendid view over the lagoon and western coast of Viti Levu. It's open daily from 9am to 5pm. Admission is F$3 (US$1.95/£1) adults, F$1 (US65¢/35p) for students. Turn west off the Queen's Road 16km (10 miles) south of Nadi Town toward **Momi Bay.** The road toward the coast is paved, since it leads to an on-again, off-again Marriott hotel project

---

⌐Fun Fact⌐ The First Village

Viseisei village, between Nadi and Lautoka, reputedly is where the great canoe *Kaunitoni* came out of the west and deposited the first Fijians some 3,000 years ago. From there, as the legend goes, they dispersed all over the islands. The yarn is helped by the local district name **Vuda,** which means "our origin" in Fijian, and Viseisei, which means "to scatter."

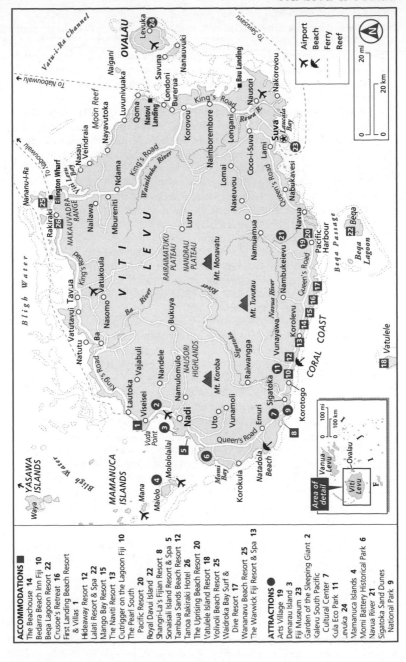

ACCOMMODATIONS ■
The Beachouse 14
Bedarra Beach Inn Fiji 10
Beqa Lagoon Resort 22
Crusoe's Retreat 16
First Landing Beach Resort
& Villas 1
Hideaway Resort 12
Lalati Resort & Spa 22
Mango Bay Resort 15
The Naviti Resort 13
Cutrigger on the Lagoon Fiji 10
The Pearl South
Pacific Resort 20
Royal Davui Island 22
Shangri-La's Fijian Resort 8
Sonaisali Island Resort & Spa 5
Tambua Sands Beach Resort 12
Tanoa Rakiraki Hotel 26
The Uprising Beach Resort 20
Vatulele Island Resort 18
Volivoli Beach Resort 25
Waidroka Bay Surf &
Dive Resort 17
Wananavu Beach Resort 25
The Warwick Fiji Resort & Spa 13

ATTRACTIONS ●
Arts Village 19
Denarau Island 3
Fiji Museum 23
Garden of the Sleeping Giant 2
Kalevu South Pacific
Cultural Center 7
Kula Eco Park 11
Levuka 24
Mamanuca Islands 4
Momi Battery Historical Park 6
Navua River 21
Sigatoka Sand Dunes
National Park 9

A Side Trip to Lautoka

Fiji's second-largest port, **Lautoka** is a pleasant town of broad avenues, green parks, and a row of towering royal palms along the middle of **Vitogo Parade**, the main drag running from the harbor along the eastern side of downtown.

Tourism may rule Nadi, but sugar is king in Lautoka. The **Fiji Sugar Corporation**'s huge mill was built in 1903 and is one of the largest crushing operations in the southern hemisphere. At the industrial port you'll also see a mountain of wood chips ready for export; the chips are a prime product of the country's pine plantations.

The stores along Vitogo Parade mark the boundary of Lautoka's business district; behind them are several blocks of shops and the lively **Lautoka Market,** which doubles as the bus station and is second in size only to Suva's Municipal Market. Handicraft stalls at the front of the market offer a variety of goods, especially when cruise ships are in port. Shady residential streets trail off beyond the playing fields of **Churchill Park** on the other side of Vitogo Parade. The Hare Krishnas have their most important temple in the South Pacific on Tavewa Avenue. I stop for lunch at **The Chilli Tree Café,** a modern coffee shop at Tukani and Nede streets (© **655 1824**). It's open Monday to Saturday 7:30am to 7pm.

The southern end of downtown gives way to a large park and picturesque promenade along the harbor. Beside it is the **Waterfront Hotel** (© **666 4777;** www.tanoahotels.com), offering Lautoka's best digs.

Local buses leave the market in Nadi Town every half-hour for the Lautoka Market from Monday to Saturday between 6am and 8pm. The fare is no more than F$3 (US$1.95/£1), depending on where you get on. The one-way taxi fare to Lautoka is about F$25 (US$16/£8.35) from Nadi. Rosie the Travel Service has a half-day Lautoka excursion from Nadi; book at any hotel activity desk.

If you're driving from Nadi, you will come to two traffic circles on the outskirts of Lautoka. Take the second exit off the first one and the first exit off the second. That will take you to the post office and the southern end of Vitogo Parade.

being developed on Momi Bay. Turn right at the signpost beside a school, and follow a rough dirt track another 4km (2½ miles) to the park. *Note:* The park does not have toilets or drinking water.

FLIGHTSEEING & SKYDIVING

Island Hoppers Fiji (© **672 0410;** www.helicopters.com.fj) and **Pacific Islands Seaplanes** (© **672 5643;** www.fijiseaplanes.com) both offer sightseeing flights over Denarau Island, Nadi Bay, the Mamanucas, and Vuda Point north of Nadi between Viseisei village and Lautoka. Call them or inquire at any hotel activities desk for prices and reservations.

I've never had the courage to put my life in someone's hands while falling to Denarau Island from 10,000 feet up in the air, but you can with **Skydive Fiji** (© **672 8166;** www.skydivefiji.com.fj). You'll pay at least F$350 (US$227/£117).

EXPLORING VITI LEVU FROM NADI

Although I wouldn't spend my entire vacation in Nadi, it does make a good base from which to explore more of Fiji. In fact, you can make day trips from Nadi to key Coral Coast and Pacific Harbour area activities, which provide transportation from the Nadi area hotels. See "What to See & Do on the Coral Coast" and the "Pacific Harbour & Beqa Island" sections, later in this chapter, for details.

A prime example is a full-day rafting trip on the **Navua River,** between Pacific Harbour and Suva on Viti Levu's south coast. The tour visits a Fijian village that puts on a *yaqona* ceremony, a lunch of local-style foods, and a traditional dance show. Price is about F$150 (US$97/£50) from the Nadi hotels. Be sure to opt for the variation of this tour that includes a ride down the river on a *bilibili* (bamboo raft).

Other fine outdoor excursions are the waterfall and cave tours offered by **Adventures in Paradise Fiji** (© **652 0833;** www.adventuresinparadisefiji.com), on the Coral Coast. You can also go for a ride on the **Coral Coast Railway Co.** (© **652 0434**), based outside Shangri-La's Fijian Resort. I'm most fond of the trip to lovely Natadola Beach, where you swim (bring your own towel) and have a barbecue lunch. Another Coral Coast tour visits the town of Sigatoka and the meandering river and fertile valley of the same name. The best part of this trip for animal lovers is **Kula Eco Park.** These full-day trips cost about F$150 (US$97/£50) from Nadi.

Robinson Crusoe Island (© **628 1999;** www.robinsoncrusoeislandfiji.com), on an islet off Natadola Beach, offers a day trip from Nadi, including bus transportation to its jetty, a jungle river cruise (on the mainland), snorkeling trips, lunch, and an island dance show for F$89 (US$58/£30). Jet Fiji has one of its high-speed jet boats stationed at the island (see "Boating, Golf, Hiking & Other Outdoor Activities," below). You also will pay extra for waterskiing, tube rides, hair braiding, and massages.

Suva day trips pick up guests at both Nadi and Coral Coast hotels. From Nadi, you'll spend a total of 8 hours riding in the bus for a 4-hour stay in Suva, so think about staying overnight and riding the Fiji Express back to Nadi the next day. You'll pay about F$90 (US$58/£30) per person from Nadi, less from Coral Coast hotels.

BOATING, GOLF, HIKING & OTHER OUTDOOR ACTIVITIES

The Nadi area offers a host of sporting and outdoor activities to suit almost every interest. Most are near Nadi, but some require a boat trip to the Mamanuca Islands or a bus ride to other locations, such as white-water rafting on the Navua River (see "River Rafting," under "Pacific Harbour & Beqa Island," later in this chapter).

Adrenalin Watersports (© **675 1288;** www.adrenalinfiji.com) provides diving, jet-skiing, wakeboarding, sailing, parasailing, game fishing, and other watersports at the resorts on Denarau Island.

Tips **Take a Day Trip to a Small Island**

No visit to Fiji is complete without exploring a small offshore island, so put at least a day trip to one of the Mamanuca or Yasawa islands high on your list of things to do while you're in Nadi.

FISHING 🎣🎣 The Denarau Island hotels and all the resorts in the Mamanucas offer sportfishing as a pay-extra activity for their guests. Based at Port Denarau, **Crystal Blue Adventures** (© 675 0950; www.crystalbluefiji.com) has a fleet of fishing boats that ply the waters off the Mamanucas for wahoo, giant trevally, mahimahi, tuna, and other game fish.

GOLF & TENNIS The 18-hole, 7,150-yard, par-72 links at the **Denarau Golf & Racquet Club** 🎾🎾 (© 675 0477; www.denaraugolf.com.fj) occupy most of Denarau Island, with the clubhouse opposite the Sheraton Fiji Resort. Its barbecue-style restaurant and bar serve breakfast, lunch, and dinner at moderate prices. It also has locker rooms with showers. Greens fees for 18 holes are F$110 (US$71/£37) for guests of the two big resorts and F$120 (US$78/£40) for those of us who can't afford to stay there. Lessons are available. It's open daily from 7am to dark.

The club's six Wimbledon-standard grass tennis courts are open daily from 7am to dark, and its four all-weather courts stay open until 10pm. Per player fees are F$25 (US$16/£8.35) per hour on grass, F$20 (US$13/£6.65) per hour on the hard courts. Lessons are available, and proper tennis attire is required.

The **Novotel Nadi Hotel** (© 672 2000) has a 9-hole executive course, and the hotel tour desks can arrange for you to play at the 18-hole **Nadi Airport Golf Club** (© 672 2148) near Newtown Beach, behind the airport. The latter is a 5,882-yard, par-70 course that isn't particularly challenging or well kept, but the setting, on the shores of Nadi Bay, is attractive.

HIKING In addition to Adventures in Paradise's waterfall hikes on the Coral Coast (see "The Coral Coast" section, later in this chapter), **Adventure Fiji** (© 672 2935 or 672 2755; www.rosiefiji.com), an arm of Rosie Holidays, takes trekkers (as hikers are known in these parts) on 1-day walks some 600m (1,969 ft.) up into the Nausori Highlands above Nadi. I found this hike to be fascinating but strenuous; in fact, you have to be between 10 and 45 years old to sign up. Wear walking shoes with excellent traction that you don't mind getting wet, for the sandy trail goes into and out of steep valleys and crosses streams. Most of this walk is through grasslands with no shade, so wear sunscreen. We had a long midday break in a Fijian village, where we shared a local-style lunch sitting cross-legged in a simple Fijian home. The cost is about F$95 (US$62/£32) per person. The company also has 4-, 6-, and 10-day hikes across the Sigatoka Valley and Nausori Highlands, ranging from about F$777 to F$1,739 (US$505–US$1,129/£259–£580), including transfers, guide, accommodation, and meals provided by Fijian villagers along the way.

HORSEBACK RIDING You can ride along Wailoaloa Beach in Nadi with a local man known as **Babba** (© 679 3652), who charges about F$25 (US$16/£8.35) an hour.

Fun Fact **Where "V. Singh" Started Swinging**

The Nadi Airport Golf Club plays second fiddle to the manicured links at the Denarau Golf & Racquet Club these days, but it was here that one V. Singh won the Grade A Open Championship in 1981. That would be **Vijay Singh,** one of the world's top professional golfers. Before he started playing, the Fiji native served as caddy for his father, who was club president. Vijay Singh now lives in the United States and is seldom seen hereabouts.

A 20-minute drive south of Nadi Town, **Sonaisali Island Resort** (© **670 6011;** www.sonaisali.com) has guided horseback rides through the tropical vegetation on its 105-acre private island. A 1-hour ride costs F$20 (US$13/£6.65). Reservations are required. See "Where to Stay in Nadi," later in this chapter.

JET BOATS   For a thrill-a-minute ride, **Jet Fiji** (© **675 0400;** www.jetfiji.com) will take you twisting and turning through the mangrove-lined creeks behind Denarau Island. Heart-stopping 360-degree turns are guaranteed to get the adrenaline flowing and the clothes wet. The half-hour rides depart every 30 minutes daily from Port Denarau. A shuttle connects the nearby Sheratons; there are scheduled pickups from other area hotels, so call for reservations. Price is about F$80 (US$52/£27) for adults, half-fare for children under 15, free for kids under 6. Jet Fiji also has a boat stationed at Robinson Crusoe Island, off Natandola Beach (see "The Coral Coast," later in this chapter).

SCUBA DIVING & SNORKELING   Serious divers go elsewhere (see the "Diving in Fiji" box on p. 73.), but you can go underwater with **Aqua Blue** (© **672 6111;** www.aquabluefiji.com), on Wailoaloa Beach, which provides guides and instruction. You'll pay about F$130 (US$84/£43) for a single-tank dive. You can also snorkel with Aqua Blue for F$60 (US$39/£20). **Adrenalin Watersports** (© **675 1288;** www. adrenalinfiji.com) offers diving on Denarau Island.

SHOPPING IN NADI

Haggling is not considered polite when dealing with Fijians, and the better stores have fixed prices. Bargaining is still acceptable, however, when dealing with Fiji Indian merchants in many small shops. They will start high, you will start low, and somewhere in between you will find a mutually agreeable price. I usually knock 40% off the asking price as an initial counteroffer and then suffer the merchants' indignant snickers, secure in the knowledge that they aren't about to kick me out of the store. After all, the fun has just begun.

To avoid the hassles of bargaining, visit **Jack's of Fiji** (Fiji's largest merchant), **Prouds,** and **Tappoo,** all of which have branches in Nadi Town, Port Denarau, Sigatoka, Suva, and in the shopping arcades of the larger hotels. The upstairs rooms in Jack's of Fiji in Nadi Town are filled with clothing and leather goods. Tappoo carries a broad range of merchandise, including electronics, cameras, and sporting goods. Prouds concentrates on perfumes, watches, and jewelry, including Fiji's own J. Hunter black pearls (see "Savusavu" in chapter 6).

In addition to being the shove-off point for cruises and transfers to the islands, **Port Denarau** is the shopping mecca on Denarau Island. This mall has a Jack's of Fiji branch, a surf shop, two banks, and a FourEx currency exchange, a grocery and wine store, an ice cream parlor, and restaurants (see "Where to Dine in Nadi," below).

"DUTY-FREE" SHOPPING

Fiji has the most developed shopping industry in the South Pacific, as will be obvious when you walk along the main thoroughfare in Nadi Town. The Fiji government charges an import tax on merchandise brought into the country, however, so despite their claims to the contrary, the stores aren't "duty-free." I have found better prices and selections on the Internet and at large-volume dealers such as Best Buy and Circuit City in the United States, so shop at home first to compare the price in Fiji. Also, the models offered in the duty-free shops here are seldom the latest editions.

> ### ⟨Tips⟩ Beware of Sword Sellers
>
> Fijians are friendly people, but beware of so-called **sword sellers**. These are men who carry bags under their arms and approach you on the street. "Where you from, 'Stralia? States?" will be their opening line, followed by, "What's your name?" If you respond, they will quickly inscribe your name on a sloppily carved wooden sword. They expect you to buy it, whether you want it or not. They are numerous in Nadi, and may also come up to you in Suva, where government efforts to discourage the practice have had more success. The easiest way to avoid this scam is to not tell any stranger your name and walk away as soon as you see the bag.

HANDICRAFTS

Fijians produce a wide variety of handicrafts, such as carved *tanoa* (kava) bowls, war clubs, and cannibal forks; woven baskets and mats; pottery (which has seen a renaissance of late); and *masi* (tapa) cloth. Although generally not of the quality of those produced in Tonga, they are made in prolific quantities. Be careful when buying souvenirs and some woodcarvings, however, for many of today's items are machine-made, and many smaller items are imported from Asia. Only with masi can you be sure of getting a genuine Fijian handicraft.

The larger shops sell some very fine face masks and *nguzunguzus* (noozoo-noozoos), the inlaid canoe prows carved in the Solomon Islands, and some primitive art from Papua New Guinea. (Although you will see plenty hanging in the shops, the Fijians never carved masks in the old days.)

The largest and best-stocked shop on Queen's Road is **Jack's of Fiji** ⟨⟩ (© 670 0744). It has a wide selection of handicrafts, jewelry, T-shirts, clothing, and paintings by local artists. The prices are reasonable and the staff is helpful rather than pushy. The Chefs The Restaurant complex is on premises (see "Where to Dine in Nadi," later in this chapter). Jack's of Fiji has other outlets including the shopping arcade of the Sheraton Fiji Resort (© 670 1777) and in Sigatoka and Suva.

Other places to look are **Nadi Handicraft Center** (© 670 2357) and **Nad's Handicrafts** (© 670 3588). Nadi Handicraft Center has an upstairs room carrying clothing, leather goods, jewelry, and black pearls. Nad's usually has a good selection of Fijian pottery. **Nadi Handicraft Market** (no phone) is a collection of stalls on the Queen's Road near the south end of Nadi Town. The best are operated by Fijian women who sell baskets and other goods woven of pandanus.

WHERE TO STAY IN NADI

Most Nadi-area hotels are on or near the Queen's Road, either near the airport or in **Martintar,** a suburban area between the airport and Nadi Town. An advantage of Martintar is that you can walk from your hotel to several restaurants and bars. Only the resorts on **Denarau Island** and beside **Wailoaloa Beach** sit beside a beach. Even if they do, runoff from the mountains, hills, cane fields, and coastal mangrove swamps perpetually leaves Nadi Bay less than clear and its beaches more gray than white.

This area has a host of backpacker hostels, all of them in fierce competition with each other. The **Fiji Backpackers Association** (www.fiji-backpacking.com) is an organization of reputable hostel owners.

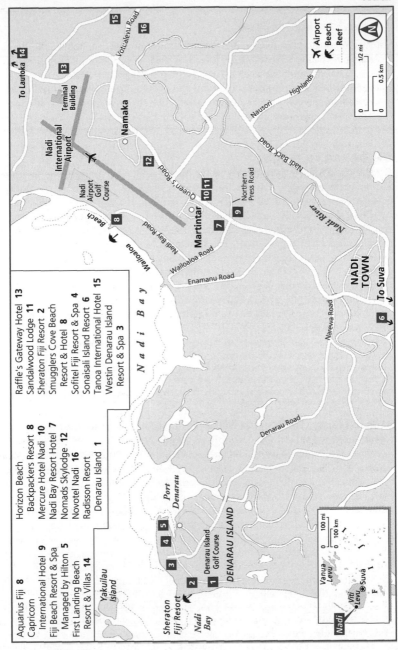

Nadi

Legend:
- ✈ Airport
- 🏖 Beach
- Reef

1/2 mi
0.5 km

Aquarius Fiji **8**
Capricorn International Hotel **9**
Fiji Beach Resort & Spa Managed by Hilton **5**
First Landing Beach Resort & Villas **14**

Horizon Beach Backpackers Resort **8**
Mercure Hotel Nadi **10**
Nadi Bay Resort Hotel **7**
Nomads Skylodge **12**
Novotel Nadi **16**
Radisson Resort Denarau Island **1**

Raffle's Gateway Hotel **13**
Sandalwood Lodge **11**
Sheraton Fiji Resort **2**
Smugglers Cove Beach Resort & Hotel **8**
Sofitel Fiji Resort & Spa **4**
Sonaisali Island Resort **6**
Tanoa International Hotel **15**
Westin Denarau Island Resort & Spa **3**

To Lautoka

Terminal Building

Nadi International Airport

Namaka

Nadi Airport Golf Course

Martintar

Northern Press Road

Vunavau Road

Votualevu Road

Nausori Highlands

Nadi Back Road

Queen's Road

Nadi River

Nadi Bay Road

Wailoaloa Beach

Wailoaloa Road

Enamanu Road

NADI TOWN

To Suva

Narewa Road

Nadi Bay

Yakuilau Island

Port Denarau

Denarau Island Golf Course

DENARAU ISLAND

Sheraton Fiji Resort

Nadi Bay

Denarau Road

Vanua Levu

Viti Levu

Suva

Nadi

FIJI

100 mi
100 km

Tips Last-Minute Plans

If you're making last-minute plans, contact **Impulse Fiji**, P.O. Box 10000, Nadi Airport (© **800/953-7595**; 672 3952; fax 672 5064; www.impulsefiji.com), which sells "unused" hotel rooms at reduced rates. It saves you the trouble of asking the front desk for a discount on rooms that would otherwise go unused. You can also get discounts on airline tickets and hotel rooms if you book in advance on the company's website.

ON DENARAU ISLAND

Fiji Beach Resort & Spa Managed by Hilton 𝄞𝄞   Extending along the northeastern point of Denarau Island, this resort opened in 2007 and was a work in progress during my recent visit (a new central building and more units could be open by the time you arrive). Two-story buildings hold the accommodations, which are two-bedroom, two-bathroom condos designed so that one bedroom and bathroom can be rented as a standard room. The remaining bedroom, kitchen, and living area are known as "villas." High-tech prevails, including flatscreen TVs and PlayStations in each unit. Sliding doors close off the bathrooms, which have showers and soaking tubs, from the bedrooms. Each villa has a gas barbecue grill on its balcony, most of which look out to a long beachside pool divided into seven separate areas. The main restaurant is by the pool, but the star is **Lépicier**, a coffee shop/deli with superb fresh breads and pastries.

P.O. Box 11185, Nadi Airport. © **800/HILTONS** [445-8667] or 675 8000. Fax 675 6801. www.fijibeachresortby hilton.com. 225 units. F$485–F$675 (US$315–US$438/£162–£225). AE, DC, MC, V. **Amenities:** 2 restaurants; 1 bar; 7 outdoor pools; fitness center; spa; Jacuzzi; watersports equipment rentals; children's programs; game room; activities desk; car rental desk; wireless Internet access in public areas; 24-hr. room service; babysitting; laundry service; free coin-op washers and dryers; concierge-level rooms. *In room:* A/C, TV, kitchen (in 1-bedroom. villas), high-speed Internet access, fridge, coffeemaker, iron, safe.

Radisson Resort Fiji Denarau Island 𝄞𝄞   Denarau Island's newest resort boasts a sophisticated and streamlined design. An extraordinary pool complex (the 4 pools are designed like lagoons—some sand-surrounded, others with waterfalls and green islands) is the highlight here. An open and airy *bure*-style lobby welcomes guests with an expansive view of the resorts' lush grounds, the pool, and the South Pacific. Spagoers can request specialized wellness menus in addition to the offerings of the hotel's restaurants, which feature a pizza kitchen as well as traditional island fare and Western dishes. Individualized service is par for the course, as the staff is obliging and ready to help at a moment's notice. Decorated in calming colors, the guest rooms have white porcelain tiled floors, practical for back-and-forth activity between the pool, beach, and hotel rooms. Each room has an outdoor furnished patio or balcony to enjoy night views of the Southern Hemisphere skies. Families and large parties should consider renting condolike suites, which offer kitchens with washers and dryers.

P.O. Box 9347, Nadi Airport. © **888/201-1718** or 675 1264. Fax 675 1117. www.radisson.com/fiji. 270 units. F$180–F$500 (US$117–US$325/£60–£167). AE, DC, MC, V. **Amenities:** 3 restaurants; 3 bars; 4 swimming pools; fitness center; spa; Jacuzzi; watersports equipment rentals; children's programs; concierge; activities desk; car-rental desk; business center; wireless Internet access; 24-hr. room service; babysitting; coin-op washers and dryers. *In room:* A/C, TV, minibar, coffeemaker, iron, safe.

Sheraton Fiji Resort ✸✸   This 1987-vintage hotel was scheduled to be closed between May and November 2008 for a major renovation, including installation of a new swimming pool complex and a state-of-the-art spa and workout center. The central building is reminiscent of a U.S. shopping mall (and it does have some very fine shops). In contrast to the Fijian-style of its nearby sister, The Westin Denarau Island Resort & Spa (see below), it could be put down in any tropical resort location. In two-story buildings flanking the central complex, the large rooms here have ocean views from their private terraces or balconies. The food choices (none of them inexpensive) include fine dining in the swanky **Ports O' Call.** There's a private island across the lagoon where guests can swim, snorkel, and sunbathe.

The resort also manages the 184 adjacent condos known as the **Sheraton Denarau Villas.** Built around a courtyard, one end of which opens to a beachside swimming pool and bar, these are among Nadi's fanciest digs. They come in various sizes, ranging from a single room to a three-bedroom apartment, and are appointed with all the comforts, including full kitchens and washers and dryers.

P.O. Box 9761, Nadi. (©) 800/325-3535 or 675 0777. Fax 675 0818. www.sheraton.com/fiji. 292 hotel units, 184 condos. US$330–US$535 (£165–£267) double; US$435–US$1,065 (£217–£532) condo. AE, DC, MC, V. **Amenities:** 4 restaurants; 3 bars; outdoor pool; exercise room; watersports equipment rentals; children's programs; concierge; activities desk; car-rental desk; business center; shopping arcade; salon; 24-hr. room service; massage; babysitting; laundry service. In room: A/C, TV, dataport, kitchen (in condos), minibar, coffeemaker, iron, safe.

Sofitel Fiji Resort & Spa ✸✸✸   One of Fiji's largest outdoor swimming pools and some of its best big-hotel dining highlight this luxury resort. The central building sports a gleaming open-air lobby overlooking the pool and beach. The spacious guest quarters are in three-story buildings lined up along the beach. Furnished and equipped in European style, they range from oceanview rooms to presidential suites. I prefer the "junior suites" with Jacuzzis hidden behind louvered windows on their balconies. Under the direction of European chefs, the kitchen provides excellent fare for three food outlets, including a fine-dining seafood restaurant. Meeting space in the central building is high-tech, including wireless Internet access. Although it lacks the Fijian charm of The Westin Denarau Island Resort & Spa, and the pool isn't as spectacular as the Radisson Fiji Denarau Island's, I admire the food and modern amenities here.

Private Mail Bag 396, Nadi Airport. (©) 800/763-4835 or 675 1111. Fax 675 1122. www.sofitel.com.fj. 296 units. F$430–F$2,000 (US$279–US$1,299/£143–£667). AE, DC, MC, V. **Amenities:** 3 restaurants; 5 bars; outdoor pool; fitness center; spa; Jacuzzi; watersports equipment rentals; children's programs; game room; concierge; activities desk; 24-hr. business center; wireless Internet access throughout; shopping arcade; 24-hr. room service; babysitting; laundry service; free coin-op washers and dryers; concierge-level rooms. In room: A/C, TV, dataport, minibar, fridge, coffeemaker, iron, safe.

The Westin Denarau Island Resort & Spa ✸✸✸   Originally known as The Regent of Fiji, and more recently as the Sheraton Royal Denarau Resort, this venerable property opened its doors in 1972. Starwood Hotels, which now owns it as well as the nearby Sheraton Fiji, recently upgraded it to luxury status. Fortunately, it still maintains more Fijian charm than any other large hotel here. Covered by a peaked wooden roof and laden with artifacts, the dark, breezy foyer opens to an irregularly shaped pool and the gray-sand beach. The rooms are in a series of two-story, motel-style blocks grouped in "villages" surrounded by thick, lush tropical gardens and linked by covered walkways to the central building. All but two of these buildings face the beach. With lots of varnished wood trim, exposed timbers, and masi cloth accents,

---

Tips Check the Hotel Websites for Rates & Specials

Hotel room rates in Fiji have been in a state of major flux since the coup in December 2006. Most resorts have been offering substantial discounts to lure visitors back to the country. The practice is so widespread that many large hotels were unwilling to tell me their rack rates. Therefore, the rates in these pages are useful primarily to tell if one hotel is more expensive than another. Frankly, you won't know what you will pay until you select a date and try to book a room. Be sure to check the hotel websites to see if specials or Internet-only rates are being offered when you plan to visit.

---

the spacious units ooze tropical charm. Guests can use the private island shared with the Sheraton Fiji, while guests there can use the fitness center and full-service spa here. While families will be at home here, The Westin is the most tranquil resort on Denarau Island, which make it more attractive to couples than its competition.

P.O. Box 9761, Nadi Airport. ℂ 800/325-3535 or 675 0000. Fax 675 0259. www.westin.com. 274 units. F$310–390 (US$475–US$600 double, £237–£300); F$735 (US$1,130/£565) suite. AE, DC, MC, V. **Amenities:** 4 restaurants; 4 bars; outdoor pool; 2 Jacuzzis; exercise room; watersports equipment rentals; children's programs; game room; concierge; activities desk; car-rental desk; shopping arcade; 24-hr. room service; massage; babysitting; laundry service. *In room:* A/C, TV, high-speed Internet access, minibar, coffeemaker, iron, safe.

AT WAILOALOA BEACH

Wailoaloa Beach, 3km (2 miles) off the Queen's Road, is a long strip of grayish brown sand fringing Nadi Bay. Although it was built as a housing development, the area known as **Newtown Beach** houses locals and several inexpensive establishments.

Aquarius Fiji 🏵 Canadian Terrence Buckley merged these two beachside condos into Fiji's first "flashpacker" budget-priced resort. Although backpackers usually occupy the five downstairs rooms with 2, 6, or 10 bunk beds (each is air-conditioned and has its own bathroom), the eight spacious rooms upstairs are suitable for anyone searching for an inexpensive beachside stay. The four upstairs rooms facing the bay are particularly attractive, as they have large balconies overlooking the beach and a small outdoor swimming pool. The other four upstairs units have smaller balconies facing the mountains. Downstairs, a restaurant, bar, and TV lounge open to the pool.

P.O. Box 7, Nadi. ℂ 672 6000. Fax 672 6001. www.aquarius.com.fj. 8 units (all with bathroom), 18 dorm beds. F$89–F$99 (US$58–US$64/£30–£33) double; F$28–F$30 (US$18–US$19/£9.35–£10) dorm bed. AE, MC, V. **Amenities:** Restaurant; bar; outdoor pool; activities desk; laundry service. *In room:* A/C, no phone.

Horizon Beach Backpackers Resort Although it's not directly on the beach, this two-story clapboard house is a less-expensive alternative to the nearby Aquarius Fiji and Smugglers Cove Beach Resort & Hotel next door. The rooms are spacious, if not luxurious, and have their own bathrooms with hot-water showers. Superior units are air-conditioned; the others have fans. The dorm beds are in two rooms; the smaller one with eight bunks is air-conditioned. There's a pool and an open-air restaurant serving inexpensive meals. Fijian musicians perform at night at the bar. Guests here can use the facilities at Smugglers Cove Beach Resort & Hotel, with which it shares owners.

P.O. Box 1401, Nadi (Wasawasa Rd., Newtown Beach). ℂ 672 2832. Fax 672 4578. www.horizonbeachfiji.com. 14 units (all with bathroom), 16 dorm beds. F$50–F$155 (US$32–US$101/£17–£51) double; F$15–F$22

(US$9.75–US$14/£5–£7.35) dorm bed. Rates include continental breakfast. AE, MC, V. **Amenities:** Restaurant; bar; outdoor pool; activities desk; laundry service. *In room:* A/C (all rooms and 8 dorm beds), no phone.

Smugglers Cove Beach Resort & Hotel 𝒜𝒜 *Value*   Opened in 2006, this three-story hotel is larger than Aquarius Fiji, and its medium-size rooms are equipped with amenities found at more expensive hotels. A family suite also has a kitchen. Best are four rooms on the front of the building with balconies overlooking the swimming pool, the beach, and Nadi Bay. Arranged in four-bed coed cubicles, the 34 beds in the first-floor Pirates Dormitory are often full (overflow heads to the owners' Horizon Beach Backpackers Resort next-door). The young guests keep the restaurant and bar—which open to the deck-surrounded pool—busy and sometimes noisy at night. Another plus here is a large, air-conditioned Internet room.

P.O. Box 5401, Nadi. © 672 6578. Fax 672 8740. www.smugglersbeachfiji.com. 22 units (all with bathrooms), 34 dorm beds. F$98–F$198 (US$64–US$129/£33–£66) double; F$28 (US$18/£9.35) dorm bed. Rates include continental breakfast. AE, MC, V. **Amenities:** Restaurant; bar; outdoor pool; activities desk; laundry service; coin-op washers and dryers. *In room:* A/C, TV, kitchen (in family suite), fridge, coffeemaker, safe.

IN THE MARTINTAR AREA

Capricorn International Hotel *Value* *Kids*   Cleanliness and firm mattresses are trademarks at this budget property, along with its Suva sister, the Capricorn Apartment Hotel (see "Where to Stay in Suva," later in this chapter). Least expensive are the standard rooms, which are entered from the rear and have window walls instead of balconies overlooking a lush tropical courtyard with a pool and a hot tub (they are the highlight here). I would opt for a unit with a balcony or patio. Six family units have kitchens and two bedrooms. The fan-cooled dorm is an afterthought here.

P.O. Box 9043, Nadi Airport. © 672 0088. Fax 672 0522. www.capricornfiji.com. 68 units, 14 dorm beds. F$100–F$170 (US$65–US$110/£33–£57) double; F$25 (US$16/£8.35) dorm bed. Rates include continental breakfast. AE, DC, MC, V. **Amenities:** Restaurant; bar; outdoor pool; spa; Jacuzzi; activities desk; limited room service; massage; babysitting; laundry service. *In room:* A/C, TV, kitchen (family units), fridge, coffeemaker, iron (family units), safe.

Mercure Hotel Nadi   Formerly the Dominion International, this motel now sports modern European decor and furniture, thanks to a facelift when it recently became a Mercure property. The spacious rooms are in two white three-story buildings that flank a tropical garden surrounding a swimming pool and wooden deck. The rooms have desks, shower-only bathrooms with French-style "bowl" hand basins, and glass doors sliding open to patios or balconies. Some have king-size beds, others both queen-size and single beds. A few units are equipped for guests with disabilities.

P.O. Box 9178, Nadi Airport. © 800/637-2873 or 672 0272. Fax 672 0187. www.accorhotels.com.au/Mercure-Nadi/default_en.aspx 85 units. F$138–F$234 (US$90–US$152/£46–£78) double. AE, DC, MC, V. **Amenities:** Restaurant; bar; outdoor pool; tennis court; spa; game room; activities desk; limited room service; massage; babysitting; laundry service. *In room:* A/C, TV, fridge, coffeemaker.

Nadi Bay Resort Hotel   Although suitable for any cost-conscious traveler, 110 dormitory beds make this Nadi's largest backpacker destination. Behind its walls you'll find three bars, two sophisticated restaurants serving reasonably priced meals, an air-conditioned TV lounge, and courtyards with two swimming pools (usually surrounded by a multitude of nubile young bodies!). There's even a hair salon, a massage parlor, and a 70-seat theater for watching movies and sporting events on TV. In addition to the dormitories, its five buildings hold standard motel rooms and apartments. The property is directly under Nadi Airport's flight path, however, so jets occasionally roar overhead in the middle of the night. Lower priced units and dorms are not air-conditioned.

NAP 0359, Nadi Airport. ℭ **672 3599.** Fax 672 0092. www.fijinadibayhotel.com. 42 units (19 with bathroom), 110 dorm beds. F$80–F$150 (US$52–US$97/£27–£50) double; F$25–F$28 (US$16–US$18/£8.35–£9.35) dorm bed. AE, MC, V. Room rates include continental breakfast; dormitory rates do not. **Amenities:** 2 restaurants; 3 bars; 2 outdoor pools; activities desk; salon; massage; laundry service. *In room:* A/C (most units), fridge, coffeemaker, no phone.

Nomads Skylodge   This 11-acre property is part of Nomads World, an Australian company specializing in accommodations and tours for backpackers and other budget-minded travelers, although it's expertly managed by Fiji's Tanoa hotels. Thirteen hotel rooms are air-conditioned dormitories, each with four or six bunk beds, private lockers (bring a lock), and its own bathroom, but no other amenities such as TVs and phones. One cottage has cooking facilities. Imported sand forms a small faux beach by the swimming pool, which has its own bar.

P.O. Box 9222, Nadi Airport. ℭ **672 2200.** Fax 671 4330. www.nomadsskylodge.com.fj. 53 units. F$78–F$153 (US$51–US$99/£26–£51) double; F$25–F$31 (US$16–US$20/£8.35–£10) dorm bed. AE, DC, MC, V. **Amenities:** Restaurant; 2 bars; outdoor pool; activities desk; game room; laundry service; coin-op washers and dryers. *In room:* A/C, fridge, coffeemaker.

Sandalwood Lodge 🐾 *Value*   "Clean and comfortable at a sensible price" is the appropriate motto at John and Ana Birch's establishment (now managed by their charming daughter, Angela), which I have long considered to be Nadi's best value, provided you don't need a restaurant on the premises. Quietly situated about 300 yards off the Queen's Road behind the Mercure Hotel Nadi, the New Zealand–style motel consists of three two-story buildings that flank a nicely landscaped lawn with a rock-bordered pool. Units in the Orchid Wing are somewhat larger than the others and have queen-size beds instead of a double. Every unit has a kitchen and sofa bed.

P.O. Box 9454, Nadi Airport. ℭ **672 2044.** Fax 672 0103. sandalwood@connect.com.fj. 34 units. F$80–F$96 (US$52–US$62/£27–£32) double. AE, DC, MC, V. **Amenities:** Outdoor pool; babysitting; laundry service; coin-op washer and dryer. *In room:* A/C, TV, kitchen, coffeemaker, iron (in Orchid Wing).

NEAR THE AIRPORT

Novotel Nadi   Formerly the Fiji Mocambo, this sprawling hotel atop a hill received a much-needed facelift after being taken over by Accor Hotels in 2006 and is once again a fitting competitor to the nearby Tanoa International Hotel (see below). All rooms have excellent views across the cane fields to the mountains. Best are on the top floor; their peaked ceilings give them the feel of bungalows. There's a main restaurant plus an open-air coffee shop by the swimming pool. You can practice your swing at the hotel's 9-hole executive golf course.

P.O. Box 9195, Nadi Airport. ℭ **800/942-5050** or 672 2000. Fax 672 0324. www.novotel.com.fj. 117 units. F$201–F$276 (US$131–US$179/£67–£92) double. AE, DC, MC, V. **Amenities:** 2 restaurants; 2 bars; outdoor pool; 9-hole golf course; 2 tennis courts; spa; game room; activities desk; business center; shopping arcade; limited room service; babysitting; laundry service. *In room:* A/C, TV, high-speed Internet access; fridge, coffeemaker, iron.

Raffle's Gateway Hotel *Kids*   This older property (no connection whatsoever to Singapore's famous Raffles Hotel) is my favorite place to wait for a flight at the airport just across Queen's Road. You can slip yourself down a water slide into a figure-eight swimming pool, the larger of two here. All units recently received a facelift and now sport attractive tropical furniture and improved, shower-only bathrooms. The best have sitting areas and patios or balconies next to the large pool. The tiny, least-expensive "standard" rooms can barely hold their double beds and are devoid of most amenities. The main building houses an open-air, 24-hour coffee shop and an air-conditioned nighttime restaurant. Passengers departing on late-evening flights to Los Angeles can check out late without paying extra.

P.O. Box 9891, Nadi Airport. © 672 2444. Fax 672 0620. www.rafflesgateway.com. 95 units. F$95–F$206 (US$62–US$134/£32–£69) double. AE, DC, MC, V. **Amenities:** 2 restaurants; bar; 2 outdoor pools; Jacuzzi; tennis court; game room; activities desk; 24-hr. room service; babysitting; laundry service. *In room:* A/C, TV, fridge, coffeemaker, safe.

Tanoa International Hotel 𝒜   This motel and the Novotel Nadi are top places to stay near the airport. The public areas open onto a garden with a waterfall splashing into a swimming pool. Shingle-covered walkways lead to medium-size, motel-style rooms in two-story blocks. The Tanoa was built in the 1970s as a TraveLodge, so its rooms are somewhat smaller than the Novotel's. Most have a double and a single bed, combination tub/shower bathrooms, and balconies or patios. Superior rooms have king-size beds, large desks, sofas, and walk-in showers. Dignitaries often take the two luxurious one-bedroom suites. The open-air restaurant by the pool is open 24 hours.

P.O. Box 9203, Nadi Airport. © 800/835-7742 or 672 0277. Fax 672 0191. www.tanoahotels.com. 135 units. F$220–F$280 (US$143–US$182/£73–£93) double; F$350–F$500 (US$227–US$325/£117–£167) suite. AE, DC, MC, V. **Amenities:** Restaurant; bar; outdoor pool; 2 tennis courts; spa; Jacuzzi; exercise room; activities desk; salon; 24-hr. room service; babysitting; laundry service; coin-op washers and dryers. *In room:* A/C, TV, dataport, fridge (stocked in suites), coffeemaker, iron, safe.

SOUTH OF NADI

Sonaisali Island Resort   You drive through cane fields and ride a boat across a narrow channel to this modern resort on a flat, 105-acre island. The lagoon is shallow here at low tide, so imported sand held in place by a seawall serves as the main beach. You can frolic in an attractive rock-lined pool with a swim-up bar. A shingled roof covers all other common facilities, including an air-conditioned fine-dining restaurant. The tropically-attired guest quarters include spacious hotel rooms, but the top choice are the airy duplex bungalows out in the gardens—some of the largest *bures* on Viti Levu. Beachside bungalows small Jacuzzi tubs on their front porches (these are *duplex* units, however, so don't expect the ultimate in privacy). Three of the units have two bedrooms each and are attractive to families. I wouldn't spend my entire vacation here (as many do), but this is a viable alternative to the Denarau Island resorts for a bayside stopover. Getting into Nadi Town for shopping requires a rental or taxi ride.

P.O. Box 2544, Nadi (Sonaisali Island, 20 min. south of Nadi Town). © 670 6011. Fax 670 6092. www.sonaisali.com. 123 units. F$477 (US$310/£159) double; F$558–F$653 (US$362–US$424/£186–£218) bungalow. Rates include full breakfast. AE, DC, MC, V. **Amenities:** 2 restaurants; 4 bars; outdoor pool; tennis court; spa; Jacuzzi; watersports equipment rentals; game room; activities desk; business center; 24-hr. room service; massage; babysitting; laundry service. *In room:* A/C, TV, minibar, coffeemaker, iron, safe.

NORTH OF NADI

First Landing Beach Resort & Villas   The creation of American Jim Dunn and Australian George Stock, this little resort sits beachside at Vuda Point, near where the first Fijians came ashore 3 millennia ago. Vuda Point Marina and the country's major oil storage tanks are nearby, but the grounds here are festooned with coconut palms and other tropical plants. The foliage and picturesque waterside setting make the resort's restaurant a favorite weekend lunch retreat for local residents. There's an attractive outdoor swimming pool, and Jim and George have dredged the shallow reef to create a swimming hole and small islet offshore. The duplex guest bungalows are comfortably furnished with both king-size and single beds, and their bathrooms have whirlpool tubs. The bures also sport charming screened porches, and four beachside bures also have decks. The resort also has three two-bedroom, two-bathroom villas with their own pools. Although not as spacious as Sonaisali Island Resort, this is a more charming choice for a layover. As there, getting into Nadi Town requires a rental or taxi.

P.O. Box 348, Lautoka (at Vuda Point, 15km/9⅓ miles north of Nadi Airport). (℃ 666 6171. Fax 666 8882. www.first landingfiji.com. 39 units. F$325–F$820 (US$211–US$532/£108–£273) double. Rates include full breakfast. AE, DC, MC, V. **Amenities:** Restaurant; bar; outdoor pool; spa; activities desk; car-rental desk; 24-hr. room service; babysitting; laundry service. *In room:* A/C, dataport, kitchen (in villas), fridge (stocked on request), coffeemaker, safe.

WHERE TO DINE IN NADI
ON DENARAU ISLAND

There's an **Esquires** coffee shop with wireless Internet access in front of the Sheraton Denarau Villas (℃ 675 0989). It's open daily 7am to 10pm. The best breads and pastries on Denarau are at **Lépicier,** a coffee shop/deli in the Fiji Beach Resort & Spa Managed by Hilton (℃ 675 8000). It's open daily 8am to 10pm. Port Denarau has a branch of **Mama's Pizza** (℃ 675 0533), which has the same menu as the Nadi Town outlet (see below). It's open daily 9am to 11pm.

Cardo's Steakhouse & Cocktail Bar STEAKS/SEAFOOD/PIZZA   Owner Cardo is known throughout Fiji for providing quality chargrilled steaks and fish, and they're his best offerings here, taken at a multitude of tables on the large deck beside the marina waterway—which can be problematic if it's raining. I usually have breakfast here before a cruise or a hair-raising ride on a Jet Fiji, or chill over a cold stubbie (beer) afterwards. Lunch specials, such as chargrilled chicken salad, are posted on a blackboard. The pizzas are wood-fired, but I go around the corner to Mama's Pizza for my pies.

Port Denarau. (℃ 675 0900. Reservations accepted. Breakfast F$4.50–F$10 (US$2.90–US$6.50/£1.50–£3.35); pizza F$17–F$32 (US$11–US$21/£5.65–£11); main courses F$22–F$49 (US$14–US$32/£7.35–£16). AE, MC, V. Daily 7am–10:30pm.

Hard Rock Cafe Fiji INTERNATIONAL   I am tempted to wear my earplugs to Fiji's first franchise of the famous chain, for it's like the others: loud, hip, relatively expensive, and adorned with rock-and-roll memorabilia. In fact, you could be in a Hard Rock in Berlin or Beirut, New York or New Orleans. The menu offers the usual selection of nachos, blackened chicken pasta, huge burgers, and grilled steaks and fish. Unlike many restaurants in Fiji, where you'll get poor imitations, everything here is up to international standards. The fajitas really taste like Mexican fare, for example, and the pulled-pork barbecue sandwiches could be from South Carolina.

Port Denarau. (℃ 675 0032. Reservations accepted. Burgers and sandwiches F$13–F$27 (US$8.45–US$18/£4.35–£9); main courses F$18–F$48 (US$12–US$31/£6–£16). AE, MC, V. Daily 11am–10:45pm.

Indigo 𝕂𝕂𝕂 *(Value* INDIAN/ASIAN   This excellent restaurant, with mostly outdoor tables, is the creation of Executive Chef Eugene Gomes, who left the Sheraton Fiji to open the dining outlets at Jack's of Fiji in Nadi Town (see below). Along with his Saffron restaurant, Indigo serves the country's best and most authentic Indian cuisine. The top–and most expensive–offering is mangrove crab marsala, but I prefer the Goan pork curry (an import from Eugene's home of Goa, a former Portuguese and predominately Catholic colony, where people actually eat pork in mostly Hindu and Muslim India). Butter chicken is excellent, too. The Asian side of the menu features Thai-style crab and Rendang curry. Vegetarians can choose from at least eight dishes here.

Port Denarau. (℃ 675 0026. Reservations recommended. Main courses F$11–F$48 (US$7.15–US$31/£3.65–£16). AE, MC, V. Daily 11am–9:30pm.

IN NADI TOWN

Bullacino 🌶️🌶️🌶️ *Value* COFFEE SHOP/DELI/BAKERY   Esquires had the corner on Fiji's coffee shop business until this urbane establishment opened its doors in 2007. The coffee is rich and steamy, the pastries—including the best bagels in Fiji—are fresh from **Nutmeg & Tulips** bakery next door, and the lunchtime offerings are among the finest I've had in Fiji. I am in love with the warm roasted chicken over a salad of mesclun greens with a lemon-tinged dressing. Grilled swordfish with Italian salsa, yellowfin tuna with wasabi mayonnaise, and vegetarian ratatouille are winners, too. You can dine at tables in the air-conditioned shop or under fans out on a deck overlooking the muddy Nadi River. Unfortunately, they are not open for dinner!

Queen's Rd. (at Nadi River bridge.). © 672 8638. Reservations not accepted. Breakfast F$5–F$15 (US$3.25–US$9.75/£1.65–£5); lunch F$10–F$17 (US$6.50–US$11/£3.35–£5.65). MC, V. Daily 8am–6pm.

Chefs The Restaurant 🌶️🌶️🌶️ *Value* INTERNATIONAL   The first of Executive Chef Eugene Gomes' creations is still one of Fiji's top restaurants. The service is attentive, and the cuisine is well presented. Menus vary with the season but always include grilled beef tenderloin and rack of lamb to satisfy Australian and New Zealand patrons. Breakfast is served, and the lunch menu offers salads, burgers, curries, and fish and chips. You get a 10% discount if you purchase F$100 (US$65/£33) worth of merchandise from Jack's (bring your receipt).

Sangayam Rd. (behind Jack's of Fiji). © 670 3131. Reservations recommended. Breakfast F$5.50–F$8 (US$3.55–US$5.20/£1.85–£2.65); lunch F$8.50–F$30 (US$5.50–US$19/£2.85–£10); dinner main courses F$29–F$69 (US$19–US$45/£9.65–£23). AE, DC, MC, V. Daily 9am–10pm.

Corner Cafe 🌶️ *Value* CAFETERIA   Another of Eugene Gomes's operations, this cafeteria is a fine place to stop for a snack, an ice cream, or a quick lunch in Nadi Town. The menu is varied: pastries and coffee (you can get a latte), hot dogs and hamburgers, sandwiches and salads, chicken, pastas, and fish and chips. I prefer the Thai curry chicken. You can also order from the adjacent Saffron's menu (see below).

Queen's Rd. (in Jack's of Fiji building). © 670 3131. Most items F$5–F$12 (US$3.25–US$7.80/£1.65–£4. AE, DC, MC, V. Mon–Sat 8am–6pm.

Mama's Pizza ITALIAN   If you need a tomato sauce fix, follow the aroma of garlic to Robin O'Donnell's establishment. Her wood-fired pizzas range from a small plain model to a large deluxe version with all the toppings. Just remember that this is Nadi, not New York or Naples, so adjust your expectations accordingly. She also has spaghetti with tomato-and-meat sauce, lasagna, and fresh salads. There're Mama's Pizzas at Port Denarau (© 675 0533) and in the Colonial Plaza shopping mall on the Queen's Road, north of Martintar (© 672 0922).

Queen's Rd., Nadi Town, opposite Mobil Station. © 670 0221. Pizzas F$7–F$27 (US$4.55–US$18/£2.35–£9); pastas F$10–F$12 (US$6.50–US$7.80/£3.35–£4). MC, V. Daily 10am–11pm.

Saffron 🌶️🌶️🌶️ NORTHERN INDIAN/VEGETARIAN   Sharing quarters in Jack's Handicrafts with the Corner Cafe (see above), this is executive chef Eugene Gomes's ode to the tandoori cooking of northern India and Pakistan, although his menu also features vegetarian and other dishes from around the subcontinent. This is the best Indian cuisine in Fiji. The Punjabi chicken *tikka* is great, and I'm addicted to the smooth butter chicken curry. You'll be greeted with a complimentary basket of crispy *papadam* with dipping sauce (an Indian version of Mexican tortilla chips and salsa).

Queen's Rd., Nadi Town (in Jack's of Fiji building). © **670 1233.** Reservations accepted. Main courses F$11–F$42 (US$7.15–US$27/£3.65–£14). AE, DC, MC, V. Mon–Sat 11am–2:30pm and 5:30–9:30pm; Sun 5:30–9:30pm.

IN THE MARTINTAR AREA

The suburban version of **Mama's Pizza** is in the rear of the Colonial Plaza shopping center on the Queen's Road between Martintar and Namaka (© **672 0922**). It has the same menu, prices, and hours as its Nadi Town mama (see above). **McDonald's** is on the Queen's Road at Emananu Road, between Nadi Town and Martintar.

Daikoku ✿ JAPANESE   There are two dining areas at this authentic restaurant, which was prefabricated in Japan and reconstructed here. Downstairs is the sushi bar, which uses the freshest salmon, tuna, and lobster. Upstairs is the teppanyaki room, where the chef will stir-fry vegetables, shrimp, chicken, or tender beef as you watch. You can also order sukiyaki, udon, and other Japanese dishes. It's Fiji's best Japanese.

Queen's Rd., Martintar (at Northern Press Rd.). © **672 3622.** Reservations recommended. Sushi and sashimi F$5–F$26 (US$3.25–US$17/£1.65–£8.65); main courses F$12–F$33 (US$7.80–US$21/£4–£11). AE, DC, MC, V. Daily noon–2pm and 6–9:30pm.

Nadina Authentic Fijian Restaurant ✿✿✿ FIJIAN   Nadi lacked a really good Fijian restaurant until Amy Suvan opened this one in late 2007. In a small wooden cottage with a wraparound porch, it excels in traditional fare such as *kokoda* (raw fish marinated in lime juice, served with fresh vegetables) and *kovu walu* (Spanish mackerel steamed with coconut milk in banana leaves). Nadina is the only place I know which regularly serves *ota miti*, the crunchy young shoots of the wood fern, which are delicious served with coconut milk. Some dishes are spiced up for Western tastes, and you can get a good curry here, too.

Queen's Rd., Martintar (opposite Capricorn International Hotel). © **672 7313.** Reservations recommended. Main courses F$18–F$22 (US$12–US$14/£6–£7.35). MC, V. Daily 7am–10pm.

The Outer Reef Seafood Café/Sandbar Restaurant ✿✿ SEAFOOD   Allan Watters relocated to Fiji and opened this cafe and restaurant, for which he imports the same fresh seafood he used to sell back in Australia. Open for lunch, his store doubles as a fish market and **The Outer Reef Seafood Café,** serving sandwiches, sashimi, and fish and chips. On the other hand, you'll feel like someone sneaking into a 1920s speakeasy when you follow a narrow passage to the **Sandbar Restaurant,** an alfresco dining patio and bar out back. The specialty under the stars is a two-level stack of hot or cold crab, shrimp, oysters, mussels, scallops, and the Australian crustaceans known as Balmain bugs. It's big enough to serve two adults. Steaks cooked over a gas grill are very good. The Outer Reef has live music on weekends, but don't head here if it's raining.

Queen's Rd. north of Nomads Skylodge, between Martintar and Namaka. © **672 7201.** Reservations recommended. Cafe items F$5–F$9 (US$3.25–US$5.85/£1.65–£3); main courses F$20–F$45 (US$13–US$29/£6.65–£15). MC, V. Cafe Mon–Sat 8am–7pm; Sun 11am–7pm. Restaurant daily 11am–11pm.

ISLAND NIGHTS IN NADI

The large hotels usually have something going on every night. As noted in the "Tips on Dining," in chapter 4, this might be a special meal followed by a Fijian dance show. The large hotels also frequently have live entertainment in their bars during the cocktail hour. Check with any hotel activities desk to see what's happening.

With several pubs, Martintar is Nadi's nightlife center. **The Bounty Bar & Restaurant** (© 672 0840) draws many expatriate residents and has live music on weekend nights (see "Where to Dine in Nadi," above). Across the Queen's Road, the outdoor tables at **Ed's Bar** (© 672 4650) are popular with locals.

On Denarau Island, **Cardo's Upstairs** is a sophisticated lounge, bar, and retro dance floor above Cardo's Steakhouse and Cocktail Bar (© 675 0900; see "Where to Dine in Nadi," above).

2 The Mamanuca & Yasawa Islands ⭐⭐

by Bill Goodwin & Valerie Haeder

The Great Sea Reef off northwest Viti Levu encloses a huge lagoon. Here, usually calm waters surround the Mamanuca and Yasawa island groups with speckled shades of yellow, green, and blue as the sea changes from shallow to deep. With ample sunshine and some of Fiji's best beaches, they are great places to escape for a day or so.

The **Mamanuca Group,** as it's officially known, consists of small flat atolls and hilly islands, ranging from 8km to 32km (5–20 miles) west of Nadi. Day cruises have been going to the Mamanucas since the dawn of Fiji's modern tourism in the early 1960s. The Mamanucas have some of the country's oldest offshore resorts, which are still very popular with Australians and New Zealanders on 1- or 2-week holidays.

North of the Mamanucas, the **Yasawa Islands** stretch as much as 100km (62 miles) from Nadi. Lt. Charles Wilkes, commander of the U.S. expedition that charted Fiji in 1840, said the Yasawa Islands reminded him of "a string of blue beads lying along the horizon." For the most part, Fijians still live in small villages among the curving coconut palms beside some of the South Pacific's most awesomely beautiful beaches. But the Yasawas are changing rapidly, with more than two dozen small resorts in all price ranges, and especially in the low-budget category aimed at young backpackers, who now see a bit of beach time in the Yasawas as an essential part of their Fiji experience. Rather than tour around Fiji, many backpackers today simply head for the Yasawas.

GETTING TO THE ISLANDS

The Mamanuca and Yasawa resorts arrange transfers for their guests (all of them require reservations), either by boat from the Port Denarau marina, or by seaplane or helicopter from Nadi. See "Getting There & Getting Around," in chapter 4.

The quickest, easiest, and most expensive way to the islands is via seaplane or helicopter. **Pacific Island Seaplanes** (© 672 5643; www.fijiseaplanes.com) provides seaplane service to the islands; the flights are on a charter basis, arranged by the resorts. It's even more expensive, but **Island Hoppers** (© 672 0140; www.helicopters.com.fj) flies helicopters to most of the moderate and expensive resorts. **Pacific Sun** (© 672 0888) flies nine-seat planes several times a day from Nadi Airport to Malololailai, home of Plantation and Musket Cove Island Resorts, and to Mana Island.

Most folk, however, take one of the fast, air-conditioned catamarans that provide daily ferry service from Port Denarau to and from the islands. The *Malolo Cat* (© 672 0774) runs from Port Denarau to Musket Cove or Plantation Island resorts on Malololailai Island. One-way fares are about F$50 (US$32/£17).

South Sea Cruises (© 675 0500; www.ssc.com.fj) operates three fast catamarans from Port Denarau. The *Tiger IV* and the *Cougar* depart for most of the Mamanuca

---

Tips Take a Big Boat

Some inexpensive properties will offer to take you to the islands in their own small craft for less than you would pay on the *Tiger IV,* the *Cougar,* or the *Yasawa Flyer.* These rides take at least an hour to the Mamanucas, several hours to the Yasawas, and the boats can be small, poorly equipped, and perhaps lacking covers to protect you from the elements. One of them sank a few years ago (without the loss of life). My advice: Take the fast catamaran.

---

resorts three times daily, usually 9am, and 12:15 and 3:15pm. The bright yellow *Yasawa Flyer* departs daily at 8:30am for the Yasawas and goes as far north as Nacula Island, a 4½-hour voyage from Port Denarau. A few resorts have docks, but most send small boats to pick up their guests, so you may have to wade ashore in your bare feet. Round-trip fares range up to F$100 (US$65/£33) per person to the Mamanucas and F$120 (US$78/£40) to the Yasawas. For a bit more, you can ride up in the captain's lounge and have someone bring you refreshments.

A subsidiary of South Sea Cruises, **Awesome Adventures Fiji** (② 670 5006; www. awesomefiji.com) has a "Bula Pass," allowing unlimited island-hopping via the *Yasawa Flyer* for 7, 14, and 21 days. These cost about F$270 (US$175/£90), F$390 (US$253/£130), and F$420 (US$273/£140) per person, respectively.

SeaFiji (② 672 5961; www.seafiji.net) provides 24-hour water-taxi service to the Mamanuca islands from Port Denarau.

SEEING THE ISLANDS ON DAY TRIPS FROM NADI

Even if you're laying over in Fiji for just a short time, you should get out to the islands for a day from Nadi or the Coral Coast. Most of the trips mentioned below depart from the Port Denarau marina on Denarau Island. Bus transportation from the Nadi or Coral Coast hotels to the marina is included in their prices (you'll pay more from the Coral Coast). Children pay half-fare on all the day trips.

My favorite is **Beachcomber Day Cruises** 𝕽𝕽𝕽 (② 666 1500; www.beachcomber fiji.com), which goes to youth-oriented Beachcomber Island Resort (see "Resorts in the Mamanucas Islands," below). Despite the advent of so many inexpensive properties elsewhere, Beachcomber still is a popular stop for young people seeking sand, sun, and suds—but be warned (or alerted) that young European women have been known to bathe topless at Beachcomber. You'll pay F$82 (US$53/£27) for bus transportation, the cruise, and a buffet lunch on Beachcomber Island. Swimming is free, but snorkeling gear, scuba diving, and other activities cost extra.

You can sightsee through the Mamanucas on the *Tiger IV* (② 675 0500; www. ssc.com.fj; see "Getting to the Islands," above). The half-day sightseeing-only voyage costs about F$90 (US$58/£30). I prefer the morning voyage, getting off at **South Sea Island, Malolo Island Resort, Castaway Island Resort, Mana Island Resort,** or **Bounty Island** (see "Resorts in the Mamanuca Islands," below, before making your decision). These include a buffet lunch, swimming and sunbathing. Depending on where you spend the day, these cost between F$120 and F$135 (US$78–US$88/£40–£45).

It's a long day (8:30am–6pm), but you can ride the *Yasawa Flyer* (② 675 0500; www.ssc.com.fj) on its daily voyages through the Yasawas and back for about F$125

(US$81/£42) round-trip. You won't be able to relax on any beaches, as the boat stops at each property only long enough to put off and pick up passengers and their luggage. It's the only way to take in the Yasawas in 1 day. Or you can get off at beautiful **Waya Island** in the southern Yasawas for lunch and a tour of a Fijian village, which will give you more of a glimpse into Fijian life than the Mamanuca day trips.

Captain Cook Cruises (© 670 1823; www.captaincook.com.au) uses the *Ra Marama,* a 33m (108-ft.) square-rigged brigantine, built in Singapore during the 1950s and once the official yacht of Fiji's colonial governors-general, for the 1-hour sail out to Tivua Island, an uninhabited 4-acre islet in the Mamanucas. A traditional Fijian welcoming ceremony greets you, then you can swim, snorkel, and canoe over 500 acres of coral gardens (or see the colors from a glass-bottom boat). Lunch and drinks are included in the F$97 (US$63/£32) charge. I've never done it, but you can stay overnight on Tivua for about F$300 (US$195/£100) per person, double occupancy, including meals. Accommodation is in two bures with cool freshwater showers.

Malamala Island (© 670 2444) is a 6-acre islet studded with palm trees and circled with white-sand beaches. The only inhabitants will be you and your fellow passengers, who will use Malamala's thatch bure for a barbecue lunch. The F$89 (US$58/£30) price includes lunch, a drink, snorkel gear, and coral viewing.

You will have more options on **Malololailai Island,** home of Plantation Island, Musket Cove, and Lomani resorts. You can visit them on a day cruise via the *Malololo Cat* (© 672 0744) for about F$50 (US$32/£17) round-trip, or fly over on **Pacific Sun** (© 672 0888) for F$122 (US$79/£41) round-trip. You can hang out at the two resorts, shop at Louis and Georgie Czukelter's **Art Gallery** on the hill above Musket Cove (no phone), and dine at **Anandas Restaurant and Bar** (© 672 2333) by the airstrip. You can book at the restaurant to play the island's short 9-hole golf course; fees are F$20 (US$13/£6.65).

Seafari Cruise is what South Sea Cruises (© 675 0500) calls its rent-a-boat service at Port Denarau. You design your own cruise to the Mamanuca Islands, such as picnicking at a deserted beach or snorkeling in your chosen spots. Prices depend on the size of the boat. The largest can hold up to 20 passengers.

SAILING THROUGH THE ISLANDS

I hesitate to use such a well-worn cliché as "reef-strewn," but that's the best way to describe Fiji's waters—so strewn, in fact, that the government does not allow bareboat yacht chartering. It's just too dangerous. You can rent both boat and skipper or local guide for extended cruises through the islands. The marina at **Musket Cove Island Resort** (see "Resorts in the Mamanuca Islands," below) is a mecca for cruising yachts, some of whose skippers take charters for a living. Contact the resort for details.

On the other hand, you can easily get out on the lagoons under sail for a day. Most interesting to my mind is the **MV** *Seaspray* 🐠🐠 (© 675 0500; www.ssc.com.fj), a

---

Moments **Sand Between My Toes**

Nothing relaxes me more than feeling sand between my toes at one of Fiji's small get-away-from-it-all resorts. If I have a spare day in Nadi, I head to Beachcomber Island Resort, where the floor of the bar and dining room is sand. And with all those young folks out on the beach, I feel like I'm 25 again.

25m (82-ft.) schooner that starred in the 1960s TV series *Adventures in Paradise,* based on James A. Michener's short stories. Based at Mana Island, it sails through the outer Mamanucas and stops for swimming and snorkeling at the same beach on rocky **Monuriki Island,** upon which Tom Hanks filmed the movie *Castaway*—Hanks did *not* live on the islet all by himself during production. The cruises range from F$140 to F$175 (US$91–US$114/£47–£58) for adults, depending on where you board, including morning tea, lunch, beer, wine, and soft drinks. You pay more to come out from Port Denarau to Mana on the *Tiger IV,* less from the Mamanuca resorts.

The ***Whale's Tale*** (© 672 2455; funcruises@connect.com.fj), a luxury, 30m (98-ft.) auxiliary sailboat owned by American Paul Myers, takes no more than 12 guests on day cruises from Port Denarau through the Mamanucas. The F$170 (US$110/£57) per-person cost includes a continental breakfast with champagne; a buffet lunch prepared on board; and all beverages, including beer, wine, liquor, and sunset cocktails. The *Whale's Tale* is also available for charters ranging from 1 day in the Mamanucas to 3 days and 2 nights in the Yasawas. Rates depend on the length of trip.

A subsidiary of Captain Cook Cruises (see "Cruising Through the Islands," below), **Fiji Windjammer Barefoot Cruises** (© 670 1823; www.fijisailingsafari.com.fj) has 3- and 4-day "sailing safaris" to the Yasawas on its tall-ship *Spirit of the Pacific.* It sails during daylight but deposits you ashore at its Barefoot Lodge at night. These start at F$535 (US$347/£178) per person, double occupancy.

CRUISING THROUGH THE ISLANDS

Started with a converted American crash vessel in the 1950s by Capt. Trevor Withers, who had worked on the original *Blue Lagoon* movie starring Jean Simmons, **Blue Lagoon Cruises** 🟎🟎🟎 (© 818/554-5000 or 666 1622; fax 666 4098; www.blue lagooncruises.com) is one of the South Pacific's best.

Newest of Blue Lagoon's vessels is the *Fijian Princess,* a 60-meter (197-ft.) catamaran with 34 air-conditioned cabins and a spa. The 47m (154-ft.) *Nanuya Princess,* carries up to 66 passengers in 33 staterooms, while the sleek 56m (184-ft.) *Mystique Princess,* looks as if she should belong to a Greek shipping magnate; and her 35 staterooms do indeed approach tycoon standards. Oldest is the 38m (125-ft.) *Lycianda,* which carries 54 passengers in 26 air-conditioned cabins.

Most cruises range from 3 to 7 nights through the Yasawas, with one of the 7-night voyages designed especially for scuba divers. They depart Lautoka and arrive in the Yasawas in time for a welcoming cocktail party and dinner on board. They then proceed to explore the islands, stopping in little bays for snorkeling, picnics or lovo feasts on sandy beaches, and visits with the Yasawans in their villages. The ships anchor in peaceful coves at night, and even when they cruise from island to island, the water is usually so calm that only incurable landlubbers get seasick. In the one major variation from this theme, the week-long "historical and cultural" cruises go to Northern Fiji, with stops at Levuka, Savusavu, Taveuni, and several remote islands.

Rates range from about F$2,000 to F$5,200 (US$1,299–US$3,377/£667–£1,733) per cabin double occupancy, depending on the length of the voyage, the season, and the cabin's location. Diving cruises cost more. All meals, activities, and taxes are included. Singles and children staying in parents' cabins pay supplements.

A less-expensive alternative is **Captain Cook Cruises** (© 670 1823; www.captain cook.com.fj). This Australian-based firm uses the 120-passenger MV *Reef Escape* for most of its 3- to 7-night cruises from Port Denarau to the Mamanucas and Yasawas.

The *Reef Escape* has a swimming pool, spa, and sauna. Compared to the sleek vessels of *Blue Lagoon Cruises,* it's more like a floating hotel. Prices begin at F$1,450 (US$942/£483) per person double occupancy.

RESORTS IN THE MAMANUCA ISLANDS

The **Mamanuca Hotel Association,** Private Mail Bag, Nadi Airport (© **670 0144;** fax 670 2336; www.fijiresorts.com), has information about all the resorts.

They all have watersports and scuba dive operators on premises. **Subsurface Fiji Diving and Watersports** (© **666 6738;** www.subsurfacefiji.com), a PADI five-star operation, staffs more than a dozen of the resorts, while **Awesome Adventures Fiji** (© **670 5006;** www.awesomefiji.com) is at Mana Island Resort. See the "Diving in Fiji" box, in chapter 4, for more information.

EXPENSIVE

Another top-end resort is the super-private **Wadigi Island Resort** (© **672 0901;** www.wadigi.com), which attracts celebrities to its three spacious bungalows atop a tiny islet. The 360-degree view from up there rocks. **Lomani Island Resort** (© **666 8212;** www.lomaniisland.com) is a boutique hotel that shares the picturesque beach on Malololailai with Plantation Island Resort.

Castaway Island Resort 🎿🎿 *Kids*   Built in the mid-1960s of logs and thatch, Castaway maintains its rustic, Fijian-style charm despite many improvements over the years. The central activities building, perched on a point wrapped by a white beach, has a thatch-covered roof, and its ceilings and those of the guest bures are lined with genuine masi cloth. Although the bures sit close together in a coconut grove, their roofs sweep low enough to provide some privacy. Upstairs at the beachside watersports shack, the Sundowner Bar faces west toward the Great Sea Reef. Guests have wood-fired pizzas there or dine in the central building, usually at umbrella tables on a stone beachside patio. This is a very good family resort, with a nurse on duty, and the staff provides a wide range of activities, from learning Fijian to sack races. Couples seeking a romantic retreat should look elsewhere during school holidays. Australian restaurateur Geoff Shaw owns this resort and the Outrigger on the Lagoon Fiji on the Coral Coast (see "The Coral Coast," below), and the two often have attractive joint packages, including helicopter transfers between them.

Private Mail Bag, Nadi Airport (Qalito Island). © 800/888-0120 or 666 1233. Fax 666 5753. www.castawayfiji.com. 66 units. F$625–F$1,690 (US$406–US$1,097/£208–£5563 bungalow. AE, DC, MC, V. **Amenities:** 2 restaurants; 3 bars; outdoor pool; tennis court; watersports equipment rentals; children's programs; game room; activities desk; massage; babysitting; laundry service. *In room:* A/C, fridge, coffeemaker, iron, no phone.

Likuliku Lagoon Resort 🎿🎿🎿   Opened in 2007, this exquisitely designed resort is the first in Fiji to have overwater bungalows, and is thus the first to compete with Bora Bora and other French Polynesian islands for honeymooners and others seeking these romantic cottages on stilts over the lagoon. Looking out at Castaway Island from a half-moon, beach-fringed bay on the northwestern corner of Malolo Island, Likuliku shows Fijian touches throughout, with *magimagi* (sennit, or coconut rope) lashing the log beams under the thatched roofs of its buildings. Likuliku was built and is owned by the Fiji-bred Whitten family, who made sure it reflects their country's indigenous culture. The 10 overwater bures aren't as large as the huge new units at Bora Bora, but they have glass fish-viewing floor panels flanking their coffee tables, and more glass behind the sinks in their spacious bathrooms makes your resting toiletries seem to float on air.

Each unit has a deck with steps leading into the lagoon, which can be shallow at low tide—the high and low tides here can differ by as much as 1.5m (5 ft.). The overwaters are close to a reef edge, so you can easily reach deep water at all tides. The split-level bungalows ashore all face the beach and are identical except for plunge pools in the front decks of the deluxe models. Overlooking the sea and a large swimming pool, the restaurant serves good (and sometimes exotic) Pacific Rim fare. The service is attentive, efficient, and friendly; I met several veteran staffers who came here from other top-end Fijian resorts. Only the overwater bures have TVs; but there's a big screen in the air-conditioned library lounge. You can pamper yourself but not your children in Likuliku's full-service spa; it's an adults-only property.

P.O. Box 10044, Nadi Airport (Malolo Island). (C) 672 4275 or 666 3344. Fax 664 0014. www.likulikulagoon.com. 45 units. F$1,300–F$1,950 (US$844–US$1,266/£43–£650) bungalow. AE, DC, MC, V. Rates include all meals and non-motorized watersports. Children under 17 not accepted. **Amenities:** Restaurant; 2 bars; outdoor pool; spa; fitness center; watersports equipment; concierge; activities desk; wireless Internet access in public areas; limited room service; massage; laundry service. In room: A/C, TV (in overwater bungalows), fridge (stocked on request), coffeemaker, iron, safe.

Tokoriki Island Resort   This adults-only property sits beside a wide beach stretching 1.5km (1 mile) on hilly Tokoriki Island, which it shares with Amanuca Island Resort. (The latter is an eclectic property I do not recommend for the time being). Although it doesn't have deep sand, once you get past rock shelves along the shoreline, the bottom slopes gradually into a safe lagoon with colorful coral gardens protected by a barrier reef. The resort itself sits on a flat shelf of land backed by a steep hill (a 4km/2.5-mile hiking trail leads up to the ridgeline). Lined up along the beach, most of the spacious units have separate sleeping and living areas equipped with wet bars, and both indoor and outdoor showers. Five much more luxurious Sunset Pool units have daybeds under thatched roofs next to their own plunge pools. A central thatch-topped bar divides the one-room central building into lounge and dining areas. Other than scuba diving, there are no motorized watersports here. I should caution that some guests have complained about the stench from seaweed washing up on the beach.

P.O. Box 10547, Nadi Airport (Tokoriki Island). (C) 666 1999. Fax 666 5295. www.tokoriki.com. 34 units. F$848–F$1,130 (US$551–US$734/£283–£377) bungalow. AE, MC, V. No children under 12 accepted. **Amenities:** Restaurant; bar; 2 outdoor pools; tennis court; spa; watersports equipment rentals; game room; massage; laundry service. In room: A/C, minibar, coffeemaker, iron, safe.

Vomo Island Resort   One of the most interesting aspects of this luxury resort is Vomo Island itself. An unusual clump of land, it features a steep, 168m-high (550-ft.) hill on one end and a flat, 200-acre shelf surrounded by a reef edged by colorful corals on the other. Offshore, **Vomolailai** (Little Vomo) is a rocky islet where you can go for private picnics. The restaurant sits adjacent to the beach, a deck-surrounded pool, and a stylish bar. Some of the luxurious guest bungalows climb the hill to provide views of the reef and sea, although I prefer those along a fine stretch of beach. Some of the beach bures are in duplex buildings, so ask for a self-standing one so you won't hear your next-door neighbors. Honeymooners take note: About half of the duplex units interconnect, making them popular choices for well-heeled families with children, especially during Australian school holidays. So is the two-bedroom, two-bathroom Royal Deluxe Villa. All of the units have sitting areas with sofas, and their large bathrooms have showers and two-person Jacuzzis. Sitting on the border between the Mamanuca and Yasawa islands, Vomo is served by the *Yasawa Flyer* as well as by seaplane and helicopter.

P.O. Box 5650, Lautoka (Vomo Island). © 666 7955. Fax 666 7997. www.vomofiji.com. 29 units. F$1,500–F$2,000 (US$974–US$1,299/£500–£667) bungalow. Rates include meals, soft drinks, and activities except scuba diving and deep-sea fishing. AE, DC, MC, V. **Amenities:** Restaurant; bar; outdoor pool; pitch-and-putt golf course; tennis court; spa; watersports equipment; children's program (during Australian school holidays); limited room service; massage; babysitting; laundry service. In room: A/C, minibar, coffeemaker, safe.

MODERATE

The 10-unit **Navini Island Resort** (© **666 2188;** www.navinifiji.com.fj) and 66-unit **Treasure Island Resort** (© **666 6999;** www.fiji-treasure.com) occupy tiny atoll-like islets. Treasure is within sight of Beachcomber Island.

Malolo Island Fiji *Kids* Although it draws mostly couples, this resort is a good choice for families with children. Among adults, it's notable for an outdoor spa, a grownups-only lounge, and one of the best beachside bars in Fiji—a thatched-roof building with a lagoonside deck and a lunchtime dining area under a sprawling shade tree. Two other restaurants and bars occupy a building at the base of a hill at the rear of the property. They open to two swimming pools, one especially suited for children because it has a walk-in sand bottom under a tarp to provide shade, the other good for grown-ups as it sports a swim-up bar. Most of the bungalows are duplexes. Of these, 18 have separate bedrooms; the others are studios. An upstairs family unit can sleep eight persons. Malolo is around a headland from its sister, Likuliku Lagoon Resort.

P.O. Box 10044, Nadi Airport (Malolo Island). © 666 9192. Fax 666 9197. www.maloloisland.com. 49 units. F$556–F$649 (US$361–US$421/£185–£216) double; F$1,082 (US$703/£361) family unit. AE, DC, MC, V. **Amenities:** 3 restaurants; 3 bars; 2 outdoor pools; spa; watersports equipment rentals; children's programs; activities desk; massage; babysitting; laundry service. In room: A/C, fridge, coffeemaker, iron, no phone.

Mana Island Resort & Spa *Kids* One of the largest off Nadi, this lively resort attracts Japanese singles and honeymooners, plus Australian and New Zealand couples and families. It's a popular day-trip destination from Nadi (see "Seeing the Islands on Day Trips From Nadi," earlier in this chapter). Seaplanes, planes, and helicopters also land here. In other words, you'll have a *lot* of company on Mana. Accommodations include varied bungalows, town houses, and hotel rooms. Least expensive are the few original "island" bures, which have been upgraded and air-conditioned. Situated by themselves on the beach north of the airstrip, seven honeymoon bures feature Jacuzzis and butler service. Six executive beachfront bures have their own hot tubs. Two-story, town house–style oceanfront suites come with mezzanine bedrooms and two bathrooms, one with claw-foot tub. A good children's program makes Mana a fine family choice.

P.O. Box 610, Lautoka (Mana Island). © 665 0423. Fax 665 0788. www.manafiji.com. 160 units. F$400 (US$260/£133) double room, F$270–F$1,200 (US$175–US$779/£90–£400) bungalow. Rates include full buffet breakfast. AE, DC, MC, V. **Amenities:** 3 restaurants; 3 bars; outdoor pool; 2 tennis courts; Jacuzzi; watersports equipment rentals; children's programs; game room; activities desk; business center; massage; babysitting; laundry service; coin-op washers and dryers. In room: A/C, fridge, coffeemaker, iron, safe.

Tips Keeping You Entertained

Don't worry about staying busy at the offshore resorts. You can do as much or as little as you like. All the resorts have canoes, kayaks, sailboards, snorkeling gear, and other equipment for your use, and each has a scuba diving operation. In addition, Fijians make music most evenings and stage meke feasts at least 1 night a week at all the resorts.

Matamanoa Island Resort ⚤⚤   The farthest of all Mamanuca resorts off Nadi, this intimate, adults-oriented complex (no kids under 12 can stay here) sits on a small island consisting of two steep hills. The bungalows, a motel-like block of rooms, a horizon-edge pool, and a central building with bar and open-air dining room occupy a small flat point on one end of the island overlooking the deep white sand on one of Fiji's best beaches. The reef shelf falls away steeply here, resulting in great snorkeling even at low tide. For scuba divers, this is the closest of all Mamanuca resorts to the outer reef. They aren't the most luxurious in Fiji, but each of the spacious, rectangular bungalows is spacious and comfortable. The 13 motel rooms are much smaller than the bungalows and do not face the beach. Australian, American, and European couples keep this well-managed resort busy year-round, so book as early as possible.

P.O. Box 9729, Nadi Airport (Matamanoa Island). ℂ **666 0511**. Fax 666 0069. www.matamanoa.com. 33 units. F$375 (US$244/£125) double room; F$565 (US$367/£188) bungalow. Rates include breakfast. AE, DC, MC, V. Children under 12 not accepted. **Amenities:** Restaurant; bar; outdoor pool; tennis court; watersports equipment rentals; activities desk; massage; laundry service. *In room:* A/C, fridge, coffeemaker, iron, safe.

Musket Cove Island Resort   One of three Australians who own Malololailai Island, Dick Smith founded this retreat in 1977. It has grown considerably since then, and now has a marina where yachties call from June to September. They congregate at an open-air bar under a thatched roof on a man-made island reached by the marina's pontoons. "Dick's Place" is the name of the pleasant bar and restaurant next to two swimming pools, one with a yacht protruding from its side, as if it has run aground. Although a mud bank appears here at low tide, Dick has dredged out a swimming beach area. Accommodations range from charming one-room bures to luxury villas with living rooms, full kitchens, and master bedrooms downstairs and two bedrooms upstairs, each with its own bathroom. Musket Cove also manages Armstrong Villas at Musket Cove, a group of two-bedroom condo bungalows on a man-made island. These have kitchens and phones. Check the website and confirm with the reservationist when booking to make sure you get the in-room amenities you desire.

Private Mail Bag, Nadi Airport (Malololailai Island). ℂ **877/313-1464** or 672 2371. Fax 672 0378. www.musketcove fiji.com. 55 units. F$474–F$551 (US$308–US$358/£158–£184) bungalow; F$680 (US$442/£227) villa. AE, DC, MC, V. **Amenities:** 2 restaurants; 2 bars; 3 outdoor pools; spa; watersports equipment rentals; bike rentals; activities desk; massage; babysitting; laundry service; coin-op washers and dryers. *In room:* A/C (in villas only), kitchen (villas only), fridge, coffeemaker, iron, safe, no phone (in bungalows).

Plantation Island Resort 🄺🄸🄳🅂   The oldest, largest, and most diverse of the Mamanuca resorts, Plantation primarily attracts Australian couples and families, plus day-trippers from Nadi. Like Mana Island, it has a Club Med–style atmosphere of nonstop activity. It shares Malololailai Island with Musket Cove Island Resort, but this end boasts one of Fiji's most picturesque palm-draped beaches, shallow though the lagoon may be at low tide. The resort has several types of accommodations: duplex bures suitable for singles or couples, two-bedroom bungalows for families, and motel-style rooms. Some are next to the beach, others surround a swimming pool, and others are removed from the action. A central building beside the beach has a bar, dance floor, lounge area, restaurant, and coffee shop. Guests can also wander over to Musket Cove or to Ananda's, a barbecue-oriented restaurant near the airport. A children's playroom, with a full-time babysitter, makes this a good choice for families.

P.O. Box 9176, Nadi Airport (Malololailai Island). ℂ **666 9333**. Fax 666 9200. www.plantationisland.com. 192 units. F$250–F$375 (US$162–US$244/£83–£125) double; F$375–F$550 (US$244–US$357/£125–£183) bungalow. AE, DC, MC, V. **Amenities:** 2 restaurants; 2 bars; 3 outdoor pools; 9-hole golf course; tennis courts; watersports equipment rentals; children's programs; game room; activities desk; salon; massage; babysitting; laundry service; coin-op washers and dryers. *In room:* A/C (in hotel rooms), fridge, coffeemaker.

INEXPENSIVE

While Beachcomber Island continues to be the most popular Mamanuca resort with low-budget travelers, you can get away from the crowds at nearby **Bounty Island** (© 666 7461; www.fiji-bounty.com), which has 22 bures and 50 dorm beds. Its flat 19-hectare (48-acre) island is much larger than Beachcomber's, and much of it is a nature preserve.

Also occupying a tiny islet, **South Sea Island** (© 675 0500; www.ssc.com.fj) has accommodations, but it is more of a day-trip destination.

Near the main pass through the Great Sea Reef, the American-operated **Tavarua Island Resort** (© 805/687-4551 in the U.S.; www.tavarua.com) began as a surfer camp but now caters to everyone.

On Mana Island, the backpacker-oriented **Mana Island Lodge** (© 620 7030; mana lodge2@yahoo.com) is on the beach, just south of the luxurious Mana Island Resort. Rooms in simple bungalows cost F$180 to F$250 (US$117–US$162/£60–£83), dorm beds F$60 (US$39/£20), including meals. Next door is **Ratu Kini Backpackers** (© 672 1959; www.ratukini.com), offering dormitories for F$38 (US$25/£13) per person, F$100 (US$65/£33) for units with bathrooms, and rooms with shared facilities F$85 (US$55/£28), including breakfast. Ratu Kini's restaurant all but hangs over the beach. Guests at these hostels cannot use Mana Island Resort's watersports facilities, but both have their own dive shops. Accommodations are much more basic than at Beachcomber Island Resort and Bounty Island.

Beachcomber Island Resort 🌟🌟 *Value* Back in 1963, Fiji-born Dan Costello bought an old Colonial Sugar Refining Company tugboat, converted it into a day cruiser, and started carrying tourists on trips out to a tiny atoll known as Tai Island. The visitors liked it so much that some didn't want to leave. Although the Yasawa Islands have stolen some of its thunder, this resort still packs in the young, young-at-heart, and other like-minded souls in search of fun, members of the opposite sex, and a relatively inexpensive vacation (all-you-can-eat meals are included in the rates). The youngest-at-heart cram into the coed dormitories. If you want more room, you can have or share a semiprivate lodge. And if you want your own charming bure, you can have that, too—just don't expect luxury. Rates also include a wide range of activities; you pay extra for sailboats, canoes, windsurfing, scuba diving, water-skiing, and fishing trips.

P.O. Box 364, Lautoka (Tai Island). © 800/521-7242 or 666 1500. Fax 666 4496. www.beachcomberfiji.com. 36 units, 102 dorm beds. F$391–F$436 (US$254–US$283/£130–£145) double bure; F$300 (US$195/£100) double lodge; F$83 (US$54/£28) dorm bed. Rates include all meals. AE, DC, MC, V. **Amenities:** Restaurant; bar; outdoor pool; miniature golf; watersports equipment rentals; activities desk; massage; laundry service. *In room:* Fridge, coffeemaker, no phone.

RESORTS IN THE YASAWA ISLANDS

Once quiet, sleepy, and devoid of tourists (except a few backpackers and well-heeled guests at Turtle Island and Yasawa Island Resort and Spa), this gorgeous chain has seen an explosion of accommodations in recent years, many of them owned by villagers and aimed at backpackers and other cost-conscious travelers. In fact, the Yasawas are one of the hottest backpacker destinations, not just in Fiji but the entire South Pacific.

West Side Waters Sports (© 666 1462; westside@connect.com.fj) provides daily dive trips for all of the central Yasawa retreats and teaches introductory and PADI certification courses.

EXPENSIVE

Turtle Island 𝒜𝒜𝒜   Enjoying one of the most picturesque settings of any resort in Fiji, this venerable little getaway nestles beside an idyllic, half-moon-shaped beach and looks out on a nearly landlocked body of water dubbed "the Blue Lagoon." Supplied by the resort's own garden, the kitchen serves excellent meals dinner-party fashion in the beachside dining room. If you don't want company, you can dine alone on the beach or on a pontoon floating on the lagoon. The beach turns into a sand bar at low tide, but you can swim and snorkel off a long pier. Everything is included in the rates except Hawaiian-style therapeutic massage. A dozen of the superluxe, widely spaced bungalows have two-person spa tubs embedded in the floors of their enormous bedrooms or bathrooms. In a few bungalows, the front porch has a lily pond on one side and a queen-size bed under a roof on the other. A few are more modest (no spa tubs), but one of these, on a headland with a 360-degree view of the lagoon and surrounding islands, is the most private of all. Every unit has its own kayaks and a hammock strung between shade trees by the beach. Only couples and singles are accepted here, except during certain family weeks in July and at Christmas. Instead of a phone in your bungalow, you will have a two-way radio to call for room service.

P.O. Box 9317, Nadi Airport (Nanuya Levu Island). ℭ 877/288-7853 or 672 2921 for reservations, 666 3889 on the island. Fax 672 0007. www.turtlefiji.com. 14 units. US$1,632–US$2,390 (£816–£1,195) per couple. Rates include meals, drinks, all activities including game fishing and 1 scuba dive per day. 6-night stay required. AE, DE, MC, V. Children under 12 not accepted except during family weeks in July and at Christmas. **Amenities:** Restaurant; bar; limited room service; massage; laundry service. *In room:* minibar, coffeemaker, iron, safe, no phone.

Yasawa Island Resort and Spa 𝒜𝒜𝒜   This luxurious resort sits in a small indention among steep cliffs that line the west coast of skinny, relatively dry Yasawa Island, northernmost of the chain. The Great Sea Reef is far enough offshore here that surf can slap against shelves of black rock just off a terrific beach of deep white sand. Or you can dip in a saltwater swimming pool. Most of the large, air-conditioned guest bures are long, 93 sq. m (1,002 sq. ft.) rectangular models with thatched roofs over white stucco walls. A door leads from the bathroom, which has an indoor shower, to an outdoor shower and a private sunbathing patio. A few other one- and two-bedroom models are less appealing but are better arranged for families (although children under 12 are allowed here only during Jan, mid-June to mid-July, and Dec) and have fine views from the side of the hill backing the property. Best of all is the remote, extremely private Lomolagi honeymoon bure, which has its own beach and pool. Guests all dine together for once-weekly Fijian-style lovos, but otherwise they can choose their own spacious seating arrangements or dine in their bungalows on the beach.

P.O. Box 10128, Nadi Airport (Yasawa Island). ℭ 672 2266. Fax 672 4456. www.yasawa.com. 18 units. US$900–US$1,800 (£450–£900) double. Rates include room, all meals, and nonmotorized watersports, but no drinks. AE, DC, MC, V. Children under 12 not accepted except in Jan, mid-June to mid-July, Dec. **Amenities:** Restaurant; bar; outdoor pool; tennis court; spa; limited room service; massage; laundry service. *In room:* A/C, kitchen (2 units), minibar, coffeemaker, iron, safe.

MODERATE

Nanuya Island Resort 𝒜   Nanuya sits amid clear, calm waters on, by far, the best beach in the Yasawas, a long stretch of white sand that wraps around a narrow point. Next to the resort is West Side Water Sports' headquarters, and you can choose any number of water activities, from kayaking to diving to caving to snorkeling—just be careful of nibbling fish! Upscale bures are nestled in the wooded hills, requiring a hike but offering stunning views of the ocean; you can't beat waking up to views of the South Pacific just feet ahead! No children under 7 years old are accepted here.

P.O. Box 7136, Lautoka (Nanuya Island). ⓒ **666 7633.** Fax 666 1462. www.nanuyafiji.com. 12 units. F$235–F$402 (US$153–US$261/£78–£134). MC, V. **Amenities:** Restaurant; bar; watersports equipment rentals; massage. *In room:* Fridge, coffeemaker, no phone.

Navutu Stars 🦋🦋🦋   Owned and operated by a young Italian family, Navutu Stars combines the best of Mediterranean flare with Fijian relaxation. From the frangipani welcome and departure leis to a personalized flower petal greeting placed on your bed, no detail is overlooked. There's a high staff-to-guest ratio, and staff look after you like you're royalty. Bures are exquisitely decorated, painted a stark white, with bedding and cushions providing splashes of color throughout the spacious rooms. Enjoy laying out on bedlike chaise lounges on your own patio as you watch the dramatic ebb and flow of the tide. With Italian and Fijian dishes served, dinner is a gastronomic delight (don't miss the homemade fish ravioli—yes, you read that right: homemade ravioli in Fiji—in garlic butter sauce)! A complimentary 30-minute massage is offered to all guests, but if you stay at Navutu any longer than a day, it's a safe bet you'll return to the masseuse with the softest hands anywhere. Navutu Stars lives up to any vision of paradise and will haunt your dreams for years to come. Six of the nine bures are beachfront. Two grand bures have in-room soaking tubs.

P.O. Box 1838 Lautoka (Yaqeta Island). ⓒ 664 0553. Fax 679 666 0807. www.navutustarsfiji.com. 9 units. F$500–F$850 (US$325–US$552/£167–£283). MC, V. **Amenities:** Restaurant; bar spa; watersports massage. *In room:* No phone.

INEXPENSIVE

Mantaray Island Resort 🦋   Mantaray is a backpacker's hangout, with good dorm accommodations and a selection of private rooms. The 32-bed dorm room clusters four beds to a group, giving quite a lot of privacy in an otherwise open area. The private bures, three of which are en suite, are bare-bones: There's a bed with mosquito net and chair . . . that's it. All three meals are served buffet-style in an open-air lodge amidst the treetops. It's a trek to climb up, but once you get there, you're treated to a good meal and one of the best views the Yasawas can offer. Mantaray's waters offer great snorkeling, but the sand is a bit pebbly; be sure to walk around in flip-flops.

P.O. Box 405, Lautoka (Naviti Island). ⓒ 664 0520. www.mantarayisland.com. 13 units (3 with bathrooms), 32 dorm beds, 20 tent sites. F$115–F$175 (US$75–US$114/£38–£58); F$40 (US$26/£13) dorm bed; F$35 (US$23/£12) per-person camping. MC, V. **Amenities:** Restaurant; bar; watersports equipment rentals; massage. *In room:* No phone.

Oarsman's Bay Lodge 🦋 🄑𝑎𝑙𝑢𝑒   Although owned by Fijians, Oarsman Bay Lodge was designed and built by Richard Evanson, owner of Turtle Island (see above), so in some respects, this is an inexpensive version of that super-luxury resort. A live tree helps support the central building with a sand-floor dining room and bar (there is no communal kitchen here). Steep stairs lead upstairs to a one-room coed dorm, whose residents share toilets and warm-water showers with guest camping on the grounds. Although the tin-roof guest bungalows are a bit cramped, they are nicely appointed with wooden cabinets, full-length mirrors, reading lights over their double beds, porches with hammocks and chairs, screened louvered windows, and bathrooms with solar-heated showers. Paddle boats and canoes are available, plus gear for fabulous snorkeling. Backpacking or not, you'll find this no-frills resort to be a very good bargain.

> ⟨**Tips**⟩ **Consider a Package Deal with Awesome Adventures Fiji**
>
> **Awesome Adventures Fiji** (⟨ⓒ⟩ **670 5006;** www.awesomefiji.com) has packages including transportation on the *Yasawa Flyer* and accommodation at several resorts and hostels in the Yasawas. It inspects all accommodations it sells to make sure they are clean and safe. Frankly, several Yasawa hostels are operated by Fijian families and can be very basic. One of us became ill when staying and eating at one such Yasawa establishment, and we have heard similar stories about others. We like to recommend Fijian-owned businesses whenever possible, but would stick to those approved by Awesome Adventures Fiji. The packages are easily arranged at any Nadi area hotel or hostel, but since the choices are complex, check the website or pick up a current Awesome Adventures Fiji brochure as soon as you can (they're widely available at the airport tour offices and at many hotel activities desks).

P.O. Box 9317, Nadi Airport (Nacula Island). ⟨ⓒ⟩ **672 2921.** Fax 672 0007. www.fijibudget.com. 6 units, 13 dorm beds. F$132–F$265 (US$86–US$172/£44–£88) double; F$23 (US$15/£7.65) dorm bed; F$36 (US$23/£12) per-person campsite with tent rental; F$25 (US$16/£8.35) per-person campsite without tent. MC, V. **Amenities:** Restaurant; bar; watersports equipment rentals. *In room:* No phone.

Octopus Resort 🐾🐾   Of all the resorts in the Yasawas, Octopus has the broadest appeal to all age groups. Typically, the Yasawas are couples- and singles-friendly, attracting honeymooners and backpackers and not children, but Octopus welcomes everyone and provides activities for singles and families alike. Many visitors island-hop, but for the traveler who wants to stay in one place for a more relaxed vacation, Octopus is our clear choice. It offers a variety of accommodations—ranging from a 14-bed dorm room to private en suite bures to deluxe, private hotel-style rooms with televisions and decorated with flowers from the resort's gorgeous gardens. Octopus is one of the few resorts in the Yasawas that has a swimming pool. Right in the center of the resort, it's used for training in its PADI-certified dive course. Rare among the Yasawas, Octopus offers a free guided visit to a traditional Fijian village, where you can buy homemade crafts and experience life like the locals. Take part in quiz night, held every Thursday; snack on homemade pastries and delicious Fijian fare; and snorkel in the turquoise waters. Don't miss a 1-hour massage on the beach (book early—appointments go fast!). It's the best F$30 (US$19/£10) you'll spend!

P.O. Box 1861, Lautoka (Waya Island). ⟨ⓒ⟩ **666 6442** or 666 6337. Fax 666 6210. www.octopusresort.com. 14 units (all with bathrooms), 13 dorm beds, 2 tents. US$104–US$175 (£52–£88) bungalow; US$25 (£13) dorm bed. 2-night minimum stay required. MC, V. **Amenities:** Restaurant; bar; outdoor pool; watersports equipment rentals; massage; laundry service. *In room:* TV (hotel rooms), no phone.

3 The Coral Coast ⟨★⟩

Long before big jets began bringing loads of visitors to Fiji, many affluent local residents built cottages on the dry southwestern shore of Viti Levu as sunny retreats from the rain and humidity of Suva. When visitors started arriving in big numbers during the early 1960s, resorts sprang up among the cottages, and promoters gave a new, more appealing name to the 70km (43-mile) stretch of beaches and reef on either side of the town of Sigatoka: the Coral Coast.

The appellation was apt, for coral reefs jut out like wide shelves from the white beaches that run between mountain ridges all along this picturesque coastline. In most spots, the lagoon just reaches snorkeling depth at high tide, and when the water retreats, you can put on your reef sandals or a pair of old sneakers and walk out nearly to the surf pounding on the outer edge of the shelf.

Frankly, the Coral Coast is now overshadowed by other parts of Fiji. Its large hotels cater primarily to meetings, groups, and families from Australia and New Zealand on 1-week holidays. Nevertheless, it does have some dramatic scenery, it has some of the country's better historical sites, and it's a central location from which to see both the Suva and Nadi sides of Viti Levu.

GETTING TO THE CORAL COAST: THE QUEEN'S ROAD

Visitors can reach the Coral Coast from Nadi International Airport by taxi, bus, or car along the Queen's Road (see "Getting There & Getting Around" in chapter 4).

The drive from Nadi to Shangri-La's Fijian Resort takes about 45 minutes. After a right turn at the south end of Nadi Town, the highway runs inland, first through sugar cane fields undulating in the wind and then past acre after acre of pine trees planted in orderly rows, part of Fiji's national forestry program. The blue-green mountains lie off to the left; the deep-blue sea occasionally comes into view off to the right.

GETTING AROUND THE CORAL COAST

Since the Coral Coast is a strip running for 70km (43 miles), a rental car is the easiest way to get around. The large hotels have car-rental desks and taxis around their main entrances. Express buses between Nadi and Suva stop at Shangri-La's Fijian Resort, the Outrigger on the Lagoon Fiji, the Hideaway Resort, the Naviti Resort and the Warwick Fiji Resort & Spa. Local buses ply the Queen's Road and stop when you hail them. **Westside Motorbike Rentals** (© **672 6402;** www.motorbikerentals fiji.com) has an outlet on the Queen's Road at the Korotonga traffic circle. See "Getting There & Getting Around," in chapter 4, for more information.

FAST FACTS: The Coral Coast

This information applies to the Coral Coast. If you don't see an item here, see "Fast Facts: Nadi," earlier in this chapter, and "Fast Facts: Fiji," in chapter 4.

Camera/Film **Caines Photofast** has a shop on Market Road in Sigatoka (© **650 0877**). Most hotel shops sell color print film and provide 1-day processing.

Currency Exchange **ANZ Bank, Westpac Bank,** and **Colonial National Bank** all have branches with ATMs on the riverfront in Sigatoka. The Outrigger on the Lagoon Fiji, the Warwick Fiji Resort & Spa, and the Naviti resorts have ATMs in their lobbies (see "Where to Stay on the Coral Coast," below).

Drugstores **Patel Pharmacy** (© **650 0213**) is on Market Road in Sigatoka.

Emergencies The emergency phone number for **police** is © **917**; for **fire** and **ambulance** dial © **911**. The Fiji **police** has posts at Sigatoka (© **650 0222**) and at Korolevu (**653 0322**).

Healthcare The government-run **Sigatoka Hospital** (© **650 0455**) can handle minor problems.

Mail Post offices are in Sigatoka and Korolevu.

WHAT TO SEE & DO ON THE CORAL COAST

Hotel reception or tour desks can make reservations for most of the activities and day cruises mentioned under "Nadi" and "The Mamanuca & Yasawas Islands," earlier in this chapter. You will likely pay more for Nadi-based activities than if you were staying on the west coast. On the other hand, you are closer to such activities as the rafting trips on the Navua River (see "Pacific Harbour & Beqa Island," later in this chapter). You also can easily take advantage of the golf, fishing, and diving at Pacific Harbour and see the sights in Suva.

I have organized the attractions below from west to east; that is, in the order in which you will come to them from Nadi.

NATADOLA BEACH

Off the Queen's Road 35km (22 miles) south of Nadi, the paved Maro Road runs down to **Natadola Beach** 𝄃𝄃𝄃, the only exceptionally beautiful beach on Viti Levu. A big resort is going up here, although land disputes and other problems had stopped construction during my recent visit. It was to have included a golf course designed by Fiji-native Vijay Singh, but he reportedly has backed out. I have no idea what will be going on by the time you arrive. One thing is for sure: A gap in the reef allows some surf to break on Natadola Beach, especially on the south end. Already here is **Natadola Beach Resort** (© 672 1001; www.natadola.com), a small, Spanish-style hotel with a dining room and bar in a shady courtyard. Rather than drive, I would wait and take the Coral Coast Railway train from Shangri-La's Fijian Resort (see below).

ROBINSON CRUSOE ISLAND

On Likuri, a small islet north of Natadola Beach, the backpacker-oriented **Robinson Crusoe Island** (© 628 1999; www.robinsoncrusoeislandfiji.com) has a lovely beach, a pool, restaurant, bar, small bures, and two dorms. It's a relaxing stop on the low-budget trail around Viti Levu. Jet Fiji has one of its high-speed jet boats stationed at the island (see "Boating, Golf, Hiking & Other Outdoor Activities," in the Nadi section, above). Snorkeling, waterskiing, tube rides, hair braiding, and massages are available to overnight guests and day-trippers. Accommodations range from F$82 (US$53/£27) for a dorm bed to F$120 (US$78/£40) for a bure, double occupancy. Rates include all meals.

CORAL COAST RAILWAY 𝄃

Based outside Shangri-La's Fijian Resort, the **Coral Coast Railway Co.** (© 652 0434) uses two restored sugar cane locomotives for a variety of tours on narrow-gauge railroads through the cane fields, across bridges, and along the coast. The best pulls you to lovely Natadola Beach, where you swim (bring your own towel) and have a barbecue lunch at the beach. These outings cost about F$115 (US$75/£38) including lunch. These "Natadola BBQ Bash" trips run daily, departing Shangri-La's Fijian resort at 10am and returning at 4pm.

A variation of the Natadola Beach trip includes a boat ride to Robinson Crusoe Island (see above) for swimming, snorkeling, and a picnic lunch. It costs about F$135 (US$88/£45). Water-skiing is extra. The boat doesn't run daily, so call ahead.

The other locomotive makes trips east to Sigatoka on the Coral Coast. A half-day version takes you to Sigatoka town for shopping and sightseeing. It costs F$59 (US$38/£20). It also makes all-day "Ratu's Scenic Inland" tours into the Sigatoka Valley for F$125 (US$81/£42) and sundown tours, which include a kava welcoming ceremony and dinner, for F$75 (US$49/£25).

Children pay half-price, and all fares are somewhat more expensive if you staying at a Nadi-area hotel.

KALEVU SOUTH PACIFIC CULTURAL CENTRE ⚑

Well worth a visit, the **Kalevu South Pacific Cultural Centre,** opposite Shangri-La's Fijian Resort (© **652 0200;** www.fijiculturalcentre.com), presents demonstrations of traditional kava processing, handicrafts, lovo cooking, and fishing. The exhibits include not just Fiji but Samoa, Kiribati (in the central Pacific), and New Zealand. The center offers 3-hour tours daily at 9am and 1pm for F$45 (US$29/£15), including a traditional island lunch cooked in an earth oven. Or you can take a 1-hour tour of the grounds and Fiji historical museum for F$15 (US$9.75/£5). Call for schedules and reservations. The center is open daily from 9am to 4pm. You can also get refreshment here, or attend a Fijian meke nightly. It's all part of a project known as "Gecko's Resort," though why anyone would want to stay in a room here beats me.

SIGATOKA SAND DUNES NATIONAL PARK

The pine forests on either side of the Queen's Road soon give way to rolling fields of mission grass before the sea suddenly emerges at a viewpoint above Shangri-La's Fijian Resort on Yanuca Island. After you pass the resort, watch on the right for the visitor center for **Sigatoka Sand Dunes National Park** (© **652 0243).** Fiji's first national park protects high sand hills, which extend for several miles along the coast. About two-thirds of them are stabilized with grass, but some along the shore are still shifting sand (the surf crashing on them is dangerous). Ancient burial grounds and pieces of pottery dating from 5 B.C. to A.D. 240 have been found among the dunes, but be warned: Removing them is against the law. Exhibits in the visitor center explain the dunes and their history. Rangers are on duty daily from 8am to 5pm. Admission to the visitor center is free, but adults pay F$8 (US$5.20/£2.65), students F$3 (US$1.95/£1) to visit the actual dunes. Call ahead for a free guided tour. (*Note:* You *must* go to the visitor center before visiting the dunes.)

SIGATOKA TOWN

About 3km (2 miles) from the sand dunes visitor center, the Queen's Road enters **Sigatoka** (pop. 2,000), the commercial center of the Coral Coast. This quiet, predominantly Fiji Indian town is perched along the west bank of the **Sigatoka River,** Fiji's longest waterway. The broad, muddy river lies on one side of the main street; on the other is a row of stores. The river is crossed by the Melrose Bridge, built in 1997 and named in honor of Fiji's winning the Melrose Cup at the Hong Kong Sevens rugby matches. The old bridge it replaced is now for pedestrians only.

SIGATOKA VALLEY

From Sigatoka, you can go inland along the west bank of the meandering river, flanked by a patchwork of flat green fields of vegetables that give the **Sigatoka Valley** its nickname: "Fiji's Salad Bowl." The pavement ends about 1km (a half-mile) from the town; after that, the road surface is poorly graded and covered with loose stones.

The residents of **Lawai** village at 1.5km (1 mile) from town offer handicrafts for sale. Two kilometers (1¼ miles) farther on, a small dirt track branches off to the left and runs down a hill to **Nakabuta,** the "Pottery Village," where the residents make and sell Fijian pottery. This art has seen a renaissance of late, and you will find bowls, plates, and other items in handicraft shops elsewhere. Tour buses from Nadi and the Coral Coast stop there most days.

Past Nakabuta the road climbs steeply along a narrow ridge, commanding panoramic views across the large Sigatoka Valley with its quiltlike fields to the right and much smaller, more rugged ravine to the left. It then winds its way down to the valley floor and the **Sigatoka Agricultural Research Station,** on whose shady grounds some tour groups stop for picnic lunches. The road climbs into the interior and eventually to Ba on the northwest coast; it intersects the **Nausori Highlands** Road leading back to Nadi, but it can be rough or even washed out during periods of heavy rain. Unless you have a four-wheel-drive vehicle or are on an organized tour with a guide, I would turn around at the research station and head back to Sigatoka.

JET BOAT TOURS   An alternative to driving up the valley is a thrill ride in a jet boat operated by **Sigatoka River Safari** (© **0800 650 1721** in Fiji or 650 1721; www.sigatokariver.com). Similar to Jet Fiji in Nadi (p. 107), these half-day rides cost F$179 (US$116/£60) for adults, F$89 (US$58/£30) for children 4 to 15. Add F$20 (US$13/£6.65) from Nadi.

TAVUNI HILL FORT

A dirt road runs from the eastern end of the Sigatoka River bridge inland 5km (3 miles) to the **Tavuni Hill Fort** (© **650 0818**), built by an exiled Tongan chief as a safe haven from the ferocious Fijian hill tribes. Those highlanders fought wars with the coastal Fijians, and they were the last to give up cannibalism and convert to Christianity. When they rebelled against the Deed of Cession to Great Britain in 1875, the colonial administration sent a force of 1,000 men up the Sigatoka River. They destroyed all the hill forts lining the river, including Tavuni. Part of the fort has been restored. The visitor center has exhibits explaining the history, and rangers will lead 30-minute tours if you ask. The fort is open to the public Monday to Saturday 8am to 4pm. Admission is F$12 (US$7.80/£4) for adults and F$6 (US$3.90/£2) for children.

KULA ECO PARK 𝕂𝕂

Opposite the Outrigger on the Lagoon Fiji, **Kula Eco Park** *(Kids* (© **650 0505;** www. fijiwild.com) is Fiji's only wildlife park. Along the banks of a stream in a tropical forest, it has a fine collection of rainbow-feathered tropical birds and an aquarium stocked with examples of local sea life. Allow 2 hours here, since this is one of the South Pacific's best places to view local flora and fauna in a natural setting. Children will love it. It's open daily 10am to 4pm. Admission is F$20 (US$13/£6.65) for adults, F$10 (US$6.50/£3.35) for children under 12.

WATERFALL & CAVE TOURS 𝕂𝕂

Try to take a waterfall and cave tour with **Adventures in Paradise Fiji** (© **652 0833;** www.adventuresinparadisefiji.com), near the Outrigger on the Lagoon Fiji. The waterfall tour goes to Biausevu in the Korolevu Valley. A bus takes you to the village, where you'll be welcomed at a traditional yaqona ceremony. Then comes a 30-minute hike along a rocky stream to the falls, which plunge over a cliff into a swimming hole. The sometimes-slippery trail fords the stream seven times, so wear canvas or reef shoes or a pair of strap-on sandals. Wear a bathing suit and bring a towel if you want to take a cool, refreshing dip after the hike. You'll be treated to a barbecue lunch.

On the other excursion, you'll spend 45 minutes inside the Naihehe Cave, which was used as a fortress by Fiji's last cannibal tribe, and then return via a bilibili raft on the Sigatoka River (the cave is a 35-minute drive up the Sigatoka Valley). You'll have a picnic lunch before the raft ride.

Either tour costs F$99 (US$64/£33) per person. Each runs on alternate days. Add F$20 (US$13/£6.65) from Nadi. Book at any hotel activities desk.

SHOPPING ON THE CORAL COAST

In Sigatoka Town, you can do some serious hunting at **Sigatoka Indigenous Women's Handicraft Centre** (no phone), in a tin-roof shack on the main street beside the river. Operated by local women, it has carvings, shell jewelry, masi cloth, and other items made in Fiji. **Jack's of Fiji, Prouds,** and **Tappoo** are across the street.

Prices at "browse-in-peace" **Baravi Handicrafts** *&& ((© 652 0364)*, in Vatukarasa village 13km (8 miles) east of Sigatoka, are somewhat lower than you'll find at the larger stores, and it has a snack bar that sells coffee made from Fijian-grown beans (you should get a freebie cup). The shop buys woodcarvings and pottery directly from village artisans. It's open Monday to Saturday 7:30am to 6pm and Sunday 8:30am to 5pm. Vatukarasa also has a roadside stall where you might find unusual seashells.

WHERE TO STAY ON THE CORAL COAST

Most hotels have abundant sports facilities, including diving, and those that don't will arrange them. Nonguests can use the facilities at most resorts—at a fee, of course.

EXPENSIVE

Outrigger on the Lagoon Fiji *&& Kids*   This lagoonside resort compensates for Mother Nature's having robbed its beach of most sand with one of the most attractive swimming pools in Fiji. You can go kayaking, spy-boarding (which is riding on a small surfboard with a glass panel in it for fish viewing), and snorkeling at high tide, but the gorgeous pool is the center of attention. In a way, the Outrigger is two hotels in one. A majority of the accommodations are hotel rooms in five-story hillside buildings at the rear of the property. They all have balconies, with spectacular views from the upper-floor units. The resort also offers thatched-roof bungalows and restaurants that resemble a traditional Fijian village in a coconut grove by the lagoon. Hotel rooms in the Reef Wing, a three-story lagoonside building (the last remnant of the Reef Resort, which once stood here), are smaller than their hillside counterparts and better suited to couples than families. You'll have butler service in the guest bures, which have masi-lined peaked ceilings. The beachfront bungalows are the pick of the litter. A few others are joined to make family units. The owner, Australian restaurateur Geoff Shaw (who also owns Castaway Island Resort; see "Resorts in the Mamanuca Islands," earlier this chapter), sees to it that everyone is well fed in either a fine-dining restaurant, a large open-air, buffet-style dining room, or a midday restaurant by the pool. The wedding chapel sits high on a hill with a stunning lagoon and sea view.

P.O. Box 173, Sigatoka (Queen's Rd., 8km/5 miles east of Sigatoka). © 800/688-7444 or 650 0044. Fax 652 0074. www.outrigger.com. 254 units. F$340–F$425 (US$221–US$276/£113–£142) double; F$500–F$1,000 (US$325–US$649/£167–£333) bungalow. AE, DC, MC, V. **Amenities:** 3 restaurants; 4 bars; outdoor pool; 2 tennis courts; exercise room; spa; Jacuzzi; watersports equipment rentals; children's programs; game room; activities desk; car-rental desk; business center; shopping arcade; salon; massage; babysitting; laundry service; coin-op washers and dryers. In room: A/C, TV, high-speed Internet access, fridge (stocked in bures), coffeemaker, iron, safe.

Shangri-La's Fijian Resort & Spa *&&&*   Fiji's largest hotel, "The Fijian" occupies all 105 acres of flat Yanuca Island, which is joined to the mainland by a short, one-lane causeway. Yanuca is bordered by a crystal-clear lagoon and a coral-colored sand beach, both superior to those at Denarau Island near Nadi. Needless to say, there is a host of watersports activities here, including diving, or you can play tennis or knock around the 9-hole golf course. Covered walkways wander through thick tropical foliage to link the hotel blocks to three main restaurant-and-bar buildings, both adjacent to swimming pools. The spacious rooms and suites occupy two- and three-story buildings, all on the shore of the island. Each room has a view of the lagoon and sea from its own private balcony or patio. The suites have separate bedrooms and two bathroom sinks. While The Fijian draws many families, its Ocean Premier units on one end of the sprawling property are reserved for couples. The Fijian's restaurants have something for everyone's taste, if not necessarily for everyone's pocketbook, and four bars are ready to quench any thirst. Away from the throngs at the end of the island, the **Chi Spa Village** is a knock-out, with bungalowlike treatment rooms where you can spend the night after being pampered. Great for honeymooners, a half-dozen luxurious Premier Ocean bures sit between the spa and the resort's glass-walled wedding chapel.

Private Mail Bag (NAPO 353), Nadi Airport (Yanuca Island, 10km/6 miles west of Sigatoka). ℂ 866/565-5050 or 652 0155. Fax 652 0402. www.shangri-la.com. 442 units. F$400–F$520 (US$260–US$338/£133–£173) double; F$650–F$750 (US$422–US$487/£217–£250) suite; F$950 (US$617/£317) bungalow. AE, DC, MC, V. **Amenities:** 4 restaurants; 4 bars; 3 outdoor pools; 9-hole golf course; 4 tennis courts; fitness center; watersports equipment rentals; bike rentals; children's programs; game room; concierge; activities desk; car-rental desk; business center; shopping arcade; salon; 24-hr. room service; massage; babysitting; laundry service. *In room:* A/C, TV, dataport, fridge, coffeemaker, iron, safe.

The Warwick Fiji Resort & Spa   Sitting on a palm-fringed beach with a bit more sand than you'll find at the Outrigger or the Hideaway, this complex reflects distinctive architecture from its origins as the Hyatt Regency Fiji. A sweeping roof supported by wood beams covers a wide reception and lobby area bordered on either end by huge carved murals depicting Capt. James Cook's discovery of Fiji in 1779. A curving staircase descends from the center of the lobby into a large square well, giving access to the dining and recreation areas on the lagoon level. The medium-size guest rooms are in two- and three-story blocks that flank the central building. Each room has its own balcony or patio with a view of the sea or the tropical gardens surrounding the complex. The most expensive units are suites, which face the lagoon from the ends of the buildings. The sand-floored **Wicked Walu,** under a thatched roof on a tiny island offshore, is the choice dining spot here. A free shuttle runs between the Warwick and its more family-oriented sister, the Naviti Resort.

P.O. Box 100, Korolevu (32km/20 miles east of Sigatoka). ℂ 800/203-3232 or 653 0555. Fax 653 0010. www.warwick fiji.com. 250 units. F$412–F$647 (US$268–US$420/£137–£216) double; F$861 (US$559/£287) suite. AE, DC, MC, V. **Amenities:** 5 restaurants; 5 bars; 2 outdoor pools; 4 tennis courts; exercise room; spa; Jacuzzi; watersports equipment rentals; children's programs; activities desk; car-rental desk; business center; shopping arcade; salon; 24-hr. room service; massage; babysitting; laundry service; coin-op washers and dryers; concierge-level rooms. *In room:* A/C, TV, dataport, minibar, coffeemaker, iron, safe.

MODERATE

Crusoe's Retreat   Only the foot-shaped swimming pool reminds me of when this low-key resort was known as Man Friday. It's one of the Coral Coast's oldest hotels, but much has been done in recent years to improve it, including installation of new bathrooms with his-and-her shower heads and sinks in all units. It's a rough but scenic 4km (2½ mile) ride along a dirt road and a steep downhill descent to reach the resort. In fact, you'll have to climb uphill to guest units numbered 12 through 29. They have stunning views, but I prefer those down near the beach, especially the thatch-encased "seaside luxury" bungalows. They're not that luxurious by modern standards, but they are much more charming than the other, A-frame units here, and they'll be air-conditioned and have outdoor showers by the time you arrive. In the meantime, all units have fans. The skimpy beach in front of the resort is augmented by sand behind a rock wall; it's much better in front of Namaqumaqua, the adjoining Fijian village. Crusoe's has what appears to be a grass tennis court, but don't bother bringing your racquet.

P.O. Box 20, Korolevu (45km/28 miles east of Sigatoka). ⓒ 650 0185. Fax 650 0666. www.crusoesretreat.com. 29 units. F$258–F$310 (US$168–US$201/£86–£103) double. AE, MC, V. **Amenities:** Restaurant; 2 bars; outdoor pool; grass tennis court; activities desk; watersports equipment rentals; massage; babysitting; laundry service. *In room:* Fridge, coffeemaker, safe.

Hideaway Resort ⓐⓐ ⓥalue   This is my favorite all-bungalow resort on the Coral Coast. It occupies a narrow strip of land between the Queen's Road and the lagoon that's long enough so that families, singles, and couples don't get in each other's way or disturb each other's sleep (or lack thereof). For the most peace and quiet, opt for a duplex "deluxe villa" on the far western end of the property. They have his-and-her indoor showers as well as outdoor showers. The 16 original, A-frame bungalows here are much closer to the action. Other units are in modern, duplex bungalows with tropical furnishings and shower-only bathrooms. A few larger family units here can sleep up to five persons. The main building opens to a beachside pool with a waterfall and a water slide. Evening entertainment features a Fijian meke feast once a week, Beqa island fire-walking, and Club Med–style cabaret shows. As has happened at the Outrigger on the Lagoon Fiji (see above), most of the beach disappears at high tide, but you can follow a trail out on the reef and observe a coral restoration project being undertaken in cooperation with local villagers.

P.O. Box 233, Sigatoka (Queen's Rd., 21km/13 miles east of Sigatoka). ⓒ 650 0177. Fax 652 0025. www.hideaway fiji.com. 112 units. F$340–F$540 (US$221–US$351/£113–£180) bungalow. AE, DC, MC, V. Rates include full breakfast buffet. **Amenities:** 2 restaurants; 2 bars; outdoor pool; miniature golf; tennis court; exercise room; watersports equipment rentals; children's programs; game room; concierge; activities desk; car-rental desk; salon; massage; babysitting; laundry service; coin-op washers and dryers. *In room:* A/C, dataport, fridge, coffeemaker, iron, safe.

The Naviti Resort ⓥalue   A sister of the Warwick Fiji Resort & Spa (see above), this sprawling resort attracts mainly Australians and New Zealanders lured by its activities and optional all-inclusive rates, which include all the beer and booze you can drink. The resort sits on 38 acres of palms waving in the trade wind beside a beach and dredged lagoon (you can wade to two islets). Or you can lounge beside two swimming pools, one with a swim-up bar. Double-deck covered walkways lead from the central complex to two- and three-story concrete block buildings, two of them constructed in 2005. The older wings hold some of Fiji's largest hotel rooms (bathrooms have both tubs and walk-in showers). The two-room suites on the ends of the older buildings are especially spacious. The best units, however, are 16 beachside bungalows, ranging from studios to two-bedrooms. Fijian-shaped shingle roofs cover a coffee shop, a restaurant for fine dining, and a lounge where a band plays for dancing most evenings. A fine Chinese restaurant looks out on an unchallenging 9-hole golf course.

P.O. Box 29, Korolevu (Queen's Road, 26km/16 miles east of Sigatoka). ⓒ 800/203-3232 or 653 0444. Fax 653 0099. www.navitiresort.com.fj. 224 units. F$268–F$296 (US$174–US$192/£89–£99) double; F$482–F$595 (US$313–US$386/£161–£198) suite or bungalow. Rates include breakfast. All inclusive rates available. AE, DC, MC, V. **Amenities:** 3 restaurants; 3 bars; outdoor pool; 9-hole golf course; 5 tennis courts; exercise room; spa; Jacuzzi; watersports equipment rentals; bike rentals; children's programs; game room; activities desk; car-rental desk; salon; limited room service; babysitting; laundry service. *In room:* A/C, TV, dataport, fridge, coffeemaker, iron, safe.

INEXPENSIVE

Although not nearly as charming as the Beachouse or as well-equipped as Mango Bay Resort, the simple, almost staid **Tubakula Beach Bungalows** (© 650 0097; www. fiji4less.com) sits in a lagoonside coconut grove near the Outrigger on the Lagoon Fiji, thus putting the restaurants on Sunset Strip within beach-walking distance. The downstairs of each A-frame bungalow has a lounge, kitchen, bathroom, bedroom and front porch; upstairs is a sleeping loft, which can be hot in the midday sun. Each can sleep 6 persons, so sharing one represents good value. The 32 dorm beds are in European-style houses. Rates range from F$109 to F$156 (US$71–US$101/£36–£52) per bungalow, F$25 (US$16/£8.35) for a dorm bed.

The Beachouse 𝒢   Andrew Waldken-Brown, a European who was born in Fiji, and his Australian wife, Jessica, have turned his family's old vacation retreat—beside one of the finest beaches on the Coral Coast—into this excellent backpacker resort. The British TV show "Love Island" took over the premises in 2006 and built a charming South Seas stage set and swimming pool, which now serves as lounge, bar, and dining room providing inexpensive meals. Each dorm is screened and has its own ceiling fan, and all beds have reading lights. Upstairs is aimed at couples, with partitions separating roomettes, but the walls don't reach the ceiling; the accommodations also have ceiling fans and mosquito-netted double beds. Better for couples are bungalowlike garden units; each has a double bed. All guests, including campers who can pitch their tents on the spacious lawn, share clean toilets and a modern communal kitchen. Although it lacks bures with bathrooms, the Beachouse is more intimate than the rocking Mango Bay Resort (see below).

P.O. Box 68, Korolevu (37km/23 miles east of Sigatoka). © 0800/653 0530 toll-free in Fiji, or 653 0500. www. fijibeachouse.com. 12 units (none with bathroom), 48 dorm beds. F$93 (US$60/£31) double; F$30 (US$19/£10) dorm bed; F$23 (US$15/£7.65) per-person camping. MC, V. **Amenities:** Restaurant; bar; outdoor pool; activities desk; bike and watersports equipment rentals; games room; massage; coin-op washers and dryers. *In room:* No phone.

Bedarra Beach Inn Fiji 𝒢 *Value*   This comfortable inn began life as a private home with bedrooms on either end of a great, two-story central hall, which opened to a veranda overlooking a swimming pool and the lagoon. The beach is across a dead-end road known as Sunset Strip, which was the main drag before the Queen's Road was diverted around the new Outrigger on the Lagoon Fiji, a short walk from here. Today a bar, lounge furniture, and potted palms occupy the great hall, and two restaurants have taken over the verandas (see "Where to Dine on the Coral Coast," below). Upstairs, four rooms open to another veranda wrapping around the house. Inside, guests can opt for two-bedroom family rooms capable of sleeping up to four persons. To the side of the house, a two-story motel block holds 16 air-conditioned rooms, all with large bathrooms with walk-in showers. Four of these also have cooking facilities.

P.O. Box 1213, Sigatoka (Sunset Strip, 8km/5 miles east of Sigatoka). © 650 0476. Fax 652 0166. www. bedarrafiji.com. 24 units (all w/bathroom). F$145–F$180 (US$94–US$117/£48–£60) double. AE, MC, V. **Amenities:** 2 restaurants; bar; outdoor pool; babysitting; laundry service. *In room:* A/C, dataport, fridge, coffeemaker, no phone.

Mango Bay Resort   This beachside resort is the most popular on the Coral Coast among 25- to 35-year-olds, although its small bungalows and African safari-style tents appeal to travelers of any age who don't mind a lot of action, or a poolside bar that can rock past midnight. Fortunately it's all spread out over several acres of lawn and palm trees, so the beat shouldn't seriously interfere with sleeping. Mango Bay is an eco-friendly place, so none of the natural thatched-roof units or dorms have energy-consuming air conditioners. They do have ceiling fans, and both the bures and tents have their own bathrooms (the bures have outdoor showers). The tents have wood floors, front porches, and double and single beds. The more expensive dorm has double beds separated by dividers, while the other has over-and-under bunk beds. Only the tents are screened, but every bed here has its own mosquito net.

P.O. Box 1720 Sigatoka (Sunset Strip, 40km/25 miles east of Sigatoka). ℭ **653 0069.** Fax 653 0138. www.mango bayresortfiji.com. 19 units (all with bathroom), 70 dorm beds. F$189–F$270 (US$123–US$175/£63–£90) double; F$36–F$45 (US$23–US$29/£12–£15) dorm bed. Rates include continental breakfast. AE, MC, V. No children under 12 accepted. **Amenities:** Restaurant; 2 bars; outdoor pool; massage; laundry service. **In room:** Safe, no phone.

Tambua Sands Beach Resort This hotel sits in a narrow, 17-acre grove of coconut palms beside a better white sand beach than fronts the nearby Hideaway Resort. All virtually identical, the bungalows here have high peaked ceilings with tin roofs, and their front porches all face the lagoon (those closest to the beach cost slightly more than the oceanview units). Each has both a queen bed and single bed. A footbridge crosses a stream flowing through the grounds and connects the bungalows with a swimming pool and plantation-style central building. The low-ceiling, open-air restaurant and bar are somewhat dark, but they do look out to the pool and the sea.

P.O. Box 177, Sigatoka (20km/12 miles east of Sigatoka). ℭ **650 0399.** Fax 650 0265. www.tambuasandsfiji.com. 25 units. F$185–F$195 (US$120–US$127/£62–£65) double. AE, MC, V. **Amenities:** Restaurant; bar; outdoor pool; grass tennis court; activities desk; game room; watersports equipment rentals; massage; babysitting; laundry service. **In room:** Fridge, coffeemaker, no phone.

Waidroka Bay Surf & Dive Resort The easternmost of the Coral Coast resorts, this lagoonside retreat has more in common with those at Pacific Harbour, which is much closer to here than is Korotogo. The lagoon has no beach, so owners Boris and Karin Kaz—a German-Israeli couple who relocated from New York City—specialize in diving, snorkeling, fishing, and surfing (Waidroka Bay is closer to Frigate's Passage than either Pacific Harbour or Beqa Island). The guest bungalows flank their spacious, Mediterranean-style main building with restaurant, bar, and large front porch opening to a swimming pool (with its own bar) set into a grassy lawn beside the palm-fringed lagoon. Guest quarters are either in bungalows (some have 2 bedrooms) or in a motel-like building. They are devoid of most island charms but all have sea views. Waidroka is 4km (2½ miles) south of the Queen's Road via a dirt track which literally climbs over a mountain before descending through a development of modest vacation homes.

P.O. Box 323 Pacific Harbour (50km/30 miles east of Sigatoka). ℭ **330 4605.** Fax 330 4383. www.waidroka.com. 11 units (all w/bathroom), 70 dorm beds. F$165–F$250 (US$107–US$163/£54–£83) double. MC, V. **Amenities:** Restaurant; 2 bars; outdoor pool; massage; babysitting; laundry service. **In room:** No phone.

A RESORT ON VATULELE ISLAND

A flat, raised coral atoll 48km (31 miles) south of Viti Levu, **Vatulele Island** is known for its unusual red shrimp—that is, they're red while alive, not just after being cooked. The only way to see them, however, is to stay at Vatulele Island Resort, which is accessible only from Nadi Airport,

Vatulele Island Resort Long a favorite haunt of Hollywood stars (it was built by Australian movie producer Henry Crawford), this super-luxe resort was recently bought by the Bangkok-based **Six Senses Resorts & Spas** (www.sixsenses.com), which plans to add a spa and to make other major changes. Accordingly, I personally would opt for another high-end resort until the dust settles here. Whatever happens, it still will reside beside one of Fiji's best beaches, a gorgeous, 1km-long (half-mile) beach of white sand. In a blend of Santa Fe and Fijian native architectural styles, the bures and main building have thick adobe walls supporting Fijian thatched roofs. Most of the large L-shaped bungalows have a lounge and raised sleeping areas under one roof; another roof covers an enormous bathroom that can be entered both from the bed/dressing area and from a private, hammock-swung patio. At the far end of the property, the private, exquisitely designed Vale Viqi (Pink House) delights honeymooners with its own private beach, plunge pool, and a unique two-person, face-to-face tub in the middle of its large bathroom. The Point, a 2-story villa with its own pool, has a terrific view of the beach from its super-private perch atop a headland.

P.O. Box 9936, Nadi Airport (Vatulele Island, 50km/31 miles south of Viti Levu, a 30-min. flight from Nadi). © 800/ 828-9146 or 672 0300. Fax 672 0062. www.vatulele.com. 19 units. US$924–US$2,079 (£462–£686) bungalow. Rates include room, food, bar, all activities except sport fishing and scuba diving. 4-night minimum stay required. AE, DC, MC, V. Children under 12 not accepted. **Amenities:** Restaurant; bar; tennis court; 24-hr. room service; massage; laundry service. *In room:* Minibar, coffeemaker, safe, no phone.

WHERE TO DINE ON THE CORAL COAST

In Sigatoka Town next to Jack's of Fiji, Roshni and Jean-Pierre Gerber's clean **Le Cafe Town** (© **652 0668**) offers a menu of inexpensive sandwiches, salads, curries, pizzas, fish and chips, and other snacks. It's cash only. Le Cafe is open Monday to Saturday from 9am to 5pm. The Gerbers—she's from Fiji, he's Swiss, both are chefs—also serve dinners at Le Cafe in Korotogo (see below). Although her original restaurant is better (see below), **Vilisite's Seafood Restaurant No. 2** is on the Queen's Road in Sigatoka, west of the river (© **650 1030**). It's open daily from 10am to 9:30pm.

In addition to Le Cafe, the Ebb Tide Cafe and Ocean Terrace Restaurant (see below), Sunset Drive west of the Outrigger on the Lagoon Fiji, has a few other restaurants.

Many Coral Coast hotels have special nights, such as meke feasts of Fijian foods cooked in a lovo, served buffet style, and followed by traditional dancing.

Le Cafe ☆☆ INTERNATIONAL   In addition to running Le Cafe Town in Sigatoka, Roshni and Jean-Pierre Gerber turn their attention to this establishment, where they offer fish and chips, Indian curries, Italian pastas, and some reasonably good pizzas. The specials board features the likes of fresh fish filet with lemon butter sauce, pepper or garlic steak, garlic prawns, and local lobster with Mornay sauce. A special lunch and dinner menu offers substantial servings of fish and chips, spaghetti, or burgers for F$7 (US$4.55/£2.35). Even if you don't dine here, the thatch-topped bar is a great place for a sunset cocktail during happy hour from 5 to 8pm daily.

Sunset Strip, Korotogo, west of the Outrigger on the Lagoon Fiji. © 652 0877. Reservations accepted. Breakfast F$5.50–F$7.50 (US$3.55–US$4.85/£1.85–£2.50); lunch F$7 (US$4.55/£2.35); pizzas F$8.50–F$17 (US$5.50–US$11/ £2.85–£5.50); main courses F$7–F$16 (US$4.50–US$10/£2.35–£5.35). No credit cards. Daily 8am–10pm.

Ocean Terrace Restaurant/EbbTide Cafe ☆ INTERNATIONAL   These two restaurants occupy the verandas overlooking the swimming pool at the Bedarra Beach Inn Fiji (see "Where to Stay on the Coral Coast," above) and utilize the same kitchen. The downstairs Ebb Tide Cafe serves a daytime menu of salads, sandwiches, burgers, a few main courses, and 12-inch pizzas with a limited selection of toppings. At night the upstairs veranda turns into the romantic Ocean Terrace Restaurant, where the chef takes flight with his own versions of chicken and seafood curries, reef fish with a creamy lemon and coriander sauce, and beef with a vegetable and peanut stuffing. The evening menu is available in both restaurants.

Sunset Strip, Korotogo, in Bedarra Beach Inn Fiji. © 650 0476. Reservations accepted. Ocean Terrace main courses F$17–F$27 (US$11–US$18/£5.65–£9). Ebb Tide sandwiches and burgers F$10 (US$6.50/£3.35), pizzas F$18

(US$12/£6), main courses F$9–F$20 (US$5.85–US$13/£3–£6.65). AE, MC, V. Ocean Terrace daily 6–9pm. Ebb Tide daily 10am–9pm.

Vilisite's Seafood Restaurant ★★ *Value* SEAFOOD/INDIAN/CHINESE Vilisite (sounds like "Felicity"), a friendly Fijian who lived in Australia, operates one of the few nonhotel places in Fiji where you can dine by the lagoon's edge. Come in time for a sunset drink and bring a camera, for the westward view from Vilisite's veranda belongs on a postcard. Her well-prepared cuisine is mostly fresh local seafood—fish, shrimp, lobster, octopus—in curry, garlic, and butter, or coconut milk (the Fijian way). She offers five full seafood meals at dinner, or you can choose from chop suey, curry, shrimp, or fish and chips from a blackboard menu. Vilisite will arrange rides for dinner parties of four or more from as far away as the Outrigger, but be sure to ask about the cost. You won't soon forget the view or this extraordinarily friendly Fijian, who certainly knows how to cook.

Queen's Road, Korolevu, between the Warwick and the Naviti. ℂ 653 0054. Reservations recommended. Lunch F$2.50–F$15 (US$1.60–US$9.75; 85p–£5); full dinners F$10–F$45 (US$6.50–US$29/£3.35–£15). MC, V. Daily 8am–10pm.

ISLAND NIGHTS ON THE CORAL COAST

Coral Coast nightlife centers around the hotels and whatever Fiji meke shows they are sponsoring.

The **Fijian fire walkers** from Beqa, an island off the south coast (remember, it's pronounced M-*bengga*, not *Beck*-a), parade across the steaming stones to the incantations of "witch doctors" at least once a week at the **Hideaway Resort** (ℂ 650 0177), **Outrigger on the Lagoon Fiji** (ℂ 650 0044), and the Warwick Fiji Resort & Spa (ℂ 653 0010). Call them or ask at your hotel for the schedule.

Gecko's Restaurant (ℂ 652 0200) in the Kalevu South Pacific Cultural Center has a 1-hour Fijian dance show Monday to Friday nights and a 3-hour version on Sunday evening. Call for reservations. The **Hideaway Resort** (ℂ 650 0177) has a South Pacific show on Sunday and excellent cabaret shows during the week.

4 Pacific Harbour & Beqa Island

Pacific Harbour was begun in the early 1970s as a recreation-oriented, luxury residential community and resort (translated: a real-estate development). A number of expatriates have built homes here and have their own tourist information website at **www.pacificharbour-fiji.com**. Given the heat, humidity, and amount of rain it gets, Pacific Harbour is not the place for a typical beach vacation, although you can swim at all tides off 3km (2 miles) of deep, grayish sand. On the plus side, it has an excellent golf course, fine deep-sea fishing, fabulous scuba diving both out in the **Beqa Lagoon** and along the coast (this is one place in Fiji where you can go on shark-feeding dives), and white-water rafting trips on the nearby **Navua River.** Local promoters aren't far wrong when they describe Pacific Harbour as "The Adventure Capital of Fiji."

It's also my favorite place to experience Fijian culture outside a village. Formerly known as the Pacific Harbour Cultural Centre & Market Place; now called the **Arts Village,** a shopping center on the Queen's Road serves both tourists and residents. Although still financially troubled, it consists of colonial-style clapboard buildings joined by covered walkways leading to restaurants, a grocery store, boutiques, handicraft shops, a swimming pool complex, and a cultural center (see below).

Offshore, rugged **Beqa Island** is nearly cut in two by Malumu Bay, making it one of Fiji's more scenic spots. Most of Fiji's famous fire walkers come from Dakuibeqa, Naceva, and Ruka villages on Beqa. The island is surrounded by Beqa Lagoon, where more than a dozen dive sites feature both soft and hard corals. Among them is **Frigate Passage,** which has a 48-meter (157-foot) wall for divers but is even better known for its powerful left-handed surf break over a relatively smooth coral reef.

GETTING TO PACIFIC HARBOUR & GETTING AROUND

Pacific Harbour is on the Queen's Road, 30km (19 miles) west of Suva. The express buses between Nadi and Suva stop at the Pearl South Pacific Resort, where you'll also find taxis waiting in the parking lot. See "Getting There & Getting Around," in chapter 4, for more information. **Thrifty Car Rental** (② 345 0655) and **Hertz** (② 338 0981) have agencies in Pacific Harbour. There is no regular ferry service between Pacific Harbour and Beqa Island; the resorts out there arrange transfers for their guests, by boat from Pacific Harbour or by seaplane from Nadi.

VISITING THE ARTS VILLAGE 🐠🐠

The centerpiece of the **Arts Village Cultural Centre** 🐠🐠 (② 345 0065; www.arts village.com), on the Queen's Road, is a lakeside Fijian village, complete with thatched roofs over the grand chief's bure and the tallest traditional temple in Fiji. The shows and tours here tend to change. For example, the general manager outlined one set of tours for me, but when I got home, the website said something else. Accordingly, I hesitate to tell you the schedule and cost. Let's just say there are firewalking shows, boat trips around the village, and tours into the village for visits with Fijians working at carving, weaving, boat building, and other crafts. All are worth doing, so call ahead to see what's going on. Prices range from F$15 to F$75 (US$9.75–US$49/£5–£25). Children 6 to 16 are charged half-price.

SCUBA DIVING, RIVER RAFTING & OTHER OUTDOOR ACTIVITIES

FISHING   The waters off southern Viti Levu are renowned for their big game fish, especially when the tuna and mahimahi are running from January to May and when big wahoos pass by in June and July. The women's world records for wahoo and trevally were set here. **Xtasea Charters** (② 345 0280; www.xtaseacharters.com) can tailor excursions—from going for big ones offshore to trolling for smaller but exciting catch inshore. A full day of big-game fishing costs about F$1,860 (US$1,208/£620). Reef fishing is less expensive at F$1,050 (US$682/£350). Xtasea also has snorkeling trips to Beqa Lagoon for F$950 (US$617/£317). Up to six can go on each trip.

GOLF   Robert Trent Jones, Jr. designed the scenic 18-hole, par-72 **Pearl South Pacific Championship Golf Course** (② 345 0905), on the north side of the Queen's Road. Some of its fairways cross lakes; others cut their way through narrow valleys surrounded by jungle-clad hills. Greens fees are F$40 (US$26/£13), and the pro shop has equipment for rent. The clubhouse restaurant is open daily 7am to 7pm.

JET-SKIING   An adventurous way to see Beqa lagoon is on a 60km (37¼ miles) excursion led by **Jetski Safari** (② 345 0933; www.jetski-safari.com). Depending on weather conditions, you will speed across Beqa Passage and explore Beqa Island's picturesque Malumu Bay. The boats also stop for snorkeling on a tiny sand islet in the lagoon. Up to three persons can ride on each boat (realistically, two adults and 1 child) for F$285 (US$185/£95) per craft.

JUNGLE CANOPY RIDES ZIP Fiji (© 930 0545; www.zip-fiji.com) has strung wires in a rainforest between Pacific Harbour and Suva, where you are strapped into a harness and ride from platform to platform high up in the jungle canopy, sometimes as fast as 50kmph (31mph). Some wires are 200 meters (656 feet) long and 30 meters (98 feet) up in the trees. The rides cost F$115 (US$75/£38) per adult, half-price for children. Reservations are required.

RIVER RAFTING & KAYAKING ☆☆☆ The South Pacific's best white-water rafting is with **Rivers Fiji** ☆☆☆ (© 800/446-2411 in the U.S., or 345 0147; fax 345 0148; www.riversfiji.com). This American-owned outfit uses inflatable rafts and kayaks for trips through the Upper Navua River Gorge, the "Grand Canyon of Fiji" and an official conservation area. I have met experienced rafters who say the Navua Gorge was one of their top experiences. The adventures cost about F$110 (US$170/£85) per person. It also has inflatable kayaking trips—"funyacking," it calls them—on the Luva River, another picturesque waterway up in the Namosi Highlands, for F$85 (US$130/£65) per person. And it has 6-day multisport trips, including kayaking down the Luva, sea kayaking in the Beqa Lagoon, and white-water rafting the Navua Gorge. Prices for the long trips start at F$1545 (US$2,375/£1,288). Reservations are essential.

Videos and brochures often feature tourists lazily floating down a Fijian river on a raft made of bamboo poles lashed together. In the old days, mountain-dwelling Fijians really did use *bilibilis*—flimsy bamboo rafts—to float their crops down river to market. They would discard the rafts and walk home. The Suva-based **Wilderness Ethnic Adventures Fiji** (© 359 9320; www.wildernessfiji.com.fj) takes you upriver by motorized canoe and usually brings you back on a bilibili (ask if the bilibili ride is included before you sign up). These 7-hour trips cost about F$96 (US$62£32) per person. Reservations and a minimum of 3 passengers are required.

The Navua River is a scenic delight as it cuts its way through the foothills. Depending on how much it has rained recently, you'll have a few gentle rapids to negotiate, and you'll stop for dips in waterfalls that tumble right into the river. Wear swimsuits and sandals, but bring a sarong to wear in a typical Fijian village, where you'll be welcomed at a yaqona ceremony.

SCUBA DIVING ☆☆☆ Pacific Harbour is famous for its **shark-feeding dives,** especially over the nearby Shark Reef Marine Reserve. You're almost guaranteed to come close to large bull and tiger sharks as well as six reef species. You watch from behind a man-made coral wall while the divemaster does the feeding. Only experienced divers need apply for these exciting excursions.

Beqa Adventure Divers (© 345 0911; www.fiji-sharks.com) pioneered the shark-feeding dives and charges F$110 (US$71/£37) for a one-tank dive, F$200 (US$130/£67) for two tanks. San Francisco–based **Aqua-Trek** (© 800/541-4334 or 345 0324; fax 345 0324; www.aquatrek.com) also has shark-feeding dives among its repertoire. Both companies also dive in Beqa Lagoon, and Aqua-Trek teaches resort diving and a full range of PADI courses.

WHERE TO STAY IN PACIFIC HARBOUR

Tsulu Luxury Backpackers & Apartments (© 345 0065; www.tsulu.com) has a collection of dorms, rooms, and apartments upstairs in one of the Arts Village buildings (see above). The fully air-conditioned quarters range from F$28 (US$18/£9) for a dorm bed to F$199 (US$129/£66) for an apartment, including continental breakfast. Guests can use the Arts Centre's pool.

Another option is the **Lagoon Resort** (© **345 0100;** www.lagoonresort.com), a 21-room hotel about 2km (1¼ miles) inland, beside the Qaraniqio River and near the Pearl South Pacific Championship Golf Course. It attracts primarily divers and ardent golfers who don't care about a beachside location. The crew of the movie *Anaconda* stayed at the Lagoon and left behind the *Bloody Mary,* the rickety boat that played a leading role (it's now part of the bar). Rates range from about F$175 (US$114/£58) for a room to F$335 (US$218/£112) for a suite.

The Pearl South Pacific   This three-story resort is so cool, sexy, and stylish that it would be more at home in New York or Sydney—or even Suva—than here beside this long beach of deep, gray sand. Jazz music permeates the public areas, from the lobby bar before a waterfall wall to the huge day-bed loungers, where you can literally stretch out while enjoying a drink or reading a book. Most units are standard hotel rooms, but some have been transformed into luxurious, one-bedroom "Penthouse Suites," each with hardwood floors, its own decor, and butler service. Dining choices include an informal restaurant, a fine-dining outlet, and a bar out by the beach and swimming pool, where Sunday jazz brunches draw crowds of well-heeled locals.

P.O. Box 144, Deuba. © 345 0022. Fax 345 0262. www.thepearlsouthpacific.com. 78 units. F$310–F$370 (US$201–US$240/£103–£123) double; F$650–F$700 (US$422–US$455/£217–£233) suite. AE, DC, MC, V. **Amenities:** 4 restaurants; 4 bars; outdoor pool; golf course; 3 tennis courts; spa; watersports equipment rentals; fitness center; game room; activities desk; 24-hr. room service; laundry service. *In room:* A/C, TV, high-speed dataport, minibar, fridge, coffeemaker.

The Uprising Beach Resort   Opened in 2007, this "flashpacker" resort shares Pacific Harbour's long beach with The Pearl South Pacific. The 12 spacious guest bungalows have queen and single beds plus sitting areas, wet bars, and small front porches. You must go outside to reach their outdoor showers and cramped bathrooms, however, so a Fijian *sulu* (sarong) will come in handy. Consisting of one large, fan-cooled room with over-and-under bunk beds, the 24-bed dorm is quietly situated at the rear of the property. The central building, with a bar and inexpensive restaurant, opens to an outdoor pool and the beach. Young guests and imbibing locals can keep the bar rocking until 1am, so I would avoid bures 1, 2, 3, 7, 8, and 9, which are closest to the action. You can camp here and share the dorm's facilities, but bring your own tent. A full range of outdoor activities includes horseback riding and "horse-boarding" (you and your boogie board are pulled over the lagoon by a horse trotting along the beach).

P.O. Box 416, Pacific Harbour. © 345 2200. Fax 345 2059. www.uprisingbeachresort.com. 12 units, 24 dorm beds, 20 tent sites. F$135–F$155 (US$88–US$101/£45–£52) double; F$30 (US$19/£10) dorm bed; F$10 (US$6.50/£3.35) per-person camping. MC, V. **Amenities:** Restaurant; bar; outdoor pool; watersports equipment rentals; laundry service. *In room:* Fridge, coffeemaker.

WHERE TO STAY ON OR NEAR BEQA ISLAND

Cost-conscious travelers can stay at **Lawaki Beach House** (© **992 1621** or 926 9229; www.lawakibeachhouse.com), on Beqa's southwestern coast. It has two simple bures with bathrooms and porches, a six-person dormitory, and space for campers. Rates range from F$52 (US$34/£17) to F$95 (US$62/£32) per person, including meals. Lawaki Beach House does not accept credit cards.

You don't have to be a surfer dude to hang out at little **Batiluva Beach Resort** (© **345 0384** or 992 0019; www.batiluva.com), on hilly Yanuca Island near the western edge of Beqa Lagoon, but the big breaks on nearby Frigate's Passage are its main attraction. Accommodations are in simple bungalows and dormitories. Rates are F$175 (US$114/£58) per person, including meals.

Beqa Lagoon Resort   On the island's north shore and once known as Marlin Bay Resort, this is the oldest hotel on Beqa. One advantage is that you can go scuba diving off the beach. Accommodations are in a variety of bungalows, from beachfront units with their own plunge pools to half a dozen beside a man-made pond with lily pads. Many feature Indian and Asian furniture. Least expensive are four rooms in a two-story building.

P.O. Box 112, Deuba. (©) 800/592-3454 or 330 4042. Fax 330 4028. www.beqalagoonresort.com. 25 units. F$438– F$585 (US$284–US$380/£146–£195) bungalow. AE, MC, V. **Amenities:** Restaurant; bar; outdoor pool; watersports equipment rentals; limited room service; massage; babysitting; laundry service. *In room:* A/C, fridge, coffeemaker, safe, no phone.

Lalati Resort & Spa ✿   This pleasant little resort sits near the mouth of narrow Malumu Bay, which nearly slices Beqa in two. As a result, it enjoys one of the most picturesque views of any Fiji resort. A jagged peak gives way to the azure Beqa Lagoon, while Viti Levu's southern coast lines the horizon (the lights of Suva can illuminate the far-off sky at night). All buildings have tin roofs and ship-plank siding, lending a South Seas plantation ambience. Bathrooms in the spacious guest bures open to both living rooms and bedrooms, and the larger honeymoon bure has a Jacuzzi and an outdoor shower. The bures lack air-conditioning, but ceiling fans whip up a breeze. A swimming pool fronts the full-service spa, which has an air-conditioned lounge with TV and DVD player. The beach becomes almost nonexistent at high tide, but you can snorkel in deepwater anytime from the resort's long pier, or kayak over to a lovely white-sand beach across the bay. Smoking is not allowed in any of the buildings here.

P.O. Box 166, Deuba. (©) 347 2033. Fax 347 2034. www.lalati-fiji.com. 7 units. F$200 (US$310/£102) per person. Rates include all meals and nonmotorized watersports. AE, MC, V. Children under 14 not accepted. **Amenities:** Restaurant; bar; outdoor pool; exercise room; spa; Jacuzzi; watersports equipment rentals; limited room service; massage; laundry service. *In room:* Minibar, coffeemaker, no phone.

Royal Davui Island Fiji ✿✿   On a rocky, 3-hectare (8-acre) islet off Beqa's southwestern coast, Royal Davui provides competition for Fiji's other top-end, luxury resorts. The island has no flat land, however, so all but one of the bungalows sit up on the hillside. The tradeoff for not being able to step from your bure onto the beach is that you will have a wonderful view. (Westward-facing units espy the sunset but can become warm in the afternoon sun, so I prefer one looking east toward Beqa.) Individually designed to fit among the rocks and old-growth forest, these spacious units have living rooms and bedrooms in separate buildings joined by a hallway. Each has a private plunge pool off the living room balcony, while their bedroom balconies hold two lounge chairs. There are whirlpool tubs as well as showers in the bathrooms. Part of each bathroom roof retracts to let in fresh air or sunshine. A walkway leads from the four-level reception building up to the open-air restaurant and bar. Guests can dine under the shade of a huge banyan tree (a remote, private space for honeymooners is facetiously dubbed the "fertilizer table").

P.O. Box 3171, Lami. (©) 330 7090. Fax 331 1500. www.royaldavui.com. 16 units. US$1,571–US$1,892 (£786–£946) double. Rates include meals, nonalcoholic beverages, all activities except scuba diving, game fishing, spa treatments. **Amenities:** Restaurant; bar; outdoor pool; spa; watersports equipment; limited room service; massage; laundry service. *In room:* A/C, dataport, minibar, coffeemaker, iron, safe.

Kadavu & the Great Astrolabe Reef

No other Fiji island is as rich in wildlife as is rugged **Kadavu,** about 100km (60 miles) south of Viti Levu. The country's third-largest island, skinny Kadavu is about 60km (37 miles) long by just 14km (8½ miles) wide—and that's at its widest point, for several bays almost cut it into pieces. No cane toads, no iguanas, no mongooses, and no mynah birds live on Kadavu to destroy the native flora and fauna in its hills and valleys. As a result, bird-watchers stand a good chance of seeing the endemic Kadavu musk (or shining) parrot, the Kadavu fantail, the Kadavu honeyeater, and the Kadavu whistling dove.

The **Great Astrolabe Reef** forms a barrier along the eastern and southern sides of the islands, and there are other fine dive sights off the north coast. Much coral inside the Great Astrolabe is dead, but its outside slopes have plentiful hard and soft corals and sea life, including a veritable herd of manta rays that gather at the so-called Manta Pass on the south coast.

The north coast is skirted by several kilometers of **Long Beach,** one of the finest in Fiji. Taking full advantage of it are Bob and Rena Forster's **Dive Kadavu/Matana Beach Resort** (© 368 3502; www.divekadavu.com), which has been in business since 1983, and the more upscale **Pagageno Resort** (© 866/862-0754 or 600 3128; www.papagenoresortfiji.com).

The south coast is rugged and exposed to strong southeast trade winds; thus it has no beaches. But here you will find **Matava—The Astrolabe Hide-away** (© 333 6222; www.matava.com), a small resort that's so eco-friendly it has no air conditioners and turns on the solar-powered lights only at night. Made primarily of thatch and other natural materials, its bungalows are both basic and charming. It's close to many Great Astrolabe Reef dive sights, but it also specializes in kayaking trips and bird-watching.

Pacific Sun and Air Fiji fly to Kadavu daily from Nadi and Suva, respectively. The airstrip is at **Vunisea,** the government station on a narrow isthmus about midway along the island. You'll have to take a boat to the resorts—from 10 minutes to Dive Kadavu/Matana Beach Resort to 45 minutes to Matana. There's no bank on Kadavu, but the resorts accept Master-Card and Visa.

WHERE TO DINE IN PACIFIC HARBOUR

Oasis Restaurant REGIONAL   Owned by English ex-pats Monica Vine and Colin Head, this airy dining room with widely spaced tables makes an excellent stop if you're driving between Nadi and Suva. The house specialty is vinegary London-style fish and chips. You can get burgers, sandwiches, salads, curries, omelets, and English-style breakfasts all day. Evening sees the likes of pan-fried mahimahi, perhaps caught by one of the skippers having a cold one at the corner bar. Monica and Colin will let you use their computer with Internet access for F20¢ (US13¢/7p) per minute.

Queen's Rd., in Arts Village. © **345 0617.** Reservations accepted. Breakfast F$6–F$13 (US$3.90–US$8.45/£2–£4.35); snacks, sandwiches, and lunch F$5.50–F$16 (US$3.55–US$10/£1.85–£5.35); main courses F$15–F$35 (US$9.75–US$23/£5–£12). MC, V. Mon–Sat 9:30am–2:30pm and 6–9:30pm; Sun 10am–2:30pm and 6–9:30pm.

5 Suva ⟨★

Neither the likelihood of frequent showers nor an occasional deluge should discourage you from visiting Suva, Fiji's vibrant, sophisticated capital city. Grab your umbrella and wander along its broad avenues lined with grand colonial buildings and orderly parks left over from the British Empire. Its streets will be crowded with Fijians, Indians, Chinese, Europeans, Polynesians, and people of various other ancestries.

Suva sprawls over a hilly, 26 sq. km (10 sq. mile) peninsula jutting like a thumb from southeastern Viti Levu. To the east lies windswept **Laucala Bay** and to the west, Suva's busy harbor and the suburbs of **Lami Town** and **Walu Bay.** Jungle-draped mountains rise to heights of more than 1,200m (3,937 ft.) on the mainland to the north, high enough to condense moisture from the prevailing southeast trade winds and create the damp climate that cloaks the city in lush green foliage all year.

Suva was a typical Fijian village in 1870, when the Polynesia Company sent a group of Australians to settle land it acquired in exchange for paying Chief Cakobau's foreign debts. The Aussies established a camp on the flat, swampy, mosquito-infested banks of **Nubukalou Creek,** on the western shore of the peninsula. When they failed to grow first cotton and then sugar, speculators convinced the new British colonial administration to move the capital from Levuka in 1882.

The business heart of the city still sits near Nubukalou Creek, and you can see most of the city's sights and find most of its shops, interesting restaurants, and lively nightspots along historic **Victoria Parade,** the main drag.

GETTING TO SUVA

Suva is served by **Nausori Airport,** 19km (12 miles) northeast of downtown near the Rewa River town of Nausori. Express buses operated by **Nausori Taxi & Bus Service** (② **347 7583** in Nausori, or 330 4178 in Suva) are scheduled to depart the airport for downtown Monday to Friday at 8:30, 9:30, and 11:30am and 2:30, 5, and 6:30pm. The fare is F$3 (US$1.95/£1) each way. That having been said, I always take one of several taxis waiting at the terminal, whose fares to downtown Suva officially are F$25 (US$16/£8.35). Allow at least 30 minutes for the taxi ride during midday, an hour during morning and evening rush hours. See "Getting There & Getting Around," in chapter 4, for more information.

I never leave Nadi without a good map of Suva, which has a confusing maze of streets, especially at night. It has taken me more than 2 decades to learn my way around the Suva area by car, and even now, I seldom drive here after dark.

GETTING AROUND SUVA

Hundreds of **taxis** prowl Suva's streets. Some have meters, but don't count on it. As a rule of thumb, F$2 to F$3.50 (US$1.30–US$2.25/65p–£1.15) will get you to the sites of interest, F$7 (US$4.55/£2.35) to the Raintree Lodge. If the taxi has a meter, make sure the driver drops the flag. The main **taxi stand** is on Central Street, behind the Air Pacific office in the CML Building on Victoria Parade (② **331 2266**), and on Victoria Parade at Sukuna Park (no phone). I have been satisfied with **Black Arrow Taxis** (② **330 0541** or 330 0139 in Suva, or 347 7071 in Nausori) and **Nausori Taxi & Bus Service** (② **347 7583** in Nausori, or 330 4178 in Suva), which is based at the Holiday Inn Suva parking lot. Others gather at the Suva Municipal Market.

Usually crowded, local **buses** fan out from the municipal market from before daybreak to midnight Monday to Saturday (they have limited schedules on Sun). The fares vary but should be no more than F$2 (US$1.30/65p) to most destinations in and around Suva. If you're going to ride the bus for the fun of it, do it in Nadi, where you won't get lost and aren't as likely to be robbed.

See "Getting There & Getting Around," in chapter 4, for the phone numbers of the major **car rental** firms.

FAST FACTS: Suva

The following facts apply to Suva. If you don't see an item here, see "Fast Facts: Fiji," in chapter 4.

Bookstores The region's largest store is **University Book Centre** (© 331 2500; www.uspbookcentre.com), on the University of the South Pacific campus on Laucala Bay Road (you can order online). Downtown, **Dominion Book Centre,** in Dominion Arcade on Thomson Street behind the Fiji Visitors Bureau (© 330 4334), has the latest news magazines and books on the South Pacific. Another good downtown choice is the book section of **Proud's** department store (© 331 8686), in the Suva Central building on Renwick Road at Pratt Street.

Camera/Film **Caines Photofast,** corner of Victoria Parade and Pratt Street (© 331 3211), sells a wide range of film, provides 1-hour processing of color-print film, and downloads and prints your digital photos.

Currency Exchange **ANZ Bank, Westpac Bank,** and **Colonial National Bank** have offices with ATMs on Victoria Parade, south of the Fiji Visitors Bureau. ANZ has a walk-up currency exchange window, which is open Monday to Friday 9am to 6pm and Saturday 9am to 1pm. **GlobalEX,** on Victoria Parade at Gordon Street, cashes traveler's checks.

Drugstores **Suva City Pharmacy,** on Victoria Parade in the General Post Office building (© 331 7400), is the city's best drugstore. It's open Monday to Friday 8:30am to 5:30pm and Saturday 8:30am to 2pm.

Emergencies/Police The emergency phone number for **police** is © 917. For **fire** and **ambulance,** dial © 911. Fiji Police's **central station** is on Joske Street, between Pratt and Gordon streets (© 331 1222).

Eyeglasses Dr. Guy Hawley, an American eye specialist, practices at **Asgar & Co. Ltd.,** Queensland Insurance Centre, Victoria Parade (© 330 0433).

Healthcare Most expatriate residents go to the **Suva Private Hospital,** 120 Amy St. (© 331 3355). It's open 24 hours a day. **Colonial War Memorial Hospital,** at the end of Ratu Mara Road at Brown Street (© 331 3444), is the public hospital, but go to Suva Private Hospital if at all possible.

Internet Access Suva has dozens of Internet cafes, many on Victoria Parade, and wireless hotspots are being set up. **Connect Internet Cafe,** in the General Post Office building (© 330 0777), has high-speed broadband access for F$3 (US$1.95/£1) an hour. It's open Monday to Friday 8:30am to 8pm, Saturday 9am to 8pm, and Sunday 10am to 6pm. You can print, scan, and burn CDs. **Esquires** on Renwick Road at Pratt Street (© 330 0082) has a hotspot. It's open Monday to Friday 7am to 10pm, Saturday 8am to 10pm, and Sunday 9am to 7pm.

Laundry/Dry Cleaning **Flagstaff Laundry & Drycleaners,** 62 Bau St. (© 330 1214), has full 1-day service.

Libraries **Suva City Library** on Victoria Parade (© 331 3433) has a small collection of books on the South Pacific. It's open Monday, Tuesday, Thursday, and Friday 9:30am to 6pm; Wednesday noon to 6pm; and Saturday 9am to 1pm. The library at the **University of the South Pacific** (© 331 3900) has one of the largest collections in the South Pacific. The university is on Laucala Bay Road.

Mail Fiji Post's General Post Office is on Thomson Street, opposite the Fiji Visitor's Bureau. It's open Monday to Friday 8am to 4:30pm and Saturday 9am to noon.

Restrooms **Sukuna Park,** on Victoria Parade, has attended (and therefore reasonably clean) public restrooms, on the side next to McDonald's. You must pay F70¢ (US45¢/23p) to use the toilets, or F$1.20 (80¢/40p) for a shower. Open Monday to Saturday 8am to 3:45pm.

Safety Street crime is a serious problem in Suva, so be alert at all times. Do not wander off Victoria Parade after dark; take a taxi. The busy blocks along Victoria Parade between the Fiji Visitors Bureau and the Holiday Inn Suva are relatively safe during the evenings (a local wag says the many prostitutes on the main drag keep the robbers away!), but protect valuables from pickpockets. See "Safety," under "Fast Facts: Fiji," in chapter 4.

Telephone/Fax You can make international calls, send faxes, and surf the Net at **Fiji International Telecommunications Ltd. (FINTEL),** in its colonial-style building on Victoria Parade. It's open Monday to Saturday 8am to 8pm.

Visitor Information & Maps The **Fiji Visitors Bureau** (© 330 2433) has an information center in a restored colonial house at the corner of Thomson and Scott streets, in the heart of Suva. It's open Monday to Thursday 8am to 4:30pm, Friday 8am to 4pm, and Saturday 8am to noon. The excellent *Suva and Lami Town,* from the Department of Lands & Surveys, is often available at Dominion Book Centre (see "Bookstores," above).

Water The tap water is safe to drink.

EXPLORING SUVA

Although you could easily spend several days poking around the capital, most visitors come here for only a day, usually on one of the guided tours from Nadi or the Coral Coast. That's enough time to see the city's highlights, particularly if you make the walking tour described below.

Sitting on a ridge about 1km (a half-mile) southeast of downtown, the **Parliament of Fiji,** on Battery Road off Vuya Road (© 330 5811), resides under a modern shingle-covered version of a traditional Fijian roof. If, and when, Fiji Islanders choose another elected government, you might see a debate or two here.

THE TOP ATTRACTIONS

Fiji Museum ✸✸✸ You'll see a marvelous collection of war clubs, cannibal forks, tanoa bowls, shell jewelry, and other relics here, in one of the South Pacific's finest museums. Although some artifacts were damaged by Suva's humidity while they were hidden away during World War II, much remains. Later additions include the rudder and other relics of HMS *Bounty,* burned and sunk at Pitcairn Island by Fletcher Christian and the other mutineers in 1789 but recovered in the 1950s by the famed *National Geographic* photographer Luis Marden. Don't miss the masi cloth and Indian art exhibits in the air-conditioned upstairs galleries. The gift shop is worth a browse.

In Thurston Gardens, Ratu Cakobau Rd. off Victoria Parade. Ⓒ **331 5944.** www.fijimuseum.org.fj. Admission F$7 (US$4.55/£2.35) adults, F$5 (US$3.25/£1.65) students with IDs. Guided tours by donation. Mon–Thurs and Sat 9am–4:30pm; Fri 9:30am–4pm.

Suva Municipal Market 𝕲𝕲𝕲   A vast array of tropical produce is offered at Suva's main supply of food, the largest and most lively market in the South Pacific. If they aren't too busy, the merchants will appreciate your interest and answer your questions about the names and uses of the various fruits and vegetables. The market teems on Saturday morning, when it seems as if the entire population of Suva shows up to shop and select television programs for the weekend's viewing. The bus station is behind the market on Rodwell Road.

Usher St. at Rodwell Road. No phone. Free admission. Mon–Fri 5am–6pm; Sat 5am–1pm.

WALKING TOUR   SUVA

Start:	The Triangle
Finish:	Government House
Time:	2½ hours
Best Time:	Early morning or late afternoon
Worst Time:	Midday, or Saturday afternoon and Sunday, when the market and shops are closed and downtown is deserted

---

Begin at the four-way intersection of Victoria Parade, Renwick Road, and Thomson and Central streets. This little island in the middle of heavy traffic is called the Triangle.

❶ The Triangle

Now the center of Suva, in the late 1800s this spot was a lagoon fed by a stream that flowed along what is now Pratt Street. A marker in the park commemorates Suva's becoming the capital, the arrival of Fiji's first missionaries, the first public land sales, and Fiji's becoming a colony. Three of the four dates are slightly wrong.

From the Triangle, head north on Thomson Street, bearing right between the Fiji Visitors Bureau and the old Garrick Hotel (now the Sichuan Pavilion Restaurant), whose wrought-iron balconies recall a more genteel but non-air-conditioned era. Continue on Thomson Street to Nubukalou Creek.

❷ Nubukalou Creek

The Polynesia Company's settlers made camp beside this stream and presumably drank from it. A sign on the bridge warns against eating fish from it today—with good reason, as you will see and smell. Across the bridge, smiling Fijian women wait under a flame tree in a shady little park to offer grass skirts and other handicraft items for sale.

Pass to the left of the Fijian women across the bridge for now, and head down Cumming Street.

❸ Cumming Street

This area, also on reclaimed land, was home of the Suva market until the 1940s. Cumming Street was lined with saloons, yaqona grog shops, and curry houses known as lodges. It became a tourist-oriented shopping mecca when World War II Allied servicemen created a market for curios. When import taxes were lifted from electronic equipment and cameras in the 1960s, Cumming Street merchants quickly added the plethora of duty-free items you'll find there today. Browse for a while.

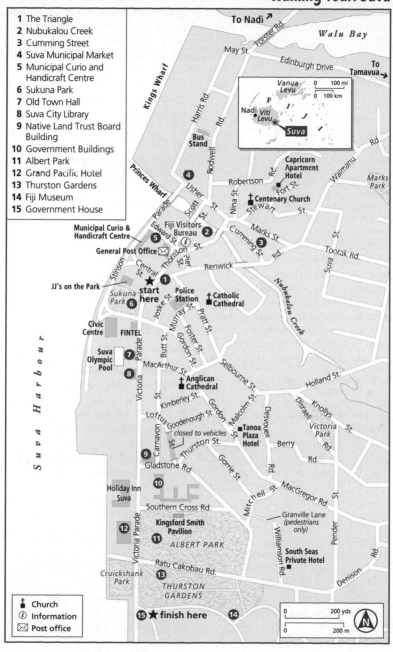

Walking Tour: Suva

1 The Triangle
2 Nubukalou Creek
3 Cumming Street
4 Suva Municipal Market
5 Municipal Curio and Handicraft Centre
6 Sukuna Park
7 Old Town Hall
8 Suva City Library
9 Native Land Trust Board Building
10 Government Buildings
11 Albert Park
12 Grand Pacific Hotel
13 Thurston Gardens
14 Fiji Museum
15 Government House

To Nadi ↗

Walu Bay

May St.
Edinburgh Drive
To Tamavua →
Forster Rd.

Kings Wharf
Harris Rd.
Rodwell Rd.

Vanua Levu
0   100 mi
0   100 km
F I J I
Nadi
Viti Levu
Suva

Bus Stand

Princes Wharf

Capricorn Apartment Hotel
Robertson
Fort St.
Waimanu Rd.
Marks Park

Usher
Scott St.
Nina St.
Stewart St.
† Centenary Church

Parade
Edward St.
Fiji Visitors Bureau ②
Marks St.
St.
Toorak Rd.

Municipal Curio & Handicraft Centre ⑤
General Post Office ✉
Thomson St.
Pier St.
Cumming St. ③

Stimson
Central St.
Renwick

JJ's on the Park
★ ① start here
Joske St.
Police Station ■
Murray St.
† Catholic Cathedral

Sukuna Park ⑥
Pratt St.

Suva Harbour

Civic Centre
FINTEL
Butt St.
Foster St.
Gordon St.
Selbourne St.
Holland St.

Suva Olympic Pool ⑦
Parade
⑧
MacArthur St.
Victoria St.
† Anglican Cathedral ■
Malcolm St.
Desvoeux Rd.
Disraeli Rd.
Knollys St.
Victoria Park

Kimberley St.
Loftus St.
Goodenough St.
Gordon St.
Carnavon St.
closed to vehicles
Thurston St.
■ Tanoa Plaza Hotel
Berry Rd.

⑨
Gladstone Rd.
Gorrie St.
Mitchell St.
MacGregor Rd.
Pender St.

Holiday Inn Suva
⑩
Southern Cross Rd.
Granville Lane (pedestrians only)

⑫
Kingsford Smith Pavilion ⑪
ALBERT PARK
Williamson Rd.
South Seas Private Hotel ■

Cruickshank Park
Victoria Parade
Ratu Cakobau Rd.
⑬
THURSTON GARDENS
Denison Rd.

† Church
ⓘ Information
✉ Post office

⑮ ★ finish here   ⑭

0   200 yds
0   200 m
N

Return to Thomson Street, turn right, and then turn left on Usher Street. Follow Usher Street past the intersection at Rodwell Road and Scott Street to the Suva Municipal Market.

4 Suva Municipal Market

This market hums with activity, especially on Saturday mornings (see "The Top Attractions," above). Big ships from overseas and small boats from the other islands dock at Princes Wharf and Kings Wharf beyond the market on Usher Street.

Head south along Stinson Parade, back across Nubukalou Creek and along the edge of Suva's waterfront to Edward Street and the gray tin roofs of the Municipal Curio and Handicraft Centre.

5 Municipal Curio and Handicraft Centre

In yet another bit of cultural diversity, you can haggle over the price of handicrafts at stalls run by Indians. (Don't try to haggle at those operated by Fijians.) It's best to wait until you have visited the Government Handicraft Centre before making a purchase (see "Shopping in Suva," below).

Continue on Stinson Parade past Central Street. The gray concrete building on the corner is the YWCA. When you get there, cut diagonally under the palms and flame trees across Sukuna Park.

6 Sukuna Park

This park is named for Ratu Sir Lala Sukuna, founding father of independent Fiji. This shady waterfront park is a favorite brown-bag lunch spot for Suva's office workers. On the west side is the harbor and on the east, Victoria Parade. For many years only a row of flame trees separated this broad avenue from the harbor, but the shallows have been filled and the land has been extended into the harbor by the width of a city block. The large auditorium that stands south of the park is the Suva Civic Centre.

Head south on the seaward side of Victoria Parade and pass the cream-colored colonial-style headquarters of FINTEL, the country's electronic link to the world. You'll come to the old Town Hall.

7 Old Town Hall

A picturesque Victorian-era building, it features an intricate, ornamental wrought-iron portico. Built as an auditorium in the early 1900s and named Queen Victoria Memorial Hall, this structure was later used as the Suva Town Hall (city offices are now in the modern Suva City Hall). The stage still stands at the rear of the Chinese restaurant.

Continue south on Victoria Parade until you come to the Suva City Library.

8 Suva City Library

The U.S. industrialist and philanthropist Andrew Carnegie gave Fiji £1,500 sterling to build this structure. The central portion of the colonnaded building opened in 1909, with an initial collection of 4,200 books. The wings were added in 1929. Books on Fiji and the South Pacific are shelved to the left of the main entrance. (See "Fast Facts: Suva," above, for the library's hours.)

Keep going along Victoria Parade, past Loftus Street, to the corner of Gladstone Road, locale for the Native Land Trust Board Building.

9 Native Land Trust Board Building

This site is known as Naiqaqi (the Crusher) because a sugar-crushing mill sat here during Suva's brief, unsuccessful career as a cane-growing area in the 1870s. Ratu Sir Lala Sukuna, who prepared his people for independence (see "Fiji Yesterday: History 101," in chapter 4), served as chairman of the Native Land Trust Board, which collects and distributes rents on the 80% of the country that is owned by the Fijians.

Across Gladstone Road, you can't miss the imposing gray edifice and clock tower of the Government Buildings.

10 Government Buildings

Erected between 1937 and 1939 (although they look older), these British-style gray stone buildings house the High Court, the prime minister's office, and several government ministries. Parliament met here until 1987, when Colonel Rabuka and gang marched in and arrested its leaders; Parliament now meets in a new complex on Ratu Sukuna Road in the Muanikau suburb. The clock tower is known as "Fiji's Big Ben." When it works, it chimes every 15 minutes from 6am to midnight.

Walk past the large open field on the south side of the building; this is Albert Park.

⓫ Albert Park

This park is named for Queen Victoria's consort, Prince Albert. The pavilion opposite the Government Buildings, however, is named for Charles Kingsford Smith, the Australian aviator and first person to fly across the Pacific. Smith was unaware that a row of palm trees stretched across the middle of Albert Park, his intended landing place. A local radio operator figured out Smith's predicament, and the colonial governor ordered the trees cut down immediately. The resulting "runway" across Albert Park was barely long enough, but Smith managed to stop his plane within a few feet of its end on June 6, 1928.

Opposite the park on Victoria Parade stands the Grand Pacific Hotel.

⓬ Grand Pacific Hotel

Vacant for years, this historic hotel was scheduled for restoration at press time. The Union Steamship Company built the "GPH" in 1914 to house its transpacific passengers during their stopovers in Fiji. The idea was to make them think they had never gone ashore, for rooms in the GPH were like first-class staterooms, complete with saltwater bathrooms and plumbing fixtures identical to those on an ocean liner. All rooms were on the second floor, and guests could step outside on a 15-foot-wide veranda overlooking the harbor and walk completely around the building—as if walking on the deck. When members of the British royal family visited Fiji, they stood atop the wrought-iron portico, the "bow" of the Grand Pacific, and addressed their subjects massed across Victoria Parade in Albert Park.

Continue south on Victoria Parade to the corner of Ratu Cakobau Road, and enter Thurston Gardens.

⓭ Thurston Gardens

Originally known as the Botanical Gardens, this cool, English-like park is named for its founder, the amateur botanist Sir John Bates Thurston, who started the gardens in 1881. Henry Marks, scion of a family who owned a local trading company, presented the drinking fountain in 1914. After G. J. Marks, a relative and lord mayor of Suva, was drowned that same year in the sinking of the SS *Empress* in the St. Lawrence River in Canada, the Marks family erected the bandstand in his memory. Children can climb aboard the stationary *Thurston Express*, a narrow-gauge locomotive once used to pull harvested cane to the crushing mill.

Walk to the southeast corner of the gardens, where you will find the Fiji Museum.

⓮ Fiji Museum

At this fascinating museum, you can see relics and artifacts of Fiji's history (see "The Top Attractions," above). After touring the complex, take a break at the museum's cafe, under a lean-to roof on one side of the main building; it serves soft drinks, snacks, and curries.

Backtrack through the gardens to Victoria Parade and head south until, just past the greens of the Suva Bowling Club on the harbor, you arrive at the big iron gates of Government House.

⓯ Government House

This is the home of Fiji's president, guarded by spit-and-polish *sulu*-clad Fijian soldiers. The original house, built in 1882 as the residence of the colonial governor, was struck by lightning and burned in 1921. The present mansion was completed in 1928 and opened with great fanfare. It is closed to the public, but a colorful ceremony marks the changing of the guard the first week of each month. Ask the Visitors Bureau whether one will take place while you're there.

From this point, Victoria Parade becomes Queen Elizabeth Drive, which skirts the peninsula to Laucala Bay. With homes and gardens on one side and the lagoon on the other, it's a lovely walk or drive. The manicured residential area, in the rolling hills behind Government House, is known as the Domain. An enclave of British civil servants in colonial times, it is now home to the Fiji parliament, government officials, diplomats, and affluent private citizens.

COLO-I-SUVA FOREST PARK

At an altitude of 121 to 182m (397 to 597 feet), **Colo-I-Suva Forest Park,** on the Prince's Road 11km (6¾ miles) from downtown Suva (℃ **332 0211**), provides a cool, refreshing respite from the heat—if not the humidity—of the city below. You can hike the system of trails through the heavy indigenous forests and stands of mahogany to one of several lovely waterfalls that cascade into swimming holes. Bring walking shoes with good traction because the trails are covered with gravel or slippery soapstone. The park is open daily 8am to 4pm. Admission is F$5 (US$3.25/£1.65). Take a taxi or the Sawani bus, which leave Suva Municipal Market every 30 minutes. Do not leave valuables in your vehicle or unattended anywhere else.

SHOPPING IN SUVA

If you took the walking tour of Suva, you already have a good idea of where to shop for handicrafts, cameras, electronic gear, and clothing. The largest and most reliable merchants are **Jack's of Fiji,** at Thomson and Pier streets, opposite the Fiji Visitors Bureau; **Prouds,** in the Suva Central building on Renwick Road at Pratt Street; and **Tappoo,** which has a large store at the corner of Thomson and Usher streets. Note that Jack's has a very small handicraft section here; it's mostly a clothing and accessories outlet. The prices are fixed in these stores.

Before buying handicrafts, be sure to visit the Fiji Museum and its excellent shop (see "The Top Attractions," above).

Government Handicraft Centre 𝒦 *Value*   Founded in 1974 to continue and promote Fiji's handicrafts, this shop has a limited selection of authentic merchandise (no war clubs carved in Asia are sold in this shop). Special attention is given to rural artisans who cannot easily market their works. You will see fine woodcarvings, woven goods, pottery, and masi cloth, and you will learn from the fixed prices just how much the really good items are worth. The Fijian staff is friendly and helpful. It's open Monday to Thursday 8am to 4:30pm, Friday 8am to 4pm, and Saturday 8am to 12:30pm. Corner of Victoria Parade and MacArthur St., in rear of Ratu Sukuna House. ℃ **331 5869.**

Municipal Curio and Handicraft Centre   Having checked out the government center, you can visit these stalls and bargain with the Indian merchants (but not with the Fijians) from a position of knowledge, if not strength. Be careful, however, for some of the work here is mass-produced and aimed at cruise-ship passengers who have only a few hours to do their shopping in Fiji. It's open Monday to Thursday 8am to 4:30pm, Friday 8am to 4pm, Saturday 8am to noon, and Sunday when cruises ships are in port. Municipal Car Park, Stinson Parade, on the waterfront. ℃ **331 3433.**

WHERE TO STAY IN SUVA
MODERATE

Holiday Inn Suva 🖋 Formerly the Centra Suva and before that the Suva Travelodge, this is the unofficial gathering place for the city's movers and shakers. The waterfront location couldn't be better, for Suva Harbour laps one side, the government buildings sit across Victoria Parade on the other, and the business district is a 3-block walk away. All units have been upgraded in recent years, which makes the mustiness, caused by Suva's humidity, less apparent. Upstairs over the lobby, rooms 263 to 281 face the harborside lawn and pool, but they are less humid. The *Fiji Times* is delivered to your room daily on request. One room is equipped for guests with disabilities.

P.O. Box 1357, Suva (Victoria Parade, opposite government buildings). © 800/465-4329 or 330 1600. Fax 330 0251. www.holiday-inn.com. 130 units. F$325–F$425 (US$211–US$276/£108–£142) double, F$585 (US$380/£195) suite. AE, DC, MC, V. **Amenities:** Restaurant; bar; outdoor pool; access to nearby health club; fitness center; activities desk; business center; wireless Internet access; 24-hr. room service; babysitting; laundry service; coin-op washers and dryers. *In room:* A/C, TV, high-speed Internet access, minibar, coffeemaker, iron, safe.

JJ's on the Park Suva's only boutique hotel, JJ's on the Park isn't much to look at from the outside, since it occupies the former YWCA Building, a stained concrete structure five stories high on the north side of Sukuna Park. But go inside and you'll find its comfortable rooms and suites are among Suva's best equipped. JJ's attracts business travelers seeking more luxuries and services than elsewhere. Accommodations range from smaller rooms without balconies to suites with two balconies and separate bedrooms. Balcony or not, every unit has a harbor view.

P.O. Box 12499, Suva (Stinson Parade, north side of Sukuna Park). © 330 5055. Fax 330 5002. www.jjsfiji.com.fj. 22 units. F$257 (US$167/£86) double; F$457–F$657 (US$297–US$427/£152–£219) suite. AE, DC, MC, V. No children accepted. **Amenities:** Restaurant; bar; access to nearby health club; activities desk; wireless Internet access; 24-hr. room service; laundry service. *In room:* A/C, TV, fax machine (some units), high-speed Internet access, fridge (stocked on request), coffeemaker, iron, safe.

Tanoa Plaza Hotel Even *sans* balcony, you will have a commanding view over Suva, the harbor, and the south coast of Viti Levu from the top floors of this curving, nine-story building. Best of all are the executive suites on the top floor, which are larger and better appointed than the smallish regular rooms, and they have small balconies, which the rooms do not. The neighborhood is quiet and residential, yet the hotel is a 3-block walk from the shops on Victoria Parade (during the day, anyway; take a taxi at night). A pleasant first-floor restaurant serves breakfast, lunch, and dinner. There's a swimming pool on the shady side of the building.

P.O. Box 112, Suva (corner Malcolm and Gordon sts.). © 331 2300. Fax 331 1300. www.tanoahotels.com. 60 units. F$210–F$235 (US$136–US$153/£70–£78) double; F$425 (US$276/£142) suite. AE, DC, MC, V. **Amenities:** Restaurant; bar; outdoor pool; wireless Internet access (in lobby); 24-hr. room service; babysitting; laundry service. *In room:* A/C, TV, high-speed Internet access, minibar, coffeemaker, iron, safe.

INEXPENSIVE

Capricorn Apartment Hotel (Value) Although it's a steep, 2-block walk uphill from Cumming Street, Mulchand Patel's super-clean establishment is popular with Australians and New Zealanders who like to do their own cooking. The three-story, L-shaped building looks out on Suva Harbour and down the mountainous coast. Private balconies off each apartment share the view, as does a pear-shaped swimming pool on the Capricorn's grounds. Tropical furniture adorns all units, and the mattresses are new and among the firmest in Fiji. Mulchand and his friendly staff make sure these roomy efficiencies are kept spotless. Each unit has air-conditioning, although (unscreened) windows on both sides of the building let the cooling trade winds blow through. The reception staff will sell you canned goods from its small on-premises store or have "Dial-A-Meal" delivered to your room.

P.O. Box 1261, Suva (top end of Saint Fort St.). ℂ 330 3732. Fax 330 3069. www.capricorn-hotels-fiji.com. 34 units. F$95–F$125 (US$62–US$82/£32–£42) double. AE, DC, MC, V. **Amenities:** Outdoor pool; babysitting; laundry service. *In room:* A/C, TV, dataport; kitchen, coffeemaker, safe.

Homestay Suva ★★★ *Value* One of the top bed-and-breakfasts in the South Pacific islands, this gorgeous 1920s-vintage colonial home sits atop a ridge in the Tamavua suburb. You will enjoy a stunning view while having breakfast or lounging on the veranda, which overlooks a ridge-top swimming pool and the south coast of Viti Levu. The choice room is appropriately named Harbor View. Another upstairs room, the Nukulau, looks eastward across Laucala Bay to Nukulau Island on the far-off reef. Three other rooms in the main house lack a view. Four more private and spacious "lodge" units in a building a few steps from the main house have kitchens and private balconies with sea views. Many guests here are business types, including women traveling alone. Call for directions if you're driving, or take a taxi from downtown for F$3.50 (US$2.25/£1.15). Neighborhood dogs can disturb the peace at night, but that's common in residential areas throughout Fiji.

265 Prince's Rd. (P.O. Box 16172, Suva). ℂ 337 0395. Fax 337 0947. www.suvahomestay.com. 9 units (all with bathroom). F$168–F$200 (US$109–US$130/£56–£67) double. Rates include full breakfast. AE, MC, V. **Amenities:** Outdoor pool; laundry service. *In room:* A/C, TV, kitchen (in lodge units), fridge, no phone.

Nanette's Homestay Suva *Finds* Almost hidden away on a side street behind Colonial War Memorial Hospital, Nanette MacAdam's two-story, white concrete house looks smaller from the road than it is. Upstairs she has a lounge, kitchen, and four breezy rooms, all with private bathrooms. One has its own balcony. Downstairs are three apartments. Two of these have two bedrooms, and one of these has two bathrooms. All three have fully modern kitchens. The apartments are popular with overseas workers on assignment to the hospital. Guests are treated to continental breakfast, and they can barbecue on the big veranda off the guest lounge.

56 Extension St. (behind Colonial War Memorial Hospital). ℂ 331 6316. Fax 331 6902. nanettes@connect.com.fj. 7 units (all with bathroom). F$110 (US$71/£37) double, F$120–F$190 (US$78–US$123/£40–£63) apartment. Rates include continental breakfast. MC, V. **Amenities:** Wireless Internet access; laundry service. *In room:* A/C, TV (apartments only), kitchen (apartments only), no phone.

Raintree Lodge Backpackers flock to this rustic lodge beside a nearly round, quarry-turned-lake high in the hills near Colo-I-Suva Forest Park (see above). The climes are cool up here, and although "Raintree" refers to an acacia tree, it can rain a lot in this forest. Except for the vehicles passing on Prince's Road, you'll hear very little except the songs of tropical birds and insects. Built of pine and overlooking the lake, the bungalows are spacious, and their beds have mosquito nets (the windows are screened, too). All have ceiling fans and bathrooms with showers. Dormitories range in size from seven private rooms with double beds to a hall with 21 bunk beds. Their occupants share toilets, hot-water showers, and a kitchen. Locals love to drive up here for Sunday barbecue at the rustic and inexpensive **Raintree Restaurant,** where they vie for tables on the lakeside veranda. The lodge is F$7 (US$4.55/£2.35) by taxi or F95¢ (US60¢/30p) by public bus from downtown Suva.

P.O. Box 11245, LBE, Suva (Prince's Rd., Colo-I-Suva, opposite post office). © **332 0562**. Fax 332 0113. www.raintree lodge.com. 4 units, 45 dorm beds. F$165 (US$107/£55) bungalow; F$65 (US$42/£22) double dorm room; F$24 (US$16/£8) dorm bed. AE, MC, V. **Amenities:** Restaurant; bar; outdoor pool; laundry service; coin-operated washers and dryers. *In room:* TV, fridge, coffeemaker, no phone.

South Seas Private Hotel   Many backpackers stay at the Raintree Lodge (see above), but those who opt for the city usually end up at this large wooden structure with a long sunroom across the front (it can get hot in the afternoons). It's a friendly establishment with dormitories, basic rooms, a communal kitchen, a TV lounge, and hand-wash laundry facilities. Bed linen is provided, but bring your own towel or pay a deposit to use one of theirs. There's a refundable key deposit, too. Showers have hot and cold water. The rooms have fans that operate from 4pm to 7am.

P.O. Box 2086, Government Bldgs., Suva (Williamson Rd. off Ratu Cakobau Rd., behind Albert Park). © **331 2296**. Fax 330 8646. www.fiji4less.com. 34 units (one with bathroom), 42 dorm beds. F$58 (US$38/£19) double; F$18 (US$12/£6) dorm bed. AE, MC, V. *In room:* No phone.

A SUPER-LUXURY RESORT ON WAKAYA ISLAND

The Wakaya Club, Fiji's most luxurious and exclusive resort, is on Wakaya Island, an uplifted, tilted coral atoll in the Koro Sea. Beaches fringe Wakaya's north and east coasts, and cliffs fall into the sea on its western side. There are still relics of a Fijian fort on the cliffs. Legend says a chief and all his men leapt off the cliff to their deaths from there rather than be roasted by a rival tribe. The spot is known as Chieftain's Leap.

The Wakaya Club & Spa ✦✦✦   A 20-minute flight by private plane from Nausori Airport, 50 minutes from Nadi, this super-deluxe beachside facility is the brainchild of Canadian entrepreneur David Gilmour, who also introduced us to "Fiji" bottled water. Gilmour has sold off pieces of Wakaya for deluxe getaway homes. For a small fortune you can rent one of these villas, including *Vale O*, Gilmore's own Japanese-influenced mansion high on a ridge overlooking the resort. Nicole Kidman (a regular guest) and other Hollywood types who don't own a private villa—or can't borrow a friend's—feel right at home in the club's large, super-luxurious bungalows. The food here is of gourmet quality and outstandingly presented. Guests dine in a huge thatched-roof beachside building or outside, either on a patio or under two gazebolike shelters on a deck surrounding a pool with its own waterfall. The Fijian staff delivers excellent, unobtrusive service. Your wish is their command. This is Fiji's most luxurious resort. Only the humongous Governor's and Ambassador's bures have TVs for DVD viewing. The latter is a 4,500-square-foot retreat, the largest bure here.

P.O. Box 15424, Suva (Wakaya Island, Lomaviti Group). © **344 0128**. Fax 970/920-1225 or 344 0406. www. wakaya.com. 9 units. US$1,900–US$7,600 (£950–£3,800) bungalow. Rates include meals, bar, all activities except deep-sea fishing, scuba diving courses, and massages. Round-trip transfers US$960 (£480) per couple from Nadi, US$480 (£240) from Suva. AE, DC, MC, V. **Amenities:** Restaurant; bar; outdoor pool; 9-hole golf course; tennis courts; 24-hr. room service; massage; babysitting; laundry service. *In room:* High-speed Internet access, minibar, coffeemaker.

WHERE TO DINE IN SUVA

The city has two shopping mall–style food courts serving inexpensive European, Chinese, and Indian dishes. **Dolphins Food Court** is in the high-rise FNPF Place building on Victoria Parade at Loftus Street. The other is on the second floor of **Suva Central,** a modern building on Renwick Road at Pratt Street.

A Side Trip Back in Time to Levuka

You might think you've slipped into *The Twilight Zone* as you stroll down historic Beach Street in **Levuka,** Fiji's first capital, on the ruggedly beautiful island of **Ovalau.** Everything in Levuka seems to be frozen at 1882, when the colonial administration moved to Suva: ramshackle dry-goods stores with false fronts, clapboard houses with tin roofs to keep dry, shaded verandas to keep cool, and round clocks in the baroque tower of Sacred Heart Catholic Church.

The 360m (1,181-ft.) walls of basalt create a soaring backdrop to the town and put Ovalau in the big leagues of dramatic tropical beauty. The island has very little flat land and no decent beach, however, so it has not attracted resort or hotel development and is off the well-beaten tourist track.

Air Fiji (© 877/247-3454 in the U.S. or 672 2251 in Nadi; www.airfiji. com.fj) has an early-morning flight from Nausori airport to Buresala, on western Ovalau, and a late-afternoon flight back to Nausori. Rainy weather or delays can cause the late-afternoon flight to be canceled, so bring your toothbrush just in case. The round trip fare from Suva to Levuka is about F$128 (US$83/£42).

Patterson Shipping Services (© 331 5644; patterson@connect.com.fj) has bus-ferry connections from Suva to Buresala Landing. The airstrip and landing are 45-minute rides from Levuka, on very rough roads.

Begin your tour at the **Levuka Community Centre** (© 344 0356), where you can get information and explore the town's small but interesting history museum. The center occupies the quaint old **Morris Hedstrom** store built by Levukans Percy Morris and Maynard Hedstrom in 1878. Also check in next door with the German-operated **Ovalau Watersports** (© 344 0166;

If you're hankering for a Big Mac, head for the **McDonald's** on Victoria Parade at the northern edge of Sukuna Park. If it's bird you want, there's a **KFC** on Victoria Parade next to the General Post Office.

Hare Krishna Restaurant 🔆 *Value* VEGETARIAN INDIAN This clean, casual restaurant specializes in a wide range of very good vegetarian curries—eggplant, cabbage, potatoes and peas, okra, and papaya to name a few—each seasoned delicately and differently from the others. Interesting pastries, breads, side dishes, and salads (such as cucumbers and carrots in yogurt) cool off the fire set by some of the curries. The items are displayed cafeteria-style near the entrance to the second-floor dining room, or get the all-you-can-eat *thali* sampler and try a little of everything. Downstairs has an excellent yogurt and ice cream bar; climb the spiral stairs to reach the air-conditioned dining room. The Hare Krishnas allow no alcoholic beverages or smoking.

16 Pratt St., at Joske St. © 331 4154. Curries F$2–F$9 (US$1.30–US$5.85/65p–£3). No credit cards. Dining room Mon–Sat 11am–2:30pm. Downstairs snack bar Mon–Thurs 8am–7pm; Fri 8am–8pm; Sat 8am–3pm.

JJ's on the Park INTERNATIONAL On the harbor side of JJ's hotel, this lively bistro sports a Southwestern theme, but that's as far it goes; the menu here is curries

www.owlfiji.com), which, in addition to offering snorkeling tours and scuba diving (there are some terrific sites nearby, including a wreck in the harbor), arranges hiking excursions and tours. I highly recommend a stroll around town led by Ovalau-born Nox Wueti.

A waterside park at **Nasova** village, south of town past a smelly tuna cannery, commemorates Chief Cakobau's ceding Fiji to Great Britain in 1874. To the north, a British warship showed the Fijians how much firepower it packed in 1849 by shelling a headland known as **Gun Rock.** In between are many historic buildings, including **Levuka Public School,** founded in 1879 and still one of Fiji's best educational institutions.

Don't miss the **Royal Hotel** (✆ 344 0024; www.royallevuka.com), built around 1860. The basic but charming rooms in the old building all have private bathrooms (added in 1969). The Royal also has modern cottages out front.   The town's best digs are the four rooms in John and Marilyn Milesi's **Levuka Homestay** (✆ 344 0777; www.levukahomestay.com), which enjoys a marvelous view over the town. Newest are at **New Mavida Lodge** (✆ 344 0477; newmavidalodge@connect.com.fj), on Beach Street, where 11 air-conditioned motel-style rooms all have TVs and phones, and a 10-bed dorm is fan-cooled. A rustic backpacker option is **Mary's Holiday Lodge** (✆ 344-0013), also on Beach Street.

You get decent inexpensive meals at the **Whale's Tale Restaurant** (✆ 344 0235), in one of Beach Street's old stores, and **Levuka Pizza Restaurant** (✆ 344 0429), on the south end of downtown. **Westpac Bank** has an ATM. For advance information, go to **www.levukafiji.com.**

and other regional fare. Best bets are substantial servings of fish and chips, salads, steaks, and rack of lamb. At dinner check the specials board for the fresh fish of the day. The bar here is a good place to slake a thirst during your walking tour of Suva.

In JJ's on the Park, Stinson Parade, north side of Sukuna Park. ✆ 330 5005. Reservations recommended at dinner. Breakfast F$7.50–F$15 (US$4.85–US$9.75/£2.50–£3); burgers and salads F$12–F$18 (US$7.80–US$12/£4–£6); main courses F$18–F$39 (US$12–US$25/£6–£13). AE, DC, MC, V. Mon–Wed 7am–10pm; Thurs–Sat 7am–11pm (bar later).

L'Opera Ristorante Italiano ⭐⭐   ITALIAN   A long corridor hung with historic photographs leads to this elegant restaurant and Suva's most refined dining. The chef ranges up and down the Italian "boot" but always reflects a Tuscan origin. Dinners are served in Italian fashion, beginning with an *apertivo* drink, followed by antipasto, pasta, and a fish or meat *secondi* (main course). The weekday fixed price lunch is good value at F$29 (US$19/£9.65). There's an extensive Sunday brunch.

59 Gordon St. at Kimberly St. ✆ 331 8602. Reservations highly recommended. Pasta F$19–F$25 (US$12–US$16/£6.35–£8.35); main courses F$29–F$40 (US$19–US$26/£9.65–£13). AE, MC, V. Mon–Fri noon–2:30pm and 6–10pm; Sat 6–10pm.

Maya Dhaba *★★* *Finds* INDIAN   This chic, noisy Victoria Parade bistro is Suva's hottest and most urbane restaurant. Local couples and families all flock here for authentic Indian fare at reasonable prices. The menu runs the gamut of the Subcontinent, from Punjabi tandoori chicken tikka to vegetarian masala dosa (rice-flour pancakes wrapped crepelike around potato curry) from Madras. In fact, vegetarians will have many choices. My old standby, butter chicken, has a wonderful smoked flavor here. There's little guesswork, as the menu explains every dish.

281 Victoria Parade, between MacArthur and Loftus sts. (©) 331 0045. Reservations recommended. Main courses F$9–F$16 (US$5.85–US$10/£3–£5.35). MC, V. Daily 11am–3pm and 5:30–10pm.

Old Mill Cottage *★★★* *Value* FIJIAN/INDIAN/EUROPEAN   One of the few remaining late-19th-century homes left in Suva's diplomatic-government section, these adjoining two-room clapboard cottages offer some of the most extraordinary home cooking in the South Pacific. You'll order at the cafeterialike counters, one for breakfast, one for lunch. You'll have a choice of daily specials such as Fijian palusami, mild Indian curries, or European-style mustard-baked chicken with real mashed potatoes and peas. The vegetable plate is good value, as you can pick and choose from more than a dozen European, Fijian, and Indian selections. Diplomats (the U.S. Embassy is out the back door) and government executives pack the place at midday.

47–49 Carnavon St., near corner of Loftus St. (©) 331 2134. Breakfasts F$3–F$8 (US$1.95–US$5.20/£1–£2.65); meals F$2.50–F$9.50 (US$1.60–US$6.15/85p–£3.15). No credit cards. Mon–Fri 7am–6pm; Sat 7am–5pm.

Tiko's Floating Restaurant SEAFOOD/STEAKS   Locals like to take out-of-town guests to this floating restaurant, which served years ago with Blue Lagoon Cruises. One hopes they don't tend to seasickness, for the old craft does tend to roll a bit when freighters kick up a wake going in and out of the harbor. Your best bets are the seafood specials, such as *walu* (Spanish mackerel) and pakapaka (snapper). It's not the best in town, but the fish is fresh, the service is attentive, and Jesse Mucunabitu, a terrific musician-singer, usually performs at dinner—all of which makes for a pleasant night.

Stinson Parade at Sukuna Park. (©) 331 3626. Reservations recommended. Main courses F$17–F$40 (US$11–US$26/£5.65–£13). AE, MC, V. Mon–Fri noon–2pm and 6–10pm; Sat 6–10pm.

ISLAND NIGHTS IN SUVA

Nocturnal activities in Suva revolve around going to the movies and then hitting the bars—until the wee hours on Friday, the biggest night out.

Movies are a big deal, especially the first-run Hollywood and "Bollywood" Indian flicks at **Village 6 Cinemas,** on Scott Street at Nubukalou Creek, a modern, American-style emporium with six screens and a games arcade upstairs. Check the newspapers for what's playing and show times. You can pig out on popcorn, candy, and soft drinks. Locals flock here on Sunday afternoon, when these plush, air-conditioned theaters offer a comfortable escape from Suva's daytime heat and humidity.

Suva's most sophisticated pub for both slaking a thirst and having a meal is the **Bad Dog Cafe,** on Victoria Parade at MacArthur Street; (©) 331 2884). **Trap's Bar,** 305 Victoria Parade, north of Loftus Street ((©) 331 2922), is another popular watering hole where you're not likely to witness a fight. A band usually plays in the back room on weekends. **O'Reilly's,** on MacArthur Street off Victoria Parade ((©) 331 2968), is an Irish-style pub with Guinness stout and sports on TVs (and it can get a bit rough, depending on who's winning the rugby matches).

Victoria Parade has a number of loud discotheques frequented by the young, noisy crowd. Just walk along; you'll hear them.

6 Rakiraki & Northern Viti Levu

Few travelers will be disappointed by the scenic wonders on the northern side of Viti Levu. Cane fields climb valleys to green mountain ridges. Cowpokes round up cattle on vast ranches. Dramatic cliffs and spires bound a stunning bay. A narrow mountain road winds along the Wainibuka River, once called the "Banana Highway" because in preroad days Fijians used it to float their crops down to Suva on disposable bilibili rafts made of bamboo. A relatively dry climate beckons anyone who wants to catch a few rays, and there's great diving on the reefs off Viti Levu's northernmost point.

The **King's Road** runs for 290km (180 miles) from Nadi Airport around the island's northern side to Suva—93km (58 miles) longer than the Queen's Road to the south. The King's Road is paved all the way to Viti Levu Bay on the island's north side, but an unsealed portion through the central mountains can be treacherous. I would not drive through the mountains during the rainy season from November through April, when bridges can wash out, and never at night.

From Lautoka, it first crosses a fertile plain and then ascends into hills dotted with cattle ranches before dropping to the coast and entering the gorgeous **Ba Valley,** Fiji's most productive sugar-growing area. Populated mostly by Fiji Indians, this valley of steep hills is second only to Suva in population and economic importance. Many of the country's most successful businesses are in the town of **Ba,** a farming community on the banks of the muddy Ba River. Indeed, the commercial center of Ba is a mirror image of many towns in India. From Ba, the King's Road continues to **Tavua,** another predominantly Fiji Indian sugar town backed by its own smaller valley that reaches up to the mountains and the **Vatukoula Gold Mine.** Later it runs through the rolling hills of **Yaqara Cattle Ranch,** from whence Fiji gets its beef—and we get our Fiji-brand water.

The enchanting peaks of the **Nakauvadra Range** keep getting closer to the sea as you proceed eastward toward Rakiraki. Legend says the mountains are home to Degei, the prolific spiritual leader who arrived with the first Fijians and later populated the country. As the flat land is squeezed between foothills and sea, cane fields give way to the grasslands and mesas of the 17,000-acre Yaqara Estate, Fiji's largest cattle ranch. Offshore, conelike islands begin to dot the aquamarine lagoon.

Although everyone calls this area Rakiraki, the chief commercial town is actually **Vaileka,** about 1km (a half-mile) off the King's Road. Vaileka itself is home to the **Penang Mill,** the only one of Fiji's five sugar mills that produces solely for domestic consumption (the others export all their sugar). There also is a 9-hole **Penang Golf Course** near the mill, which visitors may play (arrange at the Rakiraki Hotel; see "Where to Stay in Rakiraki," below).

Rakiraki itself is a Fijian village (with the usual car-destroying road humps) on the King's Road, about 1km (a half-mile) past the Vaileka junction. It's home of the *Tui*

Fun Fact **900 Men for Dinner**

Just before you reach the well-marked junction of the King's Road and the Vaileka cut-off, look on the right for the **Grave of Udre Udre.** Legend says the stones at the base of the tombstone represent every one of the 900 men this renowned cannibal chief had for dinner.

Ra, the high Fijian chief of Ra district, which encompasses all of northern Viti Levu. He likes to stroll over to the Rakiraki Hotel, on the village's eastern boundary.

After the village, a paved road leads to **Ellington Wharf,** the jumping-off point for **Nananu-I-Ra,** a semiarid island about 15 minutes offshore, which has budget-priced retreats (see "Where to Stay in Rakiraki," below).

GETTING TO RAKIRAKI   Scheduled local and express buses run the entire length of the King's Road, as do unscheduled share taxis (see "Getting There & Getting Around," in chapter 4). From the Nadi side, the buses depart from the Lautoka Market. The hotels and backpackers' resorts provide their guests with transportation from Nadi (see "Where to Stay in Rakiraki," below).

SCUBA DIVING, WINDSURFING & OTHER WATER SPORTS

Although not as dramatic or scenic as in northern Fiji (see chapter 6), the reefs off northern Viti Levu are possessed of colorful soft corals, and they are relatively undiscovered. The top dive operators up here are **Kai Viti Divers** (✆ 669 3600; www.kaiviti divers.com), next to Wananavu Beach Resort, and **Ra Divers** (✆ 669 4622; www. ra-divers.com), at Volivoli Beach Resort (see below).

The strong trade winds, especially from June to August, put this area on the world's windsurfing maps, and **Ellington Wharf Water Sports Activity Center,** at Ellington Wharf (✆ 669 3333; www.safarilodge.com.fj), rents windsurfers and teaches lessons. It also has sea kayaks, Hobie Cats, snorkeling gear, and other toys, and leads guided kayak trips, most in connection with Safari Island Lodge (see "Nananu-I-Ra Island," below).

WHERE TO STAY IN RAKIRAKI

Tanoa Rakiraki Hotel 🏔   Frequented primarily by business travelers, this establishment is one of the few remaining colonial-era hotels in Fiji. The two clapboard roadside buildings were built as guesthouses when U.S. soldiers were stationed at an airstrip nearby during World War II. One houses a tongue-and-groove-paneled bar and dining room (with a very limited menu). The other has an old-fashioned hall down the middle with five rooms to either side. They have private bathrooms but not phones. Two rooms have four beds each, and are rented on a dormitory basis. Out in the back, three modern two-story motel blocks have 36 rooms outfitted to international standards, with air-conditioning units, phones, and tiled shower-only bathrooms. The staff will arrange excursions to Vaileka and to Fijian villages, horseback riding, golfing, scuba diving, and treks into the highlands.

P.O. Box 31, Rakiraki (Rakiraki village, on King's Rd., 2.5km/1½ miles east of Vaileka, 132km/82 miles from Nadi Airport). ✆ 800/448-8355 or 669 4101. Fax 669 4545. www.tanoahotels.com. 41 units. F$60–F$130 (US$39–US$84/ £20–£43) double; F$30 (US$19/£10) dorm bed. AE, DC, MC, V. **Amenities:** Restaurant; bar; outdoor pool; tennis court; babysitting; laundry service. *In room:* A/C (in most units), TV, fridge, coffeemaker.

Volivoli Beach Resort   Opened in 2005, this is the top backpacker place in Rakiraki. Its sand-floor restaurant and bar face a mangrove swamp, but they are just around a bend from one of Fiji's best beaches, a strip of sand leading directly into deep water (no tidal flat), with a great view across a bay to Viti Levu's mountains. Although more bungalows were being added, I found it with a lodge building containing four rooms (sharing two bathrooms) and 32 dorm beds, all on a hill with sea views.

P.O. Box 417, Rakiraki. ✆ 669 4511. Fax 669 4611. www.volivoli.com. 4 units, 32 dorm beds. F$100 (US$65/£33) double; F$25–F$27 (US$16–US$18/£8.35–£9) dorm bed. MC, V. All rates plus taxes. **Amenities:** Restaurant; bar; watersports equipment rentals; laundry service; coin-op washers and dryers. *In room:* No phone.

Wananavu Beach Resort   The area's most luxurious accommodations are here near Viti Levu's northernmost point. "Beach Resort" is a bit of a misnomer: The beach was created by removing a chunk of mangrove forest, leaving gray sand and a mud flat. Wananavu's prime appeal is to divers headed to the colorful reefs offshore, not to beach vacationers. The dining room, bar, and most of the duplex bungalows have fine ocean views. A few bures are down by the beach, but most occupy hillside perches.

P.O. Box 305, Rakiraki. ℂ **669 4433.** Fax 669 4499. www.wananavu.com. 31 units. F$220–F$450 (US$143–US$292/ £73–£150) double. AE, MC, V. Rates include breakfast. **Amenities:** Restaurant; bar; outdoor pool; tennis court; spa; babysitting; laundry service. *In room:* A/C, fridge, coffeemaker, no phone.

NANANU-I-RA ISLAND
Hilly, anvil-shaped Nananu-I-Ra island, a 15-minute boat ride from Ellington Wharf, has long been popular as a sunny retreat for local Europeans who own beach cottages there (the island is all freehold land), and three local families still own low-key resorts beside a fine beach: **Betham's Beach Cottages** (ℂ/fax **669 4132;** www.bethams. com.fj), **MacDonald's Nananu Beach Cottages** (ℂ **669 4633;** www.macsnananu. com), and **Charlie's Place** (ℂ **669 4676;** charlie's@connect.com.fj). On Nananu-i-Ra's exposed eastern side, **Safari Island Lodge** (ℂ **669 3333;** www.safarilodge.com.fj) takes advantage of the strong trade winds to specialize in windsurfing. All have cottages with kitchens as well as dining rooms and bars, and they charge about F$85 (US$55/£28) double for a room, F$125 (US$81/£42) for a bungalow, and F$28 (US$18/£9.35) for a dorm bed.

6

Northern Fiji: Savusavu & Taveuni

To me, the pristine islands of northern Fiji are what the old South Seas are all about. Compared to busy Viti Levu, "The North" takes us back to the old days of *copra* (dried coconut meat) planters and Fijians living in small villages in the hills or beside crystal-clear lagoons. You will feel the slow, peaceful pace of life up here as soon as you get off the plane.

The plains of northern **Vanua Levu,** the country's second-largest island, are of little interest to anyone who has visited Nadi. **Labasa,** a predominantly Indo-Fijian town and Vanua Levu's commercial center, reminds me of Gertrude Stein's quip about Oakland: "There is no there there."

But Vanua Levu's southern side is quite another story. Over here, rugged mountains drop to coconut plantations, to an old trading town with the singsong name **Savusavu** and villages where smiling people go about life at the ageless pace of tropical islands everywhere.

Across the Somosomo Strait lies **Taveuni,** Fiji's lush "Garden Isle," where the country's largest population of indigenous plants and animals makes things even more like they used to be. One of my favorite beachside inns resides on Taveuni, and I am a great fan of two off-shore resorts almost within hailing distance: on **Qamea** and **Matagi** islands.

The north is where I come to experience the natural wonders of Fiji—to "ecotour" in today's terminology. It's also where you'll find some of the world's best scuba diving, for the strong currents in and around the Somosomo Strait feed a vast collection of colorful soft corals. Northern Fiji is unsurpassed for coral viewing.

1 Savusavu ★★

Savusavu is Vanua Levu's major sightseeing attraction, primarily because of its volcanic hot springs and magnificent scenic harbor—a bay so large and well protected by surrounding mountains that the U.S. Navy chose it as a possible "hurricane hole" for the Pacific Fleet during World War II. Today it is one of Fiji's major sailing centers and a popular stop for cruising yachties, who can clear Customs and Immigration here. The blue waters of the bay also are home to Fiji's first black pearl farm.

The paved Cross-Island Road from Labasa runs along the eastern shore, through Savusavu town. From there, a rough road leads to **Lesiaceva Point** at the end of a peninsula forming the southern side of the bay and protecting it from the Koro Sea.

The **Hibiscus Highway** starts at Savusavu and cuts south across the hilly peninsula to the airstrip before continuing along the south shore to Buca Bay. Although 19km (12 miles) of it is paved, this road is neither a highway nor lined with hibiscus (grazing cows ate them all), but it does run along a picturesque, island-dotted lagoon

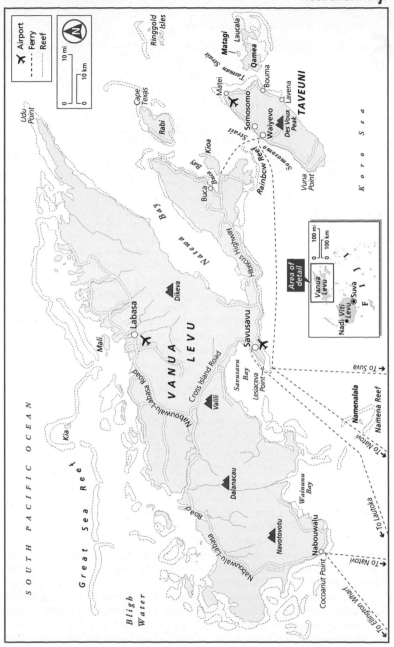

Legend:
- ✈ Airport
- - - - - Ferry
- · · · · · Reef

10 mi
10 km

N

Ringgold Isles

Cape Texas

Rabi

Udu Point

Laucala

Matagi

Qamea

Bouma

Matei

TAVEUNI

Somosomo

Waiyevo

Des Voux Peak

Lavena

Tasman Strait

Somosomo Strait

Rainbow Reef

Kioa

Buca Bay

Naviu Bay

Labasa

Dikeva

VANUA LEVU

Cross Island Road

Nabouwalu-Labasa Road

Valili

Savusavu

Savusavu Bay

Lesiaceva Point

Hibiscus Highway

Vuna Point

Koro Sea

SOUTH PACIFIC OCEAN

Great Sea Reef

Mali

Kia

Bligh Water

Nabouwalu-Labasa Road

Dalanacau

Wainunu Bay

Navotovotu

Nabouwalu

Cocoanut Point

Area of detail

100 mi
100 km

Vanua Levu

F I J I

Nadi Viti Levu

Suva

To Suva →

Namenalala

Namena Reef

← To Natovi

← To Lautoka

To Natovi →

← To Ellington Wharf

(Moments **The Way It Used to Be**

The old South Pacific of copra plantation and trading boat days still lives in Savusavu and Taveuni. It rains more in Fiji's north, but that makes the steep hills lushly green. The diving and snorkeling here are world-class.

---

through the heart of Vanua Levu's copra region. This area has one of Fiji's largest concentrations of freehold land, which Americans have been buying in recent years. So many Yanks have bought here, in fact, that some in Fiji facetiously refer to Savusavu as "Little America." Although you'll drive past thousands of coconut palms, there are now as many housing developments as copra plantations along the Hibiscus Highway.

The coastal plain here is primarily a raised limestone shelf, meaning that the reef is shallow and the beaches cannot hold a candle to the sands on Taveuni (see "Taveuni," later in this chapter). Keep that in mind as you plan your vacation.

GETTING TO SAVUSAVU

Air Fiji and **Pacific Sun** both fly from Nadi to Savusavu, and Air Fiji comes here from Suva. Air Fiji's flights between Nadi and Taveuni usually stop here briefly, so don't let your travel agent send you back to Nadi in order to get to Taveuni. The tiny Savusavu airstrip is on Vanua Levu's south coast. The hotels meet guests who have reservations.

Bligh Water Shipping Ltd. and **Venu Shipping Ltd.** operate ferries to Savusavu from Suva. **Patterson Shipping Services** has bus-ferry connections from Natovi Wharf (north of Suva on eastern Viti Levu) to Nabouwalu on Vanua Levu. You connect by bus from Suva to Natovi and from Nabouwalu to Labasa. Local buses connect Labasa to Savusavu.

See "Getting There & Getting Around," in chapter 4, for more information.

The small ferry *Amazing Grace* (© 927 1372 in Savusavu, 888 0320 on Taveuni) crosses the Somosomo Strait between Buca (*Boo*-tha) Bay and Taveuni 4 days a week. One-way fare is F$25 (US$16/£8.35), including the bus ride between Savusavu and Buca Bay. Call for schedules and reservations.

GETTING AROUND SAVUSAVU

Budget Rent-A-Car (© 800/527-0700 or 885 0377 in Savusavu, 672 2735 in Nadi; www.budget.com) and **Carpenters Rentals** (© 885 0122 in Savusavu, 672 2772 in Nadi; rentals@carpenters.com.fj) both have offices in Savusavu. **Trip n Tour,** a travel agency in the Copra Shed (© 885 3154; tripntours@connect.com.fj), rents bikes, scooters, cars, and SUVs. **Rock 'n Downunder Divers,** on the main street (© 885 3054; rockndownunder@connect.com.fj), rents bicycles.

An incredible number of **taxis** gather by the market in Savusavu. The cars of **Paradise Cab** (© 885 0018 or 956026), **Michael's Taxi** (© 995 5727) and **Blue Lagoon Cab** (© 997 1525) are air-conditioned. Fares from Savusavu are F$4.50 (US$2.95/£1.50) to the airstrip, F$7 (US$4.55/£2.35) to Namale Resort, F$12 (US$7.80/£4) to Koro Sun Resort, and F$6 (US$4/£2) to the Jean-Michel Cousteau Fiji Islands Resort on Lesiaceva Point.

Local buses fan out from the Savusavu market to various points on the island. Most of them make three or four runs a day to outlying destinations, but ask the drivers when they will return to town. The longest runs should cost about F$6 (US$3.90/£2), with local routes in the F55¢ to F$1 (US35¢–US65¢/18p–35p) range.

FAST FACTS: **Savusavu**

The following facts apply to Savusavu. If you don't see an item here, check "Fast Facts: Fiji," in chapter 4.

Currency Exchange **ANZ Bank, Westpac Bank,** and **Colonial National Bank** have offices with ATMs on the main street.

Emergencies In an emergency phone © **917** for police, © **911** for **fire** or **ambulance.** The **police station** (© **885 0222)** is east of town.

Healthcare **Dr. Joeli Taoi** has an office and pharmacy in the Palm Court shops (© **885 0721),** on the main street. The **government hospital** (© **885 0800)** is east of town, in the government compound.

Internet Access **Xerographic Solutions,** in the Copra Shed (© **885 3253),** has broadband access (and A/C!) for F10¢ (US7¢/3p) a minute.

Mail The post office is on the main street near the east of the downtown commercial district. It's open Monday to Friday 8am to 5pm and Saturday 8am to noon.

Safety Savusavu is a generally safe place to visit. Still, keep an eye on your personal belongings.

Visitor Information Best bet for local information is **Trip n Tour,** in the Copra Shed (© **885 3154),** a travel agency that arranges tours and rents bikes, scooters, and cars. You can find information on the Web at the Savusavu Tourism Association's site (www.fiji-savusavu.com).

Water The tap water in town and at the resorts is safe to drink.

EXPLORING SAVUSAVU

For practical purposes, Savusavu has only one street, and that runs along the shore for about 1.5km (1 mile). The modern **Copra Shed,** an old warehouse that has been turned into modern shops and a cafe, stands about midway along the shore. The airlines have their offices in the Copra Shed, along with the Savusavu Yacht Club and restaurants. A bit farther along is **Waitui Marina,** where cruising yachties come ashore.

Highlights of a stroll along the bay-hugging avenue are the gorgeous scenery and the volcanic **hot springs.** Steam from underground rises from the beach on the west end of town, and you can see more white clouds floating up from the ground between the sports field and the school, both behind the Shell station. A concrete pot has been built to make a natural stove in which local residents place meals to cook slowly all day. Overlooking the springs and bay, the **Savusavu Hot Springs Hotel** has great views (see "Where to Stay in Savusavu," below).

ORGANIZED TOURS

More than likely your hotel will have a choice of guided excursions in and around Savusavu. If not, **Trip n Tour,** in the Copra Shed (© **885 3154;** tripntours@ connect.com.fj), has a series of tours and excursions. One goes in search of red prawns, which grow in lakes on southeastern Vanua Levu, for F$55 (US$36/£18) per person. Another takes you to a copra and beef plantation, where you can see the modern-day version of the old South Seas coconut plantation. It costs F$35 (US$23/£12) per person. A full-day trip goes to **Waisali Rainforest Reserve,** a 116-hectare (287-acre) national forest up in the central mountains, which includes a hike to a waterfall. It costs F$125 (US$81/£42). Reservations are essential.

Rock 'n Downunder Divers, on the main street (© 885 3054; rockndownunder@ connect.com.fj), has half-day Fijian village visits for F$60 (US$39/£20). It also offers half- and full-day boat tours around Savusavu Bay for F$70 (US$45/£23) and F$120 (US$78/£40), respectively, and full-day cruises up a river on the bay's north shore for F$80 (US$52/£27).

SHOPPING IN SAVUSAVU

Marine biologist Justin Hunter spent more than 10 years working in the U.S. before coming home to Savusavu and founding Fiji's first black-pearl farm out in the bay. You can shop for the results—including golden pearls grown only here—at **J. Hunter Pearls** 🐟🐟, on the western end of town (© 885 0821; www.pearlsfiji.com). Prices range from F$20 up to F$2,000 (US$13–US$1,299/£6.65–£667) for loose pearls. Justin has them set in jewelry, too, as well as some interesting items made from the mother-of-pearl shells (I prize my salad forks made from gleaming shells with tree branch handles). Open Monday to Friday 8am to 5pm and Saturday 8am to 1pm. For F$25 (US$16/£8.35) you can take a 30-minute boat tour of the farm at 9:30am and 1:30pm weekdays.

The mother-son team of Karen and Shane Bower display their paintings and sculpture, respectively, at **The Art Gallery,** in the Copra Shed (© 885 3054). They also carry black pearls and shell jewelry. The gallery is open Monday to Friday 9:30am to 1pm and 2 to 4:30pm and Saturday 9:30am to 12:30pm. Next door, **Taki Handicrafts** (© 885 3956) sells woodcarvings, tapa cloth, shell jewelry, and items made in Fiji. It's open Monday to Friday 8am to 1pm and 2 to 4:30pm and Saturday 9:30am to noon. Another place to browse is the **Savusavu Municipal Market,** on main street (no phone), especially the handicraft stalls on the eastern side of the building. It's open Monday to Friday 7am to 5pm and Saturday 6:30am to 3pm.

MOUNTAIN BIKING, FISHING, SCUBA DIVING & SAILING

The beaches around Savusavu aren't the main reason to come here. The nearest beach to town is a shady stretch on Lesiaceva Point outside the Jean-Michel Cousteau Fiji Islands Resort, about 5km (3 miles) west of town, which is the end of the line for westbound buses leaving Savusavu market. There is a half-moon beach at **Naidi Bay,** an extinct volcanic crater, west of Namale Resort on the Hibiscus Highway. The road skirts the bay, but the beach is not easy to see. Take a taxi or ask the bus driver to let you off at Naidi Bay—not Naidi village or Namale Resort. The bar and restaurant at Namale Resort are for guests only, so bring something to drink and eat.

FISHING   Ika Levu Fishing Charters (© 944 8506; www.fishinginfiji.com) uses 24- and 41-foot boats for sport fishing excursions in the bays and offshore. Rates range from F$1,013 for half a day to F$1,688 (US$658–US$1,096/£338/£563) for a full day. Each boat can take up to four fishers.

MOUNTAIN BIKING   The best way to explore Vanua Levu's mountains by bike is on a tour offered by **Naveria Heights Lodge** (© 885 0348; www.naveriaheightsfiji. com), whose three modern bungalows all have views of Savusavu Bay as well as private bathrooms. Daily rates are F$125 (US$81/£42) double, including breakfast, but

> **Tips When to Go Diving in Northern Fiji**
>
> Diving in northern Fiji is best from late May through October, when visibility reaches 120 feet or more. Because of the strong currents, dives to such sites as the Great White Wall and Rainbow Reef can be strenuous any time of year.

they also offer "Adventure Weeks" for F$1,450 (US$942/£483) double, including meals and five biking and hiking excursions.

SCUBA DIVING & SNORKELING   A very long boat ride is required to dive on the Rainbow Reef and Great White Wall, which are more easily reached from Taveuni than from Savusavu. But that's not to say that there aren't plenty of colorful reefs near here, especially outside the bay. The beautifully preserved Namena Barrier Reef, a wonderful formation nearly encircling Moody's Namena (see "A Resort on Namenalala Island," below), is a 2½-hour ride away. Most of the resorts have complete diving facilities (see "Where to Stay in Savusavu," below).

In town, **Rock 'n Downunder Divers** (© **885 3054;** rockndownunder@connect.com.fj) has diving and snorkeling trips, teaches PADI diving courses, and rents snorkeling gear, kayaks, and bicycles.

Curly's Cruising/Bosun's Locker, on the main street opposite Waitui Marina (© **885 0122**), has snorkeling trips to reefs offshore for F$55 (US$36/£18) per person.

SAILING   Most sailboats vacate Savusavu during hurricane season from November through March, but a few stay, including *SeaHawk* **Yacht Charters** (© **885 0787;** www.seahawkfiji.com). The *SeaHawk* is a cruising yawl built for famed yacht designer Ted Hood in 1969. It can carry eight passengers and is used for half- and full-day sails, sunset cruises, and longer charters (3-day minimum). Rates range from US$150 to US$250 (£75–£125) per person per day plus food and beverages.

ADVENTURE CRUISES 🎇🎇🎇

Ecotourism takes to sea with **Active Fiji** (© **885 3032;** www.tuitai.com or www.activefiji.com), which uses the luxurious, 140-foot sailing schooner *Tui Tai* to make 7- and 10-day voyages from Savusavu. The boat goes to Taveuni, where you visit Bouma Falls; Kioa, where you spend time in that island's one village; and to Rabi Island, inhabited by Micronesians relocated here after World War II when their home island of Banaba (Ocean Island) was made uninhabitable by phosphate mining. Some cruises go into the Lau Group in eastern Fiji. The *Tui Tai* carries mountain bikes for land excursions and kayaks and dive and snorkel gear. The *Tui Tai* can accommodate 24 guests in air-conditioned cabins. Rates range from F$3,739 to F$8,722 (US$2,428–US$5,664/£1,246–£2,907) per person double occupancy, depending on length of voyage and stateroom, including all meals and activities.

WHERE TO STAY IN SAVUSAVU
EXPENSIVE

Jean-Michel Cousteau Fiji Islands Resort 🎇🎇🎇 *Kids*   The finest family resort in the South Pacific bears the name of Jean-Michel Cousteau (son of the late Jacques Cousteau), who convinced the owners that a tropical resort could be both environmentally friendly and profitable. It is indeed environmentally friendly, from wastewater treatment ponds inhabited by frogs (nature's mosquito control) to the lack of energy-guzzling air conditioners in most buildings. Its outstanding Bula Camp teaches children about the tropical environment. My cousin Eve Silverman, who was 9 years old and had never gone snorkeling or picked up a frog, did both and much more in the Bula Camp, and had great fun doing it. She was assigned a Fijian "buddy" during her stay. Children under 5 get full-time nannies at no extra cost. With the kids thoroughly occupied and mostly out of sight from 8:30am until 9pm, depending on their parents' wishes, this also is a fine couples' resort. Guests of any age can take part in environmentally oriented activities such as visits to rain and mangrove forests. An onsite marine biologist gives lectures and leads bird-watching expeditions and visits to Fijian villages. And divers are accompanied by guides skilled in marine biology.

The thatched-roof guest bures have ceiling fans to augment the natural breezes flowing through floor-to-ceiling wooden jalousie windows making up the front and rear walls. Most have porches strung with hammocks, and some of the smaller units have been enlarged to include a separate sleeping area, a plus for families. It's worth paying extra for more space and privacy in the split-level "villas" isolated at the end of the property. A award-winning honeymoon villa has its own swimming pool and a spa tub in its large bathroom. Only the honeymoon villa has a phone and is air-conditioned.

A full-service spa is planned; in the meantime, you can get massages and treatments in beachside bures, which become private dining venues after dark. Even the kids' cuisine is outstanding here.

Post Office, Savusavu (Lesiaceva Point, 5km/3 miles west of town). ℰ **800/246-3454** or 885 0188. Fax 885 0430. www.fijiresort.com. 25 units. US$575–US$2,200 (£288–£1,100) double. Rates include meals, soft drinks, airport transfers, and all activities except scuba diving. AE, MC, V. **Amenities:** Restaurant; bar; 3 outdoor pools; tennis court; watersports; scuba diving; children's program; activities desk; wireless Internet access (in main bldg.); limited room service; massage; babysitting; laundry service. *In room:* A/C (in honeymoon villa), minibar, coffeemaker, iron, safe, no phones (except honeymoon villa).

Koro Sun Resort   This property on Vanua Levu's southern coast has been upgraded in recent years by its American owners, who will sell you a piece of paradise and build a custom-designed home on it (the resort rents villas already built by its landowners). The Hibiscus Highway runs along the shoreline, separating the property from the lagoon. There is a bit of beach, and a swimming hole has been dredged into the shallow reef. A lagoonside restaurant and bar sit on a landfill by a marina, also blasted into the reef. Koro Sun sports two outdoor pools (the more attractive reserved for adults only), and a 9-hole, par-3 golf course. A dirt track leads around the golf course and through a rainforest to the resort's refreshing cascades, where there's a spa in two screened bungalows. On the way are six "Raintree Villas" beside one of the fairways; these units have two bedrooms, a bathroom, their own pools, and full kitchens. The land turns quickly from flat coastal shelf to hills, where most of the guest bungalows are perched, thus commanding views through the palms to the sea. All the hillside units have screened porches. One has a separate bedroom, another has two bedrooms. The octagonal honeymoon bure is the most deluxe and private. Down at sea level, the "garden" units lack views but have small yards behind picket fences, plus four-poster beds with mosquito nets. All bungalows have outdoor showers behind high rock walls.

Private Bag, Savusavu (Hibiscus Hwy., 16km/10 miles east of town). ℰ **877/567-6786** or 885 0262. Fax 885 0355. www.korosunresort.com. 24 units. US$320–US$550 (£160–275) bungalow, US$800–US$1,200 (£400–£600) villa. Rates include meals, nonmotorized watersports. AE, MC, V. **Amenities:** 2 restaurants; 2 bars; 2 outdoor pools; 9-hole golf course; 2 tennis courts; spa; complimentary mountain bikes, snorkeling gear, and sea kayaks; scuba diving; children's programs; massage; babysitting; laundry service. *In room:* A/C, TV (in villas), high-speed Internet access (in villas), kitchen (in villas), fridge, coffeemaker, no phone.

Namale Fiji Islands Resort & Spa *ϾϾϾ* Both luxurious and eclectic, this resort is owned by American motivational guru Anthony Robbins, who visits several times a year and conducts some of his "get-a-grip" seminars here (most participants sleep across the road, but those willing to pay a lot extra stay in the resort). Robbins obviously finds any dull moment distasteful, for he has built an air-conditioned gym with a wall-size TV for watching sports via satellite, an indoor basketball court, an electronic golf simulator, and a full-size bowling alley (really!). These indoor toys will come in handy, as the climate is borderline rainforest, and the pebbly beaches are not reason alone to spend your entire vacation here. Nevertheless, Namale has excellent scuba diving and deep-sea fishing (the only two activities costing an extra fee), plus windsurfing, horseback riding, and hiking. After all that, you can be pampered in the full-service spa, the most beautiful in Fiji. As my travel-writing friend John (Johnny Jet) DiScala once wisecracked, this is "the kind of place Americans come when they really don't want to leave home."

This area has been geologically uplifted, so all buildings are on a shelf 3 to 6m (10–20 ft.) above sea level. The guest quarters are scattered in the blooming tropical gardens, thus affording honeymoon-like privacy if not a setting beside the lagoon. Crown jewel is the "Dream House," a two-bedroom, two-bathroom minimansion with a kitchen, its own small pool, a whirlpool bathtub, and indoor and outdoor showers. Similarly equipped, the "Bula House" has one bedroom, but there are two guest bungalows outside, and it has a Jacuzzi on its deck. Both the Dream and Bula houses have drop-down movie screens with wraparound sound systems. Two more "Grand Villas" have their own pools, separate buildings for sleeping and living, and a treehouselike platform for lounging with sea views. Children can stay in these houses if they're at least 12 years old (they are allowed in the other bungalows only if you rent one just for them).

Among the bungalows, the deluxe honeymoon bure has its own swimming pool. Four more honeymoon bures have bathrooms with Jacuzzi tubs, separate showers with indoor and outdoor entrances, and their own ceiling fans. Six older bures are less spectacular, but are attractively appointed. If you're traveling solo, you can stay in one of these, but not in the larger units. You'll have a walkie-talkie instead of a phone.

P.O. Box 244, Savusavu (Hibiscus Hwy., 11km/6¾ miles east of town). (Ⓒ) 800/727-3454 or 885 0435. Fax 885 0400 or 619/535-6385 in the U.S. www.namalefiji.com. 15 bungalows, 3 houses. US$850–US$1,250 (£425–£625) double; US$1,950–US$2,100 (£975–£1,050) house. Rates include meals, drinks, all activities except spa services, scuba diving, and fishing. No children under 12 accepted. AE, MC, V. **Amenities:** Restaurant; 2 bars; 2 outdoor pools; tennis court; exercise room; Jacuzzi; watersports; free bikes; game room; spa; massage; free laundry service; basketball court. *In room:* A/C (in houses and deluxe bungalows), kitchen (in houses), minibar, coffeemaker, iron, safe, no phone.

INEXPENSIVE

Daku Resort *Ⓥalue* This former church camp is now owned by Britons John ("J.J.") and Delia Rothnie-Jones, who renovated all of its accommodations. They also use it as a base for a variety of educational courses such as creative writing, quilting, birdwatching, sketching, and gospel singing (see their website for more). The tin-roof accommodations, main building with restaurant and bar, and outdoor pool sit in a lawn across Lesiaceva Point Road from a small beach. Ranging from hotel rooms to three-bedroom houses, the units are simple but clean and comfortable. Two "lodge" rooms share hot-water showers; all other units have their own bathrooms, some with outdoor showers. Savusavu town is a 25-minute walk from here.

P.O. Box 18, Savusavu (Lesiaceva Point Rd., 2km/1¼ mile west of town). © 885 0046. Fax 885 0334. www.daku resort.com. 19 units (18 with bathroom). F$95–F$250 (US$62–US$162/£32–£83) double. AE, MC, V. **Amenities:** Restaurant; bar; outdoor pool; complimentary kayaks, canoes, and snorkel gear; wireless Internet access; babysitting; laundry service. *In room:* A/C (2 units), fridge, coffeemaker.

Savusavu Hot Springs Hotel *(Value*   Once a Travelodge, this three-story structure sits on a hill in town, and its motel-style rooms grab the view through glass doors opening to balconies. Units on the third and fourth floors have the best vantage. The less-expensive rooms on the lower levels are equipped with ceiling fans but lack air conditioners. Ground-floor rooms are devoted to dormitory-style accommodation, which makes this my local backpacker's choice. Most of these have double beds, while two are equipped with four bunk beds each. The **Decked Out Restaurant** serves all meals and opens to an outdoor pool surrounded by a deck overlooking the bay. This isn't a fancy establishment, but it's clean, comfortable, friendly, and a very good value.

P.O. Box 208, Savusavu (in town). © 885 0195. Fax 885 0430. www.hotspringsfiji.com. 48 units. F$95–F$125 (US$62–US$81/£32–£42) double; F$35 (US$23/£12) dorm bed. AE, MC, V (plus 4%). **Amenities:** Bar; outdoor pool; babysitting; laundry service; coin-op washers and dryers. *In room:* A/C (most units), fridge, coffeemaker.

COTTAGE RENTALS

As on Taveuni (see "Where to Stay on Taveuni," later in this chapter), a number of expatriates have purchased land and built homes in or near Savusavu. Some live here permanently and have constructed rental cottages on their properties. One is **Tropic Splendor** (© 851 0152 or 991 7931; www.tropic-splendor-fiji.com), on the north shore of Savusavu Bay, a 20-minute drive from town. Deserting the deserts of New Mexico, owners Susan Stone and Jeffery Mather relocated to this lush setting in 2001, and they make sure you have all the comforts of home in their guest bungalow beside a beach of powdery cocoa-color sand. It has ceiling fans, a TV with DVD player, wireless Internet access, a king-size bed, a big wraparound porch with hammock, outdoor shower, and other amenities. They charge F$360 (US$234/£120) per day, with discounts for longer stays. They accept MasterCard and Visa credit cards.

Another is **Fiji Beach Shacks** (© 885 1002; www.fijibeachshacks.com), whose "House of Bamboo" between town and Lesiaceva Point is anything but a shack. This two-level, two-bedroom, two-bathroom luxury home is perched high on a hill overlooking Savusavu Bay. You can dip in the outdoor pool. Rates are F$225 (US$146/£75) double per night, with a 3-night minimum stay required.

A RESORT ON NAMENALALA ISLAND

Covered with dense native forest and bush, dragon-shaped Namenalala is a 45-hectare (110-acre) rocky ridge protruding from the Koro Sea about 32km (20 miles) south of Vanua Levu. The huge Namena barrier reef sweeps down from Vanua Levu and surrounds it with a gorgeous lagoon, which is an officially protected marine reserve. A large colony of boobies nest on the island, and **sea turtles** climb onto some of the South Pacific's most gorgeous beaches to lay their eggs from November through February.

Moody's Namena *Value*   Originally from Pennsylvania, Tom and Joan Moody (she pronounces her name "Joanne") opened this peaceful, remote resort in 1986. The Moodys have perched all but one of their comfortable bungalows up on the ridge so that they have views of the ocean but not of one another. The walls of the hexagonal structures slide back to offer both views and cooling breezes, so you will sleep under a mosquito net. Solar power runs the reading lights and fans, but you won't be able to plug in your hairdryer or shaver. Instead of treading sandy paths among palm trees, you climb crushed-rock pathways along the wooded ridge to the central building, where the Moodys provide excellent meals. They serve wine with dinner and sell beer, but they do not have a license, so bring some duty-free booze if you drink spirits. OCCUPIED/UNOCCUPIED signs warn guests that someone else is already cavorting on four of the island's five private beaches. Other activities include hiking, kayaking, swimming, snorkeling, deep-sea fishing, and scuba diving among the colorful reefs and sea turtles. Tom does not teach scuba, so you must be certified in advance. The Moodys will have you brought out from Savusavu on a fast sportfishing boat, a voyage of 1½ hours, or arrange to charter a seaplane for the 1-hour flight from Nadi.

Private Mail Bag, Savusavu. ℃ 881 3764. Fax 881 2366. www.moodysnamenafiji.com. 6 units. US$1,375 (£688) per person double occupancy for 5-night minimum stay (required). Rates include meals, boat transfers from Savusavu, all activities except scuba diving. MC, V. Closed Mar–Apr. No children under 16 accepted. **Amenities:** Restaurant; bar; game room; massage; laundry service. *In room:* Coffeemaker, no phone.

WHERE TO DINE IN SAVUSAVU

Bula-Re Cafe ℛ INTERNATIONAL   For the money, this German-operated restaurant facing the harbor serves some of the best food in town. That's especially true of its awesome toasted sesame-seed salad dressing. The house special is chicken schnitzel-style, but the menu ranges all over the world, from British fish and chips to Fijian *palusami*. Spicy Indian-style curry prawns with almond rice will excite your taste buds. Vegetarians will have several choices here, including veggie pasta with a spicy cheese and curry sauce. Wednesday is *lovo* night here, featuring a buffet of earth-oven Fijian foods for F$17 (US$11/£5.65) per person. You can get an espresso or latte to accompany breakfast or to recharge later on.

Main street, east end of town opposite the post office. ℃ 885 0377. Reservations recommended for dinner. Breakfast F$5–F$7 (US$3.25–US$4.55/£1.65–£2.35); main courses F$7.50–F$19 (US$4.85–US$12/£2.50–£6.35). No credit cards. Mon–Sat 9am–9:30pm; Sun 5–10pm.

Captain's Cafe INTERNATIONAL   With seating inside the Copra Shed or outside on a deck over the bay, this cafe is a pleasant place for a morning coffee, an outdoor lunch, and good steaks at dinner. Fresh fish is surprisingly good, too, especially the mahimahi in lemon butter. Other offerings are sandwiches, burgers, side salads, garlic bread, and reasonably good pastas and pizzas.

Main street, in the Copra Shed. ℃ 885 0511. Breakfast F$4–F$8 (US2.60–5.20/£1.35–£2.65); burgers and sandwiches F$8–F$12 (US$5.20–US$7.80/£2.65–4); pizza F$10–F$24 (US$6.50–US$16/£3.35–£8); main courses F$9–F$11 (US$5.85–US$7.15/£3–£3.65). No credit cards. Daily 7:30am–10:30pm.

Surf 'n' Turf ℛℛ INTERNATIONAL   Formerly a chef at Jean-Michel Cousteau Fiji Islands Resort, Vijendra Kumar now puts his skills to good use at this waterfront restaurant in the Copra Shed. As the name implies, a combination of steak and tropical lobster tail leads the list here, often accompanied by *ota miti*, the young shoots of the wood fern, my favorite Fijian vegetable. Vijendra also cooks very good Indian curries. His specialty is a six-course dinner cooked at your bayside table.

Main street, in Copra Shed. ℃ 881 0966. Reservations required for fixed-priced dinner. Main courses F$12–F$50 (US$7.80–US$32/£4–£17); fixed course dinner F$50 (US$32/£17) No credit cards. Daily 10am–2pm and 6–10pm.

ISLAND NIGHTS IN SAVUSAVU

The resorts provide nightly entertainment for their guests. Otherwise, there's not much going on in Savusavu except at one local nightclub, which I have not had the courage to sample, and three local drinking establishments, which I have. Step back in time at **The Planter's Club** ℛ (℃ 885 0233), an ancient clapboard building near the western end of town. It's a friendly holdover from the colonial era, with a snooker table and a bar, where you can order a cold young coconut (add gin or rum, and you've got a genuine island cocktail). It's open Monday to Thursday 10am to 10pm, Friday and Saturday 10am to 11pm, and Sunday 10am to 8pm. You'll be asked to sign the club's register.

Yachties and the numerous expatriates who live here congregate at the wharfside bars of the **Savusavu Yacht Club,** in the Copra Shed (ⓒ **885 0685**), and the nearby **Waitui Club** (ⓒ **885 0536**), upstairs at Waitui Marina. The yacht club is open Monday to Saturday 10am to 10pm and Sunday noon to 10pm. Waitui Club is open Monday to Thursday 10am to 8pm, and Friday and Saturday 10am to 11pm.

2 Taveuni ★★★

One of my favorite places to hang out in Fiji, cigar-shaped Taveuni, the country's third-largest island, lies 6.5km (4 miles) from Vanua Levu's eastern peninsula across the Somosomo Strait, one of the world's most famous scuba-diving spots. Although the island is only 9.5km (6 miles) wide, a volcanic ridge down Taveuni's 40km (25-mile) length soars to more than 1,200m (3,937ft.), blocking the southeast trade winds and pouring as much as 10m (30 ft.) of rain a year on the mountaintops and the island's rugged eastern side. Consequently, Taveuni's 9,000 residents (three-fourths of them Fijians) live in a string of villages along the gently sloping, less-rainy but still lush western side. They own some of the country's most fertile and well-watered soil—hence Taveuni's nickname: The Garden Isle.

Thanks to limited land clearance and the absence of the mongoose, Taveuni is the best place in Fiji to explore the interior on foot. It still has all the plants and animals indigenous to Fiji, including the unique Fiji fruit bat, the Taveuni silktail bird, land crabs, and some species of palm that have only recently been identified. The **Ravilevu Nature Preserve** on the east coast and the **Taveuni Forest Preserve** in the middle of the island are designed to protect these rare creatures.

With dozens of fabulous dive sites, including the Rainbow Reef and its Great White Wall, Taveuni also is the best place to explore Fiji's soft coral underwater paradise.

The little airstrip and most of Taveuni's accommodations are at **Matei,** on the northeastern corner of the island facing the small, rugged islands of **Qamea** and **Matagi,** homes of two of my favorite little offshore resorts (see "Resorts on Qamea & Matagi Islands," later in this chapter).

GETTING TO TAVEUNI & GETTING AROUND
Both **Air Fiji** and **Pacific Sun** fly to Taveuni from Nadi, and Air Fiji has service from Suva and Savusavu. The hotels send buses or hire taxis to pick up their guests.

Tips **Rough Road**

Budget Rent-A-Car (ⓒ 800/527-0700 or 888 0291; www.budget.com) has an agency on Taveuni, but I always hire a taxi and driver rather than a vehicle here. Taveuni's main road, which runs along the west and north coasts, is paved between Waiyevo and Matei, but elsewhere it's rough gravel, winding, often narrow, and at places carved into sheer cliffs above the sea. A taxi and driver cost about F$150 (US$98/£50) for a full day, or about the same as a rental with insurance and gas.

The ferries from Suva stop at Savusavu before arriving at Waiyevo, and the small *Amazing Grace* crosses the Somosomo Strait between Waiyevo and Buca Bay daily.

See "Getting to Savusavu," earlier in this chapter, and "Getting There & Getting Around," in chapter 4, for details.

Taxis don't ply the roads here, but your hotel staff can call one. I have been satisfied with **Taveuni Island Tours** (© **888 0221**), **Nan's Taxi** (© **888 0705**), and **Ishwar's Taxi** (© **888 0464**). None of the taxis have meters, so negotiate for a round-trip price if you're going out into the villages and having the driver wait for you. The official fare from the airstrip is F$2 (US$1.30/65p) to Maravu Plantation and Taveuni Island resorts, F$17 (US$11/£5.65) to Bouma Falls, and F$20 (US$13/£6.65) to Navakoca (Qamea) Landing, or Waiyevo.

Local **buses** fan out from Waiyevo to the outlying villages about three times a day from Monday to Saturday. For example, a bus leaves Waiyevo for Bouma at 8:30am, 12:15pm, and 4:30pm. The one-way fare is no more than F$4 (US$2.60/£1.35). Contact **Pacific Transport** (© **888 0278**) opposite Kaba's Supermarket in Nagara.

Coconut Grove Beachfront Cottages, in Matei (©/fax **888 0328**), rents bicycles for F$25 (US$16/£8.35) a day. See "Where to Stay on Taveuni," below.

FAST FACTS: Taveuni

The following facts apply to Taveuni. If you don't see an item here, see "Fast Facts: Fiji," in chapter 4.

Currency Exchange **Colonial National Bank** has an office and an ATM at Nagara (© **888 0433**). It's open Monday to Friday 9:30am to 4pm.

Electricity The resorts and hotels have their own generators because only Taveuni's villages have public electricity. Most generators are 220 volts but a few are 110 volts, so ask before plugging in your electric shaver.

Emergencies In an emergency phone © **917** for the **police,** © **911** for **fire** or **ambulance.** The **police station** (© **888 0222**) is in the government compound. Taveuni is relatively safe, but exercise caution if you're out late.

Healthcare The **government hospital** (© **888 0222**) is in the government compound in the hills above Waiyevo. To get there, go uphill on the road opposite the Garden Island Resort, then take the right fork.

Internet Access **Lani's Digital Services,** in Nagara opposite Colonial National Bank (© **888 0259**), has Internet access for F$1.20 (US80¢/40p) each 10 minutes. It also will burn your digital photos to CDs. It's open Monday to Saturday 7am to 7pm.

Mail The post office is in Waiyevo. It's open Monday to Friday 8am to 4pm and Saturday 8am to noon.

Water The tap water is safe to drink only at the hotels on Taveuni.

EXPLORING TAVEUNI

Taveuni is famous for shallow **Lake Tagimaucia** (*Tangi*-maw-thia), home of the rare *tagimaucia* flower bearing red blooms with white centers. Its sides ringed with mud

---

Moments **Yesterday & Today**

The 180th Meridian would have been the International Date Line were it not for its dividing the Aleutians and Fiji into 2 days, and for Tonga's wish to be on the same day as Australia. Even so, I love to stand here on Taveuni with one of my feet in today, the other in yesterday.

---

flats and thick vegetation, the lake sits in the volcanic crater of **Des Voeux Peak** at more than 800m (2,625 ft.) altitude. It's a rare day when clouds don't shroud the peak.

The three-level **Bouma Falls** are among Fiji's finest and most accessible waterfalls, and the area around them is included in the **Bouma National Heritage Park** (see below). Past Bouma at the end of the road, a sensational coastal hiking track begins at **Lavena** village and runs through the Ravilevu Nature Reserve.

By tradition, Taveuni's **Somosomo** village is one of Fiji's most "chiefly" villages; that is, its chief is one of the highest-ranking in all of Fiji, and the big meeting house here is a prime gathering place of Fiji's Great Council of Chiefs. Although Somosomo has a modern Morris Hedstrom supermarket, the predominately Indo-Fijian **Nagara** village next door is the island's commercial center.

The village of **Waiyevo** sits halfway down the west coast. A kilometer (half-mile) south, a brass plaque marks the **180th Meridian** of longitude, exactly halfway around the world from the Zero Meridian in Greenwich, England. In addition to the aptly named Meridian Cinema, the village of **Waikiki** sports the **Wairiki Catholic Mission,** built in the 19th-century to reward a French missionary for helping the locals defeat a band of invading Tongans. There's a painting of the battle in the presbytery.

The main road is rough, slow-going gravel from Wairiki to **Vuna Point** on Taveuni's southeastern extremity. On the way it passes **Taveuni Estates,** a real estate development with a 9-hole golf course (you, too, can own a piece of this paradise).

BOUMA NATIONAL HERITAGE PARK 𝕮𝕮𝕮

One attraction on everyone's list is **Bouma National Heritage Park** (© 888 0390) on Taveuni's northeastern end, 18km (11 miles) from the airstrip, 37km (23 miles) from Waiyevo. The government of New Zealand provided funds for the village of Bouma to build trails to the three levels of **Bouma Falls**. It's a flat, 15-minute walk along an old road from the visitor center to the lower falls, which plunge some 20m (66 ft.) into a broad pool. From there, a trail climbs sharply to a lookout with a fine view of Qamea and as far offshore as the Kaibu and Naitoba islands east of Taveuni. The trail then enters a rainforest to a second set of falls, which are not as impressive as the lower cascade. Hikers ford slippery rocks across a swift-flowing creek while holding onto a rope. This 30-minute muddy climb can be made in shower sandals, but be careful of your footing. A more difficult track ascends to yet a third falls, but I've never followed it, and people who did have told me it isn't worth the effort.

Another trail, the **Vidawa Rainforest Walk,** leads to historic hill fortifications and more great views. Guides lead full-day treks through the rainforest, but you'll need to book at your hotel activities desk or call the visitor center (© **888 0390**) at least a day in advance. The trek ends at Bouma Falls. The hikes cost F$60 (US$39/£20) for adults, F$40 (US$26/£13) for children 12 to 17.

The park is open daily from 8am to 5pm. Admission is F$8 (US$5.20/£2.65) per person without a guide, F$15 (US$9.75/£5) with a guide. See "Getting to Taveuni & Getting Around," above, for information about how to get here.

HIKING *$$$*

In addition to the short walks in the Bouma National Heritage Park (see above), three other treks are worth doing, depending on the weather. The relatively dry (and cooler) season from May to September is the best time to explore Taveuni on foot.

Best of all is the **Lavena Coastal Walk** *$$$*. It follows a well-worn, easy-to-follow trail from the end of the road past the park for 5km (3 miles), then climbs to **Wainibau Falls.** The last 20 minutes or so of this track are spent walking up a creek bed, and you'll have to swim through a rock-lined canyon to reach the falls (stay to the left, out of the current). The creek water is safe to drink, but bring your own bottled water. You can do it on your own, but it's a much more rewarding to go with a Bouma National Heritage Park guide for F$60 (US$39/£20) adults, F$40 (US$26/£13) children 12 to 17, including the F$12 (US$7.80/£4) per-person admission you would otherwise have to pay to the village and walking track. Sitting on a peninsula, Lavena village has one of Taveuni's best beaches and a lodge where hikers can overnight for F$25 (US$16/£8.35) per person (② **923 9080;** ask for Maria).

An alternative to walking is to ride a boat along this spectacular coast with **Lavena Coastal Tour** (② **920 5834**). This half-day excursion costs F$50 (US$32/£17) per person and includes a picnic lunch at a waterfall. If the sea is calm, you may get to see **Savulevu Yavonu Falls,** which plunge precipitously into the sea.

High in the center of the island, a rough leads to the top of **Des Voeux Peak** and **Lake Tagimaucia,** home of the famous flower that blooms from the end of September to the end of December. This crater lake is surrounded by mud flats and filled with floating vegetation. Beginning at Somosomo village, the hike to the lake takes about 8 hours round-trip. The trail is often muddy and slippery, and given the usual cloud cover hanging over the mountains by midmorning, you're not likely to see much when you reach the top. Only hikers who are in shape should make this full-day trek. You must pay a F$25 (US$16/£8.35) per person "custom fee" to visit the lake, which includes a guide—an absolute necessity. Your hotel will make the arrangements. An alternative is to take a four-wheel-drive vehicle up Des Voeux Peak for a look down at the lake. The drive is best done early in the morning, when the mountain is least likely to be shrouded in clouds.

SCUBA DIVING, SNORKELING & OTHER OUTDOOR ACTIVITIES

The hotels and resorts will arrange all of Taveuni's outdoor activities, although you should book at least a day in advance.

FISHING   Two charter boats will take you in search of big game fish offshore: American John Llanes's **Makaira Charters** (② **888 0686;** makaira@connect.com.fj) and New Zealander Geoffrey Amos's **Matei Game Fishing** (② **888 0371**). They charge about US$325 (£163) for half a day, US$525 (£263) for a full day for up to four fishers. Call for reservations, which are required.

GOLF   **Taveuni Estates,** about 7km (4¼ miles) southeast of 180th Meridian, has a scenic 9-hole golf course skirting the island's eastern shore. Reserve at the clubhouse (② **888 0044**), which serves lunch and has a bar. The greens fee is F$40 (US$26/£13), including clubs and a pizza.

HORSEBACK RIDING   Maravu Plantation Beach Resort & Spa (© 888 0555) has horseback riding along a trail leading to the resort's wedding chapel on a ridge with views of both sides of Taveuni. **Vatuwiri Farm Resort** (© 888 0316; www.vatuwirifiji.com) also has horses. See "Where to Stay on Taveuni," below.

JET-SKIING   **Paradise Taveuni** (© 888 0125; www.paradiseinfiji.com) has jet-skiing expeditions across the Somosomo Strait to Vanua Levu, a 45-minute ride each way. These cost F$400 (US$260/£133) per person, including lunch. Reserve at least 2 days in advance. See "Where to Stay on Taveuni," below.

KAYAKING   It's great fun to kayak to the three little rocky islets off the north shore, near the airstrip. You can land on the islands for a bring-your-own picnic. **Coconut Grove Beachfront Cottages & Restaurant** (© 888 0328), opposite the airstrip (see "Where to Stay on Taveuni," below), rents two-person ocean kayaks for F$35 (US$23/£12) per half-day, F$55 (US$36/£18) all day. Owner Ronna Goldstein will prepare a picnic lunch, with advance notice.

You can also rent kayaks and outrigger canoes from **Little Dolphin,** in Matei east of the airport (© 888 0130; www.littledolphinontaveuni.com), for F$25 (US$16/£8.35) per day. It's across the main road from the lagoon.

SCUBA DIVING 🐠🐠🐠   The swift currents of the Somosomo Strait feed the soft corals on the Rainbow Reef and its White Wall between Taveuni and Vanua Levu, making this one of the world's most colorful and famous dive sites. A diver I met said, "It's like when you buy a pack of coloring pencils, except there aren't enough colors."

The Rainbow Reef and its Great White Wall are only 4 miles off Waiyevo, so the Garden Island Resort (see "Where to Stay on Taveuni," below) is the closest dive base, a 20-minute boat ride across the Somosomo Strait. The U.S. firm **Aqua-Trek** (© 800/541-4334 or 888 0286; www.aquatrek.com) manages the resort and has its dive base here. This five-star PADI operation has full equipment rental, NITROX, and teaches courses from beginner to dive master. Aqua-Trek's prices start at F$165 (US$107/£55) for a two-dive excursion.

With offices at Taveuni Estates and Wairiki, Carl Fox's **Taveuni Dive** (© 866/217-3438 or 888 0063; www.taveunidive.com) also is within reach of the Rainbow Reef. Carl charges US$95 (£48) for a two-tank dive.

At Matei on the northern end of Taveuni are Fijian-owned **Jewel Bubble Divers** (© 888 2080; www.jeweldivers.com) and **Unibokoi Divers** (© 888 0560; www. tovutovu.com).

Based at Paradise Taveuni on the island's southeastern end (see "Where to Stay on Taveuni," below), **Pro Dive Taveuni** (© 888 0125; www.paradiseinfiji.com) specializes in diving the Vuna Lagoon, which has less soft corals but bigger fish.

SNORKELING & SWIMMING   If they aren't too busy with serious divers, most of the scuba operators will take snorkelers along. For example, **Aqua-Trek,** at the Garden

---

⌒Tips It All Depends on the Tides

Because of the strong currents in the Somosomo Strait, dives on Taveuni's most famous sites must be timed according to the tides. You can't count on making the dives you would like if the tides are wrong. A friend of mine spent 10 days on Matagi and Qamea islands and never got out to Rainbow Reef.

> ### ⌒Tips   Beware of "Jaws"
>
> Ancient legend says that Taveuni's paramount chief is Fiji's highest ranking because sharks protect the island from enemies. True or not, shark attacks have occurred here, so be careful when you're swimming and snorkeling in the Somosomo Strait, and don't, under any circumstances, swim out to the edge of the reef. Swim and snorkel between 9am and 3pm to minimize the risk.

Island Resort, has snorkeling trips to **Korolevu,** a rocky islet off Waiyevo (be careful out there, for the currents can be very strong). The company will even take you snorkeling out to the Rainbow Reef, but book these trips well in advance.

You can also snorkel from a Fijian *bilibili* (bamboo raft) over the **Waitabu Marine Park** (ⓒ 888 0451), a preserved reef which is part of Bouma National Heritage Park. These half-day *bilibili* ventures cost F$40 (US$26/£13) per person for four or more, F$20 (US$13/£6.65 for snorkeling only.

Some of the best do-it-yourself snorkeling is at the foot of the cliff off **Tramontu Bar & Grill** (see the "Where to Dine on Taveuni" section), and the three little rocky islets off the north shore, near the airstrip, provided kelp from the nearby seaweed farms isn't drifting by. Also good for both snorkeling and swimming are **Prince Charles Beach, Valaca Beach,** and the lovely, tree-draped **Beverly Beach,** all south of the airstrip.

A fun outing is to **Waitavala Sliding Rocks,** near Waiyevo (no phone), where you can literally slide over the rocks down a freshwater cascade. Be prepared to get a few bruises! The rocks are off the side road leading to Waitavala Estates. Admission is free.

WHERE TO STAY ON TAVEUNI

The majority of Taveuni's accommodations are near the airstrip at Matei, on the island's northeastern corner. A few small planes arrive and depart about 9:30am and again about 2:30pm, so it's not like you're under the flight path of an international airport. I like to stay here because I can walk to the airstrip-area hotels and restaurants in no more than 20 minutes. Elsewhere you can't go out to lunch or dinner this easily.

AT MATEI

Other inexpensive options in Matei include **Little Dolphin** (ⓒ 888 0130; www. littledolphinontaveuni.com), where one upstairs unit rents for F$100 (US$65/£33) a night; and **Bibi's Hideaway** (ⓒ 888 2014 or 888 0443), where retired teacher Jim Bibi has a variety of bungalows for F$50 to F$100 (US$32–US$65/£17–£33), a dorm at F$25 (US$16/£8.35) per bed, and campsites at F$15 (US$9.75/£5) per person, all in a coconut grove. Jim does not accept credit cards.

Coconut Grove Beachfront Cottages 🌴🌴🌴 *Value*   Ronna Goldstein, who named this little gem not for the palm trees growing all around it but for her hometown in Florida, has three bures set beside a fine beach next to her restaurant (see "Where to Dine on Taveuni," below). Ronna lives here, and the restaurant is on her big, breezy front porch with a terrific view of the sea and offshore islets. You can dine here or down by the beach. Next door, her Mango cottage has a great sea view from its front porch. Down below, her Banana bure lacks the great view, but it's right by the beach and is more private. Almost on the beach, the Papaya bure is the smallest, but it's also the most private. All three have CD players and outdoor showers. Ronna's veteran staff will make you feel right at home, while Sophia, her friendly Doberman, is in charge of guest relations. Your children younger than 7 won't be petting Sophia, however, as they are not accepted here. Ronna provides complimentary kayaks, snorkeling fins (bring your own mask), a half-hour massage, and village visits. This is one of Fiji's great values.

Postal Agency, Matei, Taveuni (opposite airstrip). ©/fax **888 0328**. www.coconutgrovefiji.com. 3 units. US$155–US$195 (£78–£98) double. Rates include tropical breakfast, afternoon tea and 30-min. massage. MC, V. No children under 7 accepted. **Amenities:** Restaurant; bar; bicycle rentals; massage; laundry service. *In room:* CD player, fridge, no phone.

Maravu Plantation Beach Resort & Spa ✿ *Value*   Although it has its own lovely beach across the road (a 5-min. downhill walk), this unusual retreat is set among 90 acres of palms on a former copra plantation. Most of the bures are laid out among grounds carefully planted with bananas, papayas, and a plethora of ginger plants and wild orchids. This plantation setting means the property can get warm and humid during the day. Built in the style of South Seas planters' cottages, the guest bungalows have thatch-covered tin roofs and reed or mat accents that lend a tropical ambience. Situated about 5 minutes away from the main complex via wooden walkways spanning a small valley, six units have sea views and outdoor Jacuzzis. Nearby is the crown jewel, a treehouse bungalow. Four honeymoon bures have four-person-size whirlpool tubs under their outdoor showers, while four more honeymoon suites feature two rooms, outdoor showers, Jacuzzis, and sun decks surrounded by rock privacy walls. Only the older, "planters bures" don't have outdoor showers. With an emphasis on very good "nouvelle Fijian" cuisine, the dining room is under the high thatched roof and looks out to the lawns and a pool surrounded by an expansive deck. Wine lovers are in for a treat here, for owner Jochen Kiess, a former German lawyer, has accumulated a fine list. Because most of Maravu isn't directly on the beach, Jochen doesn't charge an arm and a leg, which makes it a good value. You can go horseback riding here.

Postal Agency, Matei, Taveuni (1km/½ mile south of airstrip). © **866/528-3864** or 888 0555. Fax 888 0600. www.maravu.net. 21 units. US$130–US$325 (£65–£163) per person, double occupancy. Rates include full breakfast. AE, DC, MC, V. **Amenities:** Restaurant; bar; outdoor pool; exercise room; spa; free bicycles; activities desk; limited room service; babysitting; laundry service. *In room:* A/C, minibar, coffeemaker, no phone.

Nakia Resort & Dive   Jim and Robin Kelly were stuck in a traffic jam in Hawaii one morning when they decided to relocate to Taveuni and build this resort in a coconut grove with a view of Somosomo Strait. Their restaurant, with excellent home cooking utilizing produce from an organic garden, overlooks a swimming pool and is flanked by plantation-style guest bungalows. Three of them have queen beds suited to couples, while the larger family unit has king and double beds. All have porches with hammocks. A stairway leads down to a small beach (at low tide, at least), but this is not the place for a beachside vacation. The Kellys have their own dive operation.

P.O. Box 204, Waiyevo, Taveuni (7km/4¼ miles south of the airport). © **888 1111**. Fax 888 1333. www.nakiafiji.com. 4 units. US$175–US$275 (£88–£138). AE, MC, V. **Amenities:** Restaurant; bar (beer and wine only); outdoor pool; complimentary snorkel gear, kayaks, mountain bikes; massage; babysitting; limited room service; laundry service. *In room:* Fridge, no phone.

Taveuni Island Resort   Once known as Dive Taveuni, this resort now relies on honeymooners for the bulk of its business (no kids under 15). If you are among these romantic souls, you're in for a very private, pampered stay with a fabulous view. You

will be disappointed if you expect to step out of your bungalow onto the beach, however, for this property sits high on a bluff overlooking Somosomo Strait, and you will have to climb down it to reach the sand. STEEP DESCEND. [sic] PLEASE MIND YOUR STEP, a sign at the top of the walkway warns. To compensate, a hilltop pool commands a stunning view over the strait, as do the central building and the guest bungalows. Six of the units are hexagonal models built of pine with side wall windows that let in the view and the breeze. The most stunning view is from the spacious deck of the Veidomoni bure—or you can take in the vista from its open-to-the-sea outdoor shower. All other units also have outdoor showers as well as separate sleeping and living areas. One deluxe unit has a separate bedroom, and the luxurious Matalau villa has two master bedrooms and its own private pool.

Postal Agency, Matei, Taveuni (1.5km/1 mile south of airstrip). © 866/828-3864 or 888 0441. Fax 888 0466. www.taveuniislandresort.com. 12 units. US$995 (£498) per person double; US$1,539 (£770) villa. Rates include all meals. AE, MC, V. Children under 15 not accepted. **Amenities:** Restaurant; bar; outdoor pool; spa; free bicycles; limited room service; laundry service. *In room:* A/C, minibar, coffeemaker, safe.

Taveuni Palms 🏵️🏵️   This private little retreat in a coconut grove specializes in pampering guests in its two private bungalows, each of which has its own expansive deck, swimming pool, and small beach among the rocks and cliffs lining the coast here. Owners Tony and Kelly Acland have no restaurant and bar. Instead, the staff prepares and serves your meals in your own dining room, on your deck, down by the beach, or just about any place you choose. The bungalows have sea views from their perches above the shoreline. Each also has two air-conditioned bedrooms with king beds, a big-screen TV to play DVDs, and an outdoor shower, an intercom for ordering your next meal, and its own kayaks and snorkeling gear. Taveuni Palms has its own dive master, and you can have your massage or spa treatment down by the beach.

P.O. Box 51, Matei, Taveuni (1km/½ mile south of airstrip). © 888 0032. Fax 888 2445. www.taveunipalms.com. 2 units. US$995 (£498) double. Minimum 5-night stay required. Rates include meals, nonalcoholic beverages, airport transfers, most activities. AE, MC, V. **Amenities:** 2 outdoor pools; spa treatments; complimentary kayaks; wireless Internet access; massage; babysitting; laundry service. *In room:* A/C, TV (DVDs only), kitchen, fridge, coffeemaker.

Tovu Tovu Resort   Spread out over a lawn across the road from the lagoon, the Peterson family's simple bungalows have front porches, reed exterior walls, tile floors, ceiling fans, and bathrooms with hot-water showers. Three of them also have cooking facilities. The Vunibokoi Restaurant is here, and it's a scenic walk to Coconut Grove Restaurant and others near the airport (see "Where to Dine on Taveuni," below).

Postal Agency, Matei, Taveuni (1km/½ mile east of airstrip). © 888 0560. Fax 888 0722. www.tovutovu.com. 5 bungalows. F$85–F$125 (US$55–US$81/£28–£42) bungalow. AE, MC, V. **Amenities:** Restaurant; bar; laundry service. *In room:* Kitchen (in 3 units), no phone.

AT WAIYEVO

Garden Island Resort 🏵️ (Value)   Built as a Travelodge in the 1960s, this waterside motel is operated by the San Francisco-based dive company Aqua-Trek, which has its Taveuni base here. Most of the clientele are divers, as this is the closest accommodation to the White Wall and its Rainbow Reef (a 20-minute boat ride away in normal conditions), but the friendly staff welcomes everyone. There is no beach, but all rooms face a fine view over the Somosomo Strait to Vanua Levu. Each medium-size unit has a queen and a single bed, tropical-style chairs, a desk, and a tub/shower combo bathroom. All rooms except the dormitories are air-conditioned (the dorms have ceiling fans). Opening to a strait-side pool, the dining room serves meals, which include vegetarian selections, at reasonable prices. Guests and nonguests can rent kayaks and go on snorkeling trips to Korolevu islet and even to the Rainbow Reef with Aqua-Trek. The hotel also arranges hiking trips and other excursions.

P.O. Box 1, Waiyevo, Taveuni (Waiyevo village, 11km/6¾ miles south of airstrip). ℂ 800/541-4334 or 888 0286. Fax 888 0288. www.aquatrek.com. 28 units, 8 dorm beds. F$240 (US$156/£80) double room; F$40 (US$26/£13) dorm bed. Room rate includes breakfast; dorm rate does not. AE, MC, V. **Amenities:** Restaurant; bar; outdoor pool; watersports; limited room service; massage; babysitting; laundry service. *In room:* A/C (except in dorms), fridge, coffeemaker, hairdryer, safe.

IN SOUTHEASTERN TAVEUNI

Paradise Taveuni 𝒦𝒦 An hour's drive south of the airport (or by jet ski, if you prefer), this pleasant property sits on the site of Susie's Plantation, a backpacker resort until present owners Allan and Terri Gorten took over and seriously upgraded it. There's no beach here; instead, you can climb down the rocky shoreline directly into the lagoon. Or you can swim in the pool or walk 5 minutes to a black-sand beach. The thatched-roof guest bures are spacious, with king-size beds and combination tub/shower bathrooms. The oceanfront models add Jacuzzis and outdoor showers. Allan is a chef, so the Pacific Rim cuisine served in the central building is very good. Pro Dive Taveuni is based here. This also is the departure point for jet ski tours to Vanua Levu.

P.O. Box 69, Waiyevo, Taveuni (near Vuna Point). ℂ fax 888 0125. www.paradiseinfiji.com. 10 units. F$300 (US$195/£100) per person. AE, MC, V. Rates include meals. **Amenities:** Restaurant; bar; outdoor pool; spa; wireless Internet access; massage; babysitting; limited room service; complimentary laundry service. *In room:* Fridge, coffeemaker, safe, no phone.

Vatuwiri Farm Resort On a flat plateau at Vuna Point, this is not a resort but a farm stay, where you reside in one of two simple seaside bungalows while sharing a 1,800-acre copra plantation, ranch and farm with the Tarte family, whose ancestor, Englishman James Valentine Tarte, bought the land in 1871. He intended to raise cotton, but a precipitous drop in prices after the American Civil War halted that notion. Today the fifth generation of Tartes produces some 300 British tonnes of copra a year and graze several hundred head of cattle beneath the coconut palms. You will share meals with the Tartes in their home overlooking the sea. Their bungalows sit on a rocky promontory, but the property has a long black-sand beach. You can go horseback riding here. Paradise Taveuni and its dive base are about 5 minutes away.

C/O S. Tarte, Waiyevo, Taveuni. ℂ 888 0316. www.vatuwirifiji.com. 2 units. US$300 (£150) double. Rates include all meals. MC, V. **Amenities:** Restaurant; bar. *In-room:* No phone.

COTTAGE RENTALS

As in Savusavu, several expatriate landowners on Taveuni rent out their own homes when they're away, or they have cottages on their properties to let.

One owner who did not move here from someplace else is Fiji-born May Goulding, who has two cottages at **Todranisiga,** her property south of the airstrip. The land slopes through coconut palms from the road down to the top of a seaside cliff, from where her planter-style bungalows look out over the Somosomo Strait. One of them has an alfresco shower—and I do mean alfresco, because nothing blocks you from the view, or the view from you! Or you can wash off in a claw-foot tub sitting on the lawn. You'll spend most of your time out on the porches enjoying the breeze, taking in the view, and perhaps cooking a light meal on a gas camp stove. May charges F$155

(US$101/£52) double. She does not accept credit cards. Contact May at Postal Agency, Matei, Taveuni (© 888 0680; makaira@connect.com.fj).

Two others cottages with views are at American Roberta Davis's **Makaira By the Sea** (© 888 0686; www.fijibeachfrontatmakaira.com), sitting above a cliff with a 180-degree view down over Prince Charles Beach and the sea (despite the URL, this is not a beachfront property). Built of pine, they have queen beds, kitchens, porches, and both indoor and outdoor showers. Tramontu Bar & Grill is across the road (see "Where to Dine on Taveuni," below). Roberta charges F$125 to F$165 (US$81–US$107/£42–£55) double, with discounts for long stays. She does not accept credit cards.

Less appealing but also with the view is the one cottage at **Karin's Garden** (© 888 0511; www.karinsgardenfiji.com), which Peter and Karin Uwe rent for US$185 (£93) per night. It's near the airstrip.

CAMPING
Campers who like to sleep by the sea can find a beautiful (if not insect-free) site at Bill Madden's **Beverly Campground** (© 888 0326 or 888 0684), on Beverly Beach about 1.5km (1 mile) south of the airstrip. Maravu Resort's beach is next door to one side, Jewel Bubbles dive base on the other. Monstrous trees completely shade the sites and hang over portions of the lagoon-lapped shore. The ground has flushing toilets, cold-water showers, and a rudimentary beachside kitchen. Rates are F$10 (US$6.50/£3.35) per person if you bring your own tent, F$20 (US$13/£6.65) if you rent one of theirs. There's also a forgettable dorm for F$20 (US$13/£6.65) per bed.

WHERE TO DINE ON TAVEUNI
East of the airstrip, **Audrey's Island Coffee and Pastries** (© 888 0039) really isn't a restaurant; it's the home of American Audrey Brown, Taveuni's top baker. She charges F$10 (US$6.50/£3.35) a serving for coffee and cakes, but she but doesn't accept credit cards. Audrey's is open daily from 10am to 6pm.

Coconut Grove Restaurant 🐟🐟 INTERNATIONAL   American Ronna Gold-stein consistently serves Taveuni's best fare at her little enclave, where she also rents cottages (see "Where to Stay on Taveuni," above). She offers breakfasts (her banana, coconut, and papaya breads are fabulous) and salads, soups, burgers, and sandwiches for lunch. Dinner sees a variety of local seafood dishes, spicy Thai and mild Fijian curries (I love the Thai fish), and homemade pastas. Saturday night features a buffet and Fijian musicians. Dining is on Ronna's veranda, which has a great view of the little islands off Taveuni, making it a fine place not just for lunch or dinner but also to sip a great fruit shake or juice while waiting for your flight. Or she will set you up for a romantic dinner under a cabana by her beach.

Matei, opposite airstrip. © 888 0328. Reservations strongly advised by noon for dinner. Main courses F$14–F$25 (US$9.10–US$16/£4.65–£.35). MC, V. Daily 8am–5pm and 6–9pm.

Karin's Garden EUROPEAN   Karin and Peter Uwe prepare meals from their native Europe in the dining room of their home overlooking Somosomo Strait. Reservations are required by noon.

Matei, south of airstrip. © 888 0511. http://karinsgardenfiji.com/en/intro.htm. Reservations required by noon. Full meals F$30–F$35 (US$19–US$23/£10–£12). No credit cards. Seatings daily 7pm.

Tramontu Bar & Grill REGIONAL   The best thing about this open-air, Fijian-owned cafe is its spectacular perch atop a cliff overlooking the Somosomo Strait, which makes it a fabulous spot to have a cold drink while watching the sun set. The local fare consists of the usual curries, grilled steaks, and chicken stir-fries, but I prefer the wood-fired pizzas. Tell them a day in advance, so they can acquire fresh lobster or fish; otherwise, don't eat seafood here.

Matei, south of airstrip. ⓒ 888 2224. Reservations recommended. Lunch F$15 (US$9.75/£5); pizza F$20–F$30 (US$13–US$19/£6.65–£10); main courses F$10–F$30 (US$6.50–US$19/£3.35–£10). No credit cards. Tues–Thurs 11am–2pm and 6–9:30pm; Fri–Sun 10am–10pm. Bar daily 11am–10pm.

Vunibokoi Restaurant   On the front porch of the main house at the Petersen family's Tovu Tovu Resort (see above), this plain but pleasant restaurant serves breakfast, lunch, and dinner, with a blackboard menu featuring home-cooked Fijian, Indian, and Western fare. I always make it here for the Friday-night buffet of Fijian *lovo food,* one of the most extensive and authentic in the islands.

Matei, in Tovu Tovu Resort, 1km/½ mile east of airstrip. ⓒ 888 0560. Reservations recommended. Main courses F$15–F$20 (US$9.75–US$13/£5–£6.65). AE, MC, V. Daily 8am–2pm and 6–9pm.

3 Resorts on Qamea & Matagi Islands ⓧⓧⓧ

The northern end of Taveuni gives way to a chain of small, rugged islands that are as beautiful as any in Fiji, especially Matagi and Qamea. Their steep, jungle-clad hills drop to rocky shorelines in most places, but here and there little shelves of land and narrow valleys are bordered by beautiful beaches. The sheltered waters between the islands cover colorful reefs, making the area a hotbed for scuba diving and snorkeling. It's unfortunate that geography places them at the end of my coverage of Fiji, for they are home to two of my favorite resorts.

Matangi Island Resort ⓧⓧⓧ *Value*   Matangi ranks high because of proprietors Noel and Flo Douglas and their daughter, Christine. Of English-Fijian descent, they own all of hilly, 105-hectare (260-acre) Matagi Island, a horseshoe-shaped remnant of a volcanic cone, where in 1987 they built their resort in a beachside coconut grove on the western shore. A lounge building with a deck hanging out over the lagoon takes full advantage of sunset views of Qamea and Taveuni. At first the Douglases catered to low-budget Australian divers, but as their business grew, their clientele shifted to a mix of diving and nondiving American, Australian, and European adults (children under 12 are not accepted). Honeymooners can escape to three romantic bures 20 feet up in the air, one of them *in* a shady Pacific almond tree. These units all have outdoor showers, as do some of the deluxe units in the coconut grove beside the beach. You can also be taken to the spectacular half-moon beach in aptly-named Horseshoe Bay and be left alone for a secluded picnic. Other nondiving activities include hiking, kayaking, bird-watching, sailing, windsurfing, and sportfishing. Except for the honeymoon bures, Matangi's bungalows are round, in the Polynesian-influenced style of eastern Fiji. Umbrella-like spokes radiating from hand-hewn central poles support reed-lined conical roofs. One bure is equipped for disabled guests. The tin-roofed restaurant and bar building overlooks a swimming pool.

P.O. Box 83, Waiyevo, Taveuni (Matagi Island, 20 min. by boat from Taveuni). ⓒ 888/628-2644 or 888 0260. Fax 888 0274. www.matangiisland.com. 13 units. US$525–US$900 (£263–£450) double. Rates include meals and all excursions and activities except scuba diving, water-skiing, sportfishing, and island trips. AE, DC, MC, V. Children under 12 not accepted. **Amenities:** Restaurant; bar; spa; watersports; wireless Internet access (near office); limited room service; massage; laundry service. *In room:* Minibar, coffeemaker, safe, no phone.

Qamea Resort and Spa ✴✴✴ *(Value*   This luxury property has the most stunning main building and some of the most charming bures of any resort in Fiji. In the lagoonside coconut grove beside a beach, this entire property shows remarkable attention to Western comfort and Fijian detail. If I were to build a set for a South Seas movie, it would feature the original bungalows, all covered by a foot-thick Fijian thatch. Spacious and rectangular, each has an old-fashioned screen door that leads out to a porch that's complete with a hammock. Each is large enough to swallow the king-size bed, two oversize sitting chairs, a coffee table, and several other pieces of island-style furniture, some of it handcrafted by the staff. Their bathrooms include outdoor showers. If you need more space, you can rent one of two honeymoon villas at the end of the property, or a split-level model, which is twice the size of the regular units. Two large, luxuriously appointed "premium villas," which have swimming pools sunken into their front porches, are even more spacious. Qamea's centerpiece is a soaring 16m (52-ft.) high priest's bure supported by two huge tree trunks. Orange light from kerosene lanterns hung high under the roof lends romantic charm for feasting on gourmet meals. Kids under 16 are not accepted here.

P.O. Matei, Taveuni (Qamea Island, 15 min. by boat from Taveuni). ⓒ **866/867-2632** or 888 0220. Fax 888 0092. www.qamea.com. 16 units. US$690–US$995 (£345–£498) double. Rates include meals; airport transfers; and all activities except diving, sportfishing, and island tours. AE, MC, V. Children under 16 not accepted. **Amenities:** Restaurant; bar; outdoor pool; exercise room; spa; laundry service. *In room:* A/C, minibar, coffeemaker, iron, safe, no phone (except in premium villas).

7

Introducing French Polynesia

Tahiti has evoked the image of an idyllic tropical paradise since 1767, when canoeloads of young *vahines* gave uninhibited, bare-breasted receptions to a British navy captain named Capt. Samuel Wallis and his crew on the HMS *Dolphin*. Sent in search of a mysterious southern continent, Wallis instead discovered Tahiti. It was the beginning of the world's long romance with the magical islands we know as French Polynesia.

Even today you are likely to encounter bare breasts on the beaches, for Tahiti and her sister islands are indeed French as well as Polynesian. Unlike other South Pacific countries, where the preaching of puritanical missionaries took deeper root, here you will discover a marvelous combination of both *joie de vivre* and *laissez-faire*. Add the awesome beauty of its islands and you'll quickly see why French Polynesia is one of the world's top honeymoon destinations.

Tahiti is both one of the most gorgeous and one of the most developed South Pacific islands. Don't be surprised when you take a freeway from the airport into the bustling capital of Papeete. Chic bistros and high-rise shopping centers long ago replaced Papeete's wooden Chinese stores, and glass-and-steel luxury resorts on the edge of town supplanted its cheap waterfront hotels. If you're into cities, Papeete will be up your alley. Even if you're not, Tahiti is worth seeing, especially its museums devoted to painter Paul Gauguin, the writer James Norman Hall, and to the islanders themselves.

Most visitors bypass these jewels and head to Moorea, Bora Bora, Huahine, and Raiatea. These high, mountainous islands are much less developed than Tahiti and even more blessed with the otherworldly peaks, multihued lagoons, and palm-draped beaches that have come to symbolize the South Pacific. The late James A. Michener thought Bora Bora was the most beautiful island in the world. I give that title to Moorea. It's all a matter of degree, for these are the world's most dramatically beautiful islands.

Out in the atolls of Rangiroa, Tikehau, Manihi, and Fakarava, you'll find marvelous snorkeling and diving in lagoons stocked with a vast array of sea life. As I wrote when suggesting a French Polynesian itinerary in chapter 3, the atolls may seem anticlimactic after the high islands, so come out here first.

1 French Polynesia Today: The Islands in Brief

French Polynesia sprawls over an area of 5.2 million sq. km (2 million sq. miles) in the eastern South Pacific. That's about the size of Europe, excluding the countries of the former Soviet Union, or about two-thirds the size of the continental United States, or of Australia. The 130 main islands consist of only 3,885 sq. km (1,500 sq. miles), an area smaller than the smallest American state of Rhode Island. Only 260,000 or so souls inhabit these specs.

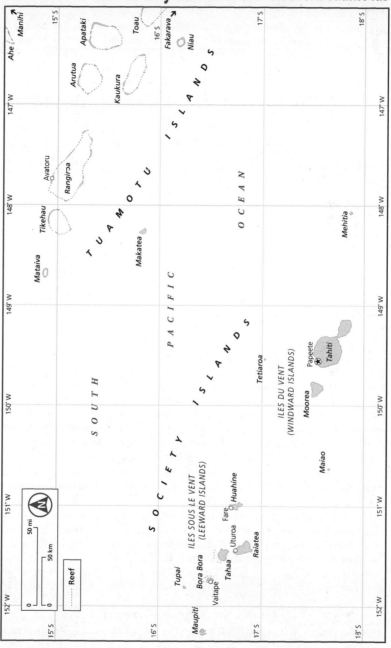

THE ISLANDS IN BRIEF

The territory's five major island groups differ in terrain, climate, and to a certain extent, people. With the exception of the Tuamotu Archipelago, an enormous chain of low coral atolls northeast of Tahiti, most are "high" islands; that is, they are the mountainous tops of ancient volcanoes eroded into jagged peaks, deep bays, and fertile valleys. All have fringing or barrier coral reefs and blue lagoons.

THE SOCIETY ISLANDS   The most beautiful and most frequently visited are the **Society Islands,** so named by Capt. James Cook, the great English explorer, in 1769 because they lay relatively close together. These include **Tahiti** and nearby **Moorea,** which also are known as the Windward Islands because they sit to the east, the direction of the prevailing trade wind. To the northwest lie **Bora Bora, Huahine, Raiatea, Tahaa, Maupiti,** and several smaller islands. Because they are downwind of Tahiti, they also are called the Leeward Islands.

Moorea and Bora Bora are the most developed from a tourism standpoint. Bora Bora is French Polynesia's tourism dynamo, with more resorts than any other island. Although Huahine is almost as beautiful as Moorea and Bora Bora, it has only a handful of hotels and retains its old Polynesian charm. The administrative center of the Leeward Islands, Raiatea lacks beaches, but the deep lagoon it shares with Tahaa makes it the sailing capital of French Polynesia. Tahaa has only recently opened to tourism, with one of French Polynesia's top resorts sitting out on a small islet. Maupiti has a few locally owned pensions. It can be visited on a day trip from Bora Bora.

THE TUAMOTU ARCHIPELAGO   Across the approaches to Tahiti from the east, the 69 low-lying atolls of the **Tuamotu Archipelago** run for 1,159km (720 miles) on a line from northwest to southeast. The early European sailors called them the "Dangerous Archipelago" because of their tricky currents and because they cannot be seen until a ship is almost on top of them. Even today they are a wrecking ground for yachts and interisland trading boats. Two of them, Moruroa and Fangataufa, were used by France to test its nuclear weapons between 1966 and 1996. Others provide the bulk of Tahiti's well-known black pearls. **Rangiroa,** the world's second-largest atoll and the territory's best scuba-diving destination, is the most frequently visited. Neighboring **Tikehau,** with a much smaller and shallower lagoon, also has a modern resort hotel, as does **Manihi,** the territory's major producer of black pearls. To the south, the reef at **Fakarava** encircles the world's third-largest lagoon.

THE MARQUESAS ISLANDS   Made famous by the *Survivor* television series, the **Marquesas** are a group of 10 high islands some 1,208km (751 miles) northeast of Tahiti. They are younger than the Society Islands, and because a cool equatorial current washes their coasts, protecting coral reefs have not enclosed them. The people live in a series of deep valleys radiating out from central mountain peaks. The Marquesas have lost their once-large populations to 19th-century disease and the 20th-century economic lure of Papeete; today their sparsely populated, cloud-enshrouded valleys have an almost haunting air about them. The best way to visit the Marquesas is via the *Aranui 3* (see "Seeing the Islands by Cruise Ship & Yacht," later in this chapter). Only **Nuku Hiva** and **Hiva Oa** have international-standard hotels.

THE AUSTRAL AND GAMBIER ISLANDS   The seldom-visited **Austral Islands** south of Tahiti are part of a chain of high islands that continues westward into the Cook Islands. The people of the more temperate Australs, which include Rurutu, Raivavae, and Tubuai, once produced some of the best art objects in the South Pacific,

Impressions

It is no exaggeration to say, that to a European of any sensibility, who, for the first time, wanders back into these valleys—away from the haunts of the natives—the ineffable repose and beauty of the landscape is such, that every object strikes him like something seen in a dream; and for a time he almost refuses to believe that scenes like these should have a commonplace existence.

—Herman Melville, 1847

but these skills have passed into time. Far on the southern end of the Tuamotu Archipelago, the **Gambier Islands** are part of a semisubmerged, middle-aged high island similar to Bora Bora. **Mangareva** is the largest of the hilly remnants of the old volcano scattered in a huge lagoon partially enclosed by a barrier reef.

GOVERNMENT

French Polynesia is a "community" within the French system of overseas territories. France sends a high commissioner from Paris and controls foreign affairs, defense, justice, internal security, and currency. French Polynesians have considerable autonomy over their internal affairs through a 49-member Assembly, which selects a president, the country's highest-ranking local official. The Assembly decides all issues that are not reserved to the metropolitan French government.

Local voters also cast ballots in French presidential elections and choose two elected deputies and two senators to the French parliament in Paris. The city of Papeete and a few other *communes* have local police forces, but the French *gendarmes* control most law enforcement (they are as likely to be from Martinique as from Moorea).

Local politics breaks down generally into two camps: those who favor remaining French but with increased local autonomy (pro-autonomy), and those who seek complete independence from France (pro-independence). They have swapped control since 2000. See "French Polynesia Yesterday: History 101," below.

THE ECONOMY

French Polynesia has only two significant industries: tourism and black pearls. Vanilla, copra, coconut oil cosmetics (you will see the *Monoi* brand everywhere), and an elixir made from the *noni* fruit are minor exports. About 80% of all food consumed here is imported. Paris pours billions of euros into French Polynesia each year, including an economic restructuring fund, set up after France closed its nuclear testing facility in 1996, to foster self-sufficiency by developing the local infrastructure.

All this money translates into both a high standard of living and high prices. If there is a saving grace for us visitors, it's the lack of tipping and no direct sales tax, which together can add 25% to your bill elsewhere.

2 French Polynesia Yesterday: History 101

Surely Capt. Samuel Wallis of HMS *Dolphin* could hardly believe his eyes in 1767 when more than 500 canoes greeted him at Matavai Bay on Tahiti. Many were loaded with pigs, chickens, coconuts, fruit, and topless young women "who played a great many droll and wanton tricks" on his scurvy-ridden crew.

The French explorer Louis Antoine de Bougainville was similarly greeted a year later. Bougainville stayed at Hitiaa only 10 days, but he took back to France a young

Tahitian named Ahutoru, who became a sensation in Paris as living proof of Jean-Jacques Rousseau's theory that man was at his best a "noble savage." Indeed, Bougainville and Ahutoru contributed mightily to Tahiti's hedonistic image.

In 1769, Capt. James Cook arrived to measure the transit of the planet Venus across the face of the sun. If successful, his survey would enable navigators for the first time to measure longitude accurately on the earth's surface. Cook set up an observation point on a sandy spit on Tahiti's north shore, a locale he appropriately named Point Venus. His measurements were of little use, but Cook remained in Tahiti for 6 months. Cook also used Tahiti as a base during two subsequent voyages, during which he discovered numerous islands and charted much of the South Pacific.

THE MUTINY ON THE *BOUNTY* Capt. William Bligh, one of Cook's navigators, returned to Matavai Bay in 1788 in command of HMS *Bounty,* on a mission to procure breadfruit as cheap food for plantation slaves in Jamaica. One of Bligh's hand-picked officers was a former shipmate, Lt. Fletcher Christian.

Bligh waited on Tahiti for 6 months until his cargo was ready. Christian and some of the crew apparently enjoyed the island's women and lifestyle so much that they mutinied on April 28, 1789, off the Ha'apai islands in Tonga. Set adrift, Bligh and 18 of his loyal officers and crewmen eventually returned to England after one of history's epic longboat voyages. Christian sailed the *Bounty* back to Tahiti, where he put ashore 25 other crewmembers who were loyal to Bligh. Christian, eight mutineers, their Tahitian wives, and six Tahitian men then disappeared.

Royal Navy's HMS *Pandora* eventually rounded up the *Bounty* crewmen still on Tahiti and returned them to England. Three were hung, four were acquitted, and three were convicted but pardoned; one of the latter was Peter Heywood, who wrote the first English-Tahitian dictionary while awaiting court martial.

The captain of an American whaling ship happened upon remote Pitcairn Island in 1808 and was astonished when some mixed-race teenagers rowed out and greeted him not in Tahitian but in perfect English. They were the children of the mutineers, only one of whom was still alive.

Bligh collected more breadfruit on Tahiti a few years later, but his entire venture was for naught when the slaves on Jamaica insisted on rice.

THE FATAL IMPACT The discoverers brought many changes to Tahiti, starting with iron. The Tahitians figured out right away that iron was much harder than stone and shells, and that they could swap pigs, breadfruit, bananas, and the affections of their young women for it. So many iron nails soon disappeared from the *Dolphin* that Wallis restricted his men to the ship out of fear it would fall apart in Matavai Bay. A rudimentary form of monetary economy was introduced to Polynesia, and the English word *money* entered the Tahitian language as *moni.*

The *Bounty* mutineers hiding on Tahiti loaned themselves and their guns to rival chiefs, who for the first time were able to extend their control beyond their home valleys. With the mutineers' help, a chief named Pomare II came to control half of Tahiti and all of Moorea.

Much more devastating European imports were diseases, such as measles, influenza, pneumonia, and syphilis, to which the islanders had no resistance. Captain Cook estimated Tahiti's population at some 200,000 in 1769. By 1810, it had dropped to fewer than 8,000.

CONVERTS & CLOTHES The opening of the South Pacific coincided with a fundamentalist religious revival in England. In 1797, members of the London Missionary

I've Got Tattoo Under My Skin

The United States isn't the only place where it's cool to have a tattoo. With their increasing interest in ancient Polynesian ways, many young Tahitian men and women are getting theirs—but not necessarily with modern electric needles.

The 18th-century explorers who arrived on Tahiti were amazed to find many Polynesians on Tahiti and throughout the South Pacific to be covered from face to ankle with a plethora of geometric and floral designs. In his journal, Capt. James Cook described in detail the excruciatingly painful tattoo procedure, in which natural dyes are hammered into the skin by hand. The repetitive tapping of the mallet gave rise to the Tahitian word *tatau,* which became *tattoo* in English.

Members of the opposite sex rejected anyone with plain skin, which may explain why members of Cook's crew were so willing to endure the torture to get theirs. At any rate, thus began the tradition of the tattooed sailor.

Appalled at the sexual aspects of tattoos, the missionaries stamped out the practice on Tahiti in the early 1800s. Although the art continued in the Marquesas and in Samoa, by 1890 there were no tattooed natives left in the Society Islands.

When a British anthropologist undertook a study of tattooing in 1900, the only specimen he could find was on the skin of a Tahitian sailor, who died in England in 1816. Before he was buried, an art-loving physician removed his hide and donated it to the Royal College of Surgeons.

Society (LMS) arrived to save the souls of the "heathens." They toiled for 15 years before making their first convert, and that was only accomplished with the help of Chief Pomare II. The missionaries thought he was king of Tahiti, but in reality, he was locked in battle to extend his rule and to become just that. By converting to Christianity, he won the missionaries' support, and with it, he gained control of the island. The people then made the transition from their primary god Taaroa to the missionaries' supreme being. They put on clothes and began going to church.

TRICKING THE CHIEFS   The Protestant missionaries enjoyed a monopoly until the first Roman Catholic priests arrived from France in the 1830s. The Protestants immediately saw a threat, and in 1836 they engineered the interlopers' expulsion by Queen Pomare IV, the illegitimate daughter of Pomare II. When word of this reached Paris, France demanded a guarantee that Frenchmen would be treated as the "most favored foreigners" in Tahiti. Queen Pomare agreed, but asked Queen Victoria for British protection. Britain declined, and in 1842 a Frenchman tricked several Tahitian chiefs into signing a document that, in effect, made Tahiti a French protectorate.

Queen Pomare fled and continued to resist from Raiatea, which was not under French control. On Tahiti, her subjects launched an armed rebellion against the French. This war continued until 1846, when the last native stronghold was captured and the remnants of their guerrilla bands retreated to Tahiti Iti, the island's eastern peninsula. A monument to the fallen Tahitians now stands beside the round-island road near the airport at Faaa, a village still noted for its strong pro-independence sentiment.

(Fun Fact Picking Up a Few Extra Bucks

Neither Clark Gable nor Charles Laughton came to Tahiti to film the 1935 version of *Mutiny on the Bounty.* While background scenes were shot on Tahiti, the stars were filmed on Catalina Island, off southern California. The Mexican actress Maria "Movita" Castenada, who played the chief's young daughter, was later married to Marlon Brando, star of the 1962 remake. A young actor named James Cagney, who was vacationing on Catalina at the time, picked up a few extra bucks by playing a sailor for a day.

Giving up the struggle, the queen returned to Papeete in 1847 and ruled as a figurehead until her death 30 years later. Her son, Pomare V, remained on the throne 3 years until abdicating in return for a sizable French pension for himself, his family, and his mistress. In 1903 all of eastern Polynesia was consolidated into a single colony known as French Oceania.

A BLISSFUL LITERARY BACKWATER   Except for periodic invasions by artists and writers. the islands remained an idyllic backwater until the early 1960s. French painter Paul Gauguin gave up his family and his career as a Parisian stockbroker and arrived in 1891; he spent his days reproducing Tahiti's colors and people on canvas until he died in 1903 on Hiva Oa in the Marquesas Islands. W. Somerset Maugham, Jack London, Robert Louis Stevenson, Rupert Brooke, and other writers added to Tahiti's romantic reputation during the early 20th century. In 1932, two Americans— Charles Nordhoff and James Norman Hall—published *Mutiny on the Bounty,* which became a bestseller. Three years later, MGM released the first movie version, with Clark Gable and Charles Laughton in the roles of Christian and Bligh.

In 1942, some 6,000 U.S. sailors and marines built the territory's first airstrip on Bora Bora and remained there throughout World War II. A number of mixed-race Tahitians claim descent from those American troops.

MOVIES & BOMBS   The sleepy years ended in 1960, when Tahiti's new international airport opened at Faaa. Marlon Brando and a movie crew arrived shortly thereafter to film a remake of *Mutiny on the Bounty.* This new burst of fame, coupled with the ability to reach Tahiti overnight, transformed the island into a jet-set destination, and hotel construction began in earnest.

Even more changes came in 1963, when France established the *Centre d'Experimentation du Pacifique* and began exploding nuclear bombs on the Moruroa and Fangataufa atolls in the Tuamotus, about 1,127km (700 miles) southeast of Tahiti. A huge support base was constructed on the eastern outskirts of Papeete. Thousands of Polynesians flocked to Tahiti to take the new construction and hotel jobs, which enabled them to earn good money and experience life in Papeete's fast lane. The nuclear tests continued aboveground until 1974, then deep beneath the atolls until 1996. Their health repercussions are still being debated.

TO BE—OR NOT TO BE—INDEPENDENT   In 1977, the French parliament created the elected Territorial Assembly with powers over the local budget. A high commissioner sent from Paris retained authority over defense, foreign affairs, immigration, the police, civil service, communications, and secondary education.

An additional grant of local control followed in 1984, and in 2007 the islands shifted status from an "overseas territory" of France to an "overseas community." The local assembly gained increased powers over land ownership, labor relations, civil aviation, immigration, education, and international affairs (within the South Pacific, that is). The 2004 law also called for fresh assembly elections. In a surprise upset, a coalition led by Oscar Temaru, the mayor of independence-leaning Faaa, narrowly ousted long-time pro-autonomy President Gaston Flosse. Temaru was in office less than 5 months before being toppled by Flosse, who ruled for only 4 months until special elections on Tahiti and Moorea removed him and returned Temaru to the presidency. Votes of no confidence shifted power between the parties several more times, and more elections were scheduled for 2008. Although the local government has been unstable, the French state still ensures that everything operates as normal from a visitor's standpoint.

3 The Islanders

About 70% of French Polynesia's population of 260,000 or so are pure Polynesian. They are called Tahitians because more than 70% of the territory's population lives on Tahiti, and because the Polynesian language originally spoken only on Tahiti and Moorea has become the territory's second language (French is the official language).

Of almost 200,000 persons who live on Tahiti, some 150,000 reside in or near Papeete. No other village in the islands has a population in excess of 4,000.

THE TAHITIANS

Many Tahitians now refer to themselves as *Maohi* (the Tahitian counterpart of *Maori*), a result of an increasing awareness of their unique ancient culture. Their ancestors came to Tahiti as part of a Polynesian migration that fanned out from Southeast Asia to the South Pacific. Early settlers brought along food plants, domestic animals, tools, and weapons. By the time Capt. Samuel Wallis arrived in 1767, Tahiti and the other islands were lush with breadfruit, bananas, taro, yams, sweet potatoes, and other crops. Most of the people lived on the fertile coastal plains and in the valleys behind them, each valley or district ruled by a chief. Wallis counted 17 chiefdoms on Tahiti alone.

TAHITIAN SOCIETY   Tahitians were stratified into three classes: chiefs and priests, landowners, and commoners. Among the commoners was a subclass of slaves, mostly war prisoners. One's position in society was hereditary, with primogeniture the rule. In general, women were equal to men, although they could not act as priests.

A peculiar separate class of wandering dancers and singers, known as the *Arioi*, traveled about the Society Islands, performing ritual dances and shows—some of them sexually explicit—and living in a state of total sexual freedom. Family values were the least of their concerns; in fact, members killed any children born into their clan.

Impressions

I was pleased with nothing so much as with the inhabitants. There is a mildness in the expression of their countenances, which at once banishes the idea of a savage, and an intelligence that shows that they are advancing in civilization.

—Charles Darwin, 1839

The Polynesians had no written language, but their life was governed by an elaborate set of rules that would challenge modern legislators' abilities to reduce them to writing. Most of these rules were prohibitions known as *tabu*, a word now used in English as *taboo*. The rules differed from one class to another.

A HIERARCHY OF GODS   The ancient Tahitians worshipped a hierarchy of gods. At its head stood **Taaroa,** a supreme deity known as Tangaroa in the Cook Islands and Tangaloa in Samoa. *Mana*, or power, came down from the gods to each human, depending on his or her position in society. The highest chiefs had so much mana that they were considered godlike, if not actually descended from the gods.

The Tahitians worshipped their gods on *maraes* (ancient temples or meeting places) built of stones. Every family had a small marae, which served the same functions as a chapel would today. Villages and entire districts—even islands—built large maraes that served not only as places of worship but also as meeting sites. Elaborate religious ceremonies were held on the large central marae. Priests prayed that the gods would come down and reside in carved tikis and other objects during the ceremonies (the objects lost all religious meaning afterward). Sacrifices were offered to the gods, sometimes including humans, mostly war prisoners or troublemakers. Despite the practice of human sacrifice, cannibalism apparently was never practiced in the Society Islands, although it was fairly widespread in the Marquesas.

The souls of the deceased were believed to return to Hawaiki, the homeland from which their Polynesian ancestors had come. In all Polynesian islands, the souls departed for it from the northwest corner of each island. That's in the direction of Taiwan, which a recent DNA study has indicated may be the origin of the Polynesians.

THE CHINESE

The outbreak of the American Civil War in 1861 resulted in a worldwide shortage of cotton. In September 1862, an Irish adventurer named William Stewart founded a cotton plantation at Atimaono, Tahiti's only large tract of flat land. The Tahitians weren't the least bit interested in working for Stewart, so he imported a contingent of Chinese laborers. The first 329 of them arrived from Hong Kong in February 1865. Stewart ran into financial difficulties, which were compounded by the drop in cotton prices after the American South resumed production after 1868. His empire collapsed.

Nothing remains of Stewart's plantation (a golf course occupies much of the land), but many of his laborers decided to stay. They grew vegetables for the Papeete market, saved their money, and invested in other businesses. Their descendants and those of subsequent immigrants from China now influence the economy far in excess of their numbers. They run nearly all of French Polynesia's grocery and general merchandise stores, which in French are called *magasins chinois*, or Chinese stores.

Impressions

He had once landed [in the Marquesas], and found the remains of a man and a woman partly eaten. On his starting and sickening at the sight, one of Moipu's young men picked up a human foot, and provocatively staring at the stranger, grinned and nibbled at the heel.

—Robert Louis Stevenson, 1890

Sex & the Single Polynesian

The puritanical Christian missionaries who arrived in the South Pacific during the early 19th century convinced the islanders that they should clothe their nearly naked bodies. They had less luck, however, when it came to sex. To the islanders, sex was as much a part of life as any other daily activity, and they engaged in it with a variety of partners from adolescence until marriage.

Even today, they have a somewhat laissez-faire attitude about premarital sex. Every child, whether born in or out of wedlock, is accepted into one of the extended families that are the bedrock of Polynesian society. Mothers, fathers, grandparents, aunts, uncles, and cousins are all part of the close-knit Polynesian family. Relationships sometimes are so blurred that every adult woman within a mile is known as a child's "auntie"—even the child's mother.

Male transvestitism, homosexuality, and bisexuality are facts of life in Polynesia, where families with a shortage of female offspring will raise young boys as girls. Some of these youths grow up to be heterosexual; others are homosexual or bisexual and, often appearing publicly in women's attire, actively seek out the company of tourists. In Tahitian, these males are known as *mahus;* in Samoan, *magus;* and in Tongan, *fakaleitis.*

4 Languages

With the exception of some older residents who speak only **Tahitian,** the primary local Polynesian dialect, everyone speaks **French. English** is also taught as a third language in most schools (and all of those operated by the Chinese community), and it's a prerequisite for getting a hotel job involving guest relations. You can converse in English with your hotel's professional staff, but not necessarily with the housemaids.

Many young Tahitians are eager to learn English, if for no other reason than to understand the lyrics of American songs, which dominate the radio in French Polynesia. Accordingly, you can get by with English in shops, hotels, restaurants, and other businesses frequented by tourists. Once you get off the beaten path, however, an ability to speak what I call *Francais touristique*—tourist French, as in asking directions—will be very helpful if not outright essential. I really need my schoolbook French on Maupiti, and it comes in handy in the Marquesas, too.

Not to fear: Tahitians are friendly folk, and most will warm to you when they discover you don't speak French, or you speak it haltingly or with a pronounced accent.

TAHITIAN PRONUNCIATION

If for no other reason, a little knowledge of Tahitian will help you correctly pronounce the tongue-tying place names here.

The Polynesian languages, including Tahitian, consist primarily of vowel sounds, which are pronounced in the Roman fashion—that is, *ah, ay, ee, oh,* and *ou,* not *ay, ee, eye, oh,* and *you,* as in English. Almost all vowels are sounded separately. For example,

Tahiti's airport is at Faaa, which is pronounced Fah-*ah*-ah, not Fah. Papeete is Pah-pay-*ay*-tay, not Pa-*pee*-tee. Paea is Pah-*ay*-ah.

Some cultural activists advocate the use of apostrophes when writing Tahitian to indicate glottal stops—those slight pauses between some vowels similar to the tiny break between "Oh-oh!" in English. Apostrophes already appear in written Tongan and Samoan. Moorea, for example, is pronounced Moh-*oh*-ray-ah and is often spelled Mo'orea. Consequently, you may see Papeete spelled Pape'ete.

The consonants used are *f, h, m, n, p, r, t,* and *v.* There are some rules regarding their sounds, but you'll be understood if you say them as you would in English.

USEFUL WORDS

To help you impress the locals with what a really friendly tourist you are, here are a few Tahitian words you can use on them:

English	Tahitian	Pronunciation
hello	**ia orana**	ee-ah oh-*rah*-na (sounds like "your honor")
welcome	**maeva**	mah-*ay*-vah
goodbye	**parahi**	pah-*rah*-hee
good	**maitai**	*my*-tie
very good	**maitai roa**	*my*-tie *row*-ah
thank you	**maruru**	mah-*roo*-roo
thank you very much	**maruru roa**	mah-*roo*-roo *row*-ah
good health!	**manuia**	mah-*new*-yah
woman	**vahine**	vah-*hee*-nay
man	**tane**	*tah*-nay
sarong	**pareu**	pah-*ray*-oo
small islet	**motu**	*moh*-too
take it easy	**hare maru**	*ha*-ray *mah*-roo
fed up	**fiu**	few

5 Visitor Information & Maps

The best source of up-to-date information and maps in advance is the territory's tourism promotion bureau: **Tahiti Tourisme,** B.P. 65, 98713 Papeete, French Polynesia (© **50.57.00;** fax 43.66.19; www.tahiti-tourisme.pf).

You can also contact Tahiti Tourisme's overseas offices or representatives:

- **United States:** 300 N. Continental Blvd., Ste. 160, El Segundo, CA 90245 (© **310/414-8484;** fax 310/414-8490; www.tahiti-tourisme.com)
- **Australia:** The Unique Tourism Collection, 362 Riley St., Surry Hills, NSW 2010 (© **1300/655-563** toll-free in Australia or 02/9281-6020; fax 02/9211-6589; www.tahiti-tourisme.com.au)
- **New Zealand:** 200 West Victoria St., Suite 2A (P.O. Box 106192), Auckland (© **09/368-5262;** fax 09/368-5263; www.tahiti-tourisme.co.nz)
- **United Kingdom:** Hills Barfour Synergy, Northcutt House, 36 Southwark Bridge Rd., London SE1 9EU (© **20/7922-1100;** fax 20/7202-6361; www.tahiti-tourisme.co.uk)

- **France:** 28, bd. Saint Germain, 75005 Paris (© **01/5542-6434;** fax 01/ 5542-6120; www.tahiti-tourisme.fr)
- **Germany:** Travel Marketing Romberg, Swartzbachstrasse, 32 40822, Mettman bei Dusseldorf (© **2104/286-672;** fax 2104/912-673; www.tahititourisme.de)
- **Italy:** Aigo, Piazza Castello, 3-20-124 Milano (© **02/66-980317;** fax 02/ 66-92648; www.tahiti-tourisme.it)
- **Chile:** Officina de turismo de Tahiti y sus islas, Av. 11 de Septiembre 2214, Of. 116, Casila 16057, Santiago 9 (© **251-2826;** fax 233-1787; www.tahititourisme.cl)
- **Japan:** Kokusai Bldg., 1F 3–1–1 Marunouchi, Chiyoda-ku Tokyo 100-0005 (© **3/5220-3877;** fax 3/5220-3888; www.tahiti-tourisme.jp)

Once you're in Papeete, you can get information at Tahiti Tourisme's **Fare Manihini** visitor center (© **50.57.**12), on the waterfront on boulevard Pomare at the foot of rue Paul Gauguin. See "Fast Facts: Tahiti," in chapter 8.

Local tourism committees have information booths on Moorea, Bora Bora, Huahine, and Raiatea (see the "Fast Facts" boxes in the following chapters).

Be sure to pick up the *Tahiti Beach Press,* a free weekly English-language newspaper that lists special events and current activities. It has artistic island and Papeete maps. Copies also are available in most hotel lobbies.

MAPS   Libraire Vaima, a large bookstore in Papeete's Vaima Centre (© **45.57.**57), sells several *cartes touristiques,* or tourist maps. The most detailed map is *Tahiti: Archipel de la Société,* published by the Institut Géographique National. It dates to 1994 and doesn't include all new roads on Tahiti, but it shows all the Society Islands in detail, including topographic features. See "Visitor Information & Maps," in chapter 2, for ordering maps before you leave home.

USEFUL WEBSITES   Useful websites include **www.airtahitimagazine.com**, with articles from Air Tahiti's in-flight magazine; **www.tahitisun.com**, with links to several other sites with a host of information about each island; **www.tahiti-explorer.com** and its affiliated **www.tahiti-guide.com**, with details about most resorts; **www.tahiti.com**, which has been around since 1994; the Moorea-based **www.tahitiguide.com**; and **www.polynesianislands.com**, with coverage of all the South Pacific islands. And you can see what other travelers have to say on the South Pacific travel talk boards at **www.frommers.com**.

The Tahiti Diving Guide at **www.diving-tahiti.com** has general information and links to dive operators in all the islands.

6 Entry Requirements

PASSPORTS & VISAS

All visitors except French nationals are required to have a **passport** that will be valid for 6 months beyond their intended stay, as well as a **return or ongoing ticket.** French citizens must bring their national identity cards.

Citizens and nationals of the United States, Canada, New Zealand, Argentina, Bermuda, Brunei, South Korea, Croatia, Hungary, Japan, Malaysia, Mexico, Poland, the Czech Republic, Singapore, Slovakia, Slovenia, Uruguay, Bolivia, Chile, Costa Rica, Ecuador, Estonia, Guatemala, Honduras, Latvia, Lithuania, Nicaragua, Panama, Paraguay, and El Salvador may visit for up to 1 month without a visa.

Nationals of Australia, the European Union countries, Belgium, Luxembourg, Monaco, Switzerland, Andorra, the Vatican, Cyprus, Iceland, Liechtenstein, Malta, Norway, and St. Martin can stay up to 3 months without a visa.

Citizens from all other countries (including foreign nationals residing in the United States) must get a visa before leaving home. French embassies and consulates overseas can issue "short stay" visas valid for 1 to 3 months, and they will forward applications for longer visits to the local immigration department in Papeete.

In the United States, the **Embassy of France** is at 4102 Reservoir Road NW, Washington, DC 20007 (© **202/944-6000;** www.info-france-usa.org). There are French consulates in Boston, Chicago, Detroit, Houston, Los Angeles, New York, Miami, San Francisco, and New Orleans. Go to **www.embassyworld.com** for French embassies in other countries.

No **vaccinations** are required unless you are coming from a yellow-fever-, plague-, or cholera-affected area.

CUSTOMS

See "Fast Facts: French Polynesia," at the end of this chapter, for what you can bring into Tahiti and "Fast Facts: South Pacific," in chapter 2, for what you can bring home.

7 When to Go: Climate, Holidays & Events

There is no bad time to go to French Polynesia, but some periods are better than others. The weather is at its best—comfortable and dry—in July and August, but this is the prime vacation and festival season. July is the busiest month because of the *Heiva Nui* festival (see "French Polynesia Calendar of Events," below). School holidays are the same as in the Northern Hemisphere, which means that both inter-island flights and hotels are most full during August, the traditional French vacation month. So book your air tickets and hotel rooms for July and August as *far* in advance as possible.

THE CLIMATE

Tahiti and the rest of the Society Islands have a balmy tropical climate. Tropical showers can pass overhead at any time of the year. Humidity averages between 77% and 80% throughout the year. The most pleasant time is the May through October austral winter or **dry season,** when midday maximum temperatures average a delightful 82°F (28°C), with early morning lows of 68°F (20°C) often making a blanket necessary. Some winter days, especially on the south side of the islands, can seem quite chilly when a strong wind blows from Antarctica.

November through April is the austral summer or **wet season,** when rainy periods can be expected between days of intense sunshine. The average maximum daily temperature is 86°F (30°C) during these months, while nighttime lows are about 72°F (22°C).

Average Daytime Temperatures in Tahiti

	Jan	Feb	Mar	Apr	May	June	July	Aug	Sept	Oct	Nov	Dec
Temp °F	81	81	81	81	80	77	77	76	77	78	79	80
Temp °C	27	27	27	27	26	25	25	25	25	26	26	27

The central and northern Tuamotus have hotter temperatures and less rainfall. Because there are no mountains to create cooling night breezes, they can experience desertlike hot periods any time of year. The Marquesas are closer to the equator, and temperatures and humidity tend to be slightly higher than in Tahiti. The climate in the Austral and Gambier islands is more temperate.

French Polynesia is on the far eastern edge of the South Pacific cyclone (hurricane) belt, and storms occur infrequently between November and March.

For the local weather, including current satellite images, visit **Meteo France's** official website at **www.meteo.pf**. You can see what the weather is like right now at **www.tahiti-nui.com**, which has live Web cams overlooking the Papeete waterfront and the Bora Bora Pearl Beach Resort.

PUBLIC HOLIDAYS

Like all Pacific Islanders, the Tahitians love public holidays and often extend them past the official day. For example, if Ascension Day falls on a Thursday, don't be surprised if some stores and banks are closed through the weekend.

Public holidays are New Year's Day (government offices also are closed on Jan 2), Good Friday and Easter Monday, Ascension Day (40 days after Easter), Whitmonday (the 7th Mon after Easter), Missionary Day (Mar 5), Labor Day (May 1), Pentecost Monday (the 1st Mon in June), Bastille Day (July 14), Internal Autonomy Day (Sept 8), All Saints Day (Nov 1), Armistice Day (Nov 11), and Christmas Day.

Tahiti Tourisme publishes an annual list of the territory's leading special events on its website, **www.tahiti-tourisme.pf**.

FRENCH POLYNESIA CALENDAR OF EVENTS

January

Chinese New Year. Parade, musical performances, demonstrations of martial arts, Chinese dances, and handicrafts. Between mid-January and mid-February.

Oceania International Documentary Film Festival (FIFO). Films produced by Pacific islanders are shown and judged in Papeete. Last weekend in January.

February

Tahiti-Moorea Marathon. Prizes of up to US$15,000 entice some of the world's best runners to trot 42km (26 miles) around Moorea. Second Saturday in February.

March

Coming of the Gospel. Gatherings on Tahiti commemorate the anniversary of the arrival of the London Missionary Society. March 5.

May

Billabong Pro Surfing. World-class surfers compete on the waves off Teuhupo'o on Tahiti Iti. First 2 weeks of May.

Tahiti Pearl Regatta. Yachts sail among Raiatea, Tahaa, Huahine, and Bora Bora. Mid-May.

June

Miss Tahiti, Miss Heiva, Miss Moorea, and Miss Bora Bora Contests. Candidates from around the islands vie to win the titles. It is among the biggest annual events on outer islands. Early to mid-June.

Tahiti International Golf Open. Local and international golfers vie at Atimaono Golf Course, Tahiti. Mid-June.

July

Heiva Nui $\mathcal{R}\mathcal{R}\mathcal{R}$. This is the festival to end all festivals in French Polynesia. Originally a celebration of Bastille Day on July 14, the islanders have extended the shindig into a month-long blast (it is commonly called *Tiurai*, the Tahitian word for July). They pull out all the stops, with parades, outrigger canoe races, javelin-throwing contests, fire walking, games, carnivals, festivals, and reenactments of ancient Polynesian ceremonies at restored maraes. A highlight for visitors: An extraordinarily colorful contest to determine the best Tahitian dancing troupe for the year—never do the hips gyrate more vigorously. Airline and hotel reservations are difficult to come by during July, so book early and take your written confirmation with you. Last weekend in June through July.

August
Mini Fêtes. Winning dancers and singers from the *Heiva Nui* perform at hotels on the outer islands. All month long.

September
World Tourism Day. Islanders pay homage to overseas visitors, who get discounts. Last weekend in September.

October
Rotui's Tour. Runners race 15km (9¼ miles) around Moorea's Mount Rotui. Late October.

Hawaiki Nui Va'a. Outrigger canoe racing, the national sport, takes center stage as international teams race from Huahine to Raiatea, Tahaa, and Bora Bora over 3 days. Late October to early November.

Tahiti Carnival. Parades, floats, and much partying on the Papeete waterfront. Last week of October.

November
Tatoonesia. Local and foreign tattoo artists gather in Papeete to share designs and techniques. Early November. Followed by **Exhibition "Tattoo"** in late November.

All Saints Day. Flowers are sold everywhere to families who put them on graves after whitewashing the tombstones. November 1.

December
Tiare Tahiti Flower Festival (The Tiare Days on Tahiti). Everyone on the streets of Papeete and in the hotels gets a *tiare Tahiti,* the fragrant Tahitian gardenia. Dinner and dancing later. First week in December.

New Year's Eve. A big festival in downtown Papeete leads territory-wide celebrations. December 31.

8 Money

The local currency is the *Comptoirs Français du Pacifique Franc,* or **French Pacific franc,** which comes in coins up to 100 CFP and in colorful notes ranging from 500 CFP into the millions. The Pacific franc is abbreviated "XPF" by the banks, but in this book I use **CFP,** the French abbreviation.

U.S. dollar and European euro notes (but not coins) are widely accepted as cash in the islands, although at less-favorable exchange rates than at banks.

Tips Converting in Your Head

No decimals are used with Pacific franc units, so prices at first can seem even more staggering than they really are. Many locals think of 100 CFP as US$1 and often give prices that way to visitors. For example, the price of something is 1,000 CFP, they might say it costs US$10. Using that method, you can make a quick conversion by thinking of 100 CFP as US$1; 500 CFP as US$5; 1,000 CFP as US$10; and so on. Drop the last two zeros, then add or subtract the percentage difference between the actual rate and 100 CFP. In the case of US$1 = 80 CFP, for example, you would add 20%.

The CFP, the U.S. Dollar, the Canadian Dollar & the British Pound

The value of the CFP is pegged directly to the European euro at a rate of 1€ = 119.33 CFP. At this writing, US$1/C$1 = approximately 80 CFP (or, the other way around, 100 CFP = US$/C$1.24), which is the exchange rate used to calculate the dollar values given in this chapter. **For British readers:** At this writing, £1 = approximately 158 CFP (or CFP100 = 63p), the rate used to calculate the pound values below. *Note:* International exchange rates fluctuate depending on economic and political factors. Thus, the values given in this table may not be the same when you travel to Fiji. Use the following table only as a guide. Find the current rates at **www.xe.com**.

CFP	US$/C$	UK£	CFP	US$/C$	UK£
100.00	1.25	0.63	1,500.00	18.75	9.49
150.00	1.86	0.95	2,000.00	25.00	12.66
200.00	2.50	1.27	3,000.00	37.50	18.99
300.00	3.75	1.90	4,000.00	50.00	25.32
400.00	5.00	2.53	5,000.00	62.50	31.65
500.00	6.25	3.16	6,000.00	75.00	37.97
600.00	7.50	3.80	7,000.00	87.50	44.30
700.00	8.75	4.43	8,000.00	100.00	50.63
800.00	10.00	5.06	9,000.00	112.50	56.96
900.00	11.25	5.70	10,000.00	125.00	63.29
1,000.00	12.50	6.33	20,000.00	250.00	126.58

HOW TO GET LOCAL CURRENCY   Banque de Polynésie, Banque Socredo, and Banque de Tahiti have offices on the main islands. See the "Fast Facts" section in the following chapters for bank and ATM locations. This is essential, as some of the smaller islands do not have ATMs. All banks charge 500 CFP (US$6.25/£3.15) or more per transaction to cash traveler's checks, regardless of the amount, so you should change large amounts each time to minimize this bite.

Automated teller machines (ATMs) are usually reliable at giving cash. Visa credit and debit/ATM cards are more likely to work than the MasterCard version. Bring some cash or traveler's checks just in case, and be prepared to put as many purchases as you can on your credit cards. ATM operating instructions are given in French and English. You will need your personal identification number (PIN) for credit and debit cards. See "Money," in chapter 2, for more information.

You will probably get a better rate if you change your money in French Polynesia rather than before leaving home.

CREDIT CARDS   MasterCard and Visa are widely accepted on the most visited islands. American Express cards are taken only by the major hotels and car-rental firms and by some restaurants. Don't count on using your Diners Club card except at the major hotels. Discover cards are not accepted in the islands.

9 Getting Around

Air Tahiti Nui, Air New Zealand, Air France, and **Hawaiian Airlines** fly between Tahiti and North America, with Air New Zealand and Air Tahiti Nui going on to Auckland, New Zealand, and Sydney, Australia. Air Tahiti Nui, Air New Zealand and **Qantas Airways** fly between Sydney and Tahiti. Air Tahiti Nui links the islands to Japan. See "Getting There & Getting Around," in chapter 2, for details.

ARRIVING & DEPARTING

All international flights arrive at **Tahiti-Faaa International Airport (PPT),** 7km (4¼ miles) west of downtown Papeete. Once you've cleared Customs, you will see a **visitor information booth** to the right. Group tour operators will be holding signs announcing their presence. Pick up some pocket money at **Banque de Polynésie,** to the left as you exit Customs, or at **Banque Socredo** to the right. They are open during normal banking hours, so you'll have to rely on their ATMs after hours. Banque Socredo has a machine that will change U.S. dollars and other major notes to CFP.

I have spent many an hour waiting for flights at the open-air, 24-hour **snack bar** to the right. There's a **McDonald's** next to Air Tahiti's domestic departure lounge.

See "Getting Around," in chapter 8, for information about local transportation on Tahiti.

GETTING TO YOUR HOTEL   Unless you're on a package tour or your hotel has arranged a transfer, your only choice of transportation to your hotel between 10pm and 6am will be a **taxi.** Official fares from 8pm to 6am are 1,500 CFP (US$19/£9.50) to the hotels on the west coast; 2,500 CFP (US$31/£16) to downtown. Add 100 CFP (US$1.25/65p) for each bag.

During daytime and evenings you can haul your baggage across the parking lot in front of the terminal, climb the stairs to the main road, and flag down a local bus. In a rental car, take Route 1 west to the InterContinental Resort Tahiti, the Sofitel Tahiti Resort, or Le Meridien Tahiti. Route 1 east passes the Sheraton Hotel Tahiti & Spa on its way to downtown Papeete. The Route 5 expressway connects Papeete to the west coast. See "Getting Around," below, for more information.

BAGGAGE STORAGE   Most hotels will keep your baggage for free. The airport's **baggage storage room** (© 88.60.08; hmoea@yahoo.fr) is in the parking lot in front of the international departures gate. It's the building behind the pavilion where Tahitian women sell leis and flower crowns. Charges range from 640 CFP (US$8/£4.05) per day for regular-size bags to 2,700 CFP (US$34/£17) for large items such as surfboards and bicycles. The room opens 2 hours before every international flight departs. Regular hours are Monday 4am to 7pm, Tuesday to Thursday 5am to 11pm, Saturday 5am to 12:30am, and Sunday and holidays 1pm to 12:30am. MasterCard and Visa credit cards are accepted for charges in excess of 1,200 CFP (US$15/£7.60).

DEPARTING   Check-in time for departing international flights is 3 hours before flight time; for domestic flights, be there 2 hours in advance. All of your bags must be screened for both international and domestic flights leaving Papeete. (There are no security procedures at the outer island airstrips.)

Note: There is no bank or currency exchange bureau in the international departure lounge, so change your money before clearing immigration.

(*Value* **Money-Saving Air Passes**

Visitors can save by buying an **Air Tahiti Pass** over the popular routes. For example, the "Bora Bora Pass" permits travel over the Papeete–Moorea–Huahine–Bora Bora–Papeete route for about 38,800 CFP (US$485/£246), which is about 10,000 CFP (US$125/£63) less than the full adult fares. The "Bora Bora–Tuamotu Pass" adds Rangiroa, Tikihau, and Manihi. Whether it's a bargain will depend on how many islands you plan to visit, so add up the regular fares and compare to the price of the passes (prices on Air Tahiti's website). All travel must be completed within 28 days of the first flight, and other restrictions apply. See **www.airtahiti.pf** for details.

GETTING AROUND
BY PLANE

Having Air Tahiti Nui or another carrier book your domestic flights along with your international ticket will greatly simplify matters in case of a local cancellation, and you will avoid an extra fee if you have to change your flights once here.

AIR MOOREA   A subsidiary of Air Tahiti (see below), **Air Moorea** (© 86.41.41; fax 86.42.99; www.airmoorea.com) provides shuttle service between Tahiti-Faaa International Airport and Temae Airport on Moorea. Its small planes (and I do mean *small*) leave Faaa on the hour and half-hour daily from 6 to 9am, then on the hour from 10am to 3pm, and on the hour and half-hour again from 4 to 6pm. Each plane turns around on Moorea and flies back to Tahiti. The fare is about 4,200 CFP (US$53/£27) each way, half-fare for children. Air Moorea's little terminal is on the east end of Tahiti-Faaa International Airport (that's to the left as you come out of Customs). Air Moorea will take you from the airport to your Moorea hotel for 500 CFP (US$6.25/£3.15) each way, but *you must buy your transfer ticket in Papeete.* It is not available after you arrive on Moorea.

AIR TAHITI   The primary domestic carrier is **Air Tahiti** (© 86.44.42; fax 86.40.99; www.airtahiti.pf), which provides daily flights between Papeete and all the main islands, most in modern ATR turboprop planes seating 44 or 72 passengers. It's wise to reserve your seats as early as possible, especially during school holidays.

Following are approximate one-way adult fares on the usual visitor's circuit. Double the fare for round-trips between any two islands and halve the cost for children.

Tahiti to Moorea	4,200 CFP	(US$53/£27)
Moorea to Huahine	14,800 CFP	(US$185/£94)
Moorea to Bora Bora	21,240 CFP	(US$266/£134)
Huahine to Raiatea	6,300 CFP	(US$79/£40)
Raiatea to Bora Bora	7,200 CFP	(US$90/£46)
Bora Bora to Tahiti	18,100 CFP	(US$226/£115)
Bora Bora to Rangiroa	27,400 CFP	(US$343/£173)
Rangiroa to Tahiti	18,200 CFP	(US$228/£115)

Air Tahiti's central downtown Papeete walk-in reservations office is at the corner of rue du 22 Septembre and rue du Maréchal Foche (© 47.44.00). It also has an office in the Tahiti-Faaa International Airport terminal (© 86.41.84).

Pack carefully and bring evidence of your international ticket with you because the **baggage limit** on both of these airlines is 20 kilograms (44 lb.) per person if you're connecting with an international flight within 7 days, but only 10 kilograms (22 lb.) per person if you're not. You will face a substantial extra charge for excess weight. You can leave your extra belongings in the storage room at your hotel or at Tahiti-Faaa International Airport.

Check-in times vary from 1 to 2 hours, so ask Air Tahiti when you should arrive at the airport. You do not need to reconfirm your interisland flights, but I usually let Air Tahiti know where I'm staying so it can contact me in case of changes.

An alternative to taking Air Tahiti's scheduled flights is to charter a plane and pilot from **Air Moorea, Air Tahiti, Air Archepels** (© 81.30.30; www.airarchipels.com), or **Wan Air** (© 50.44.18; www.wanair.pf). **Polynesia Helicopteres** (© 86.60.29; www.polynesia-helicopter.com) charters helicopters. When the total cost is split among a large enough group, the price per person could be less than airfare on a commercial airline.

BY FERRY TO MOOREA

Two companies—**Aremiti** (© 50.57.57; www.aremiti.pf) and **Moorea Ferry** (© 86.87.47; on Tahiti, or 56.34.34 on Moorea; www.mooreaferry.pf)—run ferries between the Papeete waterfront and Vaiare, a small bay on Moorea's east coast. It can seem like madness when the boats arrive and depart at the wharves, so take your time and be sure to get on one of the fast catamarans, which take 30 minutes to cover the 19km (12 miles) between the islands. The *Aremiti V* is larger, faster, and more comfortable than the *Moorea Express.* The *Aremiti Ferry* or the *Moorea Ferry* are much slower. The one-way fare on any ferry is about 900 CFP (US$11/£5.70).

Because their times change from day to day, I usually pick up a schedule at the ferry dock and carry it with me throughout my visit. In general, one or another of them departs Papeete about 6, 7:30, and 9am, noon, and 2:40, 4:05, and 5:30pm Monday to Friday, with extra voyages on Friday and Monday (Moorea is a popular weekend retreat for Papeete residents). Weekend hours are slightly different on each ferry.

Buses meet all ferries at Vaire, except the midday departures from Papeete, to take you to your hotel or other destination on Moorea for 500 CFP (US$6.25/£3.15) per person. From Vaiare, they take about 1 hour to reach the northwest corner of Moorea.

BY SHIP TO THE OUTER ISLANDS

You can go by ship from Papeete to Huahine, Raiatea, Tahaa, and Bora Bora, but it's neither the quickest nor most comfortable way to travel, nor is it the most reliable.

Tips The Best Seats & Something to Eat

It depends on the pilots and how much sightseeing they want to do, but usually you will have the best views of the islands by sitting on the left side of the Air Tahiti aircraft when you're flying from Papeete to the Leeward Islands, on the right side returning. Make sure you have your camera and a lot of film and camera batteries at the ready.

Most hotel dining rooms open for breakfast at 7am and close by 9:30am, so for early morning flights stock up on some munchies and something to drink the night before, and bring them along on the plane.

Moments **Breaking Into Tahitian Song**

I was on the ferry from Moorea to Tahiti when a Tahitian passenger, obviously on his way home from work, started playing a guitar. Within seconds everyone on board spontaneously began singing Tahitian songs. Moments like that, unplanned and beautiful, may become some of your best memories of Tahiti.

Two cargo ferries, the *Vaeanu* (© **41.25.35;** fax 41.24.34; torehiatetu@mail.pf) and the *Hawaiki Nui* (© **45.23.24;** fax 45.24.44; sarlstim@mail.pf), make three voyages a week. Both have passenger cabins. Usually they depart Papeete about 4pm, arrive at Huahine during the night, and go on to the other Leeward Islands the next day. They return from Bora Bora over the reverse route. Contact the ship owners for fares and schedules, which are at the mercy of the weather and condition of the ships.

In the Leeward Islands, you can travel between Bora Bora and Raiatea on the *Maupiti Express* (© **67.66.69** on Bora Bora, 66.37.81 on Raiatea; maupiti express@mail.pf). This small, fast ferry departs Bora Bora for Tahaa and Raiatea at 7am on Monday, Wednesday, and Friday, returning to Bora Bora in the late afternoon. It stops at Tahaa in both directions. On Tuesday, Thursday, and Saturday it sails from Bora Bora to Maupiti, departing at 8:30am and returning in late afternoon. So it's possible to make day trips from Bora Bora to Raiatea or Maupiti. Fares on either route are 3,000 CFP (US$38/£19) one-way, 4,000 CFP (US$50/£25) return.

Except for the excellent *Aranui 3,* which is as much cruise vessel as cargo ship (see "Seeing the Islands by Cruise Ship & Yacht," below), ships to the Tuamotu, Marquesas, Gambier, and Austral groups keep somewhat irregular schedules in terms of weeks or even months, not days. Consequently I cannot recommend them.

BY RENTAL CAR

Avis and Europcar have rental-car agencies (*locations de voiture* in French) on Tahiti, Moorea, Huahine, Raiatea, and Bora Bora. Hertz is present on Tahiti and Raiatea. See "Getting Around," in the following chapters, for details.

A **driver's license** from your home country will be honored in French Polynesia.

DRIVING RULES   Driving is on the right-hand side of the road, as in North America and continental Europe. All persons in a vehicle **must wear seat belts.** If you drive or ride on a scooter or motorbike, **helmets** (*casques,* pronounced "casks") are mandatory. **Speed limits** are 40kmph (25 mph) in the towns and villages and 80kmph (50 mph) on the open road. The limit is 60kmph (37 mph) for 8km (5 miles) on either side of Papeete. The general rule on the Rte. 5 freeway between Papeete and Punaauia, on Tahiti's west coast, is 90kmph (56 mph).

Drivers on the main rural roads have the right of way. In Papeete, priority is given to vehicles entering from the right side, unless an intersection is marked with a traffic light or a stop or yield sign. This rule differs from those of most other countries, so be careful at all intersections, especially those marked with a *priorité à droite* (priority to the right) sign, and give way accordingly.

Drivers are required to **stop for pedestrians** on marked crosswalks, but on busy streets, don't assume that drivers will politely stop when you try to cross.

Traffic lights in Papeete may be difficult to see, as some of them are on the far left-hand side of the street instead of on the driver's side of the intersection.

10 Seeing the Islands by Cruise Ship & Yacht

The Society Islands are ideal grounds for cruise ships, as they are barely an hour's steam from Tahiti to Moorea, half a day's voyage on to Huahine, and less than 2 hours each among Huahine, Raiatea, Tahaa, and Bora Bora. That means the ships spend most days and nights at anchor in lovely lagoons, allowing passengers plenty of time to explore the islands and play in the water. Bear in mind, however, that you will see a lot more of the ship than you will of the islands.

Cruises could be an affordable way to see the islands in style, as the prices usually include all meals, wine with lunch and dinner, soft drinks, and most onboard activities. You might even find a deal including airfare to and from Tahiti. Likewise, these are wonderful islands for chartering a yacht and setting sail on your own.

TAKING A CRUISE

ADVENTURES ON THE *ARANUI* 𝕽𝕽𝕽

The cargo ship *Aranui 3* (© **800/972-7268** in the U.S. or 42.36.21 in Papeete; fax 43.48.89; www.aranui.com) is the most interesting way to visit the out-of-the-way Marquesas Islands. Outfitted for up to 200 passengers, this 386-foot freighter makes 14-day round-trips from Papeete to 6 of the 10 Marquesas Islands, with stops at Fakarava and Rangiroa in the Tuamotus. While the crew unloads the ship's cargo, passengers spend their days ashore experiencing the islands and islanders. Among the activities: picnicking, snorkeling, visiting villages, and exploring archaeological sites. Experts on Polynesian history and culture accompany you on most voyages.

Accommodation is in 10 suites, 12 deluxe cabins, 63 standard cabins, and dormitories. The suites and cabins all have private bathrooms. Suites and deluxe cabins have windows and doors opening to outside decks, and their bathrooms are equipped with tubs as well as showers. Standard cabins lack outside doors and have portholes instead of windows. The ship has a restaurant, bar, boutique, library, video lounge, and swimming pool.

The *Aranui's* primary job is to haul cargo, so it does not have stabilizers and other features of a luxury liner. In other words, do not expect the same level of comfort, cuisine, and service as on the other ships cruising these waters. If you only want to sit by the pool, eat prodigious quantities of fine food, and smoke cigars, the *Aranui* may not be your cup of tea. But for those of us who want to go places few people visit, and learn a lot in the process, then it is an excellent choice.

Fares for the complete voyage range from about US$2,079 (£1,040) for a dormitory bunk to US$5,445 (£2,723) per person for suites. All meals are included, but you have to pay your own bar bill and your airfare to and from Tahiti.

LUXURY ON THE *PAUL GAUGUIN* 𝕽𝕽

The 157m (515-ft.), 318-passenger *Paul Gauguin* (© **877/505-5370** or 904/776-6123 in the U.S., 54.51.00 in Papeete; www.rssc.com) is the most luxurious of Tahiti's cruise ships. It spends most of its year making 7-day cruises through the Society Islands, but occasionally extends to the Tuamotu and Marquesas islands, and it has even ventured as far west as Fiji. It also has environmentalist Jean-Michel Cousteau as guest lecturer on some cruises (see "Where to Stay in Savusavu," in chapter 6). All of the ship's seven suites and about half of its 152 staterooms have private verandas or balconies (the least expensive lower-deck units have windows or portholes). All are luxuriously appointed with minibars, TVs, and VCRs, direct-dial phones, and marble bathrooms with full-size tubs. Most have queen-size beds, although some have two twins. Per-person double-occupancy fares for the 1-week Society Islands cruises start at US$2,600 (£1,300).

A LOT OF COMPANY ON PRINCESS CRUISES

Princess Cruises (© 800/774-6237 or 904/527-6660; www.princesscruises.com) will be operating the 700-passenger *Tahitian Princess* on 7- and 10-night cruises in French Polynesia until late 2009, after which it will be renamed the *Ocean Princess* and redeployed to Asia. Its identical sister ship, the *Pacific Princess*, may cruise in French Polynesia thereafter (check the line's website for more information). They are the largest ships operating in French Polynesia, so you won't have the same intimacy as on the other vessels. Princess Cruises are also the least expensive, with prices starting as low as US$1,150 (£575) per person, double occupancy, for an interior stateroom, depending on the time of year and length of voyage. Specials including airfare may be offered during the slow seasons. Passengers can make use of a sun deck, swimming pool, fitness center, casino, cabaret lounge, two bars, and four restaurants. Shore excursions are offered, but, unlike the *Paul Gauguin* and the *Star Flyer,* Princess Cruises do not have stern platforms to support onboard watersports activities. Almost 70% of the 280 staterooms and 62 suites open to private terraces.

DINING IN THE LAGOON WITH BORA BORA CRUISES

Bora Bora Cruises, P.O. Box 40186, Papeete (© **54.45.05;** fax 45.10.65; www.boraboracruises.com) uses two sleek, luxurious yachts, the *Tu Moana* and the *Tia Moana,* which measure in at 69m (226-ft.) and can carry up to 60 passengers in 30 staterooms spread over three decks. They make 1-week "Nomade" cruises from Bora Bora to Huahine, Raiatea, and Tahaa. The boats are small enough to anchor closer to shore than the other ships here. Consequently, passengers enjoy extras such as breakfast served in the lagoon (that's right, you actually sit at tables in the water) and movies and spa treatments on a beach. Fares are 5,800€ (US$6,670/£3,335) per person, double occupancy.

UNDER SAIL ON THE *STAR CLIPPER*

As I write, the 170-passenger, 300-foot-long tall ship **Star Flyer** had just begun making 7-, 10-, and 11-day cruises from Papeete through the Society and Tuamotu islands. One of the Monaco-based **Star Clippers** fleet (© 800/442-0552; www.starclippers.com), she resembles an old-time clipper ship, including an Edwardian-style library with a Belle Époque fireplace, but is loaded with modern amenities and luxuries. Fares start at $1,845 (£923) per person, double occupancy, for an interior cabin.

FLY FISHING FROM THE *HAUMANA*

Avid fishermen and women, can cast lines from the *Haumana* (© **50.06.74;** fax 50.06.72; www.tahiti-haumana-cruises.com). This 33.5m (110-ft.), 42-passenger

---

⎛Fun Fact⎞ Phoning Like a Local

In French Polynesia, the local phone numbers are presented as three two-digit numbers—for example, 42.29.17. If you ask someone for a number, he or she will say it like this: *"quarante-deux, vingt-neuf, dix-sept"* in French or "forty-two, twenty-nine, seventeen" in English.

catamaran specializes in 3-, 4-, and 7-night cruises on the calm, shallow lagoons of Rangiroa and Tikehau in the Tuamotus. Fishing is not the primary focus of the cruises (diving, surfing, and other activities are possible), but this is one of the few vessels to carry rods, reels, and other gear. It's also a much more pleasant way to visit Rangiroa's Pink Sands and Blue Lagoon than riding a speed boat an hour each way (see chapter 11). Although the *Haumana* is smaller than other ships here, its 21 air-conditioned cabins all have large windows or portholes, queen beds, sofas or settees, minibars, TVs, VCRs, phones, and shower-only bathrooms with hairdryers. Rates range from US$2,665 to US$5,275 (£1,333–£2,638) per person, double occupancy, including all meals, drinks, fishing, and kayak excursions.

CHARTERING A YACHT

If you are an experienced sailor, you can charter a yacht—with or without skipper and crew—and knock around some of the French Polynesian islands as the wind and your own desires dictate. The best place to start is Raiatea, which shares a lagoon with Tahaa, the only French Polynesian island which can be circumnavigated entirely within a protective reef. Depending on the wind, Bora Bora and Huahine are relatively easy blue-water trips away.

The Moorings *ℛℛℛ*, a respected yacht charter company based in Florida (© **800/535-7289** or 727/535-1446; www.moorings.com), operates a fleet of monohull and catamaran sailboats based at **Apooti Marina** on Raiatea's northern coast (© **66.35.93;** fax 66.20.94; moorings@mail.pf). That's a few minutes' sail to Tahaa. Depending on the size of the boat—they range from 11- to 15m (36–49 ft.) in length—and the season, bareboat rates (that is, without skipper or crew) run about US$450 to US$1,700 (£225–£850) per vessel per day. Provisions are extra. The agency will check you out to make sure you and your party can handle sailboats of these sizes; otherwise, you must pay extra for a skipper.

Also at Apooti Marina, **Sunsail Yacht Charters** (© **800/327-2276** in the U.S., 60.04.85 on Raiatea; www.sunsail.com) has a fleet of 11- to 15m (36–49 ft.). Check its arcane website for bareboat rates.

The French-owned **Tahiti Yacht Charter** (© **45.04.00;** fax 45.76.00; www.tahiti yachtcharter.com) has 11- to 14m (36–46 ft.) yachts based at Papeete and Raiatea. It designs cruises throughout the territory, including lengthy voyages to the Tuamotus and Marquesas. Similar services are offered by **Archipel Croisiers** on Moorea (© **56.36.39;** fax 56.35.87; www.archipels.com).

11 Tips on Dining

French Polynesia has a plethora of excellent restaurants. I'm not fabricating when I say I've seldom had a really bad meal here. You are in for a special treat when ordering tomatoes and other locally grown vegetables, for they will be as fresh as if they had come from your own garden.

Many visitors are shocked at the high prices on the menus and in the grocery stores. Most foodstuffs are imported, and except for sugar, flour, and a few other necessities, are subject to stiff duties. On the other hand, you won't have sales tax added to your bill, and although the practice is widespread here these days, you will not be compelled to tip the waitstaff. In other words, Americans will not have to add up to 25% to the cost of restaurant meals. See below for how I save more money on food here.

LOCAL FARE: *MA'A TAHITI*

As would be expected, French is the dominant cuisine. Local French residents want their steaks in red wine sauces, mahimahi under a vanilla sauce, and *canard* (duck) with orange sauce, which seem to appear on every menu, as does *carpaccio* (thinly sliced raw beef or tuna) and sashimi (especially good when it's fresh yellowfin tuna).

While the Tahitians have adopted many of these, as well as Chinese dishes, they still consume copious quantities of *ma'a Tahiti* (traditional Tahitian food), especially on Sunday. Like their Polynesian counterparts elsewhere, Tahitians still cook meals underground in an earth oven, known here as an *himaa*. Pork, chicken, fish, shellfish, leafy green vegetables such as taro leaves, and root crops, such as taro and yams, are wrapped in leaves, placed on a bed of heated stones, covered with more leaves and earth, and left to steam for several hours. The results are quite tasty, as the steam spreads the aroma of one ingredient to the others, and liberal use of coconut cream adds a sweet richness.

Many restaurants serving primarily French, Italian, or Chinese cuisine also offer Tahitian dishes. One you will see virtually everywhere is *poisson cru,* French for "raw fish." It's the Tahitian-style salad of fresh tuna or mahimahi marinated in lime juice and served in coconut milk with cucumbers, onions, and tomatoes. Chili is added to spice up a variation known as Chinese poisson cru.

Most of Tahiti's big resort hotels have at least one *tama'ara'a* (Tahitian feast) a week, followed by a traditional, hip-swinging dance show (see the box "A Most Indecent Song & Dance," in chapter 8).

SNACK BARS & *LES ROULOTTES*

Tahiti has two McDonald's, but locals still prefer their plethora of snack bars, which they call "snacks." You can get a hamburger and usually poisson cru, but the most popular item is the *casse-croûte,* a sandwich made from a crusty French baguette and ham, tuna, *roti* (roast pork), *hachis* (hamburger), lettuce, tomatoes, and cucumbers— or even spaghetti. A casse-croûte usually costs about 300 CFP (US$3.75/£1.90) or less.

Also in this category are *les roulottes*—or portable meal wagons which roll out after dark on most islands. They are one of the best values here. The carnival-like ambience they create on the Papeete waterfront makes them a highlight of any visit to the city (see "Don't Miss *Les Roulottes*," in chapter 8).

MONEY-SAVING TIPS

Despite the high prices, you don't have to go broke dining here. In addition to finding the nearest "snack," here are some ways to eat well for the least money:

- Unless you have no choice, do not have breakfast at the resort hotel dining rooms, which charge 3,000 CFP (US$38/£19) or more per person. You can have a perfectly good breakfast for less than half that at a snack bar or patisserie.
- Dining out is as much a part of the French Polynesian experience as snorkeling, so do not buy a hotel meal package except on remote islands, where your resort's restaurant is your only choice.
- Order breakfast from room service if your hotel serves only an expensive buffet. Room service menus usually are *a la carte,* meaning you can order individual items whose total may be much less than the full buffet price.
- Dine at *restaurants conventionné,* which get breaks on the government's high duty on imported alcoholic beverages. Wine and mixed drinks in these establishments

cost significantly less than elsewhere. They can charge no more than 700 CFP (US$8.75/£4.45) for spirits served on the rocks, but cocktails can be more than twice that amount. I buy rum on the rocks and then add my own Coke to it. You can also order *vin ordinaire* (table wine) served in a carafe to save money. The chef buys good-quality wine in bulk and passes the savings on to you.

- Take advantage of *plats du jour* (daily specials), especially at lunch, and *prix-fixe* (fixed-priced) menus, often called "tourist menus." These three- or four-course offerings are usually made from fresh produce direct from the market.

- Consider sharing a starter course. Unlike some American menus, which list the main course as an "entree," here an entree is the first course, and it is likely to be a more substantial serving than an American appetizer. An entree could suffice as a light meal, or you can share one with your mate or a friend. I discreetly glance at other tables to check portion sizes before ordering.

- Make your own snacks or perhaps a picnic lunch to enjoy at the beach. Every village has at least one grocery store. Fresh loaves of French bread are inexpensive, and most stores carry cheeses, deli meats, vegetables, and other sandwich makings, many imported from France. Locally brewed Hinano beers, which sell for 500 CFP (US$6.25/£3.15) or more at the hotel bars, cost half that in grocery stores. Bottles of decent French wine also cost a fraction of restaurant prices.

FAST FACTS: French Polynesia

The following facts apply to French Polynesia in general. For more specific information, see the "Fast Facts" sections, in chapters 8 through 11.

Area Codes French Polynesia does not have domestic area codes. The country code for calling into Fiji is **689.**

Business Hours Although many shops in downtown Papeete stay open over the lunch period, general shopping and business hours are Monday to Friday 7:30 to 11:30am and 2 to 5pm and Saturday 8am to noon. In addition to regular hours, most grocery stores also are open Saturday 2 to 6pm and Sunday 6 to 8am.

Camera & Film Photographic film and color-print processing are widely available. Digital camera batteries are available in Papeete.

Climate See "When to Go," earlier in this chapter.

Clothing Evening attire for men is usually a shirt and slacks; women typically wear a long, brightly colored dress (slacks or long skirts help to keep biting sand flies away from your ankles). Women sunbathe topless at most beaches (although I saw more exposed bums than boobs during my recent visit). Shorts are acceptable during the day almost everywhere. Outside Papeete, the standard attire for women is the colorful wraparound sarong known, in Tahitian, as a *pareu,* which can be tied in a multitude of ways into dresses, blouses, or skirts.

Customs Customs allowances are 200 cigarettes or 100 cigarillos or 50 cigars; 2 liters of liquor, champagne, or wine; 50 grams of perfume, one-quarter liter of eau de toilette; 500 grams of coffee and 100 grams of tea; and 30,000 CPF (US$375/£190) worth of other goods. Narcotics, illegal drugs, weapons, ammunition, and copyright infringements (that is, pirated video- and audiotapes) are prohibited. Pets and plants are subject to stringent regulations (don't even think of bringing your pet).

Drug Laws Plenty of pot may be grown up in the hills, but possession and use of dangerous drugs and narcotics are subject to long jail terms.

Drugstores The main towns have reasonably well-stocked pharmacies. Their medicines are likely to be from France.

Electricity Electrical power is 220 volts, 50 cycles, and the plugs are the French kind with two round, skinny prongs. Most hotels have 110-volt outlets for shavers only, so you will need a converter and adapter plugs for other appliances. Some hotels, especially those on the outer islands, have their own generators, so ask at the reception desk what voltage is supplied.

Embassies & Consulates The **United States** has a consular agent on Tahiti in Centre Tamanu Iti in Pauaauia (© **42.65.35**; fax 50.80.96; usconsular@mail.pf), whose main function is to facilitate local residents in applying for visas from the U.S. embassy in Suva, Fiji. Australia, Austria, Belgium, Chile, Denmark, Finland, Germany, Italy, Monaco, New Zealand, Norway, the Netherlands, South Korea, Sweden, and the United Kingdom have honorary consulates in Papeete. Tahiti Tourisme has their phone numbers.

Emergencies Contact your hotel staff. Otherwise, the emergency **police** phone number is © **17** throughout the territory.

Etiquette Even though many women go topless and wear the skimpiest of bikini bottoms at the beach, the Tahitians have a sense of propriety similar to what you find in any Western nation. Don't offend them by engaging in behavior that would not be permissible at home.

Firearms French Polynesians can own shotguns for hunting, but handguns are illegal.

Gambling You can play "Lotto," the French national lottery, but there are no gambling casinos.

Healthcare Highly qualified specialists practice on Tahiti, where some clinics possess state-of-the-art diagnostic and treatment equipment; nevertheless, public hospitals tend to be crowded with local residents, who get free care. Most visitors use private doctors or clinics. English-speaking physicians are on call for larger hotels. Each of the smaller islands has at least one infirmary (see "Fast Facts," in chapters 8–11). American health insurance plans are not recognized, so remember to get receipts at the time of treatment.

Insects There are no dangerous insects in French Polynesia. The only real nuisances are mosquitoes and tiny sand flies called "no-nos," (known elsewhere as "no-see-ums.") They appear at dusk on most beaches. Wear trousers or long skirts and plenty of insect repellent (especially on the feet and ankles). All pharmacies and most grocery stores and hotel boutiques sell insect repellent.

Internet Access Most hotels and resorts have computers from which guests can send and receive e-mail and surf the Web, and you can go to post offices and cybercafes on the main islands (see "Fast Facts," in chapters 8–11). Many have ADSL connections, which are not as fast as DSL or cable access in the U.S. and other countries but are speedier than dial-up connections.

The only local Internet provider is **MANA** (© **50.88.88**; www.mana.pf). No international Internet service provider has a local access number here, but you can log on from your hotel room using MANA's "anonymous" dial-up service. When setting up a new network connection in Windows, type in **0, 368888** as the local access telephone number (0 is the number used to reach an outside line in all hotels here). When you make your first connection, enter *both* your name and your password as **anonymous.** (If your first try fails, retype both in all capital letters.) MANA charges 100 CFP (US$1.25/65p) per minute for access time, and the cost of the local call also will be billed to your room. The hotel may well add an additional charge, so it can become expensive quickly. See "Staying in Touch," in chapter 2.

Liquor Laws Regulations about where and when you can drink are liberal. Anyone over 21 can purchase alcoholic beverages at bars and grocery stores, which sell wine, beer, and spirits. Official *conventionné* restaurants and hotels pay reduced duty on imported alcoholic beverages, which will cost less there than at local bars and nightclubs.

Mail All the main towns and many Papeete suburbs have post offices. Letters usually take about a week to 10 days to reach overseas destinations in either direction. Mailing addresses in French Polynesia consist of post office boxes (*boîtes postales* in French, or B.P. for short) but no street numbers or names. Local addresses have postal codes, which are written in front of the city or town. (If you send a letter to French Polynesia from the U.S., do *not* put the postal code behind the name of the town; otherwise the U.S. Postal Service may dispatch it to a zip code within the United States.)

Newspapers & Magazines The *Tahiti Beach Press,* an English-language weekly devoted to news of Tahiti's tourist industry, runs features of interest to tourists and advertisements for hotels, restaurants, real estate agents, car-rental firms, and other businesses that cater to tourists. Establishments that buy ads in it give away copies free. The daily newspapers, *La Dépêche de Tahiti* and *Les Nouvelles,* are in French. **Le Kiosk** in front of the Vaima Centre on boulevard Pomare in Papeete sells some international newspapers and magazines.

Police The emergency **police** phone number is © **17.**

Radio & TV French Polynesia has government-operated AM radio stations with programming in French and Tahitian. Several private AM and FM stations in Papeete play mostly American and British music in English; the announcers, however, speak French. Two government-owned television stations broadcast in French. Most hotels pick up a local satellite service, which carries CNN International in English. The government-owned radio and TV stations can be received throughout the territory via satellite.

Safety Do not leave valuables in your hotel room or unattended anywhere. Street crimes against tourists are rare. You should be safe after dark in the busy parks along boulevard Pomare on Papeete's waterfront, but stay alert everywhere after dusk. Women should not wander alone on deserted beaches, because some Polynesian men may still consider such behavior to be an invitation for instant amorous activity. Hitchhiking is possible in the rural parts of

Tahiti and on the outer islands, but women traveling alone should be extremely cautious.

Smoking Although antismoking campaigns and hefty tobacco taxes have reduced the practice, cigarette smoking is still more common in French Polynesia than in Western countries. Most office buildings and the airlines are smoke-free, and you will find nonsmoking sections in some restaurants (the French law against smoking in bars and restaurants is not in effect here as I write). Not all hotels have nonsmoking rooms, so be sure to ask for one.

Taxes Local residents do not pay income taxes; instead, the government imposes stiff duties on most imported goods, and a value-added tax (VAT, or *TVA* in French) is included in the price of most goods and services. Only the TVA on set pearls is refundable in the European fashion (see "Shopping" in chapter 8). Another 12% tax will be tacked to your hotel bills (including restaurant and bar expenses) and another 50 CFP to 200 CFP (65¢–$2.50/30p–£1.25) per night for the Tahiti, Moorea, and Bora Bora communes.

Telephone All land-line communications in and out of French Polynesia are handled by the *Office des Postes et Télécommunications* (OPT).

To call French Polynesia: Dial the international access code (011 from the U.S.; 00 from the U.K., Ireland, or New Zealand; or 0011 from Australia), French Polynesia's country code **689,** and the local number (there are no area codes within French Polynesia).

To make international calls from within French Polynesia: First dial **00,** then the country code (U.S. or Canada 1, U.K. 44, Ireland 353, Australia 61, New Zealand 64), then the area code and phone number. Calls to the U.S., Europe, Australia, and New Zealand are 103 CFP (US$1.30/65p) per minute when dialed directly. You can make them through your hotel, though with a surcharge, which can more than double the fee.

For operator assistance: Dial ✆ **3600** if you need assistance making an overseas call. The operators speak English.

To make domestic calls within French Polynesia: No prefix or area code is required for domestic long distance calls, so dial the local number.

For directory assistance: Dial ✆ **3612** for local directory information (*service des renseignements*). The operators speak English. You can look up local numbers online at **www.annuaireopt.pf** (it's in French).

Toll-free numbers: There are no toll-free numbers in French Polynesia. Calling a 1-800 number in the U.S. or Canada from French Polynesia is not toll-free. In fact, it costs the same as an overseas call.

Pay phones: Public pay phones are at all post offices and are fairly numerous elsewhere, less so on the other islands. You must have a *télécarte* to call from public pay phones (coins won't work). The cards are sold at all post offices and by most hotel front desks and many shops in 1,500 CFP, 2,000 CFP, and 5,000 CFP (US$19, US$25, and US$63/£9.50, £13, and £32) sizes. Digital read-outs on the phones tell you how many *unites* you have left on a card.

Cellphones: Some international cellphone companies have roaming in French Polynesia; contact yours to see if it does. You need a GSM cellphone for it to work in French Polynesia (see "Staying in Touch," in chapter 2). You can rent a phone from **Vini** (© **48.13.13**; www.vini.pf), the local provider. Stores displaying the Vini sign sell prepaid SIM cards for your unlocked GSM phone. The least-expensive card costs about 4,500 CFP (US$56/£28) and includes 30 minutes of outgoing calls (incoming are free). **CellularAbroad** (© **800/287-3020**; www.cellularabroad.com) of Santa Monica, California, rents GSM phones and sells prepaid SIM cards for French Polynesia. The main advantage to renting a SIM card overseas is that you will have it when you arrive.

Time Local time in the most-visited islands is 11 hours behind Greenwich Mean Time. I find it easier to think of it as 5 hours behind U.S. Eastern Standard Time or 2 hours behind Pacific Standard Time. Translated: When it's noon in California, it's 10am in Tahiti. When it's noon on the U.S. East Coast, it's 7am in Tahiti. Add 1 hour to the Tahiti time during daylight saving time.

The Marquesas Islands are 30 minutes ahead of the rest of the territory.

Because French Polynesia is on the east side of the international date line, Tahiti has the same date as the United States, the Cook Islands, and the Samoas, and is 1 day behind Australia, New Zealand, Fiji, and Tonga.

Tipping Although tipping is considered contrary to the Polynesian custom of hospitality, it's a widespread practice here, especially in Papeete's restaurants (credit card forms now have a "tip" line here). Nevertheless, tipping is not expected unless the service has been beyond the call of duty. Some hotels accept contributions to the staff Christmas fund.

Useful Phone Numbers See "Fast Facts: The South Pacific," in chapter 2, for useful international numbers.

    Air Tahiti © **86.42.42**
    Air Moorea © **86.41.41**
    Tahiti Tourisme © **50.57.12**
    Arimiti Ferry © **50.57.57**
    Moorea Ferry © **86.87.47**

Water Tap water is consistently safe to drink only in Papeete and on Bora Bora. Well water in the Tuamotu islands tends to be brackish; rainwater is used there for drinking. You can buy bottled water at every grocery store. The local brands Vaimato and Eau Royal are much less expensive than imported French waters.

Weights & Measures French Polynesia is on the metric system.

8

Tahiti

Large and abundant, Tahiti is the modern traveler's gateway to French Polynesia, just as it was for the late 18th-century discoverers who used it as a base to explore the South Pacific. In later years, the capital city, **Papeete,** became a major shipping crossroads. Located on Tahiti's northwest corner, the city curves around one of the region's busiest harbors.

Where Papeete now stands, there wasn't even a village until the 1820s, when Queen Pomare set up headquarters along the shore and merchant ships and whalers began using the harbor in preference to the less-protected Matavai Bay to the east. A simple town of stores, bars, and billiard parlors sprung up quickly, and between 1825 and 1829 it was a veritable den of iniquity. It grew even more after the French made it their headquarters upon taking over Tahiti in 1842. A fire nearly destroyed the town in 1884, and waves churned up by a cyclone did severe damage in 1906. In 1914, two German warships shelled the harbor and sank the French navy's *Zélée.*

Papeete is a very different place today. Vehicles of every sort crowd **boulevard Pomare,** the broad avenue along Papeete's waterfront, and the four-lane expressway linking the city to the trendy suburban districts of **Punaauia** and **Paea** on the west coast. Indeed, suburbs are creeping up the mountains, overlooking the city and sprawling for miles along the coast in both directions. The island is so developed and traffic-clogged that many Tahitians commute up to 2 hours in each direction on weekdays. Many are moving to Moorea, a 30-minute ferry ride away.

But there is a bright side to Tahiti's development: Using money from a post-nuclear-testing economic restructuring fund, Papeete has done a remarkable job in refurbishing its waterfront, including a cruise-ship terminal and a classy park where families gather and the city celebrates its festivals. It's a real treat now to walk along the promenade fronting this storied South Seas port.

Papeete's chic shops, busy Municipal Market, and lively mix of French, Polynesian, and Chinese cultures are sure to invigorate any urbanite. If you're looking for old-time Polynesia, you will find it on Tahiti's rural east and south coasts and on its peninsula, Tahiti Iti. Its three fine museums are reason enough for me to spend a day or two here.

Even if you plan to leave for Moorea, Bora Bora, and the other less-developed islands, you will have to spend a few hours here, because all international flights land at Faaa on the northwest coast of this legendary and still very beautiful island.

1 Getting Around

Except for the Route 5 expressway between Papeete and Punaauia, the island's highway system consists primarily of a paved road running for 116km (72 miles) around Tahiti Nui and halfway down each side of Tahiti Iti. From the isthmus, a road partially lined

Impressions

Edward called for him in a rickety trap drawn by an old mare, and they drove along a road that ran by the sea. On each side of it were plantations, coconut and vanilla; now and then they saw a great mango, its fruit yellow and red and purple among the massy green of the leaves, now and then they had a glimpse of the lagoon, smooth and blue, with here and there a tiny islet graceful with tall palms.

—W. Somerset Maugham, *The Fall of Edward Barnard*, 1921

with trees heads up to the high, cool Plateau of Taravao, with pastures and pines that look more like provincial France than the South Pacific.

Be prepared to deal with numerous **traffic circles** in and near Papeete. You must give way to traffic already in the circles.

BY BUS

Although it might appear from the number of vehicles scurrying around Papeete that everyone owns a car or scooter, the average Tahitian gets around by local bus. Modern buses have replaced all but a few of Tahiti's famous *le trucks*, those colorful vehicles so named because the passenger compartments are gaily painted wooden cabins mounted on the rear of flatbed trucks. The last of them operate between downtown Papeete and the Centre Moana Nui shopping complex in Punaauia. They pass the Sheraton Hotel Tahiti & Spa, the InterContinental Resort Tahiti, and the Sofitel Tahiti Maeva Beach Resort. Elsewhere look for modern buses.

Once upon a time, les trucks would stop for you almost anywhere, but today you must catch them and the buses at official stops (called *arrêt le bus* in French).

The villages or districts served by each bus are written on the sides and front of the bus. **Fares** within Papeete are 130 CFP (US$1.65/80p) until 6pm and 200 CFP (US$2.50/£1.25) thereafter. A trip to the end of the line in either direction costs about 750 CFP (US$9.40/£4.75).

BUSES GOING WEST   The few remaining le trucks and all short-distance buses going west are painted red and white. They line up on rue du Maréchal-Foch behind the Municipal Market and travel along rue du Général-de-Gaulle, which becomes rue du Commandant-Destremeau and later route de-l'Ouest, the road that circles the island. Buses run along this route as far as the Centre Moana Nui (south of the Sofitel Tahiti Maeva Beach Resort) Monday to Friday at least every 30 minutes from 6am to 6pm, once an hour between 6pm and midnight. Except for le trucks serving tourists at the west coast hotels, there is irregular service on Saturday, none on Sunday. Trucks and buses labeled Faaa, Maeva Beach, and Outuamaru pass the airport and the Sheraton Hotel Tahiti & Spa and InterContinental Resort Tahiti.

BUSES GOING EAST   Short-distance buses going east are painted green and white. They line up in the block west of the Banque de Polynésie on boulevard Pomare, opposite the cruise ship terminal and near the Municipal Market and rue Paul Gauguin. They proceed out of town via avenue du Prince-Hinoi, passing the Le Royal Tahitien Hotel cutoff and the Radisson Plaza Resort Tahiti on their way to Pirae, Arue, and Mahina. They run frequently from 6am to 5pm as far as the Mahina.

Tahiti

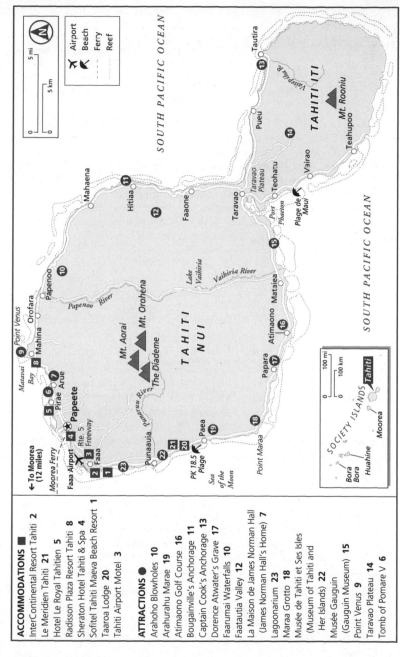

ACCOMMODATIONS ■

InterContinental Resort Tahiti **2**
Le Meridien Tahiti **21**
Hotel Le Royal Tahitien **5**
Radisson Plaza Resort Tahiti **8**
Sheraton Hotel Tahiti & Spa **4**
Sofitel Tahiti Maeva Beach Resort **1**
Taaroa Lodge **20**
Tahiti Airport Motel **3**

ATTRACTIONS ●

Arahoho Blowholes **10**
Arahurahu Marae **19**
Atimaono Golf Course **16**
Bougainville's Anchorage **11**
Captain Cook's Anchorage **13**
Dorence Atwater's Grave **17**
Faarumai Waterfalls **10**
Faatautia Valley **12**
La Maison de James Norman Hall
(James Norman Hall's Home) **7**
Lagoonarium **23**
Maraa Grotto **18**
Musée de Tahiti et Ses Isles
(Museum of Tahiti and
Her Islands) **22**
Musée Gauguin
(Gauguin Museum) **15**
Point Venus **9**
Taravao Plateau **14**
Tomb of Pomare V **6**

217

None runs at night, so you must rent a car or take a taxi to and from the Radisson and Le Royal Tahitien after dark and on weekends.

LONG-DISTANCE BUSES   Buses going in either direction to Tahiti's south coast and Tahiti Iti are painted orange and white. They line up next to the Manava Tahiti Visitors Bureau, on boulevard Pomare at rue Paul Gauguin. They run on the hour from 6am to noon Monday to Friday; there is only one afternoon trip, at 4:30pm back to the villages. They do not run nights or weekends.

BY TAXI

Papeete has a large number of taxis, although they can be hard to find during the morning and evening rush hours, especially if it's raining. You can flag one down on the street or find them gathered at one of several stations. The largest gathering points are on **boulevard Pomare near the market** (© **42.02.92**) and at the **Centre Vaima** (© **42.60.77**). Most taxi drivers understand some English.

Taxi fares are set by the government and are posted at the Centre Vaima taxi stand on boulevard Pomare. Few cabs have meters, so be sure that you and the driver have agreed on a fare before you get in. Note that *all fares are increased by at least 20% from 8pm to 6am*. A trip anywhere within downtown Papeete during the day starts at 1,000 CFP (US$13/£6.30) and goes up 120 CFP (US$1.50/75p) for every kilometer after the first one during the day, 240 CFP (US$3/£1.50) at night. As a rule of thumb, the fare from the Papeete hotels to the airport or vice versa is about 1,700 CFP (US$21/£11) during the day; from the west coast hotels to the airport, about 1,000 CFP (US$13–£6.30). A trip to the Gauguin Museum on the south coast costs 10,000 CFP (US$125/£63) one-way. The fare for a 4-hour journey all the way around Tahiti is about 16,000 CFP (US$200/£101). Drivers may charge an extra 50 CFP to 100 CFP (65¢–US$1.25/30p–65p) per bag of luggage.

BY RENTAL CAR

Avis (© **800/331-1212** or 41.93.93; www.avis.com), **Hertz** (© **800/654-3131** or 42.04.72; www.hertz.com), and **Europcar** (© **800/227-7368** or 45.24.24; www.europcar.com) all have agencies on Tahiti. The best local rental company is **Daniel Location de Voitures,** in the Faaa airport terminal (© **81.96.32;** fax 85.62.64; daniel.location@mail.pf). All charge about 9,600 CFP (US$120/£61) per day with unlimited kilometers.

DRIVING HINTS   In Papeete, priority is given to vehicles entering an intersection from the right side. This rule does not apply on the four-lane boulevard Pomare along the waterfront, but be careful everywhere else because drivers on your right will expect you to yield at intersections where there are no stop signs or traffic signals. Outside of Papeete, priority is given to vehicles already on the round-island road.

Tips Around Tahiti by Bus?

Although you had to walk across the Taravao isthmus, it once was possible to circumnavigate Tahiti by *le truck* in 1 day. Today the long distance buses run only from 6am to noon weekdays, so it is practically impossible. I recommend renting a vehicle or taking a guided tour to go around the island.

> **Tips   Get Unlimited Kilometers If Driving Around Tahiti**
>
> If you rent a car, consider the unlimited kilometer rate if you intend to drive around Tahiti, as the round-island road is 114km (71 miles) long, not counting Tahiti Iti.

The main round-island road is a divided highway east and west of Papeete, which means that to make a left turn, you will have to turn around at the next traffic circle and drive back to your destination.

PARKING   Parking spaces can be scarce in downtown Papeete during the day. You must pay to park in most on-street spaces from 8am to 5pm Monday to Saturday, which costs 100 CFP (US$1.25/65p) per hour, payable by tickets sold at shops and newsstands displaying signs saying **Parc Chec.** Put the *parc chec* ticket on the dashboard inside the vehicle. There are several municipal parking garages, including one under the Hotel de Ville (Town Hall); enter off rue Collette between rue Paul Gauguin and rue d'Ecole des Frères. Some large buildings, such as the Centre Vaima, have garages in their basements. Frankly, if I'm not staying downtown, I usually leave my car at the hotel and take a bus into the city during workdays.

FAST FACTS: Tahiti

The following facts apply specifically to Tahiti. For more information, see *"Fast Facts:* French Polynesia," in chapter 7.

American Express   The American Express representative is **Tahiti Tours,** on rue Jeanne-d'Arc (© **54.02.50;** fax 42.25.15), across from the Centre Vaima in downtown Papeete. The mailing address is B.P. 627, 98713 Papeete, Tahiti, French Polynesia.

Bookstores   **Librairie Vaima,** on the second level of the Centre Vaima (© **45. 57.57**), has some English-language novels and a wide selection of books on French Polynesia, many of them in English and some of them rare editions. It also has maps of the islands. **Le Kiosk** in front of the Centre Vaima sells the *International Herald Tribune, Time,* and *Newsweek,* as does **La Maison de la Presse,** on boulevard Pomare at Quartier du Commerce (© **50.93.93**).

Business Hours   Although some shops stay open over the long lunch break, most businesses are open Monday to Friday 8 to 11:30am and 2 to 5pm, give or take 30 minutes, as "flex hours" help alleviate Tahiti's traffic problem. Saturday hours are 8 to 11:30am, although some shops in the Centre Vaima stay open Saturday afternoon. The Papeete Municipal Market is a roaring beehive from 5 to 7am on Sunday, and many of the nearby general stores are open during those hours. Except for some small groceries, most other stores are closed on Sunday.

Camera/Film   Film and 1-hour color print processing are available at several stores in downtown Papeete. One of the best is **Tahiti Photo,** in the Centre Vaima (© **42.97.34**), where you can get help in English.

Currency Exchange **Banque de Polynésie, Banque de Tahiti,** and **Banque Socredo** each has at least one branch with ATMs on boulevard Pomare and in many suburban locations where you can cash traveler's checks. See "Money," in chapter 7, for more information.

Drugstores **Pharmacie du Vaima,** on rue du Général-de-Gaulle at rue Georges La Garde behind the Centre Vaima (© **42.97.73**), is owned and operated by English-speaking Nguyen Ngoc-Tran. Pharmacies rotate night duty, so ask your hotel staff to find out which one is open after dark.

Emergencies & Police Consult with your hotel staff. The **emergency police** telephone number is © **17** (but don't expect the person on the other end of the line to speak English). The **central gendarmerie** is at the inland terminus of avenue Bruat (© **42.02.02**).

Eyeglasses Papeete has several opticians, including **Optika** (© **42.77.54**) in the Centre Vaima.

Healthcare Both **Clinique Cardella** (© **42.80.10**), on rue Anne-Marie-Javouhey, and **Clinic Paofai** (© **43.77.00**), on boulevard Pomare, have highly trained specialists and some state-of-the-art equipment. They are open 24 hours.

Information **Tahiti Tourisme's Fare Manihini** visitor's bureau (© **50.57.12**; www. tahiti-tourisme.com), on the waterfront on boulevard Pomare at the foot of rue Paul Gauguin, is open Monday to Friday 7:30am to 5:30pm, Saturday 8am to 4pm, and Sunday and holidays 8am to 1pm.

Internet Access Every hotel here has Internet access for its guests to use. **Tahiti Tourisme** has computers in its Fare Manihini visitor center (© **50.57.12**; www. tahiti-tourisme.com), on the waterfront on boulevard Pomare at the foot of rue Paul Gauguin. It charges 300 CFP (US$3.75/£1.90) for 15 minutes of access time, 1,000 CFP (US$13–£6.35) for 1 hour. **Cybernesia Tahiti,** on the second level of the Vaima Centre (© **85.43.67**), has both dial-up and wireless access for 20 CFP (US25¢/15p) per minute for the first 10 minutes, 15 CFP (US20¢/10p) per minute thereafter. It has English keyboards and the Skype telephone program on some of its computers, and it will burn your digital photos to CD. **La Maison de la Presse,** on boulevard Pomare at Quartier du Commerce (© **50.93.93**), also has English keyboards. It charges 16 CFP (US10¢/10p) per minute.

Laundry **Lavomatic du Pont du L'Est,** Gauguin, 64 rue Paul Gauguin (© **43. 71.59**), at Pont de l'Est, has wash-dry-fold service for 1,400 CFP (US$18/£8.90) a load. Open Monday to Friday 7am to 5:30pm and Saturday 7am to noon.

Libraries The *Office Territorial D'Action Culturelle* **(Territorial Cultural Center)** on boulevard Pomare, west of downtown Papeete (© **42.88.50**), has a small library of mostly French books on the South Pacific and other topics. Hours are 8am to 5pm Monday to Friday, except on Wednesday when it closes at 4pm.

Mail The main post office is on boulevard Pomare a block west of the Centre Vaima. Open Monday through Friday 7am to 6pm and Saturday 8 to 11am. The branch post office at the Tahiti-Faaa International Airport terminal is open Monday to Friday 6 to 10:30am and noon to 2pm, and Saturday, Sunday, and holidays 6 to 9am.

Restrooms Both **Tahua Vaite** (the park by the cruise-ship terminal at rue Paul Gauguin) and **Place Toata** on the western end of downtown have free and clean public toilets.

Safety The busy parks on boulevard Pomare along the waterfront generally are safe, but be very careful if you wander onto the side streets after dark.

Telephone & Fax The main post office, the cruise-ship terminal, and Place Toata all have pay phones, where you can use a *télécarte* to make local and international calls. See "Fast Facts," in chapter 7, for more information about pay phones and international calls.

Water You can drink the tap water in Papeete and its nearby suburbs, which includes all the hotels, but not out in the rural parts of Tahiti. Bottled water is available in all grocery stores.

2 Tahiti's Top Attractions

Tahiti is shaped like a figure eight lying on its side. The "eyes" of the eight are two extinct, eroded volcanoes joined by the flat Isthmus of Taravao. The larger, western part of the island is known as *Tahiti Nui* ("Big Tahiti" in Tahitian), and the smaller eastern peninsula beyond the isthmus is named *Tahiti Iti* ("Little Tahiti"). Together they comprise about 670 sq. km (259 sq. miles), about two-thirds the size of the island of Oahu in Hawaii.

Tahiti Nui's volcano has been eroded over the eons so that now long ridges, separating deep valleys, march down from the crater's ancient rim to the coast far below. The rim itself is still intact, except on the north side, where the Papenoo River has cut its way to the sea. The highest peaks, **Mount Orohena,** 2,206m (7,238 ft.), and **Mount Aora,** 2,045m (6,709 ft.), tower above Papeete. Another summit, Mount Te Tara O Maiao, or the **Diadème,** which stands 1,308m (4,291 ft.), can be seen from the eastern suburb of Pirae but not from downtown.

Arahurahu Marae 𝕽𝕽   Arahurahu is the only *marae*—an ancient temple or meeting place—in all of Polynesia that has been fully restored, and it is maintained like a museum. Although not nearly as impressive as the great lagoonside marae on Huahine and Raiatea (see chapter 11), this is Tahiti's best example of ancient Polynesian temples and meeting places, and its exhibit boards do a good job of explaining the significance of each part. For example, the stone pens near the entrance were used to keep the pigs to be sacrificed to the gods. Arahurahu is used for the reenactment of old Polynesian ceremonies during the July *Heiva Nui* celebrations.

Paea, 23km (14 miles) west of Papeete. No phone. Free admission. Open daily 24 hr.

Impressions

To those who insist that all picturesque towns look like Siena or Stratford-on-Avon, Papeete will be disappointing, but to others who love the world in all its variety, the town is fascinating. My own judgment: any town that wakes each morning to see Moorea is rich in beauty.

—James A. Michener, *Return to Paradise,* 1951

Fun Fact **Shipwrecked**

While researching the novel *Pitcairn's Island*, which he co-authored with Charles Nordhoff, James Norman Hall disappeared for several months in 1933 after being shipwrecked near Mangareva, between Tahiti and Pitcairn.

Lagoonarium de Tahiti   If you won't be diving or snorkeling, then you will enjoy a visit to this underwater viewing room surrounded by pens containing reef sharks, sea turtles, and colorful species of tropical fish. It's part of the Captain Bligh Restaurant and Bar (see "Where to Dine," later). The view of Moorea from here is terrific.

Punaauia, 12km (7 miles) west of Papeete. ℰ **43.62.90**. Admission 500 CFP (US$6.25/£3.15) adults, 300 CFP (US$3.75/£1.90) children under 12. Daily 9am–5:30pm.

La Maison James Norman Hall **(James Norman Hall's Home)** ✮✮✮   This marvelous museum is a required stop for all of us who have ever dreamed of writing novels in a lovely lagoonside house. James Norman Hall and his wife, Sarah Teraireia Winchester Hall, lived their entire married lives here in Arue. Hall was a U.S. army pilot in France during World War I, when he was shot down behind German lines and held prisoner. He met Charles Nordhoff in Paris shortly after the war, and together they wrote *The Lafayette Flying Corp*, the story of the American unit that fought for France before the U.S. entered the war. In 1920, they moved to Tahiti, where they sailed around on copra schooners and wrote *Faery Lands of the South Seas*. In 1932, they published *Mutiny on the Bounty*, the first of their three novels about the incident and its aftermath (*Men Against the Sea* and *Pitcairn's Island* are the others). It was turned into the 1935 movie starring Clark Gable and Charles Laughton, and the 1962 remake with Marlon Brando. Hall and Nordhoff penned several more books about the islands, including *Hurricane*, which also was turned into two movies.

The Hall family manages the home and has stocked it with his typewriter, original manuscripts, and tons of heirlooms and memorabilia. (One of the three Oscars won by his son, the late Hollywood cinematographer Conrad L. Hall, is here.) His office is adorned with photographs of him with Zane Grey, Robert Dean Frisbee, and other "men of the pen" who dropped by for visits. One of Hall's grandsons still lives on the property, so you will need permission to visit his grave on the hill above the house. Staff members lead 30-minute tours and sell coffee and soft drinks. The free parking lot is across the highway beside the lagoon; if coming from Papeete you'll have to turn around at the next traffic circle and come back to reach it.

Arue, 5½km (3½ miles) east of Papeete. ℰ **50.01.60**. www.jamesnormanhallhome.pf. Admission 600 CFP (US$7.50/£3.80). Tues–Sat 9am–4pm. Closed public holidays.

Marché Municipale **(Municipal Market)** ✮✮✮   An amazing array of fruits, vegetables, fish, meat, handicrafts, and other items are sold under the big tin pavilion of Papeete's bustling public market. Unwritten rules dictate that Tahitians sell fruits and traditional vegetables, such as taro and breadfruit, Chinese sell European and Chinese vegetables, and Chinese and Europeans serve as butchers and bakers. Hogs' heads hanging in the butcher stalls could turn a weak stomach. The market is busiest early in the mornings, but it's like a carnival here from 5 to 7am every Sunday, when people from the outlying areas of Tahiti, and even from the other islands, arrive to sell their produce. (*Note:* By 8am, the pickings are slim.) A Tahitian string band plays during lunch at the upstairs snack bar, which purveys inexpensive island chow.

Papeete, between rue du 22 Septembre and rue François Cardella, 1 block inland from bd. Pomare. No phone. Free admission. Mon–Fri 5am–6pm; Sat 5am–1pm; Sun 4–8am.

Musée de Tahiti et Ses Isles (Museum of Tahiti and Her Islands) 🌾🌾🌾   Set in a lagoonside coconut grove with a gorgeous view of Moorea, this ranks as one of the best museums in the South Pacific. On display is the geological history of the islands, including a terrific topographic map; their sea life, flora, and fauna; and the history and culture of their peoples. Exhibits are devoted to traditional weaving, tapacloth making, early tools, body ornaments, tattooing, fishing and horticultural techniques, religion and maraes, games and sports, warfare and arms, deaths and funerals, writers and missionaries (note the 1938 Tahitian Bible). Most, but not all, of the display legends are translated into English. Start in the air-conditioned exhibit hall to the left as you enter and proceed outside. Give yourself at least 30 minutes here, preferably an hour.

Punaauia, 15km (9¼ miles) west of Papeete. ℂ **58.34.76**. Admission 600 CFP (US$7.50/£3.80) adults, free for children. Tues–Sun 9:30am–5:30pm. Turn toward the lagoon at the Total station and right at the museum's sign.

Musée Gauguin (Gauguin Museum) 🌾🌾🌾   This museum/memorial to Paul Gauguin, the French artist who lived in the Mataiea district from 1891 until 1893, owns a few of his sculptures, wood carvings, engravings, and a ceramic vase. It has an active program to borrow his major works, however, and one might be on display during your visit. Otherwise, the exhibits are dedicated to his life in French Polynesia. It's best to see them counterclockwise, starting at the gift shop, which sells excellent prints and reproductions of his works. The originals are in the first gallery. An interesting display in the last gallery shows who owns his works today. The museum has a lagoonside restaurant, although most visitors have lunch at the nearby Restaurant du Musée Gauguin, at PK 50.5 (see "The Circle Island Tour," below).

The museum is adjacent to the **Harrison W. Smith Jardin Botanique (Botanical Gardens),** which was started in 1919 by Harrison Smith, an American who left a career teaching physics at MIT and moved to Tahiti. He died here in 1947. His gardens, which now belong to the public, are home to a plethora of tropical plants from around the world. This is the wettest part of Tahiti, so bring an umbrella.

Mataiea, 51km (32 miles) west of Papeete. ℂ **57.10.58**. Museum admission 600 CFP (US$7.50/£3.80) adults, 300 CFP (US$3.75/£1.90) children 12–18. Gardens admission 600 CFP (US$7.50/£3.80), free for children under 12. Daily 9am–5pm.

Point Venus 🌾🌾🌾   Capt. James Cook observed the transit of the planet Venus in 1769 at Point Venus, Tahiti's northernmost extremity. The sandy peninsula covered with ironwood (casuarina) trees is about 2km (1¼ miles) from the main road. Captains Wallis, Cook, and Bligh landed here after anchoring their ships offshore, behind the reef in Matavai Bay. Captain Cook made his observations of the transit of Venus across the sun from a point between the black-sand beach and the river that cuts the peninsula in two. The beach and the parklike setting around the lighthouse, which was completed in 1868 (notwithstanding the 1867 date over the door), are popular for picnics. There is a snack bar, a souvenir and handicraft shop, and toilets.

Mahina, 10km (6¼ miles) east of Papeete. No phone. Free admission. Open daily 4am–7pm; snack bar and souvenir shop daily 8am–5pm.

WALKING TOUR   PAPEETE

Start:	Tahiti Tourisme's visitor center
Finish:	Papeete Town Hall
Time:	2 hours
Best Times:	Early morning or late afternoon
Worst Times:	Midday, or Sunday when most establishments are closed

Begin at Tahiti Tourisme's visitor center in Tahua Vaiete, the park by the cruise-ship dock, at the foot of rue Paul Gauguin. Stroll westward along Boulevard Pomare. Opposite the tuna boat dock stands Centre Vaima.

❶ Centre Vaima

The chic shops in Papeete's first shopping mall are a mecca for Papeete's French and European residents (the Municipal Market still attracts mostly Tahitians). The infamous Quinn's Bar stood in the block east of the Centre Vaima, where the Noa Noa boutique is now. The Centre Vaima takes its name from the Vaima Restaurant, everyone's favorite eatery in those days, which it replaced.

Across the four-lane boulevard from the Vaima is the wooden boardwalk along the Quay.

❷ The Quay

Cruising yachts from around the world congregate here from April to September, and resident boats are docked here all year. Beyond them, on the other side of the harbor, is **Motu Uta,** once a small natural island belonging to Queen Pomare but now home of the wharves and warehouses of Papeete's shipping port. The reef on the other side has been filled to make a breakwater and to connect Motu Uta by road to **Fare Ute,** the industrial area and French naval base to the right. The interisland boats dock alongside the filled-in reef, and their cargoes of *copra* (dried coconut meat) are taken to a mill at Fare Ute, where coconut oil is extracted and later shipped overseas to be used in cosmetics.

Walk west along the waterfront, past the main post office, next to which is Parc Bougainville.

❸ Parc Bougainville

This shady park next to the post office is named for the French explorer who found Tahiti a little too late to get credit for its discovery. Two cannons flank the statue of Bougainville: The one nearest the post office was on the *Seeadler,* Count von Luckner's World War I German raider, which ran aground in the Cook Islands after terrifying the British and French territories of the South Pacific. The other was on the French navy's *Zélée.* There's a snack bar at the rear of the park.

Walk westward to the traffic circle at the foot of avenue Bruat.

❹ Place Jacques Chirac

Few projects exemplify Papeete's vast road improvements more than the big traffic circle, under which pass the four busy lanes of boulevard Pomare, and the adjacent underground garage. On the harbor side, the semicircular park is known as Place Jacques Chirac, which created a stir because it's French tradition not to name a public place after a living president. Underneath is a garage. The park is the beginning of recent landfills, which have replaced a black-sand beach that used to run west of here.

Keep going west along the waterfront, to rue l'Arthémise, where you can't miss the big beige church on the mountain side of the boulevard.

❺ Eglise Evangélique

An impressive steeple sits atop Eglise Evangélique, the largest Protestant church in French Polynesia. The local evangelical sect grew out of the early work by the London Missionary Society. Today the pastors are Tahitian. Outrigger

Walking Tour: Papeete

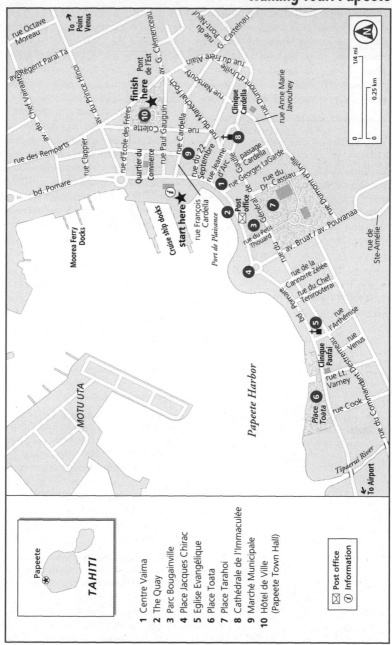

Post office
ⓘ Information

1 Centre Vaima
2 The Quay
3 Parc Bougainville
4 Place Jacques Chirac
5 Eglise Evangélique
6 Place Toata
7 Place Tarahoi
8 Cathédrale de l'Immaculée
9 Marché Municipale
10 Hôtel de Ville
   (Papeete Town Hall)

canoe racing is Tahiti's national sport, and the *va'a*—those sleek vessels seen cutting the harbor during lunchtime and after work—used to be kept on a black-sand beach across the boulevard from the church. Today a section of the landfill across the boulevard is reserved for them.

Continue west along boulevard Pomare for 6 more blocks. You'll see a few remaining stately old colonial homes across the boulevard. On the harbor side you will come to Place Toata.

⑥ Place Toata

Another project funded by the economic restructuring fund, Place Toata is another park built on the landfill, and it is a favorite gathering place for office workers during the day and families at night. They come to stroll, take in the view, and dine at inexpensive snack bars. Place Toata's outdoor amphitheater hosts concerts all year and the national dance competition during the huge *Heiva Nui* festival in July. Next door, on the banks of Tipaerui River, stands the *Office Territorial d'Action Culturelle,* Tahiti's cultural center and library.

TAKE A BREAK
Comparable to *les roulottes* (see "Where to Dine," later in this chapter) but permanently here, Place Toata's open-air snack bars are great for cold drinks, ice cream cones, or even a complete lunch. There are clean public restrooms here.

Turn around and backtrack on boulevard Pomare to Parc Bougainville (see number 3, above), cut through the park, and proceed through the park to the spacious grounds of Place Tarahoi.

⑦ Place Tarahoi

Place Tarahoi, Papeete's governmental center, was royal property in the old days and site of Queen Pomare's mansion, which the French used as their headquarters after 1842. Her impressive home is long gone but is replicated by the Papeete Town Hall (see number 10, below). As

you face the grounds, the buildings on the right house the French government and include the home of the president of French Polynesia. The modern building on the left is the Territorial Assembly. You can walk around hallways of the Assembly building during business hours. In front stands a monument to **Pouvanaa a Oopa** (1895–1977), a Tahitian who became a hero fighting for France in World War I and then spent the rest of his life battling for independence for his homeland. During the 1960s and '70s, he spent 15 years in prison in France, but he returned home in time to see more local autonomy granted to the territory. In fact, his fellow Tahitians sent him back to Paris as a member of the French Senate.

Continue 2 more blocks along rue du Général-de-Gaulle, past the rear of Centre Vaima, to Cathédrale de l'Immaculée Conception.

⑧ Cathédrale de l'Immaculée Conception

Tahiti's oldest Catholic church, Cathédrale de l'Immaculée Conception, houses a series of paintings of the Crucifixion. It's a cool, quiet, and comforting place to pray or contemplate.

Rue du Général-de-Gaulle becomes rue du Maréchal-Foch past the church. Follow it for a block. Bear left at rue Colette and continue until you come to Marché Municipale.

⑨ Marché Municipale

Take a stroll under the tin pavilion of Papeete's Municipal Market and examine the fruits and vegetables offered for sale (see "The Top Attractions," above).

After sampling the market and the marvelous handicraft stalls along its sidewalk and upstairs, walk along rue Colette 2 more blocks, until you come to Papeete Town Hall.

⑩ Hotel de Ville (Papeete Town Hall)

This is a magnificent replica of Queen Pomare's mansion, which once stood at Place Tarahoi. This impressive structure, with its wraparound veranda, captures the spirit of the colonial South Pacific.

This *Hôtel de Ville* or *Fare Oire* (French and Tahitian, respectively, for "town hall") was dedicated in 1990 by French President François Mitterand during an elaborate celebration. Walk up the grand entrance steps to catch a cool breeze from the broad balconies.

From here you can find your way back to Vaima Centre and some much-needed refreshment at its open-air cafes (see "Where to Dine," later).

3 The Circle Island Tour ★★

A **Circle Island Tour,** or a drive around Tahiti, is the best way to spend a day seeing the island's outlying sights and a bit of old Polynesia away from Papeete's bustle. The road around the Tahiti Nui is 114km (71 miles) long. It's 54km (34 miles) from Papeete to Taravao along the east coast and 60km (37 miles) along the west coast.

On the land side of the road are red-topped concrete **kilometer markers** (*pointes kilomètres* in French, or **PK** for short). They tell the distance in kilometers between Papeete and the isthmus of Taravao. That is, the distance from Papeete to Taravao in each direction—not the total number of kilometers around the island. The large numbers facing the ocean are the number of kilometers from Papeete; the numbers facing you as you drive along are the number of kilometers you have to go to Papeete or Taravao, depending on your direction. Distances between the PKs are referred to in tenths of kilometers; for example, PK 35.6 would be 35.6km from Papeete.

For a more detailed description of the tour than I give here, buy a copy of Bengt Danielsson's *Tahiti: Circle Island Tour Guide.* French and English editions are available in the local bookstores.

THE NORTH & EAST COASTS OF TAHITI NUI

Proceeding clockwise from Papeete, you'll leave town by turning inland off Boulevard Pomare and following the **avenue du Prince-Hinoi,** the start of the round-island road.

FAUTAUA VALLEY, LOTI'S POOL & THE DIADEME   It's not worth the side trip, but at PK 2.5, a road goes right into the steep-walled Fautaua Valley and the **Bain Loti,** or Loti's Pool. Julien Viaud, the French merchant mariner who wrote under the pen name Pierre Loti, used this pool as a setting for his novel *The Marriage of Loti,* which recounted the love of a Frenchman for a Tahitian woman. Now part of Papeete's water-supply system, the pool is covered in concrete. The road goes into the lower part of the valley and terminates at the beginning of a hiking trail up to the **Fautaua Waterfall,** which plunges over a cliff into a large pool 300m (984 ft.) below. The all-day hike to the head of the valley is best done with a guide (see "Golf, Hiking & Watersports," later).

Pull off the main road into the side street opposite the big seaside park at Pirae for a look inland at the **Diadème,** a rocky outcrop protruding like a crown from the interior ridge. (I think it looks like a single worn molar sticking up from a gum.)

TOMB OF POMARE V ★★   At PK 4.7 turn left at the sign and drive a short distance to a Protestant churchyard commanding an excellent view of Matavai Bay to the right. The tomb with a Grecian urn on top was built in 1879 for Queen Pomare. Her remains were removed a few years later by her son, King Pomare V, who abdicated in return for a French pension and later died of too much drink. Now he is buried there, and tour guides like to say the urn is not an urn at all but a liquor bottle, which makes it a monument not to Pomare V but to the cause of his death.

LA MAISON JAMES NORMAN HALL (JAMES NORMAN HALL'S HOME) 🐟🐟🐟   At PK 5.4, on the mountain side of the road just east of the small bridge, stands the home of James Norman Hall, coauthor with Charles Nordhoff of *Mutiny on the Bounty.* See "The Top Attractions," earlier.

> **Impressions**
>
> *Look to the Northward, stranger /*
> *Just over the hillside there / Have*
> *you in your travels seen / A land*
> *more passing fair?*
>
> —James Norman Hall
> (on his tombstone)

ONE TREE HILL 🐟🐟   At PK 8, past the new Radisson Plaza resort, you'll come to the top of One Tree Hill, so named by Capt. James Cook because a single tree stood on this headland in the late 1700s. For many years, it was the site of a luxury hotel, now closed. Pull into the roundabout at the entrance and stop for one of Tahiti's most magnificent vistas. You'll look down on the north coast from Matavai Bay to Papeete, with Moorea looming on the horizon.

POINT VENUS 🐟🐟🐟   At PK 10, turn left at Super Marché Venus Star and drive to Point Venus, Tahiti's northernmost point, where Capt. James Cook observed the transit of the planet Venus in 1769 (see "The Top Attractions," earlier).

PAPENOO VALLEY   At PK 17.1, Tahiti's longest bridge crosses its longest river at the end of its largest valley at one of its largest rural villages—all named Papenoo. The river flows to the sea through the only wall in Tahiti Nui's old volcanic crater. A new cross-island road goes up the valley, literally through the mountains (via a tunnel), and down to Tahiti's south shore. Four-wheel-drive vehicles go into the valley on their rugged excursions (see "Safari Expeditions," later).

ARAHOHO BLOWHOLES   At PK 22, the surf pounding against the headland at Arahoho has formed overhanging shelves with holes in them. As waves crash under the shelves, water and air are forced through the holes, resulting in a geyserlike phenomenon. One shoots up at the base of a cliff on the mountain side of the road, but be careful because oncoming traffic cannot see you standing there. Pull into the overlook with free parking and toilets west of the curve. There's a snack bar across the road, and a black-sand beach is within sight.

CASCADES DE TEFAARUMAI (FAARUMAI WATERFALLS) 🐟🐟   At PK 22.1, a sign on the right just past the blowhole marks a somewhat paved road that leads 1.5km (1 mile) up a small valley to the Cascades de Faarumai, Tahiti's most accessible waterfalls. The drive itself gives a glimpse of how ordinary rural Tahitians live in simple wood houses surrounded by bananas and breadfruit. Park near the stand of bamboo trees and take a few minutes to read the signs, which explain a romantic legend. Vaimahuta falls are an easy walk; Haamaremare Iti and Haamaremarerahi falls are a 45-minute climb up a more difficult trail. Vaimahuta falls plunge straight down several hundred feet from a hanging valley into a large pool. Bring insect repellent.

MAHAENA BATTLEFIELD   At PK 32.5, the Tahitian rebellion came to a head on April 17, 1844, when 441 French troops charged several times and many poorly armed Tahitians dug in near the village of Mahaena. The Tahitians lost 102 men and the French, 15. It was the last set battle of the rebellion.

BOUGAINVILLE'S ANCHORAGE 🐟   At PK 37.6, a plaque mounted on a rock on the northern end of the bridge at Hitiaa commemorates Bougainville's landing.

The French explorer anchored just offshore when he arrived in Tahiti in 1768. The two small islands on the reef, Oputotara and Variararu, provided slim protection against the prevailing trade winds, and Bougainville lost six anchors in 10 days trying to keep his ships off the reef. Tahitians recovered one and gave it to the high chief of Bora Bora, who in turn gave it to Captain Cook in 1777.

FAATAUTIA VALLEY   At PK 41.8 begins a view of Faatautia Valley, which looks so much like those in the Marquesas that in 1957 director John Huston chose it as a location for a movie version of *Typee*, Herman Melville's novelized account of his ship-jumping adventures among the Marquesans in the 1840s. The project was scrapped after another of Huston's Melville movies, *Moby Dick*, bombed at the box office. The uninhabited valley surely looks much today as it did 1,000 years ago.

TARAVAO   At PK 53, after passing the small-boat marina, the road climbs up onto the Isthmus of Taravao, separating Tahiti Nui from Tahiti Iti. At the top are the stone walls of Fort Taravao, which the French built in 1844 to bottle up what was left of the rebellious Tahitians on the Tahiti Iti peninsula. Germans stuck on Tahiti during World War II were interned there. It is now used as a French army training center. The village of Taravao with its shops, suburban streets, and churches has grown up around the military post. Its snack bars are a good place for a refueling stop.

> **Impressions**
> *It came upon me little by little. I came to like the life here, with its ease and its leisure, and the people, with their good-nature and their happy smiling faces.*
> —W. Somerset Maugham,
> *The Fall of Edward Barnard*, 1921

TAHITI ITI

Tahiti Iti is much less sparsely populated and developed than its bigger twin, Tahiti Nui. Paved roads dead-end about halfway down its north and south sides. A series of cliffs plunges into the sea on Tahiti Iti's rugged east end. While the north shore holds historical interest, the south coast has Tahiti's best beach and its top surfing spot.

TARAVAO PLATEAU   If you have to chose one of three roads on Tahiti Iti, take the one by the school and stadium. It dead-ends high up into the rolling pastures of the Taravao Plateau. It begins at the traffic signal on the north coast road to Tautira and runs up through cool pastures reminiscent of rural France, with huge trees lining the narrow paved road. At more than 360m (1,181 ft.) high, the plateau is blessed with a refreshing, perpetually springlike climate. Near the end of the road you'll come to the **Taravao Plateau Overlook,** where you'll have a spectacular view of the entire isthmus and down both sides of Tahiti Nui.

THE NORTH COAST TO TAUTIRA   The road on the north coast of Tahiti Iti goes for 18km (11 miles), to the sizable village of **Tautira,** which sits on its own peninsula. Captain Cook anchored in the bay off Tautira on his second visit to Tahiti in 1773. His ships ran aground on the reef while the crews were partying one night. He managed to get them off but lost several anchors in the process. One of them was found in 1978 and is now on display at the Museum of Tahiti and Her Islands, which we will come to on the west side of the island.

A year after Cook landed at Tautira, a Spanish ship from Peru named the *Aguila* landed here, and its captain claimed the island for Spain. It was the third time Tahiti had been claimed for a European power. He also put ashore two Franciscan priests. The *Aguila* returned a year later, but the priests had had enough of Tahiti and sailed back to Peru.

When you enter the village, bear left and drive along the scenic coast road as far as the general store, where you can buy a cold soft drink and snack.

THE SOUTH COAST TO TEAHUPOO   The picturesque road along the south coast of Tahiti Iti skirts the lagoon, passing through small settlements. Novelist Zane Grey had a deep-sea-fishing camp at PK 7.3, near the village of Toahotu, from 1928 to 1930. He caught a silver marlin that was about 4m (13 ft.) long and weighed more than 1,000 pounds—even after the sharks had had a meal on it while Grey was trying to get it aboard his boat. He wrote about his adventures in *Tales of Tahitian Waters.*

According to Tahitian legends, the demigod Maui once made a rope from his sister Hina's hair and used it to slow down the sun long enough for Tahitians to finish cooking their food in their earth ovens (a lengthy process). He accomplished this feat while standing on the reef at a point 8.5km (5¼ miles) along the south coast road. Beyond Maui's alleged footprints, now under the road, the Bay of Tapueraha provides the widest pass and deepest natural harbor on Tahiti. It was used as a base by a large contingent of the French navy during the aboveground nuclear tests at Moruroa atoll in the 1960s and 1970s. Some of the old mooring pilings still stand just offshore.

Reminiscent of the great Matira Beach on Bora Bora, **La Plage de Maui (Maui Beach)** 𝕶𝕶𝕶 borders the bay and is the best strip of white sand on Tahiti. Get out of the car and take a break at the lagoonside snack bar here. A cave, known as the *Caverne de Maui,* is a short walk inland.

Near Vairao village you'll pass the modern **IFREMER: *Le Centre Océanologique du Pacifique* (Pacific Oceanographic Center),** which conducts research into blackpearl oysters, shrimp farming, and other means of extracting money from seawater. The buildings formerly were used for France's nuclear testing program.

The south coast road ends at **Teahupoo,** the famous *"village de surf,"* whose beachside park overlooks the big waves curling around Hava'a Pass. World-class boarders compete in the Billabong Pro tournament here every May. A footbridge crosses the Tirahi River, from where a trail begins along Tahiti Iti's rugged eastern shoreline. It's a strenuous and sometimes dangerous hike done only with a guide (see "Golf, Hiking & Watersports," later in this chapter).

THE SOUTH COAST OF TAHITI NUI

As you leave Taravao, heading back to Papeete along Tahiti's south coast, note that the PK markers decrease the nearer you get to Papeete. The road rims casuarina-ringed Port Phaeton, which cuts nearly halfway across the isthmus. Port Phaeton and the Bay of Tapueraha to the south are Tahiti's finest harbors, yet European settlement and

---

Fun Fact   **R. L. S. Was Here**

Robert Louis Stevenson spent 2 months at Tautira in 1888, working on *The Master of Ballantrae,* a novel set not in Tahiti but in Scotland. Stevenson's mother was with him in Tautira. After she returned to London, she sent the local Protestant church a silver Communion service, which is still being used today. See chapter 13 for more about Stevenson's South Pacific adventures.

Tips **Take a Circle Island Break**

Shoehorned between the road and the sands of Maui Beach, **La Plage de Maui Restaurant** (© **74.71.74**) is my place to stop for refreshment while taking in the gorgeous scenery. Owners Rose Wilkinson and Alain Corre, both veterans of the Sofitel Moorea Beach Resort, offer burgers, steaks, *poisson cru* (marinated fish), ice cream, and other temptations. Burgers cost about 800 CFP (US$10/£5), while main courses range from 1,900 CFP to 2,800 CFP (US$24–US$35/£12–£18). They deal in cash only and are open daily 10am to 6pm.

The circle island tour buses deposit their passengers for lunch at the lagoon-side **Restaurant du Musée Gauguin**, at PK 50.5 (© **57.13.80**), which is worth a stop just for its phenomenal view of Tahiti Iti. The lunch buffet costs about 2,800 CFP (US$35/£18) per person Monday through Saturday, 3,700 CFP (US$46/£23) on Sunday; sandwiches are also available. It's open daily from noon to 3pm.

A less expensive option is **Beach Burger**, at PK 39 (© **57.41.03**), west of the golf course at Atimaono. In addition to burgers, it offers salads, steaks, Chinese fare, and pizzas. It's open Sunday through Thursday from 6am to 8pm, Friday and Saturday from 6am to 9:30pm.

---

most development have taken place on the opposite side of the island, around Papeete. The shrimp you'll order for dinner come from the aqua farms in the bay's shallow waters.

PAPAEARI At PK 52 stands Tahiti's oldest village. Apparently the island's initial residents recognized the advantages of the south coast and its deep lagoons and harbors, for word-of-mouth history says they came through the Hotumatuu Pass in the reef and settled at Papeari between A.D. 400 and 500. Robert Keable, author of *Simon Called Peter,* a best-selling novel about a disillusioned clergyman, lived here from 1924 until he died in 1928 at age 40. His home, now a private residence, stands at PK 55. Today Papeari is a thriving village whose residents often sell fruit and vegetables at stands along the road.

MUSEE GAUGUIN **(GAUGUIN MUSEUM)** At PK 51.2 is the entrance to the museum/memorial to Paul Gauguin, who lived near here from 1891 until 1893 (see "The Top Attractions," earlier). The museum sits in lush **Harrison W. Smith Botanical Gardens,** started in 1919 by American Harrison Smith. The museum and gardens are open daily from 9am to 5pm. There's a snack bar here, but your best bet is to continue west.

VAIHIRIA RIVER & VAIPAHI GARDENS At PK 48, in the village of Mataiea, the main road crosses the Vaihiria River. The new cross-island road from Papenoo on the north coast terminates here. An 11km (6¾ mile) track leads to **Lake Vaihiria,** at 465m (1,525 ft.) above sea level. It is Tahiti's only lake and is noted for its freshwater eels. Cliffs up to 900m (2,953 ft.) tall drop to the lake on its north side. Also in Mataiea is the lush *Jardin Vaipehi* (Vaipehi Gardens; no phone), a cool and refreshing spot with a bubbling natural spring and an oft-photographed waterfall (it's closer to the road than any other Tahitian waterfall). The garden is lush with elephant ears, tree ferns, ground orchids, jade vines, and other tropical vegetation. Signs (in

The Moon & 21 Million Pence

In 1891, a marginally successful Parisian painter named Paul Gauguin left behind his wife and six children and sailed to Tahiti. He wanted to devote himself to his art, free of the chains of civilization.

Instead of paradise, Gauguin found a world that suffered from some of the same maladies as did the one from which he fled. Poverty, sickness, and frequent disputes with church and colonial officials marked his decade in the islands. He had syphilis, a bad heart, and an addiction to opium.

Gauguin disliked Papeete and spent his first 2 years in the rural Mataiea district, on Tahiti's south coast, where a village woman asked what he was doing there. Looking for a girl, he replied. The woman immediately offered her 13-year-old daughter, Tehaamana, the first of Gauguin's early teenage Tahitian mistresses. One of them bore him a son in 1899.

Tehaamana and the others figured prominently in Gauguin's impression-istic masterpieces, which brought fame to Tahiti but did little for his own pocketbook. After 649 paintings and a colorful career, immortalized by W. Somerset Maugham in *The Moon and Sixpence,* Gauguin died penniless in 1903.

At the time of his death, on Hiva Oa in the Marquesas Islands, a painting by Gauguin sold for 150 French francs. In 2007, his *L'Homme a la Hache* (The Man at the Axe) sold for £21.2 million (US$42.4 million).

French) explains its historical importance, because ancient Tahitian nobles followed the path to the springs in order to be spiritually purified.

ATIMAONO   At PK 44 begins the largest parcel of flat land on Tahiti, site of **Atimaono Golf Course,** French Polynesia's only links. Irishman William Stewart started his cotton plantation here during the American Civil War. Nothing remains of the plantation, but it was Stewart who brought the first Chinese indentured servants to Tahiti. See "Golf, Hiking & Watersports," below.

The knobby **noni fruit**'s reputed medicinal properties have created a new industry in the islands, where folks are growing it by the boatload. You can see how it's turned into noni juice and other products at **Tahitian Noni International,** at PK 42.2 (© 80.37.50). Tours are given on Friday by reservation only. Like Castor oil, it must be good for you if it tastes this bad!

DORENCE ATWATER'S GRAVE   At PK 36, on the lagoon side of the road in Papara village, stands a Protestant church, under whose paved yard is buried Dorence Atwater, U.S. consul to Tahiti after the American Civil War. Captured while serving in the Union Army, Atwater was assigned to the hospital at the infamous Confederate POW camp at Andersonville, Georgia, where he surreptitiously recorded the names of Union soldiers who died in captivity. He later escaped and brought his lists to the federal government, thus proving that the Confederacy was keeping inaccurate records. His action made him a hero in the eyes of the Union Army. He later moved to the south coast of Tahiti, married a daughter of a chief of the Papara district, and at one time invested in William Stewart's cotton venture.

MARAA GROTTO   At PK 28.5, on Tahiti's southwest corner, the road turns sharply around the base of a series of headlands, which drop precipitously to the lagoon. Deep into one of these cliffs goes the Maraa Grotto, also called the Paroa Cave. It actually is two caves, both with water inside, and they go much deeper into the hill than appears at first glance. Park in the lot and enter at the gazebo to reach the larger of the two caves. A short trail leads from there to the smaller cave and a miniwaterfall.

THE WEST COAST OF TAHITI NUI

North of Maraa the road runs through the Paea and Punaauia suburbs. The west coast is the driest part of Tahiti, and it's popular with Europeans, Americans, and others who have built homes along the lagoon and in the hills overlooking it and Moorea.

ARAHURAHU MARAE 𝒓𝒓   At PK 22.5, a small road on the right of Magasin Laut leads to a narrow valley, on the floor of which sits the restored Arahurahu Marae (see "The Top Attractions," earlier).

MUSEE DE TAHITI ET SES ISLES **(MUSEUM OF TAHITI AND HER ISLANDS)** 𝒓𝒓𝒓   At PK 15.1, turn left at the gas station and follow the signs through a residential area to the lagoon and the *Musée de Tahiti et Ses Isles,* one of the South Pacific's best museums (see "The Top Attractions," earlier).

PUNARUU VALLEY   On a cloudless day, you will have a view up the Punaruu Valley to the Diadème as you drive from the museum back to the main road. Power lines mar the view, but it's worth stopping to take a look. Tahitian rebels occupied the valley during the 1844–48 war, and the French built a fort to keep them there (the site is now occupied by a television antenna). Later the valley was used to grow oranges, most of which were shipped to California. Villagers sell the now-wild fruit at roadside stands during July and August.

The Route 5 expressway goes as far south as the Punaruu River, just north of the Tahiti Museum. Instead of taking the overpass onto the expressway, stay in the right lane to the traffic circle under the overpass. The first exit off the circle will take you up into the Punaruu Valley. The second exit leads to the Route 5 expressway. The third is Route 1, the old two-lane coast road, which will take you to the Lagoonarium.

LAGOONARIUM   At PK 11.4, the Captain Bligh Restaurant and Bar has a terrific view of Moorea and is home to *Le Lagoonarium de Tahiti,* an underwater viewing room (see "The Top Attractions," earlier).

After the Lagoonarium, Route 1 soon joins the four-lane Route 5 expressway, which passes shopping centers and marinas in Punaauia. It splits just before the Sofitel Tahiti Maeva Beach Resort. The left lanes feed into the Route 5 expressway, which roars back to Papeete. The right lanes take you along Route 1, the old road that goes past the west coast hotels and the Tahiti-Faaa International Airport before returning to town.

Moments Watching the Sun Paint Moorea

No matter how many times I visit French Polynesia, I never tire of its incredible natural beauty. I always spend sunset of my first day at the InterContinental Resort Tahiti, on the west coast, depleting my camera battery as the sun paints another glorious red and orange sky over Moorea's purple ridges.

ORGANIZED TOURS AROUND THE COASTAL ROAD

Several companies offer tours along the coastal road around Tahiti Nui. They are a good way to see the island without hassling with traffic. I find them to be an especially fine way to recover from jet lag.

I prefer English-speaking William Leteeg's **Adventure Eagle Tours** (℡ **77.20.03**). William takes you around in an air-conditioned van and lends his experiences growing up on the island to his commentaries. Others include **Tahiti Tours** (℡ **54.02.50;** www.tahiti-tours.com), **Tahiti Nui Travel** (℡ **42.40.10;** www.tahiti-nui.com), and **Marama Tours** (℡ **50.74.74;** www.maramatours.com). They have reservations desks in several hotels. It's about 4,400 CFP (US$55/£28) for a half-day tour, 5,100 CFP (US$64/£32) for all day, plus admission to the museums, attractions and lunch, usually at the Restaurant du Musée Gauguin.

For a spectacular bird's-eye view of Tahiti or Moorea, take a sightseeing ride with **Polynesia Hélicoptères** (℡ **54.87.20;** www.polynesia-helicopter.com). The flights are anything but inexpensive, but if you can afford it, they are well worth the price of about 16,300 CFP (US$204/£103) for a flight over Tahiti Nui, 33,700 CFP (US$421/£213) for a flight over Tahiti Iti, or 26,300 CFP (US$329/£166) for a spectacular view of Moorea. Those fares are per person, with a minimum of four passengers required. The flights last between 20 and 45 minutes, depending on where you go. Reserve as far in advance as possible.

SAFARI EXPEDITIONS ✹✹✹

"Safari expeditions" into Tahiti's interior offer a different view of the island—and some spectacular views at that. Riding in the back of open, four-wheel-drive vehicles, you follow unpaved roads through Tahiti's central crater, usually via the breathtaking Papenoo Valley. Weather permitting, you'll ride up to 1,440 meters (4,724 feet) altitude on the sides of the island's steep interior ridge. The cool temperatures at the higher elevations are refreshing, as is a swim in a cold mountain stream.

⟨Tips⟩ Touring Tahiti from Moorea—& Vice Versa

You can take a circle island tour or safari expedition of Tahiti even if you're staying on Moorea. Catch an early flight or ferry to Papeete, go on the tour or safari expedition, and return to Moorea in the late afternoon. Let the tour companies know you're coming from Moorea when you make your reservation so they can meet you at the airport or ferry dock. If you do it yourself, the rental-car companies can have a vehicle waiting on Tahiti.

I would spend a day on Moorea even if I had a short layover on Tahiti. You can arrange it yourself by ferry or plane, but you will need a rental vehicle on Moorea (Avis or Europcar will have one waiting for you at the Moorea airport or ferry dock). An alternative is to take a Moorea day tour, such as those offered by **Tahiti Nui Travel** (℡ **54.02.00;** www.tahitinuitravel.com) and **Marama Tours** (℡ **50.74.74;** www.maramatours.com). They charge between 15,000 CFP and 28,500 CFP (US$188–US$356/£95–£180), depending on whether you fly or take the ferry and whether you take a circle island tour or go on a picnic on a small island, an inland safari tour, or a dolphin-watching excursion. Call or book at any hotel activities desk.

⌒Tips Pick a Clear Day

The safari expeditions do not go into the mountains when the weather is bad, and even if it's not raining, clouds atop the mountains can obscure what would otherwise be fantastic views. Pick as clear a day as possible for this thrilling outing. Your best chance will be in winter (June through early Sept).

Tahiti Safari Expedition (© **42.14.15;** www.tahiti-safari.com) has been the best since owner Patrice Bordes pioneered the concept in 1990. He charges about 5,500 CFP (US$69/£35) per person for a half-day trip, 9,500 CFP (US$119/£60) for a full day. Patrice usually stops at a restaurant in the Papenoo Valley, where you can buy lunch, or you can bring your own picnic. Don't forget your bathing suit, a towel, hat, sunscreen, insect repellent, and camera. These are popular trips with limited space, so reserve as early as possible at any hotel activities desk.

4 Golf, Hiking & Watersports

GOLF   Tahiti's mountainous interior provides a spectacular backdrop to the 27-hole **Atimaono Golf Course,** PK 40.2 (© **57.43.41**), which sprawls over the site of William Stewart's 1860s cotton plantation. A clubhouse, pro shop, restaurant, bar, locker rooms, showers, a swimming pool, a spa pool, and a driving range are on the premises. The club is open daily from 8am to dark. Greens fees are about 5,500 CFP (US$69/£35) for 18 holes. The hotel activities desks can book all-day golf outings for about 24,000 CFP (US$300/£152) for one golfer, 35,000 CFP (US$438/£222) for two, including greens fees, equipment, lunch, and transportation.

HIKING   Tahiti has a number of hiking trails, such as the cross-island Papenoo Valley–Lake Vaihiria route. Another ascends to the top of Mount Aorai, and another skirts the remote and wild eastern coast of Tahiti Iti. This is not the Shenandoah or some other American or New Zealand national park with well-marked trails, and the French gendarmes do not take kindly to rescuing some tourist who became lost trying to scale one of Tahiti's peaks. Downpours can occur in the higher altitudes, swelling the streams that most trails follow, and the nights can become bitterly cold and damp. Which side of the island is the rainy side can shift daily, depending on which way the wind blows. In addition, the quick-growing tropical foliage can quickly obscure a path that was easily followed a few days before. Permits are required to use some trails that cross government land.

Accordingly, *always* go with a guide or on organized hikes such as the ones offered by **Tahiti Evasion** (© **56.48.77;** www.tahitievasion.com). This Moorea-based company has all-day treks into the Fautaua valley, home of Loti's Pool; the Orofero Valley on Tahiti's south coast; and to the top of Mt. Aorai, the island's third-highest peak. The treks start at 5,200 CFP (US$65/£33) per person. Hikes along the wild, uninhabited east coast of Tahiti Iti take 3 days and 2 nights of camping (call for prices). All except the Mt. Aorai climb are rated as easy walks. Tahiti Evasion will also organize hiking-and-watersports trips of up to 3 weeks throughout the islands.

You can also check with the **Tourisme Tahiti's visitor bureau** in Papeete (© **50. 57.12**) for the names of guides and hiking clubs.

WATERSPORTS   Based at the InterContinental Resort Tahiti, **Aquatica Dive Centre and Nautical Activities** (© 53.34.96; www.aquatica-dive.com) offers the most comprehensive list of watersports activities, and you don't have to be an InterContinental guest to partake. Some sample prices: snorkeling gear rental, 2,000 CFP (US$25/£13); snorkeling trips, 4,000 CFP (US$50/£25); water-skiing, 6,500 CFP (US$81/£41); and kayak rental, 1,800 CFP (US$23/£11) per hour. A two-tank dive including equipment and a guide costs 12,000 CFP (US$150/£76); and introductory dive, 7,000 CFP (US$88/£44). Aquatica also has tours by jet ski and all-terrain vehicles for 19,400 CFP (US$242/£123) and 20,600 CFP (US$258/£130) per person, respectively. Also contact them about dolphin- and whale-watching tours.

Most beaches on Tahiti have black volcanic sand, not the white variety most of us expect in the South Pacific. The most convenient of these is the public beach in front of **Le Royal Tahitien Hotel** (© 50.40.40), in Pirae 4km (2½ miles) east of downtown (see "Where to Stay," below). There is some white sand among the pebbles at the **PK 18.5 Plage de Publique (Public Beach),** on the west coast at the Punaauia–Paea border. It has a restaurant and snack bar. The best beach of all is **Plage de Maui,** on Tahiti Iti (see "The Circle Island Tour," earlier).

Tahiti is famous for world-class surfing, especially **Teuhupo'o on Tahiti Iti,** home of the annual Billabong Pro championships in May. The best big waves crash on jagged reefs offshore, however, so you could be turned into hamburger if you've never surfed before. On the other hand, Tahiti is the only major South Pacific island where surf breaks on sandy beaches, upon which *Ecole de Surf Tura'i Mataare* **(Tahiti Surf School)** (© 41.91.37; www.tahitisurfschool.info) teaches a half-day surfing and bodyboarding courses for 4,800 CFP (US$60/£30), or you can take private lessons for 12,000 CFP (US$150/£76). It's a good way to find out if you have what it takes to "hang ten."

5 Shopping

There's no shortage of things to buy, especially in Papeete. Black pearls and handicrafts are sure to tempt you. The selection and prices on some items may be better on Moorea.

If you just can't live without visiting a mall, head for the **Centre Moana Nui,** on the main road in Punaauia about .5km (⅓ mile) south of the Sofitel Tahiti Maeva Beach Resort. Here you'll find a huge Carrefour supermarket, boutiques, a snack bar with excellent hamburgers, a hairdresser, a bar, banks with ATMs, and a post office (open Mon–Fri 8am–5pm and Sat 8am–noon). The local **Centre Artisinant** stands across the parking lot under a teepee-shaped roof (see "Handicrafts," below).

Duty-free shopping is limited, with French perfumes the best deal. **Duty Free Tahiti** (© 42.61.61), in the Centre Vaima, is the largest shop. Its specialties are Seiko, Lorus, and Cartier watches and Givenchy, Yves St. Laurent, Chanel, and Guerlain perfumes. The **airport departure lounge** has two duty-free shops.

BLACK PEARLS

Papeete has scores of *bijouteries* (jewelry shops) that carry black pearls in a variety of settings. Some stalls in Papeete's Municipal Market sell pearls, but buy yours from an experienced, reputable dealer. Most of these stores are in or around the Centre Vaima, along boulevard Pomare, and in the Quartier du Commerce, the narrow streets off boulevard Pomare between rue Paul Gauguin and rue d'Ecole des Frères north of the Municipal Market.

Buying Your Black Pearl ★★★

French Polynesia is the world's largest producer of cultured black pearls. They are created by implanting a nucleus into the shell of a live *Pinctada margaritifera,* the oyster used here, which then coats it with nacre, the same lustrous substance that lines the mother-of-pearl shell. The nacre produces dark pearls known as "black" but whose actual color ranges from slightly grayer than white to black with shades of rose or green. Most range in size from 10 to 17mm (slightly less than a ½ in. to slightly less than ¾ in.).

Size, color, luster, lack of imperfections, and shape determine a pearl's value. No two are exactly alike, but the most valuable are the larger ones that are most symmetrical and have few dark blemishes, and whose color is dark with the shades of a peacock showing through a bright luster. A top-quality pearl 13mm or larger will sell for US$10,000 (£5,000) or more, but there are thousands to choose from in the US$300 to US$1,000 (£150–£500) range. Some small, imperfect-but-still-lovely pearls cost much less.

Of course, the perfect pearl comes down to the eye of the beholder. Just make sure you see your dream pearl in daylight before handing over your credit card.

So many pearls were being produced a few years ago that many small pearl farms closed. Competition is still fierce among the islands' shops, some of which (or their agents—commissioned tour guides and bus and taxi drivers) will bombard you with sales pitches almost from the moment you arrive. Even at the highest-end shops, discounting is *de rigueur.* Despite the general rule to avoid haggling in French Polynesia, you shouldn't pay the price marked on a pearl or a piece of jewelry until you have politely asked for a discount.

With most tourists now spending minimum time on Tahiti in favor of the other islands, you might find pearl prices in Papeete to be lower than on Moorea and Bora Bora. That's not always the case, so you should look in shops like **Ron Hall's Island Fashion Black Pearls** on Moorea and **Matira Pearls** on Bora Bora before making a purchase in Papeete (see "Shopping," in chapters 9 and 10). Your salesperson over there is more likely to speak English fluently.

You can get a **refund** of the 16% value-added tax (TVA) included in the price of set pearls (but not on loose pearls). The TVA is not added after the purchase like an American sales tax, so you won't see it. Don't believe them if they say you can't get a refund because they've already taken the TVA off a reduced price. Truth is, they'll have to send the government 16% of whatever price you paid. Ask your dealer how to get your money back by sending them an official form after you have left the country (you can mail it after clearing Immigration at Faaa).

Your beginning point should be the **Musée de la Perle Robert Wan** (© 46.15.54), on boulevard Pomare at rue l'Arthémise, opposite Eglise Evangélique (Protestant Church). Named for Robert Wan, the man who pioneered the local industry back in the 1960s, this museum explains the history of pearls from antiquity, the method by

---

Impressions

It's a comfort to get into a pareu when one gets back from town . . . I should strongly recommend you to adopt it. It's one of the most sensible costumes I have ever come across. It's cool, convenient, and inexpensive.

—W. Somerset Maugham, *The Fall of Edward Barnard,* 1921

---

which they are cultured, and the things to look for when you buy. The museum is open Monday to Saturday from 9am to 5pm. Admission is free.

Adjoining the museum, **Robert Wan Tahiti** (℃ **46.15.54**) carries only excellent-quality pearls and uses only 18-karat gold for its settings, so the prices tend to be high. Robert Wan has outlets on all the main islands.

On the second level of the Centre Vaima, **Sibani Perles Joallier** (℃ **41.36.34**) carries the jewelry line of Didier Sibani, another local pioneer. European-style elegance is the theme here and at the other Sibani outlets throughout the islands.

One of French Polynesia's largest dealers, **Tahia Collins,** has a small outlet on boulevard Pomare at avenue du Prince Hinoi (℃ **54.06.00**). Another large dealer is **Tahiti Pearl Market,** on rue Collette at rue Paul Gauguin (℃ **54.30.60**).

HANDICRAFTS

Although most of the inexpensive souvenirs sold here are made in Asia, many local residents, especially on the outer islands, produce a wide range of seashell jewelry, rag dolls, needlework, and straw hats, mats, baskets, and handbags. I love the *tivaivai,* colorful appliqué quilts stitched together by Tahitian women, who create their works using the same techniques their great-grandmothers were taught by early missionaries. You can also buy exquisite shell chandeliers like those adorning many hotel lobbies.

The most popular item by far is the cotton *pareu,* or wraparound sarong, which everyone wears at one time or another. They are screened, blocked, or printed by hand in the colors of the rainbow. The same material is made into other tropical clothing and various items, such as bedspreads and pillowcases. Pareus are sold pretty much everywhere a visitor might wander.

The **Papeete Municipal Market** 🜚🜚🜚 is the place to shop (see "The Top Attractions," above). It has stalls upstairs and on the surrounding sidewalk, where local women's associations offer a wide selection of handicrafts at reasonable prices. The market is one of the few places where you can find pareus for 1,000 CFP (US$13/£6.35), bedspreads made of the colorful tie-dyed and silk-screened pareu material, and tivaivai quilts and pillowcases. By and large, cloth goods are sold at the sidewalk stalls; those upstairs have a broader range of shell jewelry and other items.

Several villages have *centres artisanants,* where local women display their wares. The one in Punaauia, in the Centre Moana Nui parking lot south of the Sofitel Tahiti Maeva Beach Resort, is the best place to look for tivaivai quilts, which sell for about 35,000 CFP (US$438/£222).

For finer-quality handicrafts, such as woodcarvings from the Marquesas Islands, shell chandeliers, tapa lampshades, or mother-of-pearl shells, try **Tamara Curios** (℃ **42.54.42**), on rue du Général-de-Gaulle in Fare Tony.

6 Where to Stay

With a few exceptions, Tahiti's accommodations are in four areas: on the west coast, where most properties enjoy at least a partial view of Moorea; in Faaa near the airport; in the suburbs east of Papeete, where the beaches are of black volcanic sand; and in the city of Papeete, where you can sample urban life *al la Tahitien.*

ON THE WEST COAST

InterContinental Resort Tahiti ⋆⋆⋆   This is the best all-around resort on Tahiti. Built in the 1960s as the Tahiti Beachcomber Travelodge (most folk here still call it "the Beachcomber"). It has a range of accommodations, including smaller rooms dating from its original Travelodge incarnation, newer and more spacious "Panoramic" rooms, and overwater bungalows with unimpeded views of Moorea. All are now luxuriously appointed with canopy beds and marble bathrooms, and all have private patios or balconies with views of Moorea. The original overwater units are smaller than newer models, which have separate sitting areas and steps leading from their decks into the lagoon. The resort doesn't have a natural beach, but bulkheads separate the sea from white imported sand. Or you can frolic in two pools—one adjacent to the romantic **Le Lotus,** one of Tahiti's best restaurants (see "Where to Dine," below). Features here include an all-night lobby bar, and Tahiti's top watersports center. I love to stay here between jaunts to the outer islands because I can clean my dirty clothes in the free washers and dryers, a real money-saver given the exorbitant cost of laundry services (buy your detergent before the boutique closes at 7pm). Another plus: The lobby bar serves coffee and snacks all night.

B.P. 6014, 98702 Faaa (8km/5 miles west of Papeete). ⓒ 800/327-0200 or 86.51.10. Fax 86.51.30. www.tahiti. interconti.com. 214 units. 30,000 CFP–44,000 CFP (US$375–US$550/£190–£278) double; 79,500 CFP–88,000 CFP (US$994–US$1,100/£503–£557) suite; 50,000–106,000 CFP (US$625–US$1,325/£316–£671) overwater bungalow. AE, DC, MC, V. **Amenities:** 2 restaurants; 2 bars; 2 outdoor pools; tennis courts; health club; Jacuzzi; watersports equipment rentals; concierge; activities desk; car-rental desk; 24-hr. business center with high-speed Internet access; salon; 24-hr. room service; massage; babysitting; laundry service; coin-op washers and dryers. *In room:* A/C, TV, high-speed Internet access, minibar, coffeemaker, hair dryer, iron, safe.

Le Meridien Tahiti ⋆⋆   Near the Museum of Tahiti and Her Islands, this luxury resort sits alongside one of Tahiti's few white-sand beaches. It's an excellent choice—but give yourself extra time to get to Tahiti-Faaa International Airport to catch a flight during the weekday morning traffic jam. The Melanesian-inspired architecture is stunning, with swayback shingle roofs evoking the "spirit houses" of Papua New Guinea. Imported sand surrounding the wade-in pool augments the pebbly beach and shallow lagoon here. The best accommodations are 12 overwater bungalows, but note that unlike most others, they have neither glass panels in their floors for fish-watching nor steps into the lagoon from their porches, nor are all them air-conditioned. All of the luxuriously appointed guest quarters have balconies, but try to get a north-facing unit for a Moorea view. *Le Carré* is one of the better resort dining rooms in French Polynesia. A shopping center next door has a grocery store, hairdresser, pharmacy, post office, restaurants, and a patisserie for inexpensive breakfasts.

B.P. 380595, 98718 Punaauia (15km/9⅓ miles south of Papeete, 8km/5 miles south of the airport). ⓒ 800/225-5843 or 47.07.07. Fax 47.07.08. www.lemeridien-tahiti.com. 150 units. 35,000 CFP–40,000 CFP (US$438–500/£222–£253) double; 59,000 CFP–90,000 CFP (US$738–US$1,125/£373–£570) suite; 59,000 CFP (US$738/£373) bungalow. AE, DC, MC, V. **Amenities:** 2 restaurants; 2 bars; outdoor pool; tennis court; exercise room; watersports equipment rentals; concierge; activities desk; car-rental desk; wireless Internet access; 24-hr. room service; babysitting; laundry service. *In room:* A/C, TV, dataport, minibar, coffeemaker, hair dryer, iron, safe.

Sofitel Tahiti Maeva Beach Resort *(Value*   Known for many years as the Sofitel Maeva Beach Resort, this seven-story building resembling a modern version of a terraced Mayan pyramid resides beside the gray sands of Maeva Beach. The murky lagoon off the beach isn't as good for swimming and snorkeling as it is for anchoring numerous yachts, whose masts slice the beach's view of Moorea. Equipped with modern European amenities (the bright, lime-green bathrooms nearly blinded me), the smallish rooms open to balconies. Odd-numbered rooms on the upper floors on the north (or "beach") side have views of Moorea, while those on the garden side look south along Tahiti's west coast. The Sofitel is a good value by Tahiti standards, but don't expect the same amount of space, luxuries, or amenities as at the InterContinental Resort Tahiti or Le Meridien. I like staying here because I can walk to the big Carrefour supermarket and inexpensive snack bars in Centre Moana Nui in less than 10 minutes.

B.P. 6008, 98702 Faaa (7.5km/4⅔ miles west of Papeete). © 800/763-4835 or 86.66.00. Fax 41.05.05. www. accorhotels.pf. 230 units. 21,700 CFP–24,300 CFP (US$271–US$304/£137–£154) double; 37,100 CFP (US$464/£235) suite. AE, DC, MC, V. **Amenities:** 2 restaurants; 2 bars; outdoor pool; tennis courts; watersports equipment rentals; concierge; activities desk; car-rental desk; limited room service; babysitting; laundry service. *In room:* A/C, TV, minibar, high-speed Internet access, coffeemaker, hair dryer, iron, safe.

Taaroa Lodge   Avid surfer Ralph Sanford bought the two bungalows at his humble lagoonside establishment, in ritzy Paea, as prefabricated kits in New Zealand; hence, they are larger and have more character than the cookie-cutter *fares* found at most small family-run establishments here. And their porches present million-dollar views of Moorea, especially the one sitting beside the bulkhead along the lagoon. Each has a kitchen, TV, and ceiling fan. Behind them, an A-frame chalet houses a room with a double bed downstairs and a six-bed dormitory in the loft. The communal kitchen stays busy, as do Ralph's free kayaks (bring your own snorkeling gear). Grocery stores and snack bars are short walks away. In my opinion, this is the top backpacker accommodation on Tahiti, even if you do have to stay at least 2 nights.

B.P. 498, 98713 Papeete (PK 18.2 in Paea). ©/fax 58.39.21. www.taaroalodge.com. 2 bungalows (with bathroom), 1 room (with bathroom), 6 dorm beds. 6,000 CFP (US$75/£38) double; 10,000 CFP (US$125/£63) bungalow; 2,500 CFP (US$31/£16) dorm bed. Rates include breakfast. MC, V. 2-night minimum stay required. **Amenities:** Communal kitchen; free kayaks. *In room (bungalows only):* TV, kitchen, coffeemaker, no phone.

IN FAAA

Tahiti Airport Motel   Carved into a hill across Route 1 from the airport terminal, this modern, three-story hotel offers simply furnished but comfortable rooms. A communal balcony across the front overlooks the airport and Moorea on the horizon. Although devoid of most amenities, this is a convenient and relatively cost-conscious place to sleep off your overnight flight getting here or to wait for your flight home. Restaurants and shops are steps away.

B.P. 60113, Faaa (PK 5.7, opposite Tahiti-Faaa International Airport). © 50.40.00. Fax 50.40.01. www.tahitiairport motel.com. 42 units. 12,800 CFP–22,000 CFP (US$160–US$275/£81–£139) double. AE, MC, V. **Amenities:** Wireless Internet access. *In room:* A/C, TV, fridge, coffeemaker.

IN PAPEETE

Downtown Papeete has the simple but clean **Hotel Tiare Tahiti Noa Noa,** B.P. 2359, Papeete (© **50.01.00;** fax 43.68.47; hoteltiaretahiti@mail.pf), an upstairs, five-story facility on boulevard Pomare a block west of the Centre Vaima. The rooms are minimally furnished, however, and can be noisy, as most face directly onto the busy boulevard (request one on the upper floors, which are quieter and have better views from

Guesthouses & Family Accommodations

In general, you will find a significant difference in quality between French Polynesia's moderate and inexpensive accommodations. Few establishments here are comparable in price or quality to the inexpensive motels found in abundance in the United States, Canada, Australia, and New Zealand.

The local government is encouraging the development of guesthouses and family pensions, of which there are a growing number. Many owners have used government-backed loans to acquire one-room guest bungalows with attached bathrooms. Although the bungalows are identical, the owners have added decorative touches, in some case quite tasteful, barely in others.

Tahiti Tourisme inspects these establishments and distributes lists of those it recommends. Many promote themselves through an organization known as **Haere-Mai,** whose website (**www.haere-mai.pf**) describes them.

Local families operate most of them, so if you decide to go this route, an ability to speak some French may be essential.

---

their slim balconies). It charges from 13,500 CFP to 15,000 CFP (US$169–US$188/ £85–£95) for a double room.

The Chinese-accented **Hotel Le Mandarin,** B.P. 302, Papeete (© **50.33.50;** fax 42.16.32; www.hotelmandarin.com), is a bit shopworn, but it's in a somewhat quieter location on rue Collette opposite the Town Hall. It's business-oriented and close to most offices and many restaurants. I wouldn't stay here on a Friday, when dancers can spill from the noisy nightclub onto the street. It charges between 15,500 CFP and 17,500 CFP (US$194–US$219/£98–£111) for a double room.

Fare Suisse 𝓚 *Value*   Beni Huber moved to Tahiti from Switzerland and opened this spotlessly clean guesthouse in 2006. It's uphill on rue Venus, a side street in the Paofai neighborhood and 3 blocks inland from Place Toata and the waterfront. Sea breezes cool the light, airy rooms, two of which are upstairs off a lounge and communal kitchen. One of these has over-and-under double beds and a convertible sofa; it sees double duty as a dormitory. An apartment downstairs has its own kitchen and 2 bedrooms, one of which can be rented separately. The dorm and one of the upstairs rooms share a bathroom; the other three units have their own facilities. Breakfast is available. Beni speaks German and English better than he does French.

B.P. 20355, 98713 Faaa (rue Venus, south of rue des Poilus Tahitiens). ©/fax **42.00.30.** www.fare-suisse.com. 4 units (3 with bathroom), 2 dorm beds. 9,000 CFP–12,000 CFP (US$113–US$150/£57–£76) double; 4,800 CFP (US$60/£30) dorm bed. MC, V. **Amenities:** Wireless Internet access. *In room:* Kitchen (1 unit), no phone.

Sheraton Hotel Tahiti & Spa 𝓚𝓚   A 15-minute walk to downtown and a quick drive to the airport, this state-of-the-art hotel was built in 2000 and 2001 on the site of the old Hotel Tahiti, whose massive thatched-roof public areas hosted many a local soirée. With Tahiti's largest meeting space, the Sheraton still serves as one of the city's prime gathering places. Curving steps under a huge shell chandelier lead down to **Quinn's Bar,** an overwater dining room, and a courtyard with a lagoonside swimming pool and sand piled behind a breakwater, which helps compensate for the lack of a natural beach. A whirlpool perched atop a pile of rocks beside the pool offers a terrific view of Moorea. Except for 10 suites, which have one or two bedrooms, the spacious units are almost identical—the vistas off their private balconies vary. "Superior" units face Moorea, but you pay less for them because they are slightly smaller than the "deluxe lagoon" units facing the ocean or harbor (someone who's never been to Tahiti must have devised that policy). This is a good choice for a short layover when you don't need a beach. Top Dive, one of French Polynesia's best operators, has a base here.

B.P. 416, 98713 Papeete (1km/½ mile west of downtown, 6km/3¾ miles east of the airport). (C) 800/325-3535 or 86.48.48. Fax 86.48.40. www.starwoodtahiti.com. 200 units. 33,000 CFP–41,000 CFP (US$413–US$513/£209–£259) double; 75,000 CFP–88,000 CFP (US$938–US$1,100/£475–£557) suite. AE, DC, MC, V. **Amenities:** 2 restaurants; bar; outdoor pool; health club; exercise room; spa; concierge; activities desk; car-rental desk; wireless Internet access in public areas; salon; limited room service; massage; babysitting; laundry service. *In room:* A/C, TV, high-speed Internet access, minibar, coffeemaker, hair dryer, iron, safe.

Teamo Hostel   Although it has been around for more than 2 decades, this guesthouse-cum-hostel is much improved now that friendly, English-speaking owner Gerald Teriierooiterai has added TVs and fridges to all the rooms and air conditioners to most. In a primarily residential neighborhood 6 blocks from the waterfront, it occupies a wood-frame house built around 1880. Rooms were small in those days, so don't expect them to be spacious today. Some rooms upstairs have balconies. Two downstairs units have six bunk beds each and are used for male and female dorms. There's a comfy lounge at the front of the house and a communal kitchen on a covered patio out back.

B.P. 60113, Faaa (rue du Pont-Neuf off rue du Général Castelnau). (C) 42.47.26 or 42.00.35 Fax 43.56.95. teamo hostel@mail.pf. 11 units (all with bathrooms), 12 dorm beds. 5,800 CFP–7,000 CFP (US$73–US$88/£37–£44) double; 2,300 CFP (US$29/£15) dorm bed. Rates include continental breakfast. MC, V. **Amenities:** Communal kitchen. *In room:* A/C (4 units), TV, fridge, coffeemaker.

EAST OF PAPEETE

Le Royal Tahitien Hotel (★★ (Value)   One of the top values in French Polynesia, this American-owned hotel is the only moderately priced place on the island with its own beach, a stretch of deep black sand from which its suburban neighbors fish and swim. And long-time Australian-born manager Lionel Kennedy (a die-hard baseball fan) and his English-speaking staff are Tahiti's best when it comes to friendly, personalized service. Sitting in an expansive lawn and lush garden traversed by a small stream, a swimming pool sports a Jacuzzi and a waterfall cascading over rocks. The spacious guest rooms are in contemporary two-story wood-and-stone buildings that look like an American condominium complex. Colorful bedspreads and seat cushions add a tropical ambience to the rooms, however, and the tropics definitely pervade the fine, moderately-priced **restaurant** under a 1937-vintage thatched ceiling. Both the beachside restaurant and adjacent bar are popular with local businesspeople. A band plays on Friday and Saturday evenings. Your fellow guests are likely to be businesspersons living on the other islands and travelers who have made their own arrangements (that is, few groups stay here). It's very popular, so reserve as soon as possible. As with the Radisson Plaza (see below), you will need to rent a car or take a taxi if going downtown after dark, as the last local bus passes here about 5pm.

B.P. 5001, 98716 Pirae (4km/2½ miles east of downtown). (C) 213/878-0283 in the U.S. or 50.40.40. Fax 50.40.41. www.hotelroyaltahitien.com. 40 units. 18,000 CFP (US$225/£114) double. AE, DC, MC, V. Take a Mahina bus or follow av. Prince Hinoi to the Total and Mobil stations opposite each other; turn around at next traffic circle and return; turn right to hotel. **Amenities:** Restaurant; bar; outdoor pool; Jacuzzi; laundry service. *In room:* A/C, TV, fridge, coffeemaker.

Radisson Plaza Resort Tahiti (★   This modern resort opened in 2004 beside the deep black sands of Lafayette Beach on Matavai Bay, where the 18th-century explorers dropped anchor. A huge, turtle-shaped thatched roof covers most of the central complex, which holds a restaurant, bar, arts and crafts center, full-service spa, and a cozy library devoted to author James Norman Hall. Outside is a horizon-edge pool beside the beach. Currents create an undertow here, so heed the "Dangerous Sea" signs when swimming in the lagoon. Seven hotel buildings hold the accommodations, which include standard rooms, two-story town house–style "duplexes" (their upstairs bedrooms have their own balconies), suites, and—my favorites—rooms with hot tubs romantically placed behind louvers on their balconies. Furnishings and decor are tropical with a European flair. The Radisson sends a shuttle to downtown Papeete each morning and afternoon, but public buses do not run out here after 5pm, meaning you will need to rent a car or take a taxi to get to and from downtown after dark. Like at Le Meridien Tahiti, rush-hour traffic can make for a long trek to the airport from here.

B.P. 14170, 98701 Arue (on Matavai Bay, 7km [4½ miles] east of downtown). (© 800/333-3333 or 48.88.88. Fax 43.88.89. www.radisson.com/aruefrp. 165 units. 25,600 CFP–31,200 CFP (US$320–US$390/£162–£197) double. AE, DC, MC. V. **Amenities:** Restaurant; 2 bars; outdoor pool; exercise room; spa; Jacuzzi; activities desk; car-rental desk; business center; salon; limited room service; massage; babysitting; laundry service; concierge-level rooms. *In room:* A/C, TV, high-speed Internet access, minibar, coffeemaker, iron (in suites), safe.

7 Where to Dine

Tahiti has a plethora of excellent French, Italian, and Chinese restaurants. Those I recommend below are but a few of many; don't hesitate to strike out on your own.

Food is relatively expensive in French Polynesia, whether on the shelves of grocery stores or placed before you at a restaurant or snack bar, so be sure to see my money-saving tips under "Tips on Dining" (p. 208).

Downtown Papeete has a **McDonald's** at the corner of rue du Général-de-Gaulle and rue du Dr. Cassiau behind Centre Vaima, and there's a second on the main road in Punaauia. **Champion** supermarket, on rue du Général-de-Gaulle in the block west of the Eglise Evangélique, has picnic supplies. On the west coast, head for the huge **Carrefour** supermarket in the Centre Moana Nui south of the Sofitel Tahiti Maeva Beach Resort.

As with the accommodations, I have organized the restaurants by location.

ON THE WEST COAST

Captain Bligh Restaurant and Bar ⚜ TRADITIONAL FRENCH   One of Tahiti's last large thatched-roof buildings covers this restaurant beside the lagoon (you can toss crumbs to the fish swimming just over the railing). The food is not the best on the island, but you can't beat the old Tahitian charm. Specialties are grilled steaks and lobster. Get here early to graze the all-you-can-eat lunchtime salad bar, which is so popular with locals that it quickly disappears. One of the island's top Tahitian dance troupes performs here Friday and Saturday nights after a seafood buffet—the 5,000 CFP (US$63/£32) per person price is excellent value compared to the resort hotels' buffets and dance shows. You can sample local food at the *ma'a Tahiti* buffet Sunday at noon. A pier goes out to the Lagoonarium here (see "The Top Attractions," earlier).

PK 11.4, Punaauia, at the Lagoonarium (3.9km/2½ miles south of Sofitel Tahiti Maeva Beach Resort on the round-island road; Paea buses go by it during the day; take a taxi at night). (© 43.62.90. Reservations recommended on weekends. Burgers 1,300 CFP (US$16/£8.25); lunch salad bar 1,700 CFP (US$21/£11); main courses 1,800 CFP–3,400 CFP (US$23–US$43/£11–£22). AE, MC, V. Tues–Sun 11am–2:30pm and 6:30–9pm. Bar 9am–10pm.

Casa Bianca ITALIAN   Formerly known as Casablanca Cocktail Restaurant, this now Italian establishment is perched beside the yachts moored in Marina Taina. The menu consists primarily of pizza and pasta with a few meat and fish courses. Servings are relatively small but are a good value. The food isn't as good as at either L'Api'zzeria or Lou Pescadou in Papeete (see below), but the setting is more pleasant. Try to get a table in one of the romantic gazebos out in the yard. There's live music Friday and Saturday night in the Dinghy Bar, which dispenses home brews from Papeete's Les 3 Brasseurs (see below).

PK 9, Punaauia, at Marina Taina. ℭ 43.91.35. Reservations recommended. Pizzas and pastas 1,100 CFP–1,800 CFP (US$14–US$23/£7–£11); meat courses 1,950 CFP–2,400 CFP (US$24–US$30/£12–£15). AE, MC, V. Daily noon–2:30pm and 7–10:30pm. Heading south, turn right into marina after first traffic circle.

Le Cignalon/Pacific Burger *(Value* PIZZA/SNACK BAR   Cost-conscious guests at Le Meridien Tahiti resort walk next door to Pacific Burger, the open-air snack bar side operated by Le Cignalon (an Italian restaurant) for good, reasonably priced salads, *poisson cru,* sashimi, burgers (beef, chicken, or fish), grilled rib-eye steaks, and fish with or without sauce, and very good two-person pizzas from a wood-fired oven. A big tarp covers plastic patio tables and chairs in front of the fast-food-style counter. The menu is in French and English. The Tahiti museum is a few blocks away, so this is a good place to stop for refreshment on your round-island tour.

Value Don't Miss *Les Roulottes*

Although prices in some hotel dining rooms and restaurants here can be shocking, you don't need to spend a fortune to eat reasonably well in French Polynesia. In fact, the best food bargains in Papeete literally roll out after dark on the cruise ship docks: portable meal wagons known as les roulottes.

Some owners set up charcoal grills behind their trucks and small electric generators in front to provide plenty of light for the diners, who sit on stools along either side of the vehicles. Most begin arriving about 6pm. The entire waterfront soon takes on a carnival atmosphere, especially on Friday and Saturday nights.

The traditional menu includes charbroiled steaks or chicken with french fries (known as *steak frites* and *poulet frites*), familiar Cantonese dishes, poisson cru, and *salade russe* (Russian-style potato salad, tinted red by beetroot juice) for 900 CFP to 1,700 CFP (US$11–US$21/£5.70–£11) per plate. Glassed-in display cases along the sides of some trucks hold examples of what's offered at each (not exactly the most appetizing exhibits, but you can just point to what you want rather than fumbling in French). You'll find many trucks specializing in crepes, pizzas, couscous, and waffles (*gaufres*). So many cruise-ship passengers and tourists eat here that most truck owners speak some English.

Even if you don't order an entire meal at les roulottes, stop for a crepe or waffle and enjoy the scene.

Although they now have permanent homes, the open-air restaurants at **Place Toata,** on the western end of the waterfront, were born as roulottes, and they still offer the same fare and prices as their mobile siblings. They are open for lunch **Monday to Saturday** and for dinner **Friday and Saturday.**

(*Value* Dining with a Belle View

I like to spend my last evening on Tahiti up at **Le Belvédère** (© **42.73.44**), for this innlike establishment has a spectacular view of the city and Moorea from its perch 600m (1,969 ft.) up in the Fare Ape Valley above Papeete. The restaurant provides round-trip transportation from your hotel up the narrow, one-lane, winding, switchback road that leads to it (I don't encourage anyone to attempt this drive in a rental car). Take the 5pm pickup, so you'll reach the restaurant in time for a sunset cocktail. They'll drop you back at the airport if you're leaving the same night. The specialty is fondue bourguignon served with six sauces. The 5,600 CFP (US$70/£35) fixed price includes three courses, wine, and transportation, so it is a reasonably good value. The quality of the cuisine doesn't match the view, however, so treat the evening as a sightseeing excursion, not as a fine-dining experience. Reservations are required, and American Express, MasterCard, and Visa cards are accepted. It's closed Wednesday.

PK 15, Punaauia. © **42.40.84.** Burgers 450 CFP–850 CFP (US$5.65–US$11/£2.85–£5.40); pizza and pasta 1,000 CFP–1,900 CFP (US$13–US$24/£6.35–£12); main courses 1,800 CFP–2,500 CFP (US$23–US$31/£11–£16). MC, V. Tues–Thurs 10am–3pm and 5:30–9pm; Fri–Sun 10am–3pm and 5:30–9:30pm.

Le Coco's ⚐⚐ FRENCH   Along with Le Lotus (see below), this lagoonside restaurant shares top rank as Tahiti's most romantic place to dine, especially the tables out on the lawn, where you will have a gorgeous look at Moorea (moonlit nights are awesome). Other tables shaded by a thatch cabana also share the view. The cuisine is light in the French nouvelle cuisine tradition, with island influences such as shrimp marinated in lime juice and coconut milk. If your credit card can withstand 12,400 CFP (US$155/£78) per person, you will be surprised during the five-course, fixed-price "at the humor of the chef" menu. There's also a scaled-down tourist menu. Arrive early enough for a drink or glass of fine champagne while the sun sets over Moorea.

PK 13.5, Punaauia. © **58.21.08.** Reservations recommended. Main courses 2,900 CFP–3,800 CFP (US$36–US$48/£18–£24); tourist menu 5,850 CFP (US$73/£37). AE, MC, V. Daily 11:30am–1:30pm and 7–9:30pm.

Le Lotus ⚐⚐⚐ FRENCH/CONTINENTAL   With two round, thatched-roof dining rooms extending over the lagoon and enjoying an uninterrupted view of Moorea, Le Lotus has the best setting of any restaurant in the South Pacific. The widely spaced tables are all at the water's edge (a spotlight between the two dining rooms shines into the lagoon, attracting fish in search of a handout). The gourmet French fare and attentive but unobtrusive service more than live up to this romantic scene. The resort often invites some of Europe's top master chefs to take a working vacations here. Whomever is in residence, you're in for a gastronomic delight, be it a la carte or a one- to four-course fixed menu.

In InterContinental Resort Tahiti, Faaa (7km/4½ miles west of Papeete). © **86.51.10,** ext. 5512. Reservations highly recommended. Main courses 3,100 CFP–4,800 CFP (US$39–US$60/£20–£30); fixed-price dinners 3,950 CFP–10,300 CFP (US$49–US$129/£25–£65). AE, DC, MC, V. Daily noon–2:30pm and 6:30–9:30pm.

EAST OF PAPEETE

Le Royal Tahitien Restaurant ★★ (Value INTERNATIONAL   Occupying a charming open-air building, constructed in 1937 beside the black-sand beach in Pirae, the Le Royal Tahitien Hotel's dining room provides views of the lagoon and Moorea to accompany its good international fare. Like the hotel, it also offers excellent value for the quality of its food. The cuisine is primarily French, such as fresh mahimahi in meunière sauce, but you will find island influences here, such as very good *poisson cru* and shrimp served in half a pineapple. You can also order off a snack menu, including Aussie-style burgers, the best on Tahiti. Locals flock here for the big lunchtime salads, as well as for live music in the adjacent bar on Friday and Saturday evenings. Be sure to talk baseball with Australian-born Lionel Kennedy, the hotel's general manager.

At Le Royal Tahitien Hotel, PK 4, Pirae. Reservations recommended at dinner. Snack menu 850 CFP–1,500 CFP (US$11–US$19/£5.40–£9.50); main courses 2,000 CFP–2,900 CFP (US$25–US$36/£13–£18). AE, DC, MC, V. Daily 6:30–10am, 11:30am–2:30pm, and 7–10pm.

IN PAPEETE

L'Api'zzeria ★★ (Value ITALIAN   On par with Lou Pescadou (see below) but with a garden setting, this restaurant in a grove of trees across from the waterfront has been serving very good pizza and pasta since 1968. I prefer a table outside under the trees rather than inside, which resembles an Elizabethan waterfront tavern accented with nautical relics. The food, on the other hand, is definitely Italian. Both pizzas and steaks are cooked in a wood-fired oven. The menu also features pastas, steak Milanese, veal in white or Marsala wine sauce, and grilled homemade Italian sausage.

Bd. Pomare, between rue du Chef Teriirooterai and rue l'Arthémise. © 42.98.30. Reservations not accepted. Pizzas and pastas 450 CFP–1,750 CFP (US$5.65–US$22/£2.85–£11); meat courses 1,700 CFP–2,600 CFP (US$21–US$33/£11–£16). MC, V. Mon–Sat 11:30am–10pm.

Les 3 Brasseurs FRENCH   The quality of its food tends to be up and down, but this microbrewery is the nearest thing Papeete has to an American-style bar-and-grill. The sidewalk tables are fine for a cold one while waiting for the Moorea ferry at the docks across the boulevard. The menu is all in French, but staffers speak enough English to explain offerings. Choose from sandwiches, salads, roast chicken served hot or cold, and grilled steaks, mahimahi, tuna plain or with optional sauces. *Jarret de porc,* smoked ham hocks served with sautéed potatoes and sauerkraut, reminds me of the Southern soul food of my youth. The best deal here is the *croque brasseurs,* a ham sandwich served under melted Gruyère cheese and accompanied by a glass of beer and a green salad with excellent vinaigrette dressing, all for 900 CFP (US$11/£5.70).

Bd. Pomare, between rue Prince Hinoi and rue Clappier, opposite Moorea ferry docks. © 50.60.25. Sandwiches and salads 900 CFP–1,700 CFP (US$11–US$21/£5.75–£11); main courses 1,500 CFP–2,700 CFP (US$19–US$34/£9.50–£17). MC, V. Daily 9am–1am.

L'O a la Bouche ★★★ INTERNATIONAL   One of the top restaurants in all of French Polynesia, this charming bistro's sophisticated, muted ambience would make it at home in the wine countries of Napa or Baroosa—except for the vintage labels pictured on the walls, which are all French. Although the chef offers several traditional French dishes, this is anything but a typical French restaurant. His talent soars with creations such as a moon fish steak under passion fruit and ginger sauce (the ginger perfectly tempered the fruit's sweetness). I preceded that with a smoked salmon and shrimp salad with *pampelmouse* (local grapefruit), which was delightfully refreshing after a day of tramping around Papeete. Next time I'm going with scallops marinated

Fun Fact A Most Indecent Song & Dance

The young girls whenever they can collect 8 or 10 together dance a very indecent dance which they call Timorodee singing most indecent songs and using most indecent actions in the practice of which they are brought up from their earliest Childhood.

—Capt. James Cook, after seeing his first Tahitian dance show in 1769

The Tahitian dances described by the great explorer in 1769 left little doubt as to the temptations that inspired the mutiny on the *Bounty* a few years later. At the time Cook arrived, the Tahitians would stage a *heiva* (festival) for almost any reason, from blessing the harvest to celebrating a birth. After eating meals cooked in earth ovens, they would get out the drums and nose flutes and dance the nights away. Some of the dances involved elaborate costumes, and others were quite lasciviously and explicitly danced in the nude or seminude, which added to Tahiti's reputation as an island of love.

The puritanical Protestant missionaries would have none of that and put an end to dancing in the early 1820s. Of course, strict prohibition never works, and Tahitians—including a young Queen Pomare—would sneak into the hills to dance. Only after the French took over in 1842 was dancing permitted again, and then only with severe limitations on what the dancers could do and wear. A result of these various restrictions was that most of the traditional dances performed by the Tahitians before 1800 were nearly forgotten within 100 years.

You'd never guess that Tahitians ever stopped dancing, for after tourists started coming in 1961, they went back to the old ways. Today traditional dancing is a huge part of their lives—and of every visitor's itinerary. No one goes away without vivid memories of the elaborate and colorful costumes, the thundering drums, and the swinging hips of a Tahitian *tamure,* in which young men and women provocatively dance around each other.

The tamure is one of several dances performed during a typical dance show. Others are the *o'tea,* in which men and women in spectacular costumes dance themes, such as spear throwing or love; the *aparima,* the hand dance, which emphasizes everyday themes, such as bathing and combing one's hair; the *hivinau,* in which men and women dance in circles and exclaim "*hiri haa haa*" when they meet each other; and the *pata'uta'u,* in which the dancers beat the ground or their thighs with their open hands. It's difficult to follow the themes without understanding Tahitian, but the color and rhythms (which have been influenced by faster, double-time beats from the Cook Islands) make the dances thoroughly enjoyable.

with red peppers, or perhaps scorched tuna with a light curry sauce. The list of French wines is short but excellent. The menu is in both French and English here.

Passage Cardella (between rue du Général-de-Gaulle and rue Anne-Marie Javouhey). © 45.29.76. Reservations recommended, especially on weekends. Main courses 2,950 CFP–3,700 CFP (US$37–US$46/£19–£23). AE, MC, V. Mon–Fri 11:30am–2:30pm and 7:15–10pm; Sat 7:15–10pm.

Lou Pescadou (k (*Value* ITALIAN   A lively young professional clientele packs this quintessentially Italian trattoria (red-and-white–checked tablecloths, dripping candles on each table, Ruffino bottles hanging from every nook and cranny). They come for fresh, tasty Italian fare at reasonable prices (be prepared to wait for a table). The individual-size pizzas are cooked in a wood-fire oven, and the pasta dishes include lasagna and spaghetti and fettuccine under tomato, carbonara, and Roquefort sauces.

Rue Anne-Marie Javouhey at passage Cardella. (C) **43.74.26.** Pizzas and pastas 1,000 CFP–1,750 CFP (US$13–US$22/£6.35–£11); meat courses 1,750 CFP–2,650 CFP (US$22–US$33/£11–£17). MC, V. Mon–Sat 11:30am–2pm and 6:30–11pm. Take the narrow passage Cardella, a 1-block street that looks like an alley, directly behind Centre Vaima.

Le Retrot FRENCH/ITALIAN/SNACKS   You'll find better food elsewhere, but this Parisian-style sidewalk cafe is Papeete's best place to rendezvous, or to grab a bite, a drink, or an ice cream while watching the world pass along the quay. A diverse selection of salads, sandwiches, pizzas, and pasta gets attention from the cafe crowd.

Bd. Pomare, front of Centre Vaima, on waterfront. (C) **42.86.83.** Salads, sandwiches, and burgers 500 CFP–1,450 CFP (US$6.25–US$18/£3.15–£9.20); pizza and pastas 900 CFP–1,800 CFP (US$11–US$23/£5.70–£11); main courses 1,750 CFP–2,150 CFP (US$22–US$27/£11–£14). AE, MC, V. Daily 6am–midnight.

L'Oasis du Vaima SNACK BAR   You'll find me having a small quiche or a tasty pastry with strong French coffee for breakfast at this kiosklike building on the southwest corner of Centre Vaima. In addition to dishing out ice cream and milkshakes to passersby at a sidewalk counter, it serves up varied goodies, from crispy *casse-croûtes* to two substantial *plats-du-jour* selections each day, on a covered dining terrace and in an air-conditioned dining room upstairs.

Rue du Général-de-Gaulle at rue Jeanne d'Arc (at the corner of Centre Vaima, opposite Cathédrale de l'Immaculée Conception). (C) **45.45.01.** Sandwiches, quiches, omelets, small pizzas 350 CFP–900 CFP (US$4.40–US$11/£2.20–£5.70); meals 1,500 CFP–2,100 CFP (US$19–US$26/£9.50–£13). No credit cards. Mon–Sat 5am–5pm.

8 Island Nights

A 19th-century European merchant wrote of the Tahitians, "Their existence was in never-ending merrymaking." In many respects this is still true, for after the sun goes down, Tahitians like to make merry as much today as they did in the 1820s, and Papeete has lots of good choices for visitors who want to join in the fun.

TAHITIAN DANCE SHOWS (k(k(k

Traditional Tahitian dancing isn't as indecent as it was in Captain Cook's day (see the box "A Most Indecent Song & Dance," above), but you should try to see one. You'll have plenty of chances, as nightlife on the outer islands consists almost exclusively of dance shows at the resorts, usually in conjunction with a feast of Tahitian food.

Each of Tahiti's big resort hotels has shows at least once a week. Not to be missed is the **Grande Danse de Tahiti** (k(k(k troupe, which usually performs at the InterContinental Resort Tahiti (C) **86.51.10**) on Wednesday, Friday, and Saturday evenings (the Sat-night show is a reenactment of the dance that seduced the crew of HMS *Bounty*). Call the resort to make sure. Another good place to catch a show is the **Captain Bligh Restaurant and Bar** (C) **43.62.90**), which usually has them on Friday and Saturday at 8:30pm. Expect to pay from 5,000 CFP (US$63/£32) for the show and dinner at the Captain Bligh to 8,500 CFP (US$107/£54) at the big resorts.

Impressions

They have several negative comments on the beachcombing life in Tahiti: Not much cultural life. No intellectual stimulus. No decent library. Restaurant food is disgraceful . . . But I noticed that Saturday after Saturday they turned up at Quinn's with the most dazzling beauties on the island. When I reminded them of this they said, "Well, that does compensate for the poor library."
—James A. Michener, *Return to Paradise*, 1951

PUB-CRAWLING

Papeete has a nightclub or watering hole to fit anyone's taste, from upscale private *(privé)* discotheques to down-and-dirty bars and dance halls where Tahitians strum on guitars while sipping on large bottles of Hinano beer (and sometimes engage in fisticuffs after midnight). If you look like a tourist, you'll be allowed into the private clubs. Generally, everything gets to full throttle after 9pm (except on Sun, when most pubs are closed). None of the clubs are inexpensive. Expect to pay at least 1,000 CFP (US$13/£6.35) cover charge, which will include your first drink. After that, beers cost at least 500 CFP (US$6.25/£3.15), with most mixed drinks in the 1,000 CFP to 1,500 CFP (US$13–US$19/£6.35–£9.50) range.

The narrow rue des Ecoles is the heart of Papeete's mahu district, where male transvestites hang out. The **Piano Bar** (② **42.88.24**) is the most popular of the "sexy clubs" along this street, especially for its late-night strip shows, featuring female impersonators. It's open daily from 3pm to 3am. The **Mana Rock Cafe,** at the corner of boulevard Pomare and rue des Ecoles (② **48.36.36**), draws a more mixed crowd to its bars and discotheque (you can check your e-mail between sips here).

You're unlikely to be groped or get into a fight at **Le Royal Tahitien Hotel** in Pirae (② **50.40.40**), which has a live band for dancing on Friday nights. The moderate-price seaside restaurant here has very good food for the money, so you can make Friday a dining-and-dancing evening. See "Where to Stay," earlier in this chapter.

You don't have to pay to be entertained on Friday, which is "cruise ship day" on the Papeete waterfront. Arts and crafts are on display, and Tahitians make music, from 8am to 5pm at Tahiti Tourisme's visitor center, at the foot of rue Paul Gauguin. Tahitian bands perform afterwards out on Place Vaiate, by the cruise ship docks.

9

Moorea

Like most visitors to French Polynesia, I soon grab the ferry to Moorea, just 20km (12 miles) west of Tahiti. James Michener may have thought Bora Bora the world's most beautiful island, but Moorea is my choice. In fact, it's so gorgeous that I have trouble keeping my eye on the road here. Hollywood often uses stock shots of Moorea's jagged mountains, deep bays, and emerald lagoons to create a South Seas setting for movies that don't even take place here.

Geologists attribute Moorea's rugged, otherworldly beauty to a great volcano, the northern half of which either fell into the sea or was blown away in a cataclysmic explosion, leaving the heart-shaped island we see today. In other words, Moorea is only half its old self. The rim of the crater has eroded into the jagged peaks and spires that give the island its haunting, dinosaur-like profile. Cathedral-like Mount Mouaroa—Moorea's trademark "Shark's Tooth" or "Bali Hai Mountain"— shows up on many postcards and on the 100 CFP coin.

Mount Rotui stands alone in the center of the ancient crater, its black cliffs and stovepipe buttresses dropping into Cook's Bay and Opunohu Bay, two dark blue fingers that cut deep into Moorea's interior. These mountain-shrouded bays are certainly among the world's most photographed bodies of water.

Perched high up on the crater's wall, the Belvédère overlooks both bays, Mount Rotui, and the jagged old crater rim curving off to left and right. Do not miss the Belvédère, one of the South Pacific's most awesome panoramas.

With traffic choking Tahiti and Moorea only a 30-minute ferry ride away from Papeete, the island already is a bedroom community for its big sister. Still, it has maintained its Polynesian charm to a large extent. Its hotels and resorts are spread out enough that you don't feel like you're in a tourist trap, and the locals don't feel inundated by us. They still have time to stop and talk.

Most of Moorea's 20,000 or so residents live on its fringing coastal plain, many of them in small settlements where lush valleys meet a lagoon enclosed by an offshore coral reef. This calm blue lagoon makes Moorea ideal for swimming, boating, snorkeling, and diving. Unlike the black sands of Tahiti, white beaches stretch for miles.

Impressions

From Tahiti, Moorea seems to have about 40 separate summits: fat thumbs of basalt, spires tipped at impossible angles, brooding domes compelling to the eye. But the peaks which can never be forgotten are the jagged saw-edges that look like the spines of some forgotten dinosaur.
—James A. Michener, *Return to Paradise*, 1951

1 Getting Around

All ferries from Papeete land at Vaiare, on Moorea's east coast 5km (3 miles) south of **Temae Airport.**

BY BUS   The only scheduled buses on Moorea are those that carry passengers to and from the morning and afternoon ferries at Vaiare. Tell the drivers where you're going; they will show you which vehicle is going to your hotel. The trip from Vaiare to the end of the line, at the old Club Med site, takes about 1 hour. The buses also return from the Petite Village shopping center in Haapiti to Vaiare prior to each departure. They stop at the hotels and can be flagged down along the road elsewhere. The one-way fare is 500 CFP (US$6.25/£3.15), regardless of direction or length of ride.

BY TAXI   Unless you catch a ferry bus or rent a vehicle, you're at the expensive mercy of Moorea's taxi owners, who don't run around looking for customers. The only **taxi stand** is at the airport (© 56.10.18). It's staffed daily from 6am to 6pm. The hotel desks can call one for you, or phone **Pero Taxis** (© 56.14.93), **Albert Tours** (© 56.13.53), or **Justine Taxi** (© 77.48.26). Make advance reservations for service between 6pm and 6am.

Fares are 800 CFP (US$10/£5.05) during the day, 1,700 CFP (US$21/£11) at night, plus 110 CFP (US$1.40/70p) per kilometer (half-mile). They double from 8pm to 6am. Expect to pay about 2,000 CFP (US$25/£13) one-way from the ferry or airport to the Cook's Bay area, about 4,000 CFP (US$50/£25) one-way from the airport or Cook's Bay to the Haapiti area, less for stops along the way. Be sure that you understand what the fare will be before you get in.

BY RENTAL CAR & SCOOTER   Avis (© 800/331-1212 or 56.32.68; www.avis.com) and **Europcar** (© 800/227-7368 or 56.34.00; www.europcar.com) both have booths at the Vaiare ferry wharf and at several hotels. Although I usually rent from Avis, Europcar is the more widespread and slightly less expensive of the two, with unlimited-kilometer rates starting at 9,300 CFP (US$116/£59) a day. The local firm **Albert Rent-a-Car** (© 56.19.28) is the least expensive, with unlimited-kilometer rates starting at 8,000 CFP (US$100/£51) for a day.

In addition to automobiles, Europcar also rents little "Bugsters" (noisy contraptions with two seats and no top) for about 8,800 (US$110/£56) a day. They are fun to drive on sunny days. So are scooters, which Albert rents starting at 5,000 CFP (US$63/£32) for 4 hours and 6,000 CFP (US$75/£38) for 24 hours, including gasoline, full insurance, and unlimited kilometers.

Making reservations for cars and scooters is a very good idea, especially on weekends, when many Tahiti residents come to Moorea.

BY BICYCLE   The 60km (37-mile) road around Moorea is relatively flat. The two major hills are on the west side of Cook's Bay and behind the Sofitel Moorea Ia Ora Beach Resort (the latter is worth the climb, as it has a stupendous view of Tahiti). Some resorts have bikes for their guests to use, and **Europcar** (see above) rents mountain bikes for about 1,600 CFP (US$20/£10) for 8 hours, 2,000 CFP (US$25/£13) all day.

FAST FACTS: Moorea

The following facts apply specifically to Moorea. For more information, see "Fast Facts: French Polynesia," in chapter 7.

Bookstores   **Kina Maharepa** (© **56.22.44**), in the Maharepa shopping center, has English novels and magazines. **Supersonics** (© **56.14.96**), in Le Petit Village shopping center, opposite the former Club Med, carries some English-language magazines and newspapers.

Camera & Film   The hotel boutiques, **Kina Maharepa** (© **56.22.44**), in the Maharepa shopping center, and **Supersonics** (© **56.14.96**), in Le Petit Village, opposite the old Club Med, all sell film.

Currency Exchange   **Banque Socredo, Banque de Tahiti,** and **Banque de Polynésie** have offices and ATMs in or near the Maharepa shopping center. Banque de Polynésie has an ATM and a currency exchange machine but not an office in Le Petit Village shopping center in Haapiti. Accordingly, bring cash or traveler's checks if you're staying on the northwest corner, or be prepared to put most of your expenditures on a credit card. Banks are open Monday to Friday 8am to noon and 1:30 to 4:30pm.

Drugstores   **Pharmacie Moorea** (© **56.10.51**) is in Maharepa. The owner, Tran Thai Thanh, is a Vietnamese refugee who speaks English. It's open Monday to Friday 7:30am to noon and 2:30 to 4:30pm; Saturday 8am to noon and 3:30 to 6pm; and Sunday and holidays 8 to 10am. The owner speaks English.

Emergencies & Police   The emergency police telephone number is © **17**. The telephone number for the **gendarmerie** in Cook's Bay is © **56.13.44**. Local police have offices at **Pao Pao** (© **56.13.63**) and at **Haapiti** (© **56.10.84**), near where the Club Med was.

Eyeglasses   **Optique Moorea,** in the Maharepa shopping center (© **56.55.44**), sells and can fix glasses.

Healthcare   The island's **infirmary,** which has an ambulance, is at Afareaitu on the southwest coast (© **56.24.24**). Several doctors are in private practice; ask your hotel staff for a recommendation.

Internet Access   Every hotel has Internet access for its guests. In Cook's Bay, **Top Phone** (© **56.57.57**) has fast Internet access for 200 CFP (US$2.50/£1.25) for 15 minutes. It also sells VINI cellphone SIM cards. It's open Monday to Friday 8am to 5pm and Saturday 8am to noon. In Haapiti, **Polynesian Arts** (© **70.66.38**), in Le Petit Village, also has fast access at 20 CFP (25¢/13p) a minute. It's open Monday to Saturday 8:30am to 6pm. You can burn your digital photos onto CDs at either.

Mail   Moorea's main post office is in the Maharepa shopping center. It's open Monday to Thursday 7:30am to noon and 1 to 4pm, Friday 7:30am to noon and 1:30 to 3pm, and Saturday 7:30 to 9:30am. A post office in Papetoai village is open Monday to Thursday 7:30am to noon and 1:30 to 4pm, Friday 7:30am to noon and 1:30 to 3pm, and Saturday from 8 to 10am.

Taxes   Moorea's municipal government adds 100 CFP to 150 CFP (US$1.25–US$1.90/65p–95p) per night to your hotel bill. Don't complain: The money helps keep the island litter-free.

Visitor Information The **Moorea Visitors Bureau,** B.P. 1121, 98279 Papetoai (**℡ 56.29.09;** www.gomoorea.com), has an office at Le Petit Village shopping center in Haapiti. It's open Monday to Thursday 8am to 4pm and Saturday 8am to 3pm (more or less; they sometimes change).

Water Tap water on Moorea is *not* safe to drink; buy bottled water at any grocery store. Some hotels filter their water; ask if it's safe before drinking from the tap.

2 Exploring Moorea

Where you stay and most of what you will want to see and do lie on Moorea's north coast, between the ferry wharf at **Vaiare** and the area known as **Haapiti** on the island's northwestern corner. A large Club Med dominated Haapiti until it closed in 2002, and locals still say "Club Med" when referring to this area.

The sights of Moorea may lack great historical significance, but the physical beauty of the island makes a tour—at least of Cook's and Opunohu bays and up to the Belvédère lookout—a highlight of any visit. There are few places on earth this gorgeous. As on Tahiti, the round-island road—about 60km (37 miles) long—is marked every kilometer with a PK post. Distances are measured between the intersection of the airport road with the main round-island coastal road and the village of Haapiti on Moorea's opposite side. In other words, the distances indicated on the PKs increase from the airport in each direction, reaching 30km (18½ miles) near Haapiti. They then decrease as you head back to the airport.

THE CIRCLE ISLAND TOUR ✶✶✶

The hotel activities desks offer tours around Moorea and up to the Belvédère Lookout in the interior. **Albert Tours** (℡ **56.13.53**) and **Moorea Explorer** (℡ **56.12.86**) have half-day round-island tours, including the Belvédère, for about 3,500 CFP (US$44/£22) per person. The tour buses all stop at one black pearl shop or another. See "Shopping," later in this chapter, and "Buying Your Black Pearl," in chapter 8, before making a purchase.

TEMAE & MAHAREPA   Begin at the airstrip on Moorea's northeast corner. The airstrip is on the island's only sizable area of flat land. At one time it was a *motu*, or small island, sitting on the reef by itself. Humans and nature have since filled the lagoon except for Lake Temae, which you can see from the air if you fly to Moorea.

Head west from the round-island road/airport road junction.

Fun Fact Pai's Spear

Tahitian lore says the legendary hero Pai made the hole in the top of Mount Tohiea when the god of thieves attempted to steal Mount Rotui in the middle of the night. Pai threw his spear from Tahiti and pierced Mount Tohiea. The noise woke up Moorea's roosters, whose commotion alerted the citizenry to put a stop to the dastardly plan.

Impressions

Seen for the first time by European Eyes, this coast is like nothing else on our workaday planet; a landscape, rather, of some fantastic dream.
—Charles Nordhoff and James Norman Hall, *Mutiny on the Bounty,* 1933

Temae, 1km (a half-mile) from the junction, supplied the dancers for the Pomare dynasty's court and is still known for the quality of its performers. Herman Melville spent some time here in 1842 and saw the famous, erotic *upaupa,* which he called the "lory-lory," performed clandestinely, out of sight of the missionaries. Today Moorea's golf course is here (see "Fishing, Golf, Watersports & Other Outdoor Activities," later in this chapter).

The relatively dry north shore between the airport and the entrance to Cook's Bay is **Maharepa.** The road skirts the lagoon and passes the Moorea Pearl Resort & Spa and soon reaches the island's main shopping center.

COOK'S BAY ⍟⍟⍟   As the road curves to the left, you enter **Cook's Bay,** the fingerlike body of water surrounded on three sides by the jagged peaks lining the semicircular "wall" of Moorea. The tall thumb with a small hole in its top is **Mount Tohiea.** Coming into view as you drive farther along the bay is **Mount Mauaroa,** Moorea's trademark, cathedral-like, "Shark's Tooth" mountain buttressed on its right by a serrated ridge.

Huddled along the beach at the head of the bay, the village of **Pao Pao** is the site of Moorea's public schools. The *Cooperatif de Pêche Moorea* **(Moorea Fish Market)** is open Monday to Saturday from 5am to 5pm and Sunday from 5 to 8am.

The small **St. Joseph's Catholic Church** sits on the shore on the west side of Cook's Bay, at PK 10 from the airport. Inside is a large mural that artist Peter Heyman painted in 1946 and an altar decorated with mother-of-pearl. From the church, the road climbs up the side of the hill, offering some fine views, and then descends back to the lagoon's edge.

Watch on the left for the road leading inland to *Jus de Fruits de Moorea* **(Moorea Fruit Juices)** (⍟ **56.22.33**), a factory and distillery that turns the island's produce into the Rotui juices and the potently alcoholic Tahiti Drink you will see in every grocery store. I like to refresh here by tasting the yummy fruit liqueurs. Every souvenir imaginable is for sale, too. Hours are Monday to Thursday 8:30am to 4:30pm, Friday and Saturday 8:30am to 3:30pm.

OPUNOHU BAY ⍟⍟⍟   Towering over you is jagged **Mount Rotui,** the huge green-and-black rock separating Moorea's two great bays. Unlike Cook's Bay, Opunohu is virtually devoid of development, a testament to efforts by local residents to maintain the natural beauty of their island (they have ardently resisted efforts to build a luxury resort and golf course here). As soon as the road levels out, you can look through the trees to yachts anchored in **Robinson's Cove,** one of the world's most photographed yacht anchorages. Stop here and put your camera to work.

JARDIN KELLUM   Near the cove, at PK 17.5, stands the bayside home and botanical garden of the late Medford and Gladys Kellum, an American couple that once owned all of Opunohu Valley. The Kellums arrived here in 1925, aboard his parents' converted lumber schooner, and they lived for 65 years in their clapboard colonial-style

Moorea

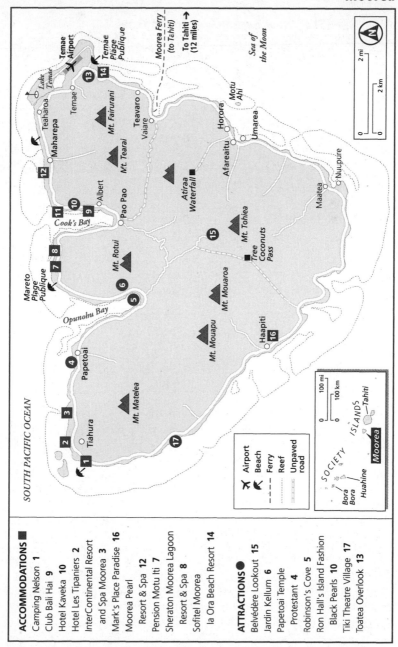

SOUTH PACIFIC OCEAN

Moorea Ferry (to Tahiti)

To Tahiti →
(12 miles)

Sea of the Moon

Temae Airport

Temae Plage Publique

Lake Temae

Teaharoa

Maharepa

Temae

Mt. Fairurani

Teavaro

Vaiare

Motu Ahi

Umarea

Horora

Afareaitu

Albert

Pao Pao

Mt. Tearai

Cook's Bay

Atiraa Waterfall ■

Maatea

Mt. Rotui

Mt. Tohiea

Mareto Plage Publique

Tree Coconuts Pass ■

Nuupure

Opunohu Bay

Mt. Mouaroa

Papetoai

Haapiti

Mt. Mouapu

Mt. Matelea

Tiahura

2 mi
2 km

ISLANDS
SOCIETY
Moorea
Tahiti
Bora Bora
Huahine

100 mi
100 km

Legend:
✈ Airport
⚓ Beach
– – – Ferry
Reef
Unpaved road

ACCOMMODATIONS ■

Camping Nelson **1**
Club Bali Hai **9**
Hotel Kaveka **10**
Hotel Les Tipaniers **2**
InterContinental Resort and Spa Moorea **3**
Mark's Place Paradise **16**
Moorea Pearl Resort & Spa **12**
Pension Motu Iti **7**
Sheraton Moorea Lagoon Resort & Spa **8**
Sofitel Moorea la Ora Beach Resort **14**

ATTRACTIONS ●

Belvédère Lookout **15**
Jardin Kellum **6**
Papetoai Temple Protestant **4**
Robinson's Cove **5**
Ron Hall's Island Fashion Black Pearls **10**
Tiki Theatre Village **17**
Toatea Overlook **13**

Moments **The View from Belvédère Lookout**

If the view from Le Belvédère restaurant on Tahiti doesn't thrill me enough, the scene from the Moorea lookout of the same name certainly does. I never tire of standing at the base of that cliff and watching dramatic Mount Rotui separate the deep blue fingers of Cook's and Opunohu bays.

---

house. Their daughter, Marimari Kellum, lives here today and gives tours of the house and garden to groups who book in advance (© **56.18.52**).

From the garden, the road soon curves right along a black-sand beach backed by shade trees and the Opunohu Valley at the head of the bay. The beach was turned into Matavai Bay on Tahiti for the 1983 production of *The Bounty*, starring Mel Gibson and Anthony Hopkins.

BELVÉDÈRE LOOKOUT *ЖЖЖ*   After the bridge by the beach, a paved road runs up Moorea's central valley through pasture land, across which Warren Beatty and Annette Benning strolled in their flop movie *Love Affair* (the scenes with Katherine Hepburn were filmed in the white house on the hill to your right). You can stop at **Lycée Agricole d'Opunohu (Opunohu Agricultural School)**, on the main road (© **56.11.34**), to see vanilla and other plantations. It's open Monday to Friday 8am to 4:30pm; Saturday 9am to 12:30pm.

At the head of the valley the road climbs steeply up the old crater wall to the restored **Titiroa Marae**, which was part of a concentration of *maraes* and other structures. Higher up you'll pass an archery platform used for competition (archery was a sport reserved for high-ranking chiefs and was never used in warfare in Polynesia). A display in the main marae parking lot explains the history of this area. You can walk among the remains of the temples, now shaded by towering Tahitian chestnut trees that have grown up through the cobblestone-like courtyards.

The narrow road then ascends to **Belvédère Lookout**, whose panorama of the valley and the bays on either side of Mount Rotui is unmatched in the South Pacific. You won't want to be without film or camera batteries here. There's a snack bar in the parking lot, so grab a cold drink or ice cream while you take in this remarkable vista.

PAPETOAI   Back on the coastal road, the village of **Papetoai** was the retreat of the Pomare dynasty in the 1800s and the base from which Pomare I launched his successful drive to take over all of Tahiti and Moorea. It was also headquarters for the London Missionary Society's work in the South Pacific. The road to the right, past the post office, leads to the octagonal **Papetoai Temple Protestant**, built on the site of a marae dedicated to Oro, son of the supreme Taaroa and the god of war. The original church was constructed in the 1820s, and although advertised as the oldest European building still in use in the South Pacific, the present structure dates from the late 1880s.

HAAPITI   From Papetoai, the road runs through the Haapiti hotel district on the northwest corner and then heads south through the rural parts of Moorea. Beginning in the 1970s, a 300-bungalow Club Med generated much business here, including Le Petit Village shopping center across the road. The area has been a bit depressed since the club closed in 2002. Still, this is your last chance to stop for refreshment before the sparsely populated southern half of Moorea (see "Where to Dine," later in this chapter).

About 4km (2½ miles) beyond Club Med, look for the **Tiki Theatre Village** ⟨⟨⟨, a cultural center consisting of thatch huts on the coastal side of the road. It's the only place to see what a Tahitian village looked like when Captain Cook arrived, so pull in. See "Tiki Theatre Village," below, for details.

When the first Europeans arrived, the lovely, mountain-backed village of **Haapiti** was home of the Marama family, which was allied with the Pomares. It became a center of Catholic missionary work after the French took over, and it is one of the few villages whose Catholic church is as large as its Protestant counterpart. Stop here and look behind the village for a view of Mount Mouaroa from a unique perspective.

THE SOUTHEAST COAST   South of Haapiti, just as the road curves sharply around a headland, is a nice view of a small bay with the mountains towering overhead (there's no place to park on the headland, so stop and walk up for the view). In contrast to the more touristy north shore, the southeast and southwest coasts have retained an atmosphere of old Polynesia.

The village of **Afareaitu,** on the southeast coast, is the administrative center of Moorea, and the building that looks like a charming hotel across from the village church actually is the island's *mairie,* or town hall.

About half a kilometer (a quarter-mile) beyond the town hall, opposite an A-frame house on the shore, an unpaved road runs straight between several houses and then continues uphill to the **Atiraa Waterfall** ⟨⟨. Often called Afareaitu Waterfall, water plunges more than 32m (105 ft.) down a cliff, into a small pool. You can drive partway to the falls, then walk 20 minutes up a steep, slippery, and muddy trail. Wear shoes or sandals that have good traction if you make this trek, for in places the slippery trail is hacked into a steep hill; if you slip, it's a long way down to the rocks below. Villagers will be waiting at the beginning of the footpath to extract a small fee.

Beyond Afareaitu, the small bay of **Vaiare** is a beehive of activity when the ferries pull in from Papeete. On workdays commuters park their vehicles at least 1km (a half-mile) in either direction from the wharf.

TOATEA OVERLOOK & TEMAE PUBLIC BEACH   Atop the hill north of the Sofitel Moorea Ia Ora Beach Resort is the **Toatea Overlook** ⟨⟨⟨. Here you'll have a magnificent view of the hotel, the green lagoon flecked with brown coral heads, the white line of the surf breaking on the reef, the deep blue of the Sea of the Moon, and all of Tahiti rising magnificently from the horizon. There's a parking area at the overlook.

The unpaved road to the right at the bottom of the hill leads to the **Temae Plage Publique (Temae Public Beach)** ⟨⟨⟨, Moorea's finest stretch of public beach. Follow the left fork through the coconut grove to the lagoon. This is a continuation of the Sofitel Ia Ora Moorea's beach, except that here you don't have a staff to rake the leaves and coral gravel from the sand. Locals often sell snacks and souvenirs here, especially on weekends. Bring insect repellent if you do your beaching here.

⟨*Moments* Tahiti in All Its Glory

My neck strains every time I cross the hill behind Moorea's Sofitel Ia Ora Moorea, for there across the Sea of the Moon sits Tahiti in all its green glory. What amazement the early explorers must have felt when those mountains appeared over the horizon!

Tiki Theatre Village 🏝🏝🏝

The best cultural experience in French Polynesia is at **Tiki Theatre Village**, at PK 31, or 2km (1¼ miles) south of old Club Med (℗ **55.02.50**; www.tikivillage. pf). Founded by Olivier Briac, a Frenchman whom the local Tahitians call *Le Sauvage Blanc* (the "White Savage"), it's built in the fashion of ancient Tahitian villages, this cultural center has old-style *fares* (houses) in which the staff demonstrates traditional tattooing, tapa-cloth making and painting, wood and stone carving, weaving, cooking, and making costumes, musical instruments, and flower crowns. There's even a "royal" house floating out on the lagoon, where you can learn about the modern art of growing black pearls.

Tiki Theatre Village will even arrange a traditional beachside wedding. The bride is prepared with flowery *monoi* oil like a Tahitian princess, and the groom is tattooed (with a wash-off pen). Both wear traditional costumes.

The village is open Tuesday to Saturday 11am to 3pm. Admission and a guided tour costs 1,500 CFP (US$19/£9.50).

Not to be missed is the authentic Tahitian feast and dance show here on Tuesday, Wednesday, Friday, and Saturday nights. They pick you up from your hotel and deposit you on the beach for a rum punch and sunset. After the staff uncovers the earth oven, they take you on a tour of the village. A buffet of both Tahitian and Western foods is followed by an energetic 1½-hour dance show with some of the most elaborate yet traditional costumes to be seen in French Polynesia. The dinner and show cost 8,700 CFP (US$109/£55) per person, or you can come for the 9pm show for 4,300 CFP (US$54/£27). Kids 3 to 12 pay half-price. Add 1,150 CFP (US$14/£7.30) for round-trip transportation.

3 Safari Expeditions, Lagoon Excursions & Dolphin-Watching

SAFARI EXPEDITIONS 🏝🏝

You can see the sights and learn a lot about the island on a four-wheel-drive excursion through Moorea's mountainous interior. Every hotel activities desk will book you on one of these adventures. **Albert Tours** (℗ **56.13.53**) and **Moorea Explorer** (℗ **56.12.86**) both have them. I've been with Alex and Gheslaine Haamatearii's **Inner Island Safari Tours** (℗ **56.20.09;** intersaf@mail.pf), which will take you through the valleys, up to Belvédère Lookout, and then down to a vanilla plantation in Opunohu Valley. They explain the island's flora and fauna along the way. The best trips end with a drive around Moorea's south coast and a hike up to Atiraa Waterfall for a refreshing swim (see "The Southeast Coast," under "The Circle Island Tour," above). Expect to visit a black pearl shop and Jus de Fruits de Moorea (see "Shopping," below). These half-day trips cost about 5,000 CFP (US$63/£32) per person.

In a variation on this theme, **Mahana ATV Tours** (℗ **56.20.44**) takes you on all-terrain vehicles into the Opunohu Valley.

LAGOON EXCURSIONS 🏝🏝🏝

The lagoon around Moorea is not as beautiful or diverse as Bora Bora's, but it's worth a day's outing. Most hotel activity desks will book you on a lagoon excursion, the best way to experience the magnificent setting. The full-day version of these excursions invariably includes a "motu picnic"—a lunch of grilled fresh fish, *poisson cru*, and salads served on a little islet (motu) out on the reef. Quite often the fresh fish is caught on the way. You'll have an opportunity to snorkel in the lagoon, and the staff will show you how to husk a coconut. Some of them also include shark- and ray-feeding, one of the most interesting and exciting things to do in the water here. Wear shoes you don't mind getting wet. The tours cost about 7,000 CFP (US$88/£44) per person.

Some lagoon excursions may take you to **Lagoonarium de Moorea,** on Motu Ahi off Afareaitu (© **78.31.15** or 23.81.23 for transfers). Like its counterpart on Bora Bora (see chapter 10), you can snorkel in a fenced area with dolphins, small sharks, and other sea life. The islet also has a snack bar and scuba diving. You can get there yourself, as the transfer boat leaves from PK 8 in Afareaitu. Transfers from the hotels to the island are 1,500 CFP (US$19/£9.50) per person, 700 CFP (US$8.75/£4.45) if you drive yourself to the landing. Admission to the island is 2,500 CFP (US$31/£16) adults, 1,800 CFP (US$23/£11) for children, including use of kayaks and snorkeling gear. It's open daily.

DOLPHIN- & WHALE-WATCHING ꝼꝼꝼ

Watching and swimming with dolphins is as much a part of the Moorea experience as is swimming with the sharks on Bora Bora (see chapter 10). And you stand a good chance of seeing humpback whales offshore from July until October, when they migrate from Antarctica to calve.

The best way to observe the animals in their natural habitat is on a dolphin- and whale-watching excursion led by American marine biologist **Dr. Michael Poole** (© **56.23.22** or 77.50.07; www.drmichaelpoole.com). An expert on sea mammals and a leader in the effort to have French Polynesian waters declared a whale sanctuary, Dr. Poole will take you beyond the reef to meet some of the 150 acrobatic spinner dolphins he has identified as regular Moorea residents. In calm conditions and if the animals are agreeable, you can don snorkeling gear and swim with them. You'll also be on the lookout for pilot whales that swim past year-round and giant humpback whales that frequent these waters from July to October. The half-day excursions cost about 7,500 CFP (US$94/£47) for adults, half-price for kids, including pickup at most hotel docks. Make reservations in advance, and be prepared not to go if the sea isn't calm.

Among the many activities at the InterContinental Resort and Spa Moorea (see "Fishing, Golf, Watersports & Other Outdoor Activities," below) and by far the most popular is the **Moorea Dolphin Center** ꝼꝼ (© **55.19.48;** www.mooreadolphin center.com). The intelligent sea mammals are sure to excite young and old alike—and many honeymooners love to have their photos taken with "smiling" dolphins. The animals live in a fenced area, although the center professes to be dedicated to their care and conservation. Kids 16 and older can join adults in snorkeling with the mammals in deeper water (all must be good swimmers) for 24,300 CFP (US$304/£154) per person. A 1-hour "dolphin discovery" excursion in shallow water costs 19,800 CFP (US$246/£125) per person. There's a 1-hour children's program (ages 5–11), which costs 12,000 CFP (US$150/£76) per kid, and there are family programs, too. They'll even take honeymooners on their own private encounter.

4 Fishing, Golf, Watersports & Other Outdoor Activities

Most hotels have active watersports programs for their guests, such as glass-bottomed-boat cruises and snorkeling in, or sailing on, Moorea's lagoon.

The most extensive array of sporting activities is at the **InterContinental Resort and Spa Moorea** (© 55.19.19), whose facilities can be used by both guests and visitors who are willing to pay. The facilities include scuba diving, parasailing (magnificent views of the bays, mountains, and reefs), water-skiing, wakeboarding, scooting about the lagoon and Opunohu Bay on jet skis, viewing coral and fish from Aquascope boats, walking on the lagoon bottom while wearing diving helmets, line fishing, and speedboat rentals. Nonguests can also pay to use the pool, snorkeling gear, tennis courts, and to be taken over to a small islet. Call the hotel for prices, schedules, and reservations, which are required.

GOLF   Encompassing Lake Temae west of the airport, the **Moorea Green Pearl Golf Course of Polynesia** (© 56.27.32; www.mooreagolf-resort.com) opened in 2007 with 18 holes designed by Jack Nicklaus. The par-70 course measures 6,564 yards. Initial greens fees were 12,000 CFP (US$150/£76) for 9 holes, 21,000 CFP (US$263/£133 for 18 holes, including a cart, but I wouldn't be surprised to see them drop. The course and clubhouse are open daily from 7:30am to 5:30pm. You can practice by driving balls into the lake. Plans call for two resorts here.

FISHING   Chris Lilley, an American who has won several sportfishing contests, takes guests onto the ocean in search of big game catch on his *Tea Nui* (© 55.19.19, ext. 1903, or 56.15.08 at home; teanuiservices@mail.pf). In keeping with South Pacific custom, you can keep the little fish you catch; Chris sells the big ones. Contact Chris for rates and reservations.

HIKING   You won't need a guide to hike from the coast road up the Opunohu Valley to Belvédère Lookout. Up and down will take most of a day. It's a level but hot walk along the valley floor and gets steep approaching the lookout. Bring lots of water. Several unmarked hiking trails lead into the mountains, including one beginning in Cook's Bay and ending on the east coast, another from the southwest coast across a pass and into Opunohu Valley. I would go with a guide on longer hikes up in the mountains. Moorea-based **Tahiti Evasion** (© 56.48.77; www.tahitievasion.com) has half-day treks to the archeological sites in the Opunohu Valley, across Three Coconuts Pass between the Belvédère and the south coast, and to the Afreaitu waterfall and the pierced Mt. Tohiea. Prices range from 4,500 CFP to 8,000 CFP (US$56–US$100/£28–£51) per person.

There's a relatively easy 15-minute hike from the shore to the top of the hill above **Painapo (Pineapple) Beach** (© 74.96.96), on Moorea's southwestern coast.

HORSEBACK RIDING   Landlubbers can go horseback riding along the beach and into the interior with **Ranch Opunohu Valley** (© 56.28.55). Rates are about 6,000 CFP (US$75/£38) for a 1½-hour ride.

SCUBA DIVING   Although Moorea's lagoon is not in the same league with those at Rangiroa, Fakarava, or even Bora Bora, its outer reef has some decent sites for viewing coral and sea life. The island's best diving operator is **TOPdive** (© 56.17.32; www.topdive.com), with bases in Cook's Bay and at the Sheraton Moorea Lagoon Resort & Spa. Also excellent is Gilles Pétré's **Moorea Diving Center** (© 55.17.50; www.bluenui.com) at the Moorea Pearl Resort & Spa. On the northwest coast, the InterContinental Resort and Spa Moorea is home to **Bathy's Diving** (© 55.19.19, ext. 1139; www.bathys.net), and **Scubapiti Moorea** (© 56.20.38; www.scubapiti.com) resides at Hotel Les Tipaniers. All charge about 6,500 CFP (US$81/£41) for a one-tank dive, including equipment (gauges are metric).

SNORKELING   Sharing the lagoon with the Sofitel Ia Ora Moorea, the **Temae Plage Publique (Tamae Public Beach)** has some of the island's best snorkeling, and it's relatively safe. Also good is the lagoon around the motus off Haapiti, but watch out for strong currents coming in and out of the nearby reef passes.

Another favorite with locals for sunning and swimming is **Mareto Plage Publique (Mareto Public Beach),** in a coconut grove west of the Sheraton Moorea between the two bays. Go around the wire fence on the eastern end.

There's good snorkeling over coral gardens off **Painapo (Pineapple) Beach** (© **74.96.96;** www.painapo.com), on the Haapiti coast. This picturesque little playground charges a one-time 2,000 CFP (US$25/£13) for a day pass, including use of snorkeling gear. I love to fill up at the restaurant here on Sunday (see "A Sunday Tahitian Feast," under "Where to Dine," later).

The lagoon off Moorea's northwest corner is blessed with offshore motu, small islets where you can sunbathe, swim, and snorkel (but be beware of strong currents), and have lunch on **Motu Moea.** You can rent a boat to get over there from **Moorea Locaboat** (© **78.13.39**), based next to Hotel Les Tipaniers, or take a transfer from **Tip Nautic** next door (© **73.76.73**) for about 700 CFP (US$8.75/£4.45) round-trip. Tip Nautic also rents snorkel gear for 500 CFP (US$6/£3) for half a day and kayaks starting at 500 CFP (US$6.25/£3.15) per hour, and it has water-skiing and dolphin-watching trips.

5 Shopping

Moorea's commercial center is at **Maharepa,** where you'll find black-pearl shops, banks, grocery stores, hairdressers, the post office, and other services. The neocolonial buildings of **Le Petit Village** shopping center anchor the northwestern corner, where stores sell *pareus,* T-shirts, and souvenirs. **Supersonics** (© **56.29.73**) carries film, batteries, stamps, magazines, and other items. There's a grocery store.

Boutiques and art galleries are numerous on Moorea, but they come and go as frequently as their owners arrive from France, then decide to go home. The shops below should still be here when you arrive.

ART

Boutique d'Art Marquisien **(Marquesan Art Boutique)**   A family from the Marquesas Islands runs this attractive shop, where they sell exquisite art and handicrafts from their native archipelago. Wood carvings top their list, including intricately carved tables that will cost a fortune to ship home. More manageable are war clubs, paintings, stone work, masks, tikis, and carved coconut shells. They're open Monday to Saturday 8am to 5:30pm. Cook's Bay, in Cooks Bay Center shops. © **56.23.37.**

Galerie van der Heyde 𝒜𝒜   Dutch artist Aad van der Heyde has lived and worked on Moorea since 1964. One of his bold impressionist paintings of a Tahitian woman was selected for French Polynesia's 100 CFP postage stamp in 1975, and his landscape of Bora Bora appeared on a 2004 stamp. Aad will sell you an autographed lithograph of the paintings. Some of his works are displayed on the gallery's garden wall. Aad has produced excellent videos of the islands and will gladly sell you a copy on DVD. He also has a small collection of pearls, wood carvings, *tapa* cloth, shell and coral jewelry, and primitive art from Papua New Guinea. The gallery is open Monday to Saturday from 8am to 5pm. East side of Cook's Bay. © **56.14.22.**

BLACK PEARLS

Moorea has more pearl shops than you can visit in a normal vacation. Tour operators are likely to deposit you at the shop offering the highest commission at the end of your excursion. But Moorea also has small, family-owned shops which carry quality pearls that cost less, as they don't have high overheads and promotion expenses. Always shop around, and re-read the "Buying Your Black Pearl" box in chapter 8 before making your purchase.

Among several stores near the old Club Med site in Haapiti is **Tahia Collins** (© 55.05.00; www.tahiacollins.com). Owner and chief designer Tahia Collins was a Miss Moorea and is a scion of the Albert Haring family (you will see the Albert name all over the island). Her husband, Marc Collins, was born in Hawaii of an American father and Tahitian mother. This is one of the more aggressive pearl shops on Moorea. Others worth visiting in this area are **Herman Perles** (© 56.42.79) and **Pai Moana Pearls** (© 56.25.25).

My favorites are on the other side of the island, to wit:

Eva Perles   Eva Frachon, the French gemologist who owns this little shop, graduated from the University of Wisconsin at Oshkosh with a bachelor's degree in photography and art metals; thus, she does her own creative settings, and speaks American-style English. She carries high-quality orbs in all price ranges. Eva and Ron Hall's Island Fashion Black Pearls (see below) are the only Cook's Bay dealers who can legally send a courtesy shuttle to pick you up. Eva's is open Monday to Saturday 9:30am to 5:30pm. Maharepa, opposite the post office. © **56.10.10.**

Ron Hall's Island Fashion Black Pearls ⟨★★★ *Value*⟩   Ron Hall sailed from Hawaii to Tahiti with the actor Peter Fonda in 1974; Peter went home, Ron didn't. Now Ron and his son, Heimata, run this air-conditioned Moorea retail outlet. It's worth a stop to see the antiques and old photos, including one of the infamous Quinn's Bar and a William Leeteg painting of a Tahitian *vahine* (Ron's wife and Heimata's mother, Josée, was herself a championship Tahitian dancer). In 15 minutes of "pearl school," you will learn the basics of picking a pearl. They will have your selection set in a mounting of your choice, their prices are fair, and they donate 10% of every pearl purchase to Dr. Michael Poole's dolphin and whale research (see "Dolphin-Watching," above). They also carry one of Moorea's best selections of bathing suits, aloha shirts, and T-shirts. They are open Monday to Saturday 9am to 6pm. East side of Cook's Bay. © **56.11.06.**

6 Where to Stay

Most of Moorea's hotels and restaurants are grouped in or near Cook's Bay, between Cook's and Opunohu bays, or in the Haapiti district on the northwest corner of the island around the old Club Med site. With the exception of the Sofitel Moorea Ia Ora Beach Resort, those in or near Cook's Bay do not have the best beaches on the island, but the snorkeling is excellent and most have unsurpassed views of the mountains. The establishments between the two bays have beaches, but they are a bit inconvenient to the facilities at Cook's Bay and Haapiti. Those on the northwest corner have generally fine beaches, lagoons like giant swimming pools, and unobstructed views of the sunset, but not of Moorea's famous mountains. The areas are relatively far apart, so you might spend most of your time near your hotel unless you rent a vehicle or otherwise make a point to see the sights. An alternative is to split your stay between the areas.

The Bali Hai Boys

Californians Jay Carlisle, Don "Muk" McCallum, and the late Hugh Kelley gave up their budding business careers as stockbroker, lawyer, and sporting goods salesman, respectively, and in 1960 bought an old vanilla plantation on Moorea. Instead of planting, they refurbished an old beachfront hotel that stood on their property (now occupied by the Moorea Pearl Resort & Spa). Taking a page from James Michener's *Tales of the South Pacific,* they renamed it the Bali Hai and opened for business in 1961. With construction of Tahiti-Faaa International Airport across the Sea of the Moon, their timing couldn't have been better. With Jay managing the money, Hugh building the resort, and Muk entertaining their guests, they quickly had a success on their hands. Travel writers soon dubbed them the "Bali Hai Boys."

Supplies and fresh produce weren't easy to come by in those days, so they put the old vanilla plantation to work producing chickens, eggs, and milk. It was the first successful poultry and dairy operation on the island.

Thank Jay, Muk, and Hugh for overwater bungalows—cabins sitting on pilings over the lagoon with glass panels in their floors so that we can watch the fish swim below. They built the world's first in 1968 on Raiatea. A novelty at the time, their romantic invention is now a staple at resorts well beyond French Polynesia.

THE COOK'S BAY AREA

Club Bali Hai *(Value*   The last property operated by Moorea's two surviving Bali Hai Boys (see the "The Bali Hai Boys" box, below), this basic hotel has an incredible view of Moorea's ragged mountains across Cook's Bay, a scene epitomizing the South Pacific. Under a bayside thatched-roof, **Snack l'Ananas Blue (The Blue Pineapple)** serves breakfast and lunch (see "Where to Dine," below). It also is the scene for Muk McCallum's bring-your-own happy hours from 5:30 to 7pm Thursday to Tuesday, when he "talks story" about the good old days on Moorea. It's worth stopping by the club's Wednesday-night Tahitian dance shows too. A swimming pool with a rock waterfall augments the manmade beach here. Half of the guest units are part of a time-share operation, but that means they come equipped with kitchens. The overwater bungalows are the least expensive in French Polynesia, while the beachfront bungalows have huge bathrooms with gardens growing in them, another trademark of the Bali Hai Boys. Most other units are in one- or two-story motel-style buildings. All are simply but comfortably furnished. The view is worth a million bucks.

B.P. 8, 98728 Maharepa, Moorea. (©) 56.13.68. Fax 56.13.27. www.clubbalihai.com. 39 units. US$175 (£88) double; US$185–US$245 (£93–£123) bungalow. AE, DC, MC, V. **Amenities:** Restaurant (breakfast and lunch); bar; outdoor pool; activities desk; car-rental desk; bicycle rentals; complimentary kayaks; coin-operated washers and dryers. *In room:* A/C, kitchen, fridge, coffeemaker, no phone.

Hotel Kaveka *(Value*   Another modest property with a fine view, this all-bungalow hotel sits behind a rock wall along the road, but its other side opens to Cook's Bay. Noted for its fish burgers, the hotel's overwater **Kaveka Restaurant** enjoys the best view of any Moorea restaurant serving an international menu. The white-sand beach here is compact (a breakwater fronts most of the property), but snorkeling is very good. The bungalows are made of timber with shingle roofs. Most have attractive mat walls, queen and single platform beds, and smallish, shower-only bathrooms. Two units have two double beds and much better bathrooms. The least expensive lanai units lack porches and air conditioners. The few-frills Kaveka often is the least expensive hotel offered in package trips to French Polynesia.

B.P. 373, 98728 Maharepa, Moorea. ⓒ 877/354-5902, or 56.50.50. Fax 56.52.63. www.hotelkaveka.com. 25 units. 11,500 CFP–23,500 CFP (US$144–US$294/£73–£149) double. AE, MC, V. **Amenities:** Restaurant; bar; bicycle rentals; watersports equipment rentals; laundry service. In room: A/C (in bungalows), TV, fridge, no phone.

Moorea Pearl Resort & Spa ⓡⓡⓡ You can easily walk from this multifaceted resort to Maharepa's shops and restaurants. Forget a great view, because the resort faces the open ocean, and its 28 overwater bungalows block most of the sea view. On the other hand, snorkeling is excellent here, especially from the decks of the 20 deluxe, overwater bungalows perched out on the edge of the clifflike reef. They and 18 beach bungalows with private pools in their courtyards are the pick of a mixed litter of accommodations. Some of the garden bungalows are standalone, while others are in less private duplex units. Sporting private backyards with plunge pools, the bungalows are identical inside, with native wood accents, ceiling fans, king-size beds, and ample shower-only bathrooms. The least expensive units are 30 spacious hotel rooms in two-story blocks away from the lagoon. They all have king-size beds and balconies or patios, and eight family rooms add two single beds. Big thatched roofs cover a large dining room and pool-level bar, which hosts Tahitian dance shows twice a week. The smallish beach and big infinity swimming pool serve as centers for numerous outdoor activities.

B.P. 3410, 98728 Maharepa, Moorea. ⓒ 800/657-3275 or 55.17.50. Fax 55.17.51. www.pearlresorts.com. 95 units. 30,200 CFP–35,800 CFP (US$378–US$448/£191–£227) double; 40,300 CFP–76,100 CFP (US$504–US$951/£255–£482) bungalow. AE, DC, MC, V. **Amenities:** 2 restaurants; bar; outdoor pool; spa; Jacuzzi; watersports equipment rentals; bike rentals; activities desk; car-rental desk; limited room service; massage; babysitting; laundry service. In room: A/C, TV, dataport, kitchen, minibar (bungalows only), fridge, coffeemaker, iron, safe.

Sofitel Moorea Ia Ora Beach Resort ⓡⓡⓡ Known as the Sofitel Moorea Beach Resort until 2005, when it was shuttered for a complete overhaul, this sprawling resort sits beside Moorea's best lagoon and beach (it's known as Temae Public Beach north of the resort). The Sofitel is the only resort with a view of Tahiti, whose green, cloud-topped mountains seem to climb out of the horizon beyond the reef. Given its already superb location, the renovations have made it the best all-around resort on Moorea. All its original, 1960s-vintage bungalows were replaced with modern, luxurious units, and 19 overwater units were added to the 20 already here. Most overwater units face the lagoon rather than Tahiti, however, so try to get bungalows 117, 119, 120, 122, or 215 through 218. Ashore, the best views are from three deluxe bungalows on the south end of the property; these are the most private units here, although the beach is much better on the north side. Least expensive are the garden bungalows whose views are squeezed through the beachfront units. The thatched-roof, sand-floor gourmet restaurant here is extremely romantic and reasonably priced (reservations are required).

B.P. 28, Maharepa, Moorea (Temae, on the northeast coast facing Tahiti). ⓒ 800/763-4835, 55.03.55, or 41.04.04 in Papeete. Fax 41.05.05. www.accorhotels.com. 119 units. 36,700 CFP–85,000 CFP (US$455–US$1,054/£231–£536) double. AE, DC, MC, V. **Amenities:** 2 restaurants; bar; outdoor pool; 2 tennis courts; spa; watersports equipment rentals; bike rentals; activities desk; car-rental desk; bicycle rentals; massage; babysitting; laundry service. In room: A/C, TV, minibar, coffeemaker, iron, safe.

BETWEEN COOK'S & OPUNOHU BAYS

Pension Motu Iti   Auguste and Dora Ienfa's little pension sits beside the lagoon about 800 meters (2,625 ft.) west of the Sheraton Moorea Lagoon Resort & Spa. They have no beach, only a bulkhead along the shore, but a pier goes to an overwater cabana for relaxing. Their five bungalows are clean, comfortable, and reasonably spacious, and they have a small dormitory over the main building. Their dining room serves breakfast, lunch, and dinner daily, although the food at Restaurant Aito next door is much more interesting (see "Where to Dine," below).

B.P. 189, 98728 Maharepa, Moorea (between Cook's and Opunohu bays). ℭ 55.05.20. Fax 55.05.21. www.pension motuiti.com. 5 units. 10,500 CFP–12,000 CFP (US$131–US$150/£66–£76) bungalow, 1,650 CFP (US$21/£10) dorm bed. AE, MC, V. **Amenities:** Restaurant; bar; free kayaks, canoes, and snorkeling gear. *In room:* TV, no phone.

Sheraton Moorea Lagoon Resort & Spa ⟨R⟩⟨R⟩   This luxury hotel is not particularly convenient to restaurants and activities, but it does provide shuttles to the Tiki Village Theatre and the Vaiare ferry dock. Two stunning, conical thatch roofs cover the reception area and a French restaurant overlooking a decent beach. Steps lead down to a beachside pool with its own sunken bar. You'll get some serious pampering in the resort's full-service Mandara spa. All the guest bungalows are identical except for their location. A Y-shaped pier—with its own sundowner bar—leads to half of them out over the lagoon. These all have glass floor panels for fish-viewing and decks with steps down into the clear, 4-foot-deep water. The others are in a coconut grove by the beach. Every unit is equipped with niceties such as CD players, complimentary snorkeling gear, plush robes, and claw-foot tubs, in addition to walk-in showers.

B.P. 1005, 98279 Papetoai, Moorea (between Cook's and Opunohu bays). ℭ 800/325-3535 or 55.11.11 in Moorea. Fax 86.48.40. www.sheraton.com. 106 units. 45,500 CFP–86,000 CFP (US$569–US$1,075/£288–£544) bungalow. AE, DC, MC, V. **Amenities:** 2 restaurants; 3 bars; outdoor pool; 2 tennis courts; health club; spa; watersports equipment rentals; bike rentals; concierge; activities desk; car-rental desk; business center; 24-hr. room service; massage; babysitting; laundry service. *In room:* A/C, TV, CD player, dataport, minibar, coffeemaker, iron, safe.

THE NORTHWEST COAST

Camping Chez Nelson   All guests share toilets, cold-water showers, and communal kitchen facilities at this campground and hostel in a beachside coconut grove about 200 yards west of the former Club Med. In addition to camping space on a shadeless lawn, basic accommodations here include tiny bungalows for couples (just enough room for a double bed), four blocks of small rooms (two beds each), and four other thatched-roof hostel bungalows down the road (and still on the beach).

B.P. 1309, 98279 Papetoai, Moorea (in Haapiti, west of old Club Med). ℭ/fax 56.15.18. www.camping-nelson.pf. 4 bungalows, 15 rooms, 20 dorm beds. 1,200 CFP–1,300 CFP (US$15–US$16/£7.60–£8.25) per camper; 1,600 CFP–2,000 CFP (US$20–US$25/£10–£13) dorm bed; 4,300 CFP–6,300 CFP (US$54–US$79/£27–£40) double; 4,500 CFP–5,000 CFP (US$56–US$63/£28–£32) per bungalow. Lower rates for stays of more than 1 night. AE, DC, MC. V. *In room:* No phone.

Hotel Les Tipaniers ⟨R⟩⟨R⟩ ⟨Value⟩   One of Moorea's best values, this friendly, French-owned establishment sits in a coconut grove beside the sandy beach wrapping around the island's northwestern corner. The widely spaced bungalows stand back in the trees, which gives the small complex an open, airy atmosphere. They also are far enough from the road to be quiet. The "standard superior" bungalows have L-shaped settees facing sliding glass doors to covered porches. Behind the settee a raised sleeping area supports a queen-size bed, and behind that, a fully tiled bathroom has a sizable shower and vanity space. To the rear of the property, other bungalows are equipped with kitchens and can sleep up to five persons. Also out back, a building houses four small hotel-style rooms equipped with twin beds (you can push them together), reading lights, and ample tiled bathrooms with showers. Okay for couples, these rooms are the least expensive yet comfortable place to stay on Moorea. Unlike the others, however, they do not have phones, fridges, or safes. All units here have ceiling fans but not air conditioners. A very good restaurant with a deck over the beach is open daily for breakfast, lunch, and afternoon snacks. The hotel is also home to a terrific beach bar and an excellent Italian restaurant (see "Where to Dine," below). Guests can make free use of canoes and bicycles, or pay Tip Nautic for kayaking, water-skiing, motu trips, and diving with Scubapiti, which is based here.

B.P. 1002, 98279 Papetoai, Moorea (in Haapiti, east of old Club Med). © 56.12.67. Fax 56.29.25. www. lestipaniers.com. 22 units. 6,900 CFP (US$86/£44) double; 13,950 CFP (US$174/£88) bungalow without kitchenette; 13,950 CFP–15,950 CFP (US$174–US$200/£88–£101) double with kitchenette. AE, DC, MC, V. **Amenities:** 2 restaurants; 2 bars; watersports equipment rentals; canoes and bicycles; babysitting; laundry service. In room: Kitchen (13 units), fridge (9 units), safe (17 units).

InterContinental Resort and Spa Moorea ⟨⟨⟨ Although relatively isolated about 2.5km (1½ miles) east of the Club Med area, Moorea's busiest resort is famous as home to the Moorea Dolphin Center (see "Safari Expeditions, Lagoon Excursions & Dolphin-Watching," earlier in this chapter). The beach and sometimes murky lagoon here aren't the island's best, but the resort has the widest range of watersports activities on the island—all of them available to guests and nonguests who are willing to pay (see "Fishing, Golf, Watersports & Other Outdoor Activities," earlier in this chapter). The airy central building with a shingle roof opens to a large pool area surrounded by an ample sunning deck. Most of the guest bungalows extend partially over the water from manmade islands. A curving two-story building holds 52 spacious hotel rooms; they all have patios or balconies facing the beach, and their tub/showers combinations are a rarity on Moorea. The Tahitian dance show on the beach is one of Moorea's most colorful. *Note:* The resort has done away with its children's program, which had made it attractive to families.

B.P. 1019, 98279 Papetoai, Moorea (between Papetoai and Haapiti). © 800/327-0200 or 55.19.19. Fax 55.19.55. www.interconti.com. 52 units, 102 bungalows. 32,900 CFP–36,500 CFP (US$411–US$456/£208–£231) double; 53,000 CFP–87,400 CFP (US$663–US$1,093/£335–£553) bungalow. AE, DC, MC, V. **Amenities:** Restaurant; bar; outdoor pool; tennis courts; spa; free snorkel gear, kayaks, and canoes; watersports equipment rentals; bike rentals; activities desk; car-rental desk; limited room service; babysitting; laundry service. In room: A/C, TV, minibar, coffeemaker, hair dryer.

Mark's Place Paradise A cabinet maker from Idaho, Mark Walker moved to French Polynesia in 1980 and has put his skills to work on the creatively rustic units at this retreat in the Haapiti Valley. No two alike, his units range in size from a honeymoon unit that has a TV with DVD player to one large enough for groups or use as a dorm. Bungalows have TVs, kitchens, and private bathrooms. Dorm residents share toilets, showers, and the communal kitchen, but everyone else has a private bathroom. Although he isn't on the beach, this is a good place for backpackers and other adventurous souls.

B.P. 41, 98279 Papetoai, Moorea (at PK 23.5 in Haapiti valley). © 56.43.02 or 78.93.65. www.marks-place-paradise.com. 5 bungalows (all with bathroom), 26 dorm beds. 8,000 CFP (US$100/£51) bungalow; 2,500 CFP (US$31/£16) dorm bed. MC, V. Minimum 2-night stay required. **Amenities:** Bike and kayak rentals; wireless Internet access. In room: TV, kitchen, coffeemaker, no phone.

7 Where to Dine

The restaurant scene changes quickly on Moorea, so I can only hope the ones I recommend below are still in business when you get here. As on Tahiti, you can save by eating at snack bars for breakfast, lunch, or an early dinner.

(*Value* **Call for Transportation**

Most Moorea restaurants will come get you or pay half if not all of your taxi fare if you make reservations for dinner. Although they restrict this service to nearby restaurants, depending on the size of your group, it pays to call ahead.

THE COOK'S BAY AREA

Nicely spiced pies come from the wood-fired oven at **Allo Pizza,** in Cook's Bay near the gendarmerie (© **56.18.22**). Carry out or call for delivery between the Sofitel Moorea Ia Ora Beach Resort and the Sheraton Moorea Lagoon Resort & Spa. It's open Tuesday to Saturday 11am to 2pm and 5 to 9pm and Sunday 5 to 9pm.

For more than 20 years I have regularly stopped at the inexpensive **Snack Rotui,** on the shore of Cook's Bay in Paopao village (© **56.18.16**), for *casse-croûte* sandwiches and homemade chocolate cake. The view from the bayside tables is awesome. It's open Tuesday to Saturday 7am to 6pm.

Another good choice is **Patisserie Caraméline,** in Maharepa next to the post office (© **56.12.06**), which offers a selection of pastries, crepes, pizzas, salads, omelets, quiches, burgers, sandwiches, *poisson cru,* shrimps in coconut curry sauce, grilled tuna and mahimahi, fruit plates, ice cream, sundaes, and other goodies. The patio tables here are a relaxing spot to write a postcard. It's open daily 7am to 3pm.

Alfredo's ITALIAN/FRENCH   French restaurateur Christian Boucheron, who worked at hotels in the Washington, D.C., suburbs for 19 years, will make you feel right at home in this old building, a short walk from the Club Bali Hai. In fact, many guests are Americans and other English-speaking visitors who come here more for the fun than the food (guitarist Ron Falconer usually plays and sings Thurs and Sun nights). The menu features pizzas, pastas, and several Italian and French main courses.

Pao Pao, near Club Bali Hai. © **56.17.71.** Reservations recommended. Pizzas 1,650 CFP (US$21/£10); main courses 2,450 CFP–3,850 CFP (US$31–US$48/£16–£24). MC, V. Daily 11am–2:30pm and 5:30–9:30pm.

Le Mahogany ⑁⑁ *Value* FRENCH/CHINESE   French chef François Courtien spent 30 years cooking at the former Hotel Bali Hai before joining Tahitian Blondine Agnia at her pleasant little dining spot next to the local gym. It's a favorite with expatriates who appreciate value and friendly service. Polished mahogany tables, art-adorned walls, and a window opening to a garden provide tropical ambience. A rich avocado-and-shrimp cocktail is a good way to start. Consistently good are Moorea-grown shrimp with curry or Provençal sauce, and shrimp and scallops in a puff pastry with a light cream sauce. The Cantonese main courses are better than those at any Chinese restaurant here. Or you can opt for the special tourist menu of a salad, mahimahi grilled or with meunière sauce, and ice cream for dessert. Otherwise, end with a *tarte tatin,* a caramelized apple pie served with vanilla ice cream.

Maharepa. © **56.39.73.** Reservations recommended. Main courses 1,450 CFP–2,950 CFP (US$18–US$37/£9.20–£19); tourist menu 3,250 CFP (US$41/£21). MC, V. Thurs–Tues 11am–2:30pm and 6–9:30pm.

Le Sud ⑁ SOUTHERN FRENCH   For a pleasant change of French pace, head to this little white house in the Maharepa shopping district for paella, Provençal-style fish dishes, and seafood pastas from *le sud* (the south) of France. The spices definitely reflect Spanish and Italian influences. The *plats du jour* here are a very good value, especially at lunch. Torches contribute to romantic nighttime dining on the patio.

Tips Check Out Moorea's *Roulottes*

For more on roulottes (see "Don't Miss *Les Roulottes,*" p. 244). The best of these meal wagons, **Roulotte Jules & Claudine,** at the fish market in Pao Pao (𝄞 **56.25.31**), serves a mixed menu of *poisson cru;* chow mein; and char-grilled steaks, chicken, and fish; but the best item is local shrimp in a tasty coconut-curry sauce. Prices range from 1,000 CFP to 1,800 CFP (US$15–US$23/£6.35–£11). No credit cards. Open Monday through Saturday from 6:30 to 8:30pm. You'll find another *roulotte* near Le Petite Village shopping center in Haapiti.

Maharepa. 𝄞 **56.42.95.** Reservations recommended. Main courses 2,200 CFP–2,950 CFP (US$28–US$37/£14–£19). MC, V. Tues–Sat 11am–2pm and 6–9pm; Sun 6–9pm.

La Petite Maison (Chez Lydie) *Finds* FRENCH/MEDITERRANEAN/CHINESE Lydie Pache worked at Le Mahogany for years before opening her own restaurant near the bridge in Pao Pao village. Ask for a bayside table on the veranda; they look north toward the yachts anchored in Cook's Bay. As at Le Mahogany, she offers Cantonese Chinese dishes (the least expensive), but her best offerings are fresh seafood treated in the Mediterranean fashion. I was impressed with her *poêlée,* a mixed seafood casserole with butter, cream, and garlic. Paella and couscous appear here, too. Lydie brings a bowl of peanuts for munching before your first course arrives.

Paopao, east side of bridge. 𝄞 **56.34.80.** Reservations recommended. Main courses 1,000 CFP–2,800 CFP (US$13–US$35/£6.35–£18). MC, V. Daily 11am–3pm and 6–10pm.

Rudy's *Finds* FRENCH/STEAKS This hacienda-style steakhouse is the latest creation of Tahiti-born Syd Pollack, who has started several restaurants and other projects both here and in Hawaii. This one's named for his son, Rudy, who oversees the kitchen here. In addition to tender New Zealand steaks and fresh local seafood, I always check the specials board for the likes of parrot fish grilled and stuffed with crab, or beef in a red wine sauce but with island influences.

Maharape, west of post office. 𝄞 **56.58.00.** Reservations recommended. Main courses 2,200 CFP–3,200 CFP (US$28–US$40/£14–£20). MC, V. Daily 11am–2:30pm and 5:30–10pm.

Snack *l'Ananas Bleu* (The Blue Pineapple) *Value* BREAKFAST/SNACKS Matahi Hunter's snack occupies what once was the bayside bar at the Club Bali Hai, where you get a stupendous view of Cook's Bay to go with your cooked or continental breakfast and lunches of big juicy beef, fish, or teriyaki burgers accompanied by french fries. Ice cream and fruit drinks provide relief from the midday heat. There's a seafood barbecue on Wednesday night following the Club's Tahitian dance show.

Pao Pao, in Club Bali Hai. 𝄞 **56.12.06.** Breakfast 600 CFP–1,650 CFP (US$7.50–US$21/£3.80–£10); burgers and sandwiches 800 CFP–1,650 CFP (US$10–US$21/£5.05–£10); main courses 1,450 CFP–2,350 CFP (US$18–US$29/£9.20–£15). MC, V. Daily 7am–3pm.

BETWEEN COOK'S & OPUNOHU BAYS

Restaurant Aito FRENCH/CORSICAN Extending out over the lagoon, this open-air cafe preserves the old South Seas ambience better than any other on Moorea. Adding to the charm are big *aito* (ironwood) trees growing through the deck and thatched roof (hence the restaurant's name). Owner Jean-Baptiste Cipriani grew up in Marseilles on the cooking of his Corsican ancestors, and he repeats some of those dishes here, including a luscious tomato sauce that requires 10 hours to prepare. You can dip your bread into some *very* spicy Corsican peppers while waiting. This isn't the cleanest place on Moorea, but it's a terrific spot for a lagoonside meal, as many celebrity visits attest.

PK 13.1, west of Sheraton Moorea between Cook's and Opunohu bays. *C* 56.45.52. Reservations recommended. Main courses 1,850 CFP–2,800 CFP (US$23–US$35/£12–£18). MC, V. Wed–Mon 11am–2:30pm and 6–9pm.

THE NORTHWEST COAST

Patisserie La Polynésienne, next door to Le Mayflower (*C* 56.20.45), is a good place to start your day with croissants-and-coffee or a full American-style breakfast. It's open daily.

La Plantation *FRENCH/CAJUN* It's not exactly New Orleans quality, but Nathalie Richard and Bertrand Jardon do a fine imitation of Louisiana fare at this large restaurant with tables inside or on a plantationlike veranda. Spicy gazpacho, jambalaya, and whole Cajun-style crab offer relief from the French sauces which rule elsewhere. Two fixed-price menus offer three courses each of either French or Cajun fare. Nathalie and Bertrand turn down the lights at night, creating romantic ambience.

Haapiti (opposite old Club Med). *C* 54.45.10. Reservations recommended. Main courses 2,400 CFP–4,500 CFP (US$30–US$56/£15–£28); fixed-price dinners 4,500 CFP–5,100 CFP (US$56–US$64/£28–£32). MC, V. Wed 6:30–9:30pm; Thurs–Mon 11:30am–9:30pm.

Le Mayflower *Value CASUAL FRENCH* This casual roadside restaurant draws mostly local residents, who rightly proclaim it to be Moorea's best for both food and value. The sauces are lighter than you will experience elsewhere, and there is always a vegetarian selection. I like to start with a salad of warm local shrimp over cool fresh greens. The house special—lobster ravioli in a cream sauce—is a worthy main choice, as are seafood pasta under pesto or the reliable shrimp in coconut curry. Mahimahi in a lobster sauce highlights a special tourist menu here.

Haapiti, west of old Club Med. *C* 56.53.59. Reservations recommended. Main courses 2,100 CFP–2,900 CFP (US$26–US$36/£13–£18). AE, MC, V. Tues–Fri and Sun 11:30am–2:30pm and 6:30–10:30pm; Sat 6:30–10:30pm.

Le Motu Pizza Grill SNACK BAR You can get grilled steak or fish with french fries at this open-air restaurant, but it's best for pizzas, crepes, and hamburgers. Light fare includes salads, crepes, and ice cream, and a selection of soft drinks, beer, and wine.

Haapiti, opposite old Club Med. *C* 56.16.70. Burgers, sandwiches, and salads 500 CFP–1,400 CFP (US$6.25–US$18/£3.15–£8.85); pizza 1,050 CFP–1,300 CFP (US$13–US$16/£6.65–£8.25). MC, V (2,000 CFP minimum [US$26/£13]). Mon–Sat 9:30am–9pm; Sun 9:30am–3pm.

Moments **A Sunday Tahitian Feast**

Locals love to partake of huge *ma'a Tahiti* feasts on Sunday afternoon, and I join them at Ron Sage's **Painapo (Pineapple) Beach** (*C* 74.96.96; www.painapo.com), on the southwestern coast. It's a lovely setting with tables under a natural thatched-roof restaurant (with a sand floor) as well as outside under the shade of a beachside tree. Ron's all-you-can-eat Sunday buffet of Tahitian foods costs 3,500 CFP (US$44/£22), a steal in these expensive islands. He also serves an a la carte menu of fresh grilled fish for 1,900 CFP–2,500 CFP (US$24–US$31/£12–£16) Monday to Thursday, when Pineapple Beach is open from 9am to 3pm. It's cash only. See "Tips on Dining," in chapter 7, for more information about Tahitian chow.

Les Tipaniers Restaurant de la Plage (Restaurant by the Beach) *♥* SNACK BAR/ITALIAN   Under a soaring thatched roof and opening to the lagoon, this is the best place in Haapiti for a lagoonside lunch or sunset cocktail. It offers a good selection of salads, some with fruit, and a big juicy burger. Or you can select one of the pastas that make Les Tipaniers' nighttime restaurant popular. Breakfast is served here.

Haapiti, at Hotel Les Tipaniers, east of old Club Med. 𝄢 **56.19.19.** Salads, sandwiches, burgers 550 CFP–1,300 CFP (US$6.90–US$16/£3.50–£8.25); pastas 1,000 CFP–1,700 CFP (US$13–US$21/£6.35–£11). AE, DC, MC, V. Daily 6:30–9:30am and noon–2:15pm. Bar 6:30am–7pm.

Restaurant Les Tipaniers *♥* *Value* ITALIAN/FRENCH   This romantic, thatched-roof restaurant is popular with visitors and Moorea's permanent residents, who come here for delicious pizzas with a variety of toppings and homemade spaghetti, lasagna, tagliatelle, and gnocchi served with Bolognese, carbonara, or seafood sauce. French dishes include pepper steak and filets of mahimahi in butter or vanilla sauce. Discounted transportation is available for Haapiti-area hotel guests.

Haapiti, at Hotel Les Tipaniers, east of old Club Med. 𝄢 **56.12.67.** Reservations recommended. Pasta and pizza 1,000 CFP–1,550 CFP (US$13–US$19/£6.35–£9.80); main courses 1,850 CFP–2,550 CFP (US$23–US$32/£12–£16). AE, DC, MC, V. Daily 6:30–9:15pm.

8 Island Nights

The one required nighttime activity here is an authentic feast and dance show at **Tiki Theatre Village** (𝄢 **55.02.50**) in Haapiti. For details, see p. 258.

Moorea's major resorts also have Tahitian feasts and dance shows at least once a week. The most elaborate is the Saturday-evening lagoonside show at the InterContinental Resort and Spa Moorea. Most charge 8,000 CFP to 9,500 CFP (US$100–US$119/£51–£60) per person for the dinner and dance show.

One notable exception is a free show at the **Club Bali Hai** (𝄢 **56.13.68**) every Wednesday at 6pm. It's followed by an a la carte seafood barbecue at Snack l'Ananas Bleu (The Blue Pineapple). Meals range from 1,800 CFP to 3,900 CFP (US$23–US$49/£11–£25). Reservations are required for the barbecue.

At PK 6, in the Cook's Bay area, the lively **Maria@Tapas** (𝄢 **55.01.70**) draws a young, well-educated clientele, especially for live entertainment on Friday and Saturday evenings. Friendly owner Julie Berten stocks a wide selection of European beers. Scottish-born guitarist Ron Falconer usually plays at **Alfredo's** (𝄢 **56.17.71**) on Thursday and Sunday. See "Where to Dine," earlier in this chapter. In the Haapiti hotel district, **PK0** (𝄢 **56.55.46**) has live music on Friday and Saturday. It's Haapiti's version of Maria@Tapas.

Moments **Sunsets with Muk at Club Bali Hai**

If I'm on Moorea, you'll find me beside Cook's Bay at the **Club Bali Hai** (𝄢 **56.13.68**), swapping yarns with Muk McCallum, one of the original Bali Hai Boys, Thursday to Tuesday between 5:30 and 7pm. Bring your own drinks (Muk usually hauls out a bucket of ice). This is one of the great vistas in the South Pacific; you'll want to become a modern Paul Gauguin in order to capture the changing colors of the bay, sky, and the jagged mountains.

10

Bora Bora

Because of its fame and extraordinary beauty, little Bora Bora is a playground for the well-to-do, occasionally the famous, and honeymooners blowing a wad. French Polynesia's tourist magnet, it has seen an explosion of hotel construction in recent years, with piers reaching out like tentacles to multitudinous overwater bungalows standing over its gorgeous lagoon. Some of the piers are so long that the Moorings has added them to its sailing charts as hazards to navigation!

Those of us who remember the island in its more natural state often bemoan that development has ruined it. But when I meet people who are here for the first time, they invariably are as blown away by Bora Bora as I was when I camped on a then-deserted Point Matira a few eons ago. If you look beyond the tourists, you will appreciate why James A. Michener wrote that this is the world's most beautiful island.

Of course, there are more tourists here than on any other French Polynesian island, and some lovers now like to finish their honeymoons on more peaceful Tahaa or Huahine.

Lying 230km (143 miles) northwest of Tahiti, Bora Bora is a middle-aged island consisting of a high center completely surrounded by a lagoon enclosed by coral reef. It has a gorgeous combination of sand-fringed *motus* (small islets) sitting on the outer reef enclosing the multihued lagoon. In turn, the lagoon cuts deep bays into the high central island. Towering over it all is Bora Bora's trademark, the basaltic tombstone known as **Mount Otemanu** (725m/2,379 ft.). Standing next to it is the more normally rounded **Mount Pahia** (660m/2,165 ft.).

One of the best beaches in French Polynesia stretches for more than 3km (2 miles) around the flat, coconut-studded peninsula known as **Point Matira,** which juts out from the island's southern end. Matira is now the island's tourist center.

Bora Bora is so small that the road around it covers only 32km (20 miles) from start to finish. All the 7,000 or so Bora Borans live on a coastal strip that gives way to the mountainous interior.

Impressions

I saw it first from an airplane. On the horizon there was a speck that became a tall, blunt mountain with cliffs dropping sheer into the sea. And about the base of the mountain, narrow fingers of land shot out, forming magnificent bays, while about the whole was thrown a coral ring of absolute perfection. . . . That was Bora Bora from aloft. When you stepped upon it the dream expanded.
—James A. Michener, *Return to Paradise,* 1951

1 Arriving & Getting Around

ARRIVING & GETTING TO YOUR HOTEL

Bora Bora's airport is on **Motu Mute,** a flat island on the northwestern edge of the barrier reef. U.S. marines built the airstrip during World War II when Bora Bora was a major refueling stop on the America-to-Australia supply line.

Some resorts send boats to pick up their guests (be sure to tell them your flight number when making your reservations). Everyone else takes Air Tahiti's launch to **Vaitape,** the only village and the center of most commerce. The major resorts have welcome desks in the terminal to greet you and steer you to the correct boat. It can be a tad confusing out on the dock, where baggage is unloaded. You do not want to end up on the wrong motu, so pay attention, and ask someone if you are not sure which boat is yours. Buses meet Air Tahiti's launch at Vaitape to take you to your hotel. Get in the bus displaying the name of your hotel, or ask the drivers if you are not sure. Bus fares from Vaitape to the Matira Point hotel district are 500 CFP (US$6.25/£3.15).

GETTING AROUND

There is no regularly scheduled public transportation system on Bora Bora. Some hotels on the main island shuttle their guests to Vaitape and back once or twice a day, but the frequency can vary depending on how many guests they have. Most resorts out on the islets run shuttle boats to the main island.

BY RENTAL CAR, SCOOTER & BICYCLE Europcar (© **800/227-7368** or 67.70.15; www.europcar.com) and a local firm, **Fare-Piti Rent a Car** (© **67.65.28**), have offices at Vaitape wharf. Europcar's rates start at 10,100 CFP (US$126/£64) a day for cars, including unlimited kilometers. Both rent open-air Bugsters for about 9,300 CFP (US$116/£59) a day, and bicycles for about 1,800 CFP (US$23/£11) all day.

The 32km (20 miles) of road around Bora Bora are paved. Most of it is flat, but drive or ride carefully and look out for pedestrians, pigs, chickens, and especially dogs.

BY TAXI   No taxis patrol Bora Bora looking for passengers, but several firms have transport licenses, which means they can get you if someone calls. The hotel desks and restaurants will do that, or you can phone **Taxi Simplet** (© **79.19.31**), **Léon** (© **70.69.16**), **Otemanu Tours** (© **67.70.49**), or **Jacques Isnard** (© **67.72.25**). Fares between Vaitape and the Matira Point hotel district are at least 1,500 CFP (US$19/£9.50) from 6am to 6pm and 2,000 CFP (US$25/£13) from 6pm to 6am. A ride between Vaitape and Anau village costs 5,000 CFP (US$63/£32). Taxis aren't metered, so agree on a fare with the diver before setting out.

If you're staying at a resort on an islet and don't want to wait for the next boat shuttle, you can call **François Ferrand Taxi Boat** (© **79.11.62**), **Dino's Land & Water Taxi** (© **79.29.65**), or **Taxi Motu** (© **67.60.61**). The ride to the main island costs about 2,500 CFP (US$31/£16).

FAST FACTS: Bora Bora

The following facts apply specifically to Bora Bora. For more information, see "Fast Facts: French Polynesia," in chapter 7.

Babysitters The hotels can arrange for English-speaking babysitters, or you can contact **Robin Teraitepo** at Chez Ben's (© **67.74.54**).

Bora Bora

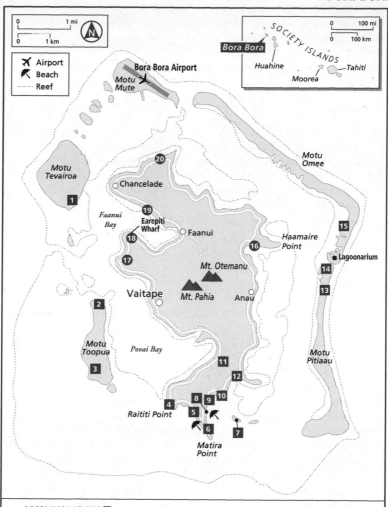

Bora Bora Airport

Motu Mute

✈ Airport
🏹 Beach
···· Reef

0 — 1 mi
0 — 1 km

N

SOCIETY ISLANDS

Bora Bora

Huahine

Moorea

Tahiti

0 — 100 mi
0 — 100 km

Motu Tevairoa

Chancelade

1

Faanui Bay

19
Earepiti Wharf

18

17

20

Faanui

Haamaire Point

16

Mt. Otemanu

Motu Omee

15

Lagoonarium

14

13

Vaitape

Mt. Pahia

Anau

Motu Toopua

2

3

Povai Bay

Motu Pitiaau

11

12

4

5

8 **9** **10**

6

7

Raititi Point

Matira Point

ACCOMMODATIONS ■

Bora Bora Lagoon
  Resort & Spa **2**
Bora Bora Nui Resort & Spa **3**
Bora Bora Pearl Beach Resort **1**
Club Med Bora Bora **12**
Hotel Bora Bora **4**
Hotel Maitai Polynesia **8**
Hotel Matira **5**
InterContinental Le
  Moana Resort **6**

InterContinental Resort
  and Thalasso Spa
  Bora Bora **13**
Le Meridien Bora Bora **14**
Novotel Bora Bora Beach Resort **9**
Rohutu Fare Lodge **11**
Sofitel Bora Bora Marara
  Beach Resort **10**
Sofitel Motu Private Island **7**
St. Regis Resort Bora Bora **15**

ATTRACTIONS ●

Aehautai Marae **16**
Marotetini Marae **18**
Old Hyatt Site **20**
U.S. guns **19**
U.S. wharf **17**

Bookstores & Newsstands **La Maison de la Press,** across the main road from the Vaitape wharf ((C) **60.57.75**), carries *The International Herald Tribune* and *USA Today,* though not the current day's edition. It also sells film, camera batteries, and prepaid SIM cards for your cellphone.

Camera & Film **Jeanluc Photo Shop,** at the Vaitape wharf ((C) **72.01.23**), offers professional photo services and overnight processing of color print film.

Currency Exchange **Banque de Tahiti, Banque Socredo,** and **Banque de Polynésie** have branches with ATMs in Vaitape.

Drugstores **Pharmacie de Bora Bora** ((C) **67.70.30**), north of the town wharf in Vaitape, is open Monday through Friday from 8am to noon and 2:30 to 6pm, Saturday from 8am to noon and 5 to 6pm, and Sunday and holidays from 9 to 11 am.

Emergencies & Police The emergency police telephone number is (C) **17.** The **gendarmerie** ((C) **67.70.58**) is opposite the Vaitape wharf.

Healthcare The island's **infirmary** is in Vaitape ((C) **67.70.77**), as is **Dr. Azad Roussanaly** ((C) **67.77.95**).

Internet Access **Aloe Cafe,** in the Centre Commercial Le Pahia just north of the Vaitape wharf ((C) **67.78.88**), has a computer terminal with Skype, which costs about 40 CFP (40¢/25p) per minute of online time. See "Where to Dine," later, for more about this pastry shop.

Mail The **Vaitape post office** is open Monday from 8am to 3pm, Tuesday through Friday 7:30am to 3pm, and Saturday 8 to 10am.

Restrooms The wharf at Vaitape has public restrooms in the small octagonal building on the wharf itself and in a small white building to the north of the visitor and handicrafts centers. It can be a long wait for a shuttle boat back to your resort, so take preventive action as necessary.

Taxes Bora Bora's municipal government adds 100 CFP to 150 CFP (US$1.25–US$1.90/65p–95p) per night to your hotel bill.

Visitor Information The **Bora Bora Comité du Tourisme,** B.P. 144, Vaitape, Bora Bora ((C) **67.76.36;** info-bora-bora@mail.pf), has a visitor center in the large building on the north side of the Vaitape wharf. It's open Monday to Friday and cruise-ship days from 9am to 4pm.

Water Bora Bora has a huge desalinization plant, so the tap water is safe to drink. Most residents still drink bottled water, available at grocery stores.

2 Exploring Bora Bora: The Circle Island Tour

THE CIRCLE ISLAND TOUR 🎫🎫

Because the round-island road is only 32km (20 miles) long, many visitors see it by bicycle (give yourself a day), scooter, or car. Some of those sights mentioned below may not be easy to find, however, so consider taking a guided sightseeing tour around the island. **Otemanu Tours** ((C) **67.70.49**) still uses one of the traditional, open-air *le truck* vehicles, which adds an extra dimension to its trips. You can book them at any hotel activities desk. The cost is about 4,000 CFP (US$50/£25) per person.

Driving or biking yourself, begin at the **wharf in Vaitape.** In the parking lot is a monument to French yachtsman Alain Gerbault, who sailed his boat around the world between 1923 and 1929 and wrote a book about it (thus adding to Bora Bora's fame).

From the wharf, head counterclockwise around the island. The road curves along the shore of **Povai Bay,** where mounts Otemanu and Pahia tower over you. Take your time along this bay; the views are the best on Bora Bora. When you reach Bloody Mary's Restaurant and Bar, go out on the pier for a killer view back across the water at Mount Otemanu.

MATIRA BEACH   The road climbs the small headland, where a huge banyan tree marks the entrance to the Hotel Bora Bora on **Raititi Point,** and then runs smoothly along curving **Matira Beach** ⚒⚒⚒, one of the South Pacific's finest. When the road curves sharply to the left, look for a narrow paved road to the right. This leads to **Matira Point,** the low, sandy, coconut-studded peninsula that extends out from Bora Bora's south end. Down this track, about 50 yards, is a **public beach** on the west side of the peninsula, opposite the InterContinental Le Moana Resort. The lagoon is shallow all the way out to the reef at this point, but the bottom is smooth and sandy.

THE EAST COAST   After rounding the point, you'll pass through the island's hotel and restaurant district before climbing a hill above the Club Med. A trail cuts off to the right on the north side of the hill and goes to the **Aehautai Marae,** one of several old temples on Bora Bora. This particular one has a great view of Mount Otemanu and the blue outlines of Raiatea and Tahaa islands beyond the motus on the reef.

You will go through a long stretch of coconut plantations before entering **Anau,** a typical Polynesian village with a large church, a general store, and tin-roofed houses crouched along the road.

The road goes over two hills at Point Haamaire, the main island's easternmost extremity, about 4km (2½ miles) north of Anau village. Between the two hills on the lagoon side of the road stands **Aehautai Marae,** a restored temple. Out on the point is **Taharuu Marae,** which has a great view of the lagoon. The Americans installed naval guns in the hills above the point during World War II.

THE NORTH & WEST COASTS   On the deserted northeast coast you will ride through several miles of coconut plantations pockmarked by thousands of holes made by *tupas* (land crabs). After turning at the northernmost point, you pass a group of overwater bungalows and another group of houses, which climb the hill. Some of these are expensive condominiums; the others are part of a defunct project that was to have been a Hyatt resort. Across the lagoon are Motu Mute and the airport.

Faanui Bay was used during World War II as an Allied naval base. It's not marked, but the U.S. Navy's Seabees built the concrete wharf on the north shore as a seaplane ramp. Just beyond the main shipping wharf at the point on the south side of Faanui Bay is the restored **Marotetini Marae,** which in pre-European days was dedicated to navigators. Nearby are tombs in which members of Bora Bora's former royal family are buried. If you look offshore at this point, you'll see the only pass into the lagoon. The remains of two **U.S. guns** that guarded it stand on the hill above but are best visited on a safari tour (see "Safari Expeditions," below).

Entering Vaitape, **Magasin Chin Lee** is a gathering place for local residents. It's a good place to soak up some island culture along with a cold bottle of Eau Royale.

A Side Trip to Maupiti

French Polynesia's last outpost is **Maupiti,** a little jewel of an island 40km (25 miles) west of Bora Bora. Like its neighbor, the much smaller Maupiti consists of an outer reef and a horseshoe of sand-edged motus enclosing a clear lagoon around a high central island. Unlike Bora Bora, Maupiti has not a hint of modern tourism; in fact, its residents voted down a proposed resort. Consequently, it reminds me of Bora Bora when I first went there almost 30 years ago. Maupiti definitely is a throwback to old Polynesia when, among other things, very few locals spoke English.

The distinguishing landmark is **Hotu Parata,** a black basaltic cliff rising 165m (540 ft.) above the wharf and Maupiti's only village. It's pockmarked with caves, which attract a multitude of nesting seabirds. On the western side is **Plage Tereia,** a gorgeous white-sand beach wrapping around a peninsula. Archaeologists have uncovered marae and petroglyphs dating to 850 A.D.

You can make a day trip to Maupiti on the fast ferry *Maupiti Express* (℃ **67.66.69;** maupitiexpress@mail.pf), which departs Bora Bora Tuesday, Thursday, and Saturday at 8:30am, arriving at Maupiti about 10:15am. It leaves Maupiti at 4pm and returns to Bora Bora about 5:30pm. Fares are 3,000 CFP (US$37/£19) one-way, 4,000 CFP (US$49.50/£25) round-trip. *One caveat:* The sole navigable pass into the Maupiti lagoon is narrow and bordered by a shifting sandbar upon which the surf breaks. If high waves come up, the *Maupiti Express* may be unable to return to Bora Bora. (Air Tahiti flies to and from Maupiti thrice weekly, from Raiatea.)

The road around Maupiti's central island is only 9.6km long (5¾ miles), so you can easily see it in half a day via bicycle (you will negotiate only one hill). Local residents will be waiting at the wharf when the *Maupiti Express* docks to rent bikes for 1,000 CFP (US$12.50/£6) per day. Because the marae and petroglyphs are not marked and thus not easily found, consider taking a tour arranged by the *Maupiti Express* or **Maupiti Loisirs** (℃ **67.80.95**) for 2,000 CFP (US$25/£12.50).

Maupiti has several family-run pensions beside incredible white-sand beaches out on the atoll-like reef islands. Most charming is **Le Kuriri** (℃ **67.82.23;** www.maupiti-lekuriri.com), on Motu Tiapaa near the pass. It's operated by Anne-Marie Badolle and Camille Majorel, who gave up the Parisian corporate life to sail around the world and then settle on Maupiti. They speak both French and English. Le Kuriri's showers dispense cold water. The most "luxurious" is **Pension Poe Iti** (℃ **67.83.14** or 74.58.76; maupiti express@mail.pf), operated by Gerard and Josephine Sachet, owners of the *Maupiti Express.* Their four bungalows have air-conditioners, hot-water showers, and TVs with DVD players powered by windmills, an incongruous site on flat Motu Tuanai off Maupiti's eastern side. Gerard speaks French and English; Josephine, only French.

Other than the pensions, the only place to dine is the inexpensive **Snack Tarona** (℃ **67.82.46**), lagoonside in the village. It serves food Monday to Saturday from 10am to 1pm and 6 to 10pm.

Le Kuriri accepts MasterCard and Visa, but the other pensions and Snack Tarona do not. Bring cash.

3 Safari Expeditions & Lagoon Excursions

SAFARI EXPEDITIONS 𝒢

The regular tours stick to the shoreline, but safari expeditions venture into the hills in open-air, four-wheel-drive vehicles for panoramic views and visits to the old U.S. Navy gun sites. Compared to safari expeditions on Moorea, Huahine, and Tahaa, which emphasize local culture as well as scenery, here they are more like scenic thrill rides. The journeys can be rough, so I do not recommend them for children, the elderly, or anyone prone to carsickness. The mountain roads are mere ruts in places, so you could become stuck if it has been raining.

Your best bet for insight into the island's history and lore is Patrick Tairua of **Patrick's Activities** (© 77.19.11 or 67.69.94; www.maohinui.nct). Son of the last Polynesian chief of Bora Bora, Patrick (pronounced Pa-*treek* in French) lived in the U.S. and speaks English fluently. He passes along stories gleaned from spending time with one of the elders responsible for protecting the island's oral history. Patrick's tours are essentially private; that is, he takes a maximum of four persons at a time for US$400 (£200) per tour. Patrick also leads private lagoon excursions (see below).

A more comfortable choice is **Vavau Adventures** (© 72.01.21; temana689@mail.pf), which has expeditions in an air-conditioned Land Rover. These tours also emphasize Bora Bora's history, culture, flora, and fauna, and they stop at a fish farm, where you will see tropical species being raised to restock the magnificent lagoon. They cost 7,400 CFP (US$93/£47) per person.

The largest operator is the Levard family's **Tupuna Four-Wheel-Drive Expeditions** (© 67.75.06). On this tour, your last stop will be at the Farm, the Levards' black-pearl operation (see "Shopping," below).

LAGOON EXCURSIONS & SHARK FEEDING 𝒢𝒢𝒢

Bora Bora has one of the world's most beautiful lagoons, and getting out on it, snorkeling and swimming in it, and visiting the islands on its outer edge are absolute musts. Although it's a widespread activity now, this is where **shark-feeding** began. That is, your guide feeds reef sharks while you watch from a reasonably safe distance.

Any hotel activity desk will book you an all-day excursion with one of several operators. My long-time favorite is Nono Levard's **Teremoana Tours** (© 67.71.38), which everyone here calls Nono's Tours. You spend the day going around the lagoon in a speedy outrigger canoe. Depending on the weather, you will go snorkeling and watch a shark-feeding demonstration in the morning. You'll stop on a motu for swimming and a picnic lunch, and then pet sting rays on your way home in the afternoon. Expect to pay about 8,500 CFP (US$106/£54) for a full-day outing.

In addition to his safari expeditions (see above), Patrick Tairua of **Patrick's Activities** (© 77.19.11 or 67.69.94; www.maohinui.net) will customize a lagoon outing for US$400 (£200) per tour for up to four persons.

If your all-day excursion doesn't feature it, you can still visit the **Bora Bora Lagoonarium** (© 67.71.34), a fenced-in underwater area near Le Meridien Bora Bora. Here you can swim with (and maybe even ride) manta rays and observe sharks (on the other side of the fence). The Lagoonarium has its own morning tour with shark-feeding and lunch on the motu, and an afternoon excursion with fish-watching. The morning excursion costs about 7,800 CFP (US$98/£49), the afternoon tour is 6,600 CFP (US$83/£42), or you can do both for 10,000 CFP (US$125/£63).

You can rent a boat and explore the lagoon yourself, but I strongly suggest you know what you are doing and understand how the color of the water tells its depth. Your hotel's activities desk will organize it.

4 Diving, Fishing & Watersports

SCUBA DIVING & SNORKELING

Certified and noncertified divers alike can swim among the coral heads, sharks, large manta rays, eels, and some 1,000 species of colorful tropical fishes out in the lagoon here. Every resort has a scuba-diving program. Both 30-minute introductory courses and one-tank lagoon dives cost about 6,500 CFP (US$81/£41), and open-water and night dives are priced at 9,000 CFP (US$113/£57).

The island's major dive operator is **TOPdive Bora Bora** (© **60.50.50;** fax 60.50.51; www.topdive.com), which has some of the best equipment and dive boats in French Polynesia. Its base is on the northern outskirts of Vaitape. **Nemo World** (© **67.71.84;** www.boradiving.com) has two bases: Nemo World Bora Bora, near the Sofitel Bora Bora Resort, and Nemo Bora Diving Center, near the Hotel Bora Bora. Two-tank dives cost about 14,500 CFP (US$181/£92).

Among the easily accessible snorkeling spots, the best is off the southern tip of Point Matira. You can walk to the outer reef from here, thus increasing your chances of seeing more fish than elsewhere. Next-best are the reefs off the Hotel Bora Bora and the Sofitel Motu, but you need to stay there to fully enjoy them.

Nondivers can walk on the bottom while wearing a diving helmet with **Aqua Safari** (© **67.71.84**).

OTHER WATERSPORTS

Every hotel has some water toys for its guests to use, and hotel activities desks can arrange fishing, diving, and other watersports. You don't have to stay at the **Novotel Bora Bora Beach Club** (© **60.59.50**) to use its equipment and facilities, but you do have to pay a fee. You can go water-skiing, sail on Hobie Cats, paddle canoes, and get a bird's-eye view of the lagoon while parasailing.

Matira Jet Tours (© **77.63.63**) has lagoon excursions by jet ski as well as inland tours by all-terrain vehicles. Many of those people riding above the lagoon went with **Bora Bora Parasail** (© **78.27.10**).

Most resorts have kayaks for their guests to paddle in the lagoon. Based at Rohotu Fare Lodge (see "Where to Stay," below), **Bora Bora Kayaks** (© **70.77.99;** www.rohotufarelodge.com) rents one- and two-person sea kayaks ranging from 1,500 CFP (US$19/£9.50) for 1 hour to 6,500 CFP (US$81/£41) for an entire day. These quality boats were made in the United States and come equipped with snorkeling and fishing gear.

Moments Like Flying Underwater

Shining with every hue on the blue end of the color spectrum, Bora Bora's watery playground is one of my favorite snorkeling spots. Hotel Bora Bora has bungalows sitting right on the edge of a reef that drops precipitously to dark depths. I experience the exhilaration of flying when I glide out over that underwater cliff.

5 Shopping

Most shopping here is in Vaitape, where you'll find several souvenir shops and upscale black pearl dealers. Other boutiques and shops are scattered along the main road, especially in the Matira hotel district.

Bora Bora I Te Fanau Tahi   Local artisans display their wares in the large hall at the wharf. It's the least expensive place to shop for straw hats, pareus, and other handicraft items. It's open Monday to Friday 8:30am to 4pm and Saturday and Sunday when cruise ships are in port. Vaitape, at the small boat landing. No phone.

The Farm   You need to know about the Farm because it's owned by the Levard family, and you are likely to be deposited here after going on one of their safari excursions. They will show you how pearls are grown, harvested, graded, and turned into jewelry. The final products are for sale in the **Bora Pearl Company,** the showroom here. It's worth a visit here to see how it's all done. The Farm is open daily from 9am to 6pm. Raititi Point, near Hotel Bora Bora. ℭ 70.06.65.

La Galerie Bora Bora   In Vaitape, this air-conditioned gallery carries excellent-quality wood and stone carvings from the Marquesas, *tivaivai* pillowcases, pottery, tapa cloth, and paintings by local artists. Black pearls, too, of course. It's open daily from 9am to 6pm.Vaitape, opposite the post office. ℭ 60.53.25.

Matira Pearls 𝘳𝘳𝘳 (Value   You will have ample opportunities to shop for black pearls here (Vaitape village alone has a dozen outlets), but this is my favorite. It's owned by Steve Fearon, whose family once had a piece of the Hotel Bora Bora, and whose brother, Tom Fearon, has a bungalow resort on Rarotonga in the Cook Islands (see "Where to Stay," in chapter 12). Steve's chief assistants are his son, Heirama, who graduated from Pepperdine University in California, and daughter-in-law Tehani, herself educated in Los Angeles (Heirama and Tehani met there, not here). Unlike some other stores, their customized settings emphasize the pearl, not the gold. Set and loose pearls start at 10,000 CFP (US$125/£63). The shop is open Monday to Saturday 9am to 5:30pm and Sunday 10am to 5pm. East side of Matira Point. ℭ 67.79.14.

Mom's Boutique   Erina Gould, wife of Bloody Mary's Restaurant and Bar maitre d' Gregg Gould (see "Where to Dine," later), sells only traditional aloha shirts, dresses, pareus, straw hats and handicrafts at her little shop. In other words, the designs are like those prevalent when I first came here in the 1970s. It's open Monday to Saturday 9am to 5pm. Vaitape, behind Fashion Bora Bora. ℭ 67.69.29.

6 Where to Stay

Bora Bora has some of the South Pacific's finest and most expensive resorts, and yet another—the super-luxe **Four Seasons Bora Bora** (www.fourseasons.com)—was scheduled to open in 2008, and, in fact, was accepting reservations for September 2008, on Motu Tehotu, on the eastern side of the lagoon.

A mainstay on the island since 1961, the luxurious Hotel Bora Bora (ℭ 800/421-1490 or 60.44.11; www.amanresorts.com) was slated to close in October 2008 for a complete rebuilding. It is expected to reopen in time for its 50th anniversary in 2011.

EXPENSIVE

Bora Bora Lagoon Resort & Spa 𝘳𝘳   Speedboats shuttle 23 times a day from the Vaitape wharf to this posh resort on the northern end of Motu Toopua, a hilly island facing the rounded peak of Mount Pahia (not Mount Otemanu's tombstone). The main building, under three interlocking thatched roofs, holds a reception area, a bar, and a gourmet restaurant. To the rear, an expansive stone deck surrounds one of French Polynesia's largest swimming pools, where you'll find another bar and daytime restaurant. Long piers with hand-carved railings lead to the 44 overwater bungalows, while the rest of the units sit ashore in tropical gardens. One is a two-bedroom villa well suited to well-heeled families. Three beachside bungalows interconnect to form suites, while three "Motu Suites" have their own swimming pools. Although very good, the accommodations do not quite live up to the resort's exceptional amenities, including an unusual spa with treatment rooms high up in a banyan tree.

B.P. 175, 98730 Vaitape, Bora Bora (on Motu Toopua, 1km/½ mile off Vaitape). © **800/860-4905** or 60.40.00. Fax 60.40.01. www.boraboralagoon.com. 77 units. 50,000 CFP–130,000 CFP (US$625–US$1,625/£315–£823) bungalow. AE, DC, MC, V. **Amenities:** 2 restaurants; 2 bars; large outdoor pool; 2 tennis courts; exercise room; spa; watersports equipment rentals; game room; concierge; activities desk; limited room service; laundry service. *In room:* A/C, TV, high-speed Internet access, minibar, coffeemaker, safe.

Bora Bora Nui Resort & Spa 𝔊𝔊𝔊   A member of Starwood Hotels' Luxury Collection, this sprawling resort occupies the southern end of hilly Motu Toopua, a 15-minute boat ride off Vaitape. It faces west toward the sea, thus depriving its public areas and all but a handful of its bungalows of the typical Bora Bora view. Only the full-service spa, perched atop the islet's central ridge, has an unimpeded view of Mt. Otemanu. A beachside, two-level infinity swimming pool serves as the focal point of activities. It's backed by two public buildings, one with a large boutique and a casual, sand-floor restaurant offering reasonably priced lunches and dinners. The other houses a fine-dining outlet, an air-conditioned library, and a fascinating photo collection of U.S. marines building the airstrip on Motu Mute during World War II. Spread out over 6.4 hectares (16 acres) and nearly a kilometer (half-mile) of lagoon (you'll soon learn to call for a golf-cart to take you to dinner), the 120 luxurious, suite-size units—84 of them overwater—are some of the largest in French Polynesia. The overwater bungalows feature separate bedrooms, huge bathrooms with tubs and walk-in showers, and big decks with privacy screens. Two three-bedroom overwater bungalows with swimming pools in their decks were being planned. Housed in a hillside hotel-style building, the "lagoon-view suites" are the least expensive units, and they interconnect to accommodate families. Top of the line are the huge royal suites.

B.P. 502, 98730 Vaitape, Bora Bora (on Motu Toopua, 1.5km/1 mile off Vaitape). © **800/782-9488** or 60.32.00. Fax 60.32.01. www.boraboranui.com. 120 units. 61,000 CFP (US$763/£386) double; 82,000 CFP–290,000 CFP (US$1,025–US$3,625/£519–£1,835) bungalow; 62,000 CFP–68,500 CFP (US$775–US$856/£392–£434) suite. AE, DC, MC, V. **Amenities:** 3 restaurants; 2 bars; large outdoor pool; tennis courts; exercise room; spa; Jacuzzi; sauna; watersports equipment rentals; bike rentals; children's programs; game room; concierge; activities desk; 24-hr. room service; massage; babysitting; laundry service. *In room:* A/C, TV, high-speed Internet access, minibar, coffeemaker, iron, safe.

Bora Bora Pearl Beach Resort 𝔊𝔊   The most traditionally Polynesian resort on Bora Bora, the Pearl Beach resides on Motu Tevairoa, the largest of the flat islets dotting the outer reef, and it has better views of Mount Otemanu across the lagoon than does the Bora Bora Lagoon Resort to its south (see above). Covered by interconnected conical thatched roofs, the open-air restaurant, main bar, and library stand on a raised earthen platform, which enhances their views over a large swimming pool to the lagoon and mountains. Guests can also enjoy splashing or snorkeling in the natural sand-bottom lagoon. Gilles Pétré, one of French Polynesia's top dive operators, is in charge of the shop here (and all other Pearl resorts). Long, curving piers extend out to 50 overwater bungalows, which ooze Polynesian charm. The 15 premium units are worth paying extra for, because they are more private and enjoy unimpeded views of Bora Bora. If privacy is more important than the sound of water under your bungalow, consider one of the garden bungalows, which have private courtyards with sun decks and splash pools. If you bring the kids, opt for a beachside bungalow with a separate bedroom. Although it lacks a sea view, the gorgeous spa is on an islet surrounded by lily ponds (among other treatments, you can get a tattoo). An annoying drawback here is that the resort's shuttle boats land at Chancelade on Bora Bora's northwestern corner, an expensive taxi ride if you don't catch an infrequent shuttle bus to Vaitape.

B.P. 169, 98730 Vaitape, Bora Bora (on Motu Tevairoa, 1km/½ mile off Farepiti). © 800/657-3275 or 60.52.00. Fax 60.52.22. www.pearlhotels.com. 80 units. 54,000 CFP–86,000 CFP (US$675–US$1,075/£342–£544) bungalow. AE, DC, MC, V. **Amenities:** 3 restaurants; 2 bars; outdoor pool; tennis court; exercise room; spa; watersports equipment rentals; game room; concierge; activities desk; limited room service; massage; babysitting; laundry service. *In room:* A/C, TV, dataport, minibar, coffeemaker, iron, safe.

InterContinental Le Moana Resort ⟨★★★⟩ On the eastern side of the Matira peninsula, this exclusive resort was formerly known as the InterContinental Bora Bora Beachcomber Resort. It's is one of the older resorts here, although much improved over the years including a recent renovation. Its bungalows, most of them overwater, are some of the most charmingly designed here. They were the first in which you could remove the tops of the glass coffee tables and actually feed the fish swimming in the turquoise lagoon below. Ashore, 11 beachside bungalows are less enchanting, but like the overwater units, they have Raiatea and Tahaa in their lagoon views. Two suites—one overwater, one ashore—have kitchenettes, making them suitable for families. Also beside the beach, a circular thatched-roof building houses the reception area, a lounge, and the restaurant and bar, both with outdoor seating. The airy, beachside dining room offers very fine French selections, with an emphasis on seafood.

B.P. 156, 98730 Vaitape, Bora Bora (east side of Matira Point). © 800/327-0200 or 60.49.00. Fax 60.49.99. www.interconti.com. 64 units. 83,000 CFP–119,000 CFP (US$1,038–US$1,488/£525–£753) bungalow; 115,000 CFP–271,000 CFP (US$1,438–US$3,388/£728–£1,715) suite. AE, DC, MC, V. **Amenities:** Restaurant; bar; outdoor saltwater pool; spa; watersports equipment rentals; bike rentals; concierge; activities desk; car-rental desk; 24-hr. room service; massage; babysitting; laundry service. *In room:* A/C, TV, dataport, kitchens (suites only), minibar, coffeemaker, iron, safe.

InterContinental Resort and Thalasso Spa Bora Bora ⟨★★★⟩ This luxury resort shares the blazing white sands of Motu Piti Aau—an atoll-like island stretching 10km (6¼ miles) along the southeastern side of the outer reef—with Le Meridien Bora Bora (see below). It has won environmental awards as the world's first resort to be air-conditioned using seawater pumped from 2,500 feet down in the ocean. The 13°C (55°F) seawater also is used by the Thalasso Spa—officially the **Deep Ocean Spa** by Algotherm, the French company which uses seawater in its beauty products and treatments. The spa is the real star, especially its three treatment rooms extending over the shallow, sand-bottom lagoon (yes, you can watch fish swimming below you while

---

Tips **Be Prepared for Mosquitoes & No-Nos**

Keep in mind that mosquitoes and "no-no" sand flies love to feast on guests on Bora Bora's motus, so you'll want a good supply of insect repellent if you opt for one of the offshore resorts.

getting your massage). You'll feel like you're floating on air as you go down the glass-floor aisle of the overwater wedding chapel. All of the 80 suite-size guest bungalows also are built over the lagoon. Extending from two pincer-shaped piers, they are identical except for three two-bedroom, two-bathroom "villa suites," which have kitchens and are good choices for well-heeled families. In addition to king-size beds, the regular bungalows also have convertible sofas in their living rooms, so families can stay in them. The thatched-roof bungalows and central building are furnished in chic, Balinese tropical style, so the resort lacks Polynesian flair. The restaurants, bars, and infinity-edge swimming pool have fine views of Mount Otemanu, whose tombstone is seen from its narrow end out here. That cannot be said of most bungalows, which face north-south along the lagoon. Guests here can use the facilities at the InterContinental Le Moana Resort (see above). The hotel's launch shuttles to Anau village.

B.P. 156, 98730 Vaitape, Bora Bora (on Motu Piti Aau, 1km/½ mile off Anau village). ℂ 800/327-0200 or 60.49.00. Fax 60.76.99. www.boraboraspa.interconti.com. 80 units. 89,000 CFP–123,000 CFP (US$1,114–US$1,538/£563–£778). AE, DC, MC, V. **Amenities:** 2 restaurants; 2 bars; outdoor pool; fitness center; spa; watersports equipment rentals; concierge; activities desk; business center; 24-hr. room service; massage; babysitting; laundry service. *In room:* A/C, TV, high-speed Internet access, kitchens (villa suites only), minibar, coffeemaker, iron, safe.

Le Meridien Bora Bora ☆☆☆

Located on the northern tip of Motu Piti Aau, this is the best family resort in French Polynesia. Its Melanesian architecture is reminiscent of its sister property on Tahiti (see "Where to Stay," in chapter 8). The architects also created a seawater-fed, lakelike lagoon, in which you can swim with endangered sea turtles, bred there as part of the resort's award-winning preservation program. Children love it. Of the 100 identical guest units, 85 are built overwater. Only a few of these have views of Mt. Otemanu's skinny side. Standing over waist-deep water, they are notable for their huge glass floors, which make it seem as if you're walking on air (maids cover the glass with carpets at evening turndown). All units here are smaller than those at Bora Bora's other resorts, however, and you could stumble over too much furniture for the space available. Ten otherwise identical "beach" bungalows actually sit beside the manmade lagoon, but most of them have fine views of Bora Bora. As the shallow manmade lagoon is safe for swimming, they are excellent for families with small children. The broad, brilliantly white main beach here has its own bar. The hotel's launch shuttles to Anau village.

B.P. 190, 98730 Vaitape, Bora Bora (on Motu Pitiaau, 1km/½ mile off Anau village). ℂ 800/225-5843 or 60.51.51. Fax 60.51.10. www.lemeridien.com. 100 units. 60,000 CFP–106,000 CFP (US$750–US$1,325/£380–£671). AE, DC, MC, V. **Amenities:** 3 restaurants; 2 bars; outdoor pool; spa; watersports equipment rentals; children's playground; game room; concierge; activities desk; 24-hr. room service; babysitting; laundry service. *In room:* A/C, TV, dataport, minibar, coffeemaker, iron, safe.

Sofitel Bora Bora Marara Beach Resort

Italian movie producer Dino De Laurentis built this resort, formerly known as the Sofitel Marara Bora Bora, in 1977 to house star Mia Farrow and the crew working on his box-office bomb *Hurricane*. It was closed for a year for an extensive rejuvenation and re-opened in 2006, with the addition of a full-service spa and 13 overwater bungalows. A beehive-shaped central building houses the restaurant and bar, both of which open to a walk-in swimming pool sunken into a deck built out over Matira Beach and the lagoon. The resort has the island's largest array of watersports activities, which it shares with the Novotel Bora Bora Beach Resort, its Accor Hotels sibling next door (the toys are available to both guests and nonguests). The overwater bungalows here have some of Bora Bora's largest decks, but be sure to ask for a unit away from the nearby round-island road or you will wonder if you're sleeping over the lagoon. Overwater units numbered 49, 50, 51, 62, and 64 are the most private and have the best views. Facing a curving beach of white sand, the land-based bungalows have views of Raiatea and Tahaa on the horizon. Guests here can dine at the Sofitel Motu (see below), but not partake of the activities there.

B.P. 6, 98730 Vaitape, Bora Bora (northeast of Matira Point). © 800/763-4835 or 41.04.04 in Papeete, or 60.55.00 on Bora Bora. Fax 41.05.05 or 67.74.03. www.accorhotels.pf. 64 units. 38,000 CFP–85,000 CFP (US$475–US$1,063/ £241–£538). AE, DC, MC, V. **Amenities:** 2 restaurants; bar; outdoor pool; tennis court; watersports equipment rentals; bike rentals; concierge; activities desk; car-rental desk; limited room service; babysitting; laundry service. In room: A/C, TV, dataport, minibar, coffeemaker, iron, safe.

Sofitel Motu Private Island 🏖🏖 More exclusive and private than its sister property, this intimate, adult-oriented resort sits on a rocky, one-hill motu and is a 3-minute shuttle boat ride from the Sofitel Bora Bora Marara Beach Resort. Unlike any other Bora Bora resort, this one has a gorgeous, picture-postcard view of Mount Otemanu's tombstone face (most but not all overwater bungalows enjoy the view, so ask for units 138, 129, or 130). Often-steep stone pathways lead up and downhill to the guest bungalows; for this reason, I don't recommend the Motu to travelers with disabilities or anyone who has trouble walking. Most of the luxurious if not overly spacious units are overwater. Those that are ashore extend on stilts from the side of the hill, rendering great lagoon views. The most expensive unit here is a large villa. Several small beaches offer hammocks and easy chairs, and one has a shower mounted on a tree. Guests here can take the free on-demand shuttle boat and use all of the facilities over there. Sofitel Bora Bora Marara Beach Resort guests, on the other hand, are allowed out here only for lunch and dinner. *Note:* The Sofitel Motu was slated for an overhaul in 2008 and 2009 during which a spa and swimming pool were to be added.

B.P. 516, 98730 Vaitape, Bora Bora (on Piti Uuuta, .5km/⅓ mile off Matira Beach). © 800/763-4835 or 41.04.04 in Papeete, or 60.56.00 on Bora Bora. Fax 41.05.05 or 60.56.66. www.accorhotels.pf. 31 units. 47,000 CFP–89,500 CFP (US$588–US$1,119/£297–£566). AE, DC, MC, V. **Amenities:** Restaurant; bar; watersports equipment rentals; activities desk; limited room service; massage; laundry service. In room: A/C, TV, dataport, minibar, coffeemaker, iron, safe.

St. Regis Resort Bora Bora 🏖🏖🏖 Nicole Kidman and Keith Urban were among the first to honeymoon at this super-luxurious resort, which opened in 2007 on Motu Omee, on the northeastern side of the lagoon. They took the 13,000-square-foot Royal Estate, a walled-off compound with its own pool. Apparently the chef even came over and prepared their meals, for reportedly no guest caught a glimpse of the celebrity duo. The Royal Estate sits on land beside its own beach. Were I a quazillionaire, however, I would have opted for one of the Royal Over Water Villas, which have their own swimming pools with terrific views of Bora Bora. I am not pulling your leg: They have swimming pools built into their overwater decks. That's really all I need to say about the St. Regis, which is over the top in all respects, even its **Hono Iti kids club,** where your little scions can surf the 'Net at high speed. The guest quarters come in eight categories, from land-based villas with pools to stripped-down overwater bungalows. Stripped down, that is, in that they do not have pools or even Jacuzzis. Shame on you if you have to settle for one of those luxurious hovels! Butlers are on call for all units. The overwater units extend from manmade islets reaching far out into the lagoon, so be prepared for some serious walking to reach the central complex. Or call for a golf cart.

B.P. 506, 98730 Vaitape, Bora Bora (on Motu Omee, 1km/½ mile off Anau village). ℂ 800/787-3447 or 60.78.88. Fax 60.78.56. www.stregis.com/borabora. 100 units. 98,000 CFP–1,500,000 CFP (US$1,225–US$18,750/£620–£9,493). AE, DC, MC, V. **Amenities:** 3 restaurants; 3 bars; 2 outdoor pools; fitness center; spa; watersports equipment rentals; children's program; concierge; activities desk; business center; 24-hr. room service; massage; babysitting; laundry service. *In room:* A/C, TV, high-speed Internet access, kitchens (villas only), minibar, coffeemaker, iron, safe.

MODERATE

Club Med Bora Bora *(Value)*   Lush tropical gardens provide the setting for this Club Med beside a good beach in a little half-moon-shaped bay north of Matira Point. The focus of attention is a large thatched-roof beachside pavilion, which houses a reception area, bar, buffet-oriented dining room, and nightclub. Guests pay extra for scuba diving and excursions, but all meals (with wine) and a wide range of activities are included in the rates. Considering the prices elsewhere on Bora Bora, this makes Club Med a good value. The accommodations are in a mix of stand-alone and duplex bungalows and two-story, motel-style buildings. The beachfront bungalows are the preferred choice here, especially for honeymooners and others seeking privacy. The rooms are comfortably if not extravagantly furnished.

B.P. 34, 98730 Vaitape, Bora Bora (northeast of Matira Point). ℂ 800/258-2633, 60.46.04, or 42.96.99 in Papeete. Fax 42.16.83. www.clubmed.com. 150 units. 16,000 CFP–30,000 CFP (US$200–US$375/£101–£190) per person. Rates include all meals, with wine, drinks, and most activities. AE, DC, MC, V. **Amenities:** Restaurant; bar; tennis courts; bike rentals; activities desk; car-rental desk; salon; massage; coin-op washers and dryers. *In room:* A/C, TV, fridge, coffeemaker, safe.

Hotel Maitai Polynesia *(Value)*   Like the nearby Novotel, this resort has hotel rooms, but here they climb a hill, giving upper-floor units spectacular lagoon views. Unlike the Novotel, it also has beachside and overwater bungalows, which are among the more reasonably priced in French Polynesia. The bungalows are smaller than those at the more expensive resorts, but they are packed with Polynesian decor, and those overwater have glass floor panels for fish-viewing. The round-island road runs through the property, separating the beach and bungalows from the thatched-roof main building and hotel rooms. Of its two restaurants, one sits beachside.

B.P. 505, 98730 Vaitape, Bora Bora (northeast of Matira Point). ℂ 60.30.00. Fax 67.66.03. www.hotelmaitai.com. 74 units. 24,200 CFP–35,500 CFP (US$303–US$444/£153–£225) double; 39,000 CFP–53,300 CFP (US$488–US$666/£247–£337) bungalow. AE, DC, MC, V. **Amenities:** 2 restaurants; 2 bars; watersports equipment rentals; bike rentals; activities desk; car-rental desk; babysitting; laundry service. *In room:* A/C (hotel rooms only), TV, dataport, minibar, coffeemaker, safe.

Hotel Matira   This is not so much a hotel as a collection of bungalows on and near the beach at the northern end of the Matira peninsula. Imported from Indonesia, the teak units have thatched roofs, porches on one corner, shower-only bathrooms, and pairs of double beds. You'll get a ceiling fan, fridge, and coffeemaker, but forget amenities like TVs, phones, and hair dryers. What you get here is essentially an unscreened cottage, so keep your insect repellent handy. The choice and most expensive models rest beside Matira Beach, while the others are back in the garden. Ask for a discount if you book directly.

B.P. 31, 98730 Vaitape, Bora Bora (on Matira Beach, south of Hotel Bora Bora). ℂ 67.70.51. Fax 67.77.02. www.hotel-matira.com. 14 units. 21,000 CFP–35,500 CFP (US$263–US$444/£133–£225). MC, V. **Amenities:** Bike rentals. *In room:* Fridge, coffeemaker, no phone.

Novotel Bora Bora Beach Resort *(Value)*   This modest but attractive property is one of the better values on the island. It sports a U-shaped tropical-style public building and an infinity swimming pool beside a palm-draped section of Matira Beach, where the Novotel shares a wide array of watersports with the Sofitel Bora Bora Marara Beach Resort next door. On the other side of the round-island road, the motel-style accommodations occupy two-story buildings dressed up in Tahitian thatch and bamboo that surround a lush courtyard with lily pond. The medium-size rooms are nicely trimmed with native woods and are comfortably furnished with a queen-size bed, a built-in settee which can double as a single bed, a desk, shower-only bathroom, and sliding doors opening to a patio or balcony. You can dine at the Sofitel Motu but not use the other facilities out there.

B.P. 943, 98730 Vaitape, Bora Bora (heart of Matira hotel district). © 800/221-4542 or 60.59.50. Fax 60.59.51. www.accorhotels.pf. 80 units. 16,200 CFP–21,600 CFP (US$203–US$270/£103–£137) double. AE, MC, V. **Amenities:** Restaurant; bar; outdoor pool; watersports equipment rentals; activities desk; car-rental desk; massage; laundry service. *In room:* A/C, TV, dataport, fridge, coffeemaker, safe.

INEXPENSIVE

On the peninsula leading to Matira Point, the pension-style **Chez Nono** (© **67.71.38;** nono.levard@mail.pf) has six simple rooms, four bungalows, and an apartment. Rates are about 6,500 CFP (US$81/£41) double, 15,000 CFP (US$188/£95) for a bungalow. Expect to share a bathroom here. Book early, because local French residents love its beachside location.

On a small part of Matira Beach in the hotel district, the no-frills **Village Temanuata** (© **67.75.61;** www.temanuata.com) has 11 thatched-roof bungalows ranging from one room to family units with kitchens and sleeping lofts. They all have private bathrooms but few other amenities. Rates are 15,000 CFP–17,000 CFP (US$188–US$213/£95–£108) double.

Rohotu Fare Lodge ☆ *Value*   Virtually hidden by 50 varieties of fruit-bearing trees, this little lodge on the mountainside overlooking Povai Bay is the creation of Nir Shalev, an Israeli expatriate whom I met shortly after he first arrived on Bora Bora wearing a backpack in 1989. With teak floors and thatched roofs, his cleverly designed bungalows are for lovers, not Puritans. In addition to suggestive paintings, statues, and other paraphernalia in the sleeping quarters, faucets in the outdoor bathrooms pour water from certain parts of nude statues. (After a night here, you may not be up to the 15-minute bike ride to Matira Beach!) Nir's two lagoon-view bungalows are more charming and have better vistas than his mountain-view unit. They all have ceiling fans, kitchens, decks with lounge furniture, and four-poster beds with mosquito nets. You will not have to leave here to enjoy a view of Mount Otemanu's tombstone face.

B.P. 400, 98730 Vaitape, Bora Bora (hillside in Povai Bay). © 70.77.99. www.rohotufarelodge.com. 3 units. 14,900 CFP–17,000 CFP (US$187–US$213/£94–£108) bungalow. MC, V. **Amenities:** Kayak rentals; free bicycles. *In room:* Coffeemaker, safe.

7 Where to Dine

Restaurants here primarily are in Matira, on the island's southern end; Povai Bay, on the southwest coast; and in Vaitape village. That's how I have organized them below.

MATIRA

At the sharp curve in the road, **Roulotte Matira** (no phone) is one of the better *roulottes* in French Polynesia, especially when owner Samuel Ruver cooks tandoori chicken and curries from recipes handed down by his East Indian father. Open daily 6am to 10pm.

Chez Ben's SNACK BAR/PIZZA   Honeymooners from the nearby Hotel Bora Bora frequently wander to this lean-to across the road from a shady portion of Matira Beach, where Bora Bora–born Ben Teraitepo and his Oklahoma-born wife, Robin, have been offering American-style cooked breakfasts, lunches, and afternoon pick-me-ups since 1988. Ben's fresh tuna-salad sandwiches, pizzas and pastas, unusually spicy *poisson cru,* tacos, and fajitas are homemade and substantial. They will shoo the dogs and cats away if they bother you.

Matira, between Hotel Bora Bora and Matira Point. ⓒ **67.74.54.** Most items 700 CFP–1,600 CFP (US$8.75–US$20/£4.45–£10). No credit cards. Daily 8am–5pm.

La Bounty 🅡 *(Value* FRENCH/ITALIAN   This casual restaurant under a thatched roof provides some of the island's best pizza and other reasonably priced Italian (and French) fare. A pie makes an ample meal for one person or can be shared as an appetizer. The spaghetti and tagliatelle are tasty, too, with either smoked salmon, carbonara, Alfredo, Neapolitan, blue cheese, or seafood sauce. Steaks and fish are served under French sauces such as mustard or creamy vanilla. Pizzas are served quickly here, but everything else is prepared to order and takes longer. Whatever you choose, it will be excellent quality for the price.

Matira, between Hotel Maitai Polynesia and Bora Bora Beach Resort. ⓒ **67.70.43.** Reservations recommended. Pizza and pasta 1,250 CFP–2,000 CFP (US$16–US$25/£7.90–£13); main courses 1,900 CFP–2,400 CFP (US$23.75–US$30/£12–£15). MC, V. Tues–Sun 11:30am–2pm and 6:30–9pm.

La Matira Beach Restaurant FRENCH   Literally hanging over the beach, this casual, bistro-style restaurant is an excellent place to have a lagoonside lunch, perhaps a salad under a slice of grilled tuna. Burgers, grilled fish, and pastas also appear at midday. Dinner switches to a somewhat overpriced French menu, with such local twists as roast pork with bananas. It's a beautiful spot on a moonlit night.

Matira, between Hotel Bora Bora and Hotel Matira. ⓒ **67.53.79.** Reservations recommended at dinner. Lunch 1,300 CFP–1,800 CFP (US$16–US$23/£8.25–£11.40); main courses 3,000 CFP–5,100 CFP (US$38–US$64/£19–£32). MC, V. Daily 7–10am, 11am–2pm, and 6–9pm.

Restaurant Fare Manuia 🅡 FRENCH   A thatched roof lends charm to this French restaurant known for large servings, such as huge slabs of prime rib served plain or with a choice of French sauces. The tender beef comes from New Zealand, as do the freshly ground hamburgers served at lunch. Other dinner main courses include mahimahi served on a wood plank with vanilla sauce, rare tuna with wasabi, and a hearty seafood soup. In addition to the American-style hamburgers, lunch sees fish burgers, salads, pastas, and grilled fish. Breakfast here is strictly continental.

Matira, between InterContinental le Moana Resort and Hotel Maitai Polynesia. ⓒ **67.68.08.** Reservations recommended. Breakfast 500 CFP–1,600 CFP (US$6.25–US$20/£3.15–£10); burgers 1,400 CFP–1,900 CFP (US$18–US$24/£8.85–£12); main courses 1,900 CFP–3,900 CFP (US$24–US$49/£12–£25). MC, V. Daily 7–10am, 11:30am–2pm, and 7–10pm.

Restaurant-Snack Moi Here REGIONAL   Tree limbs hold up the thatched roof covering this little Tahitian restaurant, which almost hangs over Matira Beach. It's more *roulotte* than restaurant, with the usual local menu of steaks and fish served with french fries, hamburgers, sashimi, chow mein, and *poisson cru.* After a tough steak, I always order fish here. Breakfast is French style, while lunch turns to burgers, sandwiches, and omelets. The view is worth more than the price of a meal here.

Matira, between Hotel Bora Bora and Matira Point. ⓒ **67.56.46.** Reservations accepted. Most items 500 CFP–2,000 CFP (US$6.25–US$25/£3.15–£13). MC, V (minimum 2,000 CFP). Daily 6am–9pm.

Tips **Call for a Ride**

The top restaurants provide free transportation for their dinner guests; always ask when making your reservations.

Snack Matira SNACK BAR   Right on Matira Beach and within hailing distance of Chez Ben's, this open-air snack bar is a favorite lunch and afternoon retreat of Bora Bora's French-speaking expatriates. It offers a roulotte-style menu of pizzas, salads, omelets, grilled steaks and fish, juicy burgers, and *casse-croûte* sandwiches, plus ice cream and milk shakes. The company is better at Chez Ben's, but not the lagoon view.

Matira, between Hotel Bora Bora and Matira Point. © **67.77.32.** Most items 450 CFP–1,900 CFP (US$5.65–US$24/ £2.85–£12). No credit cards. Tues–Sun 10am–4pm.

POVAI BAY

Bloody Mary's Restaurant & Bar ★★★ SEAFOOD/STEAKS   Having a few drinks and a slab of barbecued fish at this charming structure is as much a part of the Bora Bora experience as is taking a lagoon excursion. Ceiling fans, colored spotlights, and stalks of dried bamboo dangle from a large thatched roof over a floor of fine white sand (stash your sandals in a foot locker and dine in your bare feet). The butcher-block tables are made of coconut-palm lumber, and the seats are sections of palm trunks cut into stools. Bloody Mary's is essentially an American-style barbecued fish and steak joint—a welcome relief after a diet of lard-laden French sauces. You'll be shown the seafood and beef laid out on a bed of ice. The chef will charbroil your selection to order. Open all day, the cozy bar is cut from a beautifully polished litchi tree and is one of my favorite watering holes. The lunch menu consists of burgers, fish and chips, and salads, which are not served at dinner. You will have an evening of fun, as have the many famous faces posted on a board out by the road.

Povai Bay, 1km (½ mile) north of Hotel Bora Bora. © **67.72.86.** Reservations strongly recommended. Lunch 950 CFP–1,500 CFP (US$12–US$19/£6–£9.50); dinner main courses 2,700 CFP–3,200 CFP (US$34–US$40/£17–£20). AE, MC, V. Mon–Wed and cruise ship days 11am–3pm; Mon–Sat 6–9pm. Bar Mon–Sat 9:30am–11pm. Closed Dec.

La Villa Mahana ★★★ INTERNATIONAL   You will need one night for fun at Bloody Mary's, another for a romantic dinner at this extraordinarily fine little restaurant, the best in all of French Polynesia. Owner Damien Rinaldi Dovio, an accomplished young Corsican-born chef, started my friends and I with tuna *tartare exotique,* a luscious version of *poisson cru* with a sharp wasabi-accented sauce. My friends went on to mahimahi perfectly cooked with a subtle version of coconut-curry sauce, while I opted for filet mignon with vanilla cream gnocchi. Both were outstanding. The fixed-price menus for four or five courses will save money. The walls of this Mediterranean-style villa are adorned with the works of noted French Polynesian artist Garrick Yrondi, but Damien has only six tables, so consider calling or e-mailing for a reservation well before you get here.

Povai Bay, behind Boutique Gauguin, 1.5km (1 mile) north of Hotel Bora Bora. © **67.50.63.** damien@villamahana. com. Reservations required. Main courses 5,000 CFP–11,000 CFP (US$63–US$138/£32–£70); fixed-price dinners 10,500 CFP–15,000 CFP (US$131–US$187/£66–£95). AE, MC, V. Wed–Thurs 6–8pm.

VAITAPE

Inexpensive roulottes roll out on and near the Vaitape wharf after dark. See "Don't Miss *Les Roulottes*" in chapter 8 for details about these inexpensive food wagons. You can get an inexpensive snack in Vaitape at **Bora Bora Burger,** next to the post office (no phone). Open Monday to Saturday from 8am to 5:30pm. No credit cards.

Aloe Cafe 𝒦 *Value* FRENCH/PASTRIES   I often have breakfast here, for this patisserie bakes very good croissants, tarts, and quiches to go with the strong French coffee. Also on the menu: sandwiches, pizzas by the slice, and a *plat du jour* at lunch. Order at the counter, at a table inside, or on the shopping-center sidewalk. You can check your e-mail (see "Fast Facts: Bora Bora," earlier in this chapter).

North of the Vaitape wharf, in Centre Commercial le Pahia. ℭ **67.78.88.** Most items 500 CFP–1,950 CFP (US$6.25–US$24/£3.15–£12). No credit cards. Mon–Sat 6am–6pm.

8 Island Nights

As on all the outer islands, things are really quiet on Bora Bora after dark (this is, after all, one of the world's most romantic honeymoon hideaways, not a place to practice your dance steps). You might want to listen to a Tahitian band playing at sunset or watch the furious hips in a Tahitian dance show, which all the resorts have at least 1 night a week. The schedules change, so call ahead.

You don't have to stay at **Club Med Bora Bora** (ℭ **60.46.04**) to dine there and watch the nightclub show staged by its staff. The full meal, wine, and show together cost about 6,500 CFP (US$81/£41). Call for reservations.

I found the food to be overpriced at **Monta Restaurant & Lounge Bar,** on the site of the Bora Bora Yacht Club north of Vaitape (ℭ **67.68.68**), but on Saturday night the bar was serving finger food to accompany dancing its the sand floor.

Huahine, Raiatea, Tahaa & the Tuamotu Archipelago

Your French Polynesian experience will be much richer if you get off the usual Tahiti–Moorea–Bora Bora tourist trek and visit the less developed islands, where you will glimpse "the way Tahiti used to be," as they say in these parts. In this chapter I cover the islands that get enough visitors to warrant comfortable accommodations, but not so many as to turn off the locals' marvelous warmth, joviality, and hospitality.

One is **Huahine,** which I think is the third-most-beautiful island in French Polynesia (behind Moorea and Bora Bora). Although Bora Bora looms on the horizon, agriculture still far outweighs tourism on Huahine, and unless a cruise ship is in port, you'll have it almost to yourself.

Huahine is famous for its ancient archaeological sites, as is nearby **Raiatea,** historically the most important of Polynesian islands and today the administrative center of the Leeward Islands. Except for cruise ship visits, neither Raiatea nor neighboring **Tahaa** are on the usual tourist circuit, primarily because neither has beaches. But the deep-water lagoon surrounding them is the territory's charter yacht center. You do not have to be a world-class sailor here, for you can spend a lazy week or more circumnavigating Tahaa without venturing onto the open ocean.

The atolls of the Tuamotus offer a very different kind of experience. This immense archipelago, stretching across the northeastern approaches to Tahiti, consists not of high, mountainous islands but of low-lying necklaces of islets enclosing crystal clear lagoons. You'll find excellent accommodations and French Polynesia's best scuba diving on **Rangiroa, Tikehau, Manihi,** and **Fakarava.** You will also find drier and warmer climes than in the Society Islands, and sand so white that it alone requires sunglasses in the midday sun.

As I have noted elsewhere, Huahine and Tahaa are popular as last stops for honeymooners, who like to "come down" after the sometimes frantic pace on Bora Bora. On the other hand, I think you should go to the Tuamotus first, so as not to be "let down" after the mountainous beauty of the Society Islands.

1 Huahine ✶✶

Pronounced Wa-*ee*-nee by the French (who never sound an H) and *Who*-a-hee-nay by the Tahitians (who always do), Huahine ranks with Easter Island and Raiatea (p. 299) as the three most important Polynesian archaeological sites. Here the ancient chiefs built a series of maraes on the shores of **Lake Fauna Nui,** which separates the north shore from a long, motulike peninsula, and on Mataiea Hill above the lakeside village of **Maeva.** These have been restored, and informational markers explain their history and purposes.

Geographically, Huahine actually is two islands—Huahine Nui and Huahine Iti—enclosed by the same reef and joined by a short bridge. France did not annex Huahine until 1897, more than 50 years after it took over Tahiti, and its 5,500 residents are still independent in spirit. When the first Europeans arrived, Huahine was governed as a single chiefdom and not divided into warring tribes as were the other islands, and this spirit of unity is still strong. Pouvanaa a Oopa, the founder of French Polynesia's independence movement, hailed from here.

Of attraction to today's visitors are Huahine's Mooreaesque bays, clear lagoon, and lovely beaches. **Baie Avea (Avea Bay),** on the far southwestern coast of Huahine Iti, is fringed by one of the South Pacific's most glorious beaches. Another is right in the small hamlet of **Fare,** one of the region's best examples of what the South Seas were like in the days of trading schooners and copra planters.

GETTING AROUND HUAHINE

Huahine's airport is on the flat peninsula paralleling the north side of the island, 3km (2 miles) from Fare. Unless you have previously reserved a rental car or are willing to walk into Fare, take your hotel minibus. At other times, **Moe's Taxi** (© 72.80.60) or **Enite's Taxi** (© 68.82.37) will carry you around. Fares are about 600 CFP (US$7.50/£3.80) from the airport into Fare, about 2,500 CFP (US$31/£16) to the southern end of Huahine Iti.

Avis (© 800/230-4898 or 68.73.34; www.avis.com), **Europcar** (© 800/227-7368 or 68.82.59; www.europcar.com), and **Hertz** (© 800/654-3131 or 68.76.85; www.hertz.com) have agents in Fare. Europcar's vehicles start at 9,400 CFP (US$118/£59) a day. Avis charges about 12,000 CFP (US$150/£76) a day for air-conditioned cars. Europcar rents scooters for 6,200 CFP (US$78/£39) a day, bicycles for 2,000 CFP (US$25/£13) a day. **Huahine Lagoon,** on the Fare waterfront (© 68.70.00) has bicycles for 1,500 CFP (US$19/£9.50) for 8 hours. On Huahine Iti, **Moana Turquoise** (© 68.85.57), at Pension Mauarii, rents scooters for 6,500 CFP (US$81/£41) a day and bicycles for 2,500 CFP (US$31/£16) a day.

Each district has **local buses,** which run into Fare at least once a day, but the schedules are highly irregular. If you take one from Fare to Parea, for example, you might not be able to get back on the same day.

FAST FACTS: Huahine

The following facts apply specifically to Huahine. For more information, see "Fast Facts: French Polynesia," in chapter 7.

Camera & Film **AO Api New World,** over the Manava Huahine Visitors Bureau (© 68.70.99), burns digital photos to CDs. See "Internet Access," below.

Currency Exchange **Banque Socredo** is in Fare, on the road that parallels the main street and bypasses the waterfront. **Banque de Tahiti** is on Fare's waterfront. Both have ATMs.

Drugstore The pharmacist at the drugstore, on the main road between Fare and the airport, speaks English (© 68.80.90). Open Monday to Friday 7:30am

Huahine

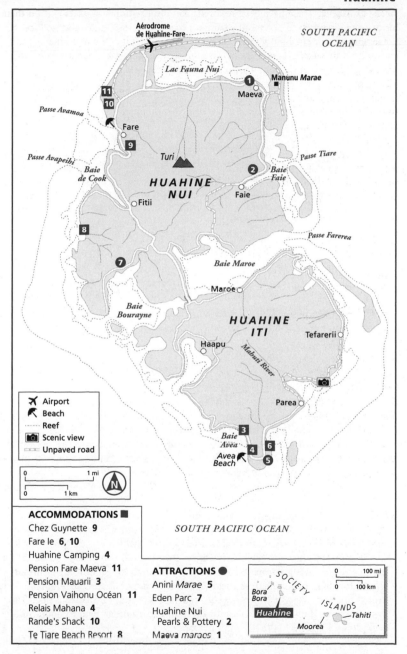

SOUTH PACIFIC OCEAN

Aérodrome de Huahine-Fare

Lac Fauna Nui

Manunu *Marae*

1 Maeva

11
10

Passe Avamoa

✕ Fare

9

Passe Avapeihi

Baie de Cook

Turi

HUAHINE NUI

Passe Tiare

2 *Baie Faie*

Faie

○Fitii

8

Passe Farerea

7

Baie Maroe

Maroe○

Baie Bourayne

HUAHINE ITI

Tefarerii○

Haapu○

Mahuti River

📷

Baie Avea

3

4

Parea○

6

Avea Beach ✕

5

✈ Airport
✕ Beach
····· Reef
📷 Scenic view
▭▭ Unpaved road

0   1 mi
0   1 km
Ⓝ

SOUTH PACIFIC OCEAN

ACCOMMODATIONS ■
Chez Guynette **9**
Fare le **6, 10**
Huahine Camping **4**
Pension Fare Maeva **11**
Pension Mauarii **3**
Pension Vaihonu Océan **11**
Relais Mahana **4**
Rande's Shack **10**
Te Tiare Beach Resort **8**

ATTRACTIONS ●
Anini *Marae* **5**
Eden Parc **7**
Huahine Nui
  Pearls & Pottery **2**
Maeva *maraes* **1**

SOCIETY
Bora Bora
ISLANDS
Huahine
Moorea
Tahiti

0   100 mi
0   100 km

to noon and 2:30 to 5pm, Saturday 8am to noon, and Sunday and holidays 8 to 9am.

Emergencies & Police The emergency **police** telephone number is ℂ **17**. The phone number of the **gendarmerie** in Fare is ℂ **68.82.61**.

Healthcare The **government infirmary** is in Fare (ℂ **68.82.48**). Ask your hotel for the name of doctors and dentists in private practice.

Internet Access You can pick up e-mail at **AO Api New World** (ℂ **68.70.99**), upstairs over the Manava Huahine Visitors Bureau. Open Monday to Friday 8:30am to noon and 4 to 7:30pm, and Saturday 4:30 to 9:30pm. Access costs 15 CFP (18¢/9p) a minute. Restaurant New Temarara, on the Fare waterfront (ℂ **68.89.31**), has wireless access for 700 CFP (US$8.75/£4.45) an hour.

Mail The colonial-style post office is in Fare, on the bypass road north of the waterfront area. Hours are Monday to Thursday 7:30am to 3pm and Friday 7am to 2pm.

Restrooms There are public toilets on the Fare wharf opposite the visitors bureau, but don't expect them to be clean. I use them for emergencies only.

Visitor Information On Fare's main street opposite the wharf, **Manava Huahine Visitors Bureau** (ℂ/fax **68.78.81**) is open Monday to Saturday 8am to noon (more or less). Some local pensions and tour operators have banded together to host **www.iaorana-huahine.com**.

Water Don't drink the tap water on Huahine. Bottled water is available at all grocery stores.

EXPLORING HUAHINE
TOURING THE *MARAES* & FARE POTEE ⟨⟨⟨

The village of **Maeva,** beside the pass where Lake Fauna Nui flows toward the sea, was a major cultural and religious center before Europeans arrived. All of Huahine's chiefly families lived here. More than 200 stone structures have been discovered between the lakeshore and **Matairea Hill,** which looms over Maeva, including some 40 maraes (the others were houses, paddocks, and agricultural terraces).

To see the maraes on your own, start west of Maeva village at the big reed-sided building known as **Fare Potee,** which houses an excellent museum (ℂ **24.16.63**). Flanked by maraes and extending out over Lake Fauna Nui, Fare Potee is modeled after a large meeting house which stood here in 1925 but was destroyed by a hurricane. Take time to read the historical markers outside, which explain the history and use of the maraes. Inside you'll observe adzes (stone axes), fishhooks, and other artifacts uncovered during restoration work by Dr. Yoshiko H. Sinoto, the chairman of the anthropology department of the Bernice P. Bishop Museum in Honolulu. He restored this and many other maraes throughout Polynesia. Fare Potee is open Monday through Friday 9am to noon and 2 to 4pm, and Saturday 9am to noon. Admission is 200 CFP (US$2.50/£1.25) per person.

Ask at Fare Potee for directions to six maraes and other structures (some were built as fortifications during the 1844–48 French-Tahitian war) on Matairea Hill. The track up the hill can be muddy and slippery during wet weather, and the steep climb is best done in early morning or late afternoon. Better yet, take a tour (see below).

Easier to reach, the large **Manunu Marae** stands on the beach about 1km (a half-mile) across the bridge on the east end of Maeva. Follow the left fork in the road after crossing the bridge. The setting is impressive.

From the bridge you will see several stone **fish traps**. Restored by Dr. Sinoto, they work as well today as they did in the 16th century, trapping fish as the tide ebbs and flows in and out of the narrow passage separating the lake from the sea.

HISTORICAL TOURS

The most informative way to see the historical sites—and much of Huahine, for that matter—is with Paul Atallah of **Island Eco Tours** ⋆⋆⋆ (© **68.79.67**). Paul is an American who graduated from the University of Hawaii with a major in anthropology and a minor in Polynesian Island archaeology. He has lived in French Polynesia for more than a decade. His is more than a typical safari expedition, for he gives in-depth commentary about the Maeva marae and other historical sites. He charges 5,000 CFP (US$63/£32) for either morning or afternoon trips from Monday through Friday. The 3½- to 4-hour trips depart daily at 8am and 1pm. He will pick you up at your hotel. Paul can also guide you to the maraes on Matairea Hill by special arrangement.

TOURING THE ISLAND

You can rent a vehicle and tour both parts of Huahine in half a day. The main roads around both islands are about 32km (20 miles) long and are paved. Be careful on the steep *traversière*, which traverses the mountains from Maroe Bay to Faie Bay on the east coast. (I would not ride a scooter or bicycle over this road). Heading clockwise from **Fare,** you skirt the shores of Lake Fauna Nui and come to the maraes outside Maeva village (see "Touring the *Maraes* & Fare Potee," above).

From Maeva the road heads south until it turns into picturesque Faie Bay. There you'll pass the landing for **Huahine Nui Pearls & Pottery** ⋆ (© **78.30.20;** www.huahinepearlfarm.com), a pearl farm and pottery studio (see "Shopping on Huahine," below). Once you're past Faie village at the head of the bay, the road starts uphill across the traversière (see above). At the top, you'll be rewarded with a view down across Mooreaesque **Maroe Bay,** which splits Huahine into two islands.

Turn right at the dead-end by the bay and drive west to the main west-coast road. Turn left and follow it across the bridge over the narrow pass separating Huahine Nui from Huahine Iti. A right turn past the bridge will take you along the winding west-coast road to **Avea Bay,** where Relais Mahana and Pension Mauarii (see "Where to Stay on Huahine," below) sit beside one of the South Pacific's greatest beaches. Either is an excellent place to stop for refreshment.

Sitting at the end of the peninsula at the south end of Huahine Iti, **Anini Marae** presents a glorious view of the island's southern coast. Nearby on the grounds of Fare Ie (see "Where to Stay on Huahine," below), another marae bears the **Taiharuru Petroglyphs.**

(Fun Fact Say Hello to Dorothy

Be sure to say hello to Dorothy Levy, who oversees the Fare Potee museum at the Maeva Maraes. Dorothy's Tahitian father came to Hollywood in the 1930s to work with Clark Gable on the original *Mutiny on the Bounty* movie. He later participated in the first film version of *Hurricane* with Dorothy Lamour, for whom he named this Dorothy.

Parea is one of Huahine's largest villages. From there, you'll skirt the shoreline until you come to the village of **Tefarerii** on the east coast. In between is a pull-off with a marvelous view over the reefs and sea. From here, it's an easy drive to Maroe Bay. The large cruise ships land their passengers at Maroe village on the south side of the bay.

VISITING THE OLD SOUTH SEAS IN FARE

The village of **Fare** ✿✿✿ (*Fa*-ray) is hardly more than a row of Chinese stores and a wharf opposite the main pass in the reef on the northwest shore, but it takes us back to the days when trading schooners were the only way to get round the islands. Even today, trucks and buses arrive from all over Huahine with passengers and cargo when the interisland boats put in from Papeete. The rest of the time, Fare lives a lazy, slow pace, as people amble down its tree-lined main street and browse through the stores facing the town wharf. A monument on the waterfront designates it as Place Hawaiki, the starting point for October's big outrigger canoe race to Raiatea and Bora Bora. Beginning at the Restaurant New Temarara (see "Where to Dine on Huahine," below), a pebbly promenade leads north along the waterfront to a sandy swimming beach, which has a daytime snack bar.

LAGOON EXCURSIONS

As on Moorea and Bora Bora, one of the most enjoyable ways to see the island is on a lagoon excursion including snorkeling and a picnic on an islet out on the reef. The biggest difference here is that with relatively few tourists around, you and your companions are likely to have the islet all to yourselves. The all-day excursion with **Huahine Nautique** (✆ 68.83.15; www.huahine-nautique.com) takes you by outrigger canoe through Maroe Bay and around Huahine Iti. You'll stop for snorkeling and a picnic featuring freshly made *poisson cru,* and you will observe shark-feeding before returning to Fare. Huahine Nautique's canoes have shade canopies, and the guides speak English as well as French. **Poetaina Cruises** (✆ 60.60.06) also does all-day trips, but I can't guarantee that you'll have shade on your outrigger. Don't be surprised if you visit Huahine Nui Pearls & Pottery (see "Touring the Island," above). The excursions cost about 8,500 CFP (US$107/£54) per person.

SAFARI EXPEDITIONS

As on most of the Society Islands, you can make four-wheel-drive expeditions into the mountains here. You will see a bit of the interior of Huahine Nui with Paul Atallah on his **Island Eco Tours** (see "Historical Tours," above), which I would take first. You will repeat seeing the Maeva maraes, but **Huahine Land** (✆ 68.89.21), which is owned by American expatriate Joel House, or **Huahine Explorer** (✆ 68.87.33) will

---

Tips Fruit Juice & an Exotic Lunch

On your way back to Fare from Huahine Iti, turn off the main road toward Bourayne Bay and drive 2km (1¼ mile) to **Eden Parc** (✆ **68.86.58**; www.eden parc.org), a lush tropical garden where you can get freshly squeezed fruit juice or enjoy an "exotic" lunch made from produce organically grown on the premises. It's a hot and steamy site, so get out your insect repellant. It's open Monday to Saturday 8am to 2pm.

> ⌢Moments **Sailboats & Sunsets at Fare**
>
> I enjoy strolling along the wharf, poking my head into the stores across the main street, observing the cruising yachts anchored in the harbor, and watching the boats come and go. With Raiatea, Tahaa, and Bora Bora resting on the western horizon, Fare is one of my favorite places to watch a sunset.

also take you to Huahine Iti on their half-day expeditions. Both charge about 5,100 CFP (US$64/£32) per person.

SWIMMING, SNORKELING, DIVING & OTHER OUTDOOR ACTIVITIES

FISHING   For lagoon or deep-sea fishing, contact **Huahine Marine Transports** (© **68.84.02;** hua.mar.trans@mail.pf), owned by American expatriate Rich Shamel, who has lived on Huahine for many years and who runs the transfer boats for Te Tiare Beach Resort (see "Where to Stay on Huahine," below). Rich charges US$800 (£400) for half a day and US$1,200 (£600) for a full day of fishing on his 11m (36-ft.) Hatteras sportfishing boat. He lives and works at the resort's transfer base, just across the bridge on the south side of Fare.

HORSEBACK RIDING   One of the best horseback-riding operations in French Polynesia is *La Petite Ferme* (**The Little Farm;** © **68.82.98;** www.huahine-lapetite ferme.com), on the main road north of Fare, just before the airport turnoff. It has Marquesas-bred horses that can be ridden with English or Western saddles along the beach and around Lake Fauna Nui. Prices range from 5,500 CFP (US$69/£35) for 2 hours to 11,000 CFP (US$138/£70) for an all-day trail ride. The farm also has accommodations, from a dormitory to bungalows.

SAILING   You can go for a half- or full-day cruise with Claude and Martine Bordier of **Sailing Huahine Voile** (©/fax **68.72.49;** www.sailing-huahine.com) on their *Eden Martin,* a 15m (49-ft.) yacht, which they sailed out from France in 1999. A half-day of sailing costs about 7,200 CFP (US$90/£46) per person; a full day is 12,500 CFP (US$156/£79). They also have sunset cruises for 6,600 CFP (US$83/£42) per person. That's assuming Claude and Martine are on Huahine and not off on a 1- or 2-week charter cruise in the Leeward or Tuamotu islands.

SCUBA DIVING   Pacific Blue Adventure (© **68.87.21;** fax 68.80.71; www.dive huahine.com) and **Mahana** Dive (© **73.07.17;** www.mahanadive.com) have offices on the Fare wharf. Both charge about 6,000 CFP (US$75/£38) for a one-tank dive. Avapeihi Pass, Huahine's most famous site, is nearby.

SNORKELING & SWIMMING   You don't have to leave Fare to find a fine little swimming and snorkeling beach; just follow the seaside promenade north past Restaurant New Temarara. Huahine's best, however, is the magnificent crescent of sand at **Avea Beach,** skirting Baie Avea on Huahine Iti. A hilly peninsula blocks the brunt of the southeast trade winds, so the speckled lagoon here is usually as smooth as glass. **Moana Turquoise** (© **68.85.57**), at Pension Mauarii (see "Where to Stay on Huahine," below), rents snorkeling gear. It also has power boats for rent.

SHOPPING ON HUAHINE

You are not as likely to be pestered to buy black pearls on Huahine as on Tahiti, Moorea, and Bora Bora—another of Huahine's appealing attributes. One stop you should make is **Huahine Nui Pearls & Pottery** ⋆ (© **78.30.20;** www.huahinepearl farm.com), a pearl farm and pottery studio run by American ex-pat Peter Owen on a motu off Baie Faie (see "Touring the Island," above). Peter offers free tours daily 10am to 4pm, with the boat leaving Faie Bay every 15 minutes. If you aren't going to the Tuamotus, this is a good place to see how black pearls are grown.

Local women sell shell jewelry, bedspreads, and other handicrafts at **Huahine Mata Aiai** (no phone), in a thatch building at the south end of the Fare waterfront. Also look into the small art galleries and other shops along the waterfront, especially **Pacific Art** (© **68.70.09**).

WHERE TO STAY ON HUAHINE

EXPENSIVE

Te Tiare Beach Resort ⋆⋆⋆ Rudy Markmiller made a fortune in the overnight courier business in California and then spent more than a decade—and a sizable chunk of his loot—building this luxury resort, one of French Polynesia's finest. Although it's on the main island, guests are ferried here from Fare, which makes this seem like a remote offshore resort (a shuttle boat makes the 10-minute run to and from Fare every hour from 5:30am–11pm). A long pier connects the thatched-roof, overwater lounge, bar, and dining to a westward-facing, white-sand beach with gorgeous sunsets over Raiatea and Tahaa out on the horizon. The lagoon is not deep here, but it's still good for swimming and snorkeling over coral heads close to shore. You can use canoes, paddle boats, and kayaks, or cool off in a beachside swimming pool equipped with a terrific bar serving libations and snacks all afternoon. The 41 spacious bungalows are as luxuriously appointed. You won't have a fish-viewing glass panel in the floor, but you can step out to huge L-shaped decks, one half of them under the shade of thatched roofs. Steps lead into the lagoon from the decks of the 11 "deep overwater" bungalows, which have spa tubs as well as showers in their bathrooms (all other units, including five "shallow overwater" models, have large showers). Six bungalows sit beside the beach, but the garden units (the least expensive here) don't have unimpeded views of the lagoon.

B.P. 36, 98731 Fare, Huahine (in Fitii District, 10 min. by boat from Fare). © **888/600-8455** or 60.60.50. Fax 60. 60.51. www.tetiarebeach.com. 41 units. 39,000 CFP–78,000 CFP (US$488–US$975/£247–£494) double. AE, DC, MC, V. **Amenities:** Restaurant; 2 bars; outdoor pool; watersports equipment rentals; activities desk; car-rental desk; limited room service; massage; babysitting; laundry service. *In room:* A/C, TV, minibar, coffeemaker, iron (overwater units only), safe.

MODERATE

Fare Ie Instead of a bungalow, you'll have your own genuine South African safari tent at this establishment's two locations. One is north of Fare and within walking distance

---

Fun Fact **The Swimsuit Models Were Here**

Those extraordinarily beautiful women seen briefly—as in both time and clothing—at Te Tiare Beach Resort recently were here to model for the 2006 swimsuit issue of *Sports Illustrated* magazine.

of town. The other is on the outskirts of Paea village, near Huahine Iti's southernmost point. The Paea location is remote, but the beach is very good, and it's actually on the grounds of an ancient marae bearing the Taiharuru Petroglyphs. The tents are all screened and have electric fans, two beds, and their own bathrooms. Two larger tents at Paea also have kitchens just outside under thatched roofs. Guests share communal kitchens at both locations.

B.P. 746, 98331 Fare, Huahine (north of Fare and in Paea village, Huahine Iti). Ⓒ/fax **60.63.77**. www.tahitisafari.com. 6 units. 16,500 CFP–27,000 CFP (US$206–US$338/£104–£171) per tent. No credit cards. **Amenities:** Communal kitchen; complimentary bicycles, kayaks, snorkeling gear. *In room:* No phone.

Relais Mahana *(Value*   This hotel offers one of the South Pacific's best beach-lagoon combinations, for half of it sits beside Avea Beach, the white sand stretching along the peninsula on Huahine's south end. A pier from the main building runs out over a giant coral head, around which fish and guests swim. Just climb down off the pier and swim with the fishes. Choice guest quarters are the deluxe models beside the beach. These were remodeled recently, and although a bit smaller than at other resorts, they have king-size beds, and their showers open to private rear gardens. Other units here are somewhat larger, but they're north of the central building where the beach has been eroded. All in all, Relais Mahana is a good value.

B.P. 30, 98731 Fare, Huahine (Avea Bay, Huahine Iti). Ⓒ **60.60.40**. Fax 68.85.08. www.relaismahana.com. 32 units. 23,900 CFP–31,600 CFP (US$299–US$395/£151–£200). AE, MC, V. **Amenities:** 2 restaurants; bar; watersports equipment rentals; bicycle rental; activities desk; car-rental desk; babysitting; laundry service. *In room:* TV, dataport, minibar, coffeemaker, iron.

INEXPENSIVE

Two family-run pensions sit on the rocky shoreline between Fare and the airport. **Pension Fare Maeva** (Ⓒ **68.75.53;** www.fare-maeva.com) is the better equipped, with a restaurant, swimming pool, and 10 modern bungalows. Rates range from 7,000 CFP to 12,100 CFP (US$88–US$151/£44–£77). **Pension Vaihonu Océan** (Ⓒ **68.87.33;** www.iaorana-huahine.com) is more basic, with beach huts, a dorm, yard space for camping, and a two-story building holding two modern units. Rates start at 1,800 CFP (US$23/£11) for a dorm bed or camp site to 8,000 CFP (US$100/£51) for a modern duplex unit. Both accept MasterCard and Visa credit cards.

American Rande Vetterli has two clean, well-equipped houses for rent at **Rande's Shack,** on the shore north of Fare (Ⓒ **68.86.27;** www.haere-mai.pf/index.php? page=detail&lg=en&id=247). Both have TVs, fans, and kitchens. One house has two bedrooms and can sleep five persons; a one-bedroom model can sleep three persons. Rates are 10,000 CFP and 15,000 CFP (US$125–US$188/£63–£95), respectively.

Chez Guynette *(Value*   Marty and Moe (*Mo*-ay) Temahahe (wife Marty is American; husband Moe is Tahitian) operate this friendly hostel across the main street from the Fare waterfront. A corridor runs down the center of the building to the kitchen and lounge at the rear. The simple but clean rooms and dorms flank the hallway to either side. The rooms are screened and have ceiling fans and their own bathrooms with hot-water showers. The dorms also have ceiling fans; they share two toilets and showers. Marty and Moe offer breakfast and lunch (sandwiches, burgers, salads, *poisson cru* on their street-side patio, plus wine and beer). It's the best place in Fare to slake a thirst and get into a good conversation—in English.

B.P. 87, 98731 Fare, Huahine (opposite the town wharf). Ⓒ **68.83.75**. chezguynette@mail.pf. 7 units (all with bathroom), 8 bunks. 1,750 CFP–2,000 CFP (US$22–US$25/£11–£13) dorm bed; 5,900 CFP–6,200 CFP (US$74–US$78/£37–£39) double (higher rates apply to 1-night stays). MC, V. **Amenities:** Restaurant; bar. *In room:* No phone.

Pension Mauarii ⭐ Beside Avea Beach, this little pension may not offer all the comforts of home, but it oozes charm. Its buildings are constructed of thatch, bamboo, tree trunks, and other natural materials. Although cleverly designed, they seem to be slapped together, which adds to the ambience. Most units are in the tropical gardens, but the rooms open to a long porch right on the beach, as does the one beachside bungalow—my favorite here. All units have ceiling fans, but not all have bathrooms, and their windows aren't screened. The pension offers a host of waterborne activities. Unless the owners haven't moved it to the inland side of the road to make room for more bungalows, the **restaurant** here is the most charming on the island (see "Where to Dine on Huahine," below).

B.P. 473, 98731 Fare, Huahine (Baie Avera, Huahine-Iti). ℂ **68.86.49.** Fax 60.60.96. www.mauarii.com. 5 bungalows (3 with bathroom), 4 rooms (2 with bathroom). 9,500 CFP (US$119/£60) double; 11,500 CFP–20,000 CFP (US$144–US$250/£73–£127) bungalow. AE, MC, V. **Amenities:** Restaurant; bar; watersports equipment rentals; bike rentals; activities desk; massage; laundry service. *In room:* No phone.

CAMPING

You can pitch a tent or rent a rudimentary thatched-roof *fare* (cabin) at Cecèle and Hubert Bremond's **Huahine Camping** (ℂ **68.85.20** or 68.83.78), on the southern end of Avea Beach. The shoreline here has as many coral ledges and sand, but the shady grounds are appealing. Guests share a communal kitchen, tables under a thatched roof, toilets, and cold-water showers (don't expect a showerhead). The cabins, which have either a double bed or two single beds, cost 6,000 CFP (US$75/£38), while tent sites are 1,800 CFP (US$23/£11) per person.

WHERE TO DINE ON HUAHINE

You will meet the locals having breakfast or lunch on the patio at **Chez Guynette.** You can also enjoy the fine-dining room at **Te Tiare Beach Resort,** though you will need to make reservations and pay 500 CFP (US$6.25/£3.15) for the boat ride there and back. See "Where to Stay on Huahine," above.

You'll find Huahine's *roulottes* on the Fare wharf. They're open for lunch and dinner. See the "Don't Miss *Les Roulottes*" box in chapter 8.

Restaurant Mauarii FRENCH/TAHITIAN Assuming the owners haven't taken leave of their senses and moved this restaurant across the road, it will still be sitting almost over the sand, with a great view along Avea Beach. It's a charmer, with a thatch-lined ceiling and tables hewn from tree trunks. Lunchtime sandwiches include a "Killer" baguette loaded with grilled fish and french fries (yes, in the sandwich) under your choice of vanilla or other sauces. For the money, this is a good place to sample Tahitian treats such as *fafa ru* (chicken with taro leaves in coconut cream), or sample different dishes on a Polynesian platter. Ask for a menu in English if the friendly staff doesn't figure you out first.

Avea Beach, Huahine Iti (at Pension Mauarii). ℂ **68.86.49.** Reservations recommended for dinner. Sandwiches and burgers 600 CFP–1,200 CFP (US$7.50–US$15/£3.80–£7.60); main courses 1,600 CFP–3,500 CFP (US$20–US$44/£10–£22). AE, MC, V. Daily noon–2pm and 6–8pm.

Restaurant New Temarara ⭐ FRENCH Facing due west beside the lagoon at the north end of Fare's wharf, this is my favorite place for a sundown cocktail or cold Hinano beer during half-price happy hour from 5:30 to 6:30pm. The *poisson cru* is outstanding, as is the coconut crumbed mahimahi, a spicy version of breaded fish. If offered, you might also try the parrot fish with lemon butter. You can get a good beef or fish burger here as well as steaks and fish with French sauces.

Fare, north end of wharf. (C) **68.89.31.** Reservations accepted. Burgers 800 CFP–900 CFP (US$10–US$11/£5.05–£5.70); main courses 1,600 CFP–2,100 CFP (US$20–US$26/£10–£13). MC, V. Mon–Sat 11:30am–9pm. Bar open all day, to 11pm Fri–Sat.

2 Raiatea & Tahaa (★

The mountainous clump of land you can see on the horizon from Huahine or Bora Bora may appear to be one island, but it is actually two, Raiatea and Tahaa, which are enclosed by a single barrier reef. Cruising yachts can circumnavigate Tahaa without leaving the lagoon, and Huahine and Bora Bora are relatively easy hauls from here. This is French Polynesia's yacht-chartering center. There are no beaches on either Raiatea or Tahaa other than a few on islets out on the reef, and except for sailing and cruise-ship visits, tourism is not an important part of their economies, which are based on agricultural produce and, in the case of Raiatea, government salaries.

Raiatea, the largest of the Leeward Islands, is by far more important than Tahaa, both in terms of the past and the present. In the old days it was the religious center of all the Society Islands, including Tahiti. Polynesian mythology has it that Oro, the god of war and fertility, was born in **Mount Temehani,** the extinct flat-top volcano that towers over the northern part of Raiatea. **Taputapuatea,** on its southeast coast, was at one time the most important marae in the islands. Legend also has it that the great Polynesian voyagers who discovered and colonized Hawaii and New Zealand left from there. Archaeological discoveries have substantiated the link with Hawaii.

Today Raiatea (pop. 10,000) is still important as the economic and administrative center of the Leeward Islands. Next to Papeete, the town of **Uturoa** (pop. 4,000) is the largest settlement and is one of the most important transportation hubs in French Polynesia. A modern cruise-ship terminal and welcome center dominate Uturoa's waterfront. Although most prefer anchoring offshore in order to use their watersports platforms, Uturoa is the only island port other than Papeete where the larger cruise ships spend their nights tied up to a wharf.

Tahaa (pronounced *Tah*-ah-ah) is much smaller than Raiatea in terms of land area, population (about 1,500), and the height of its terrain. It's a lovely island, with a few very small villages sitting deep in bays that cut into its hills. Tahaa has a few family-operated pensions, but other than sailors and guests at resorts out on its reef islets, few visitors see it, and most of those who do, see it on day tours from Raiatea.

(*Fun Fact* Delicate Petals

Found nowhere except in Raiatea's mountains, the *tiare apetahi* is a one-sided white flower of the gardenia family. Legend says that its five delicate petals are the fingers of a beautiful Polynesian girl who fell in love with a prince but couldn't marry him because of her low birth. Just before she died, heartbroken, in her lover's arms, she promised to give him her hand to caress each day throughout eternity. At daybreak each morning, accordingly, the *tiare apetahi* opens its five petals.

GETTING AROUND RAIATEA & TAHAA

The Raiatea airstrip, 3km (2 miles) north of Uturoa, serves both islands. You have to rent a vehicle or take a taxi, for there is no regular public transportation system on either Raiatea or Tahaa.

Europcar (© 800/227-7368 or 66.34.06; www.europcar.com) and **Hertz** (© 800/654-3131 or 66.44.88; www.hertz.com) have rental-car offices here. Europcar's prices start at 9,700 CFP (US$121/£61) a day, including insurance and unlimited kilometers. It also rents scooters, bicycles, and open-air Bugster vehicles. Europcar also has an office at Tupuamu Wharf on Tahaa's west coast (© **65.67.00**), so you can take the ferry there, rent a car, and drive around the island. You must take a water taxi back to Uturoa.

Trudy Tours (© **78.23.36**) provides transfers from the airport to the hotels and to Apooti Marina for 500 CFP to 700 CFP (US$6.25–US$8.75/£3.15–£4.45) per person. There is a taxi stand near the cruise-ship terminal in Uturoa, or you can contact **René Guilloux** (© **66.31.40**), **Marona Teanini** (© **66.34.62**), or **Apia Tehope** (© **66.36.41**). Fares are about 600 CFP (US$7.50/£3.80) from the airport to town and 1,200 CFP (US$15/£7.60) to the Raiatea Hawaiki Nui Hotel.

The passenger ferry *Tamarii Tahaa* (© **65.67.10**) docks in front of the Champion store on Uturoa's waterfront and runs from there to Patio on Tahaa's northern coast. It departs from Uturoa Monday to Friday, usually at 10am and 4pm, and Saturday at 10am. You had best make sure it will return to Uturoa on the same day it leaves. Fares range from 500 CFP to 750 CFP (US$6.25–US$9.40/£3.15–£4.75) one-way. **Dave's Tours** (© **65.62.42**) also runs a shuttle from Uturoa to Tahaa, departing Monday to Saturday at 9am, returning at 4:30pm. Fares are 1,500 CFP (US$19/£9.50) one-way, 2,500 CFP (US$31/£16) round-trip. **Water-taxi** service is available at the waterfront (© **65.66.64**); rides cost about 2,000 CFP (US$25/£13).

FAST FACTS: **Raiatea & Tahaa**

The following facts apply specifically to Raiatea and Tahaa. For more information, see "Fast Facts: French Polynesia," in chapter 7.

Currency Exchange French Polynesia's three banks have offices with ATMs on Uturoa's main street. There is no bank on Tahaa.

Drugstores **Pharmacie de Raiatea** (© 66.34.44) in Uturoa carries French products. Open Monday to Friday 7:30am to noon and 1:30 to 5:30pm, Saturday 7:30am to noon, and Sunday 9:30 to 10:30am.

Emergencies & Police The emergency police number is © 17. The telephone number of the **Uturoa gendarmerie** is © 66.31.07. The **Tahaa gendarmerie** is at Patio, the administrative center, on the north coast (© 65.64.07).

Eyeglasses **Optique Te Mata Ore**, on Uturoa's main street (© 66.16.19).

Healthcare Opposite the post office, the **hospital** at Uturoa (© 66.32.92) serves all the Leeward Islands. Tahaa has an **infirmary** at Patio (© 65.63.31). Drs. **Sonia Andreu** and **Pascal Diochin** (© 66.23.01) practice together on Uturoa's main street.

Internet Access **ETS**, in the Gare Maritime on the Uturoa waterfront (© 60. 25.25), has computers with Internet access for 500 CFP (US$6.25/£3.15) for 35 minutes. Open Monday to Friday 7:30am to noon and 1 to 5pm, and Saturday 7:30am to noon. The staff will burn your digital photos to CDs.

Post Office The post and telecommunications office is in a modern building north of Uturoa on the main road (as opposed to a new road that runs along the shore of reclaimed land on the north side of town). It is open Monday to Thursday 7:30am to 3pm, Friday 7am to 2pm, and Saturday 8 to 10am. There's a small branch upstairs in the Gare Maritime on the waterfront.

Restrooms The Gare Maritime on the waterfront has clean restrooms.

Telephone There are *télécarte* phones on the waterfront and at the post and telecommunications offices.

Visitor Information **Tourisme Tahiti** (*C* **60.07.77**; fax 60.07.76; www.tahiti-tourisme.pf) has a visitor information office in the Gare Maritime on the waterfront. It's open daily 8am to 4pm.

Water Don't drink the tap water on either Raiatea or Tahaa.

EXPLORING RAIATEA & TAHAA

Highlights of a visit here are visiting the ancient maraes, day trips to and around Tahaa, picnics on islands on the outer reef, and excursions into the mountains.

VISITING THE *MARAE*

On the outskirts of Opoa village 29km (18 miles) south of Uturoa, the **Taputapuatea Marae** is the second most important archaeological location in Polynesia, behind only Easter Island. Legend says that Te Ava Moa Pass offshore was the departure point for the discovery and settlement of both Hawaii and New Zealand. The large marae on the site was built centuries later by the Tamatoa family of chiefs. Vying for supremacy, the Tamatoas mingled religion with politics by creating Oro, the god of war and fertility supposedly born on Mount Temehani, and by spreading his cult. It took almost 200 years, but Oro became the most important god in the region. Likewise, the Tamatoas became the most powerful chiefs. They were on the verge of conquering all of the Society Islands when the missionaries arrived in 1797. With the Christians' help, Pomare I became king of Tahiti, and the great marae the Tamatoas built for Oro was soon left to ruin, replaced by the lovely Protestant church in nearby Opoa village.

The marae was restored in the 1960s, and more recently Tahiti Museum archaeologists discovered human bones under some of the structures, apparently the remains of sacrifices to Oro. The marae's *ahu,* or raised altar of stones for the gods, is more than 45m (148 ft.) long, 9m (30 ft.) wide, and 3.3m (11 ft.) tall. Flat rocks, used as backrests for the chiefs and priests, still stand in the courtyard in front of the ahu. The complex is in a coconut grove on the shore, opposite a pass in the reef, and legend says that bonfires on the marae guided canoes through the reef at night.

Taputapuatea is worth a visit not only for the marae itself but for the scenery there and along the way. The road skirts the southeast coast, follows Faaroa Bay to the mouth of the river, and then goes back out to the lagoon.

On the west coast, 14.5km (9 miles) from Uturoa, **Taninuu Marae** also was dedicated to Oro. Stones bordering the foundation of the ancient chief's home bear petroglyphs of turtles. This is a place of Christian history, too, as the lovely white Eglise Siloama is one of the oldest churches in French Polynesia.

WALKING AROUND UTUROA

A number of Chinese stores still line the main street, but the center of activity in Uturoa is the glistening **Gare Maritime,** a cruise-ship terminal built with money from France's economic restructuring fund. You can't miss this big Mediterranean-style building, which houses restaurants, shops, the island's visitor information office, and public restrooms. Needless to say, the waterfront is busiest when a cruise ship arrives, and handicraft and souvenir vendors occupy a number of small thatch buildings next door. Across the street is the *Marché Municipale,* the local produce market.

Just north of downtown Uturoa, the street to the left as you face the gendarmerie leads to a trail that ascends to the television towers atop 291m (955-ft.) **Papioi Hill.** (Be sure to close the gates, which keep the cows out of the station.) From the top you can see Uturoa, the reef, and the islands Tahaa, Bora Bora, and Huahine. Another trail begins with a Jeep track about 200 yards south of the bridge, at the head of Pufau Bay on the northwest coast. It leads up to the plateau atop **Mount Temehani.** The mountain itself is actually divided in two by a deep gorge.

> (*Tips* **Avoid Cruise-Ship Days**
>
> Unless you're on one of them, try to avoid visiting Raiatea when cruise ships are in port, as their passengers can monopolize all organized activities here.

SAFARI EXPEDITONS ON RAIATEA & TAHAA

Either **Raiatea 4×4** (© 66.24.16) or **Jeep Safari Raiatea** (© 66.15.73) will take you via four-wheel-drive Jeep into Raiatea's interior, including a ride into the crater of Mount Temehani, and both stop at Taputapuatea Marae before heading back to Uturoa. These expeditions are less thrill ride and more oriented to history and culture than those on Bora Bora. I would opt for Raiatea 4×4, especially if the highly informative Ronnie Moufat is to be your guide. Each has two trips a day, requires reservations a day in advance, and charges about 4,500 CFP (US$56/£28) per person.

The mountains of Tahaa offer less dramatic scenery than on Raiatea, and the island lacks the historical importance of its big sister. Consequently, safari expeditions there include visits to **La Maison de Vanille** (© 57.61.92), which explains the cultivation and uses of vanilla (Tahaa's major product), and to a black pearl farm. I thoroughly enjoyed my expedition guided by the energetic and engaging Roselyne Atiniu of **Dave's Tours** (© 65.62.42), or you can go with **Vai Poe Tours** (© 65.60.83). Either will pick you up at Uturoa.

LAGOON EXCURSIONS

If you can put together your own group (because a minimum of four persons is required), you can take a variety of **lagoon excursions** and see firsthand the Raiatea-Tahaa lagoon, one of the most beautiful in French Polynesia. All trips include snorkeling, and most include picnics on tiny islets sitting on the outer reef; unlike the mainland of Raiatea and Tahaa, they have beautiful white-sand beaches.

Marie and Tony Tucker (she's French, he's South African) of **West Coast Charters** (© 66.45.39) have a tour around Tahaa with swimming, guided snorkeling over coral gardens, shark feeding, a pearl farm visit, and lunch for 8,500 CFP (US$106/£54) a person. Andrew Brotherson at **Manava Excursions** (© 66.28.26; fax 66.28.26; maraud@mail.pf) also charges 7,500 CFP (US$94/£47) per person for an all-day trip to Tahaa, including visits to a vanilla plantation and pearl farm, a picnic on a motu, and snorkeling over a coral garden. He also offers a boat trip up the Faaroa River and on to the Taputapuatea marae for 4,500 CFP (US$56/£28) per person. Another option is Bruno Fabre's **L'Excursion Bleue** (© **66.10.90;** www.tahaa.net), whose full-day trip around Tahaa costs 9,500 CFP (US$119/£60).

DIVING & SAILING ⋩⋩⋩
The Moorings (© **800/535-7289** or 727/535-1446; www.moorings.com) and **Sunsail Yacht Charters** (© **800/327-2276** or 207/253-5400 in the U.S., or 60.04.85 on Raiatea; fax 66.23.19; www.sunsail.com) charter sailboats (see "Seeing the Islands by Cruise Ship & Yacht," in chapter 7). Both operators are based on Raiatea. If a boat is available, it can be chartered on a daily basis. Arrangements for longer charters ordinarily should be made before leaving home.

Raiatea may not have beaches, but the reef and lagoon are excellent for scuba diving, including descents of 50 to 80 feet above the wreck of the S.S. *Norby,* a three-masted Danish schooner which sunk off Uturoa in 1900. With bases at the Raiatea Hawaiki Nui Hotel and at Apooiti Marina, **Hémisphère Sub Raiatea** (© **66.12.49;** fax 66.28.63; www.multimania.com/diveraiatea) takes divers on one-tank excursions for 6,500 CFP (US$80.50/£41).

SHOPPING IN UTUROA
The Gare Maritime on the waterfront has black pearl and other shops, including **My Flower** (© **66.19.19**), where owner Flora Hart carries not just floral arrangements but excellent tapa drawings and wood carvings, some from the Marquesas Islands, others done in *hue papa'a* wood, a specialty of Raiatea's own carvers.

Other stores line the main street, where you will find the unique **Magasin Vanira** (© **66.30.06**). Owner Jeanne Chane—the *"préparatrice de vanille"*—makes many products from vanilla beans: extract, powder, even vanilla soup. The wonderful aroma alone makes it worth a visit.

WHERE TO STAY ON RAIATEA
Raiatea Hawaiki Nui Hotel ⋩   This hotel is of historical importance in its own right, for it was here in 1968 that Moorea's "Bali Hai Boys" built the world's first over-water bungalows (see the box in chapter 9). It was their way of compensating for the lack of a beach. The hotel has gone through several name changes since its days as the Hotel Bali Hai Raiatea, but those bungalows still stand out on the edge of the reef. From them you can climb into the water and get the sensation of flying as you snorkel along its clifflike face. (Snorkel gear and kayaks are free for guests here.) It's also still Raiatea's best hotel. The friendly and helpful staffers speak English, but the ambience is definitely French. The land-based bungalows, some of which have two units under their thatched roofs, are either along the seawall or in the gardens beyond. The least expensive units are hotel rooms, which have the same amenities as the bungalows and are air-conditioned.

B.P. 43, 98735 Uturoa, Raiatea (2km/1¼ miles south of town). © **800/657-3275** or 66.20.23. Fax 66.20.20. www.pearlresorts.com. 32 units. 26,000 CFP (US$325/£165) double; 26,000 CFP–36,000 CFP (US$325–US$450/£165–£228) bungalow. AE, MC, V. **Amenities:** Restaurant; bar; outdoor pool; tennis court; bike rentals; activities desk; car-rental desk; babysitting; laundry service. *In room:* A/C (some units), TV, fridge, coffeemaker, safe.

Pension Manava   Roselyne and Andrew Brotherson rent two rooms in their house and have four bungalows in their gardens, across the road from the lagoon. The two rooms share a bathroom and the Brothersons' kitchen. The bungalows have corrugated tin roofs, screened louvered windows, double and single beds, and large bathrooms with hot-water showers. Four also have kitchens. Roselyne will cook breakfast and provide free dinner transportation to town on request.

B.P. 559, 98735 Uturoa, Raiatea (6km/3¾ miles south of town). ⓒ **66.28.26.** www.manavapension.com. 6 units. 4,700 CFP (US$59/£30); 8,000 CFP (US$100/£51) bungalow. No credit cards. *In room:* Kitchen (2 units), no phone.

Sunset Beach Motel ✴ (*Value* One of the best values in French Polynesia, this is not a motel but a collection of cottages in a coconut plantation on a peninsula sticking out west of the airport. The cottages sit in a row off a palm-draped beach. The lagoon here is shallow, but the beach enjoys a gorgeous westward view toward Bora Bora, and a long pier stretches to deep water (guests can paddle free kayaks from it). Of European construction rather than Polynesian, the bungalows are spacious, comfortably furnished, and have fully equipped kitchens and covered verandas facing the sea. Part of the grove is set aside for campers, who have their own building with toilets, showers, and kitchen (bring your own tent). Manager Steve "Moana" Boubée speaks English. There is no restaurant here, but you order breakfast in your bungalow.

B.P. 397, 98735 Uturoa, Raiatea (in Apooiti, 5km/3 miles northwest of Uturoa). ⓒ **66.33.47.** Fax 66.33.08. www. sunset.raiatea.com. 22 units. 10,000 CFP (US$125/£63) double bungalow; 1,100 CFP (US$14/£7) per person camping. MC, V. **Amenities:** Free kayaks; rental bikes; laundry service. *In room:* TV, kitchen, no phone.

WHERE TO STAY ON TAHAA

Le Taha'a Private Island & Spa ✴✴✴ When I was traveling by yacht back in 1977, we anchored near *Motu* Tautau, an islet on the reef off Tahaa's west coast, and went ashore to get an unsurpassed view of Bora Bora from its outer edge. There was nothing on Tautau then except palm trees, a brackish lake, and several million mosquitoes. Since 2002, the mossies have mostly resided on the sea side of the motu, while one of French Polynesia's most luxurious and architecturally creative resorts has occupied the lagoon shoreline. A 40-minute boat ride from the Raiatea airport, or 15 minutes by helicopter from Bora Bora, this Relais & Chateau–affiliated hotel sports the territory's most tastefully decorated bungalows. Most stand out over the hip-deep lagoon, where their large decks have privacy fences screening covered sitting areas under thatched roofs. Most face hilly Tahaa, but a few have views of Bora Bora through a shallow reef pass between Tautau and its neighboring motu. Ashore beside the brilliant white-sand beach, 10 villa suites are even larger and more private. The villas all have living rooms, bedrooms, and courtyards with plunge pools hidden behind high rock walls. Two Royal Villas enlarge on them by adding a separate bungalow within their compounds, 24-hour butler service, and private shows and barbecues on the beach. At the center of it all is a stunning two-story central building, where stairs built in a tree lead up to the main bar and casual gourmet restaurant with both indoor and outdoor tables, all with a view. The most romantic tables sit by themselves on extensions from the terrace. Or you can retire to the air-conditioned fine-dining restaurant. The resort's infinity pool, a lunchtime restaurant and bar, full-service spa and air-conditioned gym are on one end of the property, thus removing most daytime activities from the vicinity of the bungalows. There's much to do here, from snorkeling to safari expeditions on Tahaa. This is a marvelous place to chill after the rigors of Bora Bora.

B.P. 67, 98733 Patio, Tahaa (on *Motu* Tautau). ⓒ **800/657-3275** or 60.84.00. Fax 60.84.01. www.letahaa.com. 60 units. 92,000 CFP–230,000 CFP (US$1,150–US$2,875/£582–£1,456) bungalow. AE, DC, MC, V. **Amenities:** 2 restaurants; 2 bars; outdoor pool; tennis court; fitness center; spa; Jacuzzi; watersports equipment rentals; concierge; activities desk; business center; limited room service; massage; babysitting; laundry service. *In room:* A/C, TV, CD player, dataport, minibar, coffeemaker, safe.

Vahine Island Private Resort 𝄢𝄢   In a coconut grove on flat Motu Tuuvahine, off Tahaa's northeastern coast, this intimate little hotel offers bungalows both beside a brilliant white-sand beach and built out over a shallow lagoon beautifully speckled with coral heads. The three thatched-roof overwater units are the pick, as they are larger and more private than the beachside units—and they have a stunning view of Bora Bora on the far horizon. The bungalows ashore have shingle roofs, but all are decorated in traditional Polynesian style, with native lumber and bamboo trim. Each sports a porch in front and a shower-only bathroom to the rear. Ceiling fans and mosquito nets make up for the lack of air-conditioning and window screens. The dining room serves good French fare with island touches. There's a guest lounge with a collection of books and videos in both English and French. Most of the guests are from Europe, but the staff makes everyone feel welcomed at this little gem.

B.P. 510, 98735 Uturoa, Raiatea (on Motu Tuuvahine). ⓒ 65.67.38. Fax 65.67.70. www.vahine-island.com. 9 units. 37,000 CFP–58,000 CFP (US$463–US$725/£234–£367) double. AE, DC, MC, V. **Amenities:** Restaurant; bar; free use of kayaks, canoes, and snorkel gear; laundry service. In room: TV, fridge, coffeemaker, hair dryer.

WHERE TO DINE ON RAIATEA

Les roulottes, Raiatea's inexpensive meal wagons, congregate after dark near the Gare Maritime, in the middle of Uturoa's business district, and in the seaside park north of the business district. They stay open past midnight on Friday and Saturday. See "Don't Miss *Les Roulottes*" in chapter 8.

Brasserie Maraamu 𝘝𝘢𝘭𝘶𝘦 CHINESE/TAHITIAN   Before it moved into the Gare Maritime, this restaurant occupied a waterfront shack and was widely known for its simple but good Chinese dishes, *poisson cru,* and fried chicken and steaks served with french fries. The chow is still good, as witnessed by the number of local office workers who head here for lunch. Local business types like to hang out here over strong cups of morning coffee served French style in soup bowls (the better to dunk your baguette).

In Gare Maritime, Uturoa waterfront. ⓒ 66.46.64. Breakfast 700 CFP–1,200 CFP (US$8.75–US$15/£4.45–£7.60); main courses 1,000 CFP–1,800 CFP (US$13–US$23/£6.35–£11.40). MC, V. Mon–Fri 7am–2pm and 6:30–9pm; Sat 10am–2pm.

Le Napoli 𝄢 ITALIAN   A stack of firewood beside a pond (note the Tahitian eels swimming about) hints that the very good pizzas and steaks are cooked in a wood-fired oven, which is dolled up with bamboo trim. The 15 varieties of pizza are all two-person size, so unless you are famished, forget the special tourist menu which adds *poisson cru* and a dessert. I like the smoked salmon and cream sauce pasta here.

Main road north of Uturoa, near airport. ⓒ 66.10.77. Reservations recommended. Pizza and pasta 1,350 CFP–1,500 CFP (US$17–US$18.75/£8.55–£9.50); main courses 1,450 CFP–2,100 CFP (US$18–US$26/£9.15–£13.29). MC, V. Tues–Fri 11am–2pm and 6:30–9pm; Sat–Sun 6:30–9pm.

Snack Moemoea SNACKS/FRENCH/CHINESE   Predating the Gare Maritime by many years, this old corner storefront has tables both outside on the sidewalk and inside on the ground floor or on a mezzanine platform. It's another good place for breakfast, from croissants to omelets. The lunch menu includes *casse-croûte* sandwiches, fine hamburgers, grilled fish and steaks, and Raiatea's best *poisson cru.* I love to slake my thirst here with an ice-cold coconut.

Waterfront, Uturoa (in Toporo Bldg.). ⓒ 66.39.84. Breakfast 600 CFP–1,500 CFP (US$7.50–US$19/£3.80–£9.50); burgers and sandwiches 400 CFP–800 CFP (US$5–US$10/£2.55–£5.05); main courses 1,500 CFP–1,900 CFP (US$19–US$24/£9.50–£12). No credit cards. Mon–Fri 6am–5pm; Sat 6am–2pm.

WHERE TO DINE ON TAHAA

Chez Louise *☆* TAHITIAN   This local restaurant beside the lagoon in Tiva village, on Tahaa's west coast, is a popular stop for cruise-ship passengers, and it's close enough to Le Taha'a Private Island & Spa that its guests come here for lunch or dinner, too (call for dinner pickup at Tapuamu wharf). The *ma'a Tahiti* fare is first rate, as are lobster and other fresh seafood items. There's a gorgeous view of Bora Bora from here, so come in time for a sunset drink.

Tiva village, lagoonside. *⌀* **65.68.88** or 72.59.18. Reservations highly recommended. Full meals 3,500 CFP–5,600 CFP (US$44–US$70/£22–£35). MC, V. Daily 11am–2pm and 6–9pm.

3 Rangiroa *☆/☆*

The largest and most often visited of the Tuamotu atolls, Rangiroa lies 312km (194 miles) northeast of Tahiti. It consists of a ring of low, skinny islets enclosing the world's second-largest lagoon. At more than 70km (43 miles) long and 26km (16 miles) wide, it's big enough so that when you stand on one side of the lagoon, you cannot see the other. In fact, the entire island of Tahiti could be placed in Rangiroa's lagoon, with room to spare.

Like all the atolls, the islets here are so low—never more than 3m (10 ft.) above sea level, not including the height of the coconut palms growing all over them—that ships can't see them until they're a few kilometers away. For this reason, Rangiroa and its Tuamotu sisters are also known as the Dangerous Archipelago. Hundreds of yachts and ships have been wrecked on these reefs, either unable to see them until it was too late or dragged ashore by tricky currents.

Schools of dolphins usually play early mornings and late afternoons in **Avatoru Pass** and **Tiputa Pass,** the two navigable passes into Rangiroa's interior lagoon, both on its north side. Currents of up to 6 knots race through the passes as the tides first fill the lagoon and then empty it during their never-ending cycle. Even at slack tide, watching the coral rocks pass a few feet under your yacht is a tense experience. Once inside the lagoon, however, you anchor in a huge bathtub whose crystal-clear water is stocked with an incredible variety of sea life (including large sharks and manta rays).

Most visitors come to Rangiroa primarily for French Polynesia's best scuba diving, snorkeling, and fishing. Others venture across the lagoon to Rangiroa's islets, where they can literally get away from civilization at a very remote resort.

GETTING AROUND RANGIROA

Rangiroa's airstrip and most of its hotels and pensions lie on the main islet, a perfectly flat, 11km-long (6¾-mile) stretch of sand and palm trees on the north side of the lagoon. The airport is about equidistant from the village of **Avatoru** on the west end and Tiputa Pass, which separates the main island from **Tiputa** village, on the east. The hotels and pensions send buses or vans to meet their guests.

Impressions

At Rangiroa you pick up a hundred natives with pigs, guitars, breadfruit and babies. They sleep on deck, right outside your bunk, and some of them sing all night.

—James A. Michener, *Return to Paradise,* 1951

Rangi Rent a Car is the local agent for **Europcar** (© **800/227-7368** or 96.08.28; www.europcar.com). It has an agency near Avatoru and a desks at the Hotel Kia Ora and Novotel Rangiroa Lagoon Resort (see "Where to Stay on Rangiroa," below). Cars rent for 12,000 CFP (US$150/£76) a day. Scooters and open-air Bugsters (the most you'll need here) cost about 6,500 CFP (US$81/£41) for 8 hours (which is longer than you'll need to see the islet). Bicycles rent for 1,500 CFP (US$19/£9.50) for half a day, 1,800 CFP (US$23/£11) for a full day. **Arehahio Locations** (© **98.82.45** or 73.92.84) in Avatoru rents cars for 8,400 CFP (US$105/£53) per day, scooters for 5,200 CFP (US$65/£33) a day, bicycles for 1,600 CFP (US$20/£10) a day.

Rangiroa's 11km-long (6¾-mile) main island actually consists of seven islets separated by narrow reef passes. The only road crosses the passes over bridges, none of them with guardrails and some of them only one lane wide. The pavement is uneven, adding to the need for constant caution when driving.

You can cross Tiputa Pass to Tiputa village via **Maurice Navette** (© **96.67.09** or 78.13.25), which operates water taxis daily from 6am to 5pm. Call or check with your hotel staff for schedules and fares.

FAST FACTS: Rangiroa

The following facts apply specifically to Rangiroa. For more information, see "Fast Facts: French Polynesia," in chapter 7.

Camera/Film **Pata Hoh'a Photo**, near Restaurant Le Kai Kai (© **93.12.85**) sells film and will burn your digital photos to CDs. It's open Monday to Saturday 9am to noon and 2 to 5:30pm.

Currency Exchange **Banque Socredo** has an agency with an ATM in Avatoru post. It's open Tuesday, Wednesday, and Friday 8am to noon; and Monday and Thursday 1:30 to 4:30pm. **Banque de Tahiti** also has a branch in Avatoru. It's open Monday and Friday 8am to 4pm, and Tuesday and Thursday 8 to 11am and 2 to 4pm.

Drugstore **Pharmacie de Rangiroa**, in Avatoru (© **93.12.35**), is open Monday to Friday 8am to 12:30pm and 3 to 6:30pm, Saturday 8am to 12:30pm and 4:30 to 6:30pm, and Sunday and holidays 10 to 11:30am.

Emergencies/Police The emergency **police** telephone number is © **17**. The phone number of the **gendarmerie** on Rangiroa is © **96.03.61**.

Healthcare There are **infirmaries** at Avatoru (© **96.03.75**) and across the pass at Tiputa (© **96.03.96**).

Internet Access **Pata Hoh'a Photo**, near Restaurant Le Kai Kai (© **93.12.85**), has Internet access for 330 CFP (US$4.15/£2.10) for 15 minutes. Open Monday to Saturday 9am to noon and 2 to 5:30pm.

Mail The post office in Avatoru is open Monday to Thursday 7am to 3pm, and Friday 7am to 2pm.

Telephone Public pay phones are at the post office in Avatoru and at the dock on the eastern end of the island. Residents in the Tuamotus tend to write their phone numbers in groups of three digits; that is, 960 375 instead of 96.03.75.

Water Except at the hotels, the tap water is brackish. Don't drink it.

Tips Come Up Here First

There isn't a lot to do in the Tuamotu Islands except snorkel and scuba dive, which makes them great for resting and recovering from your long flight before tackling Tahiti, Moorea, Bora Bora, and the other Society Islands. I recommend coming here first for a little R&R and then visiting the more developed mountainous islands and their incredible scenery.

LAGOON EXCURSIONS, SCUBA DIVING & SNORKELING ✶✶✶

Except for walks around Avatoru and Tiputa, typical Tuamotuan villages with whitewashed churches and stone walls lining the main streets, plan on either doing nothing or enjoying the fantastic lagoon. The hotels and pensions either have or can arrange lagoon excursions by boat. One favorite destination is the **Lagon Bleu (Blue Lagoon)**, a small lagoon within the big lagoon on the far eastern side of the island. It's full of colorful corals and plentiful sea life. **Les Sables Rose (The Pink Sands),** on the eastern end, are one of the most picturesque beaches in French Polynesia. These trips are not inexpensive—plan on paying to 10,000 CFP and 12,000 CFP (US$125–US$150/£63–£76) or more for a full day's outing. You're looking at an hour's boat ride in each direction to reach the Blue Lagoon or The Pink Sands.

Close to home, snorkelers and scuba divers can **"ride the rip"** tide through the passes, one of the most exhilarating waterborne experiences French Polynesia has to offer. These so-called drift snorkeling trips cost about 5,000 CFP (US$63/£32) and are worth it—if you've got a strong heart. Book at your hotel activities desk or contact **Snorkeling Rangiroa** (✆ 96.73.59 or 76.03.31).

The same operators also have **dolphin-watching** cruises, usually for about 3,000 CFP (US$38/£19) per person, but you can ride or walk to the public park at the western side of Tiputa Pass and watch them play for free.

The best **scuba diving** here is from December to March, when hammerhead sharks gather off Tiputa Pass for their mating season, and also between July and October, when the manta rays look for mates. You can see gray and black-tipped sharks all year. But be aware that dives here are deep and long compared to American standards, so bring a buddy and be prepared to stretch the limits of the dive tables in order to see the sea life. Divers must be certified in advance and bring their medical certificates.

Any of the hotels or pensions can arrange scuba dives. The best operators are **Blue Dolphins** (✆ 96.03.01; www.bluedolphinsdiving.com), at the Hotel Kia Ora (see "Where to Stay on Rangiroa," below), and **Top Dive Rangiroa** (✆ 72.39.55; www.topdive.com). Other operators here include **The Six Passengers** (✆ 96.02.60), which allows only six divers on its boat at any one time; **Raie Manta Club** (✆ 96. 04.80); and **Rangiroa Paradive** (✆ 96.05.55). One-tank day dives cost about 7,000 CFP (US$88/£44). Night dives are more expensive.

A WINERY & A BLACK PEARL FARM

Near Avarotu, **Cave de Rangiroa** (✆ 96.04.70; www.vindetahiti.pf) is the tasting room for Vin de Tahiti (Tahiti Wines), French Polynesia's only vineyard and winery. The Carignan, muscat de Hambourg, and Italia varieties were first planted in a coconut grove out on an islet in 1999. You can take a half-day tour to the motu vineyard for 6,000 CFP (US$75/£38) per person, or just stay here in the *cave* and taste the results in air-conditioned comfort for 1,800 CFP (US$23/£11). Open Monday to Saturday 9am to 1pm and 3 to 6pm.

Rangiroa does not produce black pearls in the same quantity as Manihi, but you can visit **Gauguin's Pearl Farm,** west of the airport (𝄞 **93.11.30**), and see how it's done. It's open Monday to Friday 8:30am to 5:30pm, and weekends 9am to noon and 3 to 5pm, with demonstrations Monday to Friday at 8:30am, 10:30am, and 2pm.

WHERE TO STAY ON RANGIROA

Hotel Kia Ora 𝄞𝄞   This romantic establishment in a coconut plantation has been Rangiroa's premier hotel for almost 3 decades. Its thatched-roof buildings look like a lagoonside Polynesian village. White sand is hauled over from the ocean side of the island, but the beach still is a bit pebbly; however, a long pier reaches out into deep water for excellent swimming, snorkeling, and sunset watching, and there's a canoe-shaped swimming pool beside the lagoon. Ten bungalows sit over the reef and share the sunsets. Ashore stand two-story beachside bungalows with bedrooms downstairs and up, and one-story models with only the downstairs bedroom. These beach units have Jacuzzi tubs set in their partially covered front decks, but they have not one iota of privacy. Much more luxurious are three deluxe beach units with their own small pools and bathrooms with outdoor tubs. The much smaller original bungalows are back in the gardens; they do not have window screens, but some have separate bedrooms. As at most accommodations on Rangiroa, guests here are primarily European and Japanese.

B.P. 1, 98775 Tiputa, Rangiroa (3km/2 miles east of airport, near east end of island). 𝄞 **96.02.22.** Fax 93.11.17. www.hotelkiaora.com. 58 units. 32,000 CFP–68,000 CFP (US$400–US$850/£203–£430) double. AE, DC, MC, V. **Amenities:** Restaurant; bar; outdoor pool; tennis court; Jacuzzi; watersports equipment rentals; bike rentals; activities desk; car rentals; massage; babysitting; laundry service. *In room:* A/C, dataport, fridge (stocked on request), coffeemaker, safe.

Kia Ora Sauvage   This outpost offers one of the South Pacific's most remote Robinson Crusoe–like escapes. Guests are transferred daily by a 1-hour speedboat ride from Hotel Kia Ora, which manages this retreat. Once you're out on tiny, triangle-shaped Avearahi motu, you will find a thatched main building, where the Tahitian staff cooks up the day's catch, often caught during the guests' lagoon excursions. Accommodation is in five bungalows built entirely of native materials. They have their own modern bathrooms, but they are not screened and do not have electricity. Bring reef shoes, insect repellent, SPF 60 sunscreen and an ample supply of books to read.

B.P. 1, 98775 Tiputa, Rangiroa (hotel is 1-hr. boat ride from airport). 𝄞 **96.02.22.** Fax 93.11.17. www.hotel kiaora.com. 5 units. 40,000 CFP (US$500/£253) double. Meals and drinks 8,500 CFP (US$106/£54) per person per day. Round-trip boat transfers cost 12,000 CFP (US$150/£76) per person. Minimum 2-night stay required. AE, DC, MC, V. **Amenities:** Restaurant; bar. *In room:* No phone.

Les Relais de Josephine 𝄞 *Value*   You can watch the dolphins frolic in Tiputa Pass from this comfortable inn, the creation of the charming Denise Caroggio, an English-speaking Frenchwoman who is like the grande dame of Rangiroa. Her spacious bungalows flank a Mediterranean-style villa with an expansive veranda overlooking the pass. Guests can relax there or in a lounge equipped with a TV, VCR, and CD player. At night, the veranda turns into **Le Dolphin Gourmand** restaurant, serving excellent three-course French and Mediterranean meals. Furnished with reproductions of French colonial antiques, the bungalows have thatched roofs over solid white walls. Sliding doors open to the porches, outfitted with high-quality wooden patio furniture.

Neither the doors nor the prop-up windows are screened, but the queen-size beds are covered by mosquito nets. The substantial bathrooms have double sinks and walk-in showers. Do anything possible to get one of the three units beside the pass.

B.P. 140, 98775 Avatoru, Rangiroa. ℭ and fax **96.02.00.** http://relaisjosephine.free.fr. 6 units. 14,600CFP (US$183/ £92) per person, double occupancy. Rates include breakfast and dinner. AE, MC, V. **Amenities:** Restaurant; bar; bike rentals; laundry service. *In room:* Coffeemaker, safe, no phone.

Novotel Rangiroa Lagoon Resort   This modest but attractive resort sits beside a rocky stretch of lagoon shoreline west of the airport and within walking distance of Restaurant Le Kai Kai and Vaimario Restaurant & Pizzeria (see "Where to Dine on Rangiroa," below). Brilliant white sand has been brought in to form a sunbathing strip along the property, and you can swim off a pier extending over the lagoon. The 38 bungalows and main building (with French restaurant and bar) are tightly packed on limited land. The units here come either as individual bungalows or as duplex rooms, which are narrower than the much more spacious bungalows. Both are tastefully decorated with tropical furniture and fabrics; they also have adequate bathrooms and front porches.

B.P. 17, 98775 Avatoru, Rangiroa. ℭ **800/221-4542** or 93.13.50. Fax 93.13.51. www.novotel.com. 38 units. 19,200 CFP–29,300 CFP (US$240–US$366/£122–£185) bungalow. AE, MC, V. **Amenities:** Restaurant; bar; car and bike rentals; activities desk; massage; laundry service. *In room:* A/C, TV, dataport, fridge, coffeemaker, hair dryer, safe.

WHERE TO DINE ON RANGIROA

Nonguests are welcome at Les Relais de Josephine's **Le Dolphin Gourmand** restaurant (see above), where the three-course meals cost 4,100 CFP (US$51/£26) per person. Make your reservations before noon. Outsiders are welcome at the **Hotel Kia** and the **Novotel Rangiroa Lagoon Resort,** too. You'll find a few inexpensive snack bars in Avatoru and at Tiputa Pass.

The local *roulottes* set up shop after dark at the Tiputa Pass wharf and in Avatoru village, but the best is in the center of the main island near Restaurant Le Kai Kai (it has table service). See "Don't Miss *Les Roulottes,*" in chapter 8, for details. **Snack-Restaurant Moetua,** is like a permanent *roulotte* at Tiputa Pass (ℭ **28.06.96**), and Avatoru has a few inexpensive snack bars.

Restaurant Le Kai Kai ℱ FRENCH   West of the airstrip and near the Novotel Rangiroa Lagoon Resort, Gaelle Coconnier's open-air restaurant with crushed coral floor and mat-lined ceiling is my favorite spot for a casual lunch or dinner. Midday sees a selection of omelets, salads, and *croques* (toasted sandwiches), while dinner turns to a wide-ranging menu of light French fare. A special *prix-fixe* dinner menu includes a starter such as beef carpaccio, a main of shrimps in garlic and olive oil, and a dessert (I always opt for a Tahitian sundae with coconut and honey). Reserve for a 7pm pickup from your hotel. Gaelle does all the cooking herself, so don't be in a hurry.

Main rd., west of airport. ℭ **96.30.39.** Reservations recommended. Sandwiches and omelets 300 CFP–1,000 CFP (US$3.75–US$13/£1.90–£6.35); main courses 1,500 CFP–2,000 CFP (US$19–US$25/£9.50–£13); fixed-price diner 3,200 CFP (US$40/£20). MC, V. Thurs–Tues 11:30am–2pm and 6:30–9pm; Wed 11:30am–2pm.

Restaurant Vaimario FRENCH/ITALIAN   Pizzas are the highlights at this restaurant in a thatched-roof house just west of the airport. You can dine inside, but the preferred tables are on the coral-floor veranda. The best main courses are grilled fresh fish with vanilla, coconut, or orange and ginger sauces.

Main rd., opposite Novotel Rangiroa Lagoon Resort. ℭ **96.05.69.** Reservations recommended. Pizza 1,100 CFP–1,200 CFP (US$14–US$15/£6.95–£7.60); main courses 1,950 CFP–2,950 CFP (US$24–US$37/£12–£19). MC, V. Wed–Fri and Sun–Mon 11:30am–2pm and 6:30–9pm; Sat 6:30–9pm.

4 Tikehau ★

Separated from Rangiroa by a deep-water channel, Tikehau is smaller and less developed. Its nearly circular lagoon, 26km (16 miles) across, is dotted with islets such as Ohihi, which has a pink-sand beach, and Puarua and Oeoe, the so-called Bird Islands, where noddy birds and snowy white fairy terns nest. The lagoon is no more than 30m (98 ft.) deep, which means it's unlikely to see big manta rays and sharks. A multitude of tropical fish swim in the lagoon, which makes it great for snorkelers and novice divers, but Tikehau's best diving is in the ocean beyond the reef.

Manihi Blue Nui Dive Center, based at the Tikehau Pearl Beach Resort (see below), is one of the best in French Polynesia, with top-of-the-line equipment and hard-topped boats with ladders. **Raie Manta Club** (✆ **96.22.53** or 72.89.08; www. raiemantaclub.free.fr) also is here. They charge about 6,500 CFP (US$81/£41) per one-tank dive, and they teach PADI certification courses.

Famous for a riot of hibiscus, frangipani, bougainvillea, and other colorful flowers that seem to grow everywhere, Tikehau's only village, **Tuherahera,** is one of the most picturesque in the Tuamotus. It's also one of the wealthiest, as the 400 or so residents here make more money by trapping and shipping fish to Papeete than they do from their four black pearl farms. You'll find grocery stores, a post office, and an infirmary in Tuherahera, but you won't find a bank.

WHERE TO STAY & DINE ON TIKEHAU

Relais Royal Tikihau ★★ *Finds* At low tide you can walk across the reef and another small islet to the village from this charming little hotel, the creation of the delightful Jean-Claude and Monique Varney. Jean-Claude worked in New Zealand for more than 2 decades, and Monique spent her Papeete career in tourism, so both speak English as well as French. They call this their retirement project, and a fine one it is. Their restaurant-bar building and three of their bungalows stand beside a *hoa,* a shallow pass between theirs and the next *motu.* (I watched from my porch as sting rays trolled for breakfast in the pass just after daybreak.) Four others are next to a gorgeous beach of white and pink sand. And the Varneys have four hotel-style rooms upstairs over a monstrous rain water cistern. Monique decorated each unit with bright, color-matched drapes and *tivaivai* quilts. The bungalows and central building are lined with mats and covered with plastic imitation thatch (it lasts five times as long as natural leaves). Every unit has its own bathroom here, but only the bungalows have hot-water showers.

B.P. 15, 98778 Tuherahera, Tikehau. ✆/fax **96.23.37.** www.royaltikehau.pf. 11 units. 15,750 CFP–20,570 CFP (US$197–US$257/£100–£130) double; 30,250 CFP–42,350 CFP (US$378–US$529/£191–£268) bungalow. No credit cards. Rates include breakfast and dinner. 2-night minimum stay required. **Amenities:** Restaurant; bar; laundry service. *In room:* TV (beachside units), no phone.

Tikehau Pearl Beach Resort ★★★ You may think you have made a mistake as your transfer boat approaches, for rustic Tuamotu-style thatch disguises the luxuries awaiting at this resort, which occupies all of *Motu* Tiano, a small reef islet a 10-minute boat ride from the village and the airport. Other than a concrete patio separating the lagoonside pool from the conical-roofed dining room and bar, everything about it is *très* Polynesian, with beaucoup thatch, mats, and bamboo. Strong currents in a shallow pass rip in and out beneath some of the overwater bungalows here, which means you can't go swimming from their decks. Consequently, opt for one of the "premium" suites built over quieter water; they do have ladders leading into the lagoon. The beach here has more pink and white sand than you'll find on Rangiroa and Manihi. Every unit is spacious and well appointed, and the beachside units have large outdoor bathrooms behind high rock walls. The bungalows aren't screened, but the staff closes the windows and turns on the electric mosquito repellents while you're at dinner. Ceiling fans and the trade winds usually provide plenty of ventilation, but opt for a premium overwater or deluxe beach bungalow if air-conditioning is important to you.

B.P. 20, 98778 Tuherahera, Tikehau. (C) **800/657-3275** or 50.84.54 for reservations, or 96.23.00. Fax 43.17.86 for reservations, or 96.23.01. www.pearlresorts.com. 37 units. 43,000 CFP–75,000 CFP (US$538–US$938/£272–£475) double. Meals 15,000 CFP (US$188/£95) per person per day. AE, DC, MC, V. **Amenities:** Restaurant; bar; outdoor pool; spa; free use of snorkeling gear, canoes, and kayaks; bike rentals; babysitting; laundry service. In room: A/C (in premium overwater and deluxe beach units), TV, minibar, coffeemaker, iron (some units), safe.

5 Manihi (★

Known for its black pearl farms, Manihi lies 520km (323 miles) northeast of Tahiti in the Tuamotus. At 30km (19 miles) long by 5.6km (3½ miles) wide, the lagoon is not as large—nor as deep—as Rangiroa's, but it's better for diving among colorful tropical fish, as opposed to the big rays and sharks that make diving at Rangiroa so exciting. That's not to say there are no sharks; to the contrary, the lagoon seems infested. Tairapa Pass, the main entry into the lagoon, is wider and deeper than those at Rangiroa, but it has a strong enough current to make riding-the-rip snorkeling trips a highlight.

French Polynesia's pearl farming industry began here in the late 1960s, and the 30 or so farms seem to sit atop nearly every coral head dotting the lagoon, and great lines of buoys float like crab pots atop the blue water, long strands of pearl oysters suspended below. Most of the workers stay in Turipaoa, the only village. If you visit the village, head inland from the dock for 1 block, turn right, and walk to the pass, where there's a grocery store. From there walk along the seawall for a view of the outer reef. You'll pass a picturesque Catholic church.

Note: There is no bank on Manihi.

As at Tikehau, Gilles Petrie's **Manihi Blue Nui Dive Center,** based at the Manihi Pearl Beach Resort (see below), provides top-of-the-line PADI diving. It charges about 6,700 CFP (US$84/£42) per one-tank dive.

WHERE TO STAY & DINE ON MANIHI

Manihi Pearl Beach Resort (★★)   This modern resort and the airstrip share a motu on the western end of Manihi's lagoon. As at Rangiroa, the beach is more pebbly than sandy, but guests can sun themselves on islets equipped with palm trees and chaise lounges, or on a faux beach beside a lagoonside horizon pool. A thatched-roof bar adjacent to the pool is cozy and conducive to meeting your fellow guests. In addition to diving, activities include swimming, snorkeling (you can snorkel outside the pass), canoeing, visiting pearl farms and the village, lagoon and deep-sea fishing, spending a day on a deserted motu, and cruising at sunset. The prevailing trade winds can generate a choppy lagoon under the 19 overwater bungalows here. The overwater and beachside units have mat-lined walls, natural wood floors, ceiling fans hanging from mat-lined roofs, king-size beds, writing tables, ample shower-only bathrooms, and covered porches with two recliners. Each beachfront unit also has a hammock strung between two palm trees out front, and the beachfront unit bathrooms are outdoors behind high wooden walls. Although a majority of guests here are European couples, the Tahitian staff makes English speakers feel at home.

B.P. 1, 99711 Manihi. ℂ 800/657-3275 or 50.84.54 for reservations, or 96.42.73. Fax 43.17.86 for reservations, or 96.42.72. www.pearlresorts.com. 40 units. 28,000 CFP–63,000 CFP (US$350–US$787/£177–£399) double. Meals 15,000 CFP (US$188/£95) per person per day. AE, MC, V. **Amenities:** Restaurant; bar; outdoor pool; spa; watersports equipment rentals; free bicycles; game room; activities desk; babysitting; laundry service. *In room:* A/C (in premium overwater bungalows), TV, dataport, minibar, coffeemaker, safe.

6 Fakarava

Southeast of Rangiroa and about 490km (304 miles) northeast of Tahiti, Fakarava's rectangular reef encloses French Polynesia's second-largest lagoon. This 60×24km (37×15 mile) aquamarine jewel is filled with such a rich variety of sea life that part of it has been designated a UNESCO nature preserve. Needless to say, there is some very good diving and snorkeling here.

The resort, airstrip, and main village, **Rotoava,** sit at the atoll's northeastern end, near **Garuae Pass,** the widest in the Tuamotus. It's so wide and deep that ships as large as the *Queen Elizabeth 2 (QE2)* can enter the lagoon. From there a road—facetiously dubbed "rue Flosse" because former French Polynesian President Gaston Flosse paved part of it prior to a visit by French President Jacques Chirac in 2003—runs for 30km (19 miles) along one of the South Pacific's longest motus. A smaller pass and the ancient village of **Tetamanu,** site of a restored 1834 Catholic church, lie at Fakarava's southeastern end, a 2-hour boat ride from the airport. Nondivers can spend a day on one of Fakarava's small islets surrounded by beaches of pink sand.

Rotoava village has a post office (with public phone), infirmary, school, white-washed church, and two general stores, but **no bank.**

WHERE TO STAY ON FAKARAVA

Hotel Maitai Dream   A sister of the Hotel Maitai Polynesia on Bora Bora (see "Where to Stay," in chapter 10), this unpretentious resort was showing some wear and tear during my recent visit but is still the top place to stay here. It sits beside the lagoon, a 15-minute ride by *le truck* or boat from the airstrip. A pier extends from the central building out over the multihued lagoon, but there are no overwater bunga-lows. Instead, the 28 units sit along or facing the pebbly beach, and most of their front porches have lagoon views. Built of timber with peaked shingle roofs, they are spa-cious and comfortably furnished with king-size and single beds, desks, and ceiling fans, and their ample bathrooms feature open-air showers with their own outside entry. The restaurant serves both indoor and outdoor tables and serves good French fare with Polynesian influences. Tahitians put on a dance show once a week. Kayaks, canoes, and snorkeling gear are free, but you'll pay for excellent lagoon excursions and diving.

B.P. 19, 98764 Fakarava (14km/8¾ miles from airport). ℂ 98.43.00. Fax 98.43.01. www.hotelmaitai.com. 28 units. 27,000 CFP–44,000 CFP (US$338–US$550/£171–£278). AE, MC, V. **Amenities:** Restaurant; bar; free kayaks, canoes, snorkeling gear; scooter rentals; activities desk; babysitting; laundry service. *In room:* TV, dataport, fridge, cof-feemaker, safe.

Motu Aito Paradise ⊛⊛   This remote pension is on beach-fringed Motu Aito, on the far southern end of the atoll. It's the creation of Manihi and Tila Salmon, a local couple who lived in New Zealand—where they polished their English—before retir-ing to their remote corner of paradise. Made of local materials, the thatched-roof bun-galows have enormous Polynesian charm if not luxurious amenities. Each unit has a double bed and a single bed, both on platforms. You can pull mosquito curtains over the large open windows, although the trade winds should keep the pests at bay.

Manihi and Tila do not have a bar, so BYOB. A 3-night minimum stay is required, understandable because Motu Aito is 1½-hours by truck and boat from the airport.

B.P. 12, 98763 Rotoava, Fakarava (on Motu Aito, south end of the lagoon). © **41.29.00** or 74.26.13. Fax 41.29.00. www.fakarava.org. 6 units. 15,000 CFP (US$188/£95) per person. Rates include all meals and airport transfers. No credit cards. 3-night minimum stay required. **Amenities:** Restaurant; free use of snorkeling gear. *In room:* No phone.

WHERE TO DINE ON FAKARAVA

Snack-Restaurant Teanuanua FRENCH/ITALIAN   Cecile Casseville's open-air lagoonside restaurant, on the south end of the village and a short walk north of Pension Havaiki, is a fine place for lunch while you're touring Rotoava, or for a sunset drink and early dinner anytime. Cecile, a Frenchwoman who once was a tour guide on Moorea, speaks English fluently. She offers salads, burgers, *casse-croûte* sandwiches, and grilled steak and fish for lunch. Dinner sees both French and Italian preparation of steaks and fish. Like every restaurant out here in the atolls, she serves a daily fresh fish special. I always come here for a sunset drink at a table actually in the lagoon.

Rotoava, south end of village. © **98.41.58.** Reservations recommended July–Aug. Burgers and sandwiches 700 CFP–800 CFP (US$8.75–US$10/£4.45–£5.05); main courses 1,300 CFP–2,000 CFP (US$16–US$25/£8.25–£12.65). MC, V. Daily 11:30am–2pm; Wed–Sun 6:30–8:30pm.

12

The Cook Islands: Rarotonga & Aitutaki

"**R**arotonga is cool," a French naval officer based in Papeete said to me. "It's like Tahiti—without the French."

He may have been jesting, but in many ways Rarotonga is a miniature Tahiti, and without the French, since The Cook Islands are an independent country associated with New Zealand. Like Tahiti, it has peaks and valleys surrounded by a coastal plain, beaches, an azure lagoon, and a reef extending about .5km (one-third mile) offshore.

Rarotonga's enchanting sister, Aitutaki, substitutes for Bora Bora in The Cook Islands. It is nearly surrounded by a large, shallow lagoon of multihued beauty and abundant sea life. Spending a day on the lagoon at this charming, atoll-framed outpost is a highlight of any visit here.

The Cook Islanders have more than beautiful islands in common with the people of French Polynesia, which lies some 900km (558 miles) to the east. Like the Tahitians, they enjoy having a good time, and this lust for happiness very quickly rubs off on visitors. They share almost 60% of their native language with the Tahitians, and their lifestyles and religions were similar in the old days. In fact, many Tahitians and Cook Islanders are related. Like their Tahitian cousins, the people here have a keen interest in their eastern Polynesian past, and they are very good at explaining those old ways to those of us who visit them today.

In addition to Polynesian culture, the Cooks have enough activities to satisfy almost anyone, including snorkeling, shopping, sightseeing, and diving. They have beaches of white sand, a friendly and fun-loving people who speak English, a variety of accommodations and restaurants in all price ranges, an excellent public transportation system, and some of the region's great bars and dance shows. No other place in the South Pacific packs so much to see and do into such small islands—and at relatively reasonable prices.

1 The Cook Islands Today

The 15 Cook Islands are scattered between Tahiti and Samoa, in an ocean area about one-third the size of the continental United States, yet all together they comprise only 241 sq. km (93 sq. miles) of land—a third the size of New York City. Two-thirds of that is on Rarotonga, which is only 32km (20 miles) around. With only 21 sq. km (8 sq. miles), Aitutaki is a mere speck in comparison.

THE NATURAL ENVIRONMENT The Cook Islands are divided both geographically and politically into **a Southern Group** and a **Northern Group.** The nine islands of the Southern Group are high enough to have hills, but only Rarotonga is mountainous. All but one of the remote, infrequently visited islands of the Northern Group are low-lying atolls, with circles of reef and coral islets enclosing lagoons. The few residents in the Northern Group earn their living fishing and growing black pearls.

The shoreline of **Rarotonga** consists of a slightly raised sandy bar backed by a swampy depression, which then gives rise to the valleys and mountains. Before the coming of missionaries in 1823, Rarotongans lived on the raised ground beyond the swampy flats, which they used for growing taro and other wet-footed crops. They built a remarkable road, the *Ara Metua* (back road), paved in part with stones. The route ran from village to village, almost around the island. It still exists, although the paved round-island road now runs near the shore. The area between the two roads appears to be bush but is in fact heavily cultivated with a plethora of crops and fruit trees. Otherwise the vegetation is typically tropical. The mountains and hills are covered with native brush, while the valley floors and flat coastal plains are studded with coconut and banana plantations and a wide range of flowering trees and shrubs.

THE GOVERNMENT The Cook Islands are an independent country in association with New Zealand, which provides for the national defense needs of the islands and renders substantial financial aid. Cook Islanders hold New Zealand citizenship, which means they can live there. New Zealanders, on the other hand, are not citizens of The Cook Islands and cannot live here without permission from the Immigration department. Although technically independent, the ties with New Zealand deprive the Cooks of a seat in the United Nations.

The country has a Westminster-style **parliament** led by a prime minister chosen by members of the majority party. Parliament meets twice a year, in February and March and from July to September. There is also a **House of Ariki** (that is, hereditary chiefs), which advises the government on matters of traditional custom and land tenure.

THE ECONOMY More than half of the country's gross domestic product comes from tourism, black pearls (its number-one export), and agriculture, mainly tropical fruit and juices. It relies to a large extent on overseas aid and cash sent home by islanders living abroad. Many Cook Islanders have pulled up stakes and left for better employment, education, and healthcare in New Zealand, resulting in a decrease in population. The exodus has resulted in a shortage of labor, especially in the tourism industry (don't be surprised to see Australians and Fijians working at the major hotels).

2 The Cook Islands Yesterday: History 101

Legend has it that the first Polynesians arrived in The Cook Islands by canoe from the islands of modern-day French Polynesia about A.D. 1200, although anthropologists think the first of them may have come much earlier. In any event, they discovered The Cook Islands as part of the Polynesian migrations that settled all of the South Pacific. Before Europeans arrived, feudal chiefs, known as *ariki,* ruled the islands. They owned all the land within their jurisdictions and held life-and-death power over their subjects. Like other Polynesians, the islanders believed in a hierarchy of gods and spirits, among them Tangaroa, whose well-endowed carved image is now a leading handicraft item.

The Spanish explorer Alvaro de Mendaña laid the first European eyes on The Cook Islands, sighting Pukapuka in 1595. As happened in so many South Pacific island groups, Capt. James Cook stumbled onto some of the islands during his voyages in 1773 and 1777; he named them the Hervey Islands. (A Russian cartographer later

---

Fun Fact **On Her Merry Way**

When the 19th-century missionaries sheared a woman's locks for misbehaving, she would appear in public wearing a crown of flowers and continue on her merry way.

---

changed them to the Cook Islands.) Captain Cook sailed around the Southern Group but missed Rarotonga, which apparently was visited first by the mutineers of HMS *Bounty,* under Fletcher Christian (see "French Polynesia Yesterday: History 101," in chapter 7). There is no official record of the visit, but oral history on Rarotonga has it that a great ship arrived offshore about the time of the mutiny.

MORE MISSIONARIES   The man who claimed to have discovered Rarotonga was the Rev. John Williams of the London Missionary Society. Williams came from London to Tahiti in 1818 as a missionary, and he set up a base of operations on Raiatea in the Society Islands, from which he intended to spread Christianity throughout the South Pacific. On his way to Australia in 1821, Williams left two teachers at Aitutaki. By the time Williams returned 2 years later, they had converted everyone on Aitutaki.

Pleased with this success, Williams headed off in search of Rarotonga. It took a few weeks, during which he stopped at Mangaia, Mauke, Mitiaro, and Atiu, but he eventually found Rarotonga in July 1823.

Williams established churches in the villages of Ngatangiia, Arorangi, and Avarua, but he spent most of the next 4 years forcing the locals to build a new ship, the *Messenger of Peace,* which he eventually sailed west in search of new islands and more converts. Those of us who take a dim view of proselytizing would argue that the *Messenger of Peace* extracted a measure of revenge by delivering Williams to a cannibal's oven in Vanuatu. Whatever your opinion, his reputed bones were later recovered and reburied in Samoa (see chapter 13). Meanwhile, the missionaries he left behind quickly converted all of the islanders to his rock-ribbed version of Christianity.

On Rarotonga, the missionaries divided the land into rectangular parcels, one for each family. Choice parcels were set aside for the church buildings and rectories. Rarotongans moved down from the high ground near their gardens and became seaside dwellers for the first time. All land except church and government property is still communally owned; it can be leased but not sold.

Out of the seeds planted by Williams and the London Missionary Society grew the present-day Cook Islands Christian Church, to which about 60% of all Cook Islanders belong. The churches, many of them built of coral block in the 19th century, are the center of life in every village, and the Takamoa College Bible School that the missionaries established in 1837 still teaches in Avarua. The Cook Islands Christian Church owns the land under its buildings; the churches of all other denominations sit on leased property.

THE COMING OF THE KIWIS   It was almost inevitable that the Cook Islands would be caught up in a wave of colonial expansion that swept across the South Pacific in the late 1800s. The French, who had established Tahiti as a protectorate, wanted to expand their influence west, and in 1888 they sent a warship to Manihiki in what is now the Northern Group of the Cooks. Although the British had made no claim to the islands, locals quickly sewed together a Union Jack and ran it up a pole. The

French ship turned away. Shortly thereafter the British declared a protectorate over The Cook Islands, and the Union Jack went up officially.

In 1901, Britain acceded to a request from New Zealand's prime minister, Richard Seddon, to include the Cook Islands within the boundaries of his newly independent country. In addition to engineering the transfer, Seddon is best remembered for his policy of prohibiting the Chinese—and most other Asians—from settling in the Cooks.

Otherwise, New Zealand, itself a former colony, never did much to exploit—or develop—the Cook Islands. For all practical purposes, the Cook Islands remained a South Seas backwater for the 72 years of New Zealand rule, with a brief interlude during World War II when U.S. troops built the airstrip on Aitutaki.

SIR ALBERT & SIR GEOFF The situation began to change after 1965, when the Cook Islands became self-governing in association with New Zealand. The first prime minister was Sir Albert Henry, one of the South Pacific's most colorful modern characters. He ruled for a controversial 13 years, during which time his government enlarged Rarotonga's airport (Queen Elizabeth II was on hand for the grand opening) and built the Rarotongan Resort (now the Rarotongan Beach Resort & Spa). Although Sir Albert lost the national elections in 1978 and was later indicted for bribery, he remained highly popular. When he died in 1981, his body was taken around Rarotonga on the back of a pickup truck; the road was lined with mourners.

Dr. Tom Davis, a Cook Islander who had worked in the United States for NASA, succeeded Sir Albert. The premiership returned to Henry hands in 1989, with the victory of Sir Geoffrey Henry, Sir Albert's cousin. Sir Geoffrey's tenure is best remembered

All in the Family

The missionaries weren't the only English folk to have a lasting impact on the Cook Islands.

In 1863 a farmhand from Gloucester named William Marsters accepted the job as caretaker of tiny, uninhabited Palmerston Island, an atoll sitting all by itself northwest of Rarotonga. He took his Cook Islander wife and her sister with him. A Portuguese sailor and his wife, a first cousin of Mrs. Marsters, joined them.

The Portuguese sailor skipped the island within a year, leaving his wife behind. Marsters then declared himself to be an Anglican minister and married himself to both his wife's sister and her first cousin.

Marsters had three families, one with each of his wives. Within 25 years, he had 17 children and 54 grandchildren. He divided the island into three parts, one for each clan, which he designated the "head," "tail," and "middle" families. He prohibited marriages within a clan (in a twist of logic, he apparently thought sleeping with your half-brother or half-sister wasn't incest).

Obviously there was a lot of marrying outside the clans, for today there are thousands of Marsters in the Cook Islands and New Zealand. All trace their roots to Palmerston Island, though only 50 or so live there.

> **(Tips Why Hurry?**
>
> Cook Islanders live by the old Polynesian tradition known as "island time." The clock moves more slowly here, as it does in other South Pacific islands. Everything will get done in due course, not necessarily when you want it done. In other words, service can be slow by Western standards. But why hurry? You're on vacation.

for the government-backed Sheraton Hotel project at Vaimaanga, on Rarotonga's south coast, which went unfinished after being caught up in a scandal. The project left the Cook Islands government seriously in debt. Although plans had been announced to resume work on the hotel as I write, the property has been caught up in a land dispute. Meantime, the buildings stand hauntingly unfinished.

Succeeding governments have adopted pro-business policies, and despite a dip after the terrorist attacks of September 11, 2001, record numbers of tourists, more than half of them from New Zealand, have fueled the economy. The country has seen a boom of new resorts, motels, and bungalows.

3 The Cook Islanders

The Cook Islands have a population of about 18,000, more or less, because the figure fluctuates as some islanders move to New Zealand and others return. More than half reside on Rarotonga. A majority of the population is of Polynesian descent. In culture, language, and physical appearance they are closely akin to both the Tahitians and the Maoris of New Zealand. Only on Pukapuka and Nassau atolls to the far northwest, where the residents are more like the Samoans, is the heritage significantly different.

Modern Cook Islanders have maintained the warmth, friendliness, and generosity that characterize Polynesians. Like their ancestors, they put great emphasis on family life. Within the extended family, a guiding principle remains share and share alike, and no one ever goes without a meal or a roof over his or her head. In fact, they may be generous to a fault: Many of the small grocery stores they run reputedly stay on the verge of bankruptcy.

Although not a matriarchy, Cook Islands culture places great responsibility on the wife and mother. Women are in charge of the section of land upon which their families live. They decide which crops and fruit trees to plant, they collect the money for household expenses, and, acting collectively and within the churches, they decide how the village will be run. When the mother dies, the land passes jointly to her children.

In addition to those who are pure Polynesian, a significant minority in the Cook Islands is of mixed European-Polynesian descent. There are also a number of New Zealanders and Australians plus a few Americans and Europeans, most on Rarotonga. There are very few Chinese or other Asians here.

4 Language

Nearly everyone in the Cook Islands speaks English, which is an official language along with Cook Islands Maori, a Polynesian language similar to Tahitian and New Zealand Maori. A little knowledge of the latter is helpful, primarily because nearly all place names are Maori.

Cook Islands Maori has eight consonants and five vowels. The vowels are pronounced in the Roman fashion: *ah, ay, ee, oh, oo* instead of *a, e, i, o, u* as in English. The consonants used are *k, m, n, p, r, t,* and *v*. These are pronounced much as they are in English. There is also *ng*, which is pronounced as the *ng* in "ring." The language is written phonetically; that is, every letter is pronounced. If there are three vowels in a row, each is sounded. The name of Mangaia Island, for example, is pronounced "Mahn-gah-*ee*-ah."

Generally, Cook Islanders speak English to visitors, but here are some helpful expressions with pronunciations:

English	Maori	Pronunciation
hello	kia orana	*kee*-ah oh-*rah*-nah
goodbye	aere ra	ah-*ay*-ray rah
thank you	meitaki	may-ee-*tah*-kee
how are you?	peea koe?	*pay*-ay-ah *ko*-ay
yes	ae	*ah*-ay
no	kare	*kah*-ray
good luck	kia manuia	*kee*-ah mah-*nu*-ee-ah
European person	Papa'a	pah-*pah*-ah
wraparound sarong	pareu	*pah*-ree-oo
keep out	tapu	*tah*-poo
small island	motu	*moh*-too

5 Visitor Information & Maps

VISITOR INFORMATION

The helpful staff of the Cook Islands **Tourism Corporation** provides information upon request. The address is P.O. Box 14, Rarotonga, Cook Islands (© **29-435;** fax 21-435; www.cookislands.travel). The main office and visitor center is west of the traffic circle, in the heart of Avarua. It's open Monday to Friday 8am to 4pm, and Saturday 9am to noon. Other offices are:

- **North America:** 1133-160A Street, White Rock, BC V4A 7G9, Canada (© **604/ 541-9877;** fax 604/541-9812; camadamanager@cook-islands.com)
- **New Zealand:** 1/127 Symonds St. (P.O. Box 37391), Parnell, Auckland (© **09/ 366-1199;** fax 09/309-1876; nzmanager@cook-islands.com)
- **Australia:** P.O. Box 20, Guildord, NSW 2161 (© **02/9955-0446;** fax 02/9955-0447; ausmanager@cook-islands.com)
- **United Kingdom:** Colechurch House, 1 London Bridge Walk, London SE1 2SX (© **020/7367-0928;** fax 020/7407-3810; ukmanager@cook-islands.com)
- **Germany:** Petersburgstrasse 94, 10247 Berlin (© **30/4225-6027;** fax 30/4225-6286; europemanager@cook-islands.com)

When you get to Rarotonga, stop by the visitor center and pick up brochures and other current information, especially Jason's *What's On in the Cook Islands* (www. jasons.com) and the Cook Islands *Sun,* two free tourist publications that are full of facts, advertisements, and excellent maps of the islands. The daily newspapers, the *Cook Islands News* and the *Cook Islands Herald,* provide radio and TV schedules, weather forecasts, shipping information, and advertisements for island nights and other entertainment.

6 Entry Requirements

Visas are not required for visitors, who can stay for 31 days if they have valid passports, onward or return air tickets (they will be examined at the immigration desk on arrival), and sufficient funds. New Zealand citizens do not need passports to enter the Cook Islands, but do need them to reenter New Zealand. Extensions are granted on a month-to-month basis for up to 5 more months; apply at the Immigration Department in Avarua. Visitors intending to stay more than 6 months must apply in advance from their home country to the **Principal Immigration Officer,** Ministry of Labour and Commerce, P.O. Box 61, Rarotonga, Cook Islands (© **29-363**).

No **vaccinations** are required unless you are coming from a yellow-fever-, plague-, or cholera-affected area.

CUSTOMS   See "Fast Facts: Rarotonga & the Cook Islands," later in this chapter, for what you can bring into the Cook Islands, and "Fast Facts: South Pacific," in chapter 2, for what you can bring home.

7 When to Go—Climate, Holidays & Events
THE CLIMATE

Rarotonga and Aitutaki, which are about as far south of the equator as the Hawaiian Islands are north of it, enjoy a tropical climate. Even during the summer months of January and February, the high temperatures on Rarotonga average a comfortable 84°F (29°C), although there can be hot, humid, and sticky summer days. The climes are much more pleasant during the winter, from June to August, when the average high drops to 77°F (25°C), and the ends of Antarctic cold fronts can bring a few downright chilly nights. It's a good idea to bring a light sweater or jacket for evening wear during the winter months.

December through April is both the cyclone (hurricane) and rainy season. There always is a chance that a cyclone will hit during these months (three struck almost back-to-back early in 2005), but most of the rain comes in short, heavy cloudbursts that are followed by sunshine. Rain clouds usually hang around Rarotonga's mountain peaks, even during the dry season (June to Aug).

In short, there is no bad time weather-wise to visit the Cook Islands, although the shoulder months of April, May, September, and October usually provide the best combination of sunshine and warmth.

Moments Swinging Hips

I never visit the Cook Islands without watching the hips swing at a traditional dance show. Take my word for it: Had the crew of HMS *Bounty* seen the dancing on Rarotonga instead of Tahiti, even Captain Bligh might have mutinied! The best times to see the best dancing come during the Dancer of the Year contest in mid-April and during Cook Islands National Self Governing Commemoration in early August.

HOLIDAYS & EVENTS

Legal holidays are New Year's Day, Anzac (Memorial) Day (Apr 25), Good Friday, Easter Monday, the Queen's Birthday (first Mon in June), Gospel Days (last Mon in July and Oct), Constitution Day (Aug 4), National Gospel Day (Oct 26), Aitutaki Gospel Day (Oct 27, Aitutaki only), Christmas Day, and Boxing Day (Dec 26). Government offices and many businesses are closed on Monday if a holiday falls on a weekend.

The busiest season is from late June through August, when New Zealanders and Australians escape their own winters. Make hotel reservations early for these months. Many Cook Islanders live in New Zealand and come home for Christmas; you can easily get a room, but airline seats are hard to come by during that holiday season.

The three major national festivals are the **Dancer of the Year Contest,** in mid-April; the Cook Islands **National Self Governing Commemoration,** in early August; and **Tiare Week,** the first week in December.

8 Money

Although the local government mints some unusual coins and a $3 note, the New Zealand dollar is the medium of exchange in the Cook Islands. At the time of this writing, one New Zealand dollar is worth about US80¢/40p. The exchange rate fluctuates,

The New Zealand Dollar, the U.S. & Canadian Dollars & the British Pound

At this writing, US$1/C$1 = approximately NZ$1.25 (or, the other way around, NZ$1 = US80¢), which is the exchange rate I used to calculate the dollar values given in this book. **For British readers:** At this writing, £1 = approximately NZ$2.50 (or, NZ$1 = 40p), the rate used to calculate the pound values below. *Note:* International exchange rates fluctuate daily and sometimes by a lot. So the values in this table may not be the same when you travel to the Cook Islands. Use the following table only as a guide. Find the current rates at **www.xe.com.**

NZ$	US$/C$	UK£	NZ$	US$/$C	UK£
.25	0.20	0.10	15.00	12.00	6.00
.50	0.40	0.20	20.00	16.00	8.00
.75	0.60	0.30	25.00	20.00	10.00
1.00	0.80	0.40	30.00	24.00	12.00
2.00	1.60	0.80	35.00	28.00	14.00
3.00	2.40	1.20	40.00	32.00	16.00
4.00	3.20	1.60	45.00	36.00	18.00
5.00	4.00	2.00	50.00	40.00	20.00
6.00	4.80	2.40	75.00	60.00	30.00
7.00	5.60	2.80	100.00	80.00	40.00
8.00	6.40	3.20	125.00	100.00	50.00
9.00	7.20	3.60	150.00	120.00	60.00
10.00	8.00	4.00	200.00	160.00	80.00

Fun Fact Tangaroa & Her Highness

One side of the famous Cook Islands dollar coin bears the likeness of the Polynesian god of fertility, Tangaroa—including his private part. On the other side is the image of Queen Elizabeth II, who was reportedly not at all pleased about sharing the coin with the uninhibited Tangaroa.

---

so check the business sections of most daily newspapers or find the present rate on currency conversion websites such as **www.xe.com**.

HOW TO GET LOCAL CURRENCY **Westpac Bank, ANZ Bank,** and the **Bank of the Cook Islands** have offices west of the traffic circle on the main road in Avarua. Westpac and ANZ have ATMs here and at other locations around the island. Banking hours are Monday to Friday 9am to 3pm (4pm at ANZ Bank). **GlobalEX/Western Union,** in Mana Court west of the traffic circle (② **29-907**), changes currency and traveler's checks, often at better rates than the banks.

CREDIT CARDS American Express, MasterCard, and Visa are widely accepted by hotels and restaurants on Rarotonga and Aitutaki. Only the major hotels and car-rental firms accept Diner's Club cards. Discover cards are not accepted anywhere. If you're going to Aitutaki or another outer island, you can use credit cards at the larger hotels and some restaurants, but not everywhere. Therefore, carry cash or small-denomination traveler's checks.

9 Getting to & Around the Cook Islands

GETTING THERE

Air New Zealand flies directly to Rarotonga from Los Angeles, Tahiti, Fiji, and Auckland. Its flights from and to Los Angeles stop for an hour or so in Tahiti, less than 2 hours away; accordingly, the Cook Islands can easily be combined with a visit to French Polynesia. **Polynesian Blue** has service from Sydney and Auckland. For details, see "Getting There & Getting Around" in chapter 2.

ARRIVING The terminal at **Rarotonga International Airport (RAR),** the country's only gateway, is 2km (1¼ miles) west of Avarua. Westpac Pacific Banking's terminal office is open 1 hour before and after all international flights; it has windows inside and outside the departure lounge. It has an ATM outside the arrivals door. Small shops in the departure lounge sell handicrafts, liquor, cigarettes, and stamps. Arriving passengers can purchase duty-free items before clearing Immigration.

Representatives of all the accommodations will be waiting outside Customs to usher you to a bus operated by **Raro Tours** (see below), which will take you to your hotel.

DEPARTING Raro Tours (② **25-325**) begins picking up departing passengers about 2 hours before each international flight. Your hotel or guest house can reserve a seat for you and tell you when it will arrive at your accommodation. Before clearing Immigration you must pay a **departure tax** of NZ$30 (US$24/£12) for adults, half for children between the ages of 2 and 12, in New Zealand currency at Westpac Bank's airport booth, or in advance at the bank's Avarua office. No tax is imposed for domestic departures.

Tips **How to Save If You're Going to Aitutaki**

Air Rarotonga and local travel agencies such as **Island Hopper Vacations** (© **22-026;** www.islandhoppervacations.com) will book hotels and most activities on the other islands free of charge. If you are going to Aitutaki, for example, you can save as much as NZ$100 (US$80/£40) by buying a package that includes airfare and accommodations.

GETTING AROUND THE COOK ISLANDS

Air Rarotonga (© **22-888;** www.airraro.com) is the country's only airline, and it's a good one. It has several flights from Monday through Saturday to Aitutaki and one per weekday to Atiu, Mauke, Mangaia, and Mitiaro. Regular round-trip fares are about NZ$370 (US$296/£148) to Aitutaki, slightly less to the other islands in the Southern Group. You can save with Air Rarotonga's discounted but restricted fares, which can be as little as NZ$150 (US$120/£60) round-trip to Aitutaki. Check the airline's website for special fares.

Don't forget to reconfirm your return flight.

GETTING AROUND RAROTONGA

BY BUS   When people say "catch the bus" on Rarotonga, they mean the **Cook's Island Bus** (© **25-512**), which is actually two big yellow "Cook's Passenger Transport" buses that leave the Cook's Corner shopping center in Avarua going clockwise and counterclockwise around the island, respectively. Clockwise buses depart on the hour from Avarua Monday to Saturday from 7am to 4pm, and Sunday from 8am to noon. Counterclockwise buses depart once an hour Monday to Friday beginning at 8:25am. Each takes 50 minutes to circle the island. There's less frequent, one-bus evening service Monday to Saturday from 6 to 10pm (to 1:30am on Fri night). The tourist publications available from the Cook Islands Tourism Corporation have the schedules, or ask your hotel receptionist when a bus will pass. Regardless of the length of the ride, daytime fares are NZ$3 (US$2.40/£1.20) one-way, NZ$5 (US$4/£2) round-trip. You can buy 1-day passes or a 10-ride book of tickets for NZ$20 (US$16/£8). The buses cost NZ$5 (US$4/£2) at night.

BY RENTAL CAR & SCOOTER   **Budget Rent-A-Car** (© **800/527-0700** or 20-895; www.budget.co.ck) and **Avis** (© **800/331-1212** or 22-833; rentacar@avis.co.ck), are the best companies here. Both have booths in Avarua west of the traffic circle and at several hotels, and both charge about NZ$62 (US$50/£25) per day with unlimited kilometers. Both rent convertibles, but book early for one.

Other local rental companies include **Rarotonga Rentals** (© **22-326;** www.rarotongarentals.co.ck), **Island Car & Bike Hire** (© **27-632** or 55-278; www.islandcarhire.co.ck), **BT Rentals** (© **23-586**), and **Fun Rentals** (© **22-426**).

Cook Islanders are as likely to travel by motorbike or scooter as they are by car. **Polynesian Bike Hire Ltd.** (© **20-895**) and the companies above all rent motorbikes and scooters on a daily or weekly basis. Rates start at about NZ$25 (US$20/£10) per day. Polynesian Bike Hire Ltd. and Budget Rent-A-Car share offices (see above).

Driver's Licenses   You must have a valid **Cook Islands driver's license** before operating any motorized vehicle. To get one, go to Police Headquarters (on the main road

Rarotonga

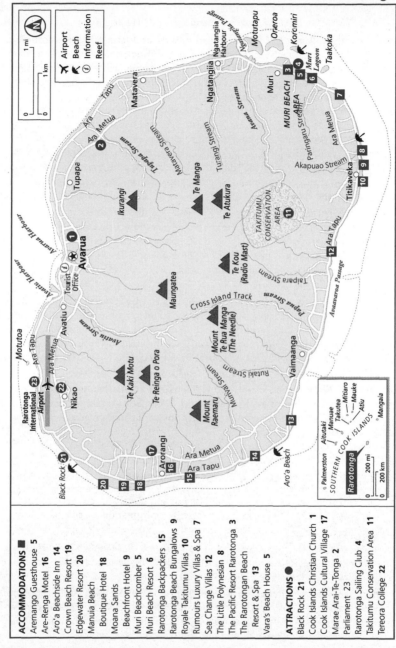

ACCOMMODATIONS ■
Aremango Guesthouse **5**
Are-Renga Motel **16**
Aro'a Beachside Inn **14**
Crown Beach Resort **19**
Edgewater Resort **20**
Manuia Beach
  Boutique Hotel **18**
Moana Sands
Beachfront Hotel **9**
Muri Beachcomber **5**
Muri Beach Resort **6**
Rarotonga Backpackers **15**
Rarotonga Beach Bungalows **9**
Royale Takitumu Villas **10**
Rumours Luxury Villas & Spa **7**
Sea Change Villas **12**
The Little Polynesian **8**
The Pacific Resort Rarotonga **3**
The Rarotongan Beach
  Resort & Spa **13**
Vara's Beach House **5**

ATTRACTIONS ●
Black Rock **21**
Cook Islands Christian Church **1**
Cook Islands Cultural Village **17**
Marae Arai-Te-Tonga **2**
Parliament **23**
Rarotonga Sailing Club **4**
Takitumu Conservation Area **11**
Tereora College **22**

just west of the Avarua traffic circle), present your valid overseas license, and pay NZ$10 (US$8/£4). If you want to rent a motorbike or scooter, and you aren't licensed to drive them at home, you have to take a driving test and pay an additional NZ$6 (US$4.80/£2.40). All drivers must be at least 16 years old. The license desk is open Monday to Saturday 8am to 3pm. (The laminated license with your photo makes a nice souvenir.)

Driving Regulations   Driving is on the **left side** of the road, as in the United Kingdom, Australia, and New Zealand. The strictly-enforced speed limit is 40kmph (25 mph) in the countryside and 30kmph (19 mph) in Avarua and the villages (I rented a Toyota here once that wouldn't go that slow!). The local cops strictly enforce the drunk-driving laws, so take public transit or a designated driver when drinking. Gasoline (petrol) is available from service stations in Avarua, at the 24-hour Oasis Energy service station west of the airport terminal, and at some village shops. The road around the island is paved but somewhat rough; always be on the alert for dogs, chickens, potholes, pigs, and tourists on motor scooters.

BY BICYCLE   There are no hills on the round-island road, so touring by bicycle (or *push bikes,* as they're called here) is a pleasure. Several hotels have bicycles available for their guests to use. **Ace Rentals** (© **22-833;** rentacar@avis.co.ck), **Polynesian Bike Hire Ltd.** (© **20-895**), **Tipani Rentals** (© **22-327**), and **BT Rentals** (© **20-331**) rent them for NZ$8 (US$6.40/£3.20) per day. The latter is at Muri Beach.

BY TAXI   A number of cars and minibuses scurry around with TAXI signs on top. Service is available daily from 7am to midnight and whenever international flights arrive. As a rule of thumb, taxi fares should be about NZ$2 (US$1.60/80p) per kilometer (half-mile), but the drivers are free to set their rates at will. Negotiate a fare before you get in. Phone **JP Taxis** (© **26-572**), **A's Taxi** (© **27-021**), **Ngatangiia Taxi** (© **22-238**), **BK Taxi** (© **20-019**), or **Muri Beach Taxi** (© **21-625**).

BY SHIP   *Adventures in Paradise,* the 1950s television series, may have glorified the South Pacific copra schooners that plied the South Seas, trading corned beef and printed cotton for copra, but to put it bluntly, you can't count on getting anywhere in the Cook Islands by ship these days.

FAST FACTS: Rarotonga & the Cook Islands

The following facts apply to the Cook Islands and to Rarotonga specifically. See "Fast Facts: Aitutaki," later in this chapter, for information specific to Aitutaki Island. Also see "Fast Facts: The South Pacific," at the end of chapter 2.

American Express   The Cook Islands have no American Express representative.

Area Codes   The Cook Islands do not have domestic area codes. The international country code is **682**.

Bookstores   **Bounty Bookshop** (© 26-660), next to the main post office in Avarua, and the Cook Islands **Trading Corporation (C.I.T.C.;** © 22-000), on the waterfront, both sell paperback novels, maps of Rarotonga and Aitutaki, and books about the Cook Islands and the South Pacific in general.

Business Hours   Most shops on Rarotonga are open Monday to Friday 8am to 4pm and Saturday 8am to noon. Some small grocery stores in the villages are open in the evenings and for limited hours on Sunday. Most government offices are open Monday to Friday 8am to 4pm.

Camera & Film A reasonable selection of color-print film is available at many shops in Avarua. One-hour processing of color-print film is available at **Cook Islands Trading Corporation (C.I.T.C.;** ℂ **22-000),** on the waterfront. Color slides are sent to New Zealand for processing.

Currency Exchange **Westpac Bank, ANZ Bank,** and the **Bank of the Cook Islands** have offices west of the traffic circle on the main road in Avarua. Westpac and ANZ have ATMs. Banking hours are Monday to Friday 9am to 3pm (4pm at ANZ). **GlobalEX,** in Mana Court west of the traffic circle (ℂ **29-907),** changes currency and travelers checks, often at better rates than the banks.

Customs **Customs** allowances are 2 liters of spirits or wine, 200 cigarettes or 50 cigars, and NZ$250 (US$200/£100) in other goods. Arriving passengers can purchase items from the duty-free shop and change money before clearing Immigration. Firearms, ammunition, and indecent materials are prohibited, as are live animals, including pets (they will be placed in quarantine until you leave the country). Personal effects are not subject to duty. All food and other agricultural products must be declared and will be inspected.

Drug Laws Dangerous drugs and narcotics are illegal; possession can land you in a very unpleasant jail for a very long time.

Drugstores **C.I.T.C. Pharmacy** (ℂ **29-292),** in the C.I.T.C. shopping center west of the traffic circle, and **Cook Islands Pharmacy** (ℂ **27-577),** beside the stream east of the traffic circle, dispense prescription medications and carry toiletries. Cook Islands Pharmacy has a small outlet at Muri Beach (ℂ **27-587).** The clinics on the outer islands have a limited supply of prescription medications.

Electricity Electricity is 230 volts, 50 cycles, so converters are necessary in order to operate U.S. appliances. The plugs, like those of New Zealand and Australia, have two angled prongs, so an adapter will also be needed. If your appliances or the table lamps in your room don't work, check to see whether the switch on the wall outlet is turned on.

Embassies & Consulates The New Zealand high commissioner's office is at the traffic circle in Avarua, but no other foreign government maintains an embassy or consulate here. In case of a problem, seek advice from the travel facilitation and consular officer in the **Ministry of Foreign Affairs** (ℂ **20-507).** The U.S. embassy in Wellington, New Zealand, has jurisdiction.

Emergencies & Police The emergency number for the **police** is ℂ **999;** for an **ambulance** or the **hospital,** ℂ **998;** for **fire,** ℂ **996.** The non-emergency **police** number is ℂ **22-499.**

Etiquette & Customs Dress in the Cook Islands is informal. Shorts of respectable length (that is, not of the short-short variety) can be worn during the day by both men and women, but beach attire should stay at the beach. Nudity is illegal, as is topless sunbathing, though some European women do it anyway. The colorful wraparound *pareu* is popular with local women. Evenings from May to September can be cool, so trousers, skirts, light jackets, sweaters, or wraps are in order after dark. The only neckties to be seen are at church on Sunday.

Eyeglasses **Cook Islands Optics** (✆ **26-605**), in the Mana Court shopping center, west of the traffic circle.

Firearms Don't even think about it—they're illegal.

Gambling There are no gambling casinos in the Cook Islands, but you can bet on the Australian and New Zealand lotteries at the C.I.T.C. shopping center.

Healthcare The **hospital,** behind the golf course (✆ **22-664,** or 998 in case of emergency), has a 24-hour emergency room. Ask your hotel to recommend a doctor in private practice.

Hitchhiking It's not illegal, but is frowned upon by the government.

Insects There are no poisonous insects in the Cook Islands. Mosquitoes are plentiful, especially during the summer and in the inland areas. Insect repellent and mosquito coils can be bought at the pharmacies and most village shops.

Internet Access All accommodations have Internet access for their guests. Avarua has several cybercafes including **Telecom Cook Islands** (✆ **29-680;** www. telecom.co.ck), the country's sole communications provider. It has access in its main office (see "Telephone," below) and in its **TelePost** outlet in the C.I.T.C. shopping center (✆ **29-940**). The main office is open 24 hours a day. TelePost is open Monday to Friday 8am to 4:30pm and Saturday 8:30am to noon. Access at both costs NZ$6 (US$4.80/£2.40) for 30 minutes.

Wi-Fi–capable laptops can tune in to **hot spots** in Telekom's two offices and at Avatiu Harbour, the airport, The Rarotongan Beach Resort & Spa, and the Edgewater Resort. The Pacific Resort Rarotonga has its own system. More hot spots are being added; look for the black-and-white bull's-eye signs. You must buy a prepaid wireless access card, available from Telekom and many shops. The cards start at NZ$15 (US$12/£6) for 50 megabytes of downloaded data (they're priced by the amount of data moved, not access time), which I found more than sufficient to check my e-mail and do my banking over 10 days.

Or you can sign up for a snail's pace "Temporary Oyster" dial-up account at Telecom's main office. There's a one-time NZ$25 (US$20/£10) connection fee, plus NZ$7 (US$5.60/£2.80) per hour spent online, which can be billed to your major credit card. In addition, your hotel will tack on the cost of the local phone calls and, quite likely, a surcharge. Sign up in the customer service office, which is open Monday to Friday 8am to 4pm.

Laundry & Dry Cleaning **Snowbird Laundry & Dry Cleaners** has 1-day laundry and dry cleaning service at its main plant in Arorangi (✆ **20-952**) and a small laundry opposite Avatiu Harbour (✆ **21-952**). It will pick up and deliver if you or your hotel staff calls in advance.

Libraries The **Cook Islands Library and Museum,** in Avarua near the Cook Islands Christian Church (✆ **26-468**), is open Monday to Friday 9am to 1pm and Saturday 9:30am to 12:30pm, with additional hours on Tuesday from 4 to 8pm. The library has a fine collection of works on the South Pacific, including many hard-to-find books.

Liquor Laws The legal drinking age is 21. Bottled liquor, beer, and wine are available from several stores. Bars and nightclubs close promptly at midnight

Saturday. Hotel bars can sell alcoholic beverages to their guests all day Sunday, and restaurants can resume service on Sunday at 6pm.

Mail **Cook Islands Post** is located at the traffic circle in Avarua. Hours are Monday to Friday 8am to 4pm and Saturday 8am to noon. There's a branch office opposite Titikaveka College on Rarotonga's south coast, which is open Monday to Friday 8am to noon and 1 to 3:30pm. Each of the other islands has a post office. There is no mail delivery, so every address includes a post office box.

Newspapers & Magazines Two local newspapers, the **Cook Islands News** (www.cookislandsnews.com) and the **Cook Islands Herald** (www.ciherald.co.ck), contain local, regional, and world news; radio and TV schedules; shipping schedules; a weather map for the South Pacific; and notices of local events, including advertisements for "island nights" at the hotels. Copies are available at the Bounty Bookshop and the large C.I.T.C. shopping center in the center of Avarua.

Radio & TV Rarotonga has one AM radio station and one FM radio station. Programming is in both English and Maori. One TV channel broadcast news, entertainment, and innumerable rugby games. Most hotels subscribe to a satellite service carrying CNN International and other channels.

Safety The streets here are safe. Burglaries and other property thefts can occur, however, so don't leave valuables in your hotel room or your belongings untended elsewhere.

Smoking Smoking is legally prohibited in many public buildings but not at hotels, businesses, and restaurants. Ask for a nonsmoking room at your hotel and an outside table at restaurants.

Taxes The government imposes a **value-added tax (VAT),** which is included in the price of most goods and services. You should ask if the VAT is included in the rates quoted by the hotels and hostels, or whether it will be added to your bill when you leave. Unlike in Europe, the VAT here is not refunded at the end of your visit. The **departure tax** on international flights is NZ$30 (US$24/£12) for adults, NZ$15 (US$12/£6) for children, which you can pay at the airport or in advance at Westpac Bank in Avarua.

Telephone Land-line telephone service is provided throughout the country by **Telecom Cook Islands** (TCI; ✆ **29-680;** www.telecom.co.ck). Although calls are exorbitantly expensive, it's a modern system.

To call the Cook Islands: Dial the international access code (011 from the U.S.; 00 from the U.K., Ireland, or New Zealand; or 0011 from Australia), the Cook Islands country code **682,** and the local number (there are no area codes within the Cook Islands).

To make international calls from within the Cook Islands: First dial **00,** then the country code (U.S. or Canada 1, U.K. 44, Ireland 353, Australia 61, New Zealand 64), and then the area code and phone number. International calls cost NZ$2.14 (US$1.71/85p) per minute to North America, NZ$3.20 (US$2.55/£1.30) to the United Kingdom and Europe. Rates to Australia and New Zealand are NZ$1.05 (US85¢/40p). Those are the per-minute fees, but you can talk up to 1 hour for NZ$10 (US$8/£4) before the minute rates resume.

Local access numbers: You cannot use a credit card to make calls in the Cook Islands, but several long-distance carriers have access numbers their customers can dial from within the Cook Islands to have international calls billed to their credit or prepaid cards, including **AT&T** (ⓒ **09111**) and **MCI** (ⓒ **09121**). You'll pay the regular local call charges on top of the international rates if you dial them from your hotel room.

To make domestic calls within the Cook Islands: No prefix or area code is required for domestic long distance calls, so dial the local number.

For directory assistance: Dial ⓒ **010** for domestic information, ⓒ **017** for international numbers.

For operator assistance: Dial ⓒ **010** for operator assistance in making a local call, ⓒ **015** for the international operator.

Toll-free numbers: Calling a 1-800 number in the U.S. or Canada from here is not toll-free. In fact, it costs the same as an overseas call.

Pay phones: Public pay phones use a Kia Orana **prepaid card.** Cards are sold in NZ$5, NZ$10, NZ$20, and NZ$50 denominations (the equivalent of US$4, US$8, US$16, and US$40/£2, £4, £8, and £20) at Telecom post offices and many shops.

Cellphones: Telecom Cook Islands rents mobile phones, and it sells prepaid SIM cards for unlocked GSM cellphones and airtime cards for NZ$25 (US$20/£10) each. Incoming calls are free, but outgoing airtime counts NZ$2 (US$1.60/80p) a minute against the cost of the card.

Time Local time is 10 hours behind Greenwich Mean Time. That's 2 hours behind California during standard time, 3 hours during daylight saving time. The Cook Islands are on the east side of the international date line, which puts them in the same day as the U.S. and a day behind New Zealand and Australia.

Tipping Tipping is considered contrary to the Polynesian way of life and is frowned upon.

Water Generally, the water on Rarotonga is safe to drink from the tap. It is filtered but not treated and can become slightly muddy after periods of heavy rain. If in doubt, boil it in the electric "jug" in your hotel room. Many hotels have their own filtration systems, and you can buy bottled water at most grocery stores and village shops. The tap water on Aitutaki is not safe to drink.

Weights & Measures The Cook Islands use the metric system.

10 Exploring Rarotonga

The Cook Islands' capital can be seen on foot, as this picturesque little South Seas town winds for only a mile or so along the curving waterfront between Avarua and Avatiu, its two harbors. Virtually every sight and most of the shops sit along or just off the main around-the-island road, which for this mile passes through town as the divided Te Ara Maire Nui (Marine Drive).

A STROLL AROUND AVARUA

Let's start at the traffic circle in the heart of town at Avarua Harbour, which is both the beginning and end of the round-island road. The rusty carcass on the reef offshore belonged to the **SS _Maitai_,** a trading ship that went aground in 1916. At the circle is the courthouse. To the west, the low-slung structure with a large veranda houses a restaurant, several shops, and the **Banana Court,** once one of the South Pacific's most infamous watering holes (see "Island Nights on Rarotonga" later in this chapter).

From the traffic circle, walk east to the modern **Beachcomber, Ltd.** ❊❊. This pearl and handicraft shop occupies a coral-block building erected in 1843 as a school for missionary children. The local legislative council met here from 1888 to 1901, but by 1968 it was condemned as unsafe. It was restored to its present grandeur in 1992 (see "Shopping on Rarotonga," later).

In a shady parklike setting across the road stand **Taputapuatea** _marae_ and the restored palace of Queen Makea Takau Ariki. Don't enter the grounds without permission, for they are _tabu_ to us commoners. The palace was reputedly a lively place when Queen Makea was around in the 19th century.

Facing the palace grounds across the road running inland is the **Cook Islands Christian Church** ❊❊❊. This whitewashed coral block structure was constructed in 1855. Just to the left of the main entrance is the grave of Sir Albert Henry, the late prime minister. A bust of Sir Albert sits atop the grave, complete with shell lei and flower crown. Robert Dean Frisbie, an American-born writer and colorful South Seas character, is buried in the inland corner of the graveyard, next to the road. Frisbee served in the U.S. army during World War I, and his gravestone is an official Department of Defense marker.

> **Impressions**
>
> _I have hunted long for this sanctuary. Now that I have found it, I have no intention, and certainly no desire, ever to leave it again._
> —Robert Dean Frisbie,
> _The Book of Puka-Puka,_ 1928

To the right, near the end of the road, is the **Cook Islands Library and Museum** ❊❊ (✆ 26-468). The museum is small but well worth a visit to see its excellent examples of Cook Islands handicrafts; a canoe from Pukapuka built in the old style, with planks lashed together; the island's first printing press (brought to Rarotonga by the London Missionary Society in the 1830s and used until the 1950s by the government printing office); and the bell and compass from the _Yankee,_ a world-famous yacht that in 1964 wrecked on the reef behind the Beachcomber, where its forlorn skeleton rusted away for 30 years. The library and museum are open Monday to Friday 9am to 1pm, Saturday 9:30am to 12:30pm, and on Tuesday also from 4 to 8pm. Admission to the museum is by NZ$2.50 (US$2/£1) donation.

Farther up the inland road stands **Takamoa Theological College,** opened in 1842 by the London Missionary Society. The original **Takamoa Mission House** still sits on the campus.

Walk a block east on Makea Tinerau Road in front of the library and museum to the **Sir Geoffrey Henry National Cultural Centre** (also known as _Te Puna Korero_), the country's showplace, built in time for the 1992 South Pacific Festival of the Arts. The large green building houses the Civic Auditorium, and the long yellow structures contain government offices as well as the **National Museum** and **National Library** (✆ 20-725). Exhibits at the National Museum feature contemporary and replicated examples of ancient crafts. The museum is open Monday to Friday from 9am to noon and 1 to 4pm. Admission is by donation. The library usually is open Monday and Wednesday 9am to 8pm and Friday 9am to 4pm.

Opposite the museum is the **Tupapa Sports Ground.** Like other South Pacific islanders formerly under New Zealand or Australian rule, the Cook Islanders take their rugby seriously. Although much of the action has shifted to the stadium at Tereora College behind the airport, Tupapa may still see a brawl or two on Saturday afternoons.

Walk back to the main road, turn left, and head to downtown. You can take a break at one of the restaurants or snack bars along the way. From the traffic circle west is a lovely stroll, either by the storefronts or along the seafront promenade. At the west end of town, stroll through **Punanga Nui Market,** where vendors sell clothing and souvenirs (see "Shopping on Rarotonga," later) and food stalls offer takeout food that you can munch at picnic tables under the shade of casuarinas whispering in the wind.

End your tour at **Avatiu Harbour,** which is Rarotonga's commercial port (the small anchorage at Avarua is strictly a small-boat refuge).

THE CIRCLE ISLAND TOUR

Traveling completely around Rarotonga and seeing the sights should take about 4 hours, with the help of a motor; allow a full day if you go by bicycle. A better idea is to take the guided tour offered by the **Cook Islands Cultural Village** (see "Cultural Experiences," below). Book at any hotel activities desk. You can do the circle island tour independently by car or motorbike, but you'll miss the informative commentary. Here's what you'll see, traveling clockwise from Avarua.

THE NORTH COAST

About 1km (a half-mile) past the Kii Kii Motel, signs mark a small dirt road to the right. It leads to the *Marae* **Arai-Te-Tonga,** one of the most sacred spots on the island. Before the coming of Europeans, these stone structures formed a *koutu,* or royal court. The investiture of high chiefs took place here amid much pomp and circumstance. Offerings to the gods and the "first fruits" of each season were also brought here and presented to the local *ariki,* or chief. The basalt investiture pillar, the major remaining structure, stands slightly offset from a rectangular platform about 3.5m (11 ft.) long, 2m (6½ ft.) wide, and 20cm (8 in.) high. Such temples, or maraes, are still considered sacred by some Cook Islanders, so don't walk on them.

The ancient Ara Metua road crosses by Arai-Te-Tonga and leads south a few yards to a small marae on the banks of **Tupapa Stream.** A trail follows the stream up to the peaks of Mounts Te Ikurangi, Te Manga, and Te Atukura, but these are difficult climbs; it's advisable to make them only with a local guide.

THE EAST COAST

Back on the main road, **Matavera** village begins about 2km (1¼ miles) beyond Tupapa Stream. Notable for the picturesque Cook Islands Christian Church and graveyard on the mountain side of the road, it's worth a stop for a photograph before continuing on to historic **Ngatangiia** village. Legend has it that a fleet of canoes left Ngatangiia sometime around A.D. 1350 and sailed off to colonize New Zealand, departing from a point across the road from where the Cook Islands Christian Church now stands in the center of the village. The canoes left on their voyage through **Ngatangiia Passage,** which lies between the mainland and **Motu Tapu,** a low island.

Ngatangiia also had its day in the sun in the early 1800s, when it was the headquarters of Charles Pitman, a missionary who came with the Rev. John Williams and later translated *The Pilgrim's Progress* into Cook Islands Maori. Unlike many of his fellow

---

Tips Take a Fruit Break

You can pull off the road, take a dip, and grab a fresh fruit juice or a smoothie at **Fruits of Rarotonga,** near The Little Polynesian (© **21-509).** This country store also sells jams, chutneys, relishes, and other fruit products, and it'll keep your bag while you're in the water. It's open Monday to Friday 7:30am to 5pm and Saturday 9am to 5pm.

---

missionaries, Pitman carefully avoided becoming involved in local politics or business, and he objected strongly when Williams forced the Cook Islanders to build *The Messenger of Peace.* The **courthouse** across from the church was the first one built in the Cook Islands.

The shore at Ngatangiia, with three small islands sitting on the reef beyond the lagoon, is one of the most beautiful parts of Rarotonga's coast. An old **stone fish trap** is visible underwater between the beach and the islands. Such traps were quite common throughout eastern Polynesia: Fish were caught inside as the tide ebbed and flowed through Ngatangiia Passage.

South of Ngatangiia begins magnificent **Muri Beach** ☆☆☆. Sailboats glide across the crystal-clear lagoon, the island's best for boating.

THE SOUTH COAST

The Cook Islands Christian Church in the village of **Titikaveka** was built in 1841 of coral blocks hand-cut from the reef (almost a mile away) and carried to the building site. Offshore, the **Titikaveka Lagoon** ☆☆☆ is the deepest on the island and has the best snorkeling. There are several public parks along the beach; the one opposite the Seventh-day Adventist church has restrooms.

Above the village, a part of the mountain is preserved in its natural state by the **Takitumu Conservation Area** (© **29-906;** kakerori@tca.co.ck). The area is the only home of the unique and endangered kakerori *(Pomarea dimidiata),* a sparrow-size yellowish bird that is native to Rarotonga. The conservation program has raised the kakerori population from 29 in 1989 to more than 130 today. Rangers lead nature walks in the forest. Call for times, prices, and reservations.

From Takitumu, the road runs along the south coast and passes the late Albert Henry's white beachside home, now home to the Queen's representative. **Mount Te Rua Manga,** the rock spire also known as "The Needle," can be seen through the palms from the main road between Vaima Restaurant and the Rarotongan Beach Resort & Spa. Assuming that construction hasn't resumed, you also will pass what may still look like a modern ruin. It's the site of the highly controversial Sheraton hotel project, which stood vacant for 10 years but is apparently back on track as the **Rarotonga Resort & Spa Managed by Hilton** (www.hiltonrarotonga.co.nz).

THE WEST COAST

The road turns the island's southwestern corner at Aroa, home of The Rarotongan Beach Resort & Spa, and heads along the west coast to the low white walls of **Arorangi,** the coastal community founded by the missionary Aaron Buzacott in 1828. Arorangi replaced the old inland village, Puaikura, where the Tahitian missionary Papeiha went to teach Christianity after he had converted all of Aitutaki. Papeiha is buried in the yard of Arorangi's Cook Islands Christian Church, built in 1849.

According to Polynesian legend, the canoes that left Ngatangiia in the 1300s stopped in Arorangi before heading off west to New Zealand. There is no reef passage near Arorangi, but the story enables the people on both sides of Rarotonga to claim credit for colonizing New Zealand.

The flat-topped mountain behind Arorangi is **Mount Raemaru.** Another legend says that mighty warriors from Aitutaki, which had no mountain, stole the top of Raemaru and took it home with them. There is a steep and somewhat dangerous trail to the top of Mount Raemaru.

The area north of Arorangi is well developed with hotels, restaurants, and shops. The shore just before the golf course is known as **Black Rock** because of the volcanic outcrop standing sentinel in the lagoon offshore. According to ancient Maori belief, the souls of the dead bid farewell to Rarotonga from this point before journeying to the fatherland, which the Cook Islanders called Avaiki.

There are two ways to proceed after passing the golf course. The main road continues around the west end of the **airport** runway (be careful; there are more road accidents on this sharp curve than anywhere else on Rarotonga). The New Zealand government built the original airstrip during World War II. It was enlarged to handle jumbo jets, and Queen Elizabeth II officially opened the new strip in 1974. The **Parliament** building is located on the shore about halfway along the length of the runway. Parliament meets from February to March and from July to September. Visitors can observe the proceedings from the gallery.

The other way to return to Avarua from Black Rock is to turn right on the first paved road past the golf course and then left at the dead-end intersection onto the Ara Metua, or "back road." Located about halfway to town, **Tereora College** was established as a mission school in 1865. An international stadium was built on the college campus for the 1985 South Pacific Mini Games held on Rarotonga and is now the site of rock 'em, sock 'em rugby games on Saturday afternoons from June through August.

SAFARI EXPEDITIONS 🐾🐾

Hooking up with **Raro Safari Tours** 🐾🐾 (© **23-629** or 61-139; www.rarosafari tours.co.ck) or **Tangaroa Tours** (© **22-200;** www.tangaroa4x4.co.ck) is the best way to see the island's mountainous interior without hiking. In fact, you'll get better views down over the reef and the sea from these four-wheel-drive vehicles than you will on foot. The open-air trucks go up the Avatiu Valley on some unbelievably narrow tracks. Guides give often humorous commentary about the native flora and its uses, about ancient legends, and about what life was like in the old days when Rarotongans lived up in the valleys instead of along the coast. Tangaroa Tours provides a meal cooked in a traditional earth oven (see the "Cook Islands Chow" box, later in this chapter) The 3½-hour tours cost NZ$60 (US$48/£24) per adult, half for kids 6 to 12.

Moments Learning a Little Culture

One of my fondest South Pacific memories was exploring Rarotonga with the entertaining and highly informative Exham Wichman, who once led the best round-island tours. He told me much of what I tell you in this chapter about the Cook Islanders' lifestyle. Today you can learn about local culture with the terrific **Cook Islands Cultural Village's** tour (see below).

(*Moments* **Magnificent Harmony**

Nearly everyone in the Cook Islands puts on his or her finest white straw hat and goes to church on Sunday morning. Many visitors join them, for even though most sermons are in Maori, the magnificent harmony of Polynesian voices in full song will not soon be forgotten. Families have been worshipping together in the same pews for generations, but the ushers are accustomed to finding seats for tourists. Cook Islanders wear their finest to church, including neckties, but visitors can wear smart casual attire.

Sunday morning services at village churches usually begin at 10am; buses leave the hotels at 9:30am. Reserve at the activities desk, or just show up at any church on the island.

CULTURAL EXPERIENCES ✰✰✰

Given their use of English and their pride in their culture, the Cook Islanders themselves offer a magnificent glimpse into the lifestyle of eastern Polynesia. They are more than happy to answer questions put to them sincerely by inquisitive visitors. Some of them also do it for money, albeit in a low-key fashion, by offering some of the finest learning experiences in the South Pacific. Unless you sit on the beach and do nothing, you won't go home from the Cook Islands without knowing something about Polynesian culture, both of yesteryear and the present.

COOK ISLANDS CULTURAL VILLAGE ✰✰✰

Plan an early visit to the Cook Islands **Cultural Village** (© 21-314; www.cookislands culturalvillage.com), on the back road in Arorangi, for it will enable you to understand what you will see during the rest of your stay. The village consists of thatch huts featuring different aspects of life, such as the making of crafts, cooking, and even dancing. Guests are guided through the huts and then enjoy a lunch of island-style foods, music, and dancing. The tour begins at 10am Monday to Friday. The Cultural Village also does its own half-day circle island historical tour. Either tour costs NZ$60 (US$48/£24). A full day combining the village tour, lunch, and a trip around the island costs NZ$90 (US$72/£36).

PA'S NATURE WALKS ✰✰✰

The best way to explore Rarotonga's mountainous interior on foot is in the company of a blond, dreadlocked Cook Islander named **Pa** (© 21-079), who leads mountain and nature walks. Along the way he points out wild plants, such as vanilla, candle nuts, mountain orchids, and the shampoo plant, and explains their everyday and medicinal uses in the days before corned beef and pharmacies. Pa's **Cross-Island Mountain Walk** costs NZ$55 (US$44/£22) for adults, NZ$30 (US$24/£12) for children under 12, while **Pa's Nature Walk** goes for NZ$55 (US$44/£22) for adults, NZ$25 (US$20/£10) for children under 12. Wear good walking or running shoes and bring a bathing suit (for a dip in an ancient pool once used by warriors). The nature walk takes 3½ hours. See "Fishing, Hiking, Diving & Other Outdoor Activities," below, for information about the cross-island hike. Reserve at any hotel activities desk, or call the phone number above.

11 Fishing, Hiking, Diving & Other Outdoor Activities

With tourism as its main business, Rarotonga has enough sporting and other outdoor activities to occupy the time of anyone who decides to crawl out of a beach chair and move the muscles. A couple of activities, such as Pa's Mountain Trek, are mentioned above, in "Cultural Experiences."

BOATING & SAILING   Captain Tama's AquaSports (© 27-350) is at the Rarotonga Sailing Club on Muri Beach, where the lagoon is the island's best spot for swimming, snorkeling, and boating. The outfit rents a variety of watersports equipment, including kayaks, sailboats, Windsurfers, canoes, and snorkeling gear. Rental rates range from NZ$5 (US$4/£2) for an hour's use of a one-person kayak to NZ$25 (US$20/£10) to rent a Windsurfer for 1 hour. You pay NZ$35 (US$28/£14) for a windsurfing lesson. Captain Tama's is open daily from 8am to 5pm.

FISHING   There have been some world-class catches of skipjack tuna (bonito), mahimahi, blue marlin, wahoo, and barracuda in Cook Islands waters. If the sea is calm enough for them to leave Rarotonga's relatively unprotected harbors, charter boats start deep-sea fishing as soon as they clear the reef. Several boat owners will take you out, but I recommend Elgin and Sharon Tetachuk's **Seafari Charters** (© 20-328; www.seafari.co.ck) and Wayne Barclay and Jenny Sorensen's **Pacific Marine Charters** (© 21-237; www.pacificmarinecharters.co.ck), which have ship-to-shore radios and safety equipment. They charge about NZ$150 (US$120/£60) per person for half a day's fishing, one of the lowest rates in the South Pacific. They like to have a day's notice, which you can probably give in person at the Cook Islands **Game Fishing Club** (© 21-419), beside the lagoon 1km (a half-mile) east of the traffic circle. Whether you fish or not, you'll be welcome to have snacks and drinks at the club while taking in the view and swapping tall tales.

Don't expect to keep your catch; fresh fish are expensive here and will be sold by the boat operator. Bring your camera or camcorder.

GOLF   Visitors can take their shots at the radio towers and guy wires that create unusual obstacles on the 9 holes of **Rarotonga Golf Club** (© 22-062). The course was once located on what is now the Rarotonga International Airport, but had to move when the runway was expanded. It now lies under Rarotonga's radio station antennae (balls that hit a tower or wire can be replayed). Greens fees are NZ$20 (US$16/£8). Rental equipment and drinks are available in the clubhouse, where "a reasonable standard of dress" is required. Open to guests Monday through Friday 8am until dark.

HIKING   There are a number of hiking trails on Rarotonga, but the most popular by far is the **Cross-Island Track** 🌺🌺🌺 from Avarua to the south coast. It's the best hike in the South Pacific. The trail begins in the Avatiu valley and follows the stream high up to the base of Mount Te Rua Manga *(The Needle)*. It's a steep and often slippery climb, but the trail is well marked. It's a more rewarding experience with **Pa's Cross-Island Mountain Walk** (see "Cultural Experiences," above).

HORSEBACK RIDING   Both adults and children will enjoy gentle rides along the beach and up to Wigmore's Waterfall with **Aroa Horse Riding** (© 25-415). The 2½-hour rides cost NZ$40 (US$32/£16) for grownups, NZ$25 (US$20/£10) for kids. Age and weight restrictions apply.

Tips **The Best Swimming & Snorkeling**

Getting into the water has to have high priority during a visit to Rarotonga. The lagoon is deep enough for snorkeling off most hotels at high tide, but you'll do better walking on the west coast reef when the tide's out. The best spot for snorkeling (and the only one at low tide) is the Titikaveka lagoon on the southeast coast. If you're not staying at the Little Polynesian, Rarotonga Beach Bungalows or the Moana Sands Beachfront Hotel (see "Where to Stay on Rarotonga," below), you can snorkel off the nearby Fruits of Rarotonga shop (see the box "Take a Fruit Break," earlier). Muri Lagoon off Rarotonga Sailing Club is the best spot for boating.

Most hotels have snorkels, fins, and masks for their guests to use for free. You can rent them from the **Edgewater Resort** (✆ 25-435) or from **Dive Rarotonga** (✆ 21-873) on the west coast, or from **Captain Tama's AquaSports** (✆ 27-350) at the Rarotonga Sailing Club on Muri Beach. Cost is NZ$10 (US$8/ £4) a day.

LAGOON EXCURSIONS   Captain Tama's AquaSports (✆ 27-350), at the Rarotonga Sailing Club on Muri Beach, has glass-bottom boat excursions on Muri Lagoon which include fish-feeding, snorkeling, and a barbecue lunch on one of the small off-shore islands. Captain Tama charges NZ$60 (US$48/£24).

SCUBA DIVING   Rarotonga's lagoon is only 1m to 3m (3¼ ft.–10 ft.) deep, but a shelf extends about 200m (656 ft.) beyond the fringing reef until it precipitously drops to more than 3,600m (11,811 ft.). Depths along the shelf range from 10m to 70m (33 ft.–230 ft.). There are canyons, caves, tunnels, and many varieties of coral. Visibility usually is in the 30m to 60m (98 ft.–197 ft.) range. Two wrecks—a 30m (98 ft.) fishing boat and a 45m (148 ft.) cargo ship—sit in depths of 24m (79 ft.) and 18m (59 ft.), respectively. Best of all for money-conscious travelers, the diving fees here are the lowest in the South Pacific.

Dive Rarotonga (✆ 21-873; fax 21-837; www.diverarotonga.com), **Cook Island Divers** (✆ 22-483; fax 22-484; www.cookislandsdivers.com), the **Dive Centre** (✆ 20-238; www.thedivecentre-rarotonga.com) on the west coast, and **Pacific Divers** (✆/fax 22-450; www.pacificdivers.co.ck) on Muri Beach charge about NZ$80 (US$64/£32) per one-tank dive, including equipment. They also teach PADI certification courses.

TENNIS   Outsiders are welcome to play at the two lighted tennis courts at the **Edgewater Resort** (✆ 22-034) for NZ$20 (US$16/£8) per hour.

12 Shopping on Rarotonga

The country's number one export is the **black pearl,** most of which are produced at Manihiki and Penrhyn atolls in the Northern Group. You'll be offered pearls at small shops and even by street vendors, but stick to dealers who are members of the local Pearl Guild, including those I recommend below. By and large, you will pay less for loose and set black pearls here than in French Polynesia. Read the "Buying Your Black Pearl" box, in chapter 8, before making your purchase here.

There is a fine assortment of **handicrafts** to choose from. Particularly good if not inexpensive are the delicately woven *rito* (white straw hats), which the women wear to church on Sunday, and the Samoan-style straw mats from Pukapuka in the Northern Group. Carvings from wood are plentiful, as is jewelry made from shell, mother-of-pearl, and pink coral. The most popular woodcarvings are small totems that represent the exhibitionist Tangaroa; they might not be appropriate for the coffee table.

Rarotonga is one of the region's best places for **tropical clothing,** especially cotton pareus, shirts, blouses, and dresses. Some of the works are more artistically creative than those in French Polynesia, especially one-of-a-kind pareus and women's apparel.

For years the Cook Islands government has earned revenue from the sale of its **stamps** to collectors and dealers overseas. The **Philatelic Bureau,** next to Cook Islands Post, at the traffic circle in Avarua, issues between three and six new stamps each year. All are highly artistic and feature birds, shells, fish, flowers, and historical events and people, including the British royal family.

I recommend some of the best stores, but you'll find many more in Avarua.

Beachcomber, Ltd.   This upscale establishment is worth a stop just to see the renovation of its 1843-vintage coral-block school house (see "A Stroll Around Avarua," earlier in this chapter). Owned by Bergman & Sons (see below), it has an excellent selection of black pearls, either loose or in exquisite settings designed and produced in the atelier behind the store. You'll also find high-quality handicrafts, including woodcarvings, and exquisite rito hats. One section is devoted to paintings and other works by local artists. It's open Monday to Friday 10am to 4pm, Saturday 9:30am to noon. Avarua, east of traffic circle. (C) 21-939.

Bergman & Sons (The Pearl Shop) ☆☆   Mike and Marge Bergman and sons Trevor and Ben helped pioneer the pearl industry in the Cook Islands, and their shops (plus Beachcomber Ltd.) are the place to see Rarotonga's largest selection of natural and cultured pearls, loose or incorporated into jewelry. The shop is open Monday to Friday 10am to 4pm, Saturday 9:30am to noon. Avarua, in Cook's Corner, and next to Banana Court. (C) 21-902.

Ellena Tavioni ☆   Check out Ellena Tavioni's workshop for one of the island's best selections of block-printed swimwear, sundresses, and other items for men, women, and children. Ellena pioneered block printing here, and she exports her clothing to the United States, Europe, the United Kingdom, and the high-end boutiques in Fiji. Here she has Rarotonga's best selection in this lovely style. Her workshop can alter items for free or make them for you from scratch. The shop is open Monday to Friday 8am to 4pm, Saturday 8am to noon. Avarua, on 2nd road inland behind Lotus China Restaurant. (C) 21-802.

Island Crafts ☆☆☆   This large store next to Westpac Bank has been Rarotonga's best place to shop for handicrafts since 1943. It has the island's largest selection—including pieces from other parts of the South Pacific—and a wide choice of carved wooden Tangaroa tikis. You can even buy a 9-karat gold pendant of the well-endowed god. The shop carries some black pearls, some set as pendants and earrings and is open Monday to Friday 8am to 5pm, Saturday 8:30am to 1pm. Avarua, in Centrepoint Building. (C) 20-919.

Kenwall Gallery ☆   Operated by Canadian-born Lorna Walters, this gallery opposite Punanga Nui Market is the best place to shop for oil and watercolor paintings by local artists, some framed, some not. Lorna also has the most artistic postcards in town. The gallery is open Monday to Friday 9:30am to 4pm, Saturday 9am to noon. Avarua, opposite Punanga Market. ℭ **25-526.**

Paka's Pearls *☆☆* *Value*   Cook Islander Paka Worthington attended American University in Washington, D.C. His specialties are tension-set designs (where tension, instead of a hole, secures the pearl in place) and enhancers, which let you clip the pearl and setting on any chain, or even a white pearl necklace. His shop is open Monday to Friday 9am to 5pm, Saturday 9am to 1pm. Avarua, at C.I.T.C. shopping center. ℭ **26-064.**

Perfumes of Rarotonga   Although their plant is at Matavera on the east coast, this showroom in the Cook's Corner shops displays perfumes, soaps, body lotions, shampoos, and other aromatic products from frangipani, gardenia, coconut, and other tropical flowers and plants. It's open Monday to Friday 9am to 5pm, Saturday 9am to 1pm. Avarua, in Cook's Corner shops. ℭ **24-238.**

Punanga Nui Market *Value*   The vendor stalls in this waterfront municipal market are the best places to look for tie-dyed bedspreads and tablecloths. You can also find good prices on T-shirts, although some may be Chinese-made cottons that will shrink (buy a size larger than you usually wear). While Saturday morning from 8am to 1pm is the best time to shop—it's market day—additional operating hours are Monday to Friday 8am to 5pm. Avatiu Harbour. No phone.

13 Where to Stay on Rarotonga

Rarotonga is blessed with too many accommodations for me to list them all, I regret to say. Because most of us desire to stay on the beach during our vacations, I have primarily confined my recommendations to waterfront locations.

I have organized the accommodations in accordance with Rarotonga's three hotel districts: **Muri Beach,** on the southeast coast; **Titikaveka** and the south coast; and the **west coast.** Marvelous Muri Beach and its shallow lagoon have more activities than the others. Titikaveka also has an even better beach, and its lagoon is the deepest and best for snorkeling on Rarotonga. The prevailing southeast trade winds, however, can make both areas chilly during the austral winter months of June through August. By the same token, these same winds provide nature's air-conditioning during the warmer summer months. You get glorious sunsets on the west coast, which the mountains shield from the prevailing trade winds, thus making the west somewhat drier than Muri Beach. The lagoon off the west coast tends to be very shallow, especially at low tide.

Camping is illegal in the Cook Islands.

IN MURI BEACH
EXPENSIVE
Muri Beachcomber *☆* *Value* *Kids*   This friendly motel sits right on Muri Beach, a short walk from the Pacific Resort, Sails Restaurant & Bar, and the Flame Tree restaurant. Ten of the one-bedroom, full-kitchen units are in five duplex buildings built of brown timber, with peaked roofs that evoke the tropics. They form two courtyards, each opening to the beach. These spacious units have French doors leading from both living rooms and bedrooms to covered verandas. Children under 12 are allowed only in the larger family units, which stand away from the beach but next to the pool, making it easy for parents to keep an eye on the kids from their shady verandas. The largest of these is a two-bedroom unit atop the motel's office. The deluxe Watergarden Villas have stucco exteriors and huge wraparound verandas that make them look like coral-block

colonial houses. Although they are behind and across a lily pond from the beachside units, they are more private and have phones, TVs, and DVD players.

P.O. Box 379, Rarotonga. (C) **21-022.** Fax 21-323. www.beachcomber.co.ck. 19 units, 3 houses. NZ$255–NZ$295 (US$204–US$236/£102–£118) double; NZ$355 (US$284/£142) house. AE, DC, MC, V. **Amenities:** Pool; bike rentals; babysitting; laundry service; coin-op washers and dryers. *In room:* A/C, TV/DVD (in villas), kitchen, coffeemaker, iron (in villas), safe, no phone (except in villas).

The Pacific Resort Rarotonga *(R)*   Sitting in junglelike grounds alongside Muri Beach, this resort was for sale during my recent visit, and it still needs improvements to its restaurant and funky beachside bar. Its spacious "villas" have two bedrooms, private entertainment areas, full kitchens, laundry facilities, minibars, and TVs with DVD players. Most other units are in one- and two-story buildings on either side of a stream crossed by foot bridges. More bungalowlike, the beachside and beachfront suites give the impression of having your own cottage. Six beachfront units in a two-story building are the largest and most expensive of the hotel-style rooms; their patios and porches are the only ones here which directly face the lagoon. Sitting near the round-island road, the swimming pool is almost an afterthought here.

P.O. Box 790, Rarotonga. (C) **20-427.** Fax 21-427. www.pacificresort.com. 56 units, 7 houses. NZ$500–NZ$960 (US$400–US$768/£200–£384) double; NZ$980–NZ$1,660 (US$784–US$1,328/£392–£664) villa. Rates include continental breakfast. AE, DC, MC, V. **Amenities:** Restaurant; bar; outdoor pool; watersports equipment rentals; bike rentals; activities desk; car-rental desk; wireless Internet access; limited room service; massage; babysitting; laundry service; coin-op washers and dryers. *In room:* A/C, TV/DVD (some units), kitchen (in villas), fridge, coffeemaker, iron, safe.

Rumours Luxury Villas & Spa *(R)(R)*   These swanky houses were two properties known as Reflections on Rarotonga and Rumours of Romance before being merged into one operation in 2007. In other words, four houses are in one location, while three are a short distance away. Built town-house style but with sound-proofed walls between them, they are all luxuriously furnished and have comfortable living rooms, full kitchens with washers and dryers, one or two separate bedrooms, beachside decks, and their own gardens with plunge pools and Jacuzzis. One unit has a movie theater with wall-size projection system, and its bathroom comes with a glass-paneled shower under skylights. A spa serves guests at both locations. As spacious as these units are, forget bringing your family because no children under 18 are accepted here.

P.O. Box 308, Rarotonga. (C) **22-551.** Fax 29-740. www.rumours-rarotonga.com, 7 units. NZ$850–NZ$1,200 (US$680–US$960/£340–£480). AE, MC, V. Children under 18 not accepted. **Amenities:** Outdoor pools (in units); Jacuzzi (in units); free use of kayaks and snorkeling equipment; spa; car rentals; wireless Internet access; coin-op washers and dryers. *In room:* A/C, TV, dataport, kitchen, coffeemaker, iron, safe.

MODERATE

Muri Beach Resort   Formerly known as the Shangri-La Beach Cottages, these adults-only cottages at Muri Beach line up in an L-shape in a beachfront yard with outdoor pool. The sailing club, The Pacific Resort Rarotonga, and the Muri restaurants are short walks away. The tropically attired cottages, which are of modern construction, have both showers and two-person whirlpool tubs. Screened doors and windows let in lots of light and fresh air. A counter separates the kitchen from the sleeping area, which has a queen-size bed. Ask about discounts if you book more than 30 days in advance.

P.O. Box 146, Rarotonga. (C) **22-779.** Fax 24-683. www.muribeachresort.com. 16 units. NZ$175–NZ$230 (US$140–US$184/£70–£92) double. MC, V. 3-night minimum stay required. Children under 18 not accepted. **Amenities:** Outdoor pool; free use of kayaks and snorkeling equipment. *In room:* A/C, TV, kitchen, coffeemaker, hair dryer.

INEXPENSIVE

Aremango Guesthouse   A good choice for cost-conscious travelers, the peaked-roof building was built here specifically with backpackers in mind, but the dorm is history. A central hallway runs between the relatively spacious rooms, which have ceiling fans, screened windows, and two or three single beds that can be combined into doubles. The fully equipped communal kitchen is large enough so that everyone gets a cupboard, and the shared bathrooms have hot-water showers and are fully tiled (as are all the floors here). Muri Beach is a short walk away.

P.O. Box 714, Rarotonga. ① 24-362. Fax 24-363. www.aremango.co.ck. 9 units (none with bathrooms). NZ$60–NZ$75 (US$48–US$60/£24–£30) double. No credit cards. **Amenities:** Communal kitchen; complimentary snorkeling gear, kayaks, bicycles; Wi-Fi; coin-op washing machines. *In room:* No phone.

Vara's Beach House ⚓   One of the most popular backpackers' hostels in the South Pacific, Vara's is usually packed with as many as 200 young travelers jammed into dorms, five rooms, four studio suites, and two small cabins right on Muri Beach, or in five houses up on the hill across the road. The studio suites have kitchens, private bathrooms, and balconies, which make them suitable for any budget traveler regardless of age. The original beach house, a lagoonside dorm, and the five houses all have communal kitchens, toilets, and showers.

P.O. Box 434, Rarotonga. ① 23-156. Fax 22-619. www.varas.co.ck. 29 units (15 with bathroom), 2 cabins (both with bathroom), 50 dorm beds (shared bathrooms). NZ$50–NZ$75 (US$40–US$60/£20–£30) double room; NZ$120 (US$96/£48) apartment; NZ$20–NZ$25 (US$16–US$20/£8–£10) dorm bed. Higher rates for stays shorter than 4 nights. MC, V. **Amenities:** Snorkeling gear rentals; bicycle and scooter rentals; coin-op washing machines. *In room:* Kitchens (studio suites only), no phone.

IN TITIKAVEKA & THE SOUTH COAST

The Little Polynesian ⚓   In a coconut grove beside Titikaveka beach, this little resort was completely rebuilt recently by sisters Dorice Reid and Joyce Peyroux, who have owned it since 1985. Now guests enter a central building opening to an infinity-edge swimming pool, near which the open-air **Little Polynesian Cafe** serves very good food. Only four of their original garden units remain, and they've been spiffed up (they have kitchens). Facing the beach are 10 identical bungalows, each with raised sleeping areas behind their lounges and porches. Every unit has an outdoor shower and whirlpool tub. Hardwood floors and hand-carved closet doors lend warmth to the white interiors of the beach bungalows, so designed to direct your eyes to the colorful lagoon.

P.O. Box 366, Rarotonga. ① 24-280. Fax 21-585. www.littlepolynesian.com. 14 units. NZ$550–NZ$950 ($440–$760/£220–£380). Rates include tropical breakfast. MC, V. Children under 12 not accepted. **Amenities:** Restaurant; bar; outdoor pool; activities desk; complimentary kayaks; limited room service; laundry service. *In room:* A/C, TV, dataport, kitchen (in garden units), fridge, coffeemaker.

Moana Sands Beachfront Hotel   Right on the beach at the deepest part of Titikaveka Lagoon, this three-story, motel-like structure has 12 rooms on its first two levels and five new suites on the top floor. Each has a balcony or patio facing the lagoon, a tropical table and chairs, a tiled shower-only bathroom, bright flower-print drapes and spreads, and a kitchenette with a fridge and microwave oven. The more spacious top-floor suites add TVs, DVD players, and glass-enclosed showers. Some units have single beds in addition to kings; others have only a king-size bed. The **Paw Paw Patch Restaurant & Bar** is here.

P.O. Box 1007, Rarotonga. ⓒ **26-189.** Fax 22-189. www.moanasands.co.ck. 17 units. NZ$295–NZ$350 (US$236–US$280/£118–£140) double. Rates include tropical breakfast. MV, V. **Amenities:** Restaurant; bar; free use of kayaks and snorkeling equipment; scooter rentals; wireless Internet access (in lobby); limited room service; massage; babysitting; laundry service. *In room:* A/C, TV (suites only), coffeemaker, safe.

Rarotonga Beach Bungalows *ᏒᏒᏒ* ⟨Value⟩   I invariably stay in one of the charming bungalows at this little complex next door to the Moana Sands Beachfront Hotel and the Paw Paw Patch Restaurant & Bar (discussed later). These are the most Tahitian units on Rarotonga, and with good reason. They were designed and built by Tom Fearon, whose family was involved with the Hotel Bora Bora in the 1970s; who lived most of his adult life in French Polynesia; whose brother, Steve Fearon, operates Matira Pearls on Bora Bora (see chapter 10); and whose Cook Islander wife, Tere, is on the staff of James Norman Hall's Home on Tahiti (see chapter 8). Tere's twin sister, Luckey, looks after the guests here, so this is very much a family affair. Built of local hardwoods, the spacious bungalows have thatch-covered roofs lined inside with pareu cloth, ceiling fans, walls of woven split bamboo, living rooms with sitting areas and full kitchens, air-conditioned bedrooms with king-size beds and televisions, and 18-foot-wide front porches with teak furniture. Borrowing from the original Bali Hai hotels in French Polynesia, Tom installed bathrooms with outdoor showers almost surrounded by gardens. Each unit has complimentary snorkeling gear and two kayaks for use in Titikaveka Lagoon, Rarotonga's best. The beachfront bungalows sit high enough off the ground to give unimpeded lagoon views. Complimentary tropical breakfast is served in an open-air lounge. Don't expect grass here; the grounds are all pure white sand—a la Bora Bora, of course. Children under 12 aren't allowed here.

P.O. Box 3045, Rarotonga. ⓒ **27-030.** Fax 27-031. www.rarotongabeachbungalows.com. 5 units. NZ$545–NZ$595 (US$436–US$476/£218/£238) double. Rates include tropical breakfast. DC, MC, V. Children under 12 not accepted. **Amenities:** Complimentary kayaks and snorkeling gear; laundry service. *In room:* A/C (in bedroom), TV (in bedroom), kitchen, coffeemaker, safe.

Royale Takitumu Villas   Another establishment catering to couples, and especially to honeymooners, this private property (you won't see a sign by the road) sits in a coconut grove with lily ponds beside the white-sand beach skirting Titikaveka Lagoon. With stucco walls and thatch-covered roofs, the villas are spacious and comfortable, although they lack the Tahitian charm of those at Rarotonga Beach Bungalows or the luxurious furnishings and private pools at Rumours Luxury Villas & Spa (see above). Their bathrooms come equipped with bidets and two-person whirlpool tubs. The six units directly facing the beach are preferable to the lagoonview models. The beachfront honeymoon units are the most private, because they sit at the ends of the complex. Their bedrooms as well as living rooms open to furnished porches, which face the beach but not their neighbors.

P.O. Box 1031, Titikaveka. ⓒ **24-682.** Fax 24-683. www.royaletakitumu.com. 10 units. NZ$445–NZ$590 (US$356–US$472/£178–£236) double. AE, DC, MC, V. Children under 15 not accepted. **Amenities:** Outdoor pool; free use of kayaks and snorkeling equipment; massage; limited room service; laundry service. *In room:* A/C, kitchen, coffeemaker, iron, safe.

Sea Change Villas *ᏒᏒ*   Midway along the south coast and within a short walk of the Saltwater Cafe (see "Where to Dine on Rarotonga," below), these luxury villas are comparable to those at Rumours Luxury Villas & Spa. There's no spa here, but the three beachfront units have small swimming pools in their decks overlooking the lagoon. The beach units are more appealing but also more expensive than five others

---

Tips Renting a Beach House

With so many residents deserting the Cook Islands for New Zealand in recent years, a multitude of houses are now for rent, ranging from simple bungalows to deluxe villas. Many of the hotels I recommend consist entirely of "self-contained" bungalows (that is, with kitchens), or they have beach houses in their inventories. If you want a place all to yourself, contact **Rarotonga Realty** (© **26-664;** fax 26-665; www.rarorealty.co.ck).

---

across the round-island road. Although they have partial or full lagoon views, their pools are in private rear patios. All units have four-poster king beds, full kitchens, and TVs with DVD players. Children under 13 aren't accepted at this honeymoon-oriented retreat.

P.O. Box 937, Rarotonga. © **22-532.** Fax 22-730. www.sea-change-rarotonga.com. 8 units. NZ$495–NZ$895 (US$396–716/£198–£358). AE, MC, V. Children under 13 not accepted. **Amenities:** Complimentary kayaks, snorkeling gear, bicycles; complimentary washers and dryers. *In room:* A/C, TV, DVD player, kitchen, coffeemaker, iron, safe.

ACCOMMODATIONS ON THE WEST COAST
EXPENSIVE
Crown Beach Resort 𝓡𝓡   This property is Rarotonga's best all-around small, full-service hotel. The best of the bungalows, or "villas" as they are known here, are the beachfront units with hot tubs on their covered front porches. Others face the swimming pool, while the least expensive are garden units between reception and Oceans restaurant. Built as duplexes, 16 "deluxe courtyard pool suites" are away from the beach, but each has a small pool in a private, wall-surrounded courtyard. All units have separate bedrooms. Honeymooners and romance-seeking couples make up the bulk of the guests, although you can bring children under 18 with advance permission. Pathways lead from the reception building through a sandy coconut grove to a swimming pool with rock waterfall, **Oceans** bar and restaurant (serving breakfast and lunch), and a full-service spa. The fine Windjammer Restaurant resides by the road here (see "Where to Dine on Rarotonga," below).

P.O. Box 738, Rarotonga. © **23-953.** Fax 23-951. www.crownbeach.com. 38 units. NZ$500–NZ$750 (US$400–US$600/£200–£300). Rates include tropical breakfast. AE, MC, V. Children under 18 accepted by request only. **Amenities:** 2 restaurants; 2 bars; outdoor pool; exercise room; spa; free use of kayaks, canoes, snorkel gear; business center; limited room service; massage; laundry service. *In room:* A/C, TV/DVD players, dataport, kitchen, fridge, coffeemaker, iron, safe.

Manuia Beach Boutique Hotel 𝓡   This intimate establishment has 24 rooms in 12 duplex bungalows set rather close together on a rectangle of beachfront land. Tropical foliage helps give the garden units some semblance of privacy, but the six beachfront units are the choice here. They have king-size beds, as opposed to queens, and a view of the reef across an infinity-edge swimming pool. Sliding glass doors lead to semiprivate wooden verandas on all units. Angled shower stalls in one corner and lavatories in another maximize space in the small bathrooms. Each garden unit has both a queen and a single bed. None of the rooms has a kitchen, but you can amble down to the **Right on the Beach Restaurant** and dig holes in its white-sand floor while enjoying a meal or snack. The facilities do not live up to the "boutique hotel" claim, but the staff will call you by your first name while providing excellent service.

P.O. Box 700, Rarotonga. (℃ **22-461.** Fax 22-464. www.manuia.co.ck. 24 units. NZ$370–NZ$540 (US$296–US$432/ £148–£216). Rates include tropical breakfast, a bottle of champagne, and afternoon tea. AE, MC, V. Children under 12 not accepted. **Amenities:** Restaurant; bar; outdoor pool; bike rentals; limited room service; laundry service. *In room:* A/C, fridge, coffeemaker, safe.

The Rarotongan Beach Resort & Spa (*R̄R̄ (Kids* After years of neglect by the government, which built it in 1977, the island's flagship resort has undergone a remarkable transformation from rundown to Rarotonga's best large resort under its present owner, Tata Crocombe, a Cook Islander who graduated from Harvard Business School. There's something for everyone here, including a full-service spa for grownups, a children's program to keep youngsters both entertained and informed, and a host of activities for all ages. A poolside stone patio and a large lagoonside deck sit beside the beach, while a swimming pool with a waterfall also draws daytime attention. The resort also has Rarotonga's widest range of accommodation, from regular hotel rooms to a romantic honeymoon bungalow with a huge outdoor bathroom (it's in the middle of the property, but a high fence provides privacy). There are even two private residences with their own pools across the road. The "deluxe beachfront junior suites" occupy one-story buildings staggered to make them seem like bungalows. Four of these have two bedrooms, a kitchen, and a private sundeck on their rooftops. Each has a bathroom with a whirlpool bathtub in addition to an outdoor shower. Although they couldn't be enlarged, the existing hotel rooms—in two-story buildings—have been vastly improved over their original versions. This is especially true of the "beachfront junior suites," which have been draped with tropical woods and mat walls (they are reserved for adults except when antipodean families invade during busy school holiday periods). The other units here are regular hotel rooms, about two-thirds of them facing the beach. A few have been turned into two-bedroom garden suites with kitchens and whirlpool tubs. Every room in the resort has either a patio or a balcony.

P.O. Box 103, Rarotonga. (℃ **800/481-9026** or 25-800. Fax 25-799. www.rarotongan.co.ck. 156 units. NZ$250–NZ$475 (US$200–US$380/£100–£190) double; NZ$550–NZ$650 (US$440–US$520/£220–£260) suite. AE, DC, MC, V. **Amenities:** 3 restaurants; 2 bars; outdoor pool; 2 tennis courts; spa; watersports equipment rentals; bike rentals; children's programs; game room; activities desk; car-rental desk; business center; wireless Internet access in bar area; limited room service; babysitting; laundry service; coin-op washers and dryers. *In room:* A/C, TV/DVD, CD player, kitchen (in some suites), minibar, coffeemaker, iron, safe.

MODERATE

Aro'a Beachside Inn Jim Bruce gave up his travel tour business in Hawaii and moved to Rarotonga, where he built this modest little resort. The best feature here is his **Shipwreck Hut,** a bar and outdoor lounge beside Aroa Beach, the same stretch of white sand wrapping around The Rarotongan Beach Resort & Spa to the south. It's a terrific spot for a sunset drink. The hut hosts barbecues and evening entertainment (reservations are required). The accommodations here are in modern one- and two-story buildings, with the best and more expensive units sitting by the beach. All are spacious and have kitchens.

P.O. Box 2160, Arorangi. (℃ **22-166.** Fax 22-169. www.aroabeach.com. 11 units. NZ$225–NZ$350 (US$180–US$280/£90–£140). Minimum stay 4 nights. MC, V. Children under 12 not accepted. **Amenities:** Restaurant; bar; free use of bicycles, kayaks, snorkeling gear; wireless Internet access; laundry service. *In room:* TV, dataport, kitchen, coffeemaker.

Edgewater Resort The Edgewater has the most units of any resort on the island, and like the Rarotongan Beach Resort & Spa (see above), it draws many visitors on package tours. Although tropical foliage helps make the grounds—just 1.6 beachside hectares (4 acres)—seem less crowded, you will have little room to roam here. Several concrete two- and three-story block structures hold most of the rooms. Each has a bougainvillea-draped patio or balcony. The more expensive beachfront suites are removed from the action and much better appointed. The majority of these have whirlpool tubs in their spacious bathrooms. Their balconies or patios open directly to the sandy beach, which the main part of the property doesn't enjoy, as rocks line most of the shore in front of the pool and expansive patio space for sunning and sitting.

P.O. Box 121, Rarotonga. ⒸⒻ 25-435. Fax 25-475. www.edgewater.co.ck. 250 units. NZ$210–NZ$410 (US$168–US$328/£84–£164) double. AE, MC, V. **Amenities:** 2 restaurants; 3 bars; outdoor pool; 2 tennis courts; spa; bike rentals; game room; activities desk; car-rental desk; limited room service; massage; babysitting; laundry service; coin-op washers and dryers. *In room:* A/C, TV, fridge, coffeemaker, iron (some units), safe (some units).

INEXPENSIVE

Are-Renga Motel   The Estall family runs this basic but clean establishment in the village of Arorangi, and the spaciousness of their units makes up for a lack of frills. Nine units are in a motel-like block at the rear of the property, which enjoys a beautiful view of the mountains. An older building beside an ancient breadfruit tree has six units in which a curtain separates the bedrooms from the living and cooking areas; the three upstairs apartments share a large veranda, and a patio does double duty for the three apartments downstairs. All units have cooking facilities. A path through a churchyard across the road leads to the beach.

P.O. Box 223, Rarotonga. Ⓒ 20-050. Fax 29-223. arerenga@oyster.net.ck. 15 units. NZ$60 (US$48/£24) double; NZ$20 (US$16/£8) per person shared unit. No credit cards. *In room:* Kitchen, no phone.

Rarotonga Backpackers   This hostel still has a chaletlike retreat up on the mountainside, but this branch down by the beach is the west coast alternative to Vara's Beach House at Muri Beach (see earlier review). Most of the rooms are in a house whose lounge has a TV and billiard table. Its large kitchen opens to an aboveground swimming pool, beyond which are two beachside cottages standing on stilts (each with two kitchen- and bathroom-equipped units) and four small "beach huts" at ground level. Suitable for couples or singles, the huts have bedrooms and bathrooms. This is a good choice for cost-conscious couples and singles as well as dorm-based backpackers.

P.O. Box 3103, Rarotonga. ⒸⒻ/fax 21-590. www.rarotongabackpackers.com. 15 units (8 with bathroom), 5 dorm beds. NZ$38–NZ$60 (US$30–US$48/£15–£24); NZ$16–NZ$20 (US$13–US$16/£6.40–£8) dorm bed. MC, V. **Amenities:** Outdoor pool; communal kitchen; bicycle rentals. *In room:* Kitchen (4 units), no phone.

14 Where to Dine on Rarotonga

Rarotonga is blessed with some good and interesting restaurants. Most make use of fresh fish caught by the country's small long-line fishing fleet. You'll see broadbill sailfish, swordfish, and other species offered alongside the usual tuna and mahimahi found everywhere in the South Pacific.

Like the hotels, above, I have arranged the restaurants by geographic location on Muri Beach, at Titikaveka and the south coast, and on the west coast, plus in the town of Avarua, where everyone goes shopping and bar-hopping.

WHERE TO DINE IN MURI BEACH

Deli-licous Internet Cafe COFFEE SHOP   This inexpensive coffee shop in a three-store shopping center in front of Vara's Beach House serves pastries, sandwiches, and other snacks. You can check your e-mail here.

Cook Islands Chow

Like their counterparts throughout Polynesia, in pre-European days the Cook Islanders cooked all their food in an earth oven—known here as an *umu*—and they still do for special occasions. The food *(umukai)* is as finger-licking good today as it was hundreds of years ago, although it's now eaten with knives and forks rather than fingers during "Island Nights" at Rarotonga's hotels, which include Cook Island dance shows (see "Don't Miss an Island Night," later). The hotels provide a wide assortment of salads and cold cuts for those who are not fond of taro, arrowroot, and *ika mata* (the local version of *poisson cru*—fish marinated in lime juice and mixed with coconut milk and raw vegetables).

Get a schedule of island nights from Cook Islands Tourism Corporation. Also check the daily *Cook Islands News* (especially the Thursday and Friday editions) or with the hotels to find out when the feasts are on. Most buffets cost about NZ$65 (US$52/£26). Some of them may charge a small admission fee to see the dance show if you don't have dinner.

Muri Beach, front of Vara's Beach House. ℂ **20-858.** Most items NZ$4–NZ$12 (US$3.20–US$9.60/£1.60–£4.80). No credit cards. Daily 8–5pm.

The Flame Tree INTERNATIONAL   Within walking distance of the Muri Beach-comber and the Pacific Resort Rarotonga, this restaurant calls on the cuisine of India and other Asian countries, but I prefer locally caught fish, coated in coconut or in a pastry with cream sauce and asparagus. Vegetarians can select from several curries.

Muri Beach, north of the Pacific Resort (11km/6¾ miles from Avarua). ℂ **25-123.** Reservations recommended. Main courses NZ$19–NZ$38 (US$15–US$30/£7.60–£15). MC, V. Daily 6–9pm. Bar 6–11pm.

Sails Restaurant & Bar ⊛ INTERNATIONAL   Occupying the main floor of the Rarotonga Sailing Club, this airy, nautically decorated restaurant offers a variety of salads, sandwiches, and "island fries"—sweet potato, taro, and banana. At dinner the chef turns his attention to fresh fish and vegetables, plus mussels and steaks flown in from New Zealand. You might be offered Cajun-style pan-seared tuna or Moroccan-style lamb shanks. Weekend afternoons are especially lively here; club members gather to sail their radio-controlled miniature yachts out on the lagoon.

Muri Beach, in Rarotonga Sailing Club, between the Pacific Resort and Muri Beachcomber. ℂ **27-349.** Reservations strongly recommended for dinner. Lunch NZ$15–NZ$22 (US$12–US$18/£6–£8.80); main courses NZ$28–NZ$32 (US$22–US$26/£11–£13). AE, MC, V. Mon–Fri 11am–9pm; Sat 9am–9pm; Sun 10:30am–3pm and 6–9pm.

WHERE TO DINE IN TITIKAVEKA & THE SOUTH COAST

Maire Nui Gardens & Cafe ⊛ (Value) SALADS/SANDWICHES   You won't appreciate Hinano MacQuarie's sophisticated cafe from the road, but wait until you walk around the thatched-roof building to the big veranda and its terrific vista of the green mountains rising beyond the flowery botanical gardens. It's the perfect spot to break a round-island tour or stop in for breakfast, a light lunch, an afternoon snack, a fruit smoothie, or a cup of espresso, cappuccino, or fresh mint tea. Hinano's breakfast offerings include muffins, fresh fruit, and omelets. You'll have more choices from her lunch-and-afternoon menu, including a marvelous papaya and chicken salad. The pineapple-lemon meringue cheesecake is well worth the calories.

Titikaveka, opposite the Little Polynesian. ⊘ 22-796. Most items NZ$6.50–NZ$17 (US$5.20–US$14/£2.60–£6.80). No credit cards. Mon–Fri 9am–4pm.

Paw Paw Patch Restaurant & Bar ⨋ INTERNATIONAL   This sophisticated cafe with an open kitchen and both indoor and outdoor seating brings a glimpse into local cuisine. The "Paw Paw Catch" of fresh fish seared and served under Hollandaise sauce over a bed of onions, coconut milk, and *rukau* (taro leaves) is a bit unusual to novice tongues, but it's a fine example of Cook Islander home cooking. Otherwise the menu tends to more familiar steaks, fish, pastas, and Thai-style chicken or vegetable curry. Be sure to check the daily specials board. The beachside Sunday night barbecue here is one of the best on the island (come early for happy hour from 6–7pm). Note that the Paw Paw is not open for lunch.

Titikaveka, in Moana Sands Beachfront Hotel. ⊘ 27-189. Reservations recommended for dinner. Breakfast NZ$7.50–NZ$14 (US$6–US$11/£3–£5.60); main courses NZ$23–NZ$28 (US$18–US$22/£9.20–£11). Sunday barbecue buffet NZ$30 (US$24/£12). MC, V. Daily 8–10:30am and 6–9pm.

Saltwater Cafe ⨋ INTERNATIONAL   Carey and Ake Hosea Winterford have created a coffeehouse atmosphere at this little cafe, exactly halfway around Rarotonga from Avarua (it's a fine place to break a round-island tour). They indeed serve excellent coffee. Both lunch and dinner see burgers, fish and chips, and outstanding local freshwater shrimp in a garlic sauce. Note that they were serving dinner Tuesday through Thursday nights during my visit, and they were not open on weekends.

South coast, halfway around the island. ⊘ 20-020. Reservations recommended for dinner. Breakfast NZ$8–NZ$16 (US$6.40–US$13/£3.20–£6.40); sandwiches and burgers NZ$8–NZ$17 (US$6.40–US$14/£3.20–£6.60); main courses NZ$18–NZ$28 (US$14–$22/£7.20–£11). AE, MC, V. Mon and Fri 9:30am–4pm; Tues–Thurs 9:30am–9pm.

Vaima Restaurant & Bar INTERNATIONAL   Lots of island ambience prevails at this bamboo-clad beachside restaurant. It offers a wide range of tastes, including spicy curry. Always check the daily blackboard specials, which feature fresh fish, but avoid anything claiming to be Cajun. There are a few tables on a veranda facing the beach plus picnic tables out by the sand.

Takitimu (1km/½ mile east of the Rarotongan Beach Resort & Spa). ⊘ 26-123. Reservations recommended. Main courses NZ$23–NZ$30 (US$18–US$24/£9.20–£12). MC, V. Mon–Sat 6:30–9pm.

> **⸤Tips⸥ Make a Reservation**
>
> Most Rarotongan restaurants are small, so reservations are essential. Folk tend to dine early, so don't show up after 8pm if you haven't booked a table.

WHERE TO DINE ON THE WEST COAST

Waterline Beach Bar & Grill ⨋ REGIONAL   This little beachside restaurant is so charming it has been used as a movie stage set. Also charming are its owners, Chris and Akisi Musselle, an English-Fijian couple. An old South Pacific fishing hand, Chris tends the bar hung with rods and reels and other nautical paraphernalia, while Akisi makes sure the kitchen provides Fijian-style curries as well as fresh seafood such as pan fried mahimahi with capers-and-coriander sauce. The most romantic tables are under palms out on the beach. This is my favorite place for Sunday night barbecue.

Tips   Sunday Night Roasts & Barbecues

Sunday is traditional New Zealand roast night on Rarotonga, and it's also popular for beach barbecues. Keep your eye out for money-saving roast and barbecue specials offered by many hotels. Note that only hotels can serve alcoholic beverages between 12:01am and 6pm on Sunday.

Arorangi, behind Joyce Peyroux Garments. ℭ 22-161. Reservations recommended. Main courses NZ$24–NZ$30 (US$19–US$24/£9.60–£12). MC, V. Tues–Sun 6–9pm.

Windjammer Restaurant ✮✮✮ ECLECTIC   Talented chef Daniel Forsyth and his partner, Maire Porter, are both of Cook Island descent but were trained in New Zealand. Together they make this roadside restaurant one of the top two in Rarotonga. The air-conditioned octagonal pine building may lack Polynesian charm, but the widely spaced tables provide the island's most elegant dining, and the wait staff renders excellent service. Maire's family owns the local meat importer, so you will be served only top-grade lamb and aged steaks, plus fresh local fish. I started with a delightful warm seafood salad with a lemon dressing, and loved the aged rib-eye filet with a pink peppercorn sauce. Vegetarians get at least two choices every night, perhaps a veggie risotto. You won't go wrong here or at the Tamarind House (see below).

Arorangi, between Manuia Beach Boutique Hotel and Edgewater Resort. ℭ 23-950. Reservations recommended. Main courses NZ$25–NZ$31 (US$20–US$25/£10–£12). MC, V. Mon and Wed–Sat 5:30–9pm; Sun 6–9pm.

WHERE TO DINE IN AVARUA

The Bus Stop Shop, a convenience store opposite the Cook's Corner bus stop (ℭ 22-787), carries very good pastries, meat pies, and packaged sandwiches, as well as groceries. It's open Monday to Friday 7:30am to 6pm and Saturday 7:30am to 4pm. If you get the late-night munchies, **Oasis Energy,** on the main road west of the airport (ℭ 22-145), is open 24/7 for sandwiches, salads, meat pies, coffee, groceries, and gasoline.

Blue Note Café SNACK BAR/REGIONAL   A fine place to take a town break and watch the traffic along the waterfront, this open-air snack bar occupies one end of the veranda of the Banana Court building. Breakfast is until 11am, but espresso, ice cream, milkshakes, and exotic cocktails are served all day. Sandwiches and big burgers are made to order for lunch.

Avarua, at the traffic circle. ℭ 23-236. Breakfast NZ$7.50–NZ$15 (US$6–US$12/£3–£6); sandwiches, salads, burgers NZ$12–NZ$19 (US$9.60–US$15/£4.80–£7.60). MC, V. Daily 8am–4pm.

The Cafe ✮✮ SALADS/SANDWICHES/SNACKS   Neil Dearlove's cafe/coffee house, which would grace Auckland's trendy Parnell district, is my favorite place to grab a papaya muffin and a latte (known as a "flat white" in this part of the world) before striking out on my rounds of Avarua. And when I have finished my walk, I often retire here and select from daily specials or a panini-style sandwich. Lots of natural wood and big canvas patio umbrellas hung from the ceiling create an outdoorsy ambience. Neil roasts his own coffee.

Avarua, east of traffic circle. ℭ 21-283. Breakfast NZ$5–NZ$14 (US$4–US$11/£2–£5.60); sandwiches and salads NZ$12–NZ$17 (US$9.60–US$14/£4.80–£6.80). AE, MC, V. Mon–Fri 8:30am–4pm; Sat 8:30am–12:30pm (breakfast only).

Cafe Salsa *☆* *(Finds* SNACK BAR   This storefront cafe with sidewalk and garden tables rivals The Cafe as Avarua's trendiest place for breakfast and lunch. You might start your day with smoked marlin hash topped by poached eggs—or if that's too exotic, regular eggs Benedict. Lunch sees salads, medium-size pizzas, and sandwiches on warm-from-the-oven focaccia. An iced coffee (iced by a scoop of vanilla ice cream) will cool you down after shopping. A blackboard dinner menu is offered from Wednesday through Friday.

Avarua, in CITC Centre. *©* **22-215.** Most items NZ$8–NZ$18 (US$6.40–US$14/£3.20–£7.20). MC, V. Mon–Tues 8am–9:30pm; Wed–Fri 8am–9:30pm; Sat 8am–2pm.

Tamarind House Restaurant & Bar *☆☆☆* INTERNATIONAL   Sue Curruthers, who grew up in Kenya and founded the Flame Tree restaurant here (see above), and partner Robert Brown renovated this 1920s seaside home and turned it into Rarotonga's top place to dine. Not only will you enjoy the first-rate food, but you will have an ocean view, as most tables are on the veranda or covered patio out front (it's very romantic at night). You can begin your day with a late breakfast featuring Sue's corn fritters with tomato, guacamole, and sour cream. She offers the fritters at lunch along with a variety of salads, sometimes including Indonesian *gado gado* with a spicy peanut sauce. She expands her globe-trotting menu at dinner, with the likes of a north Indian curry, Balinese pork, and Burmese tamarind fish with lime and chili. She also offers steaks, seafood, or fish and chips. I never visit Rarotonga without dining here.

Avarua, 1.5km (1 mile) east of traffic circle. *©* **26-487.** Reservations recommended at dinner. Breakfast NZ$4.50–NZ$19 (US$3.60–US$15/£1.80–£7.60); lunch NZ$16–NZ$27 (US$13–US$22/£6.40–£11); dinner main courses NZ$22–NZ$35 (US$18–US$28/£8.80–£14). AE, MC, V. May–Sept Mon–Fri 9am–9pm, Sat 6–9pm, Sun 9:30am–2pm; Oct–Apr Mon–Fri 9am–8pm, Sat 6–9pm.

Trader Jack's Bar & Grill *☆☆* SEAFOOD   You won't be on Rarotonga long before you hear about New Zealander "Trader Jack" Cooper's harborside joint. Floor-to-ceiling windows on three sides open to the water and give nearly everyone in the dining area a view of the harbor, the reef, and the sea and sunsets beyond. Outside, a bar dispenses libation and the island's best pizzas. A printed menu plays second fiddle to the chalkboard specials, which feature the freshest fish served on the island (Jack owns a substantial slice of Rarotonga's fish processing plant and gets the pick of the day's catch). A big seller is a seafood catch for two, including fish, shrimp, scallops, oysters, marinated mussels, and smoked marlin and salmon with dipping sauce.

Avarua, waterfront at traffic circle. *©* **26-464.** Reservations recommended for dinner. Pizza NZ$29 (US$23/£12); main courses NZ$17–NZ$29 (US$14–US$23/£6.80–£12). AE, MC, V. Mon–Sat noon–9pm. Bar Mon–Thurs and Sat 11am–midnight; Fri 11am–2am. Closed New Year's Eve.

Whatever! Bar   This is not a restaurant so much as an upstairs deck where the staff barbecues burgers, steaks, chicken, and fish on a gas grill, which you eat at picnic tables with umbrellas. There's nothing fancy at all, except the view along the north coast of Rarotonga, making this a great place for a sunset drink. Most people come up here to slake a thirst at the bar, especially on Friday and Saturday nights, when it's on the pub-crawling circuit (see "Island Nights on Rarotonga," below). To get here, follow the driveway from the bridge at the traffic circle.

Avarua, at the traffic circle. *©* **22-299.** Burgers NS$6 (US$5/£2.50); main courses NZ$15-NZ$27 (US$12–US$22/£6–£11). MC, V. Mon–Thurs and Sat noon–midnight; Fri noon–2am.

15 Island Nights on Rarotonga

Cook Islanders are some of the most fun-loving folks you will meet in the South Pacific, and you can easily catch their spirit. Every evening except Sunday is a party night—especially Friday when the pubs stay open until 2am (they close promptly when the Sabbath strikes at Saturday midnight). As with their Tahitian cousins, the infectious sound of the traditional drums starts everyone dancing.

If Rarotongans aren't performing in a show (see the "Don't Miss an Island Night" box), they seem to be dancing with each other at some of the most colorful bars in the South Pacific. No one ever explained to me why they call their tour-de-bars a "pub-crawl," although I assume it's because crawling is the method of travel after too many locally brewed Cook's Lagers. However you get around, you can pub-crawl yourself or take a Friday **nightlife bus tour,** which your hotel will book. The NZ$30 (US$24/£12) fare is worth not having to drive home after 2am.

The Friday night crawl begins—and often ends—at **Trader Jack's Bar & Grill** *&&* (© 26-464) at Avarua's old harbor, one of the best bars in all of the South Pacific. The island's affluent movers and shakers start boozing here after work.

Heading east, you can grab an outdoor beer and an ocean view at **Whatever! Bar** (© 22-299). It's behind **TJ's** (© 24-722), a disco which draws a sometimes raucous young crowd. The Trader Jack's folk then wander into the **Stair Case Restaurant & Bar** (© 22-254), an upstairs restaurant that has rock-and-roll music for dancing after 10pm and an island night show once a week.

Backtracking to the traffic circle, you'll come to **The Banana Court** (© 23-397), which for generations was *the* place to do your drinking, dancing, and fighting. It's

---

Don't Miss an Island Night *&&&*

A New Zealander once told me, only slightly tongue-in-cheek, that all Cook Islanders are deaf because they grow up 3 feet from drums you can hear from 3 miles away.

Danced to the heart-thumping beat of those deafening drums, their hip-pulsating *tamure* is very much like that in Tahiti, except it tends to be faster (which I found hard to believe until I saw it with my own eyes) and even more suggestive (which I had even more trouble believing). Indeed, dancing is high in the hearts of all Cook Islanders, and it shows every time the drums begin. Their costumes generally aren't as colorful as those in Tahiti but are as likely to be made of leaves and other natural materials as dyed synthetic fabrics.

Unadulterated Cook Islands dancing is best seen during the annual **Dance Week** in April or during the **National Self Governing Commemoration** celebrations in late July and early August. It's still good at "Island Night" feasts and shows at the hotels. Indeed, one or another will have a feast and show every night except Sunday. Although their dance shows are tailored for tourists, the participants go at it with infectious enthusiasm.

Get a schedule of island nights from Cook Islands Tourism Corporation, or check the *Cook Islands News,* especially the Thursday and Friday editions, and make reservations early. Ask the locals where the top troupes are performing.

now *the* big place to be on Wednesday night. Down the side street in Cook's Corner shops, the miniature **Hideaway Bar** (© 20-340) attracts a mature crowd of drinkers.

Near the airport are **The Nu Bar** (© 26-141) and the **RSA Club** (© 20-590), where the country's military veterans welcome everyone to drink and dance.

16 Aitutaki ★★★

The farther you get from the South Pacific's international airports, the more likely you are to find an island and a way of life that have escaped relatively unscathed by the coming of Western ways—remnants of "old" Polynesia. Although it is quickly developing as a tourist destination, this is still true of Aitutaki.

Lying 225km (140 miles) north of Rarotonga, Aitutaki is often referred to as "the Bora Bora of the Cook Islands" because it consists of a small, hilly island at the apex of a triangular barrier reef lined with skinny flat islands. This reef necklace encloses one of the South Pacific's most colorful lagoons, which appears at the end of the flight up from Rarotonga as a turquoise carpet spread on the deep blue sea. The view from the air is unforgettable.

The lagoon sides of the uninhabited, coconut-studded small islands out on the reef have some of the South Pacific's most beautiful white-sand beaches. They're perfect for a snorkel-and-picnic excursion, Aitutaki's prime attraction.

The first European to discover the lagoon was Capt. William Bligh in 1789, a few weeks before the mutinous crew of HMS *Bounty* set him adrift off Tonga.

GETTING TO AITUTAKI

Air Rarotonga (© 22-888 on Rarotonga, or 31-888 on Aitutaki; www.airraro.com) flies to and from Aitutaki Monday to Saturday. It also offers day trips for about NZ$450 (US$360/£180), which includes round-trip airfare and a lagoon excursion with a barbecue lunch (see "Lagoon Excursions," below). Regular round-trip fare is about NZ$370 (US$296/£148), but it usually is less expensive to fly at midday or at night. The early morning and late afternoon flights are often filled with day-trippers, and thus are more expensive.

Air/hotel packages to Aitutaki also can result in savings. Check with Air Rarotonga, **Island Hopper Vacations** (© 22-026; www.islandhoppervacations.com), or **Jetsave Travel** (© 27-707; www.jetsave.co.ck), which have outer island packages. The latter is owned by Melynnda Morrissette, an American expatriate who has lived in the Cook Islands longer than I've been coming here.

The airport is about 7km (4¼ miles) from most hotels and guesthouses, most of which pick up their guests who have reservations. The airline provides **airport transfers** for NZ$10 (US$8/£4) each way.

Ask the hotel desk to reconfirm your return flight to Rarotonga. **Air Rarotonga's** office is in Ureia village, just north of Arutanga (© 31-888).

GETTING AROUND AITUTAKI

There is no **public bus transportation** system on Aitutaki, but you can call **Pacifica Taxi** (© 31-220).

All hotels and guest houses can arrange **car, scooter, and bike rentals,** or you can call **Rino's Rentals** (© 31-197), north of Arutanga, or **Popoara Rentals** (© 31-735), on the mainland near the Aitutaki Lagoon Resort & Spa. Both have cars starting at

---

(*Fun Fact* **Dropping Their Rocks**

Legend has it that once Aitutaki was completely flat, but then its warriors sailed to Rarotonga and stole the top of Mount Raemaru. Pitched battles were fought on the way home, and the warriors dropped some of their rocks into the sea: Black Rock, on Rarotonga's northwest point; Rapota and Moturakau islands, in the south of Aitutaki's lagoon; and the black rocks along Aitutaki's west coast. In the end, the Aitutakian warriors were victorious, and the top of Raemaru is now **Mount Maungapu,** the highest point on Aitutaki, at 122m (400 ft.).

NZ$65 (US$52/£26) a day, scooters for NZ$25 (US$20/£10) per day, and bikes for NZ$10 (US$8/£4) per day. **Josie's Beach Lodge** (© **31-659**), also near the Aitutaki Lagoon Resort & Spa, rents scooters for that same price.

FAST FACTS: Aitutaki

These facts are specific to Aitutaki. See "Fast Facts: Rarotonga & the Cook Islands," earlier in this chapter, for general information.

Currency Exchange **ANZ Bank** has a small agency and an ATM at Mango Traders, near The Pacific Resort Aitutaki (Mon–Thurs 9am–noon and 1–3pm). **Westpac Bank** has an office and ATM at government administration building in Arutanga (Mon, Wed, and Fri 9:30am–3pm). **Bank of the Cook Islands** also is in the government administration building (Mon–Fri 9am–3pm), but no ATM.

Emergencies In case of emergency, contact your hotel staff. The **police station** is in Arutanga (© **31-015**).

Healthcare Medical and dental treatment and prescription medications are available at the island's **hospital** (© **31-002**), near Arutanga.

Internet Access You can get online (slowly and expensively) at **SpiderCo Internet Lounge,** south of the Pacific Resort Aitutaki (© **31-780**). It's open Monday to Saturday 7am to 11:30pm and Sunday 6 to 9pm. Access costs NZ30¢ (US24¢/12p) a minute.

Mail The post office in the government administration building in Arutanga is open Monday to Friday 8am to 4pm.

Safety See "Fast Facts: Rarotonga & the Cook Islands," earlier in this chapter, for general warnings and precautions.

Telephone & Fax The **Cook Island Telecentre,** in the government administration building in Arutanga, is open Monday to Friday from 8am to 4pm. It does not accept credit cards, but you can use Kia Orana prepaid calling cards.

Visitor Information Cook Islands Tourism Corporation's Aitutaki visitor information office is on Sir Albert Henry Drive near the wharf (© **31-767**). It's open Monday to Friday 9am to 3pm. Go to **www.aitutaki.com** for information.

Water Don't drink the tap water on Aitutaki. Bottled water is available at grocery stores.

EXPLORING AITUTAKI

Aitutaki has much less to offer ashore than does Rarotonga. The central island is dotted with the coconut, pineapple, banana, and tapioca plantations that are worked by most of the island's 2,100 residents. Aitutaki is a major supplier of produce and seafood to Rarotonga.

The administrative center, most of the shops, and the main wharf are on the west side of the island at **Arutanga** village, where a narrow, shallow passage comes through the reef. Trading boats cannot get through the pass and must remain offshore while cargo and passengers are ferried to land on barges. The late Sir Albert Henry was born and raised on Aitutaki, and the divided road to the wharf is named for him and his wife, Elizabeth (one lane for Sir Albert and one lane for Lady Elizabeth).

Just south of the post office in Arutanga is the **Cook Islands Christian Church,** the country's oldest church, built in 1839 of coral and limestone. The monument in front is to John Williams, the exploring missionary who came to Aitutaki in October 1821, and to Papeiha, the Tahitian teacher who came with him and converted the entire island. The interior of the church is unusual in that the altar is on one side rather than at one end. Worshippers from each village sit together during services, but visitors can take any vacancy during services at 10am on Sunday. An anchor suspended from the ceiling is a symbol of hope being a sure and steadfast anchor, as in Hebrews 6:19.

A network of mostly paved roads fans out from Arutanga to **Viapai** and **Tautu** villages on the east side and to the airport on a flat hook at the northern end of the island. About 1,000 American servicemen—with considerable help from the local residents—built the large airstrip during World War II. Many present-day Aitutakians reportedly trace their lineage to those Americans.

According to ancient legend, the first Polynesians to reach Aitutaki came in through **Ootu Pass,** on the eastern side of the lagoon between the airport and **Akitua** island, site of today's Aitutaki Lagoon Resort & Spa (see "Where to Stay on Aitutaki," below). They were led by the mighty warrior and navigator Ru, who brought 4 wives, 4 brothers, and a crew of 20 young virgins from either Tubuai or Raiatea (the legend varies as to which one) in what is now French Polynesia. Akitua island, where they landed, was originally named *Urituaorukitemoana,* which means "where Ru turned his back on the sea." The area on the north side of the pass is a major tourism center.

Aitutaki Discovery Safari (© **31-757;** safari@aitutaki.net.ck) will take you by 4×4 vehicle to an ancient marae, up Mount Maungapu, to a plantation, and to World War bunker sites. These half-day tours cost NZ$55 (US$44/£22) per person.

LAGOON EXCURSIONS ✿✿✿

The main reason I come to Aitutaki is to spend at least a day on the lagoon and one of the small islands out on the reef. The standard day trip begins at 9am and ends about 4pm. The boats spend the morning cruising and fishing on the lagoon. Midday is spent on one of the reef islands, where guests swim, snorkel, and sun while the crew cooks the day's catch and the local vegetables. The itinerary changes from day to day depending on the weather and the guests' desires.

The "Survivor: Cook Islands" TV series was filmed on **Maturaku** islet, but a more common destination is **Tapuaetai (One Foot) Island** and its adjacent sandbar, known as Nude Island (for its lack of foliage, not clothes). One Foot got its name when an ancient chief prohibited his subjects from fishing there on pain of death. One day the chief and his warriors saw two people fishing on the reef and gave chase. The two were a man and his young son. They ran onto the island, the boy carefully stepping in his

---

Tips **Don't Get Burned**

The boats all have canopies, but bring a hat and plenty of high-powered sunscreen on your Aitutaki lagoon outing—and use it! The sun out there on the water can blister you, even if you're under a canopy.

---

father's footprints as they crossed the beach. The son then hid in the top of a coconut tree. The chief found the father, who said he was the only person fishing on the reef. After a search proved fruitless, the chief decided it must have been rocks he and his men saw on the reef. He then killed the father. Ever since, the island has been known as Tapuaetai (in the local dialect, *tapuae* means footprint, and *tai* is one).

Those dark things resembling cucumbers on the bottom of the lagoon are *beche-de-mer* (sea slugs). Along with sandalwood, they brought many traders to the South Pacific during the 19th century because of high prices they fetched in China. Sea slugs are harmless—except in China, where they are considered to be an aphrodisiac.

As noted in "Getting to Aitutaki," above, Air Rarotonga has day trips from Rarotonga, which include lagoon excursions. Several operators also have full-day lagoon cruises Monday to Saturday. The oldest is **Bishop's Lagoon Cruises** (© 31-009; fax 31-493; bishopcruz@aitutaki.net.ck). It goes to One Foot Island, where it has erected a beach bar. **Teking Tours** (© 31-582; teking@aitutaki.net) goes to a sand bar, where you'll have lunch sitting at umbrella tables in the lagoon. It also has champagne brunch and sunset tours. **Kia Orana Cruise** (© 31-442; kcruises@aitutaki.net) uses a smaller boat to visit Maina Island, on the southwestern corner of the lagoon, and it has overnight "honeymoon" trips to a small motu, where you sleep under a thatched roof or under the stars on a beach mat. All charge about NZ$65 (US$52/£26) per person for the all-day excursions, including lunch.

A less strenuous way to see the lagoon is on the **Aitutaki Glass Bottom Boat** (© 31-790; story@aitutaki.net.ck), whose 6-hour excursions cost NZ$35 (US$28/£14).

BOATING, GOLF, HIKING & SCUBA DIVING

BOATING You can rent kayaks at **Samade on the Beach** (© 31-526), on the lagoon north of the Aitutaki Lagoon Resort & Spa (see "Where to Stay on Aitutaki," below), for NZ$10 (US$8/£4) per hour to NZ$20 (US$16/£8) per day. At Ranginui's Retreat, **Wet & Wild Adventure Tours** (© 31-657) rents motor boats for NZ$500 (US$400/£200) a day. It also has water-skiing and wake-boarding. Instead of going south to the resort at the Y intersection, follow the dirt track to the west.

GOLF Golfers who missed hitting the radio antennae and guy wires on the Rarotonga course (see earlier) can try again at the 9-hole course at the **Aitutaki Golf Club,** on the north end of the island between the airport and the sea. Balls hit onto the runway used to be playable, but broken clubs and increasing air traffic put an end to that. You can rent equipment at the clubhouse. The club has neither a phone nor regular hours, but the hotels and guesthouses can arrange rentals and tee times. Members are more likely to volunteer to mow the greens between May and August than during the wetter summer months.

FISHING **Aitutaki Sea Charters** (© 31-281; deepsea@aitutaki.net.ck) has half- and full-day trips offshore in search of sailfish, marlin, wahoo, tuna, and mahimahi. Call for reservations and rates.

HIKING   Hikers can take a trail to the top of **Mount Maungapu,** Aitutaki's highest point, at 124m (407 ft.). It begins across from the Paradise Cove Guest House, about 1 mile north of The Pacific Resort Aitutaki. The trail starts under the power lines and follows them uphill for about a 1.5km (1 mile). The tall grass is sharp and can be soaked after a rain, but the track is usually well tramped and should be easy to follow. Nevertheless, wear trousers. The view from the top includes all of Aitutaki and its lagoon. Sunrise and sunset are the best times.

SCUBA DIVING & SNORKELING   The lagoon here is too shallow for scuba diving, so the sites are over the edge of the reef. Divers and snorkelers can go with Neil Mitchell of **Aitutaki Scuba,** P.O. Box 40, Aitutaki (© **31-103;** fax 31-310; scuba@ aitutaki.net.ck), or Onu Hewett of **Bubbles Below** (© **31-537;** www.diveaitutaki. com). Both charge about NZ$95 (US$76/£38) per one-tank dive.

The best place to don mask, snorkel, and fins on the mainland is off the north end of the short runway at the airport, near the radio antenna. You can swim right out to the reef's edge here at high tide, but observe the usual cautions.

WHERE TO STAY ON AITUTAKI
EXPENSIVE
Aitutaki Lagoon Resort & Spa 𝕽𝕽𝕽   Another property nursed back to health by Tata Crocombe, owner of The Rarotongan Beach Resort & Spa, this excellent resort is reached by boat across Ootu Pass to Akitua, a sandy, tadpole-shaped islet south of the airport. The magnificent lagoon laps a white-sand beach, off which a channel has been dredged for swimming. The choice—and most expensive—units here are seven overwater bungalows endowed with Polynesian charm. Although the lagoon off their decks is not as deep or as clear, their amenities are on par with most overwater units in French Polynesia. Their rears sit on land, and each has an outdoor shower in a private garden. Farther apart are the deluxe beachfront bungalows, each of which has a raised sleeping area behind a sofa-equipped lounge opening through sliding, wooden louvered doors to a lagoonside deck. Other units date from the early 1970s but have been remodeled. The super-private Villa Tearau is the most cleverly designed honeymoon bungalow I've seen in the South Pacific. Its central bungalow for sleeping is flanked on one side by a living room-kitchen and on the other by a daybed, from the foot of which you can literally roll into your private pool and swim over to your private hot tub! The open-air, thatched-roof restaurant and beachside bar serve good regional fare, and a spa offers full-service pampering.

P.O. Box 99, Aitutaki (on Akitua Island, 2km/1¼ mile south of airport, 9km/5½ miles from Arutanga). © 800/481-9026 or 31-201. Fax 31-202. www.aitutakilagoonresort.com. 36 units. NZ$395–NZ$995 (US$316–US$796/£158–£398) bungalow. AE, DC, MC, V. **Amenities:** 2 restaurants; 2 bars; outdoor pool; spa; watersports equipment rentals; free kayaks and snorkel gear; scooter rentals; rental bikes; limited room service; babysitting; laundry service; coin-op washers and dryers. *In room:* A/C, TV/DVD, dataport, minibar, coffeemaker, iron, safe.

Etu Moana Beach Villas 𝕽𝕽   On a hillside terminating at a white-sand beach, this adult-oriented property is the creation of Jo-Anne and Jim Brittijn, a Canadian-Dutch couple. Jim is both an avid sailor and a carpenter, as witnessed by his nautical cabinetry, which lends many yacht touches to these comfortable bungalows. Each unit has a porch with a settee built into one side, a king-size bed facing the lagoon, a kitchen, a bathroom with walk-in shower, and another shower outside in a small courtyard. The units are grouped around a swimming pool, although the best are beside the lagoon. The complex has no restaurant, but refreshment is available at a poolside honesty bar, and Are Tamanu Village and The Pacific Resort are close at hand.

P.O. Box 123, Aitutaki (west coast, 3km/2 miles from airport). ℭ **31-458**. Fax 31-459. www.etumoana.com. 8 units. NZ$425–NZ$475 (US$340–US$380/£170–£190). Rates include continental breakfast. AE, MC, V. Children under 12 not accepted. **Amenities:** Bar; outdoor pool; scooter rentals; free bikes, kayaks, snorkeling gear; laundry service. *In room:* A/C, TV, dataport, kitchen, coffeemaker, iron, safe.

The Pacific Resort Aitutaki ★★★   This romantic, architecturally stunning sister of the Pacific Resort Rarotonga ranks with the Aitutaki Lagoon Resort & Spa as the best full-service hotels in the Cook Islands. Reception, shops, and restaurant—under a conical thatched roof—sit atop a headland overlooking a shallow but colorful lagoon. Steps lead from there down to an infinity swimming pool, daytime bar, and a white-sand beach strewn with big black rocks. The resort's 13 beachfront bungalows are on flat land by the lagoon. These spacious units have thatch-covered roofs, fans hanging from mat-lined ceilings, hardwood floors, king-size beds plus built-in settees, large bathrooms with double sinks and glass-enclosed showers, and front porches facing the beach. While the beachfront bungalows give direct access to the lagoon, the stars here are the six suites and three one-bedroom villas cleverly hidden among the rocks and old-growth tropical forest on the headland. You'll have to climb down steps to reach the beach, but these thatched-roof, stucco-sided units are much more private, and they all have outdoor and indoor showers. Asian decor and furniture, including some antique pieces, make this resort seem as much Oriental as South Seas.

P.O. Box 90, Aitutaki (1km/½ mile north of Arutanga). ℭ **31-720**. Fax 31-719. www.pacificresort.com. 22 units. NZ$795–NZ$1,470 (US$636–US$1,176/£318–£588) bungalow. AE, MC, V. **Amenities:** Restaurant; 2 bars; outdoor pool; free kayaks, rowboats, and snorkel gear; car, scooter, and bike rentals; limited room service; babysitting; laundry service. *In room:* A/C, TV, CD player, dataport, minibar, coffeemaker, iron, safe.

Tamanu Beach ★   Formerly known as Are Tamanu Beach Village, this hotel is two beachside bungalow complexes separated by a coconut grove beside the powdery white-sand beach, which stretches along the entire northwestern shore of the island. It's the creation of Mike and Stuart Henry, two grandsons of the late Prime Minister Sir Albert Henry. Both parts have their own swimming pools and bars, while a restaurant sits between them. The spacious guest bungalows face courtyards that terminate at the beach. Some units have a separate bedroom and kitchens, while others are one-room bungalows with TVs. The more expensive bungalows are on the beach.

P.O. Box 59, Aitutaki (on west coast, 3km/2 miles from airport). ℭ **31-810**. Fax 32-816. www.tamanubeach.com. 22 units. NZ$325–NZ$525 (US$260–US$420/£130–£210) bungalows. Rates include continental breakfast. AE, MC. V. Children under 12 not accepted. **Amenities:** Restaurant; 2 bars; 2 outdoor pools; free use of bikes and snorkeling equipment; coin-op washers and dryers. *In room:* A/C, TV (some units), kitchen (some units), coffeemaker, safe.

MODERATE

Samade on the Beach   These trellis-trimmed bungalows sit behind Samade on the Beach restaurant (see "Where to Dine on Aitutaki," below), where guests are served complimentary breakfast. Built of pine with cathedral ceilings under tile roofs, they are plain but well-equipped. Each has air-conditioning and a ceiling fan. They also have kitchen sinks and counter space but no cooking facilities. Lounge chairs on a section of the white-sand beach are reserved for guests, who get free use of kayaks. Although the bungalows are a bit pricey, the restaurant and beach setting make this a relaxing, friendly place to stay.

P.O. Box 75, Aitutaki (on east coast, near Ootu Pass). ℭ **31-526**. www.samadebeach.com. 12 units. NZ$300 (US$240/£120) double. Rates include breakfast. MC, V. **Amenities:** Restaurant; bar; free use of kayaks; scooter and bicycle rentals. *In room:* A/C, TV, fridge, coffeemaker, no phone.

INEXPENSIVE

Aitutaki's least expensive backpacker lodging is at **Josie's Beach Lodge** (© 31-659; josies@aitutaki.net.ck), a tin-roof house with a screened veranda a few steps from Ootu Pass between the mainland and the Aitutaki Lagoon Resort & Spa, and within walking distance of Samade on the Beach and The Boat Shed Bar & Grill (see below). Its five rooms, none with its own bathroom, range from NZ$30 to NZ$60 (US$24–US$48/£12–£24) double per night. It's cash only. You can also breakfast at Josie's.

A good choice on the west coast is the simple but clean **Amuri Guest House** (© 31-749; amuri.lodges@hotmail.com), where Ngatuaine and Maraiti Tom have four rooms flanking the central hallway of their house. All share two bathrooms, a communal kitchen, and a TV lounge. Rates are NZ$70 (US$56/£28) double, including tropical breakfast. No credit cards.

Matriki Beach Huts   On the north side of Tamanu Beach resort, the basic bungalows here are popular with backpackers, who should book as early as possible. There's nothing fancy, but you will be right beside the beach. Two of the units are over-under models, while a third stands by itself. They have double beds with mosquito nets (the units are screened), cooking facilities, and hot-water showers (hut dwellers share toilets). Attached to the rear of the owner's home, an apartment has its own bathroom but lacks the huts' charm.

P.O. Box 32, Aitutaki (Ureia Village, on west coast .5km/⅓ mile north of Arutanga). ©/fax **31-564**. www.matriki.com. 4 units (1 with bathroom). NZ$65–NZ$75 (US$52–US$60/£26–£30) double. MC, V. **Amenities:** Bike and scooter rental; coin-op washers and dryers. *In room:* Kitchen (no oven), fridge, no phone.

COTTAGE RENTALS

Aitutaki has lots of "beach bungalows." Indeed, everyone with a plot of lagoonside land seems to have put up cottages to rent. Samade on the Beach and Ranginui's Retreat, below, are two of the better examples. So is **Popoara Ocean Breeze Villas** (© 31-739; www.popoara.com), north of Ootu Pass; its four cottages are part of a complex with Popoara Rentals and The Boat Shed Bar & Grill (see "Where to Dine on Aitutaki," below). Cottages rent for NZ$135 (US$108/£54) a night.

On the west coast, **Rino's Beach Bungalows** (© 31-197; rinos@aitutaki.net.ck) has clean, comfortable New Zealand–style rooms and apartments beside the beach between Arutanga and the Pacific Resort. Although not as charming, they are more spacious than most other beach bungalows here, and you can walk to the main villages. Rooms cost NZ$85 (US$68/£34) double, while apartments range from NZ$120 to NZ$255 (US$96–US$204/£48–£102).

Ranginui's Retreat (*Value*   This no-frills bungalow complex sits on the beach across Ootu Pass from the Aitutaki Lagoon Resort & Spa (see above). You can walk to Samade on the Beach and the Boat Shed Bar & Grill (see "Where to Dine on Aitutaki," below). Although modest, tin-roof bungalows hold queen-size beds and sofas, kitchens with microwaves, and bathrooms with glass-enclosed showers. Each has a porch facing the lagoon. There's a pool, and guests get free use of kayaks.

P.O. Box 8, Aitutaki (2km/1¼ mile south of airport, 9km/5½ miles from Arutanga). © **31-657**. Fax 31-658. www. ranginuis.com. 7 units. NZ$120–NZ$160 (US$96–US$128/£48–£64) bungalow. MC, V. **Amenities:** Small outdoor pool; bike and scooter rentals; free use of kayaks; laundry service. *In room:* TV (3 units), kitchen, coffeemaker, no phone.

WHERE TO DINE ON AITUTAKI

Some Aitutaki restaurants will come and get you at your hotel and take you back after dinner, so be sure to ask about free transportation when you make reservations.

The Boat Shed Bar & Grill INTERNATIONAL   In the Popoara cottage-and-rental complex just north of Ootu Pass, Allen and Maria Mills have adorned their large dining room with nautical and fishing paraphernalia, which is fitting because their best offerings are fish and chips, grilled or pan-seared fish of the day, and coconut-crusted shrimps. Indonesian nasi goring noodles and Asian beef stir-fries also were on the menu during my visit. The big windows swing open to provide a view of the sea.

North side of Ootu Pass, near Aitutaki Lagoon Resort & Spa (turn east at the Y intersection). © 31-480. Reservations recommended at dinner. Main courses NZ$15–NZ$34 (US$12–US$27/£6–£14). MC, V. Daily noon–5pm and 6–9:30pm.

Cafe Tupuna ✿ REGIONAL   After a career as dressmaker, florist, and artist (her floral paintings adorn the walls), Tupuna Hewett opened this sand-floor charmer in an open-air addition to her home in the middle of the main island. Her blackboard menu depends on what the local fishermen have caught, plus tender steaks from New Zealand. For starters or a light meal, try her spicy version of *ika mata* (marinated raw fish) in half a coconut shell. For a main course, opt for the parrotfish cooked in banana leaves. This is the one place you will want to have dinner on Aitutaki.

Tautu Rd., in center of island. © 31-678. Reservations recommended. Main courses NZ$25–NZ$32 (US$20–US$26/£10–£13). MC, V. Mon–Sat 6–9pm. Turn inland at the post office, bear right at the roundabout at the top of the hill, bear left after the hospital and Mormon church, turn right at the sign to restaurant on left.

Kuku's REGIONAL   Order inside this roadside building, and then dine at patio tables and chairs under the shade of a breadfruit tree. The blackboard menu has everything from fresh coffee and fresh fruit smoothies to hot dogs and hamburgers—the latter accompanied by arrowroot and breadfruit chips. I make a fine late breakfast of the French toast with bacon and bananas. Everything is cooked to order.

West coast, between Arutanga and the Pacific Resort. © 31-071. Reservations not accepted. Sandwiches and burgers NZ$3–NZ$8 (US$2.40–US$6.40/£1.20–£3.20); meals NZ$9.50–NZ$11 (US$7.60–US$8.80/£3.80–£4.40). No credit cards. Mon–Fri 10am–7pm; Sat 10am–4pm.

Samade on the Beach ⟨Value⟩ REGIONAL   On Ootu Beach, a 5-minute walk from the Aitutaki Lagoon Resort & Spa, this lagoonside restaurant has a white-sand floor under a tin roof lined with coconut mats, setting the stage for hearty local-style meals. Indeed, this is a poor person's version of the famous Bloody Mary's Restaurant & Bar on Bora Bora. There's nothing fancy about the chow, but the fish and chips don't get any fresher. The name Samade is from the owners, Tongan Sam Vakalahi and his Cook Islander wife, Adrianne. They serve breakfast all day and rent kayaks and other toys, and they should have 12 well-equipped beach bungalows by the time you arrive. Tuesday sees Aitutaki's most authentic island night, and the Sunday-afternoon barbecue draws throngs of locals and visitors.

Ootu Beach, north of Aitutaki Lagoon Resort & Spa (turn west at the Y intersection). © 31-526. Reservations recommended. Main courses NZ$17–NZ$30 (US$14–US$24/£6.80–£12). MC, V (minimum NZ$30 purchase). Daily 7am–9pm.

ISLAND NIGHTS ON AITUTAKI

Island Night feasts and dance shows usually take place Monday and Friday at the **Pacific Resort Aitutaki,** Tuesday at **Samade on the Beach;** Wednesday and Saturday at the **Aitutaki Lagoon Resort & Spa** (see "Where to Stay on Aitutaki," earlier). I like the Tuesday show at **Samade on the Beach,** one of the more locally authentic feasts.

13

Samoa

The scenic 31km (19-mile) drive from Faleolo Airport into the historic capital of Apia provides a fitting introduction to Samoa. Here in this cultural storehouse, which was once known as Western Samoa, the Polynesian lifestyle known as *fa'a Samoa*—The Samoan Way—remains alive and well. On one side of the road lies an aquamarine lagoon; on the other, coconut plantations climb gentle slopes to the volcanic ridge along the middle of Upolu, the main island.

Along the shore of Upolu, Samoa's main island, sit hundreds of Samoan *fales* (houses), their big turtle-shaped roofs resting on poles, their sides open to the breeze and to passersby. Their grass trimmed and their borders marked with boulders painted white, expansive lawns make the route seem like an unending park. Samoans wrapped in *lava-lavas* shower under outdoor faucets and sit together in their fales. Only the dim glow of television screens coming from beneath tin roofs rather than thatch remind us that a century has passed since Robert Louis Stevenson lived, wrote, and died here in Samoa.

Even the town of Apia harkens back to those bygone South Seas days. Although landfills have extended the shoreline, high-rises now stand on the waterfront, and traffic lights blink at several corners, many old white clapboard buildings still sleep along Beach Road, just as they did when Stevenson stepped ashore here in 1889. Compared with the hustle and bustle of Papeete, or with the congestion and canneries of Pago Pago in American Samoa, life in Apia is slow and easy.

The old ways are even more preserved over on Savai'i, Samoa's "Big Island." The eastern and northern side of this huge shield volcano slope down to impressive beaches, which are attracting more and more visitors in search of a beautiful, little-changed escape from civilization.

If you go with an eye to exploring the culture as well as visiting some of the South Pacific's most beautiful and undeveloped beaches, Samoa will enchant you just as it did Stevenson, Maugham, and Margaret Mead, all of whom found plenty to write home about.

1 Samoa Today

The Samoa Islands, which include the independent nation of Samoa and the territory of American Samoa, stretch for some 480km (298 miles) across the central South Pacific, about 2,000km (1,243 miles) west of Tahiti and 4,000km (2,485 miles) southwest of Hawaii. The nine western islands are in Samoa; the others are in American Samoa.

GEOGRAPHY Independent Samoa, which many people still call Western Samoa, has a land area of 2,800 sq. km. (1,081 sq. miles), two-thirds of which are on **Savai'i,** the largest Polynesian island outside Hawaii and New Zealand. A series of volcanoes on a line running east to west formed **Upolu,** about 63km (39 miles) long and 21km

---

⟨Tips⟩ Both Share *Fa'a Samoa*

Although American ways have infiltrated neighboring American Samoa (see chapter 14), the people there share *fa'a Samoa* with their relatives here in Samoa. Much of the background information in this chapter, therefore, applies equally to both.

(13 miles) wide. It's considerably smaller than Savai'i, 21km (13 miles) to the west, but some 75% of Samoa's population lives on Upolu. Although geologically younger than Upolu, Savai'i in many ways is the most "old Polynesia" of any island I include in this book. It has no towns, and its villagers live very much by fa'a Samoa.

The tops of two small volcanoes, **Apolima** and **Manono** islands sit in the Apolima Strait between the two main islands. Locals like to claim that James A. Michener was inspired by them to create the romantic island of Bali Ha'i in his *Tales of the South Pacific.* (Michener said in an interview, however, that he got the idea from a cloud-draped island off Espiritu Santo in Vanuatu, where he spent much of World War II.)

GOVERNMENT   An independent nation since 1962, Samoa is ruled by a 47-member Parliament, of whom 45 are *matais,* or chiefs. Part-Samoan and non-Samoan citizens elect two nonmatai members. There are two parties: the Human Rights Protection party and the Christian Democratic party.

Parliament selects the head of state from among Samoa's four paramount chiefs. The first head of state, Malietoa Tanumafili II, served for life; that is, from independence until his death in 2007. His successors will serve 5-year terms.

ECONOMY   Samoa's only exports of any magnitude are fresh fish, *copra* (dried coconut meat), coconut cream, kava, noni juice, and beer (try a German-style Vailima brew). Tourism is of increasing importance, with the country seeing a record number of arrivals in 2007. There is some light manufacturing, including cigarettes and garments. Although there has been significant economic growth and development in recent years, mainly in and around Apia, foreign aid and remittances sent home by Samoans living elsewhere keep the country out of bankruptcy. Several thousand Samoans live and work in American Samoa, where they earn much higher wages.

2 Samoa Yesterday: History 101

Archaeologists believe that Polynesians settled in the Samoa Islands about 3,000 years ago. Their great migration halted here for some 1,000 years before voyagers went on to colonize the Marquesas, Society Islands, and other island groups farther east. Thus the Samoas are known as the "Cradle of Polynesia."

The universe known by the early Samoans included Tonga and Fiji, to which they regularly journeyed, often waging war. Tongan invaders ruled the Samoas between A.D. 950 and 1250, and there still is a friendly rivalry between the two nations—especially on the rugby field.

The first European to see the Samoas was Dutchman Jacob Roggeveen, who in 1722 sighted the Manu'a Islands in what is now American Samoa. The first Europeans to land were part of a French expedition under Jean La Pérouse in 1787. They came ashore on the north coast of Tutuila in American Samoa and were attacked by Samoan warriors. Twelve members of the landing party and 39 Samoans were killed.

The London Missionary Society's Rev. John Williams, who roamed the South Pacific in the *Messenger of Peace,* landed the first missionaries in Samoa in 1830. European-style settlements grew up at Apia on Upolu and on the shores of Pago Pago Bay on Tutuila. German businessmen established copra plantations on Upolu by the late 1850s. When steamships started plying the route between San Francisco and Sydney, the U.S. Navy negotiated a treaty with the chiefs of Tutuila in 1872 to permit the U.S. to use Pago Pago as a coaling station. The U.S. Congress never ratified this document, but it served to keep the Germans from penetrating into Eastern Samoa, as American Samoa was then known.

COLONIALISM ARRIVES   The Germans gained the upper hand over today's independent Samoa by staging a coup in 1887, backed up (unofficially) by German gunboats. They governed through Malietoa, one of Samoa's four paramount chiefs. One of his rivals, Mataafa, lost a bloody rebellion in 1888 and was exiled.

Continuing unrest turned into a major international incident—fiasco is a better word—when the United States, Britain, and Germany sent a total of seven warships to Apia in March of 1889. A hurricane arrived unexpectedly, and only a British warship survived unscathed. Of the rest, four were sunk, two others were washed ashore, and 146 lives were lost. (A newspaper story of the time is mounted in the lounge of Aggie Grey's Hotel & Bungalows in Apia.)

In December 1889, an agreement was signed in Berlin under which Germany was given today's independent Samoa, the United States was handed Eastern Samoa, and Britain created a protectorate over Tonga. The two Samoas were split apart and swept into the colonial system. The Germans in Samoa proceeded to make fortunes from their huge, orderly copra plantations.

A KIWI BACKWATER   German rule came to an abrupt end with the outbreak of World War I in 1914, when New Zealand sent an expeditionary force to Apia, and the German governor surrendered. The Germans were interned for the duration of the war, and their huge land holdings were confiscated. New Zealand remained in charge until 1962, initially under the League of Nations and then under the United Nations.

The New Zealand administrators did little in the islands except keep the lid on unrest, at which they were generally successful. In 1929, however, the Mau Movement created an uprising. It was crushed when New Zealand constables fired on a crowd of protestors outside the Courthouse, at Beach Road and Ifiifi Street in Apia, killing nine.

When opposition to colonialism flared up in the United Nations 20 years later, a Legislative Assembly of matais was established to exercise a degree of internal self-government. A constitution was drafted in 1960, and the people approved it and their

Impressions

Imagine an island with the most perfect climate in the world, tropical yet almost always cooled by a breeze from the sea. No malaria or other fevers. No dangerous snakes or insects. Fish for the catching, and fruits for the plucking. And an earth and sky and sea of immortal loveliness. What more could civilization give?

—Rupert Brooke, 1914

Fun Fact The Teller of Tales

The salvage crews were still working on the hulks of the British, American, and German warships sunk in Apia's harbor by a hurricane in 1889 when a thin, tubercular writer arrived from Scotland.

Not yet 40 years old, Robert Louis Stevenson was already famous—and wealthy—for such novels as *Treasure Island* and *Dr. Jekyll and Mr. Hyde*. He arrived in Samoa after traveling across the United States and a good part of the South Pacific in search of a climate more suitable to his ravaged lungs. With him were his wife, Fanny (an American divorcée 11 years his senior), his stepmother, and his stepson. His mother joined them later.

Stevenson intended to remain in Apia for only a few weeks while he caught up on writing a series of newspaper columns. He and his entourage stayed to build a mansion known as Vailima on the slopes of Mount Vaea, overlooking Apia, where he lived lavishly and wrote more than 750,000 published words. He learned the Samoan language and translated "The Bottle Imp," his story about a genie, into it. It was the first work of fiction translated into Samoan.

Stevenson loved Samoa, and the Samoans loved him. Great orators and storytellers in their own right, they called him *Tusitala*, the "Teller of Tales."

On December 3, 1894, almost 5 years after he arrived in Apia, Stevenson was writing a story about a son who had escaped a death sentence handed down by his own father and had sailed away to join his lover. Leaving the couple embraced, Stevenson stopped to answer letters, play cards, and fix dinner. While preparing mayonnaise on his back porch, he suddenly clasped his hands to his head and collapsed. He died not of tuberculosis but of a cerebral hemorrhage.

More than 200 grieving Samoans hacked a "Road of the Loving Hearts" up Mount Vaea to a little knoll below the summit, where they placed him in a grave with a perpetual view overlooking Vailima, the mountains, the town, the reef, and the sea he loved. Carved on his grave is his famous requiem:

This be the verse you grave for me:
Here he lies where he longed to be;
Home is the sailor, home from the sea,
And the hunter home from the hill

own independence a year later by referendum. On January 1, 1962, Samoa became the first South Pacific colony to regain its independence from the Western powers.

Samoa remained a backwater during most of its career as a colony and trusteeship territory. Only during World War II did it appear on the world stage, and then solely as a training base for thousands of Allied servicemen on their way to fight the Japanese. Tourism increased after the big jets started landing at Pago Pago in the 1960s, but significant numbers of visitors started arriving only after Samoa's Faleolo Airport was upgraded to handle large aircraft in the 1980s.

3 The Samoan People

An estimated 177,000 people live in independent Samoa, the vast majority of them full-blooded Samoans. They are the second-largest group of pure Polynesians in the world, behind only the Maoris of New Zealand.

Although divided politically in their home islands, the people of both Samoas share the same culture, heritage, and, in many cases, family lineage.

"Catch the bird but watch for the wave" is an old proverb expressing the Samoans' conservative approach, which is perhaps responsible for the extraordinary degree to which they have preserved their ancient customs while adapting it to the modern world. Even in American Samoa, where most of the turtle-shaped thatch fales have been replaced with structures of plywood and tin, the firmament of the Samoan way lies just under the trappings of the territory's commercialized surface.

The showing of respect permeates Samoans' lives. They are by tradition extremely polite to guests, so much so that some of them tend to answer in the affirmative all questions posed by a stranger. The Samoans are not lying when they answer wrongly; they are merely being polite. Therefore, visitors who really need information should avoid asking questions that call for a yes or no answer.

THE *AIGA*

The foundation of Samoan society is the extended family unit, or *aiga* (pronounced ah-*eeng*-ah). Unlike the Western nuclear family, an aiga can include thousands of relatives and in-laws. In this communal system, everything is owned collectively by the aiga; the individual has a right to use that property but does not personally own it. In a paper prepared for the government of American Samoa by the Pacific Basin Development Council, it states: "the [Samoan] attitude toward property is: if you need something which you don't have, there is always someone else who has what you need."

At the head of each of more than 10,000 aigas is a matai (*mah*-tie), a chief who is responsible for the welfare of each member of the clan. The matai settles family disputes, parcels out the family's land, and sees that everyone has enough to eat and a roof over his or her head. Although the title matai usually follows bloodlines, the family can choose another person—man or woman—if the incumbent proves incapable of handling the job.

Strictly speaking, Samoans turn all money they earn over to their matai, to be used in the best interest of the clan. The system is being threatened, however, as more and

---

Tips How to Drink Kava

Nowhere is Samoan ritual more obvious or observed than during a kava (pronounced *'ava* in Samoan) ceremony. The slightly narcotic kava brew is made by crushing the roots of the pepper plant *Piper methysticum* (see the "'Grog' Etiquette" box in chapter 4). During a Samoan ceremony, coconut shells are scooped into a large wooden bowl of the gray liquid, which looks like mud and tastes like sawdust. The host passes a cup to one person at a time. When you get yours, hold the cup straight out with both hands, and say *"Manuia"* (Good health) before gulping most of it down in one swallow. Save a little to toss on the floor mats before handing the cup back to your host. And remember, this is a solemn occasion—not a few rounds at the local bar.

more young Samoans move to the United States or New Zealand, earn wages in their own right, and spend them as they see fit. Nevertheless, the system is still remarkably intact in both Samoas. Even in Samoan outposts in Hawaii, California, Texas, and Auckland (which collectively have a larger Samoan population than do the islands), the people still rally around their aiga, and matais play an important role in daily life.

Land ownership is a touchy subject here. About 11% of the land here is freehold, which Samoan citizens can buy and sell. Non-Samoans can lease freehold and communal property, but they cannot buy it outright.

ORGANIZATION & RITUAL

Above the aiga, Samoan life is ruled by a hierarchy of matais known in English as high-talking chiefs, high chiefs, and paramount chiefs, in ascending order of importance. The high-talking chiefs do just that: talk on behalf of the high chiefs, usually expressing themselves in great oratorical flourishes in a formal version of Samoan reserved for use among the chiefs. The high chiefs are senior matais at the village or district level, and the paramount chiefs can rule over island groups. The chiefly symbol, worn over the shoulder, is a short broom that resembles a horse's tail.

MISSIONARIES & MINISTERS

Like other Polynesians, the Samoans in pre-European days worshipped a hierarchy of gods under one supreme being, whom they called **Le Tagaloa.** When the Rev. John Williams arrived in 1830, he found the Samoans willing to convert to the Christian God. He and his Tahitian teachers brought a strict, puritanical version of Christianity. About a third of all Samoans are members of the Congregational Christian Church, which he founded. His legacy can be seen both in the large white churches that dominate every settlement in all the Samoa Islands and in the fervor with which the Samoans practice religion today. Independent Samoa almost closes down on Sunday, and things come to a crawl on the Sabbath even in more Westernized American Samoa. Swimming on Sunday is tolerated in both countries only at the hotels and, after church, at beaches frequented by overseas visitors.

Christianity has become an integral part of fa'a Samoa, and every day at 6:30pm each village observes *sa,* 10 minutes of devotional time during which everyone goes inside to pray, read Scripture, and perhaps sing hymns. A gong (such as an empty acetylene tank hung from a tree) is struck once to announce it's time to get ready, a second time to announce the beginning of sa, and a third time to announce that all's clear. It is permissible to drive on the main road during sa, but it's not all right to turn off into a village or to walk around.

MISS MEAD STUDIES SAMOAN SEX

Despite their ready acceptance of much of the missionaries' teaching, the Samoans no more took to heart their puritanical sexual mores than did any other group of

---

⎛Moments Wonderful Harmony

When I first came to American Samoa in 1977, I lived for 2 months in Nu'uli village on Tuituila. Every Sunday, my girlfriend and I were treated to Samoans singing hymns in wonderful harmony in the village church. Even if you don't understand the sermon, going to church here is a rewarding experience.

(Tips   Don't Wear Skimpy Clothing

Don't wear bathing suits, short shorts, halter tops, hip-huggers, or other skimpy clothing away from the beach or hotel pool. Although shorts of respectable length are worn by young Samoan men and women in Apia and Pago Pago, it is considered very bad form for a Samoan to display his or her traditional tattoos, which cover many of them from knee to waist. Even though Samoan women went bare-breasted before the coming of Christianity, going topless is definitely forbidden today. Traditional Samoan dress is a wraparound *lava-lava* (sarong) that reaches below the knee on men and to the ankles on women.

Polynesians. In 1928, Margaret Mead, then a graduate student in anthropology, published her famous *Coming of Age in Samoa,* which was based on her research in American Samoa. She described the Samoans as a peaceable people who showed no guilt in connection with ample sex during adolescence, a view that was in keeping with practices of Polynesian societies elsewhere. Some 55 years later, New Zealand anthropologist Derek Freeman published *Margaret Mead and Samoa: The Making and Unmaking of an Anthropological Myth,* in which he took issue with Mead's conclusions and argued instead that Samoans are jealous, violent, and not above committing rape. The truth may lie somewhere in between.

The Samoans share with other Polynesians the practice of raising some boys as girls, especially in families short of household help. These young boys dress as girls, do a girl's chores around the home, and often grow up to be transvestites. They are known in Samoan as *fa'afafines.*

RULES OF CONDUCT

You should be aware of several customs of this conservative society. A briefing paper prepared by the Pacific Basin Development Council for the American Samoan Office of Tourism gives some guidelines that may be helpful:

- In a Samoan home, don't talk to people while standing, and don't eat while walking around a village.
- Avoid stretching your legs straight out in front of you while sitting. If you can't fold them beneath you, then pull one of the floor mats over them.
- If you are driving through a village and spot a group of men sitting around a fale with their legs folded, it's probably a gathering of matais to discuss business. It's polite not to drive past the meeting place. If going past on foot, don't carry a load on your shoulders or an open umbrella.
- If you arrive at a Samoan home during a prayer session, wait outside until the family is finished with its devotions. If you are already inside, you will be expected to share in the service. If you go to church, don't wear flowers.
- Whenever possible, consult Samoans about appropriate behavior and practices. They will appreciate your interest in fa'a Samoa and will take great pleasure in explaining their unique way of life.

Finally, should you be invited to stay overnight in a Samoan home, let them know at the beginning how long you will stay. Upon leaving, it's customary to give a small gift known as a *mea alofa.* This can be money—between $5 and $10 a day per person—but make sure your hosts understand that it is a gift, not a payment.

Most Samoan villages charge small **custom fees** to visitors who want to use their beaches or swim under their waterfalls. These usually are a dollar or two and are paid by local residents from other villages as well as by tourists.

In all cases, remember that almost everything and every place in the Samoas is owned by an aiga, and it's polite to ask permission of the nearby matai before crossing the property, using the beach, or visiting the waterfall. They will appreciate your courtesy in doing so.

4 The Samoan Language

Although English is an official language in both Samoa and American Samoa and is widely spoken, Samoan shares equal billing and is used by most people for everyday conversation. It is a Polynesian language that's somewhat similar to Tahitian, Tongan, and Cook Islands Maori, but with some important differences.

The vowels are pronounced not as in English (*ay, ee, eye, oh,* and *you*) but in the Roman fashion: *ah, ay, ee, oh,* and *oo* (as in kanga*roo*). All vowels are sounded, even if several of them appear next to each other. The village of Nu'uuli in American Samoa, for example, is pronounced New-u-*u*-lee. The apostrophe that appears between the vowels indicates a glottal stop—a slight pause similar to the tiny break between "Oh-oh!" in English. The consonants *f, g, l, m, n, p, s, t,* and *v* are pronounced as in English, with one major exception: The letter *g* is pronounced like "ng." Therefore, aiga is pronounced ah-*eeng*-ah. Pago Pago is pronounced "Pango Pango" as in "pong."

Here are some words that may help you win friends and influence your hosts:

English	Samoan	Pronunciation
hello	**talofa**	tah-*low*-fah
welcome	**afio mai**	ah-*fee*-oh my
good-bye	**tofa**	tow-*fah*
good health	**manuia**	mah-*new*-yah
please	**fa'amolemole**	fah-ah-*moly*-moly
man	**tamaloa**	tah-mah-*low*-ah
woman	**fafine**	fah-*fini*
transvestite	**fa'afafine**	fah-fah-*fini*
thank you	**fa'afetai**	fah-*fee*-tie
kava bowl	**tanoa**	tah-*no*-ah
good	**lelei**	lay-*lay*
bad	**leaga**	lay-*ang*-ah
happy/feast	**fiafia**	fee-ah-*fee*-ah
house	**fale**	fah-*lay*
wraparound skirt	**lava-lava**	lava-lava
dollar	**tala**	tah-*lah*
cent	**sene**	say-nay
high chief	**ali'i**	ah-*lee*-ee
small island	**motu**	mo-*too*
white person	**palagi**	pah-*lahng*-ee

5 Visitor Information & Maps

VISITOR INFORMATION

The friendly staff of the **Samoa Tourism Authority,** P.O. Box 2272, Apia, Samoa (© **63-500;** fax 20-886; www.samoa.travel), have free brochures, maps, and other publications available at their office in a handsome Samoan fale on the harbor side of Beach Road, east of the Town Clock. The bureau is open Monday to Friday 9am to 5pm and Saturday 8am to noon.

The visitors bureau has offices in:

- **Australia:** P.O. Box 611, Leumeah NSW 2560 (© **02/4627-5926;** fax 02/ 4627-5926; samoa@visitsamoa.com.au)
- **New Zealand:** Level 1, Samoa House, 283 Karangahape Rd. (P.O. Box 68423), Newton, Auckland (© **09/379-6138;** fax 09/379-8154; samoa@samoa.co.nz)

The bell captain's desk at **Aggie Grey's Hotel & Bungalows** (see "Where to Stay on Upolu," later) also has brochures and other information.

6 Entry Requirements

Except for American Samoans, who must get a permit and pay a fee, no visa or entry permit is required for visitors who intend to stay 60 days or less and who have a valid passport, a return or ongoing airline ticket, and a place to stay in Samoa. Those who want to stay longer must apply, before arrival, to the **Immigration Office,** Government of Samoa, P.O. Box 1861, Apia, Samoa (© **20-291;** www.samoaimmigration.gov.ws).

Vaccinations are not necessary unless you're arriving within 6 days of being in an infected area.

CUSTOMS See "Fast Facts: Samoa," later in this chapter, for what you can bring into the islands, and "Fast Facts: The South Pacific" in chapter 2 for what you can bring home.

7 When to Go

THE CLIMATE

The Samoas enjoy a humid tropical climate, with lots of intense sunshine, even during the wet season (Dec–May). Average daily high temperatures range from 83°F (28°C) in the drier and somewhat cooler months of June through September to 86°F (30°C) from December to April, when midday can be hot and sticky. Evenings are usually in the comfortable 70s (20s Celsius) all year round.

HOLIDAYS & EVENTS

Easter Week sees various religious observances, including hymn singing and dramas. **Independence Day** in early June features dances, outrigger-canoe races, marching

---

Fun Fact **Rise of the *Palolo***

Dawn after the full moon in October sees thousands of Samoans out on the reefs with buckets to snare the wiggling *palolo,* a coral worm which comes out to mate only then. Actually, the rear ends of the worms break off and swim to the surface, spewing eggs and sperm in a reproductive frenzy which lasts only a few hours. Pacific islanders consider the slimy palolo to be their caviar.

Impressions

Day after day the sun flamed; night after night the moon beaconed, or the stars paraded their lustrous regimen. I was aware of a spiritual change, or perhaps rather a molecular reconstitution. My bones were sweeter to me. I had come home to my own climate, and looked back with pity on those damp and wintry zones, miscalled the temperate . . . I am browner than the berry: only my trunk and the aristocratic spot on which I sit retain the vile whiteness of the north.

—Robert Louis Stevenson, 1891

competitions, and horse racing. The country's biggest event is the **Teuila Festival** ☆☆ during the first week of September (www.teuilafestival.ws). It features a variety of entertainment, including canoe races, dance competitions, traditional games, a floral parade, handicraft demonstrations, and the **Miss Samoa** beauty pageant. The second Sunday in October is observed as **White Sunday,** during which children go to church dressed in white, lead the services, and are honored at family feasts. **Christmas week** is celebrated with great gusto.

The **Samoa Tourism Authority** posts the precise dates and the schedules for these events on its website, **www.samoa.travel**.

HOLIDAYS

Offices and schools are closed January 1 and January 2 for New Year's Day; Good Friday and Easter Monday; April 25 as Anzac Day, to remember those who died in the two World Wars; the Monday after the second Sunday in May as Mothers' Day of Samoa; June 1 through June 3, for the annual Independence Celebrations; the first Monday in August as Labour Day; the Monday after the second Sunday in October, in honor of the preceding White Sunday; Christmas Day; and December 26 as Boxing Day.

8 Money

Samoa uses the *tala* (pronounced tah-*lah;* the Samoans' way of saying dollar), which is broken down into 100 *sene* (cents). Although many people will refer to them as dollars and cents when speaking to visitors, you can avoid potential confusion by making sure they mean Samoan talas, not U.S. dollars. The banks use both WST and SAT for the tala, but I have used **S$** in this chapter. Samoa's major hotels and some other firms quote their prices in U.S. dollars. U.S. dollar prices are given in this book as **US$.**

HOW TO GET LOCAL CURRENCY   ANZ Bank, Westpac Bank Samoa, National Bank of Samoa and **Samoa Commercial Bank** have offices on Beach Road in Apia. ANZ and Westpac both have ATMs at several locations in Apia and at Faleolo Airport, and ANZ has one at Salelologa on Savai'i. **GlobalEX** will exchange currency and traveler's checks at its office on Beach Road. Banking hours are Monday to Wednesday 9am to 3pm, and Thursday and Friday 9am to 4pm. All are open on Saturday 8 to 11am for foreign currency transactions.

The banks also have offices in the baggage claim area at Faleolo Airport, which are open when international flights arrive and depart, and there's an ATM outside in the main concourse.

The Samoan Tala, the U.S. & Canadian Dollars & the British Pound

At this writing, US$1/C$ = approximately S$2.50 (or, S$1 = US40¢), which is the exchange rate I used to calculate the dollar values given in this book. **For British readers:** At this writing, £1 = approximately S$5 (or, S$1 = 20p), the rate used to calculate the pound values below. *Note:* International exchange rates fluctuate depending on economic and political factors. Thus, the values given in this table may not be the same when you travel to the Cook Islands. Use the following table only as a guide. Find the current rates at **www.xe.com**.

S$	US$/C$	UK£	S$	US$/C$	UK£
.25	0.10	0.05	15.00	6.00	3.00
.50	0.20	0.10	20.00	8.00	4.00
.75	0.30	0.15	25.00	10.00	5.00
1.00	0.40	0.20	30.00	12.00	6.00
2.00	0.80	0.40	35.00	14.00	7.00
3.00	1.20	0.60	40.00	16.00	8.00
4.00	1.60	0.80	45.00	18.00	9.00
5.00	2.00	0.40	50.00	20.00	10.00
6.00	2.40	1.20	75.00	30.00	15.00
7.00	2.80	1.40	100.00	40.00	20.00
8.00	3.20	1.60	125.00	50.00	25.00
9.00	3.60	1.80	150.00	60.00	30.00
10.00	4.00	2.00	200.00	80.00	40.00

CREDIT CARDS   American Express, Visa, MasterCard, and Diner's Club credit cards are accepted by the major hotels and car-rental firms, and many restaurants accept MasterCard and Visa. Discover cards are not accepted. When traveling outside Apia and to Savai'i, you should carry enough cash to cover your anticipated expenses.

9 Getting There & Getting Around

GETTING THERE

BY PLANE   **Air New Zealand** flies between Auckland and Samoa, with one flight a week going on to Los Angeles and back. **Polynesian Blue,** a joint venture between the Samoan government and Virgin Blue, connects the country with Auckland and Sydney. **Air Pacific** flies twice weekly between Apia and Fiji (usually in the middle of the night). A less direct way to get to Apia is on **Hawaiian Airlines,** which flies between several West Coast cities and Honolulu, thence to Pago Pago in American Samoa. Connections to Samoa can then be made on **Polynesian Airlines'** small planes. See "Getting There & Getting Around," in chapter 2, for details.

Flights into and out of the Samoas are often packed with Samoans leaving and returning to the islands, so reserve a seat as soon as possible.

BY FERRY   The **Samoa Shipping Corporation** (© 20-935; www.samoashipping. com) operates the MV *Lady Naomi* ferry between Apia and Pago Pago in American

---

> ⌐ **Tips Get Rid of Your *Talas***
>
> Because the Samoan tala is virtually worthless outside the independent nation of Samoa (and that includes American Samoa), don't buy any before you get here. Be sure to change your leftover talas back to another currency before leaving Samoa. Use them to pay your hotel bill or change them at the airports.

Samoa. It usually departs Apia on Wednesday at midnight, arriving in Pago Pago at 8am on Thursday. The return voyage departs Pago Pago at 4pm Thursday, arriving at Apia at midnight. One-way fares from Pago Pago to Apia are US$60 (£30) for a seat, US$75 (£38) for a cabin.

ARRIVING   All international flights arrive at **Faleolo Airport (APW),** on the northwest corner of Upolu about 32km (19 miles) from Apia. There are duty-free shops and two currency exchange windows in the baggage claim area, or you can wait until you've cleared Customs and use ANZ Bank's ATM in the main concourse.

GETTING TO YOUR HOTEL   Aggie Grey's resorts and some other accommodation send buses to meet their guests who have reservations. Otherwise, transportation from Faleolo airport is by taxi or by buses which meet all international flights. The government-regulated taxi fare into town is S$50 (US$20/£10), but make sure you and the driver agree on the fare. The bus ride officially costs S$12 (US$4.80/£2.40) each way.

DEPARTING   Shuttle buses also transport passengers from the Apia hotels to Faleolo Airport for departing international flights. They arrive at the hotels at least 3 hours before departure time. Be sure to tell your hotel what flight you are leaving on; otherwise, the bus could leave you behind.

Everyone over 12 years old must pay a S$40 (US$16/£8) **departure tax** before leaving the country. Get your boarding pass and pay in Samoan currency at one of the banks in the main concourse, or after clearing Immigration if the banks aren't open.

There is no bank in the departure lounge, so change your leftover talas before clearing Immigration. Remember, Samoan currency cannot be exchanged outside the country, even in American Samoa.

GETTING AROUND
BY PLANE
Polynesian Airlines (℃ **800/264-0823** or 22-737; www.polynesianairlines.com) used to fly several times a day between Faleolo Airport and Maota Airstrip, near Salelologa on the southeastern corner of Savai'i, but during my recent visit it was down to one plane, which shuttled between Faleolo and American Samoa. Check with Polynesian Airlines to see if its Faleolo-Savai'i service has resumed.

BY FERRY
Two passenger-automobile ferries run between Mulifanua Wharf on Upolu and Salelologa on Savai'i every 2 hours Monday to Saturday from 6am to 4pm and Sunday 10am to 4pm. The *Lady Samoa* is larger, faster, and more comfortable than its smaller, open-air companion, with which it alternates trips. Plan on about 90 minutes each way. The one-way passenger fare is S$9 (US$3.60/£1.80). Local buses leave regularly from

The Samoa Islands

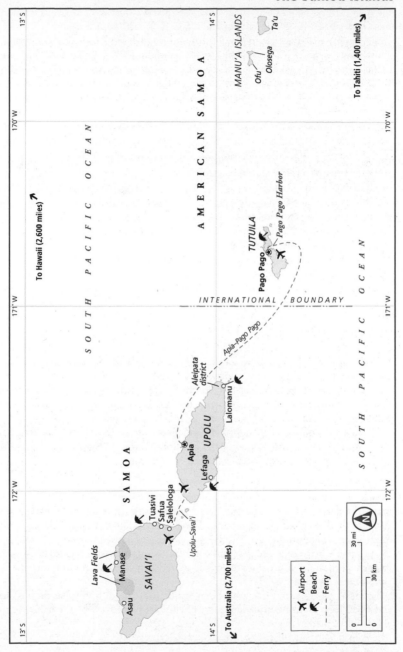

the Apia market and pass Mulifanua Wharf on their way to Pasi O Le Vaa. Taxi fare to the wharf is S$60 (US$24/£12); bus fare is S$3 (US$1.20/60p).

I bring my rental vehicle to Savai'i because it's much less of a hassle than renting another one on Savai'i. The one-way fare for vehicles is S$65 (US$26/£13), including the driver's fare. Buy your vehicle ticket in advance at **Samoa Shipping Corporation** (© 20-935; www.samoashipping.com), at Mulifanua Wharf or on Beach Road opposite the main wharf in Apia. Vehicles must be at Mulifanua Wharf at least an hour before departure.

Be sure to ask if the car rental firms will allow you to take their vehicles to Savai'i.

BY RENTAL CAR

Budget Rent-A-Car (© 800/527-0700 or 20-561; www.budget.com) and **Avis** (© 800/331-1212 or 20-486) have agencies in Apia.

Among more than 30 local firms are **Funway Rentals** (© 22-045; fax 25-008; www.funwayrentals.ws); **Apia Rentals** (© 24-244; apiarentals@ipasifika.net); **Blue Pacific Car Hire** (© 22-668; www.bluepacific.ws); **Samoana Rentals** (© 28-460; samoana@samoa.ws); and **Southpac Rentals** (© 22-074; southpac@samoa.ws).

Savai'i Car Rentals (© 51-392; fax 51-291; cars@samoa.ws) and **PK Rentals** (© 51-025; pkrentals@samoa.ws) have offices on Savai'i.

The car-rental firms will arrange to pick you up at Faleolo Airport, for an extra charge, if you have reservations. Insurance policies do not cover damage to the vehicles' undercarriages, which may occur on some rocky, unpaved roads. Depending on your own insurance policies, you might also want to buy optional personal accident coverage, which covers you and your passengers.

The main roads on both islands are paved and in reasonably good condition.

DRIVING RULES   You **drive on the right-hand side of the road,** as in the U.S., Canada, and Europe, but be extremely careful when starting out because the government has proposed changing to left-hand drive, as in Australia, New Zealand, and the U.K. You must stop for pedestrians in crosswalks and not exceed the speed limits of 35 mph on the open road or 25 mph in Apia and the villages.

Visitors are required to get a local **driver's license** from the Ministry of Transport (© 21-611), on Beach Road opposite the Old Apia Market. There is a S$12 (US$4.80/ £2.40) fee. Bring your home license. No test is required.

BY BUS

Samoa has a system of "aiga buses" which take passengers around the islands. The main **bus station** is behind the Old Apia Market on Beach Road, but the buses stop at the New Market before leaving town. They have the names of their villages written on the front. The first buses usually leave their villages between 5 and 7am, with the last departure between 2 and 2:30pm. They turn around in Apia and go back to the villages. The last departure from town is about 4:30pm. They do not run on Saturday afternoon or Sunday.

Jason's *Samoa Visitors Guide,* available at Samoa Tourism Authority, has the bus lines and fares. Here are the destinations most often visited, followed by the names of the village buses that go there:

To Robert Louis Stevenson Museum: Vaoala, Si'umu.
To Sinalei and Coconut Beach resorts: Si'umu.
To Piula Cave Pool: Falefa or Saoluafata.

To Return to Paradise Beach: Lefaga.
To Papase'a Sliding Rocks: Se'ese'e.
To Faleolo Airport: Faleolo, Pasi o le Vaa.
To Muliafanua Wharf: Pasi o le Vaa.

The Si'umu bus is the only one that goes all the way to the south coast via the Cross Island Road.

In general, 50 sene (US20¢/10p) will take you around Apia and into the hills above the town. The maximum fare is about S$4.50 (US$1.80/90p) to the most distant villages, S$2.50 (US$1/50p) to Mulifanua Wharf, where the Savai'i ferries land on Upolu's western end (see "Savai'i," later in this chapter).

BY TAXI

Apia has no shortage of taxis. The easiest way to get one is to hail a cab along Beach Road. You can also ask your hotel desk, or call **Central Taxi** (© 23-600), **Silver Star Taxis** (© 21-770), **Marlboro Taxis** (© 20-808), **Vailima Taxis** (© 22-380), **Heini Taxis** (© 24-431), and **Town Taxis** (© 21-600). They have stands at the Town Clock on Beach Road and nearby on Vaea Street. **Town Taxis** also has a stand at the airport.

The cabs do not have meters, but **fares** are set by the government. The minimum fare of S$2.70 (US$1.10/50p) will take you around Apia and its hotels. One-way fares are S$7 (US$2.80/£1.40) from Apia to Vailima; S$50 (US$20/£10) to Faleolo Airport; S$60 (US$24/£12) to Mulifanua Wharf; S$40 (US$16/£8) to Coconuts Beach Club & Spa and Sinalei Reef resorts; S$55 (US$22/£11) to Lefaga and Return to Paradise Beach; and S$25 (US$10/£5) to Piula College and Cave Pool.

FAST FACTS: Samoa

American Express There is no American Express representative in Samoa.

Area Codes Samoa does not have domestic area codes. The international country code is **685**.

Bookstores **Aggie's Gift Shop** (© 23-626), next to Aggie Grey's Hotel & Bungalows on Beach Road, carries books on Samoa and the South Pacific and a few paperback novels.

Business Hours Most shops and government offices are open Monday to Friday 9am to 5pm and Saturday 8am to 12:30pm. Except for the major hotels and restaurants, the only mom-and-pop grocery shops are open on Sunday.

Camera & Film **Image Lab** is located on Convent Street, west of Vaea Street (© 28-053).

Customs **Customs** exemptions for visitors are 200 cigarettes, 1 liter of liquor, and their personal effects. Firearms, ammunition, illegal drugs, and indecent publications are prohibited. Plants, live animals, or products of that nature, including fruits, seeds, and soil, will be confiscated unless you have prior permission from the Samoa government's Department of Agriculture and Forest. All incoming baggage is X-rayed.

Drugstores **Samoa Pharmacy** (© 22-595) and **Apia Pharmacy** (© 22-703) are both on Beach Road west of the Town Clock.

Electricity Electricity in Samoa is 240 volts, 50 cycles, and most plugs have angled prongs like those used in New Zealand and Australia.

Embassies & Consulates The **U.S. Embassy** (© 21-631) is in the ABC House on Beach Road west of the Town Clock. New Zealand and Australia both have high commissions here.

Emergencies & Police The emergency phone numbers are © **995** for police, © **994** for fire, and © **996** for an ambulance. The **police station** (© 22-222) is on Ifi'ifi Street, inland from the prime minister's office.

Etiquette & Customs See "Rules of Conduct," under "The Samoan People," earlier in this chapter, for information about fa'a Samoa and its intricate rules of etiquette and customs.

Gambling There are no casinos in Samoa, but you can play the local lottery at its office on Vaea Street.

Healthcare The best doctors are at the **MedCen Private Hospital,** a modern facility on the Cross Island Road (© 26-519). The government-run **National Hospital,** on Ifi'ifi Street in Apia (© 21-212), has an outpatient clinic open daily 8am to noon and 1 to 4:30pm. Ask your hotel staff to recommend a dentist if you need one.

Insects There are no dangerous insects in Samoa, and the plentiful mosquitoes do not carry malaria. Bring a good insect repellent with you, and consider burning mosquito coils at night.

Internet Access You can access the Internet at **Computer Services Ltd. (CSL),** at Vaea and Convent streets (© 24-149), and at **Lesamoa.net,** across the street in the Lotemanu Centre (© 20-926). You'll pay between S$2 (US80¢/40p) for 10 minutes to S$10 (US$4/£2) for 1 hour of ADSL access.

Libraries **Nelson Memorial Public Library,** on Beach Road at the Town Clock (© 21-028), is open Monday to Thursday 8:30am to 5pm, Friday 8:30am to 4:30pm, and Saturday 8:30am to 12:20pm.

Liquor Laws The legal drinking age is 21. Except for a prohibition of Sunday sale of alcoholic beverages outside the hotels or licensed restaurants, the laws are fairly liberal. Bars outside the hotels can stay open Monday to Saturday until midnight. Spirits, wine, and beer are sold at private liquor stores.

Newspapers & Magazines The daily *Samoa Observer* (www.samoaobserver.ws) carries local and world news.

Mail The main SamoaTel post office is on Beach Road, east of the Town Clock (© 23-480). It's open Monday to Friday 9am to 4:30pm.

Radio & TV Samoa has two broadcast television stations. Many homes on Upolu's north shore can receive the American Samoan channels, one of which has commercial shows, the other Public Broadcasting System programs and live news from the United States. The government also operates two AM radio stations, on which most programming is in Samoan. The world news is rebroadcast from Radio Australia and Radio New Zealand several times a day. Three privately owned FM stations broadcast lots of music.

Safety Although street crimes are rare here, remember that the communal property system still prevails in the Samoas, and items such as cameras and bags left unattended may disappear. Women should not wander alone on deserted beaches. Samoans take the Sabbath seriously, and there have been reports of local residents tossing stones at tourists who drive through some villages on Sunday. If you plan to tour by rental car, do it during the week.

Taxes Samoa imposes a 15% General Services Tax, which is included in restaurant and bar bills and is added to the cost of some other items, including rental cars, but be sure to ask if your hotel has included the tax in its room rates. Also, an airport departure tax of S$40 (US$16/£8) is levied on all passengers over 12 years of age leaving Samoa from Faleolo Airport. No tax is imposed on domestic flights or on the ferry to Pago Pago.

Telephone & Fax **SamoaTel** (www.samoatel.ws) operates both the post office and the land-line phone system here.

To call Samoa: Dial the international access code (011 from the U.S.; 00 from the U.K., Ireland, or New Zealand; or 0011 from Australia), Samoa's country code **685,** and the local number (there are no area codes within Samoa).

To make international calls from within Samoa: First dial **00,** then the country code (U.S. or Canada 1, U.K. 44, Ireland 353, Australia 61, New Zealand 64), and then the area code and phone number. International calls to North America and Europe cost about S$4.50 (US$1.80/90p) per minute. Calls to Australia and New Zealand are about half that amount.

To make domestic calls within Samoa: No prefix or area code is required for domestic long distance calls, so dial the local number.

For directory assistance: Dial ℂ **933** for domestic information, ℂ **910** for international numbers.

For operator assistance: Dial ℂ **920** for operator assistance in making international calls.

Toll-free numbers: Calling a 1-800 number in the U.S. or Canada from here is not toll-free. In fact, it costs the same as an overseas call.

Pay phones: You will need a **prepaid phone card** to make calls; buy them at post offices and most small shops. A digital readout will tell you how much money you have left on your card.

Cellphones: Two companies rent mobile phones and sell SIM cards for unlocked GMS cellphones: SamoaTel's **Go Mobile** (ℂ **44-600;** www.telecomsamoa.ws), in the post office building on Beach Road; and **Digicel Samoa** (ℂ **28-003** or 30-313; www.digicelsamoa.com), in the Chan Mow & Co. building, corner of Beach Road and Vaea Street. Both have booths at Faleolo International Airport. Phones rent for about S$6 (US$2.40/£1.20) a day, but you must buy prepaid time cards to use them. Both sell SIM cards for S$30 (US$12/£6), which includes S$10 (US$4/£2) worth of airtime—S70¢ (US28¢/14p) per minute weekdays, S25¢ (US10¢/5p) a minute nights and weekends.

Time Local time in Samoa is 11 hours behind GMT. That means it's 3 hours behind Pacific Standard Time (4 hr. behind during daylight saving time). If it's noon standard time in California and 3pm in New York, it's 9am in Apia. Samoa is east of the international date line; it shares the same date with North America and is 1 day behind Tonga, Fiji, Australia, and New Zealand. Remember that if you are going on to those countries or will be arriving from one of them.

Tipping Tipping is discouraged as being contrary to the traditional way of life.

Water All tap water should be boiled before drinking. Safe bottled water is produced locally and is available at most grocery stores.

Weights & Measures Samoa is officially on the metric system, but in their everyday lives, many residents still calculate distances by the British system used in American Samoa and in the United States. Speed limits are posted in miles per hour, and the speedometers of many local vehicles (most of which have the steering wheels on the left side, in the American and European fashion) show both miles per hour and kilometers per hour.

10 Exploring Apia & the Rest of Upolu

The town of Apia sits midway along the north coast of Upolu, which makes it a centrally located base from which to explore the main island. The Cross Island Road runs 23km (14 miles) from town, across the range of extinct volcanoes that form Upolu, thereby bringing the south coast within easy reach of town.

THE TOP ATTRACTION

Robert Louis Stevenson Museum & Grave 🌸🌸🌸 When Robert Louis Stevenson and his wife, Fanny, decided to stay in Samoa in 1889 (see the "Teller of Tales" box, earlier in this chapter), they bought 127 hectares (314 acres) of virgin land on the slopes of Mount Vaea above Apia and named the estate **Vailima**—or "Five Waters"— because five streams crossed the property. They cleared about 3.2 hectares (8 acres) and lived there in a small shack for nearly a year. The U.S. historian Henry Adams dropped in unannounced one day in 1890 and found them dressed in lava-lavas and doing dirty work about their hovel. To Adams, the couple's living conditions were repugnant. Their Rousseauian existence didn't last long, however, for in 1891 they built the first part of this magnificent mansion.

When it was completed, the big house had five bedrooms, a library, a ballroom large enough to accommodate 100 dancers, and the only fireplace in Samoa. The Stevensons shipped 72 tons of furniture from England, all of which was hauled the 5km (3 miles) from Apia on sleds pulled by bullocks. A piano sat in one corner of the great hall, in a glass case to protect it from Samoa's humidity. Among their possessions were a Rodin nude presented to Stevenson by the sculptor himself, a damask tablecloth from Queen Victoria, and a sugar bowl used by both Robert Burns and Sir Walter Scott.

The Stevensons' lifestyle matched their surroundings. Oysters were shipped on ice from New Zealand, Bordeaux wine was brought by the cask from France and bottled at Vailima, and 1840 vintage Madeira was poured on special occasions. They dressed formally for dinner every evening—except for their bare feet—and were served by Samoans dressed in tartan lava-lavas, in honor of the great author's Scottish origins.

Vailima and this lavish lifestyle baffled the Samoans. As far as they could tell, writing was not labor; therefore, Stevenson had no visible way of earning a living. Yet all this money rolled in, which meant to them that Stevenson must be a man of much *mana,* the mysterious power which Polynesians believed descended directly from heaven to their chiefs (the higher the chief, the more the mana). He was also a master at one of their favorite pastimes—storytelling—and he took interest in their own stories, as well as their customs, language, and politics. When the followers of the defeated Mataafa were released from prison, they built a road from Apia to Vailima in appreciation for Stevenson's support of their unsuccessful struggle against the Germans. And when he died in 1894, they cut the "Road of the Loving Hearts" to his grave on Mount Vaea overlooking Vailima.

Stevenson's wife, Fanny, died in California in 1914, and her ashes were brought back to Vailima and buried at the foot of Robert's grave. Her Samoan name, Aolele, is engraved on a bronze plaque.

Samoa's head of state lived in Vailima until hurricanes severely damaged the mansion in 1990 and 1991. Since then, an extraordinary renovation has returned it to its appearance when Stevenson lived here—without the Rodin. A sitting room matches exactly that seen in a photo made of Fanny on a chair. Another photo of Stevenson dictating is hung in his library, where he stood at the time.

The "Road of the Loving Hearts" leading to **Stevenson's Grave** passes a lovely cascade that Stevenson turned into a swimming pool. A short, steep trail to the grave takes about 30 strenuous minutes; a longer but easier path takes about an hour. Mount Vaea is best climbed in the cool of early morning.

Vailima, on the Cross Island Rd., 5km/3 miles south of Apia. © 20-798. Admission S$15 (US$6/£3) adults, S$5 (US$2/£1) children under 11. Mon–Fri 9am–3:30pm; Sat 8am–noon. 45-min. guided tours on hour and half-hour Mon–Fri 9am–3pm, Sat 11:30am.

A STROLL THROUGH APIA

Like most South Pacific towns, Samoa's capital and only town has expanded from one small Samoan village to include adjacent settlements and an area of several square miles, all of which is now known collectively as Apia, the name of the village where Europeans first settled. The old villages have given their names to the many neighborhoods of the sprawling metropolitan area, and much to the confusion of us visitors, the locals identify locations by neighborhood names instead of streets. The Apia area now has a population in excess of 50,000.

Most points of interest lie along **Beach Road,** the broad avenue curving along the harbor. A waterfront promenade extends along one side and churches, government buildings, and businesses line the other.

We start our walking tour of downtown at **Aggie Grey's Hotel & Bungalows,** on the banks of the Vaisigano River. This famous hotel and its founder are stories unto themselves, which are recounted in "Where to Stay on Upolu," later in this chapter. From Aggie's, head west, or to the left as you face the harbor.

> ## (Moments Walking in Apia
>
> A Hollywood set designer would be hard-pressed to top Apia as an old South Seas town. I love to stroll along the promenade fringing the perfect half-moon curve of Beach Road and let the old churches and clapboard government buildings tell me how things used to be. Locals fishing or idling the time away along the seawall tell me what's going on today.

The two large churches on the left are both Protestant, legacies of the Rev. John Williams, for whom the modern high-rise office building at the corner of Falealili Road is named. On the waterfront across Beach Road stands the **John Williams Memorial** to this missionary who brought Christianity to Samoa and many more South Pacific islands. Williams's bones are reputedly buried beneath the clapboard **Congregational Christian Church,** directly across Beach Road from the memorial. The missionary was killed and eaten on Erromango in what now is Vanuatu; the story has it that his bones were recovered and buried here.

The colonial-style **Courthouse** at the corner of Ifi'ifi Street formerly housed the Supreme Court and Prime Minister's office, before they moved into high-rise buildings across the road. In colonial times, it was headquarters of the New Zealand trusteeship administration and site of the Mau Movement demonstration and shootings in 1929.

Upstairs in the Courthouse, the small but interesting **Museum of Samoa** (© **63-444**) is worth a brief look. It's open Monday to Friday noon to 4pm. Admission is free.

When he came to Samoa, Robert Louis Stevenson first stayed in an old clapboard building in what is now the center of dining and drinking in Apia (it's the one with the upstairs veranda). The Marist Brothers' Primary School is on the banks of Mulivai Stream. Across the bridge stands **Mulivai Catholic Cathedral,** begun in 1885 and completed some 20 years later. Farther along, the imposing **Matafele Methodist Church** abuts the stores in the **Wesley Arcade.** According to a monument across Beach Road, Tongan Chief Saivaaia brought Methodism to Samoa in 1835.

The remains of the German warship *Adler* are buried under the reclaimed land, now the site of two huge, fale-topped government office buildings, built in the mid-1990s with foreign aid from China. On the water side of Beach Road stands a memorial to the Samoans who fought alongside the New Zealanders during World War II.

The center of modern Apia's business district is the **Town Clock,** the World War I memorial at the foot of Vaea Street. Across the street, the **Chan Mow & Co.** building is a fine example of late South Seas colonial architecture; its arches and red-tile roof make it look almost Spanish. Between the clock and the water stands a large Samoan fale known as **Pulenu'u House,** where local residents can be seen lounging or eating their lunches. Facing the clock, **Nelson Memorial Public Library** is named for Olaf Nelson, son of a Swedish father and Samoan mother. Olaf Nelson was exiled to New Zealand in 1928 for his leadership role in the Mau Movement.

Continuing west on Beach Road, you come to the sprawling **Old Apia Market.** Once the vegetable market, this large covered space is now home to flea-market stalls where you can find items ranging from sandals to toothpaste. One area is devoted to handicraft vendors, and you can stop and watch local women weaving *pandanus* mats,

Apia

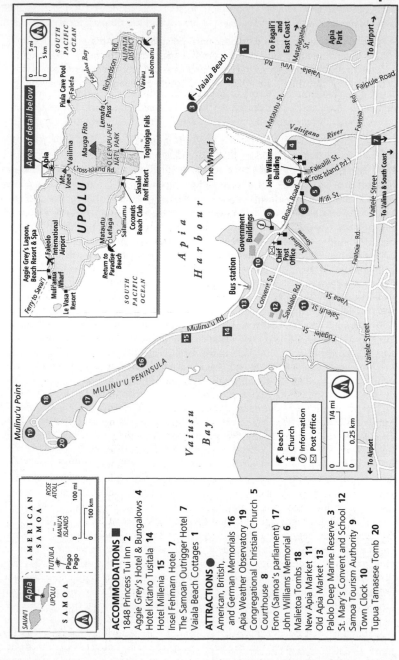

ACCOMMODATIONS ■
1848 Princess Tui Inn **2**
Aggie Grey's Hotel & Bungalows **4**
Hotel Kitano Tusitala **14**
Hotel Millenia **15**
Insel Fehmarn Hotel **7**
The Samoan Outrigger Hotel **7**
Vaiala Beach Cottages **1**

ATTRACTIONS ●
American, British,
and German Memorials **16**
Apia Weather Observatory **19**
Congregational Christian Church **5**
Courthouse **8**
Fono (Samoa's parliament) **17**
John Williams Memorial **6**
Malietoa Tombs **18**
New Apia Market **11**
Old Apia Market **13**
Palolo Deep Marine Reserve **3**
St. Mary's Convent and School **12**
Samoa Tourism Authority **9**
Town Clock **10**
Tupua Tamasese Tomb **20**

hats, and handbags. This is a good place to shop for woodcarvings and *tapa* cloth (called *siapo* here; see "Shopping," later). I haven't had the stomach for such local fare since my days as a young backpacker, but the food stalls along the market's water side are the cheapest (and dirtiest) places in town to get a meal.

Fugalei Street, which leaves Beach Road across from the market, goes to the airport and the west coast. Walk down it a block, and turn left and go east on Convent Street past picturesque **St. Mary's Convent and School.** At the next corner, turn right on Saleufi Street and walk inland 2 blocks to the **New Apia Market,** a modern, tin-roofed pavilion where Samoan families sell a wide variety of tropical fruits and vegetables, all of which have the prices clearly marked (there is no bargaining). Like everywhere else in the islands, the market is busiest on Saturday morning.

THE MULINU'U PENINSULA

Beyond the market, Beach Road becomes Mulinu'u Road, which runs about a mile to the end of **Mulinu'u Peninsula,** a low arm separating Apia Harbour to the east from Vaiusu Bay on the west. About halfway out on the peninsula stand the **American, British, and German Memorials,** one dedicated to the German sailors who died in the 1889 hurricane, one to the British and American sailors who were drowned during that fiasco, and one to commemorate the raising of the German flag in 1900.

The Mulinu'u Peninsula is home of the **Fono,** Samoa's parliament. The new Fono building sits opposite a memorial to Samoa's independence, the two separated by a wide lawn. The Fono's old home is next to the road in the same park. A tomb on the lawn holds the remains of Iosefa Mataafa, one of the paramount chiefs.

Between the Apia Yacht Club and Sails at Mulinu'u restaurant stand the **Malietoa Tombs,** the freshest being that of Malietoa Tanumafili II, Samoa's first head of state, who was buried here in 2007. The **tombs** of Tuimalaeali'ifano and Tupua Tamasese, two other paramount chiefs, are on the western side of the peninsula. At the end of the peninsula stands the **Apia Weather Observatory,** originally built by the Germans in 1902 (apparently having learned a costly lesson from the unpredicted 1889 hurricane).

EXPLORING UPOLU

To travel along the roads of Upolu away from Apia is to see Polynesia relatively unchanged from the days before the Europeans arrived. Bring your swimming gear, for you'll also visit some of the South Pacific's most stunningly beautiful beaches.

THE NORTHEAST COAST: APIA TO ALEIPATA

One of the most popular sightseeing tours makes a loop from Apia to the long, magnificent white beaches of Aleipata District on Upolu's eastern end. Most of Upolu is a volcanic shield that slopes gently to the sea, but because the eastern portion is older—and therefore more eroded and rugged than the central and western areas—this spot has the island's most dramatic scenery.

The East Coast Road follows the shore for 26km (16 miles) to the village of Falefa, skirting the lagoon and black-sand surf beaches at Lauli'i and Solosolo. Look for **Piula College,** a Methodist school on a promontory overlooking the sea about 3.3km (2 miles) before Falefa. Turn in at the playing field and drive around to the school on the right. Park there and follow the steps down to the freshwater **Piula Cave Pool** ★★. Bring snorkeling gear to swim through an underwater opening at the back of the pool into a second chamber. The cave pool is open from 8am to 4:30pm Monday through Saturday; admission is S$2 (US80¢/40p). There is a rudimentary changing room for visitors. No alcoholic beverages are allowed on the grounds.

To the left of the bridge beyond Falefa village, **Falefa Falls** are especially impressive during the rainy season. The road climbs toward 285m (935 ft.) **Le Mafa Pass** in the center of the island, with some great views back toward the sea. Another rugged, winding road to the left just before the pass dead-ends at **Fagaloa Bay**, once a volcanic crater that exploded seaward, leaving a mountain-clad bay. Although paved, the Fagaloa Bay road is steep and winding, so drive with caution.

Once you're over the pass, the main road crosses a bridge. Just beyond, an unmarked road goes to the right and cuts through the forests down to the south coast. We will come back this way, road conditions permitting, but for now go straight ahead on the **Richardson Road.** Once a bush path, this paved road crosses a refreshingly cool high plateau and skirts **Afulilo Lake,** formed by the country's hydroelectric dam.

LALOMANU BEACH ✹✹✹

From Afulilo Lake, the road gently descends into **Aleipata,** an enormously picturesque district. As you turn the corner to the south coast, stop at the overlook on the small promontory overlooking **Lalomanu Beach** ✹✹✹, one of the most gorgeous in the South Pacific. Your photos from here will be among the best you'll take in Samoa, for the view includes a clifflike escarpment behind a narrow shelf of land bordered by a long, white-sand beach. Four small islands offshore enliven the view, and on a clear day you can see the jagged blue outline of American Samoa on the horizon.

There's not enough space at Lalomanu for a village, but a collection of rustic **beach fales,** available for camping, stands on these sands (see "Beach Fales at Lalomanu," later in this chapter). They have restaurants, so stop for refreshment here.

Keep going along the southeast shore to Vavau village, where the paved Le Mafa Pass Road begins (don't take the road to the left; it dead-ends at a river). Le Mafa Pass Road climbs steadily uphill to a viewpoint overlooking 53m (174 ft.) **Sopo'aga Falls** ✹. The villagers have built a small park on a cliff overlooking the deep and narrow gorge, complete with picnic tables and toilets. They charge S$3 (US$1.20/60p) per vehicle, but that's a small price to pay for this view.

THE CROSS ISLAND ROAD

The Cross Island Road runs for 23km (14 miles) from the John Williams Building on Beach Road in Apia to the village of Si'umu on the south coast. Along the way it passes first the Robert Louis Stevenson Museum at Vailima and then the **Malololeilei Scenic View,** a park on the eastern side of the road. Pull off here and take the short walks to views over Apia, the sea, and a waterfall. Back on the road, you'll later pass the modern, nine-sided **House of Worship,** one of six Baha'i Faith temples in the world. Open for meditation and worship, the temple was dedicated in 1984. An information center outside the temple makes available materials about the Baha'i Faith.

After passing the temple, the road winds through cool, rolling pastures. Near the top of the island, a rough road leads off the Cross Island Road westward to the new **Lake Lanoto'o National Park.** The 400-hectare (988-acre) preserve is home to rare endemic bird species, including the red-headed parrot finch and the crimson-crowned fruit dove. Lake Lanoto'o, Samoa's largest lake, is filled with goldfish introduced by German settlers in the 19th century. Unless and until the often muddy trail is improved, it will take at least an hour to hike into the park, a feat best done with a guide (see "Watersports, Golf & Other Outdoor Activities," below). For more information contact the Ministry of Natural Resources and Environment (✆ **23-800;** www.mnre.gov.ws).

Moments **A Day on a Beautiful Beach**

A Sunday afternoon at one of the South Pacific's most beautiful beaches is on my agenda every time I come here. Paradise Beach is what all beaches should be like: surf breaking around black rock outcrops, palm trees draped over white sand. But I'm even more enamored of Lalomanu Beach on the island's southeastern corner, where a clifflike mountain provides a backdrop and offshore islands enhance the sea view.

On your way down to the south coast, watch on the right for a parking area overlooking **Papapai-tai Waterfalls,** which plunge 90m (295 ft.) into one of the gorges that streams have cut into central Upolu's volcanic shield. Of the many waterfalls on Upolu, Papapai-tai is the most easily seen.

THE SOUTHWEST COAST 𝒜𝒜

A left turn at the end of the Cross Island Road in Si'umu village on the south coast leads to **O Le Pupu-Pue National Park** and the **Togitogiga National Forest** 𝒜. The park contains the best remaining tropical rain forest on Upolu, but you'll have to hike into the valley to reach it. Some 51 species of wildlife live in the park: 42 species of birds, five of mammals, and four of lizards. Lovely **Togitogiga Falls** is a short walk from the entrance, from where a trail to **Peapea Cave** also begins. It's a 2-hour round-trip hike to the cave, which is a lava tube (it's dangerous to enter during heavy rains). Another walking trail leads seaward to arches cut by the surf into the south coast. **Mount Le Pu'e,** in the northwest corner of the park, is a well-preserved volcanic cinder cone. The park and reserve are open daily during the daylight hours, and there's no admission fee. Contact the Ministry of Natural Resources and Environment (✆ **23-800;** www.mnre.gov.ws) for more information.

Heading west from Si'umu, the road soon passes the Sinalei and Coconuts Beach Club & Spa resorts and then the nearby **Togo Mangrove Estuary,** a tidal waterway that's alive with birds, flowers, bees, and other wildlife.

Some of Upolu's most beautiful beaches await on the southwest coast, particularly in the Lefaga district. One of these is at the village of **Salamumu.** Farther on the south coast road, Matautu village boasts **Return to Paradise Beach** 𝒜𝒜𝒜. Palms hang over this sandy beach punctuated by large boulders that confront the breaking surf. It gets its name from the movie starring Gary Cooper that was filmed here in 1951. The S$5 (US$1.65/80p) per-person custom fee charged by Matautu village is well worth it.

From Matautu the main road winds across the island to the north coast.

ORGANIZED TOURS

Based at the two Aggie Grey's hotels, **Samoa Scenic Tours** (✆ **22-880;** www.samoascenictours.com) offers a variety of trips which stop for photographs and a swim at beautiful beaches and waterfalls. A half-day Apia township tour will take you around town and up to the Robert Lewis Stevenson Museum for about S$85 (US$34/£17) per person. A morning excursion goes to Piula Cave Pool and Falefa Falls for the same price. A full-day trip goes to either Lalomanu or Lefaga (Return to Paradise) beaches for S$120 (US$48/£24). Another full-day excursion goes out to Manono Island, for about S$160 (US$64/£32). On Sunday a half-day outing heads to Lolomanu beach on the southeast coast, with juice and towels included for S$150

(US$60/£30) per person. Each day's offerings are written on a notice board in the lobby at Aggie's in town.

Oceania Travel & Tours, at the Hotel Kitano Tusitala (© 24-443) has similar excursions, as does Samoa Tours (© 30-089; www.samoatours.com) and Polynesian Xplorer (© 26-940; www.polynesianxplorer.com).

11 Watersports, Golf & Other Outdoor Activities

Most watersports are headquartered at Aggie Grey's Lagoon, Beach Resort & Spa near the airport; on the south coast at Sinalei Reef Resort & Spa and Coconuts Beach Club & Spa; and at the beach fales on Lalomanu Beach on Upolu's southeastern corner (see "Where to Stay on Upolu," below). You need not be a guest to partake of the activities because everyone must pay.

At Aggie Grey's beach resort, Aqua Samoa Watersports (© 45-662 or 777-4744; www.aquasamoa.com) offers resort-front activities such as jet- and water-skiing, kayaking, banana boat rides, wake- and kite-boarding, Hobie Cat sailing, snorkeling trips, game fishing, and scuba diving (including PADI courses). Also at Aggie's, Samoa Adventure (© 26-107 or 777-0272; www.samoa-adventure.com) uses the *Shiloh II*, a 35-ft. catamaran to sail out in the Apolima Strait, including a trip to Amnono Island.

At Lalomanu Beach, Moanalei Dive 'n' Surf (© 41-015; www.moanaleidiven surf.com) rents kayaks, surfboards, and snorkeling gear, and it has scuba diving, snorkeling trips, fishing, and surfing excursions.

GOLF   The 18 holes at the par 72 Le Penina Golf Course (© 770-GOLF [4653]; www.peninaresortandgolfclub.com) virtually wrap around Aggie Grey's Lagoon, Beach Resort & Spa. Greens fees are S$135 (US$54/£27) for 18 holes, including cart. In a sports complex at Tuanaimato, in the highlands above Apia, the Faleata Golf Course (© 23-964) has 18 holes, a driving range, and golf cart rental. Greens fees are S$20 (US$8/£4). The Royal Samoan Golf Club (© 20-120) has a 9-hole course at Fagali'i, on the eastern side of Apia, and visitors are welcome to use the facilities. Call the club's secretary for greens fees and starting times. Sinalei Reef Resort & Spa (© 25-191) on the south coast has a 9-hole course (see "Where to Stay on Upolu," below).

HIKING   Upolu has a number of very good hiking trails. The most picturesque is the Coastal Trail in O le Pupu-Pue National Park (see "Exploring Apia & the Rest of Upolu," earlier in this chapter). This relatively flat track runs along the top of the park's sea cliffs and has some spectacular views. Another trail in the park goes through rainforests to the Peapea cave. The most exciting track leads to Lake Lanoto'o in the

---

Tips **Start Early by Watching the Police Band Parade**

Apia can be brutally hot at midday, so the best time to walk around it is right after the **Samoa Police Brass Band** marches along Beach Road (daily between 7:30 and 8am) to Government House, where it raises the national flag. It's worth watching the cops in their white helmets, light blue uniforms, and lava-lavas. If you take photos, don't get between the band and the flagpole.

new **Lake Lanoto'o National Park** (see "The Cross Island Road," above). This difficult hike takes at least 90 minutes each way is best done with a guide, such as **Samoa
on Foot** (© 31-252 or 26-592).

KAYAKING   Mats Arvidsson, a Swede who lives in Samoa, operates **Island
Explorer** (© 32-663 or 777-1814; www.islandexplorer.ws), which has guided day
tours into the Togo Mangrove Estuary on the south coast, or to the Aeipata coast.
These trips cost S$180 (US$72/£36) per person. He also has overnight expeditions to
Manono Island for S$360 (US$144/£72) plus the cost of a beach fale, and multiday
paddling trips along the Aleipata coast.

SWIMMING & SNORKELING   The best swimming and snorkeling are on the
beaches of Aleipata and the southwest coast (see "Exploring Apia & the Rest of
Upolu," earlier in this chapter). In town, just east of the main wharf, canyons in the
reef at **Palolo Deep Marine Reserve** ⋆ (© 26-942) make for good snorkeling without having to leave town. The snorkeling is best at high tide, when you can swim
rather than walk across the reef to the deep-water canyons. Don't expect to see colorful coral here; it's best for sea life. The small sandy beach is good for sunning at any
tide. This city park has changing rooms, and it rents snorkeling gear. Admission is S$3
(US$1.20/60p). The reserve is open daily from 8am to 6pm.

You of strong bottom can slip down the waterfall known as **Papase'a Sliding Rocks**
into a dark pool. Take a taxi or the Se'ese'e village bus. The rocks are about 2 kilometers (1¼ miles) from the paved road; the bus driver may go out of his way to take you
there, but you will have to walk back to the bus route. The villagers extract a S$2
(US80¢/40p) custom fee per person.

Another popular outing away from Apia is to **Piula Cave Pool** and the outlying
beaches. See "Exploring Apia & the Rest of Upolu," earlier in this chapter, for details.

12 Shopping

Although not in the quantity you'll find in Tonga, Samoans turn out excellent hand-
made baskets, sewing trays, purses, floor mats, napkin rings, placemats, and fans
woven from pandanus and other local materials, plus some woodcarvings.

Aggie's Gift Shop, next to Aggie Grey's Hotel & Bungalows (© 23-626), has Apia's
best selection of quality handicrafts and Samoan products such as sandalwood soap,
small bags of kava, and watercolors by local artists. The handicrafts include shell jewelry and siapo cloth, carved wooden war clubs, ceremonial kava bowls, and high-talking chiefs' staffs (known as *tootoo*). Clothing items include hand-screened lava-lavas,
T-shirts, shorts, and dresses. The shop also carries books about the Samoas and has a
snack bar just inside the front door.

The widest array of handicrafts is on display at the **Old Apia Market,** on Beach
Road west of the Town Clock (no phone). Once Apia's vegetable market, this giant
shed is now a crowded, very active flea market, with vendors selling everything from
cosmetics to shoes (local wags say it's better stocked than Apia's regular stores because
some goods may have been slipped past Customs on their way from American
Samoa). Your best buys here are fine mats and other Samoan handicrafts; in fact, you
can even watch local women at work in their stalls. The other handicraft shops usually have better-quality pieces, but you might find an exceptional one here. Especially
look for the merchant who sells intricately carved *tanoa* (kava) bowls.

13 Where to Stay on Upolu

ACCOMMODATIONS IN APIA

MODERATE

Aggie Grey's Hotel & Bungalows ✦✦✦ This venerable hotel has the same warm, friendly atmosphere Aggie Grey instilled when she opened it in 1943 (see the "Hot Dogs & Hamburgers" box, below). Aggie's Gift Shop next door shows what it looked like before the fire marshal ordered the old clapboard building closed. Now a modern Victorian-style building fronting Beach Road houses the reception area, the air-conditioned **Le Tamarina** restaurant (see "Where to Dine in Apia," later in this chapter), an open-air bar facing the harbor, a coffee shop, and two floors of modern rooms and suites with private verandas overlooking Apia Harbour. In some ways this modern facility has made Aggie's two hotels in one, for its rooms are designed primarily for business travelers (children under 12 cannot stay in this wing), and its presidential suites are fit for potentates. The property out back is like a resort, with its exquisite Old Fale beside the swimming pool with a palm tree growing out of an islet in the middle. Guests can still take their meals under the great turtle-shaped roof or wander over to the bar for a cold Vailima beer and a chat with friendly strangers. The efficient staff prepares feasts and barbecues in astounding quantity, as in Aggie's day, especially during the Wednesday night *fiafias* (see "Island Nights on Upolu," later).

The older hotel rooms out back are in stone-accented, two-story buildings rambling through a garden so thick with vegetation that it's easy to get lost trying to find your way from one unit to another. My favorites are the charming individual VIP fale bungalows topped by turtle-shaped roofs. Each of these units bears the name of one of Aggie's famous guests, such as Gary Cooper, William Holden, and Marlon Brando. Every unit has an old-fashioned fold-down ironing board, an Aggie Grey trademark.

P.O. Box 67, Apia (Beach Rd., on the waterfront). ℂ 800/448-8355 or 22-880. Fax 23-626. www.aggiegreys.com. 181 units. US$125–US$165 (£63–£83) double; US$270–US$350 (£135–£175) suite. AE, DC, MC, V. **Amenities:** 3 restaurants; bars; outdoor pool; exercise room; children's programs; concierge; activities desk; business center; salon; 24-hr. room service; babysitting; laundry service. *In room:* A/C, TV, minibar, fridge, coffeemaker, iron.

Hotel Kitano Tusitala Built in 1974 by the government and named the Tusitala in honor of Robert Louis Stevenson, this hotel is now owned by Kitano, a Japanese construction company. The public areas are in three Samoan-style fales with turtle-shaped roofs. They ring a tropical garden featuring a children's wading pool, from which water falls down into a larger adult swimming pool. The rooms are all in five two-story motel-style buildings grouped beyond the swimming pools. Superior and special units facing the pool are in better condition than the standard rooms. All units have a sliding glass door opening onto either a private patio or balcony. They are air-conditioned, but you won't feel any cross-ventilation unless you leave the back door open. A bar and lounge in one of the open-air fales stands next to the pool, as does a snack bar. Another of the three common buildings houses **Stevenson's Restaurant** (with portraits of R. L. S. himself). The hotel's **Seaview Restaurant,** across the main driveway, proffers good Western and Japanese fare accompanied by a harbor view.

P.O. Box 101, Apia (Beach Rd., Mulinu'u Peninsula). ℂ 800/448-8355 or 21-122. Fax 23-652. www.kitano.ws. 94 units. S$355–S$480 (US$142–US$192/£71–£96) double; S$540 S$900 (US$216 US$360/£108–£180) suite. AE, DC, MC, V. **Amenities:** 4 restaurants; 3 bars; outdoor pool; 2 tennis courts; activities desk; business center; limited room service; babysitting; laundry service; coin-op washers and dryers. *In room:* A/C, TV, fridge, coffeemaker, iron (in superior rooms).

Insel Fehmarn Hotel   This modern, well-kept motel sits on the side of the hill above Apia. Some rooms enjoy views of town and the reef from their balconies, especially those on the third (top) floor. Most of the identical rooms in this beige concrete block structure have two double beds, chairs, tables, tiled shower-only bathrooms, and kitchenettes. Some executive rooms have one king-size bed, and one suite has a separate bedroom. It's popular with business travelers looking for kitchen-equipped accommodations. Giodanno's Cafe & Pizzeria is across the road (see "Where to Dine in Apia," below). There's a complimentary shuttle to downtown Apia every 2 hours 7:45am to 4pm weekdays and 7:45am to noon Saturday.

P.O. Box 3272, Apia (on Cross Island Rd., 2km/1¼ miles uphill from Beach Rd.). ℂ 23-301. Fax 22-204. www.inselfehmarnsamoa.com. 54 units. US$98–US$150 (£49–£75) double; US$264 (£132) suite. Rates include breakfast. AE, DC, MC, V. **Amenities:** Restaurant; bar; outdoor pool; 2 tennis courts; car rentals; business center; laundry service; coin-op washers and dryers. *In room:* A/C, TV, kitchen, coffeemaker.

INEXPENSIVE

1848 Princess Tui Inn   Most of the units in this historic and charming colonial house are the original bedrooms. Although accommodations are basic by today's standards, fans hang from their high ceilings, and mosquito nets cover their beds, most queen-size. The choice units are on the front of the house; their windows face the sea across the road. One of these and a larger family unit have private bathrooms. Two rooms with six beds each serve as dormitories, one reserved for females. A modern concrete-block building next door holds four "cottage" rooms; these lack charm and share a bathroom, but they are air-conditioned. All guests share a communal kitchen. No smoking in the rooms here.

P.O. Box 9595, Apia (Vaiala Beach, 1.3km/³⁄₄ mile east of Main Wharf). ℂ 23-342. Fax 22-451. www.princesstui.ws. 12 units (7 without bathroom), 12 dorm beds. US$42–US$72 (£21–£36) double; US$18 (£9) dorm bed. Rates include breakfast. AE, MC, V. **Amenities:** Activities desk; laundry service. *In room:* A/C (cottage units); no phone.

Hotel Millenia Samoa *(Value)*   This attractive three-story colonial-style hotel opened in 2001, but it takes its name from two of its owners; thus the spelling and the pronunciation: Mel-ay-*nee*-ah. Sitting across Beach Road from Apia Harbor, the property looks and feels more like an inn than a hotel, given its large, comfortable guest lounge and veranda on the second floor. Both of these have sea views, as do some of its deluxe units, one of which opens to a front balcony. These are preferable to the standard units on the ground level and four kitchen-equipped units in a rear wing. Although most of the interior walls are of New Zealand pine, wicker chairs and bright bedspreads lend a tropical ambience. A ground floor restaurant with outdoor seating serves good regional fare at breakfast, lunch, and dinner.

P.O. Box 214, Apia (Beach Rd., Mulinu'u Peninsula). ℂ 28-284. Fax 28-285. www.hotelmilleniasamoa.com. 19 units. S$210–S$312 (US$84–US$125/£42–£62) double. MC, V. **Amenities:** Restaurant; bar; laundry service. *In room:* A/C, TV, kitchen (4 units), fridge, coffeemaker (family unit).

The Samoan Outrigger Hotel   Claus Hermansen liked what he saw so much during a visit to Samoa that he gave up a banking career in Denmark to live here and start this little hotel. There's a reading area and TV lounge with a billiards table in the great room of this colonial-style house, and to the rear is a communal kitchen and dining area. The best-equipped rooms are on the ground floor. They have their own entrances, air conditioners, phones, patios, toilets, and cold-water showers. A family unit can sleep up to five persons. The dormitories are four beach fales (see the "Beach Fales at Lalomanu" box, below), which sit out in the backyard along with an aboveground pool. All

Hot Dogs & Hamburgers

Back in 1919, a young woman of British and Samoan descent named Agnes Genevieve Grey opened the Cosmopolitan Club on a point of land where the Vaisigano River flows into Apia Harbour. It was a small pub catering to businessmen and occasional tourists who climbed off the transpacific steamers.

And then came the U.S. Marines, who landed in 1942 to train for the South Pacific campaigns against the Japanese. Aggie Grey started selling them much-appreciated hot dogs and hamburgers. Quickly her little enterprise expanded into a three-story clapboard hotel. Many of those young marines, including future U.S. Secretary of State George Shultz, left Samoa with fond memories of Aggie Grey and her hotel (and in the case of Shultz, a tattoo on his derriere).

Another serviceman was a U.S. naval historian named James A. Michener. Everyone in Samoa believes Michener used Aggie as the role model for Bloody Mary, the Tonkinese woman who provided U.S. servicemen with wine, song, and other diversions in his *Tales of the South Pacific*.

Although her hotel grew to include more than 150 rooms, Aggie always circulated among her guests, making them feel at home. Everyone sat down family style at meals in the old clapboard building on Beach Road, and afterward they all moseyed over for coffee in the lounge. Afternoon tea was a time for socializing and swapping gossip from places far away. And on fiafia nights, when the feasts were laid out, Aggie herself would dance the graceful Samoan *siva*.

Like Robert Louis Stevenson, the Samoans revered Aggie Grey. They made her the only commoner to appear on a Samoan postage stamp. And when she died in 1988 at the age of 90, Head of State Malietoa Tanumafili II and hundreds of other mourners escorted her to her final resting place in the hills above Apia.

rooms have fans as well as mosquito nets over their beds. Claus's hostel has been spotlessly clean throughout my recent visits. Giodanno's Cafe & Pizzeria is a short walk away.

P.O. Box 1922, Apia (Cross Island Rd., 1km/⅔ mile south of Beach Rd). © 20-042. Fax 30-722. www.outrigger. netfirms.com. 11 units (4 without bathroom), 4 fales with 12 dorm beds. S$130–S$180 (US$52–US$72/£26–£36) double; S$55 (US$22/£11) dorm bed. Rates include continental breakfast. AE, MC, V. **Amenities:** Communal kitchen; car rentals. *In room:* A/C (5 units), fridge (5 units), no phone (5 units).

Vaiala Beach Cottages *Value*   Across the street from Vaiala Beach, these comfortable and airy bungalows share a yard with frangipani, crotons, and other tropical plants. Except for the tropical furnishings and decor, such as cane furniture and woven floor mats, the bungalows are all identical: a full kitchen with stainless-steel sink, a bedroom with either one double or two twin beds, a spacious bathroom with a shower that dispenses hot water, and a narrow balcony off a bright living room. They are built of pine, including the varnished interior walls. The living rooms have ceiling fans hanging over the sitting area, but the large, screened, louvered windows and sliding doors leading to the balconies usually allow the trade winds to cool the house without such assistance. Rental kayaks, snorkel gear, and tennis rackets are available.

P.O. Box 2025, Apia (Vaiala Beach, 1.5km/1 mile east of Main Wharf). © **22-202.** Fax 22-008. www.western. samoa-hotels.com/vaiala/index.html 7 units. US$75 (£38) double. MC, V. **Amenities:** Laundry service. *In room:* Kitchen, coffeemaker, no phone.

ACCOMMODATIONS AT THE BEACHES

Aggie Grey's Lagoon, Beach Resort & Spa 🐸🐸🐸　Between the airport and Mulifanua Wharf on Upolu's northwestern corner, this sprawling beachside resort is the Grey family's latest contribution to Samoa. They copied many features from their historic in-town hotel and transposed them here, including fold-down ironing boards in each room and a duplicate of the huge Samoan *fale* restaurant and its weekly fiafia night (on Thurs here). The resort carries out an old South Seas theme, with **Bloody Mary's Lagoon & Courtyard Bar** honoring James A. Michener's famous character. Meanwhile, the **Solent Flying Boat Bar** pays homage to the amphibious planes which were Samoa's only air link to the world until the 1950s. The airy central building opens to a large beachside swimming pool complex with a swim-up bar. The hotel rooms are in two-story buildings facing westward, so each unit espies Savai'i and Apolima islands as well as often-glorious sunsets. Eight family suites have two bedrooms. A restored century-old church serves as the resort's wedding chapel. Treatment rooms at the full-service Manaia Polynesian Spa are in private *fales* in a stand of old-growth tropical forest. The spa also has a boutique and state-of-the-art exercise room. **Aqua Samoa Watersports** (© **45-662** or 777-4744; www.aquasamoa.com) offers a wide range of activities to all comers (see "Watersports, Golf & Other Outdoor Activities," earlier).

P.O. Box 67, Apia (1km/½ mile west of airport). © **45-611.** Fax 45-626. www.aggiegreys.com. 140 units. US$180–US$190 (£90–£95) double; US$400 (£200) suite. AE, DC, MC, V. **Amenities:** 5 restaurants; 5 bars; outdoor pool; 18-hole golf course; 2 tennis courts; exercise room; spa; Jacuzzi; sauna; watersports equipment rentals; children's program; concierge; activities desk; car-rental desk; 24-hr. room service; massage; babysitting; laundry service. *In room:* A/C, TV, dataport, fridge, coffeemaker, hair dryer, iron, safe.

Coconuts Beach Club & Spa 🐸🐸　Former Hollywood show-biz lawyers Barry and Jennifer Rose began developing this resort in the 1980s. Since then they have built an eclectic mix of motel-style rooms reached by treehouselike stairs, lagoonside bungalows, stunning "Royal Villas," and one-bedroom overwater bungalows, the only such structures in Samoa. Ashore, the beach bungalows and villas have outdoorsy bathrooms with showers pouring down rock walls into sunken tubs. Lots of natural wood creates unusual accents throughout, such as tree limbs used as posts for king-size beds. The thatched-roof bar directly beside the beach is a highlight here. The kitchen produces excellent food under the direction of former Hawaii restaurateur Michael "Mika" Pirics, whose specialties include local lobster and mud crabs from the mangrove estuary. Erosion has wiped away much of the beach, so a rock breakwater fronts most of the property. You can walk around the breakwater, and swim out to a lava wall, which creates a good snorkeling area. And there's a fine stretch of beach between here and Sinalei Reef Resort & Spa (see below), which provides a range of watersports for guests at both resorts. A gecko-shaped pool with a gecko tile mosaic bottom sits just behind the breakwater. No kids under 3 are accepted here.

P.O. Box 3684, Apia (in Si'umu, 30 min. south of Apia; turn right at end of Cross Island Rd.). © **800/726-6268** or 24-849. Fax 20-071. www.coconutsbeachclubsamoa.com. 22 units. US$199–US$239 (£100–£120) double; US$269–US$699 (£135–£350) bungalow. AE, MC, V. No children under 3 accepted. **Amenities:** Restaurant; 2 bars;

Beach Fales at Lalomanu ⭐⭐⭐

"Where in the South Pacific can I rent a little grass shack by the beach?" people often ask me. The answer is here in Samoa, and it's known as a **beach fale.**

Although included in many accommodation listings, many of these rustic structures belong in the camping category, as they are miniature Samoan fales, with oval thatched roofs covering open-air platforms with mosquito nets, foam mattresses, and pull-down canvas or plastic sides to afford some privacy and protection against the elements. A growing number have enclosed bedrooms. Guests share toilets and showers (usually cold-water) in separate buildings.

The best on Upolu are beside the great Lalomanu Beach, 1 hour by car from Apia on Upolu's southeastern corner (see "Exploring Apia & the Rest of Upolu," p. 376). **Taufua Beach Fales** (✆ 41-051; www.samoabeachfales. com) is the largest and most popular, with more than 60 fales and a lively beachside restaurant and bar. Next door, **Litia Sini Beach Resort** (✆ 41-050; www.litiasinibeach.ws) has wooden sides on its fales, a few of which have bathrooms attached. Expect to pay about S$65 (US$26/£13) per person for an open fale, S$70 to S$80 (US$28–US$32/£14–£16) for one with pull-down sides, and S$180 (US$72/£36) for one with private bathroom, including breakfast and dinner. Both accept MasterCard and Visa credit cards.

At the base of the cliff in nearby Saleapaga, Steve and Ana Harrison's **Boomerang Creek Beach Bungalows** (✆ 40-358 or 73-202; www.samoa resorts.com/boomerang/Index.html is the fanciest of the lot. It has two bars and a hillside restaurant, where you can order sandwiches, steaks, local lobster, and other simply prepared fare from a blackboard menu. Its fales—eight on the beach, seven on the mountain side of the road—are fully enclosed and much better equipped than the others. The beach units have private bathrooms. Prices range from S$60 to S$120 (US$24–US$48/£12–£24) double, including breakfast.

Based at Taufa Beach Fales, **Moanalei Dive 'n' Surf** (✆ 41-015; www. moanaleidivensurf.com) rents snorkel gear, kayaks, and bikes, and it will arrange fishing charters, boat trips to nearby islands, and mountain hikes. You can get a Samoan-style massage here, too.

outdoor pool; spa; free use of watersports equipment; free use of bikes; car rentals; activities desk; babysitting; laundry service. *In room:* A/C, fridge, coffeemaker, hair dryer, safe, no phone.

Le Vasa Resort   Once known as the Samoan Village Resort and now owned by Americans Soraya May and Scott Filipps, who rebuilt it in 2007, this small hotel sits in a coconut grove on Cape Fatuosofia, a peninsula forming Upolu's westernmost point. The Malietoa Memorial at the cape commemorates the final Samoan victory which ended Tongan occupation about A.D. 1250. Most of the bungalows sit along a rocky shoreline (a few have steps from their porches into the lagoon), and there's a small but picturesque beach for swimming and snorkeling over the surrounding reef.

The units range from single-room bungalows to the two-bedroom Villa Le Vasa, which has a full kitchen. Most private is the two-bedroom Villa Malietoa, which has a hot tub.

P.O. Box 3495, Apia (on western end of Upolu). © **46-028.** Fax 46-098. www.levasaresort.com. 11 units. US$157– US$647 (£79–£324) double. MC, V. Children under 10 accepted only during school holidays. **Amenities:** Restaurant; bar; outdoor pool; Jacuzzi; complimentary bicycles, kayaks, and snorkeling gear; limited room service; laundry service. In room: A/C, TV (on request), kitchen (1 unit), fridge, coffeemaker, iron (on request), no phone.

Sinalei Reef Resort & Spa ⑁⑁   A tad more reserved than Coconuts Beach Club & Spa, this resort sits on a rise overlooking the lagoon. A path leads down to a crescent-shaped beach—backed by the proverbial palm grove—which separates it from Coconuts. Three spacious bungalows open to this beach; they can interconnect to form Sinalei's presidential suite. There's a second, more private beach area, where reside five fales, one a honeymoon unit with a swimming pool set into its front porch. The other bungalows are up on the hill and flank the central buildings, which gives some of them fine sea views. They are of European construction, with peaked shingle roofs and glass walls across the front. Some have separate bedrooms and hot tubs set in their verandas. The beach and honeymoon fales lack air conditioners, but they do have ceiling fans. A group of three open, Samoan-style thatched-roof buildings comprise the central complex, one each covering reception and gift shop, dining room, and bar. The bar opens to a lovely hilltop pool with a waterfall and huge lava rocks at its edge, but thick foliage obscures the sea view. At the end of a pier, a second restaurant overlooks freshwater welling up from a spring beneath the lagoon. You can participate in a wide range of watersports and practice your game on the resort's 9-hole golf course.

P.O. Box 1510, Apia (in Si'umu, 30 min. south of Apia). © **25-191.** Fax 20-285. www.sinalei.com. 25 units. US$234–US$1,036 (£117–£518) bungalow. Rates include full breakfast, afternoon tea, greens fee. AE, MC, V. Children under 12 not accepted. **Amenities:** 2 restaurants; 2 bars; outdoor pool; 9-hole golf course; 2 tennis courts; spa; watersports equipment rental; limited room service; laundry service. In room: A/C (except in beachside units), fridge, coffeemaker, safe.

14 Where to Dine in Apia

After you've sampled the places I recommend below, you can explore Beach Road's "restaurant row," which has several dining choices as well as Apia's largest concentration of bars.

McDonald's is on Vaea Street, a block inland from the Town Clock. It's the only restaurant here open until 11pm Saturday to Thursday, until 1am Friday.

Bistro Tatau ⑁ INTERNATIONAL   Apia's most refined dining is at this Australian-owned bistro, where white linen covers the tables at night. The very good food features such main courses as grilled swordfish on prawn risotto, stuffed baby squid, and chargrilled beef with massaman curry from Thailand. Be sure to check the daily fish specials.

Beach Rd., at Fugalei St. © **22-727.** Reservations recommended. Main courses S$48–S$68 (US$19–US$27/£9.60–£14). MC, V. Mon–Fri noon–2pm and 6:30–9pm; Sat 6:30–9pm.

Cappuccino Vineyard COFFEE HOUSE/SNACKS   This sidewalk cafe is the best place in Apia to stop in for a cappuccino, an espresso, or a latte made from freshly roasted beans. For breakfast you can accompany it with yogurt or a pastry. Sashimi, salads, sandwiches, and American burgers appear about midday. The best tables are under umbrellas on the pedestrian mall beside the ACB House on Beach Road.

Tips Don't Miss a *Fiafia*

The Samoans gave up the use of pottery at least 1,000 years before the Europeans arrived. As did their fellow Polynesians, they cooked their foods in a pit of hot stones, which the Samoans call an *umu*. When it had steamed for hours, they dug up the dirt, unwrapped the delicacies, and sat down to a *fiafia*.

Favorite side dishes were fresh fruit and *oka* (fish marinated with lime juice and served with vegetables in coconut milk, similar to *poisson cru* in Tahiti). If you happen to be in Samoa on the seventh day after the full moon in late October or early November, the meal may include the coral worm known as *palolo*.

Aggie Grey's Hotel & Bungalows (© 22-880) has the best fiafia, promptly at 6:45pm on Wednesday. Don't miss the exciting fire dance around the swimming pool. The show is repeated on Thursday at **Aggie Grey's Lagoon, Beach Resort & Spa,** with the fire dance on the beach. The **Hotel Kitano Tusitala** (© 21-122) usually has its fiafia on Thursday. **Coconuts Beach Club & Spa** (© 24-849) and **Sinalei Reef Resort & Spa** (© 25-191) usually have theirs on Saturday. Expect to pay about S$65 (US$26/£13) per person. You'll pass a long buffet table loaded with European, Chinese, and Samoan dishes.

Beach Rd., in ACB House mall west of Town Clock. © **22-049.** Breakfast S$8–S$17 (US$3.20–US$6.80/ £1.60–£3.40); snacks S$15–S$22 (US$6–US$8.80/£3–£4.40). No credit cards. Mon–Sat 7am–11pm.

Giodanno's Cafe & Pizzeria 🎄 *Value* PIZZA/PASTA   Follow your nose around the takeout counter to Alex Stanley's romantic courtyard, where patio tables with candles sit under a breadfruit and other tropical trees. Small- or large-size pizzas are the best in town. Pasta dishes consist of lasagna with beef sauce or spaghetti under Bolognese, marinara, carbonara, or a spicy vegetarian sauce. With jazz on the speaker system, this is a very popular establishment with local expatriate residents.

Cross Island Rd., opposite Hotel Insel Fehmarn. © **25-985.** Reservations recommended. Pizza and pasta S$17–S$38 (US$6.80–US$15/£3.40–£7.60). MC, V. Tues–Sat 3–10pm; Sun 5–9pm.

Gourmet Seafood *Value* SEAFOOD/STEAKS   You can start your day with fresh fruit pies and muffins at this open-air restaurant across Beach Road from the Main Wharf. None of the seafood is gourmet here, but get a monstrous slab of fresh fish grilled and served with french fries and a salad. Get here early before the locals scarf down all of Apia's best *oka* (marinated raw fish with coconut cream and vegetables). There's another branch on Convent Street, 2 blocks behind the post office.

Beach Rd., opposite Main Wharf. © **25-962.** Breakfast S$6–S$21 (US$2.40–US$8.40/£1.20–£4.20); burgers S$9.50–S$11 (US$3.80–US$4.40/£1.90–£2.20); main courses S$9.50–S$37 (US$3.80–US$15/£1.90–£7.40). No credit cards. Mon–Sat 7am–10pm.

Le Tamarina Restaurant 🎄🎄 INTERNATIONAL   Tropical plants and furnishings lend atmosphere to this elegant, air-conditioned dining room with a view of Apia from the ground floor of Aggie's. Slacks and dresses are required for evening meals, which feature local and New Zealand produce in a variety of preparations. You may see veal saltimbocca, Pacific smoked salmon, or rack of lamb in an herb crust.

Beach Rd., in Aggie Grey's Hotel & Bungalows. ℂ 23-626. Reservations recommended. Main courses S$48–S$70 (US$19–US$28/£9.60–£14). AE, DC, MC, V. Mon–Sat 6:30–10pm.

Sails at Mulinu'u 𝕶𝕶𝕶 INTERNATIONAL   I met Ian and Lyvia Black, a charming Australian-Samoan couple, when they were managing hotels in Fiji. They returned to Samoa in the 1990s and ran Sails Restaurant on Beach Road. Now they're in this waterfront restaurant on Mulinu'u Peninsula, from which they have a terrific view of Apia Harbour. Their menu spans the globe, from English fish and chips to Bombay beef curry, from Italian pastas to New Zealand steaks. Part of the restaurant is covered by a sail-shaped roof, but you're most likely to have a table under the stars.

Mulinu'u Peninsula, north of Apia Yacht Club. ℂ 20-628. Reservations recommended for dinner. Main courses S$27–S$48 (US$11–US$19/£5.40–£9.60). AE, MC, V. Daily 11am–11pm.

Sydney Side Cafe COFFEE HOUSE/SNACKS   Although not as pleasing visually, this little cafe has better food than Cappuccino Vineyard, across the street. The chiller box at the rear usually holds Vietnamese, Greek, and other fresh salads plus the ingredients for made-to-order sandwiches. The breakfast star is French toast grilled with bananas and coconut jam. I'm also fond of the Samoan-style cocoa smoothie; it's a milkshake with tiny bits of local cocoa beans.

Convent St., at Saleufi St. ℂ 24-638. Breakfast S$12–S$24 (US$4.80–US$9.60/£2.40–£4.80); sandwiches and salads S$14–S$24 (US$5.60–US$9.60/£2.80–£4.80). MC, V. Mon–Fri 8:30am–4:30pm; Sat 8am–2:30pm; Sun 9am–2:30pm.

15 Island Nights on Upolu

Watching a traditional dance show as part of a feast night (in Samoa called a fiafia) is a highlight of any visit. Samoan dance movements are graceful and emphasize the hands more than the hips; the costumes feature more siapo cloth and fine mats than flowers. While the dances are not as lively nor the costumes as colorful as those in Tahiti and the Cook Islands, they are definitely worth seeing. See "Don't Miss a *Fiafia*," above.

PUB-CRAWLING   Sunday through Thursday nights are quiet in Apia. But on weekends, everyone with an itch to drink, dance, and socialize strolls along Beach Road, hitting one pub after another. Most of these have bands on Friday (the biggest night) and Saturday. Thanks to citizens outraged by bars opening in residential neighborhoods, pubs must close at midnight during the week (none are open on Sun). As a practical matter, some keep going into the wee hours on Friday night.

Start with a cocktail or cold Vailima beer at **Aggie Grey's Hotel & Bungalows,** and then head west along Beach Road to Apia's version of restaurant row. You'll come to the slapped-together facade and worse-than-plain furniture at **Lighthouse Bar & Grill** (ℂ 22-691), one of the more popular bars in town. You can look right into this open-air establishment. Next comes **Bad Billy's Bar** (ℂ 30-258) and **Blue Lagoon**

⟨Tips⟩ Don't Sit Near the Door

When pub-crawling along Beach Road, don't sit near the door. This is where fights are most likely to erupt as bouncers evict drunken and unruly customers who don't want to leave.

Bar & Grill (© 30-298), which share a building, and then **On the Rocks** (© 20-093), where you can actually have a good conversation at the sidewalk tables. From there everyone heads west to the **RSA Night Club** (© 20-171), where Samoa's military veterans throw open a welcome to everyone with a few talas to pay for the rock band.

16 Savai'i (★(★(★

You will wish you had stayed longer on Savai'i. Green mountains rise out of the sea and into the clouds across the 21km-wide (13-mile) Apolima Strait that separates it from Upolu. Savai'i is half as large as Upolu, yet it has only a quarter as many people as its smaller, more prosperous sister. On Savai'i, rural Samoan life is much like it always has been. People reside in villages mainly along the east and south coasts.

The northern part of Savai'i has practically deserted lava fields and forests. The last major eruption from its 450 volcanic craters occurred between 1905 and 1911. According to geologist Warren Jopling (see "Organized Tours" under "Exploring Savai'i," below), there's a cycle of activity of about 150 years, so the next eruption should be due within the 21st century.

The other attractions on Savai'i are its long, white beaches, especially on the north side around the village of Manase, home to some of Samoa's most popular beach fales.

GETTING THERE & GETTING AROUND

Air service to Savai'i is supposed to be provided by **Polynesian Airlines,** although it was not flying during my recent visit. **Samoa Shipping Corporation** operates two ferries between Mulifanua Wharf on Upolu and Salelologa, the commercial center on Savai'i. See "Getting There & Getting Around," earlier in this chapter.

You can plan a trip to Savai'i yourself, but the easiest way is to use one of the tour operators in Apia (see "Organized Tours," earlier in this chapter). **Oceania Travel & Tours** (© 24-443) has day trips for about S$350 (US$140/£70) by ferry, including breakfast and tour. It also has 2-day, 1-night packages.

Taxis meet the ferries. One-way fare from the wharf to the east-coast hotels is S$10 (US$4/£2) one-way. The one-way fare is F$60 (US$24/£12) to Manase, and S$120 (US$48/£24) to Asau village, 89km (55 miles) on the other side of Savai'i.

Local **buses** going around the east and north coasts to Manase meet the 8am and noon ferries arriving from Upolu. The fare to Manase is S$4 (US$1.60/80p).

PK Rentals (© 51-025; pkrentals@samoa.ws) has offices in both Apia and Salelogoga on Savai'i. **Savai'i Car Rentals** (© 51-392; fax 51-291; cars@samoa.ws) is based here. The round-island road is completely paved. **Sekia Rentals** (© 54-008; sekis_cars@samoa.ws) is based near Le Lagoto Beach Resort on the north shore. Expect to pay about S$115 (US$46/£23) a day in cash, not to a credit card.

EXPLORING SAVAI'I

Unless you have a week or more and plenty of energy, you should take a guided tour of this large, sparsely populated island with little public transport and few road signs. Even then, you'll need 3 days to see the sights and have no time for the beach.

ORGANIZED TOURS (★(★(★

Guided by Warren Jopling, a retired Australian geologist who has lived on Savai'i for many years and knows it like the back of his hand, **Safua Tours** (© 51-271; safua hotel@lesamoa.net) is the best way to see the island. Warren is a font of information, especially about the desertlike lava fields. He will tailor any tour to suit your interests.

Manono & Apolima

You will pass the islands of **Manono** and **Apolima** on the trip to Savai'i. The top of an extinct volcano, Apolima is the more scenic of the two. Its beachside village of Apolima-tui sits inside the crater that collapsed on one side, causing the island's half-moon shape. Small boats shuttle between Apolima Island and the village of Apolima-uta on Upolu's western end. Boats to Manono leave from Mulifanua Wharf. **Samoa Scenic Tours** (© **22-880**) at Aggie Grey's hotels operates day trips to Manono and its surrounding reef, and **Island Explorer** (© **32-663** or 777-1814; www.islandexplorer.ws) has sea-kayaking expeditions to Manono (see "Exploring Apia & the Rest of Upolu," earlier in this chapter).

It will take an energetic 2 days to see most of the sights, with 1 day spent going along the east and north coasts, the other along the south shore. His full-day excursions cost US$50 (£25) for two people, if you book directly and not through a travel agent. Reservations are required. Although Warren will meet you at the ferry wharf, he prefers that you come over to Savai'i the day before your tour and stay at the Safua Hotel (see "Where to Stay & Dine on Savai'i," below).

THE EAST & NORTH COASTS

Leaving the Safua Hotel, the east-coast road soon passes a memorial to the Rev. John Williams, and then goes up a rise to **Tuasivi**, the administrative center of the island and site of the hospital and police station. From there it drops to **Faga** and **Siufaga**, two long, gorgeous beaches. Many villages along this stretch have bathing pools fed by freshwater that runs down underground from the mountains. Only the south side of Savai'i has rivers and streams. Rainwater seeps into the porous volcanic rock elsewhere and reappears as springs along the shoreline.

Mount Matavanu last erupted between 1905 and 1911, when it sent a long lava flow down to the northeast coast, burying villages and gardens before backing up behind the reef. Today primitive ferns primarily populate the desertlike **Matavanu lava field.** The flow very nearly inundated the village of **Mauga,** which sits along the rim of an extinct volcano's cone. The villagers play cricket on the crater floor. Past Mauga is the **Virgin's Grave,** a hole left around a grave when the lava almost covered a nearby church. The steeple still sticks out of the twisted black mass. The villagers charge S$3 (US$1.20/60p) to visit the grave.

The north-coast road past the lava fields is picturesque but holds little of interest other than gorgeous tropical scenery.

On the north coast, the village of **Manase** has a gorgeous white-sand beach, which has made it the beach fale capital of Savai'i (see "Where to Stay & Dine on Savai'i," below). It also has a **Turtle Conservatory,** where you can swim with the turtles in freshwater pools—after paying a S$5 (US$2/£1) custom fee.

THE SOUTH COAST

On the south coast near Vailoa, on the Letolo Plantation, stands the ancient ruin known as **Pulemelei Mound** 𝕲𝕲. This two-tiered pyramid 72m (236 ft.) long, 58m

(190 ft.) wide, and 14m (46 ft.) high is the largest archaeological ruin in Polynesia. It is similar to the ceremonial temples, or *maraes,* in French Polynesia and the Cook Islands, but it is so old (more than 1,000 years) that the Samoans no longer have legends explaining its original function. Shortly before his death in 2002, Thor Heyerdahl, of *Kon Tiki* fame, visited the mound and organized an archaeological expedition, which cleared the pyramid of vegetation. Excavations continued through 2004. You can read about them at **www.kon-tiki.no/Research/samoa/index.html.** A narrow dirt track, which passes Olemoe Waterfall, ends some 300m (984 ft.) from the mound. A steep and often muddy track leads down to the waterfall.

From the mound, the south-coast road continues to **Gautavai Waterfall,** a lovely black-sand beach at Nu'u, and the geyserlike **Taga Blowholes** on the island's southernmost point.

SCUBA DIVING & SNORKELING

The reefs off the north shore of Savai'i provide bountiful sea life for snorkelers to view, but beware of strong currents near the reef passes. Scuba divers can find some relatively unexplored sites here, most no more than a 10-minute boat ride from shore. One of them is a missionary ship, which sank on the reef in 1881.

Fabien and Flavia Lebon of **Dive Savai'i** (℃ 54-172; www.divesavaii.com), opposite Le Lagoto Beach Resort (see below), charge S$150 (US$60/£30) for a one-tank dive, and they teach PADI open-water courses for S$1,200 (US$480/£240). They also have guided snorkeling trips for S$50 (US$20/£10) per person, and they rent snorkeling gear for S$30 (US$12/£6) a day.

On the beach in Manasee village, **Raci's Beach Club** (℃ 54-003; www.rbcltd.ws) rents snorkel gear and kayaks, and it has snorkeling tours. Owned by a Swiss couple, René Achermann and Zita-Manuela Jerg, it also dispenses Italian espresso coffee as well as libation. A branch next to the village gasoline station has Internet access.

WHERE TO STAY & DINE ON SAVAI'I
ON THE NORTH SHORE

Le Lagoto Beach Resort 🐢🐢🐢   Owners Kuki and Sara Retzlaff rebuilt this small resort into the finest on Savai'i, and one of the best in Samoa. The property faces west across Manasee Bay, with a view of the sea and mountains beyond. *Lagoto* means sunset in Samoan, and I saw the most awesome sunset of my life from here. Kuki and Sara house most of their guests in 10 traditional Samoan *fales,* whose turtle-shaped ceilings are intricately stitched together with coconut sennit. Half directly face the sea, while the others are set back but still have a lagoon view. There's also a house with one apartment upstairs, another downstairs, both of which have kitchens. The central building, also a Samoan *fale,* houses a bar and very good **restaurant,** which has tables outside beside an infinity-edge swimming pool, and a spa called Bodyworks, where you can get various massages and beauty treatments. This is one fine small resort.

P.O. Box 34, Fagamalo (Lelepa village, 45km/28 miles north of ferry wharf). ℃ 58-189. Fax 58-249. www. lelagoto.ws. 12 units. US$90–US$300 (£45–£150) double. Rates include tropical breakfast. AE, MC, V. **Amenities:** Restaurant; bar; spa; massage; laundry service. *In room:* A/C, TV, kitchen (2 units), fridge, coffeemaker.

Savai'i Lagoon Beach Resort   This is not a resort but six modern cottages, all with kitchens and front porches, on the beach next door to Le Lagoto Beach Resort, where you can get food and libation. The bedrooms in the units have windows on two sides, which catch the breeze and help compensate for the lack of air conditioners.

Post Office, Fagamalo. (C)/fax **54-168**. www.savaiilagoon.co.nz. 6 units. S$298 (US$119/£60) double. Rates include tropical breakfast. MC, V. **Amenities:** Bicycle rentals; complimentary kayaks and dinghies; laundry service. *In room:* TV, kitchen, no phone.

Stevenson's at Manase   I mention this eclectic resort primarily because it has a restaurant. Most of it sits across the road from a beach of white sand in Manase village. The best units are five air-conditioned beachside bungalows (they call them "villas"). Leaf exteriors and siapo-lined ceilings make these houses look rustic, but they are relatively modern, and they have outdoor hot-water showers enclosed by rock walls. I would not stay in the 19 smallish, motel-style rooms occupying what appear to be converted shipping containers. Guests have free use of paddle boats and canoes, but the lagoon is too shallow for such diversions at low tide. Guests also have to rent towels.

P.O. Box 210, Apia (at Manase village, 48km/30 miles north of ferry wharf). (C)/fax **58-219**. 33 units (10 without bathroom). S$120 (US$48/£24) double; S$250 (US$100/£50) bungalow. Rates include breakfast. MC, V. **Amenities:** Restaurant; bar; watersports. *In room:* A/C (bungalows and 1 room), no phone.

BEACH FALES AT MANASE ★★★

Like Upolu, Savai'i has scores of beach fales, especially in Manase village on the north shore. The best share the white-sand beach with Stevenson's at Manase (see above).

The most comfortable are at **Vacations Beach Fales** ((C) **54-024;** www.vacations beachfales.com), where two have air conditioners and bathrooms. Other beach units are enclosed for privacy. The communal toilets and showers here are more modern than at the others. The restaurant and bar extend out over the beach—great for a sunset cocktail. Rates range from S$90 (US$36/£18) per person for an open beach fale to S$300 (US$120/£60) double for an air-conditioned unit, including breakfast and dinner. MasterCard and Visa credit cards are accepted.

Jane's Beach Fales ((C)/fax **54-066;** sbec@samoa.ws), are a bit more luxurious—if that word can be applied to these rustic accommodations. Her 22 fales are larger than Tanu's. Each is about half front porch, half bedroom; they are thus much more private, and you can lock them. Most of her fales sit among palms and breadfruit trees on a lawn, as opposed to sand at Tanu, but one of them actually sits on stilts above the lagoon. It's the most private and romantic. Another has a kitchen and its own bathroom. The others share toilets, cold-water showers, and a communal kitchen. A restaurant here serves simple local-style meals daily and stages a fiafia on Friday or Saturday night. Jane charges S$50 (US$20/£10) per person per night, including breakfast and dinner, but she does not accept credit cards.

Largest and most basic is **Tanu Beach Fales** ((C)/fax **54-050**), whose 32 huts sit beside the lagoon or in a grove of tropical trees. They all have electric lights, mosquito nets, linen, mattresses, pillows, and pull-down side mats for privacy. Guests share toilets, cold-water showers, and a communal kitchen. Rates are S$50 (US$20/£10) per person, including breakfast and dinner. No credit cards.

ON THE EAST COAST

Safua Hotel   This rustic hotel in Safua village is known not so much for the quality of its accommodations as for its owner, Moelagi Jackson, who holds several chiefly titles and often represents Samoa at international conferences, especially those dealing with women's rights. Her main fale holds a bar and dining room, where most travelers have breakfast before setting out to tour the island with Warren Jopling. The fales scattered about the lawn are of clapboard construction, with front porches, screened windows, basic electric lights, and bathrooms with cold-water showers. Don't be surprised to hear a catfight or the grunts of pigs running loose at night. In other words, stay here for a Samoan village experience, not for a beachside vacation.

P.O. Box 7088, Salelologa, Savai'i (in Safua village, 6.5km/4 miles north of wharf). © 51-271. Fax 51-272. safuahotel@ lesamoa.net. 12 units. S$110 (US$44/£22) per person. Rates include breakfast. AE, MC, V. **Amenities:** Restaurant; bar. *In room:* No phone.

Siufaga Beach Resort   Dr. Peter Cafarelli, an Italian who lived on Savai'i for more than 30 years, founded this resort facing Faga Beach and an emerald lagoon speckled with coral heads, Savai's most colorful. It's now managed by his son, Paul Caferrelli, who recently added 12 modern bungalows with most of the comforts of home plus outdoor showers. You can dine inside or outside on a porch at **Parenzo's Bar/Restaurant,** notable for its wood-fired pizzas (3 nights a week) and fresh local fish. The accommodations here are as modern as any on Savai'i, you'll be more isolated than on the north shore.

P.O. Box 7112, Salelologa, Savai'i (in Tuasivi, 13km/8 miles north of ferry wharf). © 53-518. Fax 53-535. www.siufaga. com. 12 units (all with bathroom). S$120–S$210 (US$48–$84/£24–£42) double. MC, V. **Amenities:** Restaurant bar; complimentary kayaks and snorkel gear; laundry service. *In room:* A/C, TV, kitchen (some units), fridge, coffeemaker, no phone.

14

American Samoa

One of the prime reasons to visit American Samoa is to see Tutuila, one of the South Pacific's most dramatically beautiful islands, and you'll get an eyeful of gorgeous scenery on the 11km (6¾-mile) ride from the airport at Tafuna into the legendary port of Pago Pago. But first you will see the effects of American dollars, for the area around the airport is a bustling suburb with shopping centers and a modern multiscreen cinema. The road is crowded with cars and buses and patrolled by policemen in big American-style cruisers.

Yet the physical beauty of this island competes favorably with the splendor of Moorea and Bora Bora in French Polynesia. Once the road clears the shopping area at Nu'uuli, it twists and turns along the rocky coastline. At places it rounds the cliffs of headlands dropping into the sea; at others it curves along beaches in small bays backed by valleys. All the way, the surf pounds on the reef. When you make the last turn at Blount's Point, you'll behold green walls dropping precipitously into Pago Pago Harbor.

Try to ignore the mountain of rusting shipping containers and the two smelly tuna canneries on the shore of the harbor.

Despite the obvious inroads of Western ways and American loot, the local residents still cling to *fa'a Samoa*, the ancient Samoan way of life (see "The Samoan People," in chapter 13). While many young American Samoans wear Western clothes and speak only English, often with a pronounced Hawaiian or Californian accent, in the villages the older folk still converse in Samoan and abide by the old ways.

This also is the scene of the first American national park below the equator. Although it has yet to be developed, you can hike its trails and explore some of American Samoa's phenomenal beauty close up.

1 American Samoa Today

The seven islands of American Samoa are on the eastern end of the 483km-long (300-mile) Samoa Archipelago. Together they comprise a land area of 200 sq. km (77 sq. miles), almost half of which belong to **Tutuila,** the slender remains of an ancient volcano. One side of Tutuila's crater apparently blew away, almost cutting the island in two. This created the long, bent arm of **Pago Pago Harbor,** one of the South Pacific's most dramatically scenic spots.

Fewer American Samoans live in their home islands than reside in the United States. The expatriate American Samoans have been replaced at home by their kindred from independent Samoa and by some Tongans, who have swelled the population to about 68,000, up from 30,000 in the 1990s.

GOVERNMENT   American Samoa is the only U.S. territory south of the equator. American Samoans are "noncitizen nationals" of the United States. Although they carry American passports, have unrestricted entry into the United States, and can serve in the U.S. armed forces, they cannot vote in U.S. presidential elections. American Samoa has a "delegate" in the U.S. House of Representatives; that is, an elected representative who may not vote in the full House, but can cast a vote on a House committee. Eni Faleomavaega, a Democrat, is the delegate from American Samoa. The country also holds primary elections for U.S. presidential candidates, and sends delegates to the conventions, but does not have any electoral votes.

The U.S. Department of the Interior has jurisdiction over American Samoa, but American Samoans elect their own governor and members of the lower house of the **Fono,** their bicameral legislature. In accordance with Samoan custom, local chiefs pick members of the territorial senate. The Fono has authority over the budget and local affairs, although both the governor and the U.S. Department of the Interior can veto the laws it passes. American Samoans also elect a nonvoting delegate to the U.S. House of Representatives in Washington, D.C.

The territorial government's annual budget is considerably larger than that of independent Samoa, which has a population some three times larger. Washington provides about half the government's revenue. Some 80% of the taxes raised locally go to pay more than 5,000 government employees, about 42% of the local workforce. They earn more per hour than any South Pacific country other than French Polynesia.

ECONOMY   Together the local government and the two tuna canneries employ about 80% of the local workforce. The canneries account for some 80% of the territory's private sector product. About 70% of their 4,700 workers are from nearby Samoa (they earn at least three times what they can make at home). The aging canneries have survived for more than 50 years because of tax credits and duty-free access to the United States. Tourism is a minuscule part of the economy. Most visitors arrive on large cruise ships putting into Pago Pago for a day.

2 American Samoa Yesterday: History 101

As friendly as American Samoans are today, their ancestors did anything but warmly welcome a French expedition under Jean La Pérouse, which came ashore in 1787 on the north coast of Tutuila. Samoan warriors promptly attacked, killing 12 members of the landing party, which in turn killed 39 Samoans. The site of the battle is known as **Massacre Bay.** La Pérouse survived that incident, but he and his entire expedition later disappeared in what is now the Solomon Islands.

In 1872, the U.S. Navy negotiated a treaty with the chiefs of Tutuila to permit it to use Pago Pago as a coaling station. The agreement helped keep the Germans out of Eastern Samoa, as present-day American Samoa was then known.

In 1900 the chiefs on Tutuila ceded control of their island to the United States, and the paramount chief of the Manu'a Group of islands east of Tutuila did likewise in 1905. Finally ratified by the U.S. Senate in 1929, those treaties are the legal foundation for the U.S. presence in American Samoa.

PART OF THE U.S.   From 1900 until 1951, U.S. authority in Samoa rested with the U.S. Navy, which maintained the refueling station at Pago Pago and for the most part let the local chiefs conduct their own affairs. Tutuila became a base for U.S. servicemen during World War II, but things quickly returned to normal after 1945.

Control of the territory was shifted from the navy to the U.S. Department of the Interior in 1951. The department did little in the islands until 1961, when *Reader's Digest* magazine ran an article about "America's shame in the South Seas." The story took great offense at the lack of roads and adequate schools, medical care, water and sewer service, and housing. The U.S. federal government reacted by paving the roads and building an international airport, water and electrical systems, the then-modern Rainmaker Hotel, and a convention center. A 1.5km-long (1 mile-long) cable was strung across Pago Pago Harbor to build a television transmitter atop 480m (1,575 ft.) Mount Alava, from which education programming was beamed into the schools.

For fear of losing all that federal support, American Samoans were reluctant to tinker with their relationship with Washington during the 1960s and 1970s, when other South Pacific colonies were becoming independent. The United States offered local autonomy, but they refused. They changed minds in the mid-1970s, when an appointed governor was very unpopular, and elected their own governor for the first time in 1977.

3 Visitor Information & Maps

VISITOR INFORMATION

The **American Samoa Office of Tourism,** P.O. Box 1147, Pago Pago, AS 96799 (© **699-9411;** fax 699-9414; www.amsamoatourism.com), has offices inconveniently located in Tafuna, near the airport. The office is open Monday to Friday from 8am to 4pm. The brochure of the National Park of American Samoa contains the best map of the territory (see below).

The **Delegate from American Samoa** to the U.S. Congress (Eni Faleomavaega) also dispenses some tourist information. His address is: U.S. House of Representatives, 2422 Rayburn HOB, Washington, DC 20515 (© **202/225-8577;** www.house.gov/faleomavaega/index.shtml).

4 Entry Requirements

Except for Samoans, New Zealanders, and a few others, entry permits are not required for stays of up to 30 days. American citizens and nationals need valid passports or certified birth certificates (forget the birth certificate, you will need your passport to go home). Everyone else needs a valid passport and a ticket for onward passage. Women more than 6 months pregnant are not allowed entry.

Immunizations are not required.

CUSTOMS See "Fast Facts: American Samoa," later in this chapter, for what you can bring into American Samoa, and "Fast Facts: South Pacific" in chapter 2 for what you can bring home.

5 When to Go

CLIMATE

"It did not pour, it flowed," wrote W. Somerset Maugham in his 1921 short story "Rain," the famous tale of prostitute Sadie Thompson, who seduces a puritanical missionary while stranded in American Samoa. This description, however, applies mainly to Pago Pago, which, because of its location behind appropriately named Rainmaker Mountain, gets an average of over 500cm (197 in.) of rain a year. The rest of American Samoa enjoys a typically tropical climate, with lots of very intense sunshine even during the wet season from December to April. Average daily high temperatures range from 83°F (28°C) in the drier, somewhat cooler months of June through September to 86°F (30°C) from December to April, when midday can be hot and sticky. Evenings are usually in the 70s (20s Celsius) all year round.

HOLIDAYS & EVENTS

The biggest celebration is on April 17, when **American Samoa Flag Day** commemorates the raising of the Stars and Stripes over Tutuila in 1900. The second Sunday in October is observed as **White Sunday;** children attend church dressed in white and are later honored at family feasts.

Public holidays are New Year's Day, Martin Luther King Jr. Day (third Mon in Jan), President's Day (third Mon in Feb), Good Friday, American Samoa Flag Day (Apr 17), Memorial Day (last Mon in May), the Fourth of July, Labor Day (first Mon in Sept), Columbus Day (second Mon in Oct), Veteran's Day (Nov 11), Thanksgiving (fourth Thurs of Nov), and Christmas Day.

6 Money

United States currency is used in American Samoa. Samoan *tala* are not accepted, nor can they be exchanged here.

HOW TO GET LOCAL CURRENCY The **Bank of Hawaii** and the **ANZ Amerika Samoa Bank,** both in Fagatogo, are open Monday to Friday 9am to 3pm. Both have ATMs at their main offices, and ANZ has one in Pago Plaza, the shopping center at the head of the harbor.

CREDIT CARDS American Express, Visa, MasterCard, and Diners Club are accepted by the hotels, car-rental firms, and airlines. Otherwise, it's best to carry cash to cover your anticipated expenses. No one here accepts Discover.

7 Getting There & Getting Around

GETTING THERE

FROM SAMOA **Polynesian Airlines** (✆ 800/644-7659 in the U.S., 22-737 in Apia, or 633-4331 in Pago Pago; www.polynesianairlines.com), **Inter Island Airways** (✆ 42-580 in Samoa, 699-7100 in American Samoa), and **South Pacific Express** (✆ 28-901 in Apia, 699-9900 in American Samoa) fly between Faleolo Airport in Samoa and Pago Pago several times a day. I always fly on Polynesian because it is a licensed scheduled carrier while the others are charter airlines. Round-trip fares are about S$310 (US$124/£62) if purchased in Apia, US$155 to US$165 (£78–£83 plus taxes if bought in American Samoa.

For the adventurous, a relatively modern ferry, the *Lady Naomi,* makes the 8-hour voyage between Pago Pago and Apia at least once a week, usually leaving the main wharf in Apia at 11pm on Wednesday and departing Pago Pago's marine terminal at 4pm on Thursday for the return voyage. Tickets should be bought at least a day ahead. One-way fares from Pago Pago to Apia are US$60 (£30) for a seat, US$75 (£38) for a cabin. The *Lady Naomi* is operated by the **Samoa Shipping Corporation,** whose ticket office is on Beach Road, opposite the main wharf in Apia (✆ 20-935; www.samoashipping.com). The American Samoa agent is **Polynesia Shipping Services** (✆ 633-1211). Because the trade winds prevail from the southeast, the trip going west with the wind toward Apia is usually smoother.

FROM OTHER COUNTRIES The only international carrier serving American Samoa is **Hawaiian Airlines,** which flies from several U.S. West Coast cities to Pago Pago, with a change of planes at Honolulu. Otherwise, you can fly to Faleolo Airport in Samoa on **Air New Zealand, Air Pacific,** or **Polynesian Blue,** and then connect to Pago Pago. For more information, see "Getting There & Getting Around," in chapter 2.

> ### *Tips* Seeing American Samoa as a Day Trip from Apia
>
> You can see American Samoa as a 1-day side trip from independent Samoa. The easiest way is to buy a package from **Oceania Travel & Tours,** at the Kitano Tusitala Hotel in Apia (© **24-443;** fax 22-255). The US$350 (£175) per-person fee includes round-trip airfare, a guided tour of Tutuila island, and lunch. Oceania's American Samoa office is above the main post office in Pago Pago (© **633-1172**).
>
> To do it yourself, reserve a rental car in Pago Pago at least a day in advance (there is too much to see to rely on the bus system or even a taxi). Then fly early in the morning from Faleolo airport to Pago Pago. Go to the airline's office and reconfirm your afternoon return flight, then pick up your car. Drive into Pago Pago and take the stroll described in "Exploring American Samoa," below. Drive to the eastern end of the island, then back-track to Pago Pago and have lunch. If you have time, drive out to the western end. Catch the last flight back to Apia.

ARRIVING & DEPARTING   Pago Pago International Airport (PPG) is near the village of Tafuna, about 11km (6¾ miles) west of Pago Pago. Taxi fare is about US$15 (£7.50) from the airport to Pago Pago harbor. The "Tafuna" local buses stop at the airport terminal on their way into Pago Pago. Bus fare is US75¢ (38p).

Departure taxes are included in the ticket price.

GETTING AROUND

Inter Island Airways (© **42-580** in Samoa, 699-7100 in American Samoa; www.interislandair.com), the local carrier, flies to the Manu'a Islands, but don't count on it. The territory always has trouble keeping a domestic airline flying.

BY RENTAL CAR   The only international car-rental firm in American Samoa is **Avis** (© **800/331-1212** or 699-2746; www.avis.com), which rents air-conditioned models for US$70 to US$110 (£35–£55) per day, including unlimited mileage, plus an optional US$13 (£6.50) for insurance. Less reliable local firms include **Sir Amos** (© **699-4554**), **Friendly** (© **699-7186**), and **Dollar Rental Car** (© **633-7716;** dollarrentalcar@yahoo. com). The latter is not affiliated with the international rental company of the same name.

Driving Rules   Your valid home driver's license will be honored in American Samoa. **Driving is on the right-hand side of the road,** and traffic signs are the same as those used in the United States. The speed limit is 15 mph in the built-up areas and 25 mph on the open road.

BY BUS   Gaily-painted *aiga* buses prowl the roads from early morning until sunset every day except Sunday. Basically they run from the villages to the market in Pago Pago and back, picking up anyone who waves along the way. Some buses leave the market and run to Fagasa on the north coast or to the east end of the island; others go from the market to the west. None goes from one end of the island to the other, so you'll have to change at the market in order to do a stem-to-stern tour of Tutuila. Most drivers are helpful, so just ask how far they go in each direction. Fares are between US75¢ and US$2 (38p/£1) per ride.

BY TAXI   There are **taxi stands** at the **airport** (✆ 699-1179) and at the **Pago Pago market** (no phone). None of the taxis have meters, so be sure to negotiate the fare before driving off. The fares should be about US$1 (50p) per mile.

FAST FACTS: American Samoa

American Express There is no American Express representative in American Samoa.

Area Codes American Samoa does not have domestic area codes. The international country code is **684**.

Business Hours Shopping hours are Monday to Friday 8am to 5pm and Saturday from 9am to noon. Government offices are open Monday to Friday 8am to 4pm.

Customs Customs allowances are 1 liter of liquor or wine and one carton of cigarettes. Illegal drugs and firearms are prohibited, and pets are quarantined. U.S. citizens get larger customs allowances for purchases made in American Samoa than they do elsewhere in the South Pacific, provided that they have been in the territory for at least 48 hours (see "Customs," under "Fast Facts: The South Pacific," in chapter 2).

Electricity American Samoa uses 110-volt electric current and plugs identical to those in the United States and Canada.

Emergencies The emergency telephone number for the **police, fire department,** and **ambulance** is ✆ **911**. In a medical emergency, you can call or go to **Lyndon B. Johnson Tropical Medical Center** (see "Healthcare," later in this chapter). The **police station** (✆ **633-1111**) is in Fagatogo, across the *malae* (open field) from the Fono.

Etiquette & Customs See "Rules of Conduct," under "The Samoan People" in chapter 13, for information about *fa'a Samoa* and its intricate rules of etiquette and customs. Young American Samoans have adopted Western-style dress, including jeans and shorts of respectable length, although the traditional wraparound *lava-lava* is still worn by many older men and women. Visitors should not wear bathing suits or other skimpy clothing away from the hotels. Women must confine their bikini tops to the beach.

Healthcare The **Lyndon B. Johnson Tropical Medical Center** (✆ **633-5555** for emergencies, or 633-1222) in Faga'alu west of Pago Pago (turn off the main road at Tom Ho Chung's store) handles the territory's medical and dental services. The outpatient clinic is open 24 hours daily. Frankly, you will get much better treatment in Apia (see "Fast Facts: Samoa," in chapter 13).

Insects There are no dangerous insects in American Samoa, and the plentiful mosquitoes do not carry malaria.

Internet Access **DDW Internet Cafe,** in Pago Plaza at the head of the bay (✆ **633-5297**), has one computer with Internet access for US$3 (£1.50) for 15 minutes. See "Where to Dine," below.

Libraries The **Feleti-Barstow Public Library** (✆ **633-5816**), in the government buildings in Utulei, is open Monday to Wednesday and Friday 9am to 5pm, Tuesday and Thursday 9am to 7pm, and Saturday 10am to 2pm.

Liquor Laws The minimum drinking age is 21. Beer, wine, and spirits are available at the grocery stores.

Newspapers & Magazines The daily *Samoa News* (www.samoanews.com) is the dominant newspaper here.

Mail The U.S. Postal Service's main post office is in Fagatogo. U.S. domestic postage rates apply, and first-class and priority letters and packages go by air between American Samoa and the United States. Unless you pay the first-class or priority mail rate, parcel post is sent by ship and will take several weeks to reach Hawaii or the U.S. mainland. The post office is open Monday to Friday 7:30am to 3:30pm, Saturday 9am to noon. The zip code for Pago Pago is **96799**.

Radio & TV The transmitters atop Mount Alava are used during the day to send educational TV programs to the territory's public schools and to transmit CNN and live sporting events. At night they broadcast U.S. network entertainment programs. The broadcasts can be seen 129km (80 miles) away, on eastern Upolu in Samoa. Many homes in American Samoa also have cable television. The territory has three FM radio stations, which transmit American network news broadcasts on the hour.

Safety Street crime is not a serious problem in American Samoa except late at night around Pago Pago Harbor. Fa'a Samoa and its rules of communal ownership are still in effect, however, so it's wise not to leave cameras, watches, or other valuables unattended or in your rental car.

Taxes Airport departure tax is included in ticket prices. There is no sales tax.

Telephone & Fax The **American Samoa Telecommunications Authority** (**SamoaTelCo;** www.samoatelco.com) provides land-line phone service. The system is the same as in the United States.

To call American Samoa: Dial the international access code (011 from the U.S.; 00 from the U.K., Ireland, or New Zealand; or 0011 from Australia), American Samoa's country code **684,** and the local number (there are no area codes within American Samoa).

To call the United States and Canada from within American Samoa: Dial **1** followed by the area code and local number.

To make international calls from within American Samoa: First dial **011,** then the country code (U.K. 44, Ireland 353, Australia 61, New Zealand 64), then the area code and phone number. You can also place overseas calls at SamoaTelCo's office, diagonally across the Fagatogo malae from the Fono building. It is open 24 hours daily.

To make domestic calls within American Samoa: No prefix or area code is required for domestic long distance calls, so dial the local number.

For directory assistance: Dial ☏ **411** for information.

For operator assistance: Dial ☏ **0** for operator assistance in making international calls.

Toll-free numbers: Calling a 1-800 number in the U.S. or Canada from here is not toll-free. In fact, it costs the same as an overseas call.

Pay phones: Public pay phones are the same type used throughout the United States. The easiest way to call home from here is to buy a prepaid **Blue**

Sky card, available at many shops. You can use these cards from any phone as you would a prepaid card at home.

Access numbers: Several international companies have access numbers here, including AT&T (© 633-2872), MCI (© 633-2624), Sprint (© 633-1000), GTE/Verizon (© 633-1706), and Hawaii Verizon (© 633-2482).

Cellphones: Blue Sky (© 699-2759; www.bluesky.as), which has offices in Fagatogo Plaza and in the Lafou shopping center on the main road in Nu'uli, rents cellphones for US$25 (£13) a week plus airtime. You can also buy a prepaid SIM card for your own unlocked GSM phone; these cost US$20 (£10) and include US$10 (£5) worth of airtime.

Time The local time in American Samoa is the same as in independent Samoa: 11 hours behind Greenwich Mean Time. That's 3 hours behind Pacific Standard Time (4 hr. behind during daylight saving time, which American Samoa does not observe). In other words, if it's noon standard time in California and 3pm in New York, it's 9am in Pago Pago. If daylight saving time is in effect in the U.S., it's 8am in American Samoa. American Samoa is east of the international date line and shares the same date with North America, 1 day behind Tonga, Fiji, Australia, and New Zealand.

Tipping Although this is a U.S. territory, officially there is no tipping in American Samoa. A lot of American Samoans have lived in the United States, however, so the practice is not exactly uncommon.

Water The tap water is treated and is safe to drink except during periods of heavy rain.

Weights & Measures American Samoa is the only country or territory in the South Pacific whose official system of weights and measures is the same as the U.S.—pounds and miles, not the metric system of kilograms and kilometers.

8 Exploring American Samoa

A STROLL THROUGH PAGO PAGO

Although the actual village of Pago Pago sits at the head of the harbor, everyone considers Pago Pago to be the built-up area on the south shore of the harbor, including Fagatogo, the government and business center. The harbor is also called the Bay Area. Despite development that has come with economic growth of the territory, Pago Pago still has much of the old South Seas atmosphere that captivated W. Somerset Maugham when he wrote "Rain" in the 1920s.

A stroll through the Pago Pago area should take about 2 hours. Begin at **Sadie's by the Sea** hotel on the east end of the inner harbor, actually in the village of Utulei (see "Where to Stay," below). Just across the road from the hotel, a set of concrete steps climbs to **Government House,** the clapboard mansion built in 1903 to house the governor. The mansion is not open to the public, but there is a splendid view from the top of the steps looking across the harbor to flat-top Rainmaker Mountain.

Back on the main road heading toward town, you walk past a mountain of shipping containers standing idle on the main wharf. Beyond the busy port terminal and opposite the post office is the **Jean P. Haydon Museum** (© 633-4347), in an old iron-roofed building that was once the U.S. Navy's commissary. Worth a 30-minute stop, the museum has exhibits on Samoan history, sea life, canoes, kava making, and traditional tools and handicrafts, including a 400-year-old finely woven mat. A few high-quality handicrafts are for sale. Open Monday to Friday 9am to 3pm, except on holidays. Admission is free, but donations are accepted.

Every Samoan village has a **malae**, or open field, and the area across from the museum is Fagatogo's. The chiefs of Tutuila met on this malae in 1900 to sign the treaty that established the United States in Samoa. The round modern building across the road beside the harbor is the **Fono**, American Samoa's legislature; the visitors' galleries are open to the public. The ramshackle stores along the narrow streets on the other side of the malae were Pago Pago's downtown for half a century, although like any other place under the Stars and Stripes, much business is now conducted in suburban shopping centers. On the malae, the **American Samoa Archives Office** occupies the stone jail built in 1911.

Just beyond the malae on the main road stands the **Judicial Building,** home of the **High Court** of American Samoa (everyone calls it the Court House). The big white clapboard building with columns looks as if it should be in South Carolina rather than the South Pacific. Across the road on the waterfront stands **Fagatogo Plaza,** a shopping center. In contrast to Fagatogo Plaza are the **produce and fish markets** a few yards farther on. They are usually poorly stocked, and when they do have produce, it most likely comes by ferry from Samoa. The markets also serve as the bus terminal.

Continuing north along the harbor, you soon come to the historic **Sadie Thompson Building,** where W. Somerset Maugham stayed in the 1920s. Now home to the Sadie Thompson Inn and restaurant (see "Where to Stay" and "Where to Dine," below), it is the best place in town for lunch before touring the island.

A TOUR OF TUTUILA
THE NORTH COAST OF TUTUILA

A paved road turns off the main highway at Spenser's Store in Pago Pago village and leads up **Vaipito Valley,** across a ridge, and down to Fagasa, a village huddled beside picturesque Fagasa, or **Forbidden Bay,** on Tutuila's north shore. The road is steep but paved, and the view from atop the ridge is excellent. The track up Mount Alava begins on the saddle (see "National Park of American Samoa," below). Legend says that porpoises long ago led a group of three men and three women to safety in Fagasa Bay, which has long been a porpoise sanctuary.

THE EAST SIDE OF TUTUILA

The 29km (18-mile) drive from Pago Pago to the east end of Tutuila skirts along the harbor, past the canneries and their fishy odor, and then winds around one headland after another. Watch particularly for **Pyramid Rock** and the **Lion's Head,** where you can wade out to a small beach. (Never go in the water anywhere here unless the locals are already swimming there.)

From Aua, at the foot of Rainmaker Mountain, a switch-backing road runs across Rainmaker Pass (great views from up there) to the lovely north-shore village of **Vatia,** on a bay of the same name. If you're going to venture off the main road, this is the place to do it. The north-shore coastal road runs through National Park of Samoa land and is the only way to visit the park without hiking (see below). World War II pillboxes still dot the beach here. At the north end of Vatia Bay sits the skinny, offshore rock formation known as the **Cockscomb,** one of Tutuila's trademarks.

Another paved road leaves Faga'itua village and climbs to a saddle in the ridge, where it divides. The left fork goes down to Masefau Bay; the right goes to Masausi

Pago Pago

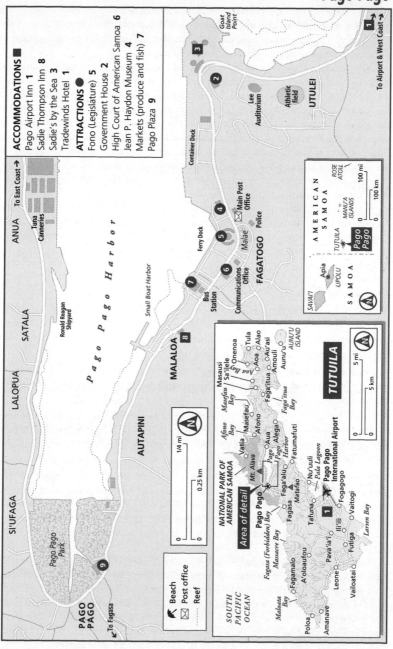

ACCOMMODATIONS ■
Pago Airport Inn **1**
Sadie Thompson Inn **8**
Sadie's by the Sea **3**
Tradewinds Hotel **1**

ATTRACTIONS ●
Fono (Legislature) **5**
Government House **2**
High Court of American Samoa **6**
Jean P. Haydon Museum **4**
Markets (produce and fish) **7**
Pago Plaza **9**

Tips A Fascinating Pit Stop

Ramshackle bars by the beach are part of the South Seas lore, but few of these establishments actually exist these days. One that does is **Tisa's Barefoot Bar** on Alega Beach (© 622-7447). This funky joint looks slapped together because it is. The owners put it together from driftwood, scrap lumber, well-worn tables, and whatever else they could find. Libation is served daily from 11am to 7pm, with seafood dinners afterward by advance reservation only. They take American Express, MasterCard, or Visa.

---

and Sa'ilele villages. Near the east end, a road from Amouli village cuts across Lemafa Saddle to **Aoa Bay** on the north coast.

To my eye, the southeastern coast road is the most scenic in American Samoa. The route twists and turns from one gorgeous little bay to the next, most of them with villages beside white-sand beaches. **Aunu'u Island** will be visible from the main road as you near the east end of Tutuila. The top of a small volcanic crater, Aunu'u has a village near a famous pink quicksand pit. Motorboats leave for it from the small-boat harbor at Au'asi, opposite it on the southeast coast.

Alao and **Tula** villages on the east end of Tutuila are the oldest settlements in American Samoa. They face a long, gorgeous surf beach, but be careful of the undertow from waves driven by the prevailing southeast trade winds. The road turns the northwestern point and climbs precipitously over a mountain ridge and down to **Onenoa,** a picturesque village tucked in a little bay. You'll have a fine view of the north shore and the Cockscombs as you descend into Onenoa.

THE WEST SIDE OF TUTUILA

You saw some of Tutuila's rugged coast on the drive from the airport west of Pago Pago, including the **Flower Pot,** a tall rock with coconut palms growing on its top sitting in the lagoon. About halfway from the airport to The Rainmaker Hotel, an inland road (at Tom Ho Chung's store) leads to the **Lyndon B. Johnson Tropical Medical Center** in the Faga'alu Valley. If you feel like taking a hike, take the left fork in the road past the medical center, and when the pavement ends, follow the track to **Virgin Falls.** It's not the easiest walk, but the falls have a nice pool beneath them. Allow several hours for this sweaty outing.

The **airport** sits on the island's only sizable parcel of relatively flat land, and the main road west from there cuts through rolling hills and shopping centers until emerging on the rugged west end.

At Pava'ia'i village a road goes inland and climbs to the village of A'oloaufou, high on a central plateau. A hiking trail leads from the village down the ridges to the north coast. From here it drops to A'asutuai on **Massacre Bay,** where Samoans attacked the La Pérouse expedition in 1787. The French have put a monument there to the members of the expedition who were slain by Samoan warriors. Don't try this hike unless you have experience on mountain trails, and if you do go, take plenty of water to drink.

Back on the main road, head west and watch for a sign on the left marking the turn to the villages of Illi'ili and Vaitogi. Follow the signs to **Vaitogi,** and when you're in the village, bear right at the fork to the beach. Take the one-lane track to the right along the beach, past some graves and the stone remains of an old church, and up a rocky headland through pandanus groves. When you reach the first clearing on the left, stop the car and walk over to the cliff. According to legend, Vaitogi once experienced such a severe famine that an old blind woman and her granddaughter jumped off this cliff and were turned into a shark and a turtle. Today the villagers can reputedly chant their names, and the turtle and the shark will appear. The view of the south coast from **Turtle and Shark Point,** with the surf pounding the rocks below you, is superb.

The Rev. John Williams chose the village of **Leone,** which sits on a white-sand beach in a small bay, as his landing place on Tutuila in 1830, and it became the cradle of Christianity here. There is a monument to Williams in the village. The road beside the Catholic church leads about 2.5km (1½ miles) to **Leone Falls,** which has a freshwater pool for swimming (but as in the equally religious Samoa, never on Sun).

The road from Leone to the western end of the island winds in and out of small bays with sandy beaches and climbs across a ridge to Poloa village on the northwest coast.

GUIDED TOURS

In addition to its day trips from Apia (see the "Seeing American Samoa as a Day Trip from Apia" box, earlier in this chapter), **Oceania Travel & Tours,** in the Lumanaʻi Building in Fagatogo (© 633-1172), has half- and full-day guided tours of Tutuila and Aunuʻu islands for about US$40 and US$80 (£20–£40) per person.

9 National Park of American Samoa

The **National Park of American Samoa** was authorized by the U.S. Congress in 1988. Although its facilities have been slow in coming (little has been developed except a few rough hiking trails), the park has amassed more than 10,000 pristine acres—3,000 of them on Tutuila and another 6,000 in the Manuʻa Islands. In all, they protect some beautiful shoreline, magnificent beaches, cliffs dropping into the sea, reefs, and rainforest reaching to serrated, mist-shrouded mountain peaks. Unlike other U.S. National Parks, in which the federal government buys property outright, here the National Park Service has leased the land from the villages for 50 years, thereby protecting both the natural environment and traditional Samoan ownership customs.

Because development is ongoing, you should stop by the **Park Visitors Center,** in the Pago Plaza shopping center at the head of the bay, or contact them at NPAS, Pago Pago, AS 96799 (© **633-7082;** fax 633-7085; www.nps.gov/npsa). The center has exhibits that explain Samoa's prehistory.

On Tutuila, the park starts along the ridge atop Mount Alava and drops down sharp ridges and steep valleys to the north coast. It includes The Cockscomb off the north coast and the scenic Amalau Valley, near the picturesque north-shore village of Vatia, where you can see many of Samoa's native bird species plus flying foxes (fruit bats). See "A Tour of Tutuila," above, for directions to Vatia.

Hikers can scale 1,575-foot Mount Alava via a trail that begins in the Fagasa Pass and ascends steeply through the rainforest. It's a 3-hour walk uphill along a seldom-used four-wheel-drive track, and it takes about 2 hours to get back down, but you'll be rewarded with a view over the entire Pago Pago Harbor and most of Tutuila Island. It's one of the most spectacular vistas in the South Pacific, if not the world. Be sure to take plenty of water.

An easier hike follows the paved road between Afono and Vatia on the north shore. This route skirts cliffs and beaches, and you'll have a view of the Cockscomb offshore. Birds, bats, and land crabs will keep you company.

Rory West of **North Shore Tours** (© **644-1416** or 733-3047) has various expeditions to the north coast, including hiking, camping, and fishing trips.

10 Where to Stay

If you are a bed-and-breakfast type, check out Dean Hudson's **Le Falepule**, P.O. Box 4179, Pago Pago, AS 96799 (© **633-5246;** fax 633-5648; www.american.samoa-hotels. com/le-falepule).

Pago Airport Inn   In a village setting west of the airport, this two-story motel is a more basic alternative to the Tradewinds Hotel (see below). The dark motel-style rooms open to verandalike walkways across the front of the white stucco building. The units are simple but clean. Each is equipped with a double or two single beds, cable TV mounted on the wall, a desk and chairs, and a tiled shower-only bathroom. A restaurant is open for breakfast and lunch only. It's a 15-minute walk to the island's McDonald's and KFC outlets, but consider renting a car.

P.O. Box 783, Pago Pago, AS 96799 (Tafuna, 3 min. from airport). © 699-6333. Fax 699-6336. www.pago airportinn.com. 19 units. US$125 (£63) double. Rates include airport transfers. AE, MC, V. **Amenities:** Restaurant (breakfast, lunch); laundry service. *In room:* A/C, TV, fridge, coffeemaker, iron.

Sadie's by the Sea 𝒜𝒜   Tom and Ta'aloga Drabble, who did a terrific job with the Sadie Thompson Inn (see below), have completely refurbished two wings of the original Rainmaker Hotel (first opened in 1965), which had gone steadily downhill until being shuttered several years ago. All their rooms have sea views, and there's a half-moon beach in front (this is the only place to stay beside a beach in American Samoa). The complex has a restaurant, bar, and swimming pool. Saturday is fiafia night here. With the beach and proximity to town, this my choice in American Samoa.

P.O. Box 3222, Pago Pago, AS 96799 (Goat Island Point, at entrance to harbor). © 633-5900. Fax 633-5988. www.sadieshotels.com. 46 units. US$149–US$164 (£75–£82). AE, DC, MC, V. **Amenities:** Restaurant; bar; outdoor pool; kayak rentals; car rentals; wireless Internet access; limited room service; laundry service; coin-op washers and dryers. *In room:* A/C, TV, dataport, fridge, iron.

Sadie Thompson Inn 𝒜𝒜   This historic wooden structure was a rooming house when W. Somerset Maugham stayed here in the 1920s, and it provided the setting for his famous short story "Rain." Present-day owners Tom and Ta'aloga Drabble have turned it into this comfortable inn. Each named for a character in "Rain," the units are upstairs over Sadie's Restaurant and Bar (see "Where to Dine," below). The best for my money is a suite at the front with a view of the harbor and Rainmaker Mountain. One of the suites has a separate bedroom, and two have large bathrooms with whirlpool tubs and showers. Most of the eight standard rooms are on the back of the building, but two others open to an open-air passageway with harbor view.

P.O. Box 3222, Pago Pago, AS 96799 (in Pago Pago). © 633-5981. Fax 633-5982. www.sadieshotels.com. 14 units. US$135–US$150 (£68–£75). Rates include airport transfers. AE, DC, MC, V. **Amenities:** Restaurant; bar; wireless Internet access; limited room service; laundry service. *In room:* A/C, TV, high-speed Internet access, minibar, coffeemaker, iron.

Tradewinds Hotel 𝒜𝒜   In an area known as Ottoville west of the airport, this plantation-style property would be terrific were it beside a beach instead of this inland setting. You won't be without a place to swim and sun here, for a white-marble floor leads through the two-story reception area to an outdoor pool in a courtyard to the rear of the three-story, stucco building. Guest quarters include Taupou rooms with two double beds, Manaia rooms with king-size beds, Maitai suites with king-size beds and dining tables, and Plaza suites with a separate bedroom. Some have patios or balconies. Teak furniture and sleigh or four-poster beds lend a bit of elegance throughout. **The Equator** restaurant and bar reside in a separate building.

P.O. Box 999, Pago Pago, AS 96799 (Ottoville Rd. off Airport Rd., 2.5km/1½ miles west of airport). ℭ **699-1000.** Fax 699-1010. www.tradewinds.as. 104 units. US$135–US$150 (£68–£75) double; US$165–US$240 (£83–£120) suite. Rates include limousine airport transfers. AE, MC, V. **Amenities:** Restaurant; coffee shop; bar; outdoor pool; exercise room; car rentals; salon; limited room service; laundry service. *In room:* A/C, TV, high-speed Internet access, fridge (stocked on request), coffeemaker, safe.

11 Where to Dine

The food doesn't match the harbor view, but a decent place to refresh during your walking tour of Pago Pago is the inexpensive **Waterfront Restaurant** (ℭ **633-1199**), in the Fagatogo Square shops opposite the High Court. It offers pizzas, fried chicken, sandwiches, hamburgers, hot dogs, nachos, fish and chips, and daily specials such as fried fish with rice and gravy, a fattening local favorite. It's open Monday to Friday 6am to 5pm and Saturday 6am to 3pm; it does not take credit cards.

The DeLuxe Cafe *(Value* AMERICAN   I usually stop for breakfast at this American-style cafe west of the airport next to the big Cost-U-Less store and near the Tradewinds Hotel. The walls are adorned with large paintings of Samoan wildlife both in and out of the sea, which adds a touch of sophistication. Among the eye-openers are fresh fruit plates and banana pancakes. Lunch sees a collection of American-style soups, salads, sandwiches, burgers, and fried chicken, shrimp, and fish, while dinner turns to fish and steaks.

Ottoville Rd., west of airport. ℭ **699-4000.** Breakfast US$4–US$13 (£2–£6.50); lunch US$5–US$15 (£2.50–£7.50); main courses US$15–US$25 (£7.50–£13). AE, MC, V (US$10/£5 minimum purchase). Mon–Sat 7am–10pm; Sun 9am–2pm.

Don't Drink the Water (DDW) Cafe AMERICAN   You can check your e-mail while having breakfast or lunch at this friendly cafe in the Pago Plaza shopping center at the head of the harbor. The hearty chow is all American: pancakes, omelets, burgers (including veggie patties), grilled sandwiches, steaks, and grilled or fried fish. The owners moved this cafe from Apia where you can't drink the water; hence its name. Everything is cooked to order, so don't be in a hurry here.

Pago Pago, in Pago Plaza. ℭ **633-5297.** Breakfast US$2.50–US$6.50 (£1.25–£3.25); lunch US$3–US$16 (£1.50– £8). MC, V. Mon–Fri 7am–2:30pm (Internet cafe to 4pm); Sat 7am–12:30pm.

Rubbles Tavern AMERICAN/MEXICAN   It's a long way from town, but this friendly air-conditioned pub is a good place to cool off while you're waiting for the last plane back to Apia. Except for the bamboo lining the walls of one dining room and the mat panels and huge Samoan war canoe rudder adorning the other, Rubbles could be in any Western city. You can even watch sports on the two TVs behind the long bar. The fare includes salads, nachos, burgers, sandwiches, wings, and grilled steaks and fish.

Nu'uuli, on main rd. in Nu'uuli Shopping Center (west of airport turnoff). ℭ **633-4403.** Burgers, sandwiches, and salads US$6–US$10 (£3–£5); main courses US$9–US$20 (£4.50–£10). AE, MC, V. Mon–Sat 10am–11pm.

Sadie's Restaurant and Bar ℱ AMERICAN   This pleasant, American-style restaurant on the ground floor of the Sadie Thompson Inn is the most refined and best place to dine in American Samoa. You can get cooked or continental breakfasts; lunches of burgers, sandwiches, salads, and a few mains such as fish and chips; and dinners ranging from prime rib to steamed Alaska crab legs with drawn butter. Freshest is the daily catch, served either grilled or poached. Wednesday is *fiafia* night, with a buffet and Samoan dance presentation.

Pago Pago, in Sadie Thompson Inn. ℭ **633-5981.** Reservations recommended for lunch and dinner. Breakfast US$9–US$14 (£4.50–£7); burgers and sandwiches US$10–US$12 (£5–£6); main courses US$12–US$42 (£6–£21). AE, DC, MC, V. Daily 6–10:30am, 11am–3pm, and 6–10pm.

15

The Kingdom of Tonga

Thanks to a quirk of humankind and not of nature, the international date line swings eastward from its north–south path down the middle of the Pacific Ocean just enough to make the last Polynesian monarch the first sovereign to see the light of each new day. When King Siaosi (George) Tupou V of Tonga greets the dawn and looks out on his realm from the veranda of his whitewashed Victorian palace, he sees a country of low but fertile islands, of gorgeous sandy beaches, and of colorful coral reefs waiting to be explored.

His nation is protected—but was never ruled—by a Western power. Like Samoa to the north, Tonga has managed to maintain its Polynesian culture in the face of modern change. The Tonga Visitors Bureau is spot on when it says the kingdom "still remains far away from it all; still different, still alone, and to the joy of those who find their way to her—essentially unspoiled."

While this description is true of the flat main island Tongatapu, it is even more applicable to Vava'u and Ha'apai. Vava'u is a group of hilly islands whose fjordlike harbor makes it one of the South Pacific's most popular yachting destinations. The low islands of the Ha'apai group seem to have changed little since the crew of HMS *Bounty* staged their mutiny just offshore in 1789. Visiting Vava'u is extremely pleasant to the eyes, and you should make every effort to see it and its multitudinous islets.

Along with my taste for adventure, I make sure to bring my sense of humor to Tonga. You may need yours, too, for things don't always go according to plan here. This is the poorest country covered in this book. The local airline might not come to get you, the electricity might suddenly quit, and the tap water might be turned off during your lukewarm shower (not that you can drink it when it's running). You'll see multitudes of dogs, chickens, and pigs almost everywhere, even wandering the streets of Nuku'alofa, the capital. But if you take the quirks of humankind with a smile, you will enjoy your time in Tonga, during which you will get a most fascinating glimpse into the way things used to be out here.

1 Tonga Today

When you drive from the airport into **Nuku'alofa,** the nation's capital, you can see why the country's main island is named **Tongatapu (Sacred Garden).** Every bit of it not occupied by a building or by the road is under cultivation with bananas, tapioca, taro, yams, watermelons, tomatoes, squash, and a plethora of other fruits and vegetables. The Tongans might be generally poor in terms of material wealth, but they own some of the South Pacific's most fertile and productive land. There just isn't much of it.

GEOGRAPHY The kingdom consists of 170 islands, 36 of them inhabited, scattered over an area of about 259,000 sq. km (100,000 sq. miles). The amount of dry land, however, is only 697 sq. km (269 sq. miles). That's smaller than New York City.

Tonga has three major island groups. Tongatapu and its neighbor, the smaller 'Eua, comprise the southernmost group. About 155km (96 miles) north are the islands of Ha'apai, where Fletcher Christian led the mutiny on the *Bounty*. About 108km (67 miles) beyond Ha'apai, beautiful Vava'u reigns as the kingdom's sailing heaven. Even farther north are the remote Niuas Islands, but you won't be going there.

The largest island in the kingdom, Tongatapu, has about a third of the country's land area and about two-thirds of its population. It's a flat island about 65km (40 miles) across from east to west and 32km (20 miles) across from north to south at its longest and widest points. In the center a lakelike lagoon is now void of most sea life.

Tongatapu and most of the islands here are raised coral atolls. The exceptions are the Niuas and, in Ha'apai, the active volcano Tofua and its sister volcanic cone, Kao. Geologists say that the weight of the Ha'apai volcanoes has caused the Indo-Australian Plate to sag like a hammock, raising Tongatapu and 'Eua on the south end of the Tongan chain and Vava'u on the north end. As a result, the sides of Tongatapu and Vava'u facing Ha'apai slope gently to the sea, and the sides facing away end in cliffs.

GOVERNMENT   It would be an understatement to say that Tonga's royal family has a hand in every important decision made here; in fact, very little gets done without the royal family's outright or tacit approval or involvement. Tonga technically is a constitutional monarchy, although in many respects the king is head of a system of hereditary Polynesian chiefs who happen to have titles derived from England. The king picks his own Privy Council of advisors and appoints nine cabinet members and the governors of Ha'apai and Vava'u. With a few exceptions they are nobles. The cabinet members and the governors hold 11 of the 30 seats in the Legislative Assembly. Of the 19 other members of the assembly, the nobles choose 10 from among their ranks, leaving 9 to be elected by the taxpaying commoners.

With more Tongans living abroad, and those at home being exposed more and more to news of the world, Tonga now has an active pro-democracy movement. It suffered a serious setback in November 2006, when one of its demonstrations turned into a riot which left eight people dead and several square blocks burned in Nuku'alofa. King George Topou V, who succeeded to the throne when his father, King Taufa'ahau Tupou IV, passed away earlier that year, has appointed a commission to move toward a parliament with a popular-elected majority. What happens next is anyone's guess.

ECONOMY   Tourism is an important component of Tonga's economy but is minuscule when compared to Fiji and French Polynesia. Tonga has few natural resources other than its fertile soil and the fish in the sea within its exclusive economic zone. The world markets for its exports—fresh fish, vanilla, kava, bananas, coconut oil, pineapples, watermelons, tomatoes, squash, and other vegetables—have been unstable and depressed at times in recent years. Money sent home by Tongans living overseas is a major source of foreign exchange.

2 History 101

Polynesians found and settled these islands sometime around 500 B.C. on their long migration across the South Pacific. Around A.D. 950, according to a myth, the supreme Polynesian god (known here as Tangaloa) came down to Tongatapu and fathered a son by a lovely Tongan maiden. Their son, Aho'eitu, thus became the first Tui Tonga—king of Tonga—and launched one of the world's longest-running dynasties.

The first *tuis* ruled from Niutoua village on the northwest corner of Tongatapu. They moved to Lapaha on the shore of the island's interior lagoon about 800 years ago, to take advantage of a safer anchorage for the large, double-hulled war canoes they used to extend their empire as far as Fiji and Samoa. At that time, a deep passage linked the lagoon to the sea; it has been slowly closing as geological forces raise the island and reduce the entrance to the present shallow bank.

Over time, the tui became more of a figurehead, and his power was dispersed among several chiefs, all of them descendants of the original tui. For centuries the rival chiefs seemed to stop warring among themselves only long enough to make war on Fiji and Samoa. The chiefs were fighting in 1798 when missionaries from the London Missionary Society landed on Lifuka in Ha'apai. Two of the missionaries were killed. The rest fled to Sydney, leaving Tonga to the heathens.

EUROPEANS ARRIVE   Although Dutch explorers had sighted Tonga in the 17th century, the missionaries knew of the islands from the visits of British captains Samuel Wallis, James Cook, and William Bligh in the late 1700s. During his third voyage in 1777, Captain Cook was feted on Lifuka by a powerful chief named Finau I. Cook was so impressed by this show of hospitality that he named the Ha'apai group "The Friendly Islands," the modern kingdom's motto. Unbeknownst to Cook, however, Finau I and his associates apparently plotted to murder him and his crew, but they couldn't agree among themselves how to do it before the great explorer sailed away.

Captain Bligh and HMS *Bounty* visited Lifuka in 1789 after gathering breadfruit in Tahiti. Before he could leave Tongan waters, however, the famous mutiny took place near the island of Ha'afeva in the Ha'apai group.

Some 20 years later Chief Finau II of Lifuka captured a British ship named the *Port au Prince,* stealing all of its muskets and ammunition, setting it on fire, and brutally slaughtering all but one member of its crew. The survivor was a 15-year-old Londoner named Will Mariner. He became a favorite of the chief, spent several years living among the Tongans, and later wrote a four-volume account of his experiences. He told how the Tongans mistook 12,000 silver coins on the *Port au Prince* for gaming pieces they called *pa'angas.* The national currency today is known as the pa'anga.

The arrival of the Wesleyan missionaries on Lifuka in the 1820s coincided with the rise of Taufa'ahau, a powerful chief who converted to Christianity in 1831. With their help, he won a series of domestic wars. By 1845, he had conquered all of Tonga and declared himself to be the new Tui Tonga.

ROYALTY ARRIVES   Taufa'ahau took a Christian name and became King George I of Tonga. In 1862 he made his subordinate chiefs "nobles," but he also freed the commoners from forced labor and instituted the policy of granting each adult male a garden plot in the countryside and a house lot in town. He created a Privy Council of his own choosing and established a legislative assembly made up of representatives of the nobles and commoners. This system was committed to writing in the Constitution of 1875, which still is in effect today. The assembly is known now as Parliament.

King George I died in 1893 at the age of 97, thus ending a reign of 48 years. His great-grandson, King George II, ruled for the next 25 years and is best remembered for signing a treaty with Great Britain in 1900, which turned Tonga's foreign affairs over to the British and prevented any further encroachments on Tonga by the Western colonial powers. Consequently, the Kingdom of Tonga was never colonized.

King George II was succeeded in 1918 by his daughter, the 6-foot-2-inch Queen Salote (her name is the Tongan transliteration of Charlotte). For the next 47 years, Queen Salote carefully protected her people from Western influence, even to the extent of not allowing a modern hotel to be built in the kingdom. She did, however, come to the world's attention in 1953, when she rode bareheaded in the cold, torrential rain that drenched the coronation parade of Queen Elizabeth II in London (she was merely following Tongan custom of showing respect to royalty by appearing uncovered in their presence). She later hosted Queen Elizabeth II and Prince Philip in Nuku'alofa.

Queen Salote died in 1965 and was succeeded by her son, King Taufa'ahau Tupou IV. Then in his late 40s, he set about bringing Tonga into the modern world. On the pretext of accommodating the important guests invited to his elaborate coronation scheduled for July 4, 1967, the International Dateline Hotel was built on Nuku'alofa's waterfront, and Fua'amotu Airport on Tongatapu was upgraded to handle jet aircraft. Tourism had arrived, albeit modestly.

DEMOCRACY DOESN'T ARRIVE   In the late 1980s, a group of commoners founded *Kele'a,* a newspaper published without the king's input. The paper created a ruckus almost from its first issue by revealing that some government ministers had rung up excessive travel expenses on trips abroad.

More scandals followed, including news that the government was selling Tongan passports to overseas nationals (which helps explains Tonga's growing Chinese population). Incensed, several hundred Tongans marched down Nuku'alofa's main street in a peaceful protest, and established the Tonga Human Rights Democracy Movement. A recent scandal included the 2001 loss of some US$20 million of Tonga's overseas trust fund through a questionable investment by the official Court Jester (actually an American businessman).

In 2005, Tonga's civil servants went on strike demanding better pay. The protest went on for 6 weeks until the government agreed to raise wages by as much as 60%. A year later a pro-democracy gathering turned into the riot which burned several square blocks of downtown Nuku'alofa. Not all of downtown was torched, for the burnings apparently were targeted at an airline, a hotel, and power, cellphone, and other businesses owned by the king and his associates.

The king has since promised to divest himself of his business interests, and he has appointed a commission to search for a path to a more popularly elected parliament.

3 The Tongans

The population of Tonga is estimated at 104,000 (no one knows for sure). Approximately 98% of the inhabitants are pure Polynesians, closely akin to the Samoans in physical appearance, language, and culture.

As in Samoa, the bedrock of the Tongan social structure is the traditional way of life—*faka Tonga*—and the extended family. Parents, grandparents, children, aunts, uncles, cousins, nieces, and nephews all have the same sense of obligation to each other as is felt in Western nuclear families. The extended-family system makes sure that no one ever goes hungry or without a place to live.

THE TONGAN SYSTEM   The extended family aside, some striking differences exist between Tonga, Samoa, and the other Polynesian islands. Unlike the others, in which there is a certain degree of upward mobility, Tonga has a rigid two-tier caste system. The king and 33 "Nobles of the Realm"—plus their families—make up a privileged class at the top of society. Everyone else is a commoner, and although commoners can hold positions in the government (a commoner serves as prime minister), it's impossible for them to move into the nobility even by marriage. Titles of the nobility are inherited, but the king can strip members of their positions if they fail to live up to their obligations (presumably including loyalty to the royal family).

Technically the king owns all the land in Tonga, which in effect makes the country his feudal estate. Although the nobles each rule over a section of the kingdom, they have an obligation to provide for the welfare of the serfs rather than the other way around. The nobles administer the villages, look after the people's welfare, and apportion the land among the commoners.

TONGAN DRESS   Even traditional dress reflects the Tongan social structure. Western-style clothes have made deep inroads in recent years, especially among young persons, but many Tongans still wear wraparound skirts known as *valas*. These come to well below the knee on men and to the ankles on women. To show their respect for the royal family and to each other, traditional men and women wear finely woven mats known as *ta'ovalas* over their valas. Men hold these up with waistbands of coconut fiber; women wear decorative waistbands known as *kiekies*. Tongans have ta'ovalas for everyday wear, but on special occasions they break out mats that are family heirlooms, some of them tattered and worn. The king owns ta'ovalas that have been in his family for more than 500 years.

Tongan custom is to wear black for months to mourn the death of a relative or close friend. Because Tongan extended families are large and friends numerous, almost everyone in traditional Tonga dress wears black.

RELIGION   Tongans converted to Christianity in the old days—apparently an easy transition, as Tongan legend holds that their own king is a descendant of a supreme Polynesian god and a beautiful earthly virgin. Today about half of all Tongans belong to the Free Wesleyan Church of Tonga, founded by early Methodist missionaries and headed by the king. The Free Church of Tonga is an offshoot that is allied with the Methodist synods in Australia and New Zealand. There are also considerable numbers of Roman Catholics, Anglicans, Seventh-day Adventists, and Mormons. Church services are usually held at 10am on Sunday, but few are conducted in English. St. Paul's Anglican Church, on the corner of Fafatehi and Wellington roads, usually has communion in English on Sunday at 8am. The royal family worships at 10am in Centenary Church, the Free Wesleyan Church on Wellington Road, a block behind the Royal Palace.

The red national flag has a cross on a white field in its upper corner to signify the country's strong Christian foundation.

As was the case throughout Polynesia, the Tongans accepted most of the puritanical beliefs taught by the early missionaries but stopped short of adopting their strict sexual mores. Today Tongan society is very conservative in outlook and practice in almost every aspect of life except the sexual activities of unmarried young men and women.

Tongan families without enough female offspring will raise boys as they would girls. They are known in Tongan as *fakaleitis* (like a woman) and live lives similar to those

---

⌐Fun Fact⌐ Buried with Banners

Tongans of all religions bury their dead in unique cemeteries set in groves of frangipani trees. The graves are sandy mounds decorated with colorful flags, banners, artificial flowers, and seashells.

⌐ *Fun Fact* What Day Is It?

Theoretically, the international date line should run for its *entire length* along the 180th meridian, halfway around the world from the prime meridian, the starting point for measuring international time. If it followed the 180th meridian precisely, however, most of the Aleutian Islands would be a day ahead of the rest of Alaska, and Fiji would be split into 2 days. To solve these problems, the date line swings west around the Aleutians, leaving them in the same day as Alaska. In the South Pacific, it swerves east between Fiji and Samoa, leaving all of Fiji a day ahead of the Samoas.

Because Tonga and Samoa lie east of the 180th meridian, both countries should logically be in the same day. But Tonga wanted to have the same date as Australia and New Zealand, so the line was drawn arbitrarily east of Tonga, putting it 1 day ahead of Samoa.

To travelers, it's even more confusing because the time of day is the same in Tonga and Samoa. When traveling from one to the other, only the date changes. For example, if everyone is going to church at 10am on Sunday in Tonga, everyone's at work on Saturday in Samoa.

---

of the *mahus* in Tahiti and the *fa'afafines* in the Samoas. In Tonga they have a reputation for sexual promiscuity and for persistently approaching Western male visitors in search of sexual liaisons.

4 Language

The official language is Tongan, but English is taught in the schools and is widely spoken in the main towns. Tongan is similar to Samoan. One major difference between them is the number of glottal stops (represented by an apostrophe in writing) in the Tongan tongue. These are short stops similar to the break between "Oh-oh" in English.

Every vowel is pronounced in the Latin fashion: *ah, ay, ee, oh,* and *oo* (as in kangaroo) instead of *ay, ee, eye, oh,* and *you* as in English. The consonants are sounded as they are in English.

An extensive knowledge of Tongan will not be necessary for English-speakers to get around and enjoy the kingdom, but here are a few words you can use to elicit smiles from your hosts and to avoid the embarrassment of entering the wrong restroom:

English	Tongan	Pronunciation
hello	**malo e lelei**	*mah*-low ay *lay*-lay
welcome	**talitali fiefia**	tah-lay-*tah*-lay fee-ay-*fee*-ah
how do you do?	**fefe hake?**	*fay*-fay *hah*-kay?
fine, thank you	**sai pe, malo**	*sah*-ee pay, *mah*-low
good-bye	**'alu a**	ah-*loo* ah
thank you	**malo**	*mah*-low
how much?	**'oku fiha?**	*oh*-koo *fee*-hah?

English	Tongan	Pronunciation
good	**lelei**	lay-*lay*-ee
bad	**kovi**	*koh*-vee
woman	**fefine**	fay-*feen*-ay
man	**tangata**	tahn-*got*-ah
house	**fale**	*fah*-lay
transvestite	**fakaleiti**	fah-ka-*lay*-tee

5 Visitor Information & Maps

The friendly staff has many brochures, maps, and other materials available at the **Tonga Visitors Bureau (TVB)**, P.O. Box 37, Nuku'alofa, Kingdom of Tonga (℃ 21-733; fax 23-507; www.tongaholiday.com). The office is on Vuna Road near the International Dateline Hotel. Especially good are the bureau's brochures on Tongan dancing, handicrafts, archaeology, construction skills, and a walking tour of central Nuku'alofa. A stop by the "TVB" is a must before setting out to see the country. Hours are Monday to Friday 8:30am to 4:30pm and Saturday 9am to noon.

Other sources of information are:

- **North America:** Tonga Consulate, 360 Post St., Ste. 604, San Francisco, CA 94108 (℃ **415/781-0365;** fax 415/781-3964; secretary@sfconsulate.gov.to).
- **Australia:** Sione Pinomi, Marketing Representative (℃ **04/1461-1080;** jpinomi@hotmail.com)
- **New Zealand:** Will Ilolahia, Marketing Representative (℃ **0276-368357;** fax 09/629-0826; will@waiatatrust.co.nz)
- **United Kingdom:** Tonga Consulate, 36 Molyneux St., London W1H 6AB (℃ **0207 245828;** fax 0207 239074; snkioa@tongahighcom.co.uk)

Once you're in Nuku'alofa, **Friends Tourist Center,** on Taufa'ahau Road between Wellington and Salote roads (℃ **26-323**), is another good source of information. Owned by Paul Johansson, a Tongan who lived overseas for many years, it arranges tours of the islands and has Internet access (see "Fast Facts: Tonga," below).

6 Entry Requirements

PASSPORTS & VISAS   Every visitor must have a valid passport. **Visas** are issued upon arrival for visitors from the United States, Canada, Australia, New Zealand, the United Kingdom, and most European and South Pacific island countries. They are permitted to stay for up to 1 month, provided they have a valid passport and proof of adequate funds. You cannot board a plane flying into Tonga unless you have a ticket out of the country.

If in doubt about whether citizens of your country need visas, contact the **Immigration Department,** Hale Salote Kolofo'ou, Nuku'alofa (℃ **26-970;** fax 26-977; www.pmo.gov.to).

Applications for stays of longer than 30 days must be made to the principal immigration officer in Nuku'alofa.

7 When to Go

THE CLIMATE

Tongatapu is far enough south of the equator to have cool, dry, and quite pleasant weather during the austral winter months (July–Sept), when temperatures range between 60°F and 70°F (16°C–21°C). However, the ends of occasional cold fronts from the Antarctic and periods of stiff southeast trade winds can make it seem even cooler during this period. During the summer (Dec–Mar), the high temperatures can reach above 90°F (32°C), with evenings in the comfortable 70s (20s Celcius). A sweater, jacket, or wrap will come in handy for evening wear at any time of the year.

The islands get about 180 centimeters (71 in.) of rainfall a year, the majority of it falling during the summer months. Vava'u to the north tends to be somewhat warmer and slightly wetter than Tongatapu.

Tonga is in the southwestern Pacific cyclone belt, and hurricanes are possible from November to April. There will be ample warning if one bears down on the islands while you're there.

HOLIDAYS & EVENTS

The largest annual festival is **Heilala**, the week of July 4, when Nuku'alofa goes all out for a week of dance and beauty competitions, parades, sporting matches, concerts, marching contests, regattas, parties, and the lovely **Night of Torches** on the waterfront. Tongans living overseas like to come home for Heilala, so hotel reservations should be made well in advance. Vava'u stages its own version of Heilala early in May.

The Tonga Visitors Bureau keeps track of festival dates.

Public holidays are New Year's Day, Good Friday and Easter Monday, Anzac (Memorial) Day (Apr 25), Independence Day (June 4), the King's Birthday (Aug 1), Constitution Day (Nov 4), King Tupou I Day (Dec 4), Christmas Day, and Boxing Day (Dec 26).

8 Money

The Tongan unit of currency is the **pa'anga**, which is divided into 100 **seniti**. The banks use "TOP" for the pa'anga but I have abbreviated if as **T$** in this book. Most Tongans refer to "dollars" and "cents" when doing business with visitors, meaning pa'angas and senitis.

Tongan coins bear the likeness of the late King Taufa'ahau Tupou on one side and such items as bananas, chickens, and pigs on the other.

HOW TO GET LOCAL CURRENCY   ANZ Bank, on Taufau'ahau Road, is open Monday to Friday 9am to 4pm and Saturday from 8:30 to 11:30am. **Westpac Bank of Tonga,** at the waterfront end of Taufa'ahau Road, Nuku'alofa's main street, is open Monday to Friday 9am to 3:30pm and Saturday 8:30 to 11:30am. Both banks have ATMs. ANZ also has an ATM at the airport. You may get a better rate for cash and traveler's checks at **GlobalEX/Western Union,** on Taufa'ahau Road. It's open Monday to Friday 8:30am to 4:30pm and Saturday 8:30am to 12:30pm.

CREDIT CARDS   The major hotels, car-rental firms, travel agencies, and Royal Tongan Airlines accept American Express, Diners Club, MasterCard, and Visa credit cards. Many restaurants and other businesses accept MasterCard or Visa, but most add 4% or 5% to your bill for doing so. Always ask first if you want to charge your purchases. Leave your Discover card at home.

The Tongan Pa'anga, the U.S. & Canadian Dollars & the British Pound

At this writing, US$1/$C1 = approximately T$2.00 (or, the other way around, T$1 = US50¢), which is the exchange rate I used to calculate the dollar values given in this book. **For British readers:** At this writing, £1 = approximately T$4 (or, T$1 = 25p), the rate used to calculate the pound values below. *Note:* International exchange rates fluctuate depending on economic and political factors. Thus, the values given in this table may not be the same when you travel to Tonga. Use the following table only as a guide. Find the current rates at **www.xe.com**.

F$	US$/C$	UK£	F$	US$/C$	UK£
.25	0.13	0.06	15.00	7.50	3.75
.50	0.25	0.13	20.00	10.00	5.00
.75	0.38	0.19	25.00	12.50	6.25
1.00	0.50	0.25	30.00	15.00	7.50
2.00	1.00	0.50	35.00	17.50	8.75
3.00	1.50	0.75	40.00	20.00	10.00
4.00	2.00	1.00	45.00	22.50	11.25
5.00	2.50	1.25	50.00	25.00	12.50
6.00	3.00	1.50	75.00	37.50	18.75
7.00	3.50	1.75	100.00	50.00	25.00
8.00	4.00	2.00	125.00	62.50	31.25
9.00	4.50	2.25	150.00	75.00	37.50
10.00	5.00	2.50	200.00	100.00	50.00

9 Getting to Tonga & Getting Around

GETTING THERE

Air New Zealand flies between Auckland and Tonga, with one flight a week going to Los Angeles and back, with a brief stop in Samoa each way. **Air Pacific** connects Tonga to its flights to Fiji from Los Angeles, Australia, and New Zealand. **Polynesian Blue** flies to Tonga from Auckland and Sydney. **Airlines Tonga** (see "Getting Around," below) flies a turbo-prop plane between Nadi and Vava'u.

No flights go into, or out of, Tonga on Sunday, when local airports are closed. For more information, see "Getting There & Getting Around," in chapter 2.

ARRIVING   Except for the few international flights destined for Vava'u, most land at **Fua'amotu Airport (TBU)** on Tongatapu, 24km (15 miles) or a 30-minute drive from Nuku'alofa. The terminal has currency exchange counters, an ATM, a duty-free shop, a snack bar, and a handicraft outlet. International passengers can purchase duty-free liquor and cigarettes after clearing Immigration but before going through Customs.

GETTING TO YOUR HOTEL   Transportation from the airport into Nuku'alofa is by hotel minibuses or taxi. The bus ride to town costs T$10 (US$5/£2.50). The one-way taxi fare into Nuku'alofa is about T$30 (US$15/£7.50); the drivers will be happy to take U.S., New Zealand, or Australian currency.

Nuku'alofa

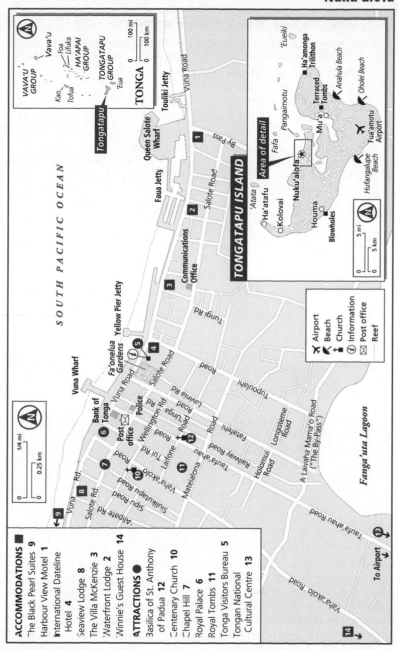

ACCOMMODATIONS ■

The Black Pearl Suites **9**
Harbour View Motel **1**
International Dateline
Hotel **4**
Seaview Lodge **8**
The Villa McKenzie **3**
Waterfront Lodge **2**
Winnie's Guest House **14**

ATTRACTIONS ●

Basilica of St. Anthony
of Padua **12**
Centenary Church **10**
Chapel Hill **7**
Royal Palace **6**
Royal Tombs **11**
Tonga Visitors Bureau **5**
Tongan National
Cultural Centre **13**

SOUTH PACIFIC OCEAN

Fanga'uta Lagoon

To Airport

Airport ✈
Beach ↙
Church ✝
Information ⓘ
Post office ✉
Reef

TONGATAPU ISLAND

TONGA

VAVA'U GROUP
Vava'u
Foa
Lifuka
HA'APAI GROUP
Kao
Tofua
TONGATAPU GROUP
'Eua

Area of detail

DEPARTING　A **departure tax** of T$25 (US$13/£6.25) is charged of all passengers leaving on international flights. You pay it in Tongan currency at Fua'amotu Airport, at a separate booth outside Immigration. There is no departure tax for domestic flights. There is no currency exchange facility in the departure lounge, so swap your money before clearing Immigration.

GETTING AROUND

BY PLANE

Domestic air service has been in a state of flux since the government-owned Royal Tongan Airlines folded in 2004. As I write, **Airlines Tonga** (© 24-506) was flying from Tongatapu to Ha'apai and Vava'u. It's a joint venture between Air Fiji (see "Getting Around," in chapter 4) and Nuku'alofa-based Teta Tours. Frankly, no one at the airline would answer the phone when I was in Tonga recently. Consequently, I get a local in-bound tour operator, such as **Pacific Travel Marketing** (© 28-304; sales@ pacifictravelmarketing.afe.to), to make my arrangements.

The one-way fare from Tongatapu to Vava'u is about T$450 (US$225/£113), and to Ha'apai, about T$300 (US$150/£75).

A more reliable option is **Chathams Pacific—The Friendly Islands Airline** (© 28-000; www.chathamspacific.com), a New Zealand–based airline that began operating in Tonga in April 2008, using comfortable, 50-seat Convair aircraft. Its unrestricted one-way fares from Tongatapu were T$278 (US$139/£70) to Vava'u and T$173 (US$87/£43) to Ha'apai.

Note: Domestic flights arrive and depart from the old terminal, not the newer international terminal.

BY RENTAL CAR

Avis (© 800/331-1212 or 21-179; www.avis.com) has an office on Taufa'ahau Road. Rates are T$82 (US$41/£21) per day, including unlimited kilometers. A subsidiary of E. M. Jones Travel, **KL2 Rental Car** (© 30-221; kl2rental@kalianet.to), Taufa'ahau Road Extended, rents cars starting at T$50 (US$25/£13) per day, including unlimited mileage. Both have a limited supply of cars, so reserve as soon as you can.

You must obtain a **local driver's license** before you can officially drive in Tonga. The rental firms will do it for you, or you can go through the rather cumbersome application process at the central police station (© 21-222), on Wellington Road just off Taufa'ahau Road in Nuku'alofa. Enter on the Railway Road side of the building. You will need your home driver's license and T$18 (US$9/£4.50) in pa'anga.

DRIVING RULES　**Driving in Tonga is on the left-hand side of the road.** Speed limits are 65kmph (40 mph) on the open road and 40kmph (25 mph) in towns and villages. You must wear your seat belt at all times, and driving under the influence of alcohol is a serious offense.

Tips　Don't Miss Your Flight Home

Try not to fly back from Vava'u or Ha'apai to Nuku'alofa on the same day your international flight is scheduled to take you home. Give yourself at least a day's cushion, just in case the local airline has an unexpected cancellation. And remember to always reconfirm your return flight as soon as possible.

BY TAXI

Taxis are plentiful in Nuku'alofa, although most are in poor condition (sometimes I think Tonga is where old cars go to die). They usually gather near Maketi Talamahu at the corner of Salote and Railway roads in Nuku'alofa, but you can flag them down anywhere. They aren't all identified as taxis except for their license plates, which begin with the letter T. Among the many firms are **Fiemalie Taxis** (© 24-270), **Wellington Taxis** (© 24-844), or **Holiday Taxis** (© 25-655 or 25-169).

Fares are T$3 (US$1.50/75p) in town. The taxis have no meters, so make sure you and the driver agree on just how much the fare will be. The fares are doubled on Sundays, when taxis are officially permitted only to take passengers to church and back (some of them will carry tourists from their hotels or guesthouses to the wharf in order for them to get to the offshore islands).

BY BUS

Local buses operate Monday to Saturday during regular business hours (that is, they stop at 5pm). They use the **Vuna Road waterfront** as their terminal. Town buses stop in front of the Tonga Visitors Bureau; long-distance ones stop in front of the government buildings. They fan out from there to all parts of Tongatapu, but there are no reliable schedules. Simply ask the bus drivers at the market where they are going. About T$2 (US$1/50p) will take you to the end of the island in either direction.

BY BICYCLE

Tongatapu is virtually flat, making it an ideal island for bicycling. "Pushbikes" can be rented from **Bicycle Hire** (no phone) on the Vuna waterfront near the International Dateline Hotel. One-speed models cost T$1 (US50¢/25p) per hour, T$10 (US$5/£2.50) for a full day. Open Monday to Saturday 8am to 6pm.

BY FERRY

It's not for everyone, but the **Shipping Corporation of Polynesia** (© 23-853; www.olovaha.com) operates weekly ferry service from Nuku'alofa to Ha'apai and Vava'u. It leaves Nuku'alofa on Tuesday and takes about 16 hours to make the 262km (163-mile) trip to Vava'u, stopping at Lifuka in the Ha'apai group on the way. The ship then turns around and arrives back in Nuku'alofa on Thursday. The one-way fare between Nuku'alofa and Vava'u is about T$70 (US$35/£18) for deck passage.

FAST FACTS: Tonga

American Express American Express has no representative in Tonga.

Bookstores **Friendly Islands Bookshop,** on Taufa'ahau Road (© 23-787), carries greeting cards made from *tapa* cloth, paperback books, postcards, international news magazines, week-old Australian newspapers, books about Tonga and the rest of the South Pacific, and maps of Tonga.

Business Hours In general, Tonga's shops are open Monday to Friday from 8am to 1pm and 2 to 5pm and Saturday from 8am to noon. Government offices are open Monday to Friday from 8:30am to 12:30pm and 1:30 to 4:30pm.

Camera & Film **Foto Fix,** on Taufa'ahau Road north of Wellington Road (© 23-466), sells Kodak and Fuji film, provides 1-hour color film processing, and has machines which will print photos from digital camera memory cards.

424   CHAPTER 15 · THE KINGDOM OF TONGA

Customs   Visitors are allowed to bring in 500 cigarettes and 2.25 liters of spirits or 4.5 liters of wine, as well as personal belongings in use at the time of arrival. Pets, dangerous drugs, indecent materials, firearms, and ammunition are prohibited, and foodstuffs must be declared and inspected. Arriving visitors can buy duty-free merchandise at Fua'amotu Airport after clearing Immigration but before going through Customs. See "Fast Facts: South Pacific," in chapter 2, for what you can bring home.

Drug Laws   A drug-sniffing dog roams the baggage claim area at the airport, so don't even think about bringing illegal drugs into Tonga.

Drugstores   **Village Mission Pharmacy,** on 'Unga Road between Wellington and Laifone roads (✆ 27-522), is the most modern drug store here. Open Monday to Friday 8:30am to 5pm and Saturday 9am to 12:30pm. **Fasi Pharmacy & Clinic,** on Salote Road between Lavina and Tupoulahi roads (✆ 22-955), is open Monday to Friday 9am to 5pm and Saturday 9am to 4pm. Both have doctors on call. See "Healthcare," below.

Electricity   Electricity in Tonga is 240 volts, 50 cycles, and the plugs are the heavy, angled type used in Australia and New Zealand. You will need a converter and adapter plug to operate American appliances.

Embassies & Consulates   The nearest U.S. embassy is in Suva, Fiji. Consular offices in Tonga are the **Australian High Commission** (✆ 21-244), the **New Zealand High Commission** (✆ 21-122), and the **People's Republic of China Embassy** (✆ 24-554).

Emergencies & Police   The emergency telephone number for the **police, fire department,** and **hospital** is ✆ **911.** The main **police station** (✆ 21-222) is on Salote Road at Railway Road.

Etiquette & Customs   It's against the law for men as well as women to appear shirtless in public. While Western men—but definitely not women—can swim and sunbathe shirtless at the hotel pools and beaches frequented by visitors, you will see most Tongans swimming in a full set of clothes. Visitors should not wear bathing suits or skimpy attire away from the hotel pools or beaches frequented by foreigners. Summer clothing is in order during most of the year, but a sweater, jacket, or wrap should be taken for evening wear.

Healthcare   **Vaiola Hospital** (✆ 21-200) provides medical, dental, and optical service, but it's considerably below the standards you're used to. The outpatient clinics are open from 8:30am to 4:30pm daily. The two drugstores have private physicians on call (see "Drugstores," above).

Insects   There are no dangerous insects in Tonga, and the mosquitoes do not carry malaria. Vava'u, warmer and more humid than Tongatapu, tends to have more mosquitoes and has tropical centipedes that can inflict painful stings if touched; watch your step if walking around with bare feet.

Internet Access   **Friends Tourist Center** (✆ 26-323), on Taufa'ahau Road between Salote and Wellington roads, has Internet access Monday to Friday 8am to 10pm and Saturday 8:30am to 7:30pm. **Dataline Internet Cafe** (✆ 27-688), on Wellington Road east of Taufa'ahau Road, is open Monday through Saturday 8am to

11pm. On Faua Jetty, **Café Reef** (© **26-777**) has two computers with access. All charge T$3 (US$1.50/75p) per hour.

Road warriors can get temporary Internet access accounts for their laptops at **Tonga Communications Corp.** (© **23-499**), on Salote Road at Takaunove Road. There's a T$41 (US$21/£10) setup fee plus T$23 (US$12/£5.75) for 2 hours of access over 1 month, or T$46 (US$23/£12) for a month's unlimited access. Go into the telephone office, which is open Monday to Saturday 8:30am to 10:30pm and Sunday 10am to 10:30pm. See "Staying Connected," in chapter 2, for information on how to configure your computer.

Laundry & Dry Cleaning **Savoy Dry Cleaners,** on Fatefehi Road (© **878-3314**), has 1-day laundry and dry-cleaning service. Open Monday to Friday 8am to 5pm and Saturday 8am to 2pm.

Liquor Laws The legal drinking age is 18. Licensed hotels can sell alcoholic beverages to their guests 7 days a week; otherwise, sale is prohibited from midnight Saturday to midnight Sunday. Ikale beer is the local brew.

Newspapers & Magazines All the local newspapers are published in Tongan. **Matangi Tonga** (www.matangitonga.to) is a fine English-language monthly magazine edited by the noted Tongan writer and publisher Pesi Fonua. It has features about the kingdom and its people. **Friendly Islands Bookstore** (see "Bookstores," above) carries international newspapers and magazines.

Mail The **Nuku'alofa Post Office** is at the corner of Taufa'ahau and Salote roads. It's open Monday to Friday 8:30am to 4pm. Many Tongan stamps in the shape of bananas and pineapples are collectors' items.

Radio & TV The government-owned radio station, A3Z (Radio Tonga), broadcasts in both AM and FM. Most programming on the AM station is in Tongan, although the music played is mostly U.S., Australian, or British popular tunes. The news in English is relayed from the BBC or Radio Australia several times a day. One privately owned FM station in Nuku'alofa plays popular music.

Safety Robberies and break-ins are on the increase, although crimes against tourists have been rare. It's a good idea to be alert if you walk down dark streets at night. Remember that the communal property system still prevails in the kingdom. Items such as cameras and bags left unattended might disappear, so take precautions. Women should not wander alone on deserted beaches.

Taxes The government adds a 15% "consumption" tax to the price of *everything* purchased in Tonga, including hotel rooms. The tax is added to most bills in the American fashion and included in the price in others. All passengers on international flights pay a departure tax of T$25 (US$13/£6.25) in Tongan currency.

Telephone & Fax **Tonga Communications Corporation (TCC),** on Salote Road at the corner of Takaunove Road, handles all land-line phones here.

To call Tonga: Dial the international access code (011 from the U.S.; 00 from the U.K., Ireland, or New Zealand; or 0011 from Australia), Fiji's country code **676,** and the local number (there are no area codes within Tonga).

To make international calls from within Tonga: First dial 00, then the country code (U.S. or Canada 1, U.K. 44, Ireland 353, Australia 61, New Zealand 64), then the area code and phone number. Direct-dial calls to anywhere in the world cost about T80¢ (US40¢/20p) a minute during the day, T68¢ (US34¢/17p) on weekends, making Tonga by far the least expensive place in the South Pacific from which to call home.

You can also make international calls at the **Tonga Communications Corporation (TCC)**, on Salote Road at the corner of Takaunove Road, which has phones in private booths. TCC is open Monday to Saturday 8am to 10:30pm and Sunday 10am to 10:30pm.

To make domestic calls within Tonga: No prefix or area code is required for domestic long-distance calls, so dial the local number.

For directory assistance: Dial 🕻 **910** or 🕻 **919** for directory assistance.

For operator assistance: Dial 🕻 **913** for operator assistance in making an international call.

Toll-free numbers: Calling a 1-800 number in the U.S. or Canada from Tonga is not toll-free. In fact, it costs the same as an overseas call.

Pay phones: Calls can be placed from any public phone using a prepaid phonecard, which can be bought at many shops and at the **Tonga Communications Corporation (TCC)**, on Salote Road at the corner of Takaunove Road.

Cellphones: The **Tonga Communications Corporation (TCC)** branch on Taufa'ahau Road (🕻 **27-335** or 27-336) rents mobile phones and sells SIM cards for unlocked GSM cellphones, starting at T$28 (US$14/£7), including T$20 (US$10/£5) of airtime. A subsidiary of Digicel Pacific, **Tonfon** (🕻 **876-1000**; www.tonfon.to) also rents cellphones and sells SIM cards.

Time Local time in Tonga is 13 hours ahead of Greenwich Mean Time. It's in the same day as Australia, New Zealand, and Fiji, and a day ahead of the United States, the Samoas, the Cook Islands, and French Polynesia. Translated, Tonga is 3 hours behind the U.S. West Coast during standard time (4 hr. behind during daylight saving time)—and 1 day ahead. If it's noon on Tuesday in Tonga, it's 3pm Pacific Standard Time on Monday in Los Angeles and 6pm Eastern Standard Time on Monday in New York.

Tipping Although it has gained a foothold, tipping is officially discouraged in Tonga because it's considered contrary to the Polynesian tradition of hospitality. One time gratuities are encouraged is during Tongan dance shows, when members of the audience rush up to the female dancers and stick notes to their well-oiled bodies.

Water Although the government proclaims the tap water in the main towns to be chlorinated and safe, I don't know anyone who drinks it. Because it comes from wells in the limestone bedrock, it's hard (laden with minerals) and doesn't easily rinse off soap and shampoo. Bottled water is available at most grocery stores in Nuku'alofa.

Weights & Measures Tonga uses the metric system.

10 Exploring Tongatapu

The government and most businesses and tourist activities are in Nuku'alofa (pop. 25,000 or so), but there is much to see outside town, including some of the South Pacific's most important and impressive archaeological sites. You'll need about half a day to stroll around Nuku'alofa and see its sights and a full day to tour the island—half a day on the eastern end, another half to see the west.

THE TONGAN NATIONAL CULTURAL CENTRE 😊😊😊

Make time to visit the **Tongan National Cultural Centre** (📞 23-022), one of the South Pacific's best cultural expositions. On Fanga'uta Lagoon about 1.5km (1 mile) south of Nuku'alofa on Taufa'ahau Road, the center's turtle-roof, Tongan *fale*-style buildings house displays of the kingdom's history, geology, and handicrafts. In fact, artisans work daily on their crafts and sell their wares to visitors. In other words, you can see how Tonga's remarkable handicrafts are made, which should help as you later scour the local shops for good buys. The center is open Monday to Friday 9am to 4pm. Admission is T$3 (US$1.50/75p) for adults, T$1 (US50¢/25p) for children. Special displays feature demonstrations of carving, weaving, tapa making, food preparation, a kava ceremony, and dancing. The dinners and dance shows on Tuesday and Thursday nights are not to be missed (see "Island Nights on Tongatapu," later in this chapter).

A STROLL THROUGH NUKU'ALOFA

Before starting out to see Nuku'alofa, drop by the Tonga Visitors Bureau office on Vuna Road and pick up a copy of the brochure "Walking Tour of Central Nuku'alofa." A morning's stroll around this interesting town will be time well spent, for in many respects it's a throwback to times gone by in the South Pacific.

Although there are no street signs, the visitors bureau has put up signs that give general directions to the main sights. In addition, Nuku'alofa is more or less laid out on a grid, so you shouldn't have trouble finding your way around. It's also flat, with no hills to climb.

Start at the **Tonga Visitors Bureau** and walk west along Vuna Road toward the heart of town. The park with a playground on the left as you leave the Visitors Bureau is known as **Fa'onelua Gardens,** at the rear of which is a convention hall. Before Railway Road, the modern three-story building houses many government ministries.

Turn left on Railway Road. The colonial-era wooden structure on the left in the first block serves as both the **Court House** and **parliament** when it meets from June to September. Both court and parliament sessions are open to the public. Now return to Vuna Road and turn left.

Vuna Wharf, at the foot of Taufa'ahau Road, Nuku'alofa's main street, was built in 1906, and for some 60 years most visitors to Tonga debarked from ships that tied up here. A railroad once ran through town along Railway Road to transport copra and other crops to Vuna Wharf.

Directly across Vuna Road from the wharf is the low **Treasury Building.** Constructed in 1928, it's a fine example of South Pacific colonial architecture. Early in its life it housed the Tongan Customs service and the post office as well as the Treasury Department.

The field to the west of the wharf is the **Pangai,** where royal feasts, kava ceremonies, and parades are held.

Overlooking the Pangai and surrounded by towering Norfolk pines is the **Royal Palace** 😊😊😊. The king lives in a sprawling mansion out on Taufa'ahau Road these days, but his mother still lives in this white Victorian building with gingerbread fretwork and gables under a red roof, and he conducts business and entertains dignitaries here. The palace was prefabricated in New Zealand, shipped to Tonga, and erected in 1867. The second-story veranda was added in 1882.

Now walk up Taufa'ahau Road past **Raintree Square,** appropriately shaded by the huge rain tree in front of the modern Westpac Bank of Tonga. The park benches at the base of the tree are a local gathering place. Across the street stands the colonial-style **Prime Minister's Office** with its quaint tower.

Turn right at the post office on Salote Road. The **Nuku'alofa Club** on the left, about halfway down the block, is another holdover from the old South Pacific: It's a private club where Tonga's elite males gather to relax over a game of snooker and a few Australian beers.

The next block of Salote Road runs behind the Royal Palace. Turn right on Vaha'akolo Road and walk along the west side of the palace toward the sea. The highest point on Tongatapu, **Chapel Hill** (or Zion Hill) to the left, part of the Royal Estate, was a Tongan fort during the 18th century and the site of a missionary school opened in 1830 and a large Wesleyan church built in 1865. The school, **Sia'atoutai Theological College,** is now located 6.5km (4 miles) west of Nuku'alofa. The church has long since been torn down.

When you get to the water, look back and take your photos of the palace framed by the Norfolk pines.

Picturesque **Vuna Road** runs west from the palace, with the sea and reef on one side and stately old colonial homes on the other. Now used for Tongan government functions, the former British High Commissioner's residence, in the second block, sports a flagpole surrounded by four cannons from the *Port au Prince,* the ship captured and burned by the Tongans at Ha'apai in 1806 after they had clubbed to death all its crew except Will Mariner. King George I had two wives—not concurrently—and both are buried in casuarina-ringed Mala'e'aloa Cemetery, whose name means "tragic field." The clapboard house at the end of the next block is known as **Ovalau** because it was built in the 1800s at Levuka, the old capital of Fiji on the island of Ovalau, and was shipped to Tonga in the 1950s.

Turn inland at the corner, walk 2 blocks on 'Alipate Road, take a left on Wellington Road, and walk 2 blocks east to **Centenary Church.** Just before the church, the large wooden building with a widow's walk atop it was reputed to have been built about 1871 by the Rev. Shirley W. Baker, a missionary who had much influence over King George I. Members of the Free Wesleyan Church of Tonga constructed Centenary Church between 1949 and 1952. While construction was going on, the town was divided into sections that fed the workers three meals a day on a rotating basis. The amount of money spent on the building was about T$80,000 (US$40,000/£20,000); the actual value of the materials and labor was many times that amount. The church seats about 2,000 persons, including the king and queen, who worship here on Sunday mornings.

Turn right past the church and proceed inland on Vaha'akolo Road. Past the church is **Queen Salote College,** a girls' school named for a wife of King George I and not for his great-great-granddaughter, the famous Queen Salote.

Turn left at the first street, known as Laifone Road, and walk along a large open space to your right. Since 1893, this area has been known as the **Royal Tombs** 𝖆𝖆. King George I, King George II, Queen Salote, King Taufa'hau Tupou IV and most of their various wives and husbands are buried at the center of the field. At the corner of Tu'i Road stands the **Free Wesleyan Church of Tonga.** Built of coral block in 1888, it is a magnificent example of early Tongan church architecture.

On Taufa'ahau Road, behind this open expanse stands the modern **Queen Salote Memorial Hall,** the country's national auditorium.

Tips **How to Survive Sunday in Tonga**

A clause in Tonga's constitution declares, "The Sabbath Day shall be sacred in Tonga forever and it shall not be lawful to work, artifice, or play games, or trade on the Sabbath." The penalty for breaking this stricture is 3 months in jail at hard labor. Although hotels can cater to their guests on the Sabbath, almost everything else comes to a screeching halt. Stores are closed, airplanes don't fly, most taxis don't operate, and most restaurants other than those in the hotels don't open. Tongans by the thousands go to church and then enjoy family feasts and a day of lounging around in true Polynesian style.

So how do the rest of us survive without "artificing" on Sunday? You can start by worshiping with the royal family at 10am in the Centenary Church on Wellington Road. Tongan men wear neckties, but tourists get by without if they're neatly dressed. Women should wear dresses that cover the shoulders and knees.

Even before church, many of us visitors—and many a Westernized Tongan, too—head for one of the offshore resorts, where we can get a meal, some libation, and a legal swim. You will find me having a few cold ones out at **Pangaimotu Island Resort,** where King George V was known to while away a Sunday after when he was still crown prince. See "Island Excursions, Watersports & Other Outdoor Activities," below.

On the other side of the road, opposite the Royal Tombs, rises the tent-shaped **Basilica of St. Anthony of Padua,** the first basilica in the South Pacific islands.

Now follow **Taufa'ahau Road** toward the waterfront. On this main street, you'll pass a few vacant lots (the result of the Nov 2006 riot) and shop after shop, some of them carrying handicrafts and clothing. Between Wellington and Salote roads, an old house now provides the setting for the **Langafonua Women's Association Handicraft Center** (see "Shopping on Tongatapu," below). The clapboard house was built by William Cocker, a local merchant, for his five daughters, who lived in New Zealand but spent each winter in Nuku'alofa.

Turn right on the next street—Salote Road—and walk past the police station on the left to **Maketi Talamahu** in the second block, the lively produce market where vendors sell a great variety of fresh produce, ranging from huge taro roots and watermelons to string beans and bananas. Tongatapu's climate is cool enough during the winter months that both European and tropical fruits and vegetables grow in great bounty. Upstairs, several stalls carry handicraft items, such as tapa cloth and straw baskets and mats. End your tour here by looking around the market and perhaps munching on a banana or sipping a fresh young coconut.

TOURING TONGATAPU

Most visitors see Tonga's main island in two parts: first the eastern side and its ancient archaeological sites, and then the western side for its natural spectacles. You can do these on your own via rental car or go with one of the local tour operators (see "Organized Tours," below). Either way, pick up a copy of the visitors bureau's "The Capital Places Tour," which covers the entire island.

THE EASTERN TOUR

Take Taufa'ahau Road out of Nuku'alofa, making sure to bear left on the paved road. If you want to see tropical birds in captivity, watch for the signs on the right-hand side of the road directing you to the **Bird Park** and follow the dirt track about 3km (1¾ miles). There you will find the **Tongan Wildlife Centre** ʕʕ (© **29-449**), which has a fine collection of colorful birds from Tonga and other South Pacific islands. They are kept in cages planted with native vegetation. A star is the Tongan **megapode,** a native only of Niuafo'ou in the Niuas islands; it buries its eggs in volcanic vents where the temperature is a constant 95°F (35°C), and then flies away, never to see its offspring. Admission is T$3 (US$1.50/75p). The center is open daily 9am to 5pm.

Now backtrack to the main road and turn right toward the airport. Keep left, especially at Malapo (where the road to the airport goes to the right), and follow the Tonga Visitors Bureau's signs, which will show you the way to **Mu'a.** When the road skirts the lagoon just before the village, watch for the stone-and-brass monument marking **Captain Cook's Landing Place** ʕʕ. The great British explorer landed and rested under a large banyan tree here when he came ashore in 1777 to meet with Pau, the reigning Tui Tonga. He attended the traditional presentation of first fruits marking the beginning of the harvest season. The banyan tree is long gone.

The next village is **Lapaha** ʕʕ, seat of the Tui Tonga for 6 centuries, beginning about A.D. 1200. All that remains of the royal compound is a series of *langa,* or ancient terraced tombs, some of which are visible from the road. A large sign explains how the supreme Polynesian god Tangaloa came down from the sky about A.D. 950 and sired the first Tui Tonga. The last Tui Tonga, who died in 1865, after being deposed by King George I in 1862, is buried in one of the tombs. The 28 tombs around Lapaha and Mu'a are among the most important archaeological sites in Polynesia, but none of them have been excavated. Take the dirt road near the sign to see more of the tombs.

From Lapaha, follow the left fork and the scenic paved road along the coast until reaching the **Ha'amonga Trilithon** ʕʕʕ, near the village of Niutoua on the island's northeast point. This huge archway, whose lintel stone is estimated to weigh 35 tons, is 4.75m (16 ft.) high and 5.75m (19 ft.) wide. Tradition says it was built by the 11th Tui Tonga about A.D. 1200, long before the wheel was introduced to Tonga. It serves as the gateway to the royal compound. The present King Taufa'ahau Tupou IV advanced a theory that it was used not only as an entrance but also for measuring the seasons. He found a secret mark on top of the lintel stone and at dawn on June 21, 1967, proved his point. The mark pointed to the exact spot on the horizon from which the sun rose on the shortest day of the year. You can stand under this imposing archway and ponder just how the ancient Tongans got the lintel stone on top of its two supports; it's the same sense of wonderment you feel while looking at Stonehenge in England or contemplating the great long-nosed heads that were carved and somehow erected by those other Polynesians far to the east of Tonga, on Easter Island.

The paved road ends at **Niutoua,** but a dirt track proceeds down the east coast. **Anahulu Beach** has a cave with stalactites near the village of Haveluliku. A gorgeous beach begins here and runs to **Oholei Beach.** 'Eua Island is visible on the horizon.

On the way back to Nuku'alofa you can take a detour to **Hufangalupe Beach** on the south coast for a look at a natural bridge carved out of coral and limestone by the sea.

THE WESTERN TOUR

Proceed out of Nuku'alofa on Mateialona Road and follow the Visitors Bureau signs to the **Blowholes** ʕʕ near the village of Houma on the southwest coast. At high tide the surf pounds under shelves, sending geysers of seawater through holes in the coral. These are the most impressive blowholes in the South Pacific, and on a windy day the coast for miles is shrouded in mist thrown into the air by hundreds of them working at once. Lime sediments have built up circular terraces like rice paddies, around each hole, and the local women come just before dusk to gather clams in the pools formed by the rings. The overlook has benches and a parking area at the end of the road near the blowholes. You'll need shoes with good soles to walk across the sharp edges of the top shelf. This once was an underwater reef, and corals are still very much visible, all of them now more than 15m (49 ft.) above sea level. (Look for what appear to be fossilized brains; they are appropriately named brain corals.) The blowholes are known in Tongan as *Mapu'a a Vaea*, "the chief's whistle."

From Houma, proceed west toward the village of Kolovai, and watch for the trees with what appears to be black, strange-looking fruit. The sounds you hear and the odors in the air are actually coming from **flying foxes,** a bat with a foxlike head found on many islands in the Pacific. Nocturnal creatures, they spend their days hanging upside down from the branches of trees like a thousand little Draculas, their wings like black capes pulled tightly around their bodies. They don't feed on blood but on fruit; hence they are known as fruit bats. On some islands they are considered a delicacy. In Tonga, where they live in trees throughout the villages of Kolovai and Ha'avakatolo, they are thought to be sacred, and only members of the royal family can shoot them. Legend says that a Samoan princess gave the first bats to a Tongan navigator.

Near the end of the island is **Ha'atafu,** site of an offshore reef preserve. The first missionaries to land in Tonga came ashore at the end of the peninsula on the northwest coast, and a sign marks the spot at the end of the road. They obviously got their feet wet—if they were not "baptized"—wading across the shallow bank just offshore.

You've now toured Tongatapu from one end to the other. Turn around and head back to town.

ORGANIZED TOURS

Several companies have half- and full-day tours around Nuku'alofa and the rest of the island, including **Joe's Friendly Island Tours** (© 21-284), **Teta Tours** (© 23-690) and **Friendly Islander Explorer** (© 29-910). You should reserve any of these tours at least a day in advance. Half-day tours cost about T$25 (US$13/£6.25) per person; full-day tours of the entire island, T$45 (US$23/£11).

11 Island Excursions, Watersports & Other Outdoor Activities

ISLAND EXCURSIONS ☆☆☆ You will have a much wider choice of watersports activities on Vava'u (see "Vava'u" later in this chapter). Here they are concentrated in the huge lagoon on Tongatapu's north shore, especially at resorts on the small islets off Nuku'alofa. In fact, the most popular way to spend a day—particularly a very slow Sunday in Tonga—is swimming, snorkeling, sunbathing, dining, or just hanging out at the flat, small islands of Pangaimotu, Fafa, or 'Atata, each of which has a resort just a few miles off Nuku'alofa. These little beachside establishments have restaurants and bars, too.

Pangaimotu Island Resort ☆☆ (© 23-759) on Pangaimotu is the oldest and closest of the offshore resorts, and it's my favorite by far. Hanging over a lovely beach, its main building oozes slapped-together, old South Seas charm. Its boat usually leaves Faua Jetty on Vuna Road at 11am Monday to Friday, and at 11am and noon on Saturday, and

10am, 11am, and noon on Sunday. They return in the late afternoon. Round-trip fare is T$15 (US$7.50/£3.75) per person. Once there, a chalkboard menu offers burgers and sandwiches, and owner Earle Emberson serves icy-cold brews from an ice box behind the bar. The lagoon here is safe for swimming, and there's a children's playground.

Fafa Island Resort (© 22-800), a German-owned, Robinson Crusoe–like establishment, operates its own sailboat from Faua Jetty daily at 11am. Round-trip transfers and lunch cost T$70 (US$35/£18).

Royal Sunset Island Resort ✿ (© 21-155) on 'Atata, the farthest from Nuku'alofa, charges T$58 (US$29/£15), including transfers and lunch.

See "Where to Stay on Tongatapu," below, for more information about these off-shore resorts.

GOLF   You won't be playing any golf on Sunday, but you can every other day at the flat 9-hole **Manamo'ui Golf Course,** home of the Tonga Golf Club. The tour desk at the International Dateline Hotel (© 21-411) can arrange equipment rentals and tee times on this somewhat-less-than-challenging course, which is on the main road between the airport and town.

SAILING   In addition to the charter yachts based in Vava'u (see "Vava'u," later in this chapter), **Sailing Tonga** ✿✿✿ (© 874-2228; www.sailingtonga.com) has the 15m (49 ft.) yacht *Impetuous* that's available for charter anywhere in Tonga. It's one of the best ways to explore the more remote islands in the Ha'apai group, and do some scuba diving while you're at it. This crewed craft has three cabins, each with its own head (restroom) with shower. Rates start at US$190 (£95) per person per day if six persons go, and increase to US$440 (£220) per person per day if only two are on board. The skipper, cook, and provisions are included.

SCUBA DIVING & SNORKELING   Although diving off Tongatapu plays second fiddle to diving off Vava'u, the reefs offshore have some colorful coral and a variety of sea life. **Deep Blue Diving Centre,** on Vuna Road at Faua Jetty (©/fax 23-379; www.deep-blue-diving.to), has dives to Hakaumana'o and Malinoa Reef Reserves, two protected underwater parks, and to nearby 'Eua Island, which has one of the largest underwater caves in the South Pacific (the entry is 28m/92 ft. deep). A two-tank dive costs about T$140 (US$70/£35), including equipment. Nondivers can go on many of his diving trips for T$40 (US$20/£10), including equipment.

12 Shopping on Tongatapu

Tonga is the best place in the South Pacific to shop for Polynesian handicrafts, such as tapa cloth, mats, carvings, shell jewelry, and other exquisite items. A large laundry basket will take at least 3 months to get home via ship if you don't send it by air freight or check it as baggage on your return flight, but the quality of the craftsmanship will be worth the wait.

Tapa cloth and finely woven pandanus mats are traditional items of clothing and gifts in Tonga, and the women of the kingdom have carried on the ancient skills, not only out of economic necessity but also out of pride in their craft. Collectively they produce thousands of items each day, each made by hand and no two exactly alike. Pick up a copy of the Tonga Visitors Bureau's brochure "Tongan Handicrafts" for an excellent description of how tapa cloth is made from the bark of the paper mulberry tree, and the process by which women weave baskets, mats, and other items.

Tips **Watch Out for Fake *Tapa* & Shoddy Carvings**

Be careful when shopping for paintings on tapa cloth, as some unscrupulous artisans have been using paper instead of real bark from the paper mulberry tree. Avoid men who approach you on the street and attempt to sell shoddy carvings and black coral jewelry; they fall into the same category as the "sword sellers" of Fiji (see chapter 4). Also be sure you get what you paid for; that is, purchase handicraft items already made and on display rather than ordering for future production and delivery after you have left Tonga. Stick to reputable shops such as those recommended in this section.

The Art of Tonga 𝒜𝒜𝒜 This sophisticated store carries excellent baskets, tapa, coral jewelry, and whale- and fish-bone scrimshaw, but the best items are the works of owner Sitiveni "Steve" Fehoko, one of Tonga's most talented wood carvers. He has another outlet in Talamahu Market, and owns **Fehoko Art Creation,** a shop on Vuna Road near the domestic wharf. He accepts MasterCard and Visa credit cards and will ship your purchases. His shop is open Monday to Friday 8:30am to 5pm, Saturday 8:30am to 2pm. Taufa'ahau Rd., in Fund Management Building between Wellington and Lafone roads. ℂ 27-667.

Blue Banana Studios 𝒜 This is the best place in town for hand-painted sarongs and T-shirts as well as watercolors on tapa, all by Sune, Shane, and Chris Egan, a family of artists. The Egans also carry Tahitian black pearls and some very clever Christmas cards. The shop is open Monday to Friday 9am to 5pm, Saturday 9am to noon. Taufa'ahau Rd., in Fund Management Building between Wellington and Lafone roads. ℂ 22-662.

Catholic Women's League Handicraft Centre This little waterfront shop carries locally made baskets, tapa, carvings, and shell jewelry. It's not as well stocked as the Langafonua center (see below), but you might find an excellent piece here. It's open Monday to Friday 9am to 5pm. Vuna Rd., opposite Faua Jetty. ℂ 27-524.

Langafonua Women's Association Handicraft Centre This shop in the charming colonial house on Taufa'ahau Road was founded by Queen Salote in 1953 in order to preserve the old crafts and provide a market for them. It has an excellent collection, but you may pay more here than elsewhere for similar items. It does not accept credit cards; the shop will pack your purchases but not ship them. It's open Monday to Friday 8:30am to 4:30pm, Saturday 8:30am to noon. Taufa'ahau Rd., second block inland. ℂ 21-014.

Maketi Talamahu 𝒜𝒜 It's fun to browse around the handicraft stalls on the second level of the Talamahu market, especially the branch of The Art of Tonga (see above). Prices here tend to be less than at the shops in town. It's open Monday to Friday 6am to 5pm, Saturday 6am to 12:30pm. ℂ 24-146. Salote Road, between Railway and Fatafehi roads.

13 Where to Stay on Tongatapu

There are no luxury resorts in Tonga, although there are comfortable hotels and island hideaways. In other words, don't set your expectations too high. On the other hand, you won't pay an arm and a leg here, either.

ACCOMMODATIONS IN NUKU'ALOFA

The Black Pearl Suites 🞰 Built by Tongans who did well in the U.S., this two-story clapboard building facing the lagoon has some of the best hotel rooms and suites in Tonga, even if their furniture is a bit overwrought, and the decor a tad gaudy in places. A guest lounge has more heavy furniture and a large-screen TV for watching movies and rugby, Tonga's national sport. Two of the units are large "executive suites" with four-poster king-size beds, oversized sofas, wet bars, kitchen table and chairs, and a mezzanine with sofa. Although called suites, the other units are standard hotel rooms with sleigh beds, desks, and tub/shower combination bathrooms. The neighborhood is primarily residential, thus peaceful and quiet. Breakfast is available in the guest lounge, and Kaati-ni Restaurant, two blocks away on Vuna Road, is part of this business.

P.O. Box 2913, Nuku'alofa (in Sopu, on Vuna Rd., 2.5km/1.5 miles west of Royal Palace). © **28-393.** Fax 28-432. www.blackpearlsuites.to. 16 units. T$150 (US$75/£38) double; T$460 (US$230/£115) suite. MC, V. **Amenities:** Wireless Internet access; laundry service. *In room:* A/C, TV, minibar, fridge, coffeemaker, iron, safe.

Harbour View Motel *Value* This three-story concrete building offers a variety of simple, clean rooms, from budget to a penthouse suite. The latter occupies all of the third floor and is the largest hotel room in Tonga. It features windows on three sides, a TV, a wet bar, two king-size beds, and a bathroom with a Jacuzzi tub. On the second floor, deluxe rooms are equipped with TVs, refrigerators, and bathrooms. Three budget rooms and two standard units share bathrooms. The budget units have phones but none of them has a TV or air conditioner. This is a walk-up establishment with external stairways leading to verandas on each floor. The location opposite the commercial wharf is not particularly scenic or convenient to downtown, and noise from the Billfish Bar and Restaurant filters in on weekend nights, but some of Nuku'alofa's better restaurants are an easy walk. Continental breakfast is available in the lobby.

P.O. Box 83, Nuku'alofa (Vuna Rd., opposite Queen Salote Wharf). © **25-488.** Fax 25-490. harbvmtl@kalianet.to. 13 units (6 without bathroom). T$92–T$155 (US$46–US$78/£23–£39) double; T$218 (US$109/£55) suite. MC, V. **Amenities:** Bar; laundry service; coin-op washers and dryers. *In room:* A/C (in some units), TV (in some units), fridge (in some units), coffeemaker, iron (penthouse only).

International Dateline Hotel Built in time for the king's coronation in 1967, this is Tonga's largest and most widely known place to stay. Its Chinese owners renovated all of the existing structure and added a three-story wing holding 50 modern units. Most of these are moderately spacious standard rooms with balconies, either a king-size bed or two doubles, and somewhat cramped bathrooms with combination tub-showers. Executive suites add a living room with sofa and easy chairs, and their bathrooms are somewhat larger than in the standard units. The royal suite has two bedrooms, two bathrooms, and an office. Cherry wood furniture from China lends more of an Asian than Pacific ambience to all the new units. Now renovated, the 76 rooms in the two original wings are once again worthy of consideration, except their beds are almost as hard as boards (which is to say, try them out before checking in, or choose a new wing room with ordinary mattresses). The Dateline is Nuku'alofa's prime place for meetings, conventions, and other functions. The property enjoys a choice location facing the harbor across Vuna Road on Nuku'alofa's waterfront, a few blocks from downtown, and it's the only hotel on Tongatapu with spacious grounds featuring a swimming pool.

P.O. Box 39, Nuku'alofa (Vuna Rd. at Tupoulahi Rd., on the waterfront). © **23-411.** Fax 23-410. www.datelinehotel.com. 126 units. T$168–T$220 (US$84–US$110/£42–£55) double; T$300–T$500 (US$150–US$250/£75–£125) suite. AE, MC, V. **Amenities:** 2 restaurants; 2 bars; outdoor pool; activities desk; salon; limited room service; massage; babysitting; laundry service. *In room:* A/C, TV, high-speed Internet access, minibar, coffeemaker, iron (in suites).

Seaview Lodge 🌟🌟   Some of Nuku'alofa's best rooms are here at the fine **Seaview Restaurant** (see "Where to Dine on Tongatapu," below). Three of these spacious, light, and airy units are upstairs over the restaurant and have balconies with views across Vuna Road to the lagoon; they are the choice ones. Two other upstairs units face over the gardens. Six more units in a building to the side of the restaurant lack any view. Each unit is equipped with a TV and a VCR, a ceiling fan over a king-size bed, and a spacious bathroom with European-style, glass-enclosed showers with large heads. Six other less attractive but still comfortable units are in another building next door. Business travelers keep this place busy, so book as early as possible. The Seaview Restaurant is open to lodge guests for breakfast. You will get a good night's sleep here, as this quiet location is well away from Nuku'alofa's noisy bars.

P.O. Box 268, Nuku'alofa (Vuna Rd. west of Royal Palace). ☏ 23-709. Fax 26-906. seaview@kalianet.to 12 units. T$140–T$180 (US$70–US$90/£35–£45) double. AE, MC, V. **Amenities:** Restaurant; bar; wireless Internet access; laundry service. *In room:* A/C, TV, dataport, minibar, coffeemaker.

The Villa McKenzie 🌟🌟   Oozing old South Seas charm, this one-story colonial clapboard home on the waterfront is one of the South Pacific's best bed-and-breakfasts. A central hallway is flanked on one side by a large lounge room (equipped with TV and VCR), an old-fashioned dining room, and a huge country kitchen. To the other side, the four rooms all have tongue-in-groove walls, and mosquito nets hang over their double or single beds. Tea, coffee, and soft drinks are available around the clock in the kitchen. The town's expatriate movers and shakers turn up here for snacks in the rear garden Friday evenings. This clean and comfortable choice is extremely popular with business travelers, so book as early as possible.

P.O. Box 1892, Nuku'alofa (Vuna Rd., at Tungi Rd.). ☏/fax **24-998.** www.tongavilla.com. 5 units. T$175 (US$88/£44) double. Rates include full breakfast. MC, V. **Amenities:** Wireless Internet access; laundry service. *In room:* A/C, dataport.

Waterfront Lodge   Taking a page from the Seaview Lodge's book, owners G. P. and Daniella Orbassano have eight units above their **Waterfront Cafe** (see "Where to Dine on Tongatapu," below). The moderately spacious rooms have high ceilings with fans, polished oak floors, a king-size bed, tropical furniture including desks, shower-only bathrooms, and sliding doors opening to balconies trimmed with plantation-style fretwork. Units on the front of the building with sea views are the most expensive and preferable, although they are subject to the beat of loud music from a bar next door on weekends. Guests can buy breakfast at the Waterfront Cafe downstairs.

P.O. Box 1001, Nuku'alofa (Vuna Rd., opposite domestic wharf). ☏ 25-260. Fax 28-059. www.waterfront-lodge.com. 8 units. T$184–T$196 (US$92–US$98/£46–£49) double. AE, MC, V. **Amenities:** Restaurant; bar; wireless Internet access; massage; laundry service. *In room:* A/C, dataport, fridge, coffeemaker, safe.

Winnie's Guest House *(finds)*   While The Villa McKenzie is a commercial operation (see above), here you share a typical Tongan home with the charming Mrs. Winnie Santos and family. Two of her rooms have twin beds, the other four have double beds. The rooms are screened, but all beds have mosquito nets anyway. Guests share three toilets, three showers, the kitchen, the large living room with satellite TV, and an enclosed veranda for reading and connecting to the Internet. The backyard offers a picnic table and a barbecue grill. The house is not air-conditioned, but on most days a breeze cools things off. Winnie's is in a residential neighborhood behind Vaiola Hospital; local buses pass in front.

P.O. Box 3049, Nuku'alofa (Vaha'akolo Rd., behind the hospital). ☏ 25-215. winnies@tonfon.to. 6 units (none with bathroom). T$40 (US$20/£10) per person. Rates include tropical breakfast. No credit cards. *In room:* No phone.

ACCOMMODATIONS AT THE BEACH

Sune, Shane, and Chris Egan of Blue Banana Studios (see "Shopping on Tongatapu," above) have **Blue Banana Beach House** (✆ **41-575;** www.bluebananastudios.com), which actually consists of two bungalows on the west coast. Both have bathrooms and kitchens. The Egans charge in Australian dollars: A$65 to A$130 (US$60–US$120/£30–£61) double per night.

White Sands Beach Resort   Facing due west, this little establishment on Tongatapu's western end takes in sunsets all year and whales swimming past from July through October. Originally from New Zealand (thus they quote their rates in Kiwi dollars), owners Gloria and Ian Skelton renovated the place in 2007 and added an outdoor swimming pool. Accommodations are in duplex buildings of concrete block with tin roofs. Each unit is spacious, and most face the beach and sea. Gloria and Ike were planning to add a restaurant and bar in a grove of shade trees near the lagoon.

P.O. Box 799, Nukua'alofa (20-min. drive west of Nuku'alofa). ✆ **878-9383** or 17-632 www.whitesandstonga.com. 6 units. NZ$174 (US$87/£44). Rates include tropical breakfast. MC, V. **Amenities:** Outdoor pool; laundry service. *In room:* Fridge, coffeemaker.

OFFSHORE RESORTS

Fafa Island Resort ✍   German Rainer Urtel has stocked his resort, on a 17-acre atoll-like island studded with coconut palms, with bungalows made entirely of natural materials. They have a South Seas charm that attracts a clientele in search of a Robinson Crusoe–like experience, albeit one with most of the comforts of home. Two deluxe fales have refrigerators and two bedrooms. The push-out windows aren't screened, so each of the platform beds has a mosquito net. The bungalows have front porches, over two of which are "honeymoon" sleeping lofts with lagoon views. All of the toilets, lavatories, and showers are in enclosed courtyards. Complimentary morning coffee and tea are delivered to the units, and the dining room in a beachside central building features excellent seafood. Guests can use snorkeling gear for free; they pay extra for Windsurfers, Hobie Cats, and trips to an uninhabited island for snorkeling.

P.O. Box 1444, Nuku'alofa (Fafa Island, 10km/6¼ miles off Nuku'alofa). ✆ **22-800.** Fax 23-592. www.fafa.to. 13 units. US$212–US$280 (£106–£140) double. Meal plans US$70 (£35) per person per day. Round-trip airport transfers US$50 (£25) per person. AE, DC, MC, V. **Amenities:** Restaurant; bar; watersports equipment rental; free use of snorkeling gear; limited room service; massage; babysitting; laundry service. *In room:* Fridge, no phone.

Pangaimotu Island Resort   Unless I were backpacking or prepared to live with no luxuries whatsoever, I wouldn't stay at Earle and Ana Emberson's lively little joint, but you will find me out here on Sunday afternoons, when it's packed with tourists, local expatriate residents, and Westernized Tongans (see "Island Excursions, Watersports & Other Outdoor Activities," above). Most of their basic guest fales are built of natural materials, while a few are of concrete blocks. Each has separate sitting and sleeping areas, a platform double bed with a mosquito net, and a simple bathroom with a cold-water shower. All the fales face the beach.

Private Bag 49, Nuku'alofa (Pangaimotu Island, 3km/1¾ miles off Nuku'alofa). ✆ **15-762.** Fax 17-257. www.pangaimotu.to. 8 units. T$80 (US$40/£20) double. Round-trip transfers T$15 (US$7.50/£3.75). MC, V. **Amenities:** Restaurant; bar. *In room:* No phone.

Royal Sunset Island Resort   This resort shares small, tadpole-shaped 'Atata Island with a native Tongan village. One of the South Pacific's finest beaches swings around the "tail" of the tadpole, and the lagoon attracts swimmers, snorkelers, scuba divers, and anyone who loves to fish. Whales often play offshore from June through October. Two shingle-roofed fales house a dining room and a sunken bar, which opens to a small pool surrounded by a deck dotted with lawn tables and umbrellas. The basic but comfortable guest bungalows face the lagoon. A few are minisuites—one room with a sitting area and tea-and-coffee facilities—and a few units have kitchens. Guests can use snorkeling gear, kayaks, sailboats, and Windsurfers for free, and they can pay to water-ski, sport fish, and scuba dive (you must be certified in advance).

P.O. Box 960, Nuku'alofa ('Atata Island, 10km/6¼ miles off Nuku'alofa). ⓒ/fax **21-254**. www.royalsunset.biz. 24 units. T$250–T$340 (US$125–US$170/£63–£85) double. Meals T$97 (US$49/£24) per person per day. Round-trip transfers T$37 (US$19/£9.25) per person. AE, DC, MC, V. **Amenities:** Restaurant; bar; outdoor pool; babysitting; laundry service. *In room:* Fridge, coffeemaker, no phone.

14 Where to Dine on Tongatapu

Nuku'alofa is blessed with a few restaurants that serve Continental cuisine of remarkably high quality for such a small and unsophisticated town. Expatriates, especially from Germany and Italy, operate most of them.

MODERATE

Billfish Bar and Restaurant INTERNATIONAL   Primarily a socializing and drinking spot (see "Island Nights on Tongatapu," below), the Billfish nevertheless serves good pub fare, especially fish and chips. Also acceptable are the spicy pepper steaks and fresh fish steamed with fresh herbs and coconut milk. For lunch you can opt for burgers, sandwiches, fish and chips, and grilled chops. Booze and food are served under a thatch-lined, lean-to roof, and there are dining tables in a gazebo to one side. The crushed coral floor helps create a tropical ambience. Sunday is roast night here.

Vuna Rd., opposite Queen Salote Wharf. ⓒ **24-084**. Reservations accepted. Lunch T$7–T$23 (US$3.50–US$12/ £1.75–£5.75); burgers T$12 (US$6/£3); main courses T$23–T$39 (US$12–US$20/£5.75–£9.75). MC, V. Mon–Fri noon–2pm and 6–10:30pm; Sat 6–10:30pm. Bar Mon–Thurs noon–10:30pm; Fri noon–2am; Sat 6pm–midnight.

Kaati-ni Restaurant ⨂ STEAKS/SEAFOOD   Operated by the Black Pearl Suites (see "Where to Stay on Tongatapu," above), this upstairs restaurant is the domain of chef Kaati (Kathy) Moehau, who trained in the United States. Although she turns out some fine seafood dishes, such as fresh swordfish with a sour cream sauce, her clientele demands American-size steaks and ribs from the chargrill in her display kitchen. The ambience is casual yet refined, and the staff provides some of Tonga's most attentive table service. The best tables are out on the porch. The Black Pearl Suites guests can have breakfast here.

Vuna Rd. (2.5km/1½ miles west of Royal Palace). ⓒ **28-393**. Reservations recommended at dinner. Main course T$26–T$65 (US$13–US$33/£6.50–£16). MC, V. Daily 6:30–10pm.

Seaview Restaurant ⨂⨂⨂ CONTINENTAL   This pleasant establishment in a colonial-style house west of the Royal Palace serves the best cuisine in Tonga. The fresh tropical lobster—especially served *au natural* with only butter—is outstanding, as are pepper steak and other dishes made with quality meats imported from New Zealand. Start with a seafood cocktail and finish with homemade Austrian pastries for dessert. Top seats are on the screened porch, which has a sea view across Vuna Road.

Vuna Rd., 3 blocks west of Royal Palace. ⓒ **23-709**. Reservations recommended. Main courses T$32–T$46 (US$16– US$23/£8–£12). AE, MC, V. Sun–Fri 6–10pm.

> ## *Tips* Dine Like a Tongan
>
> Like all Polynesians, the Tongans in the old days cooked their food over hot
> rocks in a pit—an *umu*—for several hours. Today they roast whole suckling
> pigs on a spit over coals for several hours (larger pigs still go into the umu).
> The dishes that emerge from the umu are similar to those found elsewhere
> in Polynesia: pig, chicken, lobster, fish, octopus, taro, taro leaves cooked
> with meat and onions, breadfruit, bananas, and a sweet breadfruit pudding
> known as *faikakai-lolo,* all of it cooked with ample amounts of coconut
> cream. Served on the side are *ota ika* (fish) and *vasuva* (clams), both mari-
> nated in lime juice.
>
> The best place to sample Tongan food is during the evening buffets and
> dance shows at the **Tongan National Cultural Centre** (© 23-022). Others are
> the **International Dateline Hotel** (© 23-411) and the **Good Samaritan Inn**
> (© 41-022). See "Island Nights on Tongatapu," below, for details.

Waterfront Cafe 🌟🌟 INTERNATIONAL   This stylish creation of Daniella
Orbessano, an Italian who once worked on Princess Cruises' ships, is the best place for
Italian fare here. The restaurant is on the ground floor of her Waterfront Lodge, and
the best tables are out on the long veranda fronting the colonial-style building. You
can choose from homemade pastas, freshly caught fish, and tender steaks. Many wines
from Australia, New Zealand, and Italy are available by the glass.

Vuna Rd., opposite Faua Jetty. © **24-962.** Reservations recommended Thurs–Fri. Burgers T$16 (US$8/£4); main
courses T$21–T$50 (US$11–US$25/£5.25–£13). AE, MC, V. Tues–Fri 7:30–10am, noon–3pm, and 5–10pm; Sat–Sun
7:30–10am and 5–10pm.

INEXPENSIVE

Cafe Escape   Although it has tables in plaza in front of the Funds Management
Building, this sophisticated restaurant is an air-conditioned version of Friends Cafe
(see below). Breakfast is served all day; try the fruit salad. Lunch sees beef and fish
burgers, chicken wraps, sushi, and a very good shrimp, avocado, and papaya salad with
a slightly spicy curry dressing. Dinner is a bit more mundane, with grilled fish and
steaks leading the blackboard menu.

Tauffa'ahau Rd., in Funds Management Building, between Wellington and Laifone rds. © **21-212.** Reservations not
accepted. Breakfast T$6–T$16 (US$3–US$8/£1.50–£4); lunch T$12–T$30 (US$6–US$15/£3–£7.50); main courses
T$30–T$35 (US$15–US$18/£7.50–£8.75). AE, MC. V. Mon–Fri 7:30am–9:30pm; Sat 7:30am–3:30pm.

Café Reef   Sitting in the middle of the Faua Jetty parking lot, this joint lacks any
charm whatsoever, but it's a fine place to watch Tongans going to and from the inter-
island boats. Local expats like to grab an outdoor table and a cold Ikale beer here, too.
Good coffee and teas accompany all-day breakfast. Lunch and dinner see a blackboard
menu featuring sandwiches, burgers, salads, Indian curries, grilled fish and chicken,
seared tuna, and lamb shanks in red wine sauce. It may not be the best food in town,
but this is a fun place to hang out.

Vuna Rd, at Faua Jetty. © **26-777.** Reservations recommended at dinner. Breakfast and lunch T$6–T$18
(US$3–US$9/£1.50/£4.50); main courses T$15–T$30 (US$7.50–US$15/£3.75–£7.50). MC, V. Mon–Sat 8am–10pm;
Sun 6am–9pm.

Fiesta Seafood Restaurant ★★ *Value* SEAFOOD   The owners of this casual restaurant operate a commercial fishing boat, and the best of the catch ends up here. They import mussels and prawns, but always best is the fresh tuna, snapper, and mahimahi grilled and served with lemon butter and garlic. This is the least expensive place in town for spiny tropical lobster, especially good served local-style with coconut milk. The joint is simple and bit crowded, but it's great value for seafood lovers.

Salote Rd., inland from Faua Jetty. ② **56-062.** Reservations recommended. Main courses T$20–T$28 (US$10–US$14/£5–£7). No credit cards. Mon–Sat 7am–11pm.

Friends Cafe ★★★ COFFEE HOUSE/CAFE   This outstanding coffee shop and cafe provides a modern oasis in Taufa'ahau Road's dusty business scene. Locally grown beans create great cappuccino, espresso, and latte. You can also eat the town's best cakes and pastries, fruit plates, and made-to-order sandwiches at the counter, then sip or dine inside or out on the side patio while listening to jazz or classical music on the sound system. A blackboard menu offers specials such as quiche and salad and braised lamb shanks in tomato sauce. Lunch and dinner offerings include sandwiches, cakes, pastries, and main courses such as lobster Polynesia-style and pan-fried snapper.

Taufa'ahau Rd., between Salote and Wellington rds. ② **21-284.** Reservations accepted at dinner. Breakfast T$5.50–T$19 (US$2.75–US$9.50/£1.40–£4.75); sandwiches T$7–T$8.50 (US$3.50–US$4.25/£1.75–£2.15); main courses T$12–T$30 (US$6–US$15/£3–£7.50). AE, MC, V. Mon–Fri 7:30am–10pm; Sat 8am–7:30pm.

Pizzeria Little Italy *Value* PIZZA   Angelo Crapanzano, who learned his trade as a pizza chef in Milan, Italy, oversees the open kitchen in this unusual restaurant: It's a genuine, thatched-roof Tongan fale, but empty Ruffino wine bottles dangle from the support posts, and hats of every imaginable description adorn the walls. Don't be in a hurry, for everything is made from scratch. Pastas and main courses are on the menu, too, but this is Nuku'alofa's top pizza place.

Vuna Rd., 5 blocks west of Royal Palace. ② **25-053.** Reservations recommended. Pizzas T$15–T$20 (US$7.50–US$10/£3.75–£5); pastas T$14–T$25 (US$7–US$13/£3.50–£6.25); main courses T$27–T$39 (US$14–US$20/£6.75–£9.75). MC, V. Mon–Fri noon–2pm and 6:30–10:30pm; Sat 6:30–10:30pm.

15 Island Nights on Tongatapu

As in Samoa, traditional **Tongan dancing** emphasizes fluid movements of the hands and feet instead of gyrating hips, as is the case in French Polynesia and the Cook Islands. There is also less emphasis on drums and more on the stamping, clapping, and singing of the participants. The dances most often performed for tourists are the *tau'olunga*, in which one young woman dances solo, her body glistening with coconut oil; the *ma'ulu'ulu*, performed sitting down by groups ranging from 20 members to as many as 900 for very important occasions; the *laklaka*, in which rows of dancers sing and dance in unison; and the *kailao*, or war dance, in which men stamp the ground and wave war clubs at each other in mock battle.

The best place to see it is at **Tongan National Cultural Centre** ★★★ (② **23-022**), which stages a Tongan-style feast complete with a traditional kava welcoming ceremony and dance show Tuesday and Thursday evenings. What makes the evening special is an explanation, in English, of what each dance represents. Cost is T$25 (US$13/£6.25), plus T$5 (US$2.50/£1.25) for transportation. Book by 4:30pm.

Another good choice is the Friday night feast at the **Likualofa Resort** (② **41-967**), on the beach 18km (11 miles) west of Nuku'alofa. They offer an extensive buffet of

Tongan and Western foods, followed by a dance show beside the lagoon. The meal and show costs about T$30 (US$15/£7.50). Reservations are required.

You'll also have a chance to see Tongan dancing on Wednesday night in Nuku'alofa at the **International Dateline Hotel** (© 23-411), where floor shows start around 9pm after a buffet-style dinner.

PUB-CRAWLING Because all pubs and nightclubs must close at the stroke of midnight Saturday, Friday is the busiest and longest night of the week in Tonga. That's when some establishments stay open until 2am. Many Tongans start their weekends at one of the local bars and then adjourn to a nightclub for heavy-duty revelry.

Clubs change in popularity quickly, so it's best to ask around to learn which ones are drawing the crowds. The most popular are on Vuna Road between Faua Jetty and Queen Salote Wharf. You can avoid fights by doing your drinking at the venerable **Billfish Bar and Restaurant,** where a squad of security guards keep order (see "Where to Dine on Tongatapu," above), and at **Shooters '07** (© 28-701), a hip, American-style sports bar.

16 Vava'u ★★★

The crown jewel of this little kingdom, Vava'u lies approximately 260km (162 miles) north of Tongatapu. It's one of the South Pacific's great yachting centers and one of this region's most unusual destinations.

Often mispronounced Va-*vow* (it's Va-*va*-oo), the group consists of one large, hilly island shaped like a jellyfish, its tentacles trailing off in a myriad of waterways and small, sand-ringed islets. In the middle, the fjordlike harbor known as **Port of Refuge** ranks as one of the finest anchorages in the South Pacific. From its picturesque perch above the harbor, the village of **Neiafu** (pop. 5,000) evokes scenes from the South Seas of yesteryear.

To the south of Neiafu, the reef is speckled with 33 small islands, 21 of them inhabited. The others are beautiful dots of land upon which Robinson Crusoe would fit right in. The white beaches and emerald lagoon are unsurpassed in their beauty.

When you see these protected waterways, you'll know why cruising sailors love Vava'u. But this is heaven not just to sailors but to any watersports enthusiast. Getting out on the water for a day is easy. If you like walking on unspoiled white beaches on uninhabited islands, swimming in crystal-clear water, and taking boat rides into mysterious caves cut into cliffs, you'll like Vava'u, too.

Vava'u is the most seasonal destination in the South Pacific. Virtually asleep for 6 months of the year, it comes alive during the whale-watching and yachting season from May to October, when more than 500 boats can be in port at any one time. Humpback whales migrate from the Antarctic to frolic in Tongan waters this time of year, and Vava'u is the best place in the region to see them up close and personal.

Tips **Don't Forget to Reconfirm**

It's *imperative* to reconfirm your return flight to Tongatapu as soon as possible after arriving on Vava'u, and on the morning of your flight. The staff at your hotel can take care of this for you, or drop by the airlines' offices on the main street in Neiafu.

As with Savai'i in Samoa, you will wish you had stayed longer in this most beautiful and enchanting part of Tonga.

GETTING TO VAVA'U & GETTING AROUND

GETTING THERE

Chathams Pacific—The Friendly Islands Airline (© 28-000; www.chathamspacific. com) and **Airlines Tonga** (© 24-506) fly between Tongatapu and Vava'u (see "Getting to Tonga & Getting Around," earlier in this chapter). Airlines Tonga also has service from Nadi to Vava'u, but I would let The Moorings or your whale-watching operator make my arrangements. **Lupepa'u International Airport (VAV)** is on the north side of Vauau'u, about 7km (4⅓ miles) from Neiafu. Most hotels will pick up their guests with reservations, or you can take a taxi to Neiafu for about T$20 (US$10/£5).

The ferries from Nuku'alofa land in Neiafu at Uafu Lahi, which everyone calls the "Big Wharf." From there you can walk or take a taxi ride to your hotel or guesthouse. If you're on foot, turn right on the main street to reach the center of town and the accommodations.

The road from the airport dead-ends at a T-intersection atop the hill above the wharf. The main street runs from there in both directions along the water, with most of the town's stores and government offices flanking it.

GETTING AROUND

You can explore all of Neiafu on foot, but public transportation to the outlying areas of Vava'u is limited. If you book an excursion, ask about the availability of transportation to and from the event.

Adventure Backpackers Lodge (© 70-955) rents mountain bikes for T$20 (US$10/ £5) a day. See "Where to Stay on Vava'u," below.

Taxis are not metered, so be sure you determine the fare before getting in. **Falepiu Taxi** (© 70-671) has a stand opposite the Westpac Bank of Tonga; **Liviela Taxi** (© 70-240) is opposite the Bounty Bar; and **Lopaukamea Taxi** (© 70-153) is at the market. Fares are T$3 (US$1.50/75p) per kilometer, or you can hire one for about T$50 (US$25/£13) per hour, but be sure to negotiate a fare in advance.

Buses and pickup trucks fan out from the market in Neiafu to various villages, but they have no fixed schedule and are not a reliable means of transport. If you take one, make sure you know when and whether it's coming back to town.

FAST FACTS: Vava'u

If you don't see an item here, check "Fast Facts: Tonga," earlier this chapter, or ask around. Vava'u is a small place where nearly everyone knows everything.

Currency Exchange **ANZ Bank** and **Westpac Bank of Tonga** are both on the main street in Neiafu and have ATMs. Banking hours are Monday to Friday 9am to 4pm, with Westpac also open Saturday 8 to 11am.

Drugstores **Vava'u Pharmacy** (© 70-212), on the main street opposite the Tonga Visitors Bureau, is open Monday, Tuesday, Thursday, and Friday 8:30am to 4pm and Saturday 8:30 to 11am.

Emergencies & Police The telephone number for the **police** is **70-234**.

Healthcare The government has a small **hospital** in Neiafu (℗ **70-201**).

Information The **Tonga Visitors Bureau** (℗ **70-115**; fax 70-666; www.vavau.to) has an office on the main road in Neiafu. Check there for lists of local activities while you're in town. The staff can also help arrange road tours of the island and boat tours of the lagoon. The office is open Monday to Friday 8:30am to 4:30pm. The address is P.O. Box 18, Neiafu, Vava'u.

Internet Access **Cafe Tropicana,** on the main street in Neiafu (℗ **71-322**), has Internet access at T$3 (US$1.50/75p) for 15 minutes and T$9 (US$4.50/£2.25) per hour. See "Where to Dine on Vava'u," below. Down by the harbor, **Aquarium Cafe** (℗ **70-493**) has access for T$8 (US$4/£2) an hour. It's open Monday to Saturday 8am to 8:30pm. Both have wired and wireless access.

Mail The post office opposite the wharf is open Monday to Friday 8:30am to 4pm.

Telephone Tonga Communications Corporation next to the post office is open 24 hours a day, 7 days a week for domestic and long-distance calls. It also has a card phone (there's one next to Westpac Bank of Tonga, too).

Water Don't drink the tap water.

EXPLORING VAVA'U

Be sure to take a walk along Port of Refuge from Paradise International Hotel into town, a stroll of about 15 minutes.

The flat-top mountain across the harbor, **Mo'unga Talau,** at 204m (669 ft.), is the tallest point on Vava'u and part of a Tongan national park. A hike to the top takes about 2 hours round-trip. To get there, turn inland a block past the Westpac Bank of Tonga on the airport road, and then turn left at the Old Market. This street continues through the residential area and then becomes a track, with rope handles in places. The turnoff to the summit starts as the track begins to head downhill. It's a steep climb and can be slippery in wet weather. The Tonga Visitors Bureau maintains the trail, so ask there before making this trek.

Vava'u Adventures, down by the harbor in The Moorings complex (℗ **71-493;** www.vavauadventures.com) has half-day tours of the island by all terrain vehicles for T$150 (US$75/£38) or a single-seater, T$250 (US$125/£63) for a two-seat model. You will see lovely scenery of the fingerlike bays that cut into the island, visit some beautiful beaches, and take in the sweet smell of vanilla—the principal cash crop on Vava'u—drying in sheds or in the sun.

BOAT TOURS ⭐⭐⭐

The absolute best thing to do in Vava'u is to take a boat tour out on the fabulous fjords for a day of swimming, snorkeling, and exploring of the caves and uninhabited islands.

The typical tour follows Port of Refuge to **Swallows Cave** on Kapa Island and then to **Mariner's Cave** (named for Will Mariner, the young Englishman captured with the *Port au Prince* in 1806) on Nuapapu Island. Both of these have been carved out of cliffs by erosion. Boats can go right into Swallows Cave for a look at the swallows flying in and out of a hole in the cave's top. Swimmers with snorkeling gear and a guide can dive into Mariner's Cave. Both caves face west and are best visited in the afternoon, when the maximum amount of natural light gets into them. Most trips also include a stop at one of the small islands for some time at a sparkling beach and a swim over the reefs in crystal-clear water.

Every hotel and guesthouse here will organize boat tours, or you can drop by **Vava'u Adventures** (𝓒 **71-493;** www.vavauadventures.com) or **Sailing Safaris** (𝓒 **70-650;** www.sailingsafaris.com), which will arrange all-day snorkeling trips to the caves and islets for about T$50 (US$25/£13) per person. You can rent a sailboat or powerboat (with skipper) and go where you please. Boats cost about T$400 (US$200/£100) a day.

SAILING 𝓻𝓻𝓻

The waterfront at the base of the hill in Neiafu is home to more than 30 charter yachts that you can rent for as many days as you can afford. Most Americans who visit Tonga, in fact, come here to explore Vava'u in a chartered yacht. You can spend your time sailing from one tiny islet to another in these calm waters. There are dozens of gorgeous beaches off which to anchor, and there are several restaurants to visit at night.

The Moorings 𝓻𝓻𝓻 (𝓒 **800/534-7289** or 70-016; www.moorings.com), the Florida-based pioneer of chartering sailboats in the Caribbean, has one of its two South Pacific bases here. It requires that you be qualified to handle sailboats of the size it charters, and the staff will check out your skills before turning you loose. If you don't qualify, you can hire a skipper or guide at extra cost. Boats range in length from 10m to 15m (33 ft.–49 ft.) and in price from about US$400 to US$990 (£200–£495) a night per boat for bareboat charters (that is, you hire the "bare" boat and provide your own skipper and crew). Prices are more expensive during the May to October high season, but that's far and away the best time to be here. A skipper will cost another NZ$200 (US$160/£80) per day. The Moorings will do your shopping and have the boat provisioned with food and drink when you arrive.

You can rent small sailing dinghies for T$25 (US$13/£6.25) per hour or T$125 (US$63/£31) for all day from **Vava'u Adventures** (𝓒 **70-493**), on the waterfront in the Moorings complex. These little boats were once used as dinghies by The Moorings' yachts. **Vava'u Adventures** (www.vavauadventures.com) is operated by Ben and Lisa Newton, a young American couple who sailed their own yacht to Vava'u and stayed. They also offer jet-boat tours, water-skiing, and other watersports activities, and they have an Internet cafe on premises.

Crewed charter yachts based here include **Melinda Sea Adventures** (𝓒 **70-975;** www.sailtonga.com), a 44-foot ketch which can accommodate up to four passengers on overnight and longer cruises. It charges US$350 (£175) per person per night when only two go, US$225 (£113) per person when four are on board.

In addition, American Vern Kirk provides cruises on his 38-foot trimaran sailboat *Orion* (𝓒 **12-673;** queequeq1931@hotmail.com).

WHALE-WATCHING 𝓻𝓻𝓻

Humpback whales breed in the waters off Vava'u from June to October, and going out to see them—and listen to them through hydrophones—is a highlight of a visit. Other whale-watching destinations such as Hawaii won't allow you to snorkel or scuba dive with the whales, but you can here, albeit under very tightly controlled conditions. Local operators say there's a 50% to 60% chance you'll get to swim among the whales and a 90% chance of seeing them during the season.

Almost everyone here with a boat goes out to see the whales, including the scuba diving operators and fishing charter craft mentioned below. The most experienced operator is Allan Bowe's **Whale Watch Vava'u** (© 70-747; www.whalewatchvavau.com). Allan practically launched whale-watching in Vava'u. He charges about T$220 (US$110/£55) per person. These are all-day voyages, and the sun can be brutal, so come prepared.

FISHING, KAYAKING & SCUBA DIVING

As noted above, Vava'u has a busy yachting and whale-watching season from May to October. Some of the activities mentioned operate only during this period and then clear out of Tonga during the hurricane season from November to April. It's best to ask in advance whether any particular activity is available when you will be here.

FISHING   The waters off Vava'u hold a large number of sizable blue marlin, sailfish, yellowfin and dogtooth tuna, mahimahi, and other species, and you can charter one of several boats here to go get 'em.

New Zealanders Keith and Pat McKee of *Kiwi Magic* (©/fax 70-441; kiwi fish@kalianet.to) take visitors offshore for a full day of sport-fishing, and snorkelers can go along by arrangement. The McKees operate year-round, as do their fellow Kiwis, Henk and Sandra Gross of *Target One* (©/fax 70-647; www.invited.to/target1) and Jeff and Janine Le Strange of the *Hakula* (© 70-872; fax 70-875; www.fishtonga.com). They all charge about US$500 (£250) per day, including bait, tackle, and lunch. At least two persons must be on board. Most of them do whale-watching trips during the season. The Stranges will put you up at their **Hakula Lodge,** on the edge of Neiafu.

KAYAKING   Yachties aren't the only ones who can enjoy the multitude of protected waterways. Kayakers can, too. **Friendly Islands Kayak Company** (© 70-173; www.fikco.com), a New Zealand firm, operates the **Adventure Centre** south of the Paradise International Hotel. It rents sea kayaks and conducts guided tours. It has 5-, 9-, and 11-day trips through the islands, using double- and single-seat kayaks. The tours range from about US$950 to US$2,250 (£457–£1,125) per person and must be arranged in advance.

Several firms rent kayaks, including **Adventure Backpackers Lodge** (© 70-955), the **Paradise International Hotel** (© 74-744), and the two diving operators mentioned below. Expect to pay about T$30 (US$15/£7.50) a day.

SCUBA DIVING 🐟🐟   There's good diving in these clear waters, especially because you don't have to ride on a boat for several hours just to get to a spot with colorful coral and bountiful sea life. In Port of Refuge, divers can explore the wreck of the copra schooner *Clan McWilliam,* sunk in 1906.

Beluga Diving (©/fax 70-327; www.belugadivingvavau.com), **Dive Vava'u** (© 70-492; www.divevavau.com), and the New Zealand–based **Dolphin Pacific Diving** (©/fax 70-292; www.academydivers.co.nz) offer two-tank dives for about T$180 (US$90/£45), including tanks and weight belts.

SHOPPING

Vava'u produces some of the finest handicrafts in Tonga. The best place to shop in Tonga is **South Seas Treasures** 🐟🐟🐟 (© 70-982), beside Port of Refuge in the Puataukanave International Hotel complex. It's owned by English expatriate Amecia Yeal, who collects extraordinary handicrafts, paintings, and drawings by local artisans and artists in Tonga, Papua New Guinea, Solomon Islands, and other Pacific countries. Her prices are as high as the quality, but you get what you pay for.

The local branch of **Langafonua Handicrafts,** the women's handicraft organization founded by Queen Salote (see "Shopping on Tongatapu," earlier in this chapter), is adjacent to the Tonga Visitors Bureau. It carries a good variety of baskets, mats, wood carvings, and other items at reasonable prices. Also look in the small shops along the main street for baskets, mats, wood carvings, and other items.

WHERE TO STAY IN VAVA'U
IN NEIAFU

On a bluff overlooking Port of Refuge and next door to the Paradise International Hotel, **The Sovereign Residence** (© 70-725; gray_tinley@yahoo.com) is a former home of the king's sister, Princess Salote Mafile'o Pilolevu Tuita. It's now a bed-and-breakfast and by-reservation-only restaurant. Princess Pilolevu's old bedroom has a Jacuzzi, while her daughter's room does not. Neither has a telephone.

Adventure Backpackers Lodge   In the center of Neiafu's commercial strip, Sandra and Henk Gross's excellent lodge for both backpackers and other cost-conscious travelers has a marvelous view of Port of Refuge from its large veranda. Three of the nine rooms have private bathrooms. Although it doesn't, room 6 has windows on two sides and opens to the big veranda across the water side of the building, which makes it my favorite. Two units in a separate building are more private, but they lack good ventilation. One is a family-size unit with a double bed and two twins. Everyone else shares four toilets and four hot water showers.

Private Bag 3, Neiafu, Vava'u (main st. next to Royal Tongan Airlines). © **70-955.** Fax 70-647. www.visitvavau.com/backpackers. 9 units (6 without bathroom), 6 dorm beds. T$78–T$95 (US$39–US$48/£20–£24) double; T$25 (US$13/£6) dorm bed. MC, V. **Amenities:** Bicycle rentals; complimentary washers and dryers. *In room:* No phone.

Paradise International Hotel   Although it's getting a little long in the tooth, this hotel perched on a ridge overlooking Port of Refuge has some of the largest rooms in Tonga. A large central building houses the reception area, bar, and restaurant. Next to it, a pool offers a panoramic view of the harbor. A path leads down to the water's edge, where the hotel has its own pier and kayaks for rent. The rooms, in one- and two-story buildings, are devoid of any tropical charms except the views from their balconies (the most expensive units have unimpeded views of Port of Refuge). They have various bed combinations, recliner chairs, coffee tables, and ample, American-style bathrooms with tub/shower combos.

P.O. Box 11, Neiafu, Vava'u (east end of Neiafu). © **74-744.** Fax 70-184. www.tongahost.com. 48 units. US$79–US$119 (£40–£60). AE, MC, V. **Amenities:** Restaurant; bar; outdoor pool; watersports; business center; limited room service; massage; babysitting; laundry service. *In room:* A/C, fridge, coffeemaker.

Puataukanave International Hotel   The tongue-twisting *Puataukanave* means "hibiscus" in Tongan, but locals call this property "Pua's Hotel." The restaurant and a building with 14 of the rooms sit beside the Port of Refuge in the middle of Neiafu. Another 36 units are in a second waterside building, which has shops at ground level. All their balconies face the water. The economy rooms are in a building to the rear; they have only partial views of the Port of Refuge, and two of them lack air conditioners. Another wing has simple rooms and dormitories aimed at backpackers and low-budget divers. These units are devoid of amenities; none has a view. In other words, they are much less attractive than the airy units at Adventure Backpackers (see above). It lacks charm and is understaffed, but is the most modern hotel on Vava'u.

P.O. Box 24, Neiafu, Vava'u (heart of town). ℂ **71-002.** Fax 70-080. tfpel@hotmail.com. 75 units, 20 dorm beds. T$111–T$250 (US$56–US$125/£28–£63) double; T$71 (US$36/£18) double backpacker room; T$35 (US$18/£8.75) dorm bed. AE, MC, V. **Amenities:** Restaurant; bar; outdoor pool; tennis court; bike rentals; laundry service. *In room:* A/C (69 units), TV, fridge, kitchen (super deluxe units).

ON 'UTUNGAKE ISLAND

Roads and causeways link Neiafu to 'Utangake Island, 8.8km (5½ miles) south of Port of Refuge. The establishments below sit beside a lovely narrow channel, giving guests their own swimming beach and jumping-off point for scuba diving, kayaking, and other watersports.

Mystic Sands Beachfront Bungalows The creation of Sandra and Henk Gross of Adventure Backpackers Lodge (see above), these modern cottages all have front decks with tables and chairs, kitchens equipped with microwave ovens, and king-size beds which can be unzipped into singles. Four units are by the beach, while number 5 is upstairs (it has a covered porch overlooking the lagoon). There's no restaurant, but the Tongan Beach Resort is one house away along the beach.

Private Bag 3, Neiafu, Vava'u. ℂ **59-323** or 70-955. Fax 70-647. www.mysticsands.net. 5 units. US$90–US$120 (£45–£60). MC, V. **Amenities:** Complimentary kayaks; laundry service. *In room:* Kitchen, fridge, coffeemaker.

Tongan Beach Resort The main building here is an open Tongan fale housing a restaurant. A sand-floored bar is in its own fale next door. The comfortable, motel-like guest rooms flank the main complex. They are of New Zealand–style construction and furnishings. Each has tile floors, ceiling fans, a dressing area, one queen-size and one single bed, and shower-only bathrooms.

P.O. Box 104, Neiafu, Vava'u ℂ/fax **70-380.** www.thetongan.com. 12 units. US$130–US$160 (£65/£80) double. Meals US$52 (£26) per person per day. Round-trip airport transfers US$26 (£13). MC, V. **Amenities:** Restaurant; bar; free use of kayaks and snorkeling gear; bicycle rentals; laundry service. *In room:* Fridge, coffeemaker, no phone.

OFFSHORE RESORTS

Several islets out in the lagoon have small establishments with restaurants and bars frequented by yachties, who drop anchor and go ashore for some food and libation. Among them are **Blue Lagoon Resort** (ℂ **71-300;** bllagoon@kalianet.to); **Ika Lahi International Gamefishing Lodge** (ℂ **70-611;** www.tongafishing.com); **Mala Island Resort** (ℂ **71-304;** www.malaislandresort.com); and **Treasure Island Resort** (ℂ **12-935;** www. treasureisland-vavau.com).

Mounu Island Resort 𝕲𝕲 The longtime dream of New Zealanders Allan and Lyn Bowe, this resort sits beside a wraparound beach of white sand on Mounu ("Bait Fish" in Tongan), a flat, 2.4-hectare (6-acre) islet near the southern end of the Vava'u lagoon. Cruising yachties moor their boats near the colorful corals and row ashore to imbibe and dine on freshly caught seafood in the Bowes' main building, a mat-lined Tongan fale right on the beach. Their widely-spaced guest fales are rustic but charming, with futon beds covered with mosquito nets (a necessity, as the windows aren't screened), rattan easy chairs, bathrooms with hot-water showers, and front porches facing the lagoon. Solar power generates the electricity, and rain provides the fresh water here. You can swim, snorkel, kayak, fish, go on village visits, and observe seabirds at a nearby breeding colony. This is a popular retreat during the June-to-October whale-watching season, when Allan operates Whale Watch Vava'u (see "Whale-Watching," above). It's a fine place to unwind any time of year.

Private Box 7, Neiafu, Vava'u (Mounu Island, 25 min. by speedboat from Neiafu). ✆ **70-747**. Fax 70-493. www. mounuisland.com. 4 units. US$175–US$200 (£88/£100) double. Meals US$70 (£35) per person per day. Transfers US$45 (£23) per person. MC, V. **Amenities:** Restaurant; bar; watersports; Internet access; laundry service. *In room:* No phone.

Reef Resort The creation of Teresa James and Tim Ellis, who hail from Wales and England, respectively, this little resort resides beside a beach on Kapa Island, which is large enough to have its own Tongan village. Two of their modern bungalows sit by the beach, while the other two are up on a hillside. All have bright white walls, shingle roofs, and views of the coral-speckled lagoon. Each has a king-size bed, as the resort is designed primarily for couples (children under 13 are not welcome here). A lagoonside building holds the restaurant, bar, and guest lounge.

Private bag 11, Neiafu, Vava'u (Kapa Island, 5 min. by boat from Tahihau village). ✆ **47-156** or 59-279. www.reefresort vavau.com. 4 units. T$400 (US$200/£100) double. MC, V. No children under 13 accepted. **Amenities:** Restaurant; bar; complimentary kayaks and snorkeling gear; wireless Internet access; laundry service. *In room:* A/C, fridge, coffeemaker.

WHERE TO DINE ON VAVA'U

Aquarium Cafe 🎔 SNACKS/TAPAS This outdoor cafe is part of Ben and Lisa Newton's Vava'u Adventures complex, next to the Moorings on the waterfront. Dining is out on a sail-covered deck, where I like to have banana crepes for breakfast. It's a good place for fried tofu cakes and vegetarian pasta for lunch. In season, dinner focuses on tapas. Dolmas Vava'u is an interesting twist on the Greek morsels: spicy beef, chili beans, and rice wrapped in a taro leaf.

Neiafu, main st. on the water next to The Moorings. ✆ 70-493. Breakfast and lunch T$6–T$14 (US$3–US$7/£1.50–£3.50); dinner T$7–T$13 (US$3.50–US$6.50/£1.75–£3.25). MC, V. Mon–Sat 8am–10pm (5pm off-season).

Bounty Bar REGIONAL With a great view of Port of Refuge from its rear veranda, this is one of Neiafu's more popular watering holes, with the food playing second fiddle to the cold brews. Breakfast consists of eggs, omelets, and fruit plates, while lunch features lobster salad, sandwiches, and Canadian-style hamburgers. Dinner is best taken elsewhere.

Neiafu, main st. in center of town. ✆ 70-576. Breakfast T$3–T$13 (US$1.50–US$6.50/75p–£3.25); lunch T$17–T$27 (US$8.50–US$14/£4.25/£6.75); main courses T$19–T$34 (US$9.50–US$17/£4.75–£8.50). No credit cards. Mon–Fri 8:30am–10pm; Sat 8:30am–3pm.

Cafe Tropicana 🎔 COFFEE SHOP A knockoff of Friends Cafe in Nuku'alofa, this cafe has a great view of Port of Refuge from its patio out back. Coffees, teas, juices, pastries, sandwiches, and salads are on the menu. Everything is homemade and tasty. You can check your e-mail, but smoke only outside on the patio.

Neiafu, main st. in center of town. ✆ 71-322. Breakfast T$5–T$16 (US$2.50–US$8/£1.25–£4); sandwiches and snacks T$4–T$13 (US$2–US$6.50/£1–£3.25). MC, V. Mon–Fri 7am–6pm; Sat 7am–3pm.

The Dancing Rooster 🎔 SEAFOOD Swiss chef Gunter Schnell came to cook at the Paradise International Hotel, married a local girl, settled down, and opened this restaurant in the backyard of their home opposite the Catholic church. You won't have a water view here. Gunter should have named it "The Dancing Lobster," for he's very good with fresh tropical lobsters. They're best whole with garlic butter, but he also dices them for salads or stir-fries. The bar serves a light menu during the high season.

Neiafu, main st. opposite Catholic church. ✆ 70-886. Reservations recommended. Main courses T$28–T$50 (US$14–US$25/£7–£13). MC, V. Mon–Sat 11am–10pm (bar later in season).

Tips **A Tongan Feast at the Beach**

If you missed a Tongan feast in Nuku'alofa or you just liked it so much you want to go to another, head for **Hinakauea Beach Feast** (② **12-288**), which takes place Thursday night on lovely Lisa Beach, or to **Ano Beach Tongan Feast** (② **71-135**) on Saturday. Either costs T$30 (US$15/£7.50) per person. Your hotel or the Tonga Visitors Bureau will book them.

Mango Cafe INTERNATIONAL   This open-air waterfront restaurant is a sophisticated version of the Mermaid Bar & Restaurant (see below), and because it doesn't have a bar, it does not attract a noisy drinking crowd. With widely spaced tables, it's also a good place for a bit of romance. You can opt for a pizza or pasta, but I had a tasty Thai-style curry with fish, lobster, and papaya served over rice. Whole tropical lobsters usually are available, although just the tail is sufficient for a satisfying meal. If it's offered, I'm ordering yellowfin tuna next time here.

Neiafu, main st. on the water next to The Moorings. ② **70-664.** Reservations recommended. Pizza and pasta T$10–T$20 (US$5–US$10/£2.50–£5); main courses T$20–T$60 (US$10–US$30/£5–£15). MC, V. High season daily 7am–10pm; off-season Mon–Sat 10am–10pm.

Mermaid Bar & Restaurant SNACKS/SEAFOOD   Operated by Sailing Safaris, this open-air restaurant beside the harbor is the most popular place in Neiafu for breakfast, sandwiches, burgers, salads, pizzas, and dinner choices including grilled lobster, steaks, and fish (check the "Specials" board for today's catch). For lunch try the lobster salad. This is the town's most popular drinking establishment, with local expatriates and yachties usually packing the bar during happy hour from 4 to 7pm.

Neiafu, main st. on the water next to Sailing Safaris Marine Center. ② **70-730.** Reservations recommended for dinner July–Aug. Breakfast T$6–T$17 (US$3–US$8.50/£1.50–£4.25); salads, sandwiches, and burgers T$7–T$20 (US$3.50–US$10/£1.75–£5); main courses T$20–T$50 (US$10–US$25/£5–£13). MC, V. Daily 8am–9pm (bar until midnight).

ISLAND NIGHTS ON VAVA'U

Bands play from June through August at the **Paradise International Hotel** (② **70-211**), and all year at **Tonga Bob's Cantina** (② **70-285**), an open-air waterfront joint near the western end of Neiafu. Otherwise, there's not much to do except hang out with all the expatriates and yachties down at the Mermaid, on the waterfront (see "Where to Dine on Vava'u," above).

17 Ha'apai

Off the beaten path, Ha'apai is central in both Tonga's geography and history. In the middle of the kingdom, 155km (96 miles) north of Nuku'alofa and 108km (67 miles) south of Vava'u, Ha'apai consists of numerous small, atoll-like islands scattered across the sea. Linked by a causeway, **Lifuka** and **Foa** are the largest and the only ones you can visit without being on a sailboat. On the horizon to their west sits the active volcano **Tofua,** where puffs of steam spew from the rim above its crater lake, and the perfectly shaped cone of its inactive neighbor, **Kao.**

Today Lifuka and the other islands seem much as they must have been when King George moved his capital to Tongatapu. You'll find some great beaches and fine scuba diving here, but there's not much else to do except relax, explore historical sights in **Pangai,** the only town, and go diving.

GETTING TO HA'APAI & GETTING AROUND

Chathams Pacific—The Friendly Islands Airline (© 28-000; www.chathamspacific. com) and **Airlines Tonga** (© 24-506) fly between Tongatapu and Vava'u (see "Getting to Tonga & Getting Around," earlier in this chapter). There is no public transportation system on Ha'apai.

WHERE TO STAY & DINE ON HA'APAI

Sandy Beach Resort ☆☆   This resort is aptly named, for it sits beside one of the South Pacific's great beaches, a glorious curving stretch of white sand that faces west, toward Tofua and Kao on the horizon. And unlike so many beaches in the islands, at this one you can swim and snorkel at all tides. Of modern construction but with Tongan style, each light, airy bungalow has a porch facing the beach and is equipped with a cool tile floor, either a double or two single beds, and an ample bathroom with a tiled hot-water shower. Guests can take nature walks, watch a culture show, and catch a daily shuttle to Pangai. You'll pay extra for horseback riding, boat trips, and tennis at the local Mormon church (bring your own racquet and balls). The resort is closed December and January. **Ocean Blue Adventures** (© 60-369; www.tonga-dive.com) has its dive base here.

P.O. Box 61, Pangai, Ha'apai (north end of Foa Island). ©/fax 60-600. www.sandybeachresort.de. 12 units. 70€–210€ (US$81–US$242/£40–£121) bungalow. AE, MC, V. Children under 16 accepted on request only. Closed Dec 1–Feb 1. **Amenities:** Restaurant; bar; free use of snorkeling gear, kayaks, and bikes; laundry service. *In room:* Fridge, coffeemaker, no phone.

Appendix:
The South Pacific in Depth

As you have seen in the preceding chapters, each South Pacific island group has its own history, culture, language, geography, and geology. That is the nature of such a far-flung region, where hundreds or thousands of miles separate one island from the next. On the other hand, the islands have many things in common. Their indigenous peoples are descended from Polynesians and Melanesians who migrated here several millennia ago. Many of their traditions and customs are the same, but with local quirks that have developed over the eons. Nowhere are the local variations as evident as in the Polynesian languages, which are similar but differ from one group to the next.

1 The Islanders

Early European explorers were astounded to find the far-flung South Pacific islands inhabited by peoples who shared similar physical characteristics, languages, and cultures. How had these people—who lived a late–Stone Age existence and had no written languages—crossed the Pacific long before Christopher Columbus had the courage to sail out of sight of land? Where had they come from? Those questions continue to intrigue scientists and scholars today.

THE FIRST SETTLERS
The late Thor Heyerdahl drifted in his raft *Kon Tiki* from South America to French Polynesia in 1947, to prove his theory that the Polynesians came from the Americas. Bolstered by linguistic and DNA studies linking the Polynesians to Taiwan, however, experts now believe the Pacific Islanders have their roots in eastern Asia. The accepted view is that during the Ice Age a race of humans known as Australoids migrated from Southeast Asia to Papua New Guinea and Australia, when those two countries were joined as one land mass. Another group, the Papuans, arrived from Southeast Asia between 5,000 and 10,000 years ago. Later a lighter-skinned race known as

Austronesians pushed the Papuans out into the more eastern South Pacific islands.

The most tangible remains of the early Austronesians are remnants of pottery, the first shards of which were found during the 1970s in Lapita, in New Caledonia. Probably originating in Papua New Guinea, Lapita pottery spread east as far as Tonga. Throughout the area, it was decorated with geometric designs similar to those used today on Tongan tapa cloth. Apparently the Lapita culture died out some 2,500 years ago, for by the time European explorers arrived in the 1770s, gourds and coconut shells were the only crockery used by the Polynesians, who cooked their meals underground and ate off banana leaves. Of the islanders covered in this book, only the Fijians still make pottery using Lapita methods.

MELANESIANS
The islands settled by the Papuans and Austronesians are known collectively as *Melanesia*, which includes Papua New Guinea, the Solomon Islands, Vanuatu, and New Caledonia. Fiji is the melting pot of the Melanesians to the west and the Polynesians to the east.

The name Melanesia is derived from the Greek words *melas,* "black," and *nesos,* "island." The Melanesians in general have features more akin to sub-Saharan Africans: skin color ranging from brown to black, flat or hooked noses, full lips, and wiry hair. But interbreeding among the successive waves of migrants resulted in many subgroups with varying physical characteristics. That's why the Fijians look more African-American than Polynesian. Their culture, on the other hand, has many Polynesian elements, brought by interbreeding and conquest.

POLYNESIANS

The Polynesians' ancestors stopped in Fiji on their migration from Southeast Asia but later pushed on into the eastern South Pacific. Archaeologists now believe that they settled in Samoa more than 3,000 years ago and then slowly fanned out to colonize the vast Polynesian triangle.

These extraordinary mariners crossed thousands of miles of ocean in double-hulled canoes capable of carrying scores of people, animals, and plants. They navigated by the stars, the wind, the clouds, the shape of the waves, and the flight pattern of birds—a remarkable achievement for a people who had no written languages.

Their ancestors fought each other with war clubs for thousands of years, and it stands to reason that the biggest, strongest, and quickest survived (many modern Polynesians have become professional football and rugby players). The notion that all Polynesians are fat is incorrect. In the old days, body size did indeed denote wealth and status, but obesity today is more likely attributable to poor diet. On the other hand, village chiefs are still expected to partake of food and drink with anyone who visits to discuss a problem; hence, great weight remains an unofficial marker of social status.

POLYNESIAN SOCIETY Although Polynesians frequently experienced wars among their various tribes, generally their conflicts were not as bloody as those in Fiji. Nor were their wars as likely to end with cannibalistic orgies at the expense of the losers as in Fiji and Melanesia, where cannibalism was widely practiced.

Polynesians developed highly structured societies. Strong and sometimes despotic chiefdoms developed on many islands. The royal family of Tonga continues a line of leaders who were so powerful in the 1700s that they conquered much of Fiji, where they installed Polynesian customs, including their hereditary chief system. Melanesians are more likely to choose their "big men" by consensus rather than ancestry.

In some places, such as Tahiti, the Polynesians developed a class system of chiefs, priests, nobility, commoners, and slaves. Their societies emphasized elaborate formalities. Even today ceremonies featuring **kava**—that slightly narcotic drink so loved in the islands—play important roles in Samoa, Tonga, and Fiji. Everyday life was governed by a system based on *tabu,* a list of things a person could or couldn't do, depending on his/her status. Tabu and its variants *(tapu, tambu)* are used throughout the South Pacific to mean "do not enter"; from them derives the English word *taboo.*

Western principles of ownership have made inroads, but by and large everything in Polynesia and Fiji—especially land—is owned communally by families. In effect, the system is pure communism at the family level. If your brother has a crop of taro and you're hungry, then some of that taro belongs to you. The same principle applies to a can of corned beef on a shelf in a store, which helps explain why islander-owned grocery shops often teeter on the brink of bankruptcy. It also explains why you should keep an eye on your valuables.

Although many islanders would be considered poor by Western standards, no one in the villages goes hungry or sleeps without a roof over his or her head. Most of the

---

(*Fun Fact* **Jotting It Down**

No Polynesian language was written until Peter Heywood jotted down a Tahitian vocabulary while awaiting trial for his part in the mutiny on the *Bounty* (he was convicted but pardoned). The early missionaries who later translated the Bible into Tahitian decided which letters of the Roman alphabet to use to approximate the sounds of the Polynesian languages. These tended to vary from place to place. For example, they used the consonants *t* and *v* in Tahitian. In Hawaiian, which is similar, they used *k* and *w*. The actual Polynesian sounds are somewhere in between.

---

thatch roofs in Polynesia today are actually bungalows at the resort hotels; nearly everyone else sleeps under tin. It's little wonder, therefore, that visitors are greeted throughout the islands by friendly, peaceable, and extraordinarily courteous people.

THE OLD GODS Before the coming of Christian missionaries in the 1800s, the Fijians believed in many spirits in the animist traditions of Melanesia. The Polynesians, however, subscribed to the idea of a supreme spirit, who ruled over a plethora of lesser deities, who, in turn, governed the sun, fire, volcanoes, sea, war, and fertility. Tikis were carved of stone or wood to give each god a home (but not a permanent residence) during religious ceremonies, and stone maraes were built as temples and meeting places for the chiefs. Sacrifices—sometimes human—were offered to the gods.

LANGUAGES

Like their DNA, linguists have traced the islanders' languages to present-day Taiwan.

They belong to the Austronesian family of languages spoken from Madagascar, off the coast of Africa, to Easter Island, off the coast of South America. No other group of ancient languages spread to so much of the earth's surface.

Today, the Polynesian islanders speak similar languages from one major island group to another. For example, the word for "house" is *fale* in Tongan and Samoan, *fare* in Tahitian, *'are* in Cook Islands Maori, *hale* in Hawaiian, and *vale* in Fijian. Without having heard the other's language, Cook Islanders say they can understand about 60% of Tahitian, and Tongans and Samoans can get the gist of each others' conversations.

Thanks to the American, British, New Zealand, and Australian colonial regimes, English is an official language in the Cook Islands, both Samoas, and Fiji. It is spoken widely in Tonga. French is spoken alongside Tahitian in French Polynesia, although English is understood among most hotel and restaurant staffs.

2 The Islands & the Sea

A somewhat less-than-pious wag once remarked that God made the South Pacific islands on the 6th day of creation so He would have an extraordinarily beautiful place to rest on the 7th day. Modern geologists have a different view, but the fact remains that the islands and the surrounding sea are possessed of heavenly beauty and a plethora of life forms.

HIGH, LOW & IN BETWEEN

The Polynesian islands were formed by molten lava escaping upward through cracks in the earth's crust as it has crept slowly northwestward over the eons, thus building great seamounts. Many of these—called "high islands"—have mountains soaring into the clouds. In contrast, flat atolls were formed when the islands sank back into the sea, leaving only a thin necklace of coral islets to circumscribe their lagoons and mark their original boundaries. In some cases, geologic forces have once again lifted the atolls, forming "raised" islands whose sides drop precipitously into the sea. Other, partially sunken islands, are left with the remnants of mountains sticking up in their lagoons.

The islands of Tonga and Fiji were created by volcanic eruptions along the collision of the Indo-Australian and Pacific tectonic plates. Although the main islands are quiet today, they are part of the volcanically active and earthquake-prone "Ring of Fire" around the Pacific Ocean.

FLORA & FAUNA

Most species of plants and animals native to the South Pacific originated in Southeast Asia and worked their way eastward across the Pacific, by natural distribution or in the company of humans. The number of native species diminishes the farther east one goes. Very few local plants or animals came from the Americas, the one notable exception being the sweet potato, which may have been brought back from South America by voyaging Polynesians.

PLANTS In addition to the west-to-east differences, flora changes according to each island's topography. The mountainous islands make rain from the moist trade winds and thus possess a greater variety of plants. Their interior highlands are covered with ferns, native bush, or grass. The low atolls, on the other hand, get sparse rainfall and support little other than scrub bush and coconut palms.

Ancient settlers brought coconut palms, breadfruit, taro, paper mulberry, pepper (*kava*), and bananas to the isolated midocean islands because of their usefulness as food or fiber. Accordingly, they are generally found in the inhabited areas of the islands and not so often in the interior bush.

With a few indigenous exceptions, such as the *tiare* (Tahiti gardenia) and Fiji's *tagimaucia,* tropical flowers also worked their way east in the company of humans. Bougainvillea, hibiscus, allamanda, poinsettia, poinciana (the flame tree), croton, frangipani (plumeria), ixora, canna, and water lilies all give colorful testament to the islanders' love for flowers of every hue in the rainbow. The aroma of the white, yellow, or pink frangipani is so sweet it's used as perfume on many islands.

ANIMALS & BIRDS The fruit bat, or "flying fox," and some species of insect-eating bats are the only mammals native to the South Pacific islands. The early settlers introduced dogs, chickens, pigs, rats, and mice. There are few land snakes or other reptiles in the islands. The notable exceptions are geckos and skinks, those little lizards that seem to be everywhere. Don't go berserk when a gecko walks upside-down across the ceiling of your bungalow. They are harmless and actually perform a valuable service by eating mosquitoes and other insects.

The number and variety of species of bird life also diminishes as you go eastward. Most land birds live in the bush away from settlements and their cats, dogs, and rats. For this reason, the birds most likely to be seen are terns, boobies, herons, petrels, noddies, and others that earn their livelihoods from the sea. Of the introduced birds, the Indian myna exists in the greatest numbers. Brought to the South Pacific early in the 20th century to control insects, the myna quickly became a noisy nuisance in its own right. Mynahs are extremely adept at stealing the toast off your breakfast table.

THE SEA

The tropical South Pacific Ocean teems with sea life, from colorful reef fish to the Great White sharks featured in *Jaws,* from the paua clams that make tasty chowders in the Cook Islands to the deep-sea tuna that keep the canneries going at Pago Pago.

More than 600 species of coral—10 times the number found in the Caribbean—form the great reefs that make the South Pacific a divers' mecca. Billions of tiny coral polyps build their own skeletons on top of those left by their ancestors, until they reach the level of low tide. Then they grow outward, extending the edge of the reef. The old skeletons are white, while the living polyps present a rainbow of colors. Corals grow best and are most colorful in the clear, salty water on the outer edge or in channels, where the tides and waves wash fresh seawater along and across the reef. A reef can grow as much as 2 inches a year in ideal conditions. Although pollution, rising seawater temperature, and a proliferation of crown-of-thorns starfish have greatly hampered reef growth—and beauty—in parts of the South Pacific, there still are many areas where the color and variety of corals are unmatched.

A plethora of tropical fish and other marine life fill most of the lagoons, which are like gigantic aquariums. Bookstores in the main towns sell pamphlets containing photographs and descriptions of the creatures that will peer into your face mask. Humpback whales migrate to the islands from June to October, and sea turtles lay their eggs on some beaches from November through February.

Most South Pacific countries restrict the use of spear guns, so ask before you go in search of the catch of your life. Sea turtles and whales are on the list of endangered species, and many countries, including the United States, prohibit the importation of their shells, bones, and teeth.

3 Recommended Reading

I have picked some of my favorites that are likely to be available at bookstores, online, or at your local library. A few out-of-print island classics have been reissued in paperback by **Mutual Publishing Company,** 125 Center St., Ste. 210, Honolulu, HI 96816 (© **808/ 732-1709;** fax 808/734-4094; www. mutualpublishing.com).

GENERAL
If you have time for only one South Pacific book, read *The Lure of Tahiti* (1986). Editor A. Grove Day, himself an islands expert, includes 18 short stories, excerpts of other books, and essays. There is a little here from many writers mentioned below, plus selections from captains Cook, Bougainville, and Bligh.

The National Geographic Society's book *The Isles of the South Pacific* (1971), by Maurice Shadbolt and Olaf Ruhen, and Ian Todd's *Island Realm* (1974), are somewhat out-of-date but have lovely color photographs. *Living Corals* (1979), by Douglas Faulkner and Richard Chesher, shows what you will see underwater.

HISTORY & POLITICS
Several early English and French explorers published accounts of their exploits, but *The Journals of Captain James Cook* stand out as the most exhaustive and evenhanded. Edited by J. C. Beaglehole, they were published in three volumes (one for each voyage) in 1955, 1961, and 1967. A. Grenfell Price edited many of Cook's key passages and provides short transitional explanations in *The Explorations of Captain James Cook in the Pacific* (1971).

The explorers' visits and their consequences in Tahiti, Australia, and Antarctica are the subject of Alan Moorehead's excellent study *The Fatal Impact: The Invasion of the South Pacific, 1767–1840* (1966), a colorful tome loaded with sketches and paintings.

Three good books trace Tahiti's history. Robert Langdon's *Tahiti: Island of Love*

(1979) takes the story up to 1977. David Howarth's *Tahiti: A Paradise Lost* (1985) stops with France's taking possession in 1842. *The Rape of Tahiti* (1983), by Edward Dodd, covers the island from prehistory to 1900.

Mad About Islands (1987), by A. Grove Day, follows the island exploits of literary figures Herman Melville, Robert Louis Stevenson, Jack London, W. Somerset Maugham, Charles Nordhoff, and James Norman Hall (see "Fiction," below). *A Dream of Islands* (1980), by Gavan Dawes, tells of the missionary John Williams as well as of Melville, Stevenson, and the painter Paul Gauguin.

PEOPLES & CULTURES

Perhaps the most famous book about Polynesia culture is *Coming of Age in Samoa* (1928), in which Margaret Mead tells of her year studying promiscuous adolescent girls in the Manu'a islands of American Samoa. Her interpretation of Samoan sex customs was taken to task by New Zealander Derek Freeman in *Margaret Mead and Samoa: The Making and Unmaking of an Anthropological Myth* (1983).

Bengt Danielsson, a Swedish anthropologist who arrived on Thor Heyerdahl's *Kon Tiki* raft in 1947 and spent the rest of his life in on Tahiti, painted a broader picture of Polynesian sexuality in *Love in the South Seas* (1986). Heyerdahl tells his tale and explains his theory of Polynesian migration (since debunked) in *Kon Tiki* (1950). In 1936, Heyerdahl and his wife lived for a year in the Marquesas. His book, *Fatu-Hiva: Back to Nature* (1975), provides an in-depth look at Marquesan life at the time.

Two Americans gave unscholarly but entertaining accounts of Polynesian island life during the 1920s. Robert Dean Frisbie spent several years as a trader in the Cook Islands and told about it charmingly in *The Book of Puka-Puka* (1928; Mutual, 1986). Robert Lee Eskridge spent a year on Mangareva in French Polynesia; his book is titled, appropriately, *Manga Reva* (1931; Mutual, 1986).

TRAVELOGUES

Although the novelist Robert Louis Stevenson composed little fiction about the South Pacific during his years in Samoa (see chapter 13), he wrote articles and letters about his travels and about events leading to Germany's acquisition of the islands in 1890. Many of them are available in two collections: *In the South Seas* (1901) and *Island Landfalls* (1987). The latter includes three Stevenson short stories with South Seas settings: "The Bottle Imp," "The Isle of Voices," and "The Beach at Falesá."

Sir David Attenborough, the British documentary film producer, traveled to Papua New Guinea, Vanuatu, Fiji, and Tonga in the late 1950s to film, among other things, Tongan Queen Salote's royal kava ceremony. Sir David entertainingly tells of his trips in *Journeys to the Past* (1983).

The travel writer and novelist Paul Theroux took his kayak along for a tour of the South Pacific and reported on what he found in *The Happy Isles of Oceania: Paddling the Pacific* (1992). The book is a fascinatingly frank yarn, full of island characters and out-of-the-way places. Tonga's royal family reportedly was so upset with Theroux's comments that he is banned from returning to the kingdom.

More recently, J. Maarten Troost tells some hilarious tales in *Getting Stoned with Savages: A Trip Through the Islands of Fiji and Vanuatu* (2006). He spins similar yarns about Micronesia in *The Sex Lives of Cannibals* (2004).

FICTION

Starting with Herman Melville's *Typee* (1846) and *Omoo* (1847)—semifictional accounts of his adventures in the Marquesas and Tahiti, respectively—the South Pacific has spawned a wealth of fiction.

(Though set in the South Pacific Ocean, Melville's 1851 classic *Moby-Dick* does not tell of the islands.)

After Melville came Julien Viaud, a French naval officer who fell in love with a Tahitian woman during a sojourn in Tahiti. As Pierre Loti, he wrote *The Marriage of Loti* (1880; reprinted by KPI in 1986), a classic tale of lost love.

W. Somerset Maugham's *The Moon and Sixpence* (1919) is a fictional account of the life of Paul Gauguin. Maugham changed the name to Charles Strickland and made the painter English instead of French. Gauguin's own novel, *Noa Noa*, was published in English in 1928. Maugham also produced a volume of South Pacific short stories, *The Trembling of a Leaf* (1921; Mutual, 1985). The most famous is "Rain," the tragic story of prostitute Sadie Thompson and the missionary she led astray in American Samoa. It was made into several movies. My favorite Maugham story is "The Fall of Edward Bernard," about a Chicagoan who forsakes love and fortune at home for "beauty, truth, and goodness" in Tahiti.

Next on the scene were Charles Nordhoff and James Norman Hall (more about them in chapters 7 and 8). Together they wrote the most famous of all South Pacific novels, *Mutiny on the Bounty* (1932). They followed that enormous success with two other novels: *Men Against the Sea* (1934), based on Captain Bligh's epic longboat voyage after the mutiny; and *Pitcairn's Island* (1935), about Lt. Fletcher Christian's demise on the mutineers' remote hideaway.

For a nonfiction retelling of the great tale, see Caroline Alexander's *The Bounty: The True Story of the Mutiny on the Bounty* (2003).

Nordhoff and Hall later wrote *The Hurricane* (1936), a novel set in American Samoa that has been made into two movies filmed in French Polynesia. Hall also wrote short stories and essays, collected in *The Forgotten One* (1986).

The second-most-famous South Pacific novel appeared just after World War II—*Tales of the South Pacific* (1947), by James A. Michener. A U.S. Navy historian, Michener spent much of the war on Espiritu Santo in the New Hebrides (now Vanuatu). Richard Rodgers and Oscar Hammerstein turned the novel into the musical *South Pacific*, a huge Broadway hit; it was later made into the blockbuster movie.

Michener toured the islands a few years later and wrote *Return to Paradise* (1951), a collection of essays and short stories. The essays describe the islands as they were after World War II but before tourists began to arrive—near the end of the region's backwater, beachcomber days. His piece on Fiji predicts that country's Fijian-Indian problems.

Index